Electronics and VLSI Circuits

Senior Consulting Editor
Stephen W. Director, *Carnegie Mellon University*

Consulting Editor
Richard C. Jaeger, Auburn University

Conclaser and Diehl-Nagle: *Materials and Devices for Electrical Engineers and Physicists*
DeMicheli: *Synthesis and Optimization of Digital Circuits*
Elliott: *Microlithography: Process Technology for IC Fabrication*
Fabricius: *Introduction to VLSI Design*
Ferendeci: *Physical Foundations of Solid State and Electron Devices*
Fonstad: *Microelectronic Devices and Circuits*
Franco: *Design with Operational Amplifiers and Analog Integrated Circuits*
Geiger, Allen, and Strader: *VLSI Design Techniques for Analog and Digital Circuits*
Grinich and Jackson: *Introduction to Integrated Circuits*
Hodges and Jackson: *Analysis and Design of Digital Integrated Circuits*
Huelsman: *Active and Passive Analog Filter Design: An Introduction*
Ismail and Fiez: *Analog VLSI: Signal and Information Processing*
Laker and Sansen: *Design of Analog Integrated Circuits and Systems*
Long and Butner: *Gallium Arsenide Digital Integrated Circuits Design*
Millman and Grabel: *Microelectronics*
Millman and Halkias: *Integrated Electronics: Analog, Digital Circuits, and Systems*
Millman and Taub: *Pulse, Digital, and Switching Waveforms*
Ng: *Complete Guide to Semiconductor Devices*
Offen: *VLSI Image Processing*
Roulston: *Bipolar Semiconductor Devices*
Ruska: *Microelectronic Processing: An Introduction to the Manufacture of Integrated Circuits*
Schilling and Belove: *Electronic Circuits: Discrete and Integrated*
Seraphim: *Principles of Electronic Packaging*
Singh: *Physics of Semiconductors and Their Heterostructures*
Singh: *Semiconductor Devices: An Introduction*
Singh: *Semiconductor Optoelectronics: Physics and Technology*
Smith: *Modern Communication Circuits*
Sze: *VLSI Technology*
Taub: *Digital Circuits and Microprocessors*
Taub and Schilling: *Digital Integrated Electronics*
Tsividis: *Operation and Modeling of the MOS Transistor*
Wait, Huelsman, and Korn: *Introduction to Operational and Amplifier Theory Applications*
Yang: *Microelectronic Devices*
Zambuto: *Semiconductor Devices*

Also Available from McGraw-Hill

Schaum's Outline Series in Electronics & Electrical Engineering

Most outlines include basic theory, definitions and hundreds of example problems solved in step-by-step detail, and supplementary problems with answers.

Related titles on the current list include:

Analog & Digital Communications
Basic Circuits Analysis
Basic Electrical Engineering
Basic Electricity
Basic Mathematics for Electricity & Electronics
Digital Principles
Electric Circuits
Electric Machines & Electromechanics
Electric Power Systems
Electromagnetics
Electronic Circuits
Electronic Communication
Electronic Devices & Circuits
Electronics Technology
Feedback & Control Systems
Introduction to Digital Systems
Microprocessor Fundamentals

Schaum's Solved Problems Books

Each title in this series is a complete and expert source of solved problems with solutions worked out in step-by-step detail.

Related titles on the current list include:

3000 Solved Problems in Calculus
2500 Solved Problems in Differential Equations
3000 Solved Problems in Electric Circuits
2000 Solved Problems in Electromagnetics
2000 Solved Problems in Electronics
3000 Solved Problems in Linear Algebra
2000 Solved Problems in Numerical Analysis
3000 Solved Problems in Physics

Available at most college bookstores, or for a complete list of titles and prices, write to: Schaum Division
         McGraw-Hill, Inc.
         1221 Avenue of the Americas
         New York, NY 10020

COMPLETE GUIDE TO SEMICONDUCTOR DEVICES

Kwok K. Ng
AT&T Bell Laboratories
Murray Hill, New Jersey

McGraw-Hill, Inc.

New York   St. Louis   San Francisco   Auckland   Bogotá   Caracas   Lisbon
London   Madrid   Mexico City   Milan   Montreal   New Delhi
San Juan   Singapore   Sydney   Tokyo   Toronto

The editor was George T. Hoffman;
the production supervisor was Leroy A. Young.
R. R. Donnelley & Sons Company was printer and binder.

COMPLETE GUIDE TO SEMICONDUCTOR DEVICES

This book is printed on recycled, acid-free paper containing 10% postconsumer waste.

1 2 3 4 5 6 7 8 9 0   DOC DOC   9 0 9 8 7 6 5 4

ISBN 0-07-035860-5

Library of Congress Cataloging-in-Publication Data

Ng, Kwok K., (date).
    Complete guide to semiconductor devices / Kwok K. Ng.
        p.   cm. — (McGraw-Hill series in electrical and computer
    engineering. Electronics and VLSI circuits)
    Includes index.
    ISBM 0-07-035860-5
    1. Semiconductors—Handbooks, manuals, etc.   2. Semiconductors—
History.   I. Title.   II. Series
TK7871.85.N49   1995
621.3815'2—dc20   94-32476

INTERNATIONAL EDITION

When ordering this title, use ISBN 0-07-113527-8.

ABOUT THE AUTHOR

Kwok K. Ng received his Ph.D. degree from Columbia University in 1979 and B.S. degree from Rutgers University in 1975, both in Electrical Engineering. He has been with AT&T Bell Laboratories at the Murray Hill location since 1980, engaging in different aspects of silicon VLSI devices and technologies. Dr. Ng has been active in contributing to journal papers, conference talks, book chapters, and holds various patents. He is a Publication Committee member of the IEEE Electron Devices Society, and a former Associate Editor of *IEEE Electron Device Letters.*

ABOUT THE BOOK

Complete Guide to Semiconductor Devices provides an overview of a *complete* collection of semiconductor devices. As a *guide,* the essential informations are presented for a quick, practical, and balanced survey.

Each short chapter is devoted to only one specific device and is self-contained, enabling the readers to go directly to the intended device. Chapters are written to be independent with minimum cross references to other chapters.

A special format for each chapter answers basic questions about each device: (1) History–when was it invented and by whom? (2) Structure–how is it made? (3) Characteristics–how does it work? (4) Applications–what is it for?

With a final section–Related Devices–added to many of the 67 chapters, more than 180 device structures are covered, and more than 800 references cited for further in-depth studies. Together with more than 480 illustrations and extensive appendixes, *Complete Guide to Semiconductor Devices* is a pragmatic handbook that offers an engineering approach to the study of semiconductor devices.

CONTENTS

Note: Since the standard sections of (.1) History, (.2) Structure, (.3) Characteristics, and (.4) Applications are in every chapter, they are omitted from the Contents except for Chapter 1 as an example.

CAPACITIVE DEVICES

TWO-TERMINAL SWITCHES

TRANSISTORS: I–FIELD-EFFECT

OTHER PHOTONIC DEVICES

SENSORS

PREFACE

Semiconductor devices are the basic components of integrated circuits and are responsible for the startling rapid growth of the electronics industry in the past fifty years worldwide. Because there is a continuing need for faster and more complex systems for the information age, existing semiconductor devices are being studied for improvement, and new ones are being invented. Whether it is for higher speed, lower power, higher density, higher efficiency, or new functionality, the number and types of semiconductor devices have been growing steadily in this fascinating field. While there is no shortage of journal papers and books to cover each device in detail, there lacks a single book that includes all semiconductor devices, from the older and sometimes obsolete types to the recent quantum devices; and from the common to the specialized thyristors and sensors. This handbook is designed as a complete collection of semiconductor devices, giving a quick review of each device.

Because of the unique format, this book is intended for a wide audience directly or peripherally related to the electronics industry. In academics, it is a good supplementary text for courses that are related to semiconductor device physics, VLSI technology, material science, or physical science. This book will give the students, undergraduate and graduate, a complete survey of semiconductor devices and a better perspective about the types of devices available. As a main text, it is suitable for a graduate-level seminar course where ample discussions can, hopefully, overcome the lack of problem sets in this book. For practicing engineers, the book can serve as a practical guide to learn about devices outside their field quickly.

A book of this nature will certainly generate controversy, whether it is due to some devices that are missed, or to some historical developments of devices that are overlooked. Suggestions for inclusion of these items for future editions are most welcomed and appreciated.

I would like to first acknowledge S. M. Sze, J. R. Brews, T. C. Y. Poon, and S. J. Hillenius for their personal influence and encouragement, and various helps during the course of this work. The support and the environment provided by my past and present management W. T. Lynch, R. Liu, and J. T. Clemens are very much appreciated. The computer assistance offered by T. D. Stanik, C. J. Case, and W. S. Lindenberger was very helpful to my delivering the camera-ready manuscript, prepared with a commercial desk-top publishing software.

I am indebted to the AT&T Library Network without which this book would not have been possible. Credits are also due to W. F. Wright who did all the literature search. I am grateful to my Bell Laboratories editor N. Erdos who edited the entire manuscript and made significant improvement. My interaction with McGraw-Hill editors A. T. Brown and G. T. Hoffman has been most helpful and enjoyable. I also appreciate the permissions from both publishers and authors to reproduce the published figures and tables, which have all been redrawn.

I am very thankful to the many reviewers who took their time to review selected chapters in their expertise, and made many invaluable corrections and suggestions. Such credits are due to D. A. Antoniadis, P. Bhattacharya, A. Blicher, G. Bosman, C. O. Bozler, J. C. Campbell, F. Capasso, H. C. Casey, Jr., R. Castagnetti, C. Y. Chang, T. H. Chiu, T. Y. Chiu, S. Y. Chou, T. P. Chow, N. F. de Rooij, K. Dezaki, P. W. Diodato, L. F. Eastman, J. S. Escher, E. R. Fossum, H. M. Gibbs, M. A. Green, A. Grinberg, H. K. Gummel, G. I. Haddad, M. M. Hashemi, M. Heiblum, K. Hess, M. A. Hollis, C. Hu, A. Kastalsky, R. A. Kiehl, W. F. Kosonocky, S. K. Lai, B. F. Levine, S. S. Li, S. Luryi, T. P. Ma, R. J. Malik, G. C. M. Meijer, S. Middelhoek, T. Misawa, H. Morkoc, S. R. Morrison, P. N. Panayotatos, P. Plotka, E. Rosencher, R. H. Saul, A. C. Seabaugh, S. D. Senturia, M. P. Shaw, M. Shoji, M. Shur, B. G. Streetman, T. Sukegawa, G. W. Taylor, B. Y. Tsaur, R. Tung, H. T. Weston, J. F. White, R. M. White, T. H. Wood, and C. H. Yang.

I wish to take this opportunity to thank my undergraduate advisor W. A. Anderson, then of Rutgers University, and my graduate advisor H. C. Card, then of Columbia University, for guiding me into the device field which I enjoy so much. Finally, I thank my family–my wife Linda, and my daughters Vivian and Valerie–for their kind understanding and support during this busy period of four-and-a-half years.

Kwok K. Ng

COMPLETE GUIDE TO
SEMICONDUCTOR DEVICES

INTRODUCTION

It is difficult to have a clear quantitative definition of semiconductor. Based on conductivity, materials can be classified into three groups: (1) metal (conductor), (2) semiconductor, and (3) insulator (non-conductor). A general guideline indicating their ranges of conductivity is shown in Fig. I.1. Note that one important feature of a semiconductor is that it can be doped with impurities to different concentration levels, so every semiconductor material can cover a range of conductivity. The total range of conductivity for semiconductors is from 10^{-8} S/cm to 10^3 S/cm (resistivity from 10^{-3} Ω-cm to 10^8 Ω-cm).

The conductivity of materials is ultimately related to the energy-band structure as shown in Fig. I.2. For an insulator, the energy gap E_g is large. Consequently, the valence band is completely filled with electrons, and the conduction band is completely empty. Since current is a movement of electrons, and electrons need available states to move to, current cannot be generated from a completely filled band and a completely empty band. A semiconductor has a smaller E_g. Even when the Fermi level is within the energy gap, thermal energy excites electrons into the conduction band, and some empty states are left behind in the valence band. These partially filled bands make electron movement possible. In a metal, the energy gap is even smaller, and the Fermi level resides within either the conduction band or the valence band. Another possibility for a metal is that the E_V is above the E_C so that the two bands overlap, and there is no energy gap. In such a system, the Fermi level can be in any position. Since for the semiconductor, the Fermi-Dirac statistics are necessary to determine the electron populations, temperature is also a crucial factor. At a temperature of absolute-zero, all semiconductors would become insulators. For practical consideration, at room temperature, semiconductors have energy gaps ranging from ≈ 0.1 eV to ≈ 4 eV.

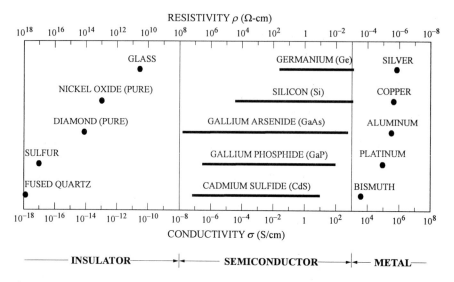

FIGURE I.1

A semiconductor is distinguished from the insulator and the metal by the range of resistivity (or conductivity) it spans. Note that, unlike the metal and insulator, each semiconductor can be doped to vary its resistivity. (After Ref. 1)

For a historic perspective, some common electronic devices with the years they were developed are shown in Fig. I.3. The earliest device, not necessarily made of semiconductor material, is probably the resistor, implied by Ohm's law back in 1826. Vacuum tubes started around 1904, and were the major electronic components in the early radio era through World War II. The real birth of the semiconductor industry was in 1947 with the invention of the bipolar transistor. Ever since, new semiconductor devices have been invented at quite a steady pace, although some are more commercially significant than others. Figure I.3 shows only the more common kinds. There are some devices whose development is too gradual to assign a milestone. An example is the solar cell. Starting from the mid-1970s, with the advent of MBE and MOCVD technologies, there are numerous heterojunction devices that are also omitted because it is too early for them to have an impact commercially.

Currently, there are more than 100 semiconductor devices. To include such a large collection, the hierarchy of semiconductor devices used in this guide needs to be clarified. This also explains why certain devices are put in separate chapters. Figure I.4 shows that, for example, the LED, laser, solar cell, and tunnel diode are all variations of a *p-n* junction. But since each of these is made for a special purpose, their designs consider different device physics, and their structures are very different. A person who wants information about a solar cell, which receives light and converts it into electrical power, does not have to understand how a *p-n* junction emits light in an LED. It is for these reasons that a total of 67 major devices are identified and put into individual chapters. For the next level of variation, the deviations are relatively minor and additional materials needed to describe them do not require separate chapters. These devices are attached to some of the major devices as "related devices." The total number of devices falling into this category is found to be 114. This, of course, will change with time and rearrangement might be necessary for future editions. It is intentional that this guide includes older devices that have become obsolete. Old information is important to avoid duplication of effort, and is often the ground for new concepts.

The word *complete* in the book title refers to the inclusion of all devices, to the best of the author's knowledge. It does not mean complete in covering details on every device. References are always given if the readers are interested in more in-depth studies. As a *guide*, this book presents only the key background, principles, and applications.

To help gain a better perspective on this large variety of devices, chapters are ordered according to their functions or structures, with group names assigned to describe them. This also provides a means for comparison among devices in the same group. These groups are:

1. Diodes: I–rectifiers
2. Diodes: II–negative resistance
3. Resistive devices
4. Capacitive devices
5. Two-terminal switches
6. Transistors: I–field-effect
7. Transistors: II–potential-effect
8. Transistors: III–hot-electron
9. Nonvolatile memories
10. Thyristors
11. Light sources
12. Photodetectors
13. Bistable optical devices
14. Other photonic devices
15. Sensors

While most of these group names are self-explanatory, a few need clarification. The name diode comes from vacuum tubes, and refers to a 2-element diode tube. Other vacuum tubes are the triode tube, tetrode tube, and pentode tube, with the number of active elements being 3, 4, and 5, respectively (see Appendix A1). Since in the diode tube, the cathode emits only one kind of carriers–electrons–the diode tube has asymmetric I-V behavior and is a rectifier. Although semiconductor diodes inherited the name, some of them actually do not have

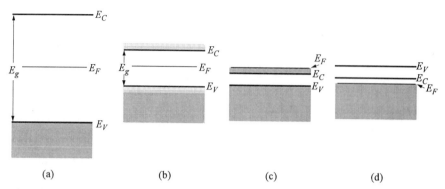

FIGURE I.2

Energy-band diagrams showing that (a) in an insulator, the bands are completely filled or completely empty, (b) in a semiconductor, both bands are partially filled, and in a metal, (c) the Fermi level resides within one of the bands, or (d) E_V is above E_C so that there is no energy gap. In (d), the E_F can be in any position.

rectifying characteristics. Examples are the tunnel diode and the Gunn diode. A more proper definition for a diode now is simply a two-terminal device having nonlinear DC characteristics.[2] Rectifiers are therefore only a subgroup of diodes. Another subgroup of diodes that are distinctively different from rectifiers are those having negative differential resistance. Within this group of negative-resistance devices, there are two types: one that has a negative dI/dV region, and the transit-time devices where the negative resistance is due to the small-signal current and voltage that are out of phase.

A switch, in semiconductor terms, is a device that has two states—a low-impedance state (on) and a high-impedance state (off). Switching between these two states can be controlled by voltage, current, temperature, or by a third terminal. A transistor, for example, is considered a three-terminal switch in digital circuits. Thyristors are also a special case of switch. They are included in a separate group from switches because they usually contain p-n-p-n layers, have more than two terminals, and are used mainly as power devices.

Unlike diode, transistor (transfer-resistor) was a new name coined at the beginning of the semiconductor era for the bipolar transistor, instead of keeping the old equivalent of triode. In the classification of devices, this book does not follow the common approach in literature to divide devices into bipolar and unipolar types. For transistors, the bipolar transistor has been used as a representative of the first type, and MOSFET and JFET of the second type. The reason behind that classification is for a bipolar transistor, the base current is due to one type of carrier while the emitter-collector current is of the opposite type; thus, both types of carriers are involved. For a MOSFET, the gate current is negligible, and the carriers in the channel are the only kind responsible for the current flow. The author, however, feels that the classification based on this

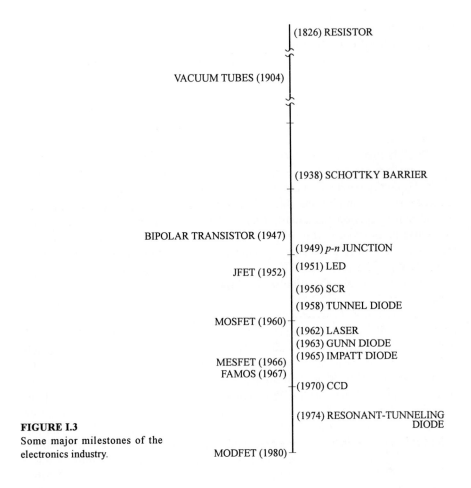

FIGURE I.3
Some major milestones of the
electronics industry.

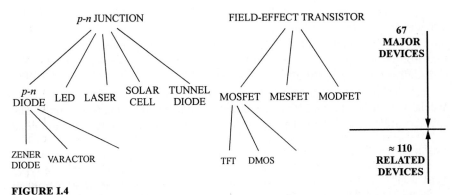

FIGURE I.4
Hierarchy of semiconductor devices. Major devices are included in individual chapters, and their
variations are included as "related devices."

bipolar-unipolar terminology is not clear, or maybe even incorrect. For example, in a bipolar transistor, the base current is a sort of leakage current. It is only a by-product of a base potential needed to modulate the emitter-collector current. If this base current is somehow made zero, the bipolar transistor would still work, and work even better. In fact, the main purpose of a heterojunction bipolar transistor is to suppress this base current, without affecting the main current. Next, let us consider an enhancement JFET. To turn the transistor on, the *p-n* junction gate is forward biased. This injects minority carriers into the channel. The JFET is therefore as "bipolar" as the bipolar transistor. This argument can also be extended to diodes. A *p-n* junction has been referred to as a bipolar device while a Schottky barrier as a unipolar device. For practical *p-n* junctions, they are usually one-sided in that one side is much more heavily doped than the other. A typical Si *p-n* junction has doping levels of 10^{20} cm^{-3} and 10^{16} cm^{-3}, and the ratio of the two types of current is $\approx 10^{-4}$. For a practical Schottky-barrier diode, even though the current is dominated by majority carriers, the minority-carrier current is not zero. It is a factor of $\approx 10^{-4}$–10^{-6} (injection efficiency) smaller. As seen from these diodes, the transition from a bipolar device to a unipolar device is not clear.

In this book, transistors are divided into three groups, following the notation used in Ref. 3. These are (1) field-effect transistor (FET), (2) potential-effect transistor (PET), and (3) hot-electron transistor (HET). The field effect is defined, originally by Shockley when the first field-effect transistor (JFET) was envisaged, as "modulation of a conducting channel by electric fields."[4] An FET differs from a PET in that its channel is coupled capacitively by transverse electric fields while in a PET, the channel's potential is accessed by a direct contact.[*] This distinction is illustrated in Fig. I.5. The capacitive coupling in an FET is via an insulator or a space-charge layer. A hot-electron transistor is a special case of PET, whose emitter-base junction is a heterostructure such that the emitted carriers in the base have high potential or kinetic energy (Fig. I.5(e)). Since a hot carrier has high velocity, HETs are expected to have higher intrinsic speed, higher current, and higher transconductance. One also notes that the energy-band diagrams of the FET and the PET (excluding HETs) are similar. This is because the way the channel is influenced, either capacitively for FET or directly for PET, is not indicated in these diagrams. One observation on FETs is that almost all have channel conduction by the drift process, and have a well-defined threshold voltage.

To achieve the goal of including this large variety of devices as a guide, a special format is created. First, each chapter is dedicated to one device only. The chapters are written to be independent, and readers can go directly to the intended

---

[*] FET and PET are defined in Ref. 3 differently by the editor (S. Sze) and by one of the contributors (S. Luryi). Sze's definition (pp. 3 and 6 in Ref. 3), adopted in this book, is based on the physical structure, while Luryi's definition (p. 400 in Ref. 3) is based on the current-control mechanism. In the latter definition, the same device can switch from an FET to a PET, depending on the bias regime.

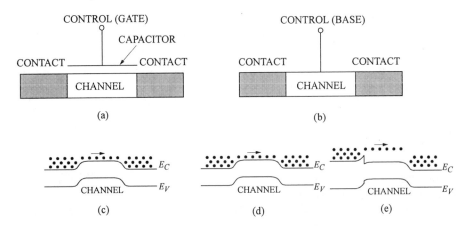

FIGURE I.5
Schematic structures of (a) FET and (b) PET. Energy-band diagrams of *n*-channel (c) FET, (d) PET, and (e) HET. Note that (c) and (d) are similar. HET is a special case of PET.

device to get an overview quickly by reading only a few pages. Second, each chapter consists of four main sections:

1. History
2. Structure
3. Characteristics
4. Applications

With these, the essential information about each device is given: When was it invented and by whom? (History) How is it made? (Structure) How does it work? (Characteristics) What is it for? (Applications) For more than half of the chapters, there is another section–5. Related Devices, to cover slightly different structures. This is necessary to account for all devices to meet the goal of completeness and yet not have more than the existing 67 chapters. This book is intended to be an engineering approach to understand semiconductor devices, giving a pragmatic overview. Because of its complete coverage, readers can also pick up the subtle differences that sometimes exist between devices. With this rigid format, the listing of sections .1–.4 are omitted from the Contents to avoid repetition in every chapter, with the exception of Chapter 1 as an example. In effect, only the device names are listed in the Contents.

The appendixes are extensive compared to those in other semiconductor-device books. Appendix A includes some non-semiconductor devices that one might encounter in this broad field. Appendix B covers the device physics and phenomena that are common to some devices, to avoid repetition. This appendix also makes up the lost opportunity in this book format to go over some

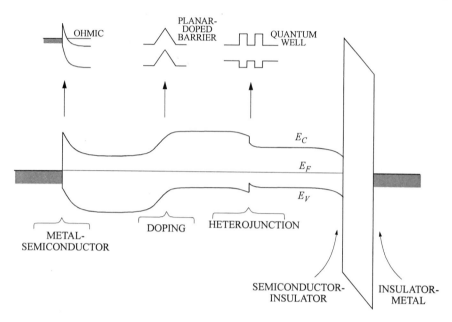

FIGURE I.6

Energy-band diagrams showing the basic device building blocks, or interfaces. Inserts indicate that ohmic contact, planar-doped barrier, and quantum well are special cases of Schottky barrier, doping interface, and heterojunction, respectively.

fundamental device physics. Appendix C covers the general applications of various device groups, again to avoid repetition in some chapters. Appendixes D and E are the more typical kind of semiconductor data and background information, but attempts have been made to collect as much information needed for a stand-alone handbook.

In the course of writing this book, several thoughts arose that are worth mentioning. Semiconductor devices can be viewed as consisting of device building blocks. In spite of the large number of devices, there are only a few building blocks, which are interfaces of two materials or doping types. These fundamental interfaces are all included in the energy-band diagram of the book cover, repeated here in Fig. I.6. They are, from left to right, a metal-semiconductor interface, doping interface, heterojunction, semiconductor-insulator interface, and an insulator-metal interface. The metal-semiconductor interface, known as the Schottky barrier, also includes the ohmic contact which is inevitable in every semiconductor device. The doping interface also includes the planar-doped barrier. The heterojunction is also the basis for quantum-well devices. A bipolar transistor, for example, is built of two *p-n* junctions. A

TABLE I.1
Current-conduction mechanisms of semiconductor devices.

Mechanisms	Examples
Drift	Resistor, most FETs
Diffusion	*p-n* junction, bipolar transistor
Thermionic emission	Schottky barrier, PDB diode
Tunneling	Tunnel diode, ohmic contact
Recombination	LED, *p-i-n* diode
Generation	Solar cell, photodetectors
Avalanche	IMPATT diode, Zener diode

MOSFET has two *p-n* junctions, one semiconductor-insulator interface, and one insulator-metal interface.

Since the compositions vary among different semiconductor devices, their current-conduction mechanisms also vary accordingly. All the current-conduction mechanisms are summarized in Table I.1 for an overview. These currents are due to drift, diffusion, thermionic emission, tunneling, recombination, generation, and avalanche.

Finally, we discuss what is meant by the recent, commonly used term high-speed device. Is it a device that has intrinsically fast response, or is it one that enables a high-speed circuit? This is important to clarify since different criterion calls for a different device design. Table I.2 summarizes the different parameters that are used to indicate the first-order estimate of the device speed, with a different amount of parasitics and loading taken into consideration. The fundamental parameter is the transit time, the time it takes for the carriers to travel between the source-drain or emitter-collector. Direct measurement of this parameter is extremely difficult. The next level is parameters deduced from two-port, small-signal S-parameter microwave measurement.[5] This is done with a single device, and thus not as a circuit. It is the highest frequency that can be

TABLE I.2
Parameters pertaining to the speed of a transistor. Using an FET as an example, C_G, C_{ip}, C_{out}, C_{run}, and C_{load} are the capacitances of the intrinsic gate, input parasitics, output, runner, and load, respectively.

Parameters	Considerations	Speed figure-of-merit of FET
Transit time	Intrinsic, no capacitance	g_m/C_G
S-para. meas. (f_T)	No output capacitance, no runner	$g_m/(C_G+C_{ip})$
(f_{max})	Optimized load, no runner	
Ring oscillator	Fan-out = 1, short runner	$g_m/(C_G+C_{ip}+C_{out})$
Real circuit	Multiple fan-outs, long runner, load capacitance	$g_m/(C_G+C_{ip}+C_{out}+C_{run}+C_{load})$

measured on the device, but certain parasitics are ignored. The cutoff frequency, for example, is a current-gain measurement. The output is shorted so that the output capacitance is not included. f_{max} includes the output capacitance but the load is matched to optimize the power transfer. The simplest circuit measurement is a ring oscillator. It is usually designed with a minimum fan-out of one, and minimum interconnect distance. A real circuit has much larger load capacitance as well as larger interconnect capacitance. From this viewpoint, if the circuit speed is to be optimized, the current drive or transconductance of a transistor is more important than the intrinsic response. It is possible to predict the ultimate circuit speed based on the transit time, microwave measurements, or ring-oscillator speed, but care has to be taken to account for realistic parasitics. For PETs, the parasitic resistance is also critical since the input current is much higher than that in FETs.

REFERENCES

1. S. M. Sze, *Semiconductor devices: Physics and technology,* Wiley, New York, 1985.
2. *The new IEEE standard dictionary of electrical and electronics terms,* 5th Ed., IEEE, 1993.
3. S. M. Sze, Ed., *High-speed semiconductor devices,* Wiley, New York, 1990.
4. W. Shockley, "A unipolar field-effect transistor," *Proc. IRE,* **40,** 1365 (1952).
5. M. Banu, private communications.

CHAPTER

1

p-n
JUNCTION
DIODE

1.1 HISTORY

The *p-n* junction diode is among the oldest semiconductor devices. It was mainly used as mixers in the 1940s during World War II. The theory for the *p-n* diode was developed later by Shockley in 1949,[1] and it was instrumental in the invention of the bipolar junction transistor. The theory was subsequently refined by Sah et al.[2] and Moll.[3] More recent review articles on the device can be found in Refs. 4–7. The *p-n* junction has been the most common rectifier used in the electronics industry. It also serves as a very important fundamental building block for many other devices.

1.2 STRUCTURE

The early version of the structure was made by pressing a metal wire onto the surface of a semiconductor. A junction was then formed by passing a pulse of current through the wire and semiconductor. It is believed that doping is diffused from the metal wire as shown in Fig. 1.1(a). Such a structure is referred to as the point contact and the metal wire as a cat's whisker. (A point contact has the characteristics of either a *p-n* junction or a Schottky barrier, depending on the forming process. See Section 3.2.) Another old process is the alloy method in which a metal containing the appropriate impurity is placed onto the semiconductor surface. Heating above the eutectic temperature would form an alloy with a thin heavily doped region at the interface. This technique, along with

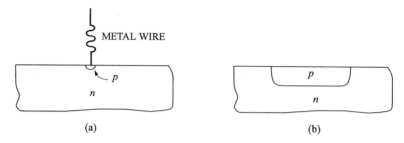

FIGURE 1.1
The cross-section structure of a *p-n* junction as in (a) point contact and (b) planar technology.

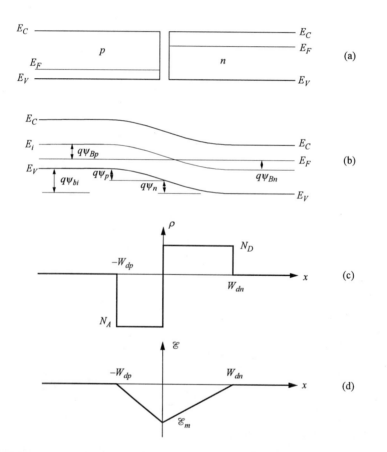

FIGURE 1.2
Formation of *p-n* junction by bringing (a) isolated materials into (b) intimate contact. The potential variation is a result of (c) charge distribution, or (d) field distribution in the depletion layer.

the point contact, is no longer used. A planar structure is shown in Fig. 1.1(b). The surface doping is usually introduced by ion implantation. Diffusion at high temperature can also be used, and the impurity source can be in a carrying gas or deposited material. A less common technique is to incorporate doping during epitaxial growth. The area of the diode is usually defined by an opening in an insulator layer.

1.3 CHARACTERISTICS

A *p-n* junction can be viewed as isolated *p*-type and *n*-type materials brought into intimate contact (Fig. 1.2). Being abundant in *n*-type material, electrons diffuse to the *p*-type material. The same process happens for holes from the *p*-type material. This flow of charges sets up an electric field that starts to hinder further diffusion until an equilibrium is struck. The energy-band diagram under equilibrium is shown in Fig. 1.2(b). (Notice that when $N_A \neq N_D$, where E_i crosses E_F does not coincide with the metallurgical junction.) Since the overall charge has to be conserved, it follows that for an abrupt (step) junction,

$$W_{dp}N_A = W_{dn}N_D \tag{1.1}$$

as shown in Fig. 1.2(c). An important parameter is the built-in potential ψ_{bi}. According to Fig. 1.2(b), it is the sum of ψ_{Bn} and ψ_{Bp}, given by

$$\psi_{bi} = \psi_{Bn} + \psi_{Bp} = \frac{kT}{q} \ln\left(\frac{N_D N_A}{n_i^2}\right) \tag{1.2}$$

which is the total band bending at equilibrium by definition.

Under bias, the following can be obtained using the Poisson equation with appropriate boundary conditions,

$$W_{dn} = \sqrt{\frac{2\varepsilon_s \psi_n}{qN_D}}$$

$$W_{dp} = \sqrt{\frac{2\varepsilon_s \psi_p}{qN_A}} \tag{1.3}$$

$$|\mathscr{E}_m| = \frac{qN_A W_{dp}}{\varepsilon_s} = \frac{qN_D W_{dn}}{\varepsilon_s} \tag{1.4}$$

$$\psi_T = \psi_p + \psi_n = (\psi_{bi} - V_f) \text{ or } (\psi_{bi} + V_r) = \frac{1}{2}\mathscr{E}_m(W_{dn} + W_{dp}) \ . \tag{1.5}$$

Equation (1.5) can be interpreted as the area under the field-distance curve in Fig. 1.2(d). The partition of band bending and depletion width between the n- and p-regions can be related by

$$\frac{W_{dn}}{W_{dn} + W_{dp}} = \frac{\psi_n}{\psi_T} = \frac{N_A}{N_A + N_D}$$

$$\frac{W_{dp}}{W_{dn} + W_{dp}} = \frac{\psi_p}{\psi_T} = \frac{N_D}{N_A + N_D} \ . \tag{1.6}$$

It can further be shown that

$$W_{dp} + W_{dn} = \sqrt{\frac{2\varepsilon_s}{q}\left(\frac{N_A + N_D}{N_A N_D}\right)}\psi_T \ . \tag{1.7}$$

In practical devices, one side usually has a doping concentration much higher than the other, and the junction can be treated as a one-sided junction. The depletion width and potential variation in the heavily doped side can then be neglected.

Figure 1.3, which shows the energy-band diagram and the carrier concentrations under bias, is used to derive the I-V characteristics. The forward current of a p-n junction under bias is determined by diffusion of injected minority carriers. The carrier concentration at the edge of the depletion region is given by

$$n_p(W_{dp}) = n_{po}\exp\left(\frac{qV_f}{kT}\right)$$

$$p_n(W_{dn}) = p_{no}\exp\left(\frac{qV_f}{kT}\right) \ . \tag{1.8}$$

Combining the continuity equation with the current equation, assuming steady state, zero generation rate and zero drift current, one gets

$$D_n\frac{d^2 n_p}{dx^2} - \frac{n_p - n_{po}}{\tau_n} = 0$$

$$D_p\frac{d^2 p_n}{dx^2} - \frac{p_n - p_{no}}{\tau_p} = 0 \tag{1.9}$$

where $x = 0$ now corresponds to the edge of the depletion region. (Notice the x-coordinate in Fig. 1.3(c).) Solving these differential equations gives the minority-carrier profiles

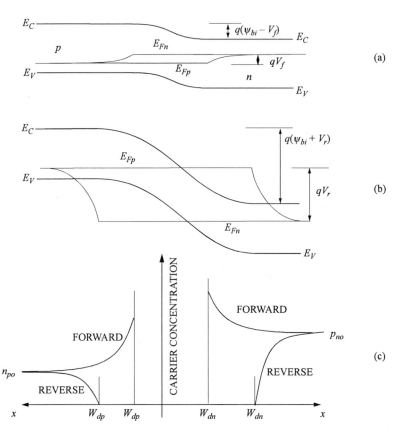

FIGURE 1.3
Energy-band diagram showing a *p-n* junction (a) under forward bias (positive voltage applied to *p*-type material and (b) under reverse bias. (c) Minority-carrier concentration profiles under forward and reverse bias.

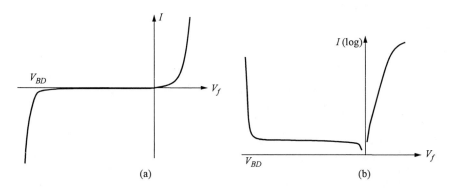

FIGURE 1.4
I-V characteristics of a *p-n* junction in (a) linear current scale and (b) logarithmic current scale.

$$n_p(x) = n_{po} + n_{po} \left[\exp\left(\frac{qV_f}{kT}\right) - 1 \right] \exp\left(\frac{-x}{L_n}\right) , \tag{1.10}$$

$$p_n(x) = p_{no} + p_{no} \left[\exp\left(\frac{qV_f}{kT}\right) - 1 \right] \exp\left(\frac{-x}{L_p}\right) . \tag{1.11}$$

The two diffusion currents give a total of

$$J = q \left(\frac{D_p p_{no}}{L_p} + \frac{D_n n_{po}}{L_n} \right) \left[\exp\left(\frac{qV_f}{kT}\right) - 1 \right]$$

$$= q n_i^2 \left(\frac{D_p}{L_p N_D} + \frac{D_n}{L_n N_A} \right) \left[\exp\left(\frac{qV_f}{kT}\right) - 1 \right] . \tag{1.12}$$

At each side of the junction the diffusion current is a function of distance. It maximizes at $x = 0$ where Eq. (1.12) is obtained. Since the current has to be continuous, the diffusion current is supplemented by the majority-carrier drift current. This equation is also valid for reverse bias when V_f is negative. In cases where the thickness of the p-type or n-type material is less than the diffusion length L_p or L_n, the latter parameter should be replaced by the corresponding thickness in Eq. (1.12) and thereby increasing the current.

The I-V characteristics described by Eq. (1.12) is shown in Fig. 1.4. In both the linear current scale and the logarithmic current scale, additional features at high forward bias and reversed bias are to be noticed. In the forward direction, currents rises exponentially with V_f until the slope becomes more gradual. This can be due to high-level injection of carriers such that the applied voltage is no longer totally developed across the depletion region. Series resistance, R_s, can also cause the same effect. At high reverse bias, breakdown can occur due to impact ionization (see Appendix B3) or Zener tunneling. These mechanisms can be separated by temperature dependence. At higher temperature, the ionization rate decreases and the breakdown voltage due to avalanche multiplication increases. The opposite dependence holds for Zener breakdown. Normally avalanche multiplication occurs first, with breakdown voltage shown in Fig. B3.3.

An additional current component besides Eq. (1.12) is due to recombination/generation through mid-gap states within the depletion region (see Appendix B2). This mechanism gives rise to a current described by

$$J = \frac{q n_i W_d}{2\tau} \left[\exp\left(\frac{qV_f}{2kT}\right) - 1 \right] . \tag{1.13}$$

If the term $q n_i W_d / 2\tau$ is comparable to or larger than the pre-exponential factor in Eq. (1.12), the current for small V_f as well as the reverse current will be increased.

A common use of the *p-n* junction requires it to switch between the on-state and the off-state. Because of minority-carrier storage under forward bias, the immediate response to reverse bias is shown in Fig. 1.5, with $I_r = V_r/R_s$,

$$t_d \approx \tau \ln\left(1 + \frac{I_f}{I_r}\right) , \tag{1.14}$$

$$\mathrm{erf}\sqrt{\frac{t_{tr}}{\tau}} + \frac{\exp\left(-t_{tr}/\tau\right)}{\sqrt{\pi t_{tr}/\tau}} = 1 + 0.1\left(\frac{I_r}{I_f}\right) . \tag{1.15}$$

This reverse recovery limits a *p-n* junction to about 1 GHz operation. In order to increase the frequency response, the carrier lifetime τ can be intentionally shortened by introducing impurities for recombination. The penalty for this is an increased leakage current. An alternative approach is to use a step-recovery diode (Section 1.5.2).

The equivalent circuit for a *p-n* junction is shown in Fig. 1.6. Since capacitance is defined by dQ/dV, the depletion-layer capacitance C_d is associated with the depletion-layer charge, while the diffusion capacitance C_D is related to injected carriers. The C_D is significant only under forward bias conditions and is proportional to the forward current, given by

$$C_D = \frac{q^2}{2kT}(L_p p_{no} + L_n n_{po})\exp\left(\frac{qV_f}{kT}\right) . \tag{1.16}$$

The C_d is determined by the depletion width and for a one-sided step junction,

$$C_d = \frac{\varepsilon_s}{W_d} = \sqrt{\frac{q\varepsilon_s N}{2(\psi_{bi} + V_r)}} \tag{1.17}$$

where N is from the lightly doped side. A measurement of $1/C^2$ vs. V_r, as shown in Fig. 1.7, can extrapolate ψ_{bi} and its slope can determine the doping

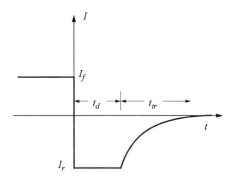

FIGURE 1.5
Transient current characteristics of a *p-n* junction when switched from forward to reverse direction. t_d and t_{tr} are called delay time and transition time, respectively.

concentration (or area). This technique can be extended to obtain nonuniform doping profile,

$$\frac{dC_d^{-2}}{dV_r} = \frac{2}{q\varepsilon_s N(x)} \quad . \tag{1.18}$$

1.4 APPLICATIONS

1. Because it is the most common rectifier, a *p-n* junction has many circuit applications. See Appendix C1–Applications of Rectifiers.
2. Many devices are special forms of *p-n* junction. Examples are LED, laser, solar cell, and photodiode. A *p-n* junction also serves as a building block for many other devices such as the bipolar transistor, MOSFET, junction FET, etc.
3. Due to the non-linear, exponential nature of the current, the *p-n* junction can be used as a varistor.
4. The variable depletion capacitance at reverse bias can be utilized as a varactor.
5. A *p-n* junction is a very common protection device for electro-static discharge (ESD). It discharges a voltage surge when it exceeds a certain value comparable to the built-in potential.
6. A *p-n* junction is a robust device and is a good choice for a diode required in power electronics.
7. The *p-n* junction can be used to isolate devices or regions of semiconductors. An example can be found in the tub isolation for CMOS circuits.

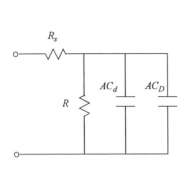

FIGURE 1.6
Equivalent circuit of a *p-n* junction. *A* is the area of the diode.

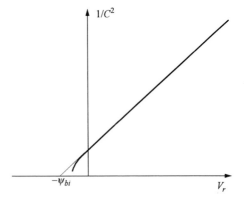

FIGURE 1.7
A plot of capacitance $(1/C^2)$ under reverse bias yields ψ_{bi} and doping concentration (or area).

8. The well-behaved forward characteristics of a *p-n* diode enable it to be used as a temperature sensor. In operation, a constant current is applied and the voltage is monitored. This forward voltage drop is a fairly linear function of temperature. GaAs diodes can be good sensors in a wide temperature range from a few degree K to ≈ 400 K, and Si diode from ≈ 20 K.

1.5 RELATED DEVICES

1.5.1 Zener Diode

A Zener diode has a well-controlled breakdown voltage, called Zener voltage, and sharp breakdown characteristics in the reverse bias regime. In spite of the name, the breakdown can be due to either impact ionization or Zener tunneling. Zener breakdown is caused by quantum-mechanical tunneling of carriers between the conduction band and the valence band (see Appendix B7–Tunneling). It occurs in junctions with higher doping concentrations and the critical field required is approximately 1 MV/cm. A Zener diode is usually used to establish a fixed reference voltage.

1.5.2 Step-Recovery Diode

The step-recovery diode is sometimes called a fast-recovery diode, a snap-off diode, or snap-back diode. The response of a standard *p-n* junction is limited by the minority-carrier storage, with the reverse recovery represented by Fig. 1.5. A step-recovery diode has a special doping profile such that the field confines the injected carriers much closer to the vicinity of the junction. This results in a much shorter transition time t_{tr} (but with the same delay time t_d). The sharp turn-off of current approaches a square waveform which contains rich harmonics, and is often used in applications of harmonic generation and pulse shaping.

1.5.3 Anisotype Heterojunction

An anisotype heterojunction is a junction not only of opposite types, but also of different semiconductor materials. The structure requires good lattice match between the two materials, and Ge–GaAs can be used as an example.[8] The distinct features are the discontinuity in the conduction band ΔE_C and the valence band ΔE_V as shown in Fig. 1.8. These values can be determined graphically to be

$$\Delta E_C = q\,(\chi_1 - \chi_2) \tag{1.19}$$

$$\Delta E_V = (E_{g2} - E_{g1}) - \Delta E_C \ . \tag{1.20}$$

The static characteristic described by Eqs. (1.1)–(1.7) have to be modified by the two dielectric constants K_1 and K_2 in the two materials. Specifically,

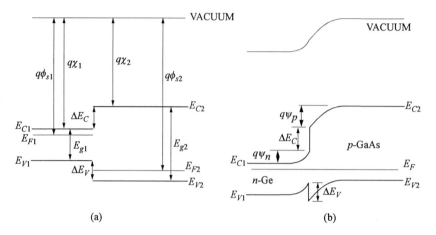

FIGURE 1.8
(a) Energy-band diagram of two isolated different semiconductor materials with opposite types. (b) Example of an anisotype heterojunction between n-type Ge and p-type GaAs. (After Ref. 8)

$K_1 \mathscr{E}_1 = K_2 \mathscr{E}_2$ has to be satisfied at the interface. The potential variation across the n-type and p-type materials are given by

$$\frac{\psi_n}{\psi_T} = \frac{K_2 N_A}{K_1 N_D + K_2 N_A}$$

$$\frac{\psi_p}{\psi_T} = \frac{K_1 N_D}{K_1 N_D + K_2 N_A} \quad . \tag{1.21}$$

According to Fig. 1.8(b), ψ_T at equilibrium is the difference between the two work functions, $q\phi_{s2} - q\phi_{s1}$.

The current conduction, however, can be either diffusion limited or thermionic-emission limited. In the example shown in Fig. 1.8, the barrier for holes is similar to a standard p-n junction, and hole transport from GaAs to Ge is diffusion limited. Under forward bias, this component is similar to a homojunction

$$J_p = \frac{q n_i^2 D_p}{L_p N_D} \left[\exp\left(\frac{qV_f}{kT}\right) - 1 \right] \quad . \tag{1.22}$$

The barrier for electrons is increased by ΔE_C and the current is greatly reduced. Unlike a homostructure p-n junction in which current is dominated by diffusion current in the lightly doped side, an anisotype heterojunction usually favors injection of carriers from the material of larger energy gap. Other current components are due to tunneling and recombination arising from a non-ideal interface. The suppression of one type of carriers improves the injection efficiency, which makes it beneficial for the emitter-base junction of a bipolar transistor.[9] Other applications include photodetectors in which a local absorption coefficient can be optimized.

1.5.4 Varactor

The word varactor comes from variable reactor. A varactor, also called a varactor diode or varicap (variable capacitance) diode, is in principle any two-terminal device whose capacitance varies with the DC bias. In practice, a *p-n* junction is the most common structure. A Schottky-barrier diode can also perform the same function, and is used especially in ultra-high-speed operations.

When a *p-n* junction is under a reverse bias, the depletion layer widens, and its capacitance changes according to Eq. (1.17). Forward bias is to be avoided from excessive current which is undesirable for any capacitor. The dependence of capacitance on the DC reverse bias is determined by the doping profile near the junction. It can be described by the form

$$C = C_1 \left(\psi_{bi} + V_r \right)^{-s} . \tag{1.23}$$

For a one-sided junction, if the profile of the lighter doping is approximated by

$$N(x) = C_2 x^m , \tag{1.24}$$

it can be shown that[6]

$$s = \frac{1}{m+2} . \tag{1.25}$$

For a one-sided step profile, $m = 0$ and $s = 1/2$. For a linearly graded junction, $m = 1$ and $s = 1/3$. If $m < 0$, the junction is said to be hyper-abrupt. Specific cases of interest are $m = -1, -3/2, -5/3$ and $s = 1, 2, 3$, respectively.

The applications of a varactor are in filters, oscillators, tuning circuits of radio and TV receivers, parametric amplifiers, and automatic frequency control circuits.

REFERENCES

1. W. Shockley, "The theory of *p-n* junctions in semiconductors and *p-n* junction transistors," *Bell Syst. Tech. J.*, **28**, 435 (1949).
2. C. T. Sah, R. N. Noyce and W. Shockley, "Carrier generation and recombination in *p-n* junctions and *p-n* junction characteristics," *Proc. IRE*, **45**, 1228 (1957).
3. J. L. Moll, "The evolution of the theory for the voltage-current characteristic of *p-n* junctions," *Proc. IRE*, **46**, 1076 (1958).

4. A. Nussbaum, "The theory of semiconducting junctions," in R. K. Willardson and A. C. Beer, Eds., *Semiconductors and semimetals*, Vol. 15, p. 39, Academic Press, New York, 1981.

5. M. P. Shaw, "Properties of junctions and barriers," in C. Hilsum, Vol. Ed., T. S. Moss, Ser. Ed., *Handbook on semiconductors*, Vol. 4, p. 1, North-Holland, Amsterdam, 1981.

6. S. M. Sze, *Physics of semiconductor devices*, 2nd Ed., Wiley, New York, 1981.

7. E. S. Yang, *Microelectronic devices*, McGraw-Hill, New York, 1988.

8. R. L. Anderson, "Experiments on Ge–GaAs heterojunction," *Solid-State Electron.*, **5**, 341 (1962).

9. H. Kroemer, "Theory of a wide-gap emitter for transistors," *Proc. IRE*, **45**, 1535 (1957).

CHAPTER
2

p-i-n
DIODE

2.1 HISTORY

The *p-i-n* diode is a refinement of the *p-n* junction for special applications. After the *p-n* junction was developed in the late 1940s, the *p-i-n* diode was first used as a low-frequency, high-power rectifier in 1952 by Hall,[1] and in 1956 by Prince.[2] The presence of an intrinsic layer can substantially increase the breakdown voltage for high-voltage application. This intrinsic layer also provides interesting properties when the device is operated at high frequencies in the microwave and radio-wave range. It was not until 1958 that the device started to be used in microwave applications by Uhlir.[3] More details on this device can be found in Refs. 4–9.

2.2 STRUCTURE

A *p-i-n* diode consists of an intrinsic layer sandwiched between the opposite types of a *p-n* junction. The intrinsic layer has a very low concentration of either *n*-type or *p*-type in the order of 10^{13} cm^{-3}, and a resistivity in the order of kΩ-cm. The intrinsic-layer thickness (x_I) ranges between 10 μm to 200 μm. The outside *p*- and *n*-layers are usually heavily doped. As shown in Fig. 2.1, the *p-i-n* diode can be realized as a planar structure or a mesa structure, both fabricated on degenerate substrate material. In the planar structure, an intrinsic epitaxial film is grown and the p^+-region is introduced by either diffusion or ion implantation. A mesa structure has epitaxially grown layers with dopants incorporated, and is capable of higher-frequency operation because the intrinsic layer can be made thinner with better control. Isolation of the device is achieved by mesa etching and

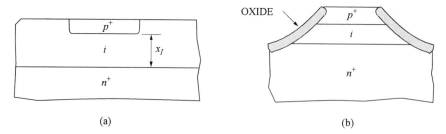

FIGURE 2.1
A *p-i-n* diode with (a) planar structure and (b) mesa structure.

surface passivation such as oxidation. The advantages of a mesa structure are reduced fringing capacitance and inductance, and improved surface breakdown voltage. The substrate material for the *p-i-n* diode has been almost exclusively silicon until the early 1980s when GaAs was also studied.

2.3 CHARACTERISTICS

The special feature of a *p-i-n* diode is a wide intrinsic layer that provides unique properties such as low capacitance, high breakdown voltage with reverse bias, and most interestingly, carrier storage for microwave applications with forward bias. Near zero or at low reverse bias, the lightly doped intrinsic layer starts to be fully depleted (Fig. 2.2(c)), and the capacitance is given by

$$C = \frac{\varepsilon_s A}{x_I} \ .$$

(2.1)

Once fully depleted, its capacitance is independent of reverse bias. Since there is little net charge within the intrinsic layer, the electric field is constant (Fig. 2.2(d)) and the reverse breakdown voltage is given by

$$V_{BD} = \mathscr{E}_{BD} x_I \ .$$

(2.2)

For silicon, the breakdown field $\mathscr{E}_{BD}$ is approximately 2×10^5 V/cm. These two equations show that the parameter x_I controls the trade-off between frequency response (from capacitance) and power (from maximum voltage).

When the *p-i-n* diode is under forward bias, both types of carriers are injected into the intrinsic layer, and the carrier profiles are shown in Fig. 2.2(f). It is usually assumed that within the intrinsic layer, the electron and hole concentrations are the same ($p_I = n_I$), and that they are uniform within the intrinsic layer. The current conduction is through recombination,

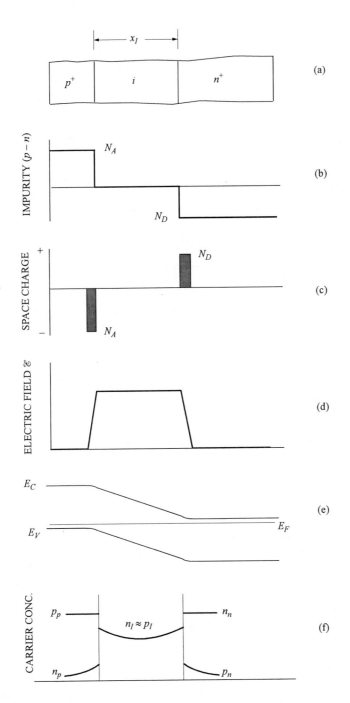

FIGURE 2.2
p-i-n diode shown in (a) structure cross-section, (b) impurity profile, (c) space charge distribution, (d) electric field, (e) energy-band diagram at equilibrium, and (f) carrier concentrations under forward bias.

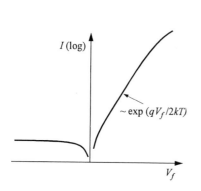

FIGURE 2.3
DC *I-V* characteristics of a *p-i-n* diode.

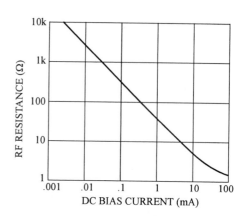

FIGURE 2.4
Typical RF resistance as a function of DC forward current. (After Ref. 5)

$$J_f = \int_0^{x_I} qU dx$$

$$= \frac{qn_I x_I}{\tau} \quad .$$

$$(2.3)$$

The carrier lifetime τ is a critical parameter in designing a *p-i-n* diode. The relationship of n_I to applied voltage is complicated, and the final *I-V* relationship is given here without proof [9–11]

$$J_f = \frac{4qn_i D_a F_L}{x_I} \exp\left(\frac{qV_f}{2kT}\right) \quad .$$

$$(2.4)$$

The parameter F_L is a further function of x_I and τ, and it has a value between 0.01 and 0.3. D_a is called the ambipolar diffusion coefficient and is given by

$$D_a = \frac{n_I + p_I}{\dfrac{n_I}{D_p} + \dfrac{p_I}{D_n}}$$

$$\approx \frac{2D_p D_n}{D_p + D_n} \quad .$$

$$(2.5)$$

The forward current is shown in Fig. 2.3. The ideality factor of 2 is a characteristic of recombination current.

A similar equation can be obtained from standard recombination/generation consideration which can provide some physical insight. The recombination current within a depletion region is given by

$$J_{re} = \frac{qx_I n_i}{2\tau} \exp\left(\frac{qV_f}{2kT}\right) \tag{2.6}$$

(see Appendix B2). Assuming that x_I is comparable to the ambipolar diffusion length,

$$x_I \approx \sqrt{D_a \tau} \quad , \quad \tau \approx \frac{x_I^2}{D_a} \quad . \tag{2.7}$$

Substitution of τ into Eq. (2.6) gives

$$J_{re} \approx \frac{qn_i D_a}{2x_I} \exp\left(\frac{qV_f}{2kT}\right) \quad . \tag{2.8}$$

This result is similar to Eq. (2.4).

It should be noted that since the *p-i-n* diode is similar to a *p-n* junction diode, the diffusion current component should also be considered. In practice, this component is small since both regions surrounding the intrinsic layers are heavily doped. High N_A and N_D result in small diffusion current, due to the relationship

$$J = qn_i^2 \left(\frac{D_p}{L_p N_D} + \frac{D_n}{L_n N_A}\right)\left[\exp\left(\frac{qV_f}{kT}\right) - 1\right] \quad . \tag{2.9}$$

The most interesting phenomenon for a *p-i-n* diode, however, is for small signals at high frequencies ($> 1/(2\pi\tau)$) at which the stored carriers within the intrinsic layer are not completely swept by the RF signal or by recombination. At these frequencies there is no rectification or distortion and the *p-i-n* diode behaves like a pure resistor whose value is solely determined by the superimposed DC bias or current. This dynamic RF resistance is simply given by

$$R_{RF} = \rho \frac{x_I}{A}$$

$$= \frac{x_I}{qn_I(\mu_n + \mu_p)A}$$

$$= \frac{x_I^2}{J_f \tau (\mu_n + \mu_p)A} \quad . \tag{2.10}$$

Here Eq. (2.3) has been assumed for J_f. The RF resistance is controlled by the DC current. Typical characteristics are shown in Fig. 2.4.

For modulation and switching applications, even the mean bias point can vary with time. The upper limit of this modulation frequency is determined by the reverse recovery characteristics. When a *p-i-n* diode is switched from forward bias to reverse bias abruptly, the stored charges continue to contribute to a large reverse current until they are fully drained away (Fig. 2.5). The reverse current is determined by the series resistance R_s ($I_r = V_r/R_s$), and the delay time t_d is given by

$$ t_d = \tau \ln\left(1 + \frac{I_f}{I_r}\right) . \tag{2.11} $$

The transition time t_{tr} is a complicated function of the doping profile and diode geometry. This reverse recovery time is the sum of t_d and t_{tr} and it puts an upper limit on the rate at which the quiescent bias point can be switched.

2.4 APPLICATIONS

1. RF switching: The RF resistance of a *p-i-n* diode is controlled by the quiescent bias. This feature makes it practical as a circuit, shown in Fig. 2.6, called a series switch. When the diode is forward biased it is considered a short. At zero or reverse bias, it is considered a capacitor or an open circuit.
2. Attenuation and modulation: Because the RF resistance is a continuous function of quiescent bias, it can be varied to attenuate and modulate the RF signal. The modulation frequency is limited by the reverse recovery given in Eq. (2.11). RF switching is an extreme case of attenuation and modulation.

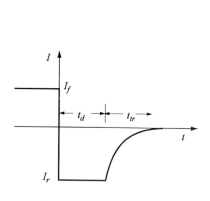

FIGURE 2.5
Reverse recovery characteristics of *p-i-n* diode. $I_r = V_r/R_s$.

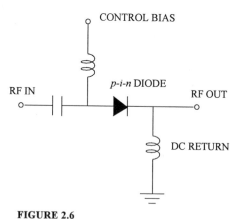

FIGURE 2.6
A simple circuit for series switch. This circuit can be used for RF switching as well as attenuation.[5]

3. Phase shifting: Phase shifting of an RF signal can be achieved by using transmission lines of different lengths. The *p-i-n* diodes can be used as switches for selecting these transmission lines.

4. Limiter: As mentioned before, at RF frequencies, a *p-i-n* diode behaves like a pure resistor. However, this is valid only when the RF signal is below a critical level. Above this level, the RF resistance drops, similar to that of the DC resistance. This property enables it to be used for protection of radar receivers, when it is connected in parallel, against excessive transmitter power.

5. Power rectifier: Due to the thick intrinsic layer, a *p-i-n* diode has a high breakdown voltage and can be used as high power rectifier.

6. Photodetector: For a photodetector, a wide region with a built-in field is advantageous such that light can be completely absorbed within this region. A *p-i-n* structure is used as a nuclear-radiation detector and is one of the most common photodetectors (see Chapter 50).

REFERENCES

1. R. N. Hall, "Power rectifiers and transistors," *Proc. IRE*, **40**, 1512 (1952).
2. M. B. Prince, "Diffused *p-n* junction silicon rectifiers," *Bell Syst. Tech. J.*, **35**, 661 (1956).
3. A. Uhlir, Jr., "The potential of semiconductor diodes in high-frequency communications," *Proc. IRE*, **46**, 1099 (1958).
4. P. N. Robson, "Microwave receivers," in T. S. Moss, Ser. Ed., C. Hilsum, Vol. Ed., *Handbook on semiconductors*, North-Holland, Amsterdam, 1981.
5. A. G. Milnes, *Semiconductor devices and integrated electronics*, Van Nostrand, New York, 1980.
6. J. F. White, *Microwave semiconductor engineering*, Van Nostrand Reinhold, New York, 1982.
7. J. F. White, "Semiconductor control devices: pin diodes," in K. Chang. Ed., *Handbook of microwave and optical components*, Vol. 2, Wiley, New York, 1990.
8. F. F. Mazda, Ed., *Electronics engineer's reference book*, Butterworths, London, 1989.
9. P. D. Taylor, *Thyristor design and realization*, Wiley, New York, 1987.
10. A. Herlet, "The forward characteristic of silicon power rectifiers at high current densities," *Solid-State Electron.*, **11**, 717 (1968).
11. S. C. Choo, "Effect of carrier lifetime on the forward characteristics of high-power devices," *IEEE Trans. Electron Dev.*, **ED-17**, 647 (1970).

CHAPTER
3

SCHOTTKY-BARRIER DIODE

3.1 HISTORY

The metal-semiconductor (MS) junction is more commonly known as the Schottky-barrier diode. It is sometimes called the surface-barrier diode. Due to the energy-band discontinuity at the interface, injected carriers possess excess energy and the structure is also referred to as a hot-carrier diode or a hot-electron diode. An MS junction is also a useful building block for many other devices. A special type of MS junction is the ohmic contact where the semiconductor is heavily doped. Obviously ohmic contacts are required for every semiconductor device because the final conductor at the chip level is always a metal.

The metal-semiconductor system is among the oldest semiconductor devices. Application of the device can be traced to before 1900. The realization of a potential barrier resulting from space charge in the semiconductor surface was initiated in 1938 by Schottky,[1] and by Mott[2] independently. The formulation of the thermionic-emission theory was established by Bethe in 1942.[3] This theory was later refined by Crowell and Sze in 1966.[4] The theory of surface states developed by Bardeen in 1947 was instrumental for better understanding of experimental results.[5] The use of silicide in place of metal on silicon substrates was pioneered by Lepselter and coworkers in 1968.[6,7] The epitaxial silicide process developed by Tung in 1984 provides new insight into intrinsic metal–semiconductor properties.[8] In-depth treatment of the Schottky-barrier structure can be found in Refs. 9–14.

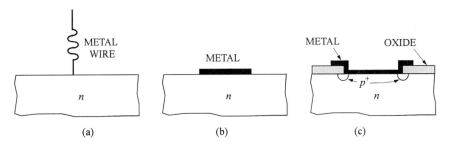

FIGURE 3.1
Schottky-barrier diode in the form of (a) point contact, (b) deposited metal, and (c) deposited metal with oxide isolation and diffusion guard ring.

3.2 STRUCTURE

The early version of the Schottky diode was in the form of a point contact (Fig. 3.1) where a metal wire, called a cat's whisker, is pressed against a clean semiconductor surface. (A point contact has the characteristics of either a Schottky barrier or a *p-n* junction, depending on the forming process.) Such a structure was unreliable and not reproducible, and was subsequently replaced by vacuum-deposited metal. A diffused guard ring shown in Fig. 3.1(c) is often used to avoid leakage and breakdown effects caused by the high electric field at the perimeter of the diode. For silicon substrates, metallic silicides can also be used in place of the metals.

A critical step in fabricating a Schottky-barrier diode is to prepare a clean surface for an intimate contact of the metal. In manufacturing, the surface is cleaned chemically. Experimentalists have also explored cleaved surfaces, as well as cleaning by back-sputtering in vacuum. The metal is usually deposited in vacuum, either by evaporation or sputtering. Chemical deposition is gaining popularity, especially for refractory metals. Plating can also be used but contamination from the solution is not controllable. Silicides on silicon substrates are usually made by metal deposition, followed by heat treatment to form the silicides. Such a system can be potentially more ideal because the reaction consumes silicon and the silicide–semiconductor interface propagates below the original surface. One advantage of a Schottky structure is the low temperature processing. The need for high temperature steps in impurity diffusion or impurity activation after ion implantation can be avoided.

3.3 CHARACTERISTICS

The formation of a Schottky-barrier junction is shown by the energy-band diagrams in Fig. 3.2. Assuming an ideal interface, the barrier height should be given by

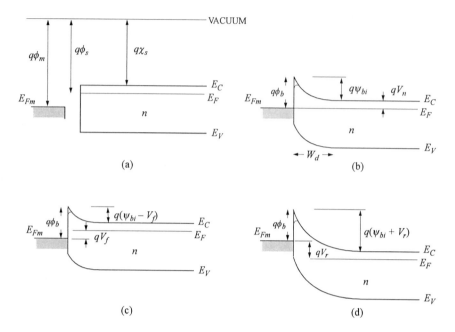

FIGURE 3.2

Energy-band diagram for metal-semiconductor structure. (a) Isolated metal and n-semiconductor. (b) Connected and under equilibrium. (c) Under forward bias (positive voltage applied to the metal for n-type substrate). (d) Under reverse bias. Also shown are rounded, reduced barrier heights due to image-force lowering.

$$\phi_b = \phi_m - \chi_s \ .$$ (3.1)

Experimentally, such a relationship is seldom realized exactly. The discrepancy is not yet fully understood. Presently, a few proposals exist, considering (1) an insulating layer at the interface (similar to that of Fig. 3.9), (2) surface traps, (3) metal-induced gap states, and (4) structure-dependent interface dipoles. As a result, the barrier formation has a weaker dependence than Eq. (3.1) on the metal work function. Typical barrier heights of metals and silicides on n-type semiconductors are listed in Table 3.1. Their corresponding barrier heights on p-type substrates, even with the above imperfections, are given by

$$q\left(\phi_{bn} + \phi_{bp}\right) = E_g \ .$$ (3.2)

This relationship is experimentally observed. The depletion width is given by

$$W_d = \sqrt{\frac{2\varepsilon_s\left(\psi_{bi} + V_r\right)}{qN}}$$ (3.3)

and the corresponding capacitance is

TABLE 3.1
Barrier heights for metals and silicides on *n*-type semiconductors ($q\phi_{bn}$ in eV) at 300 K (* at 77 K).[12] (#)[15] Barrier heights on *p*-type materials $\approx E_g - q\phi_{bn}$.

	Si	Ge	SiC	GaP	GaAs	GaSb	InP	InAs	InSb	ZnS	ZnSe	CdS	CdSe	CdTe
Al	0.68–0.74	0.48	2.0	1.05	0.73–0.80			Ohmic	0.18*	0.8	0.74	Ohmic	0.43	0.76
Ag	0.56–0.79			1.2	0.88		0.54	Ohmic	0.17*	1.65	1.22	0.35–0.56		0.66–0.78
Au	0.81–0.83	0.45	1.95	1.18	0.90	0.61	0.40–0.49	Ohmic		2.0	1.35–1.51	0.68–0.78	0.70	0.86
Au/Ti					0.89–0.92		0.53							
Bi											1.14	0.84		0.78
Ca	0.40													
Co	0.64	0.5			0.56									
CoSi2#	0.64													
Cr	0.57–0.59			1.18								0.36–0.50	0.33	
Cu	0.66–0.79	0.48		1.20	0.82					1.75	1.10			0.82
Fe	0.65	0.42			0.83									
In											1.11			0.78
Ir	0.77	0.42		1.04						0.82				0.69
Mg	0.4										0.86			
Mo	0.56–0.68				0.65						0.49			
MoSi2#	0.63–0.69													
Na	0.43				0.78–0.83									
Ni	0.66–0.70											0.45		0.83
NiSi2#	0.66											0.53		
Os	0.7	0.4									1.14			
Pb	0.6									1.87				
Pd	0.71											0.62		
Pd2Si#	0.71–0.75			1.45										
Pt	0.90				0.86					1.84	1.4	0.85–1.1	0.37	0.89
PtSi#	0.81–0.86													
Rh	0.72	0.40												
RhSi	0.70													
Ru	0.76	0.38			1.0–1.2, 0.86		0.8–0.9							
(SN)xPolymer										2.7–3.0	1.7	1.1	0.6–0.7	
Sb											1.34			0.76
Sn					0.75									
Ti	0.50				0.75–0.84									
TiSi2#	0.58–0.60													
W	0.66	0.48			0.66–0.71									
WSi2	.86													
Zn	0.75													
ZrSi2	0.55													

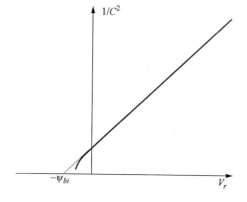

FIGURE 3.3
Capacitance characteristics vs. reverse bias.

$$\frac{A^2}{C^2} = \frac{1}{C_d^2} = \frac{2\,(\psi_{bi} + V_r)}{q\varepsilon_s N} \quad . \tag{3.4}$$

Capacitance measurement plotted in this format (Fig. 3.3) can yield the barrier height as well as the doping concentration (or area). This technique can be extended to profile non-uniform doping concentration (see Eq. (1.18)).

The current transport in a Schottky barrier is thermionic emission of majority carriers over the barrier (see derivation in Appendix B5), given by

$$J = A^* T^2 \exp\left(\frac{-q\phi_b}{kT}\right)\left[\exp\left(\frac{qV_f}{nkT}\right) - 1\right] \quad , \tag{3.5}$$

with

$$A^* = \frac{4\pi q m^* k^2}{h^3} \quad . \tag{3.6}$$

Common effective Richardson constants A^* used for Ge, Si and GaAs are shown in Table. 3.2. The n value (≥ 1) in Eq. (3.5) is called the ideality factor. The

TABLE 3.2
Commonly used values of Richardson constants (A^*)
for Si, GaAs and Ge. (A/cm²-K²)

	Si	GaAs	Ge
n-type	110	4.4	143
p-type	30	74	41

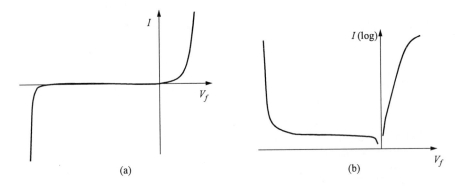

FIGURE 3.4
Typical I-V characteristics of a Schottky barrier in (a) linear current plot and (b) logarithmic current plot.

underlying cause for $n > 1$ can be an interfacial layer, barrier height inhomogeneity, or image-force lowering which is voltage dependent.

The minority-carrier hole current, on the other hand, is limited by diffusion as in the case of a p-n junction and is therefore given by

$$ J_h = \frac{q D_p p_{no}}{L_p} \left[\exp\left(\frac{q V_f}{kT}\right) - 1 \right] \ . \tag{3.7} $$

This diffusion current is usually 4–6 orders of magnitude smaller than the thermionic-emission current. It is the dominance of the majority-carrier current with minimum minority-carrier storage that enables the Schottky barrier to operate at much higher frequencies (≈ 100 GHz) compared to a p-n junction (≈ 1 GHz).

Another current component in addition is the depletion-region generation/recombination current (see Appendix B2), given in the form

$$ J = J_{re} \left[\exp\left(\frac{q V_f}{2kT}\right) - 1 \right] \ . \tag{3.8} $$

The magnitude of J_{re} depends on the quality of the semiconductor material. If J_{re} is larger than the corresponding component in Eq. (3.5), the current for small forward bias, as well as the reverse current, will be increased.

Typical I-V characteristics are shown in Fig. 3.4. The n value can be measured from the exponential rise of current with voltage. At high forward bias, current is leveled off by series resistance or high current injection. At high reverse bias, breakdown occurs whose mechanism is similar to the impact ionization breakdown in p-n junction.

After fabrication of a Schottky-barrier diode, it is often required to measure its barrier height. There are altogether five methods to do so and they are listed below:

1. *I-V* characteristics: A current level is measured when V_f is extrapolated to zero. With a known effective Richardson constant, Eq. (3.5) is used to deduce the barrier height. Due to the exponential dependence of current on ϕ_b, the accuracy of A^* is not critical.

2. Temperature dependence: The dependence of forward current on temperature can yield the barrier height (Eq. (3.5)). For a fixed V_f, a plot of $\log(J/T^2)$ vs. $1/T$ gives the activation energy of $q(\phi_b - V_f)$.

3. *C-V* characteristics: Equation (3.4) and Fig. 3.3 are used to obtain the built-in potential and doping concentration. Barrier height is then the sum of $q\psi_{bi}$ and qV_n (or qV_p).

4. Photoresponse: The quantum efficiency for carriers excited from the metal over the barrier is known to be a function of photon energy $h\nu$. If the square root of the photoresponse is plotted against the photon energy, the barrier height can be obtained as shown in Fig. 3.5.

5. Photovoltaic effect: When a Schottky barrier is exposed to light, a short-circuit current J_{sc} or an open-circuit voltage can be obtained. The relationship is given by[16]

$$V_{oc} = \frac{nkT}{q} \ln\left(\frac{J_{sc}}{J_o} + 1\right) . \tag{3.9}$$

Plotting V_{oc} vs. J_{sc} at different illumination levels provides J_o and n. The dark current J_o obtained can be used to calculate the barrier height.

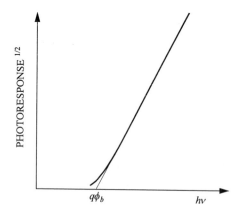

FIGURE 3.5
Photoresponse vs. photon energy to determine Schottky-barrier height.

In the presence of image-force lowering (see Appendix B6), the tip of the barrier is rounded off as shown in Fig. 3.2. The amount of barrier lowering is given by

$$\Delta\phi_b = \sqrt{\frac{q\mathscr{E}_m}{4\pi\varepsilon_s}} \qquad (3.10)$$

where $\mathscr{E}_m$ is the maximum field near the interface and is given by

$$\mathscr{E}_m = \sqrt{\frac{2qN(\psi_{bi} - V_f)}{\varepsilon_s}} . \qquad (3.11)$$

Among the above measurement methods, all yield the final effective barrier height with the exception of the C-V method where the built-in potential ψ_{bi} obtained would be overestimated by $\Delta\phi_b$ and must be corrected to obtain the exact barrier height.

The barrier height for a metal on a semiconductor is known to be independent of the semiconductor doping level, if the doping is uniform. However, it can be modified by a thin sheet of heavily doped layer at the surface, as first suggested by Shannon.[17,18] As shown in Fig. 3.6, a layer of n^+-region reduces the effective barrier height (on n-type substrate) due to increased image-force lowering and increased tunneling. A layer of p^+-region increases the barrier due to band bending in the bulk of the semiconductor.

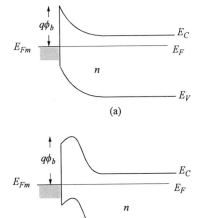

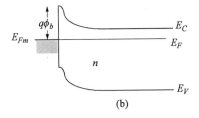

FIGURE 3.6
Modification of barrier height from (a) original value, (b) with n^+-layer to reduce ϕ_b, (c) with p^+-layer to increase ϕ_b.

3.4 APPLICATIONS

The main features of a Schottky-barrier diode are high-frequency capability and low forward-voltage drop. These features plus the ease of fabrication make the device useful in a wide range of applications.[19]

1. As a general purpose rectifier, it can be used in many circuit applications outlined in Appendix C1–Applications of Rectifiers.
2. Due to its high-frequency capability, among all rectifiers the Schottky barrier is the most widely used diode as microwave mixer and detector.
3. Due to its low loss (low voltage drop) in forward bias, it is used quite extensively in power electronics. In particular, it is used in low-voltage, high-current power supplies.
4. Due to the non-linear *I-V* characteristics, it can be used as a varistor (see Section 12.5.1).
5. It can be used as a varactor based on the variation of depletion-layer capacitance under reverse bias (see Section 1.5.4).
6. It is a fundamental building block for many other devices such as the solar cell, photodetector, metal-base transistor, MESFET, etc.
7. A special form of Schottky junction is the ohmic contact which is required to connect every semiconductor device to other devices or to the external environment.
8. In a clamped bipolar transistor, a Schottky diode is connected between the base and the collector as shown in Fig. 3.7. In the saturation regime of the transistor operation, the base-collector junction is under forward bias. When a Schottky diode is connected in parallel, most of the current passes through the Schottky device, and minority-carrier storage is eliminated in the base-collector *p-n* junction. As a result the turn-off time of the bipolar transistor is greatly reduced.

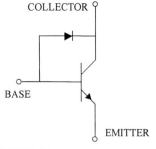

FIGURE 3.7
An *n-p-n* bipolar transistor with Schottky-diode clamp.

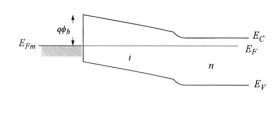

FIGURE 3.8
Energy-band diagram for Mott diode.

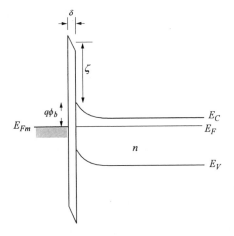

FIGURE 3.9
Energy-band diagram for MIS tunnel
diode.

9. It is also used as a clamping diode in integrated injection logic circuits and transistor-transistor logic circuits.

10. Due to the low temperature processing, a Schottky barrier is used as a tool for characterization of the semiconductor material, especially on surface properties.

3.5 RELATED DEVICES

3.5.1 Mott Barrier

A Mott barrier has a metal contact on a lightly doped surface layer on a more heavily doped substrate (Fig. 3.8). The lightly doped layer is fully depleted, and the space charge is negligible so that the electric field is constant. The capacitance of the device is small and independent of bias. The current, in this case, is diffusion limited rather than thermionic emission limited.[11]

3.5.2 Metal-Insulator-Semiconductor Tunnel Diode

In the metal-insulator-semiconductor (MIS) structure, a thin interfacial layer such as an oxide is intentionally introduced before metal deposition (Fig. 3.9).[20,21] The interfacial layer thickness lies in the range of 1–5 nm. The current is reduced from Eq. (3.5) to

$$ J = A^* T^2 \exp\left(-\sqrt{\zeta}\delta\right) \exp\left(\frac{-q\phi_b}{kT}\right)\left[\exp\left(\frac{qV_f}{nkT}\right) - 1\right] \tag{3.12}$$

where ζ is the mean barrier height in eV, and δ is the oxide thickness in nm (product is normalized to be dimensionless). The interfacial layer reduces the majority-carrier current without affecting the minority-carrier current, and this raises the minority injection efficiency. This structure is used in other devices such as the solar cell, MISS switch, and surface oxide transistor.

REFERENCES

1. W. Schottky, *Naturwissenschaften*, **26**, 843 (1938).
2. N. F. Mott, "Note on the contact between a metal and an insulator on semiconductor," *Proc. Cambr. Philos. Soc.*, **34**, 568 (1938).
3. H. A. Bethe, "Theory of the boundary layer of crystal rectifiers," *MIT Radiat. Lab. Rep. 43-12*, (1942).
4. C. R. Crowell and S. M. Sze, "Current transport in metal-semiconductor barriers," *Solid-State Electron.*, **9**, 1035 (1966).
5. J. Bardeen, "Surface states and rectification at a metal semi-conductor contact," *Phys. Rev.*, **71**, 717 (1947).
6. M. P. Lepselter and S. M. Sze, "Silicon Schottky barrier diode with near-ideal I-V characteristics," *Bell Syst. Tech. J.*, **47**, 195 (1968).
7. M. P. Lepselter and J. M. Andrews, "Ohmic contacts to silicon," in B. Schwartz, Ed., *Ohmic contacts to semiconductors*, p. 4.7"159, Electrochem. Soc., New York, 1969.
8. R. Tung, "Schottky barrier formation at single crystal metal-semiconductor interfaces," *Phys. Rev. Lett.*, **52**, 461 (1984).
9. H. K. Henisch, *Semiconductor contacts: An approach to ideas and models*, Clarendon Press, Oxford, 1984.
10. E. H. Rhoderick, "Metal-semiconductor contacts," *IEE Proc.*, **129**, 1 (1982).
11. S. M. Sze, *Physics of semiconductor devices*, 2nd Ed., Wiley, New York, 1981.
12. A. G. Milnes, *Semiconductor devices and integrated electronics*, Van Nostrand, New York, 1980.
13. E. H. Rhoderick and R. H. Williams, *Metal-semiconductor contacts*, 2nd Ed., Clarendon Press, Oxford, 1988.
14. V. L. Rideout, "A review of the theory, technology and applications of metal-semiconductor rectifiers," *Thin Solid Films*, **48**, 261 (1978).
15. K. K. Ng, "Barrier heights and contact resistances: Silicide/Si," in *Properties of silicon*, INSPEC, London, 1988.
16. P. Panayotatos and H. C. Card, "Use of V_{oc}/J_{sc} measurements for determination of barrier height under illumination and for fill-factor calculations in Schottky-barrier solar cells," *IEE Proc., Pt. I*, **127**, 308 (1980).
17. J. M. Shannon, "Increasing the effective height of a Schottky barrier using low-energy ion implantation," *Appl. Phys. Lett.*, **25**, 75 (1974).
18. J. M. Shannon, "Reducing the effective height of a Schottky barrier using low-energy ion implantation," *Appl. Phys. Lett.*, **24**, 369 (1974).
19. B. L. Sharma and S. C. Gupta, "Metal-semiconductor Schottky barrier junctions," *Solid State Technol.*, 90 (June 1980).
20. H. C. Card, "Tunnelling MIS structures," *Inst. Phys. Conf. Ser.*, **50**, 140 (1980).
21. M. Y. Doghish and F. D. Ho, "A comprehensive analytical model for metal-insulator-semiconductor (MIS) devices," *IEEE Trans. Electron Dev.*, **39**, 2771 (1992).

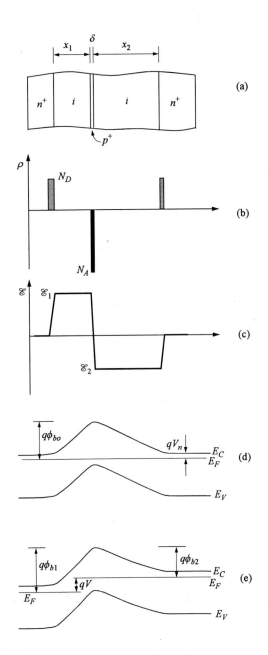

FIGURE 4.2
Properties of a planar-doped-barrier diode. (a) Doping profile. (b) Space-charge density and (c) electric-field profile in equilibrium. Energy-band diagram (d) in equilibrium and (e) under forward bias, with positive voltage applied to the top (left) layer.

and is independent of bias.

It is known that, in the injecting side of the barrier where carriers are going against the potential, if the potential variation exceeds kT/q within one mean free path, the current conduction is limited by thermionic emission. A PDB diode typically falls into this category. Under bias, the barriers faced by the two n^+-layers are no longer symmetrical, as shown in Fig. 4.2(e). With a positive voltage V applied to the surface (left) layer, the barriers are modified to

$$\phi_{b1} = \phi_{bo} + \frac{x_1 V}{(x_1 + x_2)} \quad , \tag{4.6}$$

$$\phi_{b2} = \phi_{bo} - \frac{x_2 V}{(x_1 + x_2)} \quad . \tag{4.7}$$

The thermionic-emission current under this condition is given by

$$\begin{aligned} J &= A^* T^2 \left[\exp\left(\frac{-q\phi_{b2}}{kT} \right) - \exp\left(\frac{-q\phi_{b1}}{kT} \right) \right] \\ &= A^* T^2 \left[\exp\left(\frac{-q\phi_{bo}}{kT} \right) \right] \left[\exp\left(\frac{x_2 q V}{(x_1 + x_2) kT} \right) - \exp\left(\frac{-x_1 q V}{(x_1 + x_2) kT} \right) \right] \end{aligned} \tag{4.8}$$

where A^* is the effective Richardson constant (see Chapter 3 and Appendix B5). The applied voltage V can be either positive or negative, and both polarities are valid in Eq. (4.8). Typical characteristics are shown in Fig. 4.3. The factors, also known as barrier leverage factors, $x_1/(x_1+x_2)$ and $x_2/(x_1+x_2)$ determine the portion of voltage applied to ϕ_{b1} and ϕ_{b2}, respectively. These factors control the effective

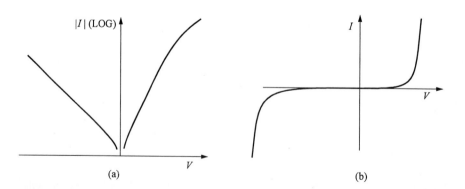

(a)   (b)

FIGURE 4.3
Typical I-V characteristics of a planar-doped-barrier diode in (a) semi-log scale and (b) linear scale. Asymmetry is due to $x_1 < x_2$.

ideality factor (n value) of the I-V characteristics. Also, in an asymmetrical structure ($x_1 \neq x_2$), the voltage polarity that forces higher current is considered the forward bias. In the above example, $x_2 > x_1$, and positive V is the forward direction.

4.4 APPLICATIONS

The PDB diode is a majority-carrier device. It has no minority-carrier storage and is capable of high-frequency operations. It has certain advantages over the Schottky-barrier diode. First, the barrier can be varied between zero to approximately the energy-gap value. The degree of symmetry between the forward and reverse directions can also be adjusted. Second, the barrier is not at the metal-semiconductor interface so that it is more stable in response to electrical stress. Third, since all the layers are semiconductors, the PDB structure is more flexible as a device building block. Applications of the PDB diode are listed below.

1. Referring to the energy-band diagram of Fig. 4.2(e), if extra minority carriers (holes) are supplied by external means, they would accumulate at the peak of the valence band. These positive charges set up a field that reduces the barrier heights ϕ_{b1} and ϕ_{b2}, resulting in a larger thermionic-emission (majority-carrier) current. This property of current gain is used in a photodetector (see Section 54.5.4) and switch (see Chapter 17).

2. Two PDB diodes back-to-back are used to form a hot-electron transistor (see Chapter 35). The planar-doped barrier has also been incorporated as the channel or the gate of various FETs.

3. As a microwave mixer and detector, it has performance similar to that of a Schottky-barrier diode.[8] It can also be used as a special subharmonic mixer that requires symmetrical I-V characteristics.[9] In this case it replaces two Schottky-barrier diodes in anti-parallel.

4. It can replace the Schottky barrier as the injecting junction in a BARITT diode[10] or a TED.

4.5 RELATED DEVICE

4.5.1 Camel Diode

A camel diode can be viewed as the extreme case of asymmetry in a PDB diode with $x_1 = 0$. It has a three-layer structure shown in Fig. 4.4. The center layer is again fully depleted. The doping concentrations of the three layers increase toward the surface. Since the heavily doped layers are very near the surface, and the sharpness of the doping profiles is less critical, ion implantation and standard

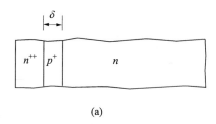

(a)

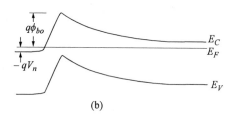

(b)

FIGURE 4.4
(a) Doping profile and (b) energy-band diagram of a camel diode.

chemical vapor deposition, instead of MBE, can be used for fabrication. The barrier height, in this case, is given by[2,4]

$$\phi_{bo} \approx \frac{qN_A\delta^2}{2\varepsilon_s} + V_n \ .$$ (4.9)

(V_n is negative for degenerate semiconductor.) Under bias, it behaves like a Schottky-barrier diode except with a small dependence of barrier height on bias, giving an ideality factor slightly larger than unity (typically $\approx$ 1.2). Both the camel diode and the PDB diode belong to what is called bulk unipolar diode.[7,11]

REFERENCES

1. J. M. Shannon, "Increasing the effective height of a Schottky barrier using low-energy ion implantation," *Appl. Phys. Lett.*, **25**, 75 (1974).
2. J. M. Shannon, "A majority-carrier camel diode," *Appl. Phys. Lett.*, **35**, 63 (1979).
3. R. J. Malik, T. R. Aucoin, R. L. Ross, K. Board, C. E. C. Wood and L. F. Eastman, "Planar-doped barriers in GaAs by molecular beam epitaxy," *Electron. Lett.*, **16**, 836 (1980).
4. S. E. D. Habib and K. Board, "Unified analysis of the bulk unipolar diode," *IEEE Trans. Electron Dev.*, **ED-30**, 86 (1983).
5. S. Luryi, "Device building blocks," in S. M. Sze, Ed., *High-speed semiconductor devices*, Wiley, New York, 1990.
6. M. Shur, *Physics of semiconductor devices*, Prentice Hall, Englewood Cliffs, 1990.
7. K. Board, "A review of bulk unipolar diodes and their applications," *Microelectron. J.*, **13**, 19 (1982).
8. M. J. Kearney, M. J. Kelly, R. A. Davies, T. M. Kerr, P. K. Rees, A. Condie and I. Dale, "Asymmetric planar doped barrier diodes for mixer and detector applications," *Electron. Lett.*, **25**, 1454 (1989).

9. R. J. Malik and S. Dixon, "A subharmonic mixer using a planar doped barrier diode with symmetric conductance," *IEEE Electron. Dev. Lett.*, **EDL-3**, 205 (1982).

10. S. Luryi and R. F. Kazarinov, "Optimum BARITT structure," *Solid-State Electron.*, **25**, 943 (1982).

11. J. M. Woodcock and J. M. Shannon, "Thermionic emission in bulk unipolar camel diodes," *Appl. Phys. Lett.*, **45**, 876 (1984).

CHAPTER
5

ISOTYPE HETEROJUNCTION

5.1 HISTORY

An isotype heterojunction is different from an anisotype heterojunction in that the dopants of the two sides are of the same type. It can be an *n-n* heterojunction or a *p-p* heterojunction. (Discussions of the anisotype heterojunction can be found in Section 1.5.3.) The first heterojunction was the anisotype, which was suggested by Shockley in 1951, to be incorporated into the emitter-base junction to increase the current gain of a bipolar transistor.[1] This application was analyzed in more detail by Kroemer in 1957.[2] The isotype heterojunction had been studied in different material systems. These include Ge–GaAs by Anderson in 1962,[3] InP–GaAs by Oldham and Milnes in 1963,[4] Ge–GaAsP by Chang in 1965,[5] and GaAs–AlGaAs by Womac and Rediker in 1972,[6] by Chandra and Eastman[7,8] and Lechner et al.[9] in 1979. Theoretical analysis of the device has been presented by some of these authors, namely Anderson,[3] Chang,[5] and Chandra and Eastman.[10]

5.2 STRUCTURE

An *n-n* isotype heterojunction is shown in the schematic cross-section of Fig. 5.1, using the GaAs–AlGaAs system as an example. The layers are grown epitaxially. For good-quality heterostructure epitaxy, the lattice constants of the two materials have to be matched within ≈ 5%. The heterointerface must be extremely abrupt to achieve rectification rather than have ohmic characteristics. This transition region has to be less than ≈ 100 Å thick.[10–12] Also, for best rectification behavior, the doping level in the wide-energy-gap material should be non-degenerate and

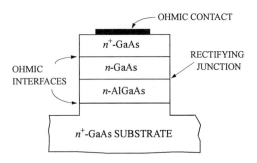

FIGURE 5.1
Schematic cross-section of an isotype heterojunction, using an *n-n* AlGaAs–GaAs system.

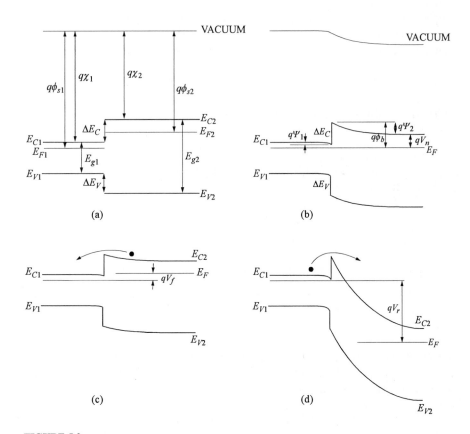

FIGURE 5.2
Energy-band diagrams of an isotype heterojunction. (a) Isolated layers. (b) Joined layers, at equilibrium. (c) Under forward bias. (d) Under reverse bias.

lighter than that in the narrow-energy-gap counterpart. Isolation between diodes can be achieved by mesa etching down to the substrate layer.

5.3 CHARACTERISTICS

For a heterojunction of two materials of different electron affinities, work functions and energy gaps, the band-edge discontinuities in Fig. 5.2(b) are related by

$$\Delta E_C = q \, (\chi_1 - \chi_2) \quad , \tag{5.1}$$

$$\Delta E_V = (E_{g2} - E_{g1}) - \Delta E_C \quad . \tag{5.2}$$

For the GaAs–AlGaAs system, GaAs is referred to as material 1. The potential barrier for the majority carriers is usually formed on the wide-energy-gap material, in this case AlGaAs. This system is similar in nature to a Schottky barrier with the narrow-energy-gap layer replacing the metal contact.

As shown in Fig. 5.2(a), the Fermi level in isolated AlGaAs is higher than that in GaAs. Conceptually, upon contact of these two materials, electrons transfer from AlGaAs to GaAs, causing a depletion layer in AlGaAs and an accumulation layer in GaAs. Such an accumulation layer does not exist in the anisotype heterojunction. In order to calculate the barrier height and band bending, the boundary condition for electric field is used,

$$K_1 \mathscr{E}_{m1} = K_2 \mathscr{E}_{m2} \quad . \tag{5.3}$$

$\mathscr{E}_{m1}$ is the maximum field in the accumulation layer, which occurs at the heterointerface, given by

$$\mathscr{E}_{m1} = \sqrt{\frac{2qN_{D1}}{\varepsilon_{s1}} \left\{ \frac{kT}{q} \left[\exp \frac{q \, (\Psi_1 - V_1)}{kT} - 1 \right] - (\Psi_1 - V_1) \right\}} \quad . \tag{5.4}$$

$\mathscr{E}_{m2}$ is the maximum field in the depletion layer, given by

$$\mathscr{E}_{m2} = \sqrt{\frac{2qN_{D2} \, (\Psi_2 - V_2)}{\varepsilon_{s2}}} \quad . \tag{5.5}$$

Ψ_1 and Ψ_2 are band bendings at equilibrium. V_1 and V_2 are the portions of applied forward voltage developed across GaAs and AlGaAs, respectively ($V_f = V_1 + V_2$). With another known relationship

$$(\Psi_1 - V_1) + (\Psi_2 - V_2) = \phi_{s1} - \phi_{s2} - V_f \quad , \tag{5.6}$$

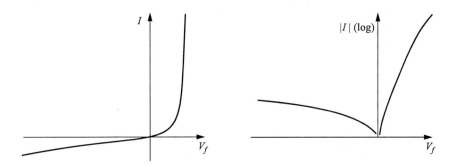

FIGURE 5.3
Typical I-V characteristics of an isotype heterojunction. (a) Linear plot. (b) Semilog plot.

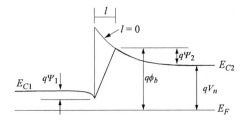

FIGURE 5.4
Energy-band diagram showing the effect of a graded layer l on the resultant barrier height.

these net potentials ($\Psi_1 - V_1$ and $\Psi_2 - V_2$), as a function of applied bias, can be obtained by iterating Eqs. (5.3)–(5.6). Of particular interest is the barrier height at equilibrium, solved with $V_f = V_1 = V_2 = 0$, giving

$$\phi_b = \Psi_2 + V_n \ . \tag{5.7}$$

The thermionic-emission current under bias can be obtained from

$$J = qN_{D2}\sqrt{\frac{kT}{2\pi m^*_2}}\ \exp\left(\frac{-q\Psi_2}{kT}\right)\exp\left(\frac{-qV_1}{kT}\right)\left[\exp\left(\frac{qV_f}{kT}\right)-1\right] \ . \tag{5.8}$$

Qualitatively, the square-root term represents the average carrier velocity, $N_{D2}\exp(-q\Psi_2/kT)$ is the number of electrons above the barrier Ψ_2, and the next two terms are due to opposite effects on the barrier exerted by V_1 and V_f. For better comparison to a Schottky barrier, this equation can be rearranged to give

$$J = A^* T^2 \exp\left(\frac{-q\phi_b}{kT}\right)\exp\left(\frac{-qV_1}{kT}\right)\left[\exp\left(\frac{qV_f}{kT}\right)-1\right] \ . \tag{5.9}$$

It can be seen that if $V_1 = 0$, the current is identical to a Schottky diode where A^* is the effective Richardson constant for the wide-energy-gap material.

To eliminate the variable V_1 in the above equation, an approximation is made from Eqs. (5.3)–(5.5)[5]

$$\exp\left[\frac{q(\Psi_1 - V_1)}{kT}\right] \approx \frac{q}{kT}(\Psi - V_f) \tag{5.10}$$

where $\Psi = \Psi_1 + \Psi_2 = \phi_{s1} - \phi_{s2}$. Substituting V_1 into Eq. (5.9) gives

$$J = \frac{q\Psi A^* T}{k}\left(1 - \frac{V_f}{\Psi}\right)\exp\left(\frac{-q\Psi_1}{kT}\right)\exp\left(\frac{-q\phi_b}{kT}\right)\left[\exp\left(\frac{qV_f}{kT}\right) - 1\right]. \tag{5.11}$$

In comparison to a standard thermionic-emission current of a Schottky-barrier diode, a few points are worthy of mentioning. The temperature dependence of the coefficient is now T instead of T^2. The term $(1 - V_f/\Psi)$ affects both the forward current and the reverse current. It causes the forward current to have a more gradual exponential rise with voltage. The reverse current also becomes non-saturating. A typical set of I-V characteristics of an isotype heterojunction is shown in Fig. 5.3.

Another important deviation from a Schottky diode is that the barrier height becomes temperature dependent. This is implied in the derivation of the barrier height from Eqs. (5.3)–(5.7). Since the temperature dependence on current is a useful technique to measure parameters for thermionic-emission current, the barrier height in Eq. (5.11) can be eliminated to give

$$J = \frac{q^2\Psi N_{D2}}{\sqrt{2\pi m^*_2 kT}}\left(1 - \frac{V_f}{\Psi}\right)\exp\left(\frac{-q\Psi}{kT}\right)\left[\exp\left(\frac{qV_f}{kT}\right) - 1\right]. \tag{5.12}$$

As mentioned in Section 5.2, the transition between the two materials at the heterointerface has to be abrupt. This transition region, indicated as l in Fig. 5.4, has been shown to decrease the barrier height. A transition region of only ≈ 150 Å can reduce the barrier to the extent that rectification vanishes and ohmic behavior results.[10–12]

A structure with two isotype heterojunctions has been reported.[13] As shown by the energy-band diagram in Fig. 5.5, the barrier is formed by a thin wide-energy-gap material (≈ 500 Å), sandwiched between two narrow-energy-gap materials. The I-V characteristics in Fig. 5.6 show that the current is symmetrical, and, at low temperature, nonlinear. The nonlinearity is due to the decrease of the effective barrier height with bias, as shown in Fig. 5.5(b).

5.4 APPLICATIONS

The isotype heterojunction is not a practical device for rectification. The fabrication requirement is quite stringent. The barrier height obtained is usually lower than that from the metal-semiconductor junction. Also, the reverse current

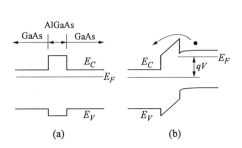

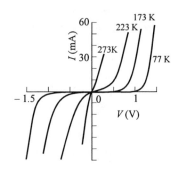

FIGURE 5.5
A rectangular barrier formed by two isotype heterojunctions. (a) Under equilibrium. (b) Under bias.

FIGURE 5.6
I-V characteristics of the rectangular barrier at different temperatures. (After Ref. 13)

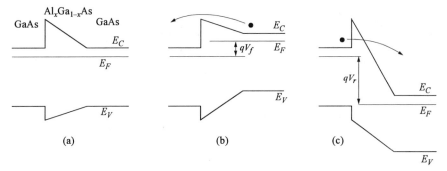

FIGURE 5.7
Energy-band diagrams of a sawtooth graded-composition barrier. (a) Equilibrium. (b) Under forward bias. (c) Under reverse bias.

does not saturate with voltage. This device, currently, has no commercial value. It is only used as a research tool to study the fundamental properties of heterojunctions.

5.5 RELATED DEVICE

5.5.1 Graded-Composition Barrier

The first graded-composition barrier was reported by Allyn et al. in 1980, with a saw-tooth barrier as shown in Fig. 5.7.[14] In this example, the energy gap is varied by the Al and Ga concentrations in the $Al_xGa_{1-x}As$ layer. This barrier layer is typically ≈ 500 Å. The outer layers are GaAs. The I-V characteristics are shown in Fig. 5.8 where the forward current is a thermionic-emission current and the reverse current is a tunneling current through the thin barrier.

A barrier of triangular shape, shown in Fig. 5.9, is also possible.[13] The electrical characteristics in Fig. 5.10 are asymmetrical, reflecting the different control of barrier height by the two polarities. This asymmetry is similar to that in a planar-doped-barrier diode. Both directions of currents are due to thermionic emission of majority carriers.

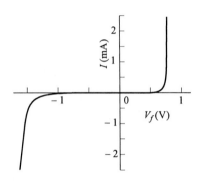

FIGURE 5.8
I-V characteristics of a saw-tooth graded-composition barrier. (After Ref. 14)

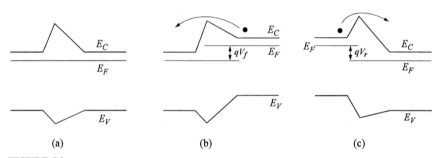

(a)   (b)   (c)

FIGURE 5.9
Energy-band diagrams of a triangular graded-composition barrier. (a) Equilibrium. (b) Under forward bias. (c) Under reverse bias. Currents in both directions are due to thermionic emission.

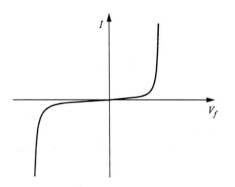

FIGURE 5.10
I-V characteristics of a triangular graded-composition barrier.

REFERENCES

1. W. Shockley, "Circuit element utilizing semiconductive material," U.S. Patent 2,569,347 (1951).
2. H. Kroemer, "Theory of a wide-gap emitter for transistors," *Proc. IRE*, **45**, 1535 (1957).
3. R. L. Anderson, "Experiments on Ge-GaAs heterojunction," *Solid-State Electron.*, **5**, 341 (1962).
4. W. G. Oldham and A. G. Milnes, "*n-n* semiconductor heterojunctions," *Solid-State Electron.*, **6**, 121 (1963).
5. L. L. Chang, "The conduction properties of Ge-GaAs$_{1-x}$P$_x$ *n-n* heterojunctions," *Solid-State Electron.*, **8**, 721 (1965).
6. J. F. Womac and R. H. Rediker, "The graded-gap Al$_x$Ga$_{1-x}$As-GaAs heterojunction," *J. Appl. Phys.*, **43**, 4129 (1972).
7. A. Chandra and L. F. Eastman, "Rectification at *n-n* GaAs:(Ga,Al)As heterojunctions," *Electronics Lett.*, **15**, 90 (1979).
8. A. Chandra and L. F. Eastman, "Rectification at *n*-GaAs–*n*-Ga$_{0.7}$Al$_{0.3}$As heterojunctions grown by liquid phase epitaxy," *J. Vac. Sci. Technol.*, **16**, 1525 (1979).
9. A. Lechner, M. Kneidinger, H. W. Thim, R. Kuch and J. Wernisch, "Microwave detection with *n*-GaAs/*N*-GaAlAs heterojunctions," *Electronics Lett.*, **15**, 254 (1979).
10. A. Chandra and L. F. Eastman, "A study of the conduction properties of a rectifying *n*GaAs–*n*(Ga,Al)As heterojunction," *Solid-State Electron.*, **23**, 599 (1980).
11. R. M. Raymond and R. E. Hayes, "Barrier height reduction for graded *n-n* heterojunctions," *J. Appl. Phys.*, **48**, 1359 (1977).
12. S. C. Lee and G. L. Pearson, "Rectification in Al$_x$Ga$_{1-x}$As–GaAs *n-n* heterojunction devices," *Solid-State Electron.*, **24**, 563 (1981).
13. A. C. Gossard, W. Brown, C. L. Allyn and W. Wiegmann, "Molecular beam epitaxial growth and electrical transport of graded barriers for nonlinear current conduction," *J. Vac. Sci. Technol.*, **20**, 694 (1982).
14. C. L. Allyn, A. C. Gossard and W. Wiegmann, "New rectifying semiconductor structure by molecular beam epitaxy," *Appl. Phys. Lett.*, **36**, 373 (1980).

CHAPTER
6

TUNNEL
DIODE

6.1 HISTORY

The tunnel diode was discovered by L. Esaki in 1958,[1] and is often called the Esaki diode. As part of his Ph.D. dissertation work, Esaki was studying heavily doped germanium *p-n* junctions for application in high-speed bipolar transistors in which a narrow and heavily doped base was required.[2] In 1973, Esaki received the Nobel prize in physics for his pioneering work in tunnel diode. Tunnel diodes were subsequently demonstrated by other researchers in other materials such as GaAs (Holonyak and Lesk)[3] and InSb (Batdorf et al.)[4] in 1960, Si (Chynoweth et al.)[5] and InAs (Kleinknecht)[6] in 1961, GaSb (Carr)[7] and InP (Burrus)[8] in 1962. For in-depth treatment of the device, the readers are refereed to Refs. 9–13.

The main attractiveness of the tunnel diode, apart from the negative differential resistance, is high-speed operation since it is a majority carrier device and it does not suffer from minority carrier storage. Quantum-mechanical tunneling inherently is a fast mechanism that is not limited by drift transit time. The drawbacks of the tunnel diode are: (1) low power for an oscillator because of low tunneling current, (2) being a two-terminal device it does not provide input and output isolation, and (3) problems in device reproducibility, especially in integrated circuits. Even though the device looked promising in the 1960s, it is being replaced by the TED and IMPATT diode as oscillators, and by FETs as switching elements.[14] Currently it finds very limited applications as microwave low-noise amplifier.

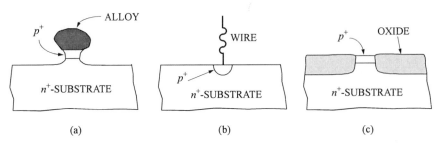

FIGURE 6.1
Structures of tunnel diode formed by (a) ball alloy, (b) pulse forming, and (c) planar technology.

6.2 STRUCTURE

A tunnel diode is similar to a *p-n* junction except that the doping levels are very high (degenerate) and abrupt. Typical concentrations are higher than 5×10^{19} cm^{-3} and the depletion width is in the range of 5–10 nm. Due to the small depletion width, the capacitance of the tunnel diode is very high. For high-frequency operations, a small diode area is required. Germanium has been the most common substrate material. One of the reasons is its small energy gap that provides more efficient tunneling.

A tunnel diode can be fabricated by one of the following methods:

1. **Ball-alloy:** An alloy containing the appropriate dopants is brought to contact with the heavily doped substrate. At temperature around 500°C, the alloy melts quickly ($\approx$ 1 minute) and dopants diffuse out from the alloy. Etching is then used to define the mesa structure as shown in Fig. 6.1(a).

2. **Pulsed bond:** A metal wire, coated with an alloy which contains the appropriate dopants, is pressed against the heavily doped substrate. A voltage pulse forms the junctions by local alloying. This method produces a small diode area, but the exact area is not controllable.

3. **Planar technology:** Here most of the heavily doped substrate is masked off by some insulating layer (Fig. 6.1(c)). In the exposed area, doping of the active area can be introduced by diffusion, alloying, or epitaxial growth. Alternatively, a uniform epitaxial layer is grown on the surface of the whole wafer, and diodes are defined by etching mesa structures.

6.3 CHARACTERISTICS

Typical *I-V* characteristics of a tunnel diode is shown in Fig. 6.2(a). It features an N-shaped negative differential resistance (voltage-controlled negative resistance) between the peak voltage V_{pe} and the valley voltage V_v. The characteristics near the origin are nearly symmetrical for both forward and reverse directions. The

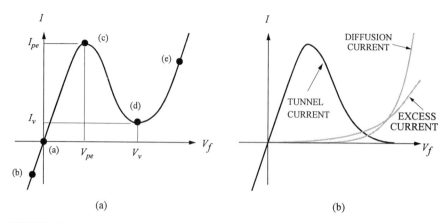

FIGURE 6.2
(a) *I-V* characteristics of tunnel diode. V_f is positive voltage applied to p-type material. Labels (a)–(e) correspond to different biases in Fig. 6.4. (b) Current components of a tunnel diode.

current is composed of different components as indicated in Fig. 6.2(b). The component giving rise to negative differential resistance is tunneling of electrons between the conduction band and the valence band.

Tunneling is a quantum-mechanical phenomenon (see Appendix B7). When a carrier faces a triangular barrier shown in Fig. 6.3, the tunneling probability is given by

$$T_t \approx \exp\left(-\frac{4a\sqrt{2m^* q\phi_b}}{3\hbar}\right).$$ (6.1)

In the case of a tunnel diode, as shown in Fig. 6.4, a is the depletion width and $q\phi_b$ is the energy gap. For high tunneling current, it is desirable to have a small effective mass, small energy gap and narrow depletion width. A stringent requirement for tunneling is that empty states must be available on the other side of the barrier for electrons to tunnel to. These empty states must be at the same energy level since tunneling requires the conservation of energy. The last two

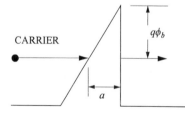

FIGURE 6.3
Parameters associated with tunneling through a triangular potential barrier.

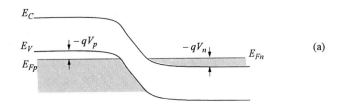

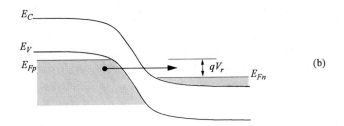

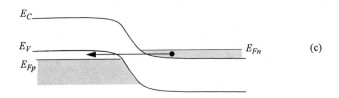

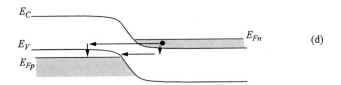

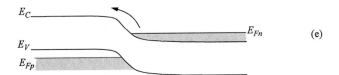

FIGURE 6.4
Energy-band diagrams of tunnel diode at different biases. (a) Equilibrium. (b) Tunneling current at reverse bias. (c) Tunneling current at forward bias, near V_{pe}. (d) Excess current at V_v. (e) Standard p-n junction diffusion current at high bias.

requirements are met only if both sides of the junctions are doped to the extent that their Fermi levels reside within the bands (degeneracy).

The general I-V characteristics in Fig. 6.2 can be explained qualitatively by the energy-band diagrams in Fig. 6.4. For the sake of simplicity, low temperature is assumed such that the Fermi distribution is abrupt, i.e., states above the Fermi level are empty and those below are full. At reverse bias, electrons tunnel from the valence band in the p-type material to the conduction band in the n-type material, and the current increases monotonically. With forward bias up to V_{pe}, electrons from the conduction band find increasing availability of empty states in the valence band, and current increases to the peak value I_{pe} when E_{Fn} lines up with E_V of the p-type material. Beyond that point, the available empty states (at the same energy level as the electrons) start to decrease. When E_C of the n-type material lines up with E_V of the p-type material (Fig. 6.4(d)), there is no empty state available and tunneling current drops to zero. This tunneling current can be approximated empirically by[15]

$$I_t = I_{pe} \left(\frac{V_f}{V_{pe}} \right) \exp \left(1 - \frac{V_f}{V_{pe}} \right) .$$

(6.2)

The peak current I_{pe} occurs at a voltage which can be approximated by

$$V_{pe} \approx \frac{|V_n| + |V_p|}{3} .$$

(6.3)

The valley voltage V_v, according to Fig. 6.4(d), occurs when

$$V_v = |V_n| + |V_p| .$$

(6.4)

In practical devices, the valley current I_v is not zero, due to the "excess" current resulting from tunneling through bulk states in the energy gap, as shown in Fig. 6.4(d). This component can also be expressed by[16]

$$I_x = I_v \exp [C_1 (V_f - V_v)]$$

(6.5)

TABLE 6.1
Typical properties of tunnel diodes for different materials.[9]

	Ge	GaAs	Si
I_{pe}/I_v	10–15	10–20	3–5
V_{pe} (mV)	40–70	90–120	80–100
V_v (mV)	250–350	450–600	400–500

where C_1 is a constant. I_v bears direct relationship to the density of trap levels within the energy gap. At still higher voltage, the standard diffusion current starts to dominate. This diffusion current is the same as the *p-n* junction current and is given by

$$I = qA\left(\frac{D_p p_{no}}{L_p} + \frac{D_n n_{po}}{L_n}\right)\left[\exp\left(\frac{qV_f}{kT}\right) - 1\right] .$$
(6.6)

A useful figure of merit for a tunnel diode is the peak-to-valley current ratio (I_{pe}/I_v). The values for different materials are shown in Table 6.1. It can be seen here that silicon, in spite of its mature technology, has the lowest peak-to-valley ratio.

6.4 APPLICATIONS

Most of the applications of tunnel diodes utilize the negative differential resistance or high-speed capability. The applications of negative resistance are summarized in Appendix C2. The high-speed capability is useful for microwave modulation, mixing and detection (see end of Appendix C1). Tunneling is also known to be insensitive to temperature and this feature is sometimes advantageous. Tunneling can be used as a research tool to study certain properties of energy-band structures, especially in indirect energy gap materials. However, the popularity of tunnel diode has dropped due to the problems in reproducibility, low peak-to-valley current ratio, low current drive, and also due to the availability of other devices to perform similar circuit functions.

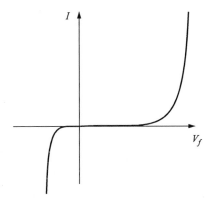

FIGURE 6.5
Typical *I-V* characteristics of a backward diode.

6.5 RELATED DEVICE

6.5.1 Backward Diode

A backward diode (back diode) is formed when one side of the junction is not as heavily doped as the other. The more heavily doped side usually remains degenerate. The characteristics shown in Fig. 6.5 are similar to a regular diode but are in a reverse direction, hence the name backward diode. In the forward direction, the tunneling current component is much reduced or negligible. In the reverse direction, tunneling current is still the dominant current and it is not affected as much by the lighter doping.

Since the backward diode is a majority carrier device, it is a fast device like the tunnel diode (and temperature insensitive). Applications include general rectification, microwave detection, mixing, and frequency conversion.

REFERENCES

1. L. Esaki, "New phenomenon in narrow germanium *p-n* junctions," *Phys. Rev.*, **109**, 603 (1958).
2. L. Esaki, "Discovery of the tunnel diode," *IEEE Trans. Electron Dev.*, **ED-23**, 644 (1976).
3. N. Holonyak, Jr. and I. A. Lesk, "Gallium arsenide tunnel diodes," *Proc. IRE*, **48**, 1405 (1960).
4. R. L. Batdorf, G. C. Dacey, R. L. Wallace and D. J. Walsh, "Esaki diode in InSb," *J. Appl. Phys.*, **31**, 613 (1960).
5. A. G. Chynoweth, W. L. Feldmann and R. A. Logan, "Excess tunnel current in silicon Esaki junctions," *Phys. Rev.*, **121**, 684 (1961).
6. H. P. Kleinknecht, "Indium arsenide tunnel diodes," *Solid-State Electron.*, **2**, 133 (1961).
7. W. N. Carr, "Reversible degradation effects in GaSb tunnel diodes," *Solid-State Electron.*, **5**, 261 (1962).
8. C. A. Burrus, "Indium phosphide Esaki diodes," *Solid-State Electron.*, **3**, 357 (1962).
9. H. C. Okean, "Tunnel diodes," in R. K. Willardson, Ed., A. C. Beer, Ed., *Semiconductors and semimetals,* Vol. 7B, p. 473, Academic Press, New York, 1971.
10. S. M. Sze, *Physics of semiconductor devices*, 2nd Ed., Wiley, New York, 1981.
11. S. Wang, *Fundamentals of semiconductor theory and device physics*, Prentice Hall, Englewood Cliffs, 1989.
12. M. P. Shaw, V. V. Mitin, E. Scholl and H. L. Grubin, *The physics of instabilities in solid state electron devices*, Plenum Press, New York, 1992.
13. P. N. Robson, "Microwave receivers," in C. Hilsum, Ed., T. S. Moss, Ed., *Handbook on semiconductor*, Vol. 4, North-Holland, Amsterdam, 1981.
14. R. G. Swartz, "In perspective: The tunnel diode," *Proc. 1986 IEEE Int. Solid-State Circuits Conf.*, 278 (1986).
15. T. A. Demassa and D. P. Knott, "The prediction of tunnel diode voltage-current characteristics," *Solid-State Electron.*, **13**, 131 (1970).
16. D. K. Roy, "On the prediction of tunnel diode *I-V* characteristics," *Solid-State Electron.*, **14**, 520 (1971).

CHAPTER
7

TRANSFERRED-ELECTRON DEVICE

7.1 HISTORY

The transferred-electron device (TED), also known as the Gunn diode, is one of the most useful microwave devices in the 1–100 GHz range. It is used mainly for microwave generation (as a transferred-electron oscillator, TEO) and for amplification (as a transferred-electron amplifier, TEA). The TED has a voltage-controlled negative differential resistance (N-shaped) but it is unique in that it depends on the bulk material properties rather than a junction or an interface. The fundamental mechanism, the transferred-electron effect, was pointed out theoretically by Ridley and Watkins in 1961,[1] and by Hilsum in 1962.[2] Independently, Gunn in 1963 observed the first transferred-electron oscillation using GaAs.[3,4] For this reason the transferred-electron effect is also known as the Ridley-Watkins-Hilsum effect, and sometimes as the Gunn effect. Kromer was the first to point out that the observed oscillation was indeed due to the transferred-electron effect.[5] Hutson et al. in 1965 presented convincing evidence of such correlation by observing the effect of applied pressure on oscillation.[6] Detailed treatment of the transferred-electron device can be found in Refs. 7–10.

7.2 STRUCTURE

One of the features of the TED is that the structure is simple and is relatively inexpensive to make. A device mounted on a heat sink is shown in Fig. 7.1(a). The most common TED materials are GaAs and InP although other materials such as Ge, CdTe, InAs, InSb, ZnSe, etc. have been used. The device is simply an n-type bar with n^+-contacts. n-type material is mandatory since the transferred-electron

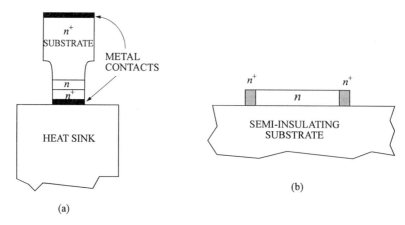

FIGURE 7.1
(a) A discrete TED with the active layer mounted onto the heat sink for efficient heat transfer. (b) A lateral device in planar technology.

effect only applies to electrons. Usually an epitaxial layer is grown on a degenerate n^+-substrate. The active layer ranges from a few microns to hundreds of microns, and has a doping between 10^{14} cm^{-3} and 10^{16} cm^{-3}. Two stringent requirements are that the material has to be of high quality (defect free), and the doping concentration must be extremely uniform. The top n^+-layer can be deposited epitaxially, or doped by ion implantation or diffusion. Samples are usually diced as discrete devices as shown in Fig. 7.1(a), sometimes after grooves are etched. In high-power operations, heat removal is critical and the TED is often mounted upside down on a heat sink for efficient heat transfer. In other configurations, planar technology can be used to make lateral devices on a semi-insulating substrate (Fig. 7.1(b)). In this case the active n-type region is grown epitaxially on material of high resistivity, and the n^+-contacts doped by masked ion implantation.

7.3 CHARACTERISTICS

Before discussing the device operation, we will examine the transferred-electron effect. In standard carrier transport by the drift process, the carrier velocity is proportional to electric field at low fields, with mobility being the proportionality constant, and it saturates with higher fields. Such a relationship is monotonic and there is no negative resistance. In certain semiconductors, the conduction band has multiple valleys, represented by the energy-band diagram in momentum space shown in Fig. 7.2. At low fields, most of the electrons reside in the central valley. However, at higher fields, electrons gain enough potential energy to be escalated to the satellite valley. If carriers in the satellite valley have lower mobility and

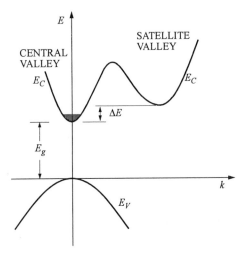

FIGURE 7.2
Energy-band diagram in k-space showing two valleys for the conduction band.

saturation velocity, an interesting relationship between carrier velocity (current) and electric field (voltage) is realized, leading to negative differential resistance.

The net current density combining the carrier transport in both valleys is equal to[7]

$$J = n_1 q \mu \mathscr{E} + n_2 q v_{sat} = n_o q v_{ave} \qquad (7.1)$$

where n_1 and n_2 are electrons in the central valley and the satellite valley, respectively, with a total electron concentration of

$$n_o = n_1 + n_2 \ . \qquad (7.2)$$

In arriving at Eq. (7.1), it is assumed that: (1) carriers in the central valley are in the mobility regime before transferring to the satellite valley, and (2) carriers in the satellite valley have already become velocity saturated when the field is high enough for the transfer. Assumption (2) is not critical for the origin of differential negative resistance but it is valid, at least for some semiconductors such as GaAs. The fraction of electrons in the satellite valley is defined as

$$F(\mathscr{E}) \equiv \frac{n_2}{n_o} \qquad (7.3)$$

and obviously is a function of the electric field. It increases from zero at low fields toward unity at high fields. The average velocity v_{ave} of electrons becomes

$$v_{ave} = \mu \mathscr{E} - F(\mu \mathscr{E} - v_{sat}) \ . \qquad (7.4)$$

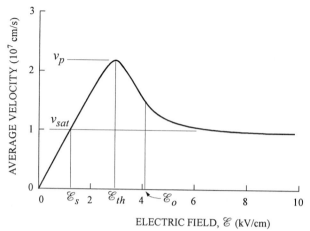

FIGURE 7.3
Average electron velocity vs. electric field in GaAs.

The v_{ave} is a direct indication of current since n_o is constant in Eq. (7.1). An example of v_{ave} as a function of field for GaAs is shown in Fig. 7.3. The threshold field $\mathscr{E}_{th}$ for negative resistance is 3.2 kV/cm for GaAs and 10.5 kV/cm for InP. For efficient transferred-electron effect, the difference in conduction-band minimum between the valleys ΔE should be smaller than the energy gap to avoid voltage near the avalanche breakdown. On the other hand ΔE has to be reasonably large compared to kT so that $F(\mathscr{E})$ is small at low fields. (ΔE for GaAs and InP is 0.31 eV and 0.69 eV, respectively.) It is also required that the mobility and saturation velocity in the satellite valley be smaller than those of the central valley.

The operation of a TED relies totally on the transferred-electron effect. The *I-V* characteristics, which have the same form as Fig. 7.3, indicate a region of negative differential resistance resulting from negative mobility, because an increase of voltage causes a decrease of current. One can presumably use these final *I-V* characteristics to incorporate a TED in a circuit for amplification and oscillation (see Appendix C2–Applications of Negative Differential Resistance). However, In most practical TED applications, the nature of the transferred-electron effect is critical. Understanding of this internal mechanism is important in order to distinguish the TED from other devices possessing negative differential resistance.

When a TED is biased in the region of negative resistance with $\mathscr{E}_o$ (Fig. 7.3), the space charge and the electrical field distribution become internally unstable. This is a unique feature of the TED since other negative-resistance devices are stable internally, but can be externally unstable when connected in certain circuit configurations. This instability in a TED starts with a dipole which consists of excess electrons (negative charge) and depleted electrons (positive charge) as shown in Fig. 7.4. The dipole may arise from many possibilities such as doping inhomogeneity, material defect, or random noise. This dipole sets up a higher field for the electrons at that location. This higher field, according to Fig. 7.3, slows down these electrons relative to the rest. As a result, the region of excess electrons will grow because electrons from the trailing path are arriving with a higher velocity. By the same token the region of depleted electrons (positive charge) also grows because electrons slightly ahead will leave with a higher velocity.

Mathematically, in a standard semiconductor, if a dipole is generated it decays rapidly according to

$$\Delta n(t) = \Delta n(0) \exp\left(\frac{-t}{\tau_D}\right) \tag{7.5}$$

where

$$\tau_D = \frac{\varepsilon_s}{q\mu n_o} \tag{7.6}$$

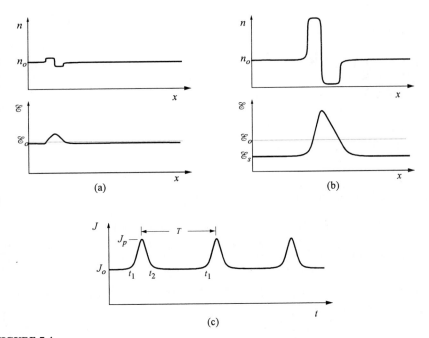

(a) (b) (c)

FIGURE 7.4
(a) A small dipole grows to (b) a mature domain when the field outside the domain equals to $\mathscr{E}_s$. (c) The output current waveform, with t_1 corresponding to (a) and t_2 corresponding to (b).

is the dielectric relaxation time. With negative mobility (μ_-) the dipole grows exponentially instead with

$$\tau_D = \frac{\varepsilon_s}{q|\mu_-|n_o} \ .$$

(7.7)

As the dipole grows, the field at that location also grows, but only at the expense of the field everywhere else. When the field outside the dipole decreases to $\mathcal{E}_s$, called the sustaining field, the velocity of electrons inside and outside the dipole are the same and equal to the saturation velocity. At this point the dipole ceases to grow and is said to mature to a domain, usually still near the cathode. At any specific time, only one domain can exist because of the high field required to drive the velocity to v_{sat} (Fig. 7.3).

The terminal current waveform is shown in Fig. 7.4(c). At t_2, a domain is formed and all electrons move with v_{sat} so that

$$J_o = qn_o v_{sat} \ .$$

(7.8)

At t_1, the domain reaches the anode and before another domain is formed, the electric field jumps to $\mathcal{E}_o$. During the formation of a domain, the field outside the dipole passes through the value of $\mathcal{E}_{th}$ where the peak velocity occurs so that

$$J_p = qn_o v_p \ .$$

(7.9)

The current pulse width corresponds to the interval between the arrival of the domain at the anode, and the formation of a new domain. The period T corresponds to the transit time of L/v_{sat} where L is the device length. It should be pointed out that this terminal current waveform of Fig. 7.4(c) is not characteristic of other negative-resistance devices.

A TED can be operated in numerous modes, depending on the frequency and field both of which are controlled mainly by the external resonant circuit and the applied voltage. These include the transit-time mode, delayed mode, quenched mode, and limited-space-charge accumulation (LSA) mode.

1. Transit-time (Gunn) mode: As the name implies, this mode operates with transit-time frequency v_{sat}/L. It is further divided into transit-time dipole-layer mode (Fig. 7.5(a)) and transit-time accumulation-layer mode. The difference in the latter is that only an accumulation layer is formed, without the depletion layer or the dipole. The criteria for dipole formation is that the transit time is larger than the τ_D in Eq. (7.7) such that a domain can have enough time to mature. Assuming a μ_- of $- 100$ cm^2/V-s, the criteria becomes

$$n_o L > 10^{12} \ (\text{cm}^{-2}) \ .$$

(7.10)

Below this critical n_oL level, the field and carriers are intrinsically stable and this condition is required for amplification applications. In the transit-time mode, a small L improves the frequency capability, but decreases the power output due to reduced total voltage across the sample. The power is given by

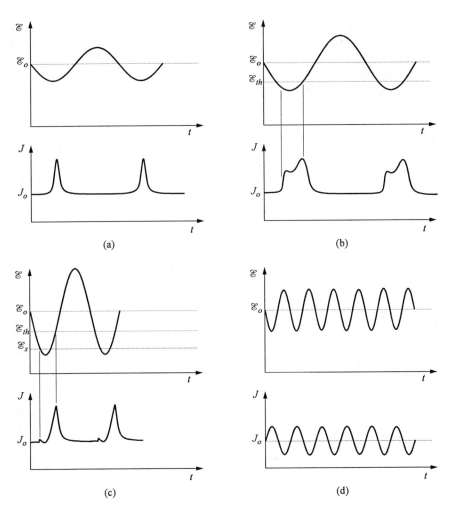

FIGURE 7.5
Field (voltage) and current waveforms for (a) transit-time dipole-layer mode, (b) delayed mode, (c) quenched mode and (d) LSA mode. Field is the average value (V/L) across the device, and it is time variant because of the resonant circuit of which part of the component is connected in series with the TED.

$$\text{Power} = \frac{V^2}{R} = \frac{\mathscr{E}^2 L^2}{R} = \frac{\mathscr{E}^2 v_{sat}^2}{Rf^2} \tag{7.11}$$

and is shown to be inversely proportional to the square of frequency. Another shortcoming of this mode is the low power efficiency due to narrow current pulses.

2. Delayed mode: In this mode the current pulse is widened for increased power efficiency. The timing is adjusted by the external circuit such that the domain arrives at the anode when the field is below $\mathscr{E}_{th}$ (Fig. 7.5(b)). Once the domain is annihilated, another one is not formed until the fields rises above $\mathscr{E}_{th}$ and during that time, current simply follows the field because it is in the positive resistance regime. The frequency of operation is slightly lower than the transit-time frequency.

3. Quenched mode: To avoid the frequency limitation due to the transit time, the domain can be quenched before it reaches the anode. This can be achieved when part of the field drops below $\mathscr{E}_s$ as shown in Fig. 7.5(c).

4. Limited-space-charge accumulation (LSA) mode: In this mode a domain is not allowed to form at all. To effectively avoid domain formation, the period of the waveform is chosen such that it is below τ_D in Eq. (7.7) to avoid domain maturity, and above τ_D in Eq. (7.6) for small dipoles to decay. These place the frequency within the range

$$\frac{\varepsilon_s}{q\mu n_o} < \frac{1}{f} < \frac{\varepsilon_s}{q|\mu_-|n_o} \tag{7.12}$$

or an n_o/f ratio of 10^4 to 10^5 s-cm^{-3}. Even though for some fixed L, the frequency can be higher than the transit-time mode, due to Eq. (7.12), one finds that the frequency range (≈ 20 GHz for GaAs and higher for InP) is not as high as the transit-time mode for state-of-the-art devices. But since the device length L is not a critical factor, the demand for a thin active layer will be relaxed. In this mode, high power output can be obtained with pulsed operations.

Although a TED is a bulk device, the nature of the contact, especially on the cathode side, can improve the performance. Above a critical current level, the field distribution of an n^+-n-n^+ structure in the active region is no longer uniform (Fig. 7.6(a)). The low field at the cathode creates a dead zone for domain formation. This can be circumvented by a Schottky-barrier (metal) contact with low barrier height (Fig. 7.6(b)). A composite contact shown in Fig. 7.6(c) can even maximize the field at the cathode.

7.4 APPLICATIONS

1. Microwave oscillation: A TEO in a tuned resonant circuit can generate microwave power with a DC bias. The n-type active region must be doped above the critical level ($n_oL > 10^{12}$ cm^{-2}) for this application. The TEO is one of the most important microwave oscillators. Compared to an IMPATT diode (see Chapter 8), it has lower power output (by a factor of ≈ 5) but it requires a lower voltage and is less noisy. The demand on power supply stability, on the other hand, is very stringent. For CW operations, a TEO can produce power from a few mW to a few W, and for pulse operations, from 1 W to several kW. The power is often limited by heating and as a result pulse operation is much more efficient. Theoretically a TEO can operate at a frequency as high as 150 GHz. It is used in radar systems, detection systems such as intrusion alarms and speedometers, remote controls such as door openers, parametric amplifiers, and general microwave test instruments.

2. Microwave amplification: A TEA is usually doped sub-critically ($n_oL < 10^{12}$ cm^{-2}) to avoid domain formation and oscillation. It utilizes the properties of negative differential resistance. Signals of frequencies close to the transit-time frequency can be applied (see Appendix C2).

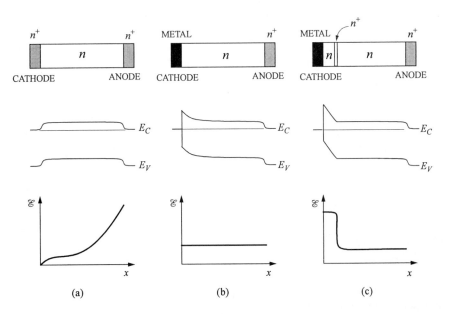

FIGURE 7.6
Structures, energy-band diagrams (without bias) and field distributions (with bias) for (a) a standard TED with n^+-cathode contact, (b) with Schottky-barrier contact and (c) with two-zone Schottky-barrier contact.

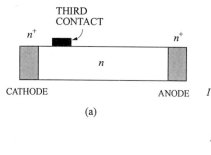

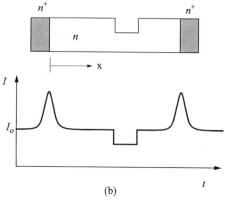

FIGURE 7.7
(a) A TED with a third contact near the cathode. (b) A TED with non-uniform cross-section and its current waveform.

3. As functional devices: For functional and logic applications, a three-terminal device is often needed to isolate the input and the output. Figure 7.7 shows a TED with a third terminal near the cathode. This additional contact can be a metal or an MIS structure. When the cathode-to-anode voltage is biased with a field below $\mathscr{E}_{th}$, a domain is not formed until triggered by the third terminal. A TED with arbitrary cross-section can also generate a corresponding current waveform as shown in Fig. 7.7(b). Since n_o is uniform (outside the domain), and current has to be continuous, velocities of the electrons must be different at different locations for non-uniform cross-section. It can be shown that carriers in the vicinity of the domain travel with the domain at v_{sat}, the current from Eq. (7.8) can be generalized to

$$I_o(t) = qn_o(x)A(x)v_{sat} \quad , \quad x = v_{sat}t \tag{7.13}$$

where $A(x)$ is the cross-section area. Equation (7.13) also implies that an n_o variation in space also produces the same effect. With proper choice of devices and connections, different functions can be realized. Examples are analog–digital converter, delay line, memory, and shift register.[11,12]

4. As logic devices: Logic operations such as OR, NOT, AND, NOR, and NAND can be realized.[11,12]

REFERENCES

1. B. K. Ridley and T. B. Watkins, "The possibility of negative resistance effects in semiconductors," *Proc. Phys. Soc. Lond.*, **78**, 293 (1961).
2. C. Hilsum, "Transferred electron amplifiers and oscillators," *Proc. IRE.*, **50**, 185 (1962).
3. J. B. Gunn, "Microwave oscillations of current in III-V semiconductors," *Solid State Comm.*, **1**, 88 (1963).
4. J. B. Gunn, "The discovery of microwave oscillations in gallium arsenide," *IEEE Trans. Electron Dev.*, **ED-23**, 705 (1976).
5. H. Kromer, "Theory of the Gunn effect," *Proc. IEEE*, **52**, 1736 (1964).

6. A. R. Hutson, A. Jayaraman, A. G. Chynoweth, A. S. Coriell and W. L. Feldman, "Mechanism for the Gunn effect from a pressure experiment," *Phys. Rev. Lett.*, **14**, 639 (1965).

7. M. Shur, *Physics of semiconductor devices*, Prentice Hall, Englewood Cliffs, 1990.

8. H. Thim, "Microwave sources," in C. Hilsum, Vol. Ed., T. S. Moss, Ser. Ed., *Handbook on semiconductor*, Vol. 4, North-Holland, Amsterdam, 1981.

9. P. J. Bulman, G. S. Hobson and B. C. Taylor, *Transferred electron devices*, Academic Press, New York, 1972.

10. B. G. Bosch and R. W. H. Engelmann, *Gunn-effect electronics*, Wiley, New York, 1975.

11. M. Shur, *GaAs devices and circuits*, Plenum Press, New York, 1987.

12. A. G. Milnes, *Semiconductor devices and integrated electronics*, Van Nostrand, New York, 1980.

CHAPTER

8

IMPACT-IONIZATION-AVALANCHE
TRANSIT-TIME
DIODE

8.1 HISTORY

The IMPact-ionization-Avalanche Transit-Time (IMPATT) diode is the most powerful solid-state microwave generator in the 3–300 GHz range. It can be built using different structures as shown in Section 8.2. The original structure proposed by Read is still one of the most common versions and is called the Read diode.[1]

The original idea of generating negative resistance via transit-time delay was given by Shockley in 1954.[2] The injection mechanism was based on forward biased p-n junction current. In 1958, Read proposed a p^+-n-i-n^+ structure (known as Read diode) that uses avalanche multiplication as the injection mechanism.[1] The first experimental observation of the IMPATT oscillation was made by Johnston et al. in 1965 on Si p^+-n structures.[3] Subsequently, the originally proposed Read diode was shown to work by Lee et al. a few months later (both of these two groups were from Bell Telephone Laboratories).[4] In 1966, Misawa showed that a p-i-n structure (Misawa diode) can also be used.[5] A historic perspective of early IMPATT diode activities is found in an article by De Loach.[6] The small signal theory of the IMPATT diode was developed by Misawa[5] and Gilden and Hines.[7] Detailed treatment of the device can be found in Refs. 8 and 9.

8.2 STRUCTURE

An IMPATT diode can be realized by different structures, schematically shown in Fig. 8.1. In general, they are variations of the p-n junction and when reverse

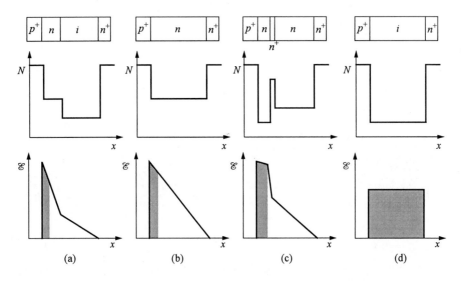

FIGURE 8.1
Schematics for common structures of IMPATT diodes with their doping and electric field profiles. (a) Read diode (hi-lo structure). (b) Step *p-n* junction. (c) Lo-hi-lo structure. (d) *p-i-n* structure (Misawa diode). In most cases ((a)–(c)), a Schottky barrier can be used as the injecting junction where the top layer of p^+-region is replaced by metal. The shaded area represents avalanche multiplication region.

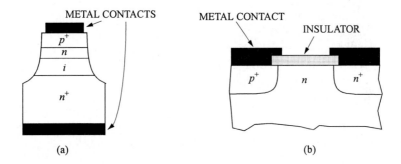

FIGURE 8.2
Cross-section for (a) a vertical IMPATT structure and (b) a horizontal structure.

biased, avalanche multiplication occurs within the high field region. In most structures, a Schottky barrier can be used as the injecting junction instead of the p^+-n junction. A common practice is to build the IMPATT diode with vertical current flow as shown in the cross-section of Fig. 8.2, although lateral devices can

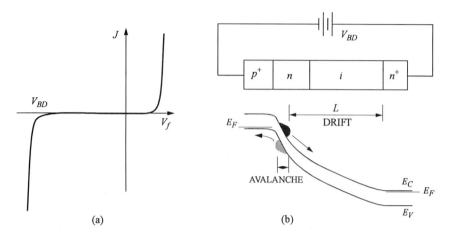

FIGURE 8.3
(a) DC characteristics for an IMPATT diode. Forward voltage V_f is voltage applied to the p^+-terminal.
(b) Energy-band diagram under reverse bias when avalanche occurs.

be built with planar technology. In the former case, the active layers are grown epitaxially on a degenerate substrate to reduce series resistance. For high frequency devices, MBE or MOCVD is required for thin layers. The dopants can be incorporated by diffusion, ion implantation or in-situ doping during epitaxial growth. These devices are usually used as discrete components, after mesa etching and dicing. When these devices are used as a power source, great care must be exercised in packaging to ensure good thermal conduction. The device is usually bonded upside down so that the active layers are closer to the heat sink. A typical Read diode has an n-layer of 1–2 μm at a doping of $\approx 10^{16}$ cm^{-3}, and an intrinsic layer of 3–20 μm. For high-frequency operation, these thicknesses have to be reduced. For frequencies above 100 GHz, they are thinner than 0.5 μm. Very often the heavily doped substrate has to be thinned down from the commercial wafer thickness of ≈ 500 μm to reduce series resistance. Most commonly used materials are Si and GaAs, but the use of other semiconductors such as Ge, InP, GaAlAs have been employed.

8.3 CHARACTERISTICS

The DC characteristics of an IMPATT diode are shown in Fig. 8.3(a). They are not different from a standard p-n junction or Schottky-barrier diode. These characteristics do not show conventional negative differential resistance (negative dV/dI). The negative resistance of an IMPATT diode is dynamic in nature such that the small signals of the terminal voltage and current waveforms are of opposite polarities. When a sinusoidal voltage is applied to an IMPATT diode, the current responds with a 180° phase lag such that when the AC component of the voltage is positive, the AC component of the current is negative. This 180° phase shift is the sum of two delays: (1) the injection phase delay and (2) the transit-time delay. The feature of an IMPATT diode is the presence of an avalanche region and a drift region (Fig. 8.3(b)). The avalanche region is very thin and is close to the p^+ or metal top region. When electrons and holes are generated by avalanche multiplication, holes are collected by the p^+-region immediately and the packet of electrons drift to the n^+-substrate with saturation velocity v_{sat}.

The terminal voltage and current waveforms of an IMPATT diode are shown in Fig. 8.4. The applied voltage has a mean value at the verge of avalanche breakdown, or V_{BD}. In the positive cycle, avalanche multiplication occurs. The generation rate of carriers, however, as shown, is not in unison with the voltage or field. This is because the generation rate is not only a function of the field, but also of the number of existing carriers. After the field passes the peak value, the generation rate continues to grow until the field is below the critical value. This phase lag is approximately 90° and is called the injection phase delay.

When the electrons traverse toward the n^+-region with a saturation velocity, an external current is induced. According to the Ramo-Shockley theorem, a charge Q moving between two parallel plates of distance L apart induces a terminal current of

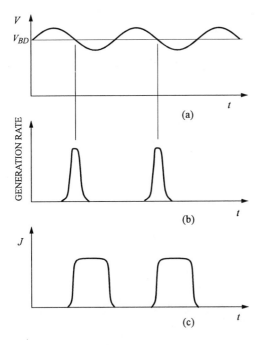

(a)

(b)

(c)

FIGURE 8.4
Terminal (a) voltage and (c) current waveforms of an IMPATT diode. In (b), the avalanche generation rate lags the applied voltage by 90°.

$$J = \frac{Q v_{sat}}{AL} \ . \tag{8.1}$$

This equation can be obtained by calculating the induced charge partitioned at the anode Q_a which is a function of the location of Q,

$$Q_a = \frac{Qx}{L} = \frac{Q v_{sat} t}{L} \tag{8.2}$$

and

$$J = \frac{dQ_a}{A dt} = \frac{Q v_{sat}}{AL} \ . \tag{8.3}$$

For maximum efficiency, the current should drop near the end of the cycle before the voltage rises above the mean value. Since the duration of the current pulse corresponds to the transit time of the charge packet, the frequency of operation is

$$f = \frac{v_{sat}}{2L} \ . \tag{8.4}$$

Figure 8.4 shows that positive current coincides with the negative AC voltage. This is the origin of dynamic negative resistance, or negative power absorbed by the device.

To calculate the magnitude of current in Fig. 8.4(c), the avalanche current has to be known precisely but the dynamic nature of the field and the number of carriers make the calculation extremely complicated. One can, however, estimate the maximum current level. The injected charge Q creates a change of field (Gauss' law), and since during the transit period the breakdown field $\mathscr{E}_{BD}$ for avalanche is to be avoided,

$$\frac{Q_{max}}{A} \approx \varepsilon_s \mathscr{E}_{BD} \tag{8.5}$$

and

$$J_{max} \approx \frac{Q_{max} v_{sat}}{AL} \approx 2 \varepsilon_s \mathscr{E}_{BD} f \ . \tag{8.6}$$

To improve the efficiency and the power, the transit of both types of carriers are utilized in the double-drift IMPATT structure shown in Fig. 8.5. The avalanche region is sandwiched between two drift regions. The lengths of the drift regions are adjusted for equal transit times for both carriers. The applied voltage can be doubled compared to the single-drift device. A disadvantage of the device is degraded thermal conduction due to the distance of the buried avalanche layer

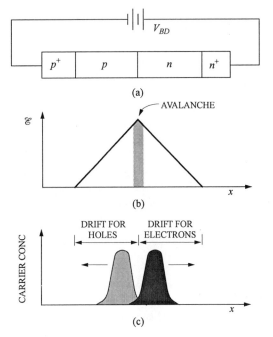

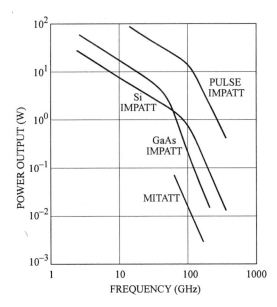

FIGURE 8.5
(a) A double-drift IMPATT diode and its (b) electric field profile and (c) generated carriers after avalanche injection.

FIGURE 8.6
Power-frequency characteristics when used as an oscillator for IMPATT and MITATT diodes. (After Ref. 9)

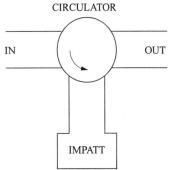

FIGURE 8.7
A reflection-type amplifier in a waveguide using a circulator.

from the surface. In a similar device, the *p-i-n* transit-time diode (Misawa diode) shown in Fig. 8.1(d), the whole intrinsic region is the avalanche injection region, and both electrons and holes participate in the drift process.

The power-frequency performance for different IMPATT diodes is summarized in Fig. 8.6. At high frequencies, L and thus the applied voltage are reduced such that the power decreases with f^2. Silicon devices have higher power capability because of their higher saturation velocity, and higher breakdown field. At low frequencies (high power levels), the power is limited by thermal constraints and it decreases with f. The efficiency of an IMPATT diode remains fairly constant below ≈ 10 GHz but it decreases continuously with higher frequencies. GaAs devices have low-frequency efficiency of $\approx 35\%$ compared to 15% for Si devices. The higher efficiency in GaAs is due to their lower critical field for velocity saturation so that a larger AC voltage swing can be applied (lower voltage in the negative cycle).

8.4 APPLICATIONS

The main application of an IMPATT diode is microwave generation, most dominantly above 3 GHz. When a properly tuned circuit is connected to the IMPATT diode, AC oscillation is obtained from a DC supply. Compared to other diodes having negative resistance such as TED or tunnel diode, it can generate much higher power at higher frequency and is quite reliable. The microwave power source is commonly used in radar systems and alarm systems. The main disadvantage of an IMPATT diode is the high noise level associated with the inherent statistical nature of the avalanche process. For this reason, an IMPATT diode is used as a local oscillator more commonly in transmitters than in receivers. In this respect GaAs is less noisy than Si because of the closer ionization coefficients for electrons and holes. Another drawback is the high operational voltage (70–150 V) required.

An IMPATT diode, based on the negative resistance, can be used as a microwave amplifier. In practice, it is usually incorporated in a reflection-type amplifier for input–output isolation as shown in Fig. 8.7. The power amplification is given by

$$P_{out} = P_{in} \left(\frac{Z_o + |R|}{Z_o - |R|} \right)^2 \tag{8.7}$$

where R is the dynamic negative resistance and Z_o is the characteristic impedance of the waveguide.

8.5 RELATED DEVICES

8.5.1 Trapped-Plasma Avalanche-Triggered Transit Diode

The TRApped-Plasma Avalanche-Triggered Transit (TRAPATT) diode was discovered experimentally by Prager et al. in 1967.[10] The structure is normally a single-drift, step junction with a p^+-n-n^+ or n^+-p-p^+ doping profile. This mode of operation is initiated by a large AC voltage swing, or equivalently by a large current step. As shown in Fig. 8.8, when the internal electric field increases to the critical value $\mathscr{E}_{BD}$ for avalanche multiplication, it collapses locally due to the generated plasma. The separation and drift of the electrons and holes are then driven by a much smaller field, as if they are "trapped" behind, with a velocity smaller than the saturation velocity. After the plasma is created throughout the entire active region, electrons and holes begin to drift to the opposite terminals, and the field (or voltage) begins to rise.

During the creation of the plasma, the terminal current is a displacement current, given by

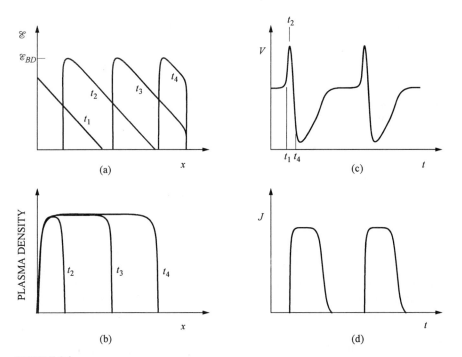

FIGURE 8.8
Operation of a TRAPATT diode. t_1–t_4 indicate different time intervals. (a) Avalanche shock front progression. (b) Growth of plasma region. Terminal (c) voltage and (d) current waveforms.

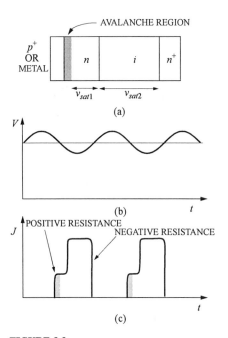

FIGURE 8.9
(a) In a DOVATT diode, the drift region consists of two materials of different v_{sat}. (b) Terminal voltage and (c) current waveforms. In this example, $v_{sat1} < v_{sat2}$.

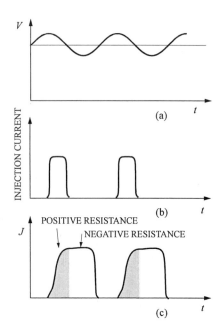

FIGURE 8.10
(a) Voltage and (c) current waveforms for a MITATT diode. (b) The injection current has a mean phase delay between 0° and 90°.

$$J = \varepsilon_s \frac{\partial \mathscr{E}}{\partial t} \quad . \tag{8.8}$$

The space dependence of the field is also governed by the Poisson equation. It can be shown that the location of $\mathscr{E} = \mathscr{E}_{BD}$ travels with a velocity

$$v = \frac{\partial x}{\partial t} = \frac{J}{qN} \quad . \tag{8.9}$$

The criterion for a TRAPATT mode is that the so-called avalanche shock front, whose velocity is given by Eq. (8.9), advances faster than the saturation velocity of carriers. A practical value can be as high as a factor of three compared to v_{sat}.

It is interesting to note that the TRAPATT mode does not depend on the injection phase delay. The advantage of a TRAPATT mode is the higher efficiency ($\approx 75\%$) and higher power than an IMPATT mode. A TRAPATT diode is usually operated in the pulse mode. It can also extend the frequency from the transit-time frequency to a lower range (1–10 GHz), which is sometimes of practical importance. The disadvantage of a TRAPATT diode is its noise level which is even higher than an IMPATT diode.

8.5.2 Double-Velocity Avalanche Transit-Time Diode

The DOuble-Velocity Avalanche Transit-Time (DOVATT) diode, as shown in Fig. 8.9, consists of a drift region in which carriers traverse with two different saturation velocities. This is usually accomplished by a heterojunction with materials of different v_{sat}. The advantage is a tailored current waveform to enhance the efficiency.

8.5.3 Mixed-Tunnel-Avalanche Transit-Time Diode

In a MIxed-Tunnel-Avalanche Transit-Time (MITATT) diode, the injection current contains a tunneling-current component that is in-phase with the applied voltage, giving rise to an overall injection phase-delay between 0° and 90° (Fig. 8.10). This results in degraded efficiency compared to an IMPATT diode. The advantage is reduced noise level due to less dependence on avalanche current. In terms of structure, the doping near the injecting junction has to be increased for tunneling to occur.

REFERENCES

1. W. T. Read, Jr., "A proposed high-frequency, negative-resistance diode," *Bell Syst. Tech. J.*, **37**, 401 (1958).
2. W. Shockley, "Negative resistance arising from transit time in semiconductor diodes," *Bell Syst. Tech. J.*, **33**, 799 (1954).
3. R. L. Johnston, B. C. De Loach, Jr. and B. G. Cohen, "A silicon diode microwave oscillator," *Bell Syst. Tech. J.*, **44**, 369 (1965).
4. C. A. Lee, R. L. Batdorf, W. Wiegmann and G. Kaminsky, "The Read diode - An avalanching, transit-time, negative-resistance oscillator," *Appl. Phys. Lett.*, **6**, 89 (1965).
5. T. Misawa, "Negative resistance in *p-n* junctions under avalanche breakdown conditions, Parts I and II," *IEEE Trans. Electron Dev.*, **ED-13**, 137 (1966).
6. B. C. De Loach, Jr., "The IMPATT story," *IEEE Trans. Electron Dev.*, **ED-23**, 657 (1976).
7. M. Gilden and M. E. Hines, "Electronic tuning effects in the Read microwave avalanche diode," *IEEE Trans. Electron Dev.*, **ED-13**, 169 (1966).
8. T. Misawa, "IMPATT diodes," in R. K. Willardson and A. C. Beer, Eds., *Semiconductors and Semimetals*, Vol. 7, Pt. B, p. 371, Academic Press, New York, 1971.
9. S. M. Sze, *High-speed semiconductor devices*, Wiley, New York, 1990.
10. H. J. Prager, K. K. N. Chang and S. Weisbrod, "High-power, high-efficiency silicon avalanche diodes at ultra high frequencies," *Proc. IEEE*, **55**, 586 (1967).

CHAPTER
9

BARRIER-INJECTION TRANSIT-TIME DIODE

9.1 HISTORY

The barrier-injection transit-time diode, more commonly known as the BARITT diode, is similar to another transit-time device, the IMPATT diode. The main difference is that the injection current here is due to thermionic emission over the barrier, as opposed to avalanche multiplication. Unlike the avalanche current, the injection current in a BARITT diode does not have an injection phase delay. The negative differential resistance comes from only the transit-time delay.

The original idea of obtaining negative differential resistance by transit-time delay was introduced by Shockley in 1954.[1] A standard *p-n* junction diffusion current was proposed as the injection mechanism. Using avalanche current to introduce additional phase delay (as in an IMPATT diode) was proposed by Read in 1958,[2] and later shown experimentally by Johnston et al. in 1965.[3] Ruegg[4] and Wright[5] in 1968 independently proposed the BARITT mode of operation. The first BARITT diode was demonstrated by Coleman and Sze in 1971.[6] For more detailed discussions of the device, readers are referred to Ref. 7.

9.2 STRUCTURE

A BARITT diode consists of two diodes back-to-back as shown in Fig. 9.1. The diodes can be either *p-n* junctions or Schottky barriers, or a combination of the two. The thickness of the middle layer has to be equal to the sum of the depletion widths for "punch-through" to occur. Depending on the doping level, a typical

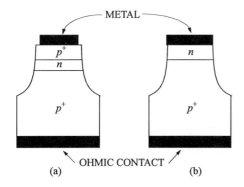

FIGURE 9.1
Cross-section showing a BARITT diode with (a) a *p-n* junction injector and (b) a Schottky-barrier injector.

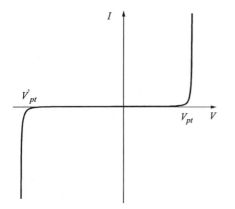

FIGURE 9.2
DC *I-V* characteristics of a BARITT diode.

range is between 0.5–10 μm. The substrate is usually degenerate for low series resistance, and the active layers are grown epitaxially. Sometimes, the substrate is even thinned to approximately 10 μm to further reduce the power dissipation from series resistance. A BARITT diode is usually diced as a discrete device and bonded upside-down in a microwave cavity that has efficient thermal conduction. Most commercial BARITT devices are made on silicon material due to its mature technology, but other semiconductors can also be used.

9.3 CHARACTERISTICS

When two rectifiers are connected back-to-back, as in the case of a BARITT diode, the applied bias is developed mainly across the reverse-biased junction. If the voltage is increased until the depletion edges meet, punch-through is said to occur. The DC characteristics of a BARITT diode is shown in Fig. 9.2. If the junctions are asymmetric, the punch-through voltages in either direction are different, $V_{pt} \neq V'_{pt}$. These characteristics do not show a negative differential resistance, or negative dV/dI. The transit-time diodes have a "dynamic" negative

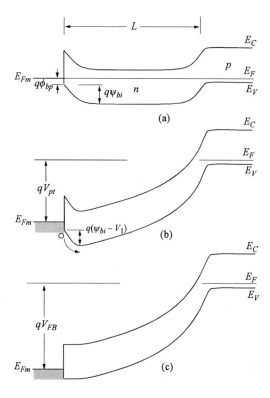

FIGURE 9.3
Energy-band diagrams of a BARITT
diode having a Schottky-barrier
injector. (a) Under thermal
equilibrium. (b) At punch-through.
(c) At flat-band condition.

differential resistance in that the small signals of the terminal voltage and current
waveforms have opposite polarities.

The energy-band diagram of a BARITT diode, taking a Schottky barrier as
an injector, is shown in Fig. 9.3. At punch-through, L equals the sum of the
depletion widths and

$$V_{pt} \approx \frac{qN_D L^2}{2\varepsilon_s} - L\sqrt{\frac{2qN_D\psi_{bi}}{\varepsilon_s}} \; . \tag{9.1}$$

At flat-band condition, ψ_{bi} at the injecting junction is reduced to zero and

$$V_{FB} \approx \frac{qN_D L^2}{2\varepsilon_s} \; . \tag{9.2}$$

For the injection cycle, the bias is usually between V_{pt} and V_{FB}. In this bias range,
the built-in potential of the injecting junction is reduced to[7]

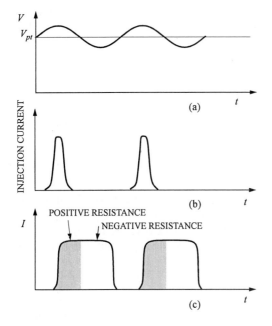

(a)

(b)

(c)

FIGURE 9.4
(a) Terminal voltage, (b) injection current and (c) terminal current waveforms for a BARITT diode.

$$\psi_{bi} - V_1 = \frac{(V_{FB} - V)^2}{4V_{FB}} \tag{9.3}$$

where V_1 is the portion of the applied voltage across the injecting junction. The injection current, in this case due to holes, is given by

$$J_p = A^*_p T^2 \exp\left[-\frac{q(\phi_{bp} + \psi_{bi})}{kT}\right]\left[\exp\left(\frac{qV_1}{kT}\right) - 1\right]$$

$$\approx A^*_p T^2 \exp\left(-\frac{q\phi_{bp}}{kT}\right)\exp\left[-\frac{q(V_{FB} - V)^2}{4kTV_{FB}}\right] . \tag{9.4}$$

In the case a p-n junction as an injector, ϕ_{bp} in Eq. (9.4) becomes zero.

The voltage and current waveforms for a BARITT diode are shown in Fig. 9.4. After a charge Q is injected, it travels to the substrate with a saturation velocity v_{sat}. According to the Ramo-Shockley theorem, a charge moving within two electrodes spaced L apart would induce a terminal current of

$$I = \frac{Qv_{sat}}{L} . \tag{9.5}$$

Notice that the injection current is in-phase with the AC voltage, giving rise to a non-ideal terminal-current waveform that contains positive resistance. This portion of the current is dissipative because the voltage is still on the positive cycle. This is the main reason for the much reduced efficiency of a BARITT diode compared to an IMPATT diode. The maximum efficiency is calculated to be about 10% whereas for IMPATT diodes it is about 15% (for Si devices). The terminal current-pulse width is determined by the transit time L/v_{sat} and it constitutes three quarters of the cycle. Therefore, the frequency of operation is required to be

$$f = \frac{3v_{sat}}{4L} \; .$$

(9.6)

Experimental power-frequency characteristics of a BARITT diode are shown in Fig. 9.5. The power decreases with f^2 because higher-frequency operation requires smaller L, which limits the applied voltage. The efficiency for low-frequency operation is around 5%, and it also decreases with frequency.

9.4 APPLICATIONS

A BARITT diode is used mainly as microwave generator. When connected to a properly tuned tank circuit, an oscillator results that produces microwave AC signals from a DC source. This microwave power source is commonly used in burglar and proximity alarm systems. The advantages of a BARITT diode are low noise level and low-voltage operation. The avalanche current associated with an IMPATT diode is very noisy and it requires high voltage, in the range of 75–150 V. Unlike an IMPATT diode, a BARITT diode can be used for local oscillator in microwave detectors because of its low noise level. An example is the Doppler radar system where the BARITT diode is used not only as the microwave transmitter, but also as a mixer-detector unit. The drawback of a

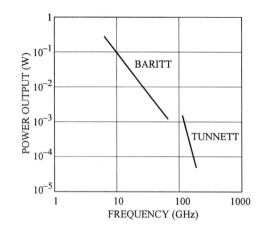

FIGURE 9.5
Power-frequency characteristics of BARITT diode and TUNNETT diode. (After Ref. 8)

BARITT diode is reduced efficiency and lower output power compared to an IMPATT diode.

From the DC characteristics shown in Fig. 9.2, a BARITT diode, sometimes called a punch-through diode, can also be used as a voltage limiter. The advantage compared to a regular Zener diode is that clipping occurs at both polarities. A punch-through diode can thus replace two Zener diodes connected back-to-back.

9.5 RELATED DEVICES

9.5.1 Double-Velocity Transit-Time Diode

A DOVETT diode operates in the DOuble-VElocity Transit-Time mode.[9] Its unique feature is that in the drift region there are two values for the saturation velocity, spatially separated as shown in Fig. 9.6. If v_{sat1} is suppressed, the current yielding positive resistance can be minimized for increased overall efficiency. The difference in saturation velocity is usually accomplished by a heterojunction. The injection current can be thermionic emission (as in a BARITT diode) or tunneling (as in a TUNNETT diode, to be discussed next). If the injection current is due to avalanche multiplication (as in an IMPATT diode), a DOVATT diode is obtained (see Section 8.5.2).

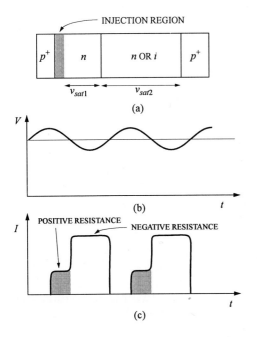

FIGURE 9.6
(a) Structure of the DOVETT diode. (b) Terminal voltage and (c) current waveforms under operation. $v_{sat1} < v_{sat2}$.

9.5.2 Tunnel-Injection Transit-Time Diode

In the tunnel-injection transit-time (TUNNETT) diode, the injection current is by tunneling, which occurs at high field of ≈ 1 MV/cm.[2,10] The structure is different from a BARITT diode in that only one junction exists. The vicinity of the injecting junction also has higher doping level (Fig. 9.7). A typical n^+-layer (for

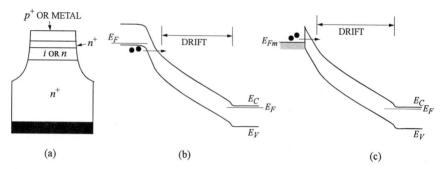

(a)   (b)   (c)

FIGURE 9.7
(a) Structure of a TUNNETT diode. Energy-band diagrams showing (b) band-to-band tunneling in a p-n junction injector, and (c) tunneling through the barrier in a Schottky-barrier injector.

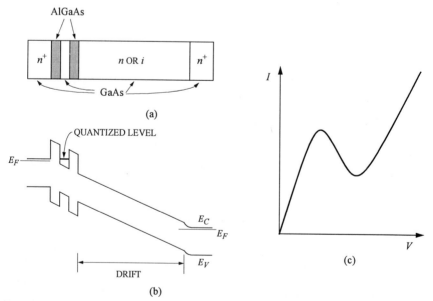

FIGURE 9.8
(a) Structure and (b) energy-band diagram (under bias) of a QWITT diode. (c) Forward I-V characteristics of the injector, resonant-tunneling diode.

an n-type drift region) near the injector has a doping of $\approx 10^{19}$ cm^{-3} and a thickness of ≈ 10 nm. Tunneling can occur band-to-band in the case of a p-n junction injector, and through the barrier in the case of a Schottky barrier as shown in Fig. 9.7. The advantages of a TUNNETT diode include the high-frequency capability that can go up to 1000 GHz theoretically. Experimental performance is summarized in Fig. 9.5. Another advantage is the low-voltage operation which can be as low as 2 V. The limitation on the device is the power capability due to low tunneling current.

9.5.3 Quantum-Well-Injection Transit-Time Diode

The quantum-well-injection transit-time (QWITT) diode also depends on tunneling as the injection current.[11,12] The resonant-tunneling mechanism is via a quantized subband inside a quantum well as shown in Fig. 9.8. The QWITT diode has higher efficiency than the TUNNETT diode. Notice that the DC characteristics of the injecting resonant-tunneling diode have a negative differential resistance (see Chapter 10). When operated within this region, the injection current peaks at the most negative voltage of the cycle so that the injection delay can be increased from 0 to π. The stringent requirement for precise thickness control necessitates MBE or MOCVD growth.

REFERENCES

1. W. Shockley, "Negative resistance arising from transit time in semiconductor diodes," *Bell Syst. Tech. J.*, **33**, 799 (1954).
2. W. T. Read, Jr., "A proposed high-frequency, negative-resistance diode," *Bell Syst. Tech. J.*, **37**, 401 (1958).
3. R. L. Johnston, B. C. De Loach, Jr. and B. G. Cohen, "A silicon diode microwave oscillator," *Bell Syst. Tech. J.*, **44**, 369 (1965).
4. H. W. Ruegg, "A proposed punch-through microwave negative-resistance diode," *IEEE Trans. Electron Dev.*, **ED-15**, 577 (1968).
5. G. T. Wright, "Punch-through transit-time oscillator," *Electron. Lett.*, **4**, 543 (1968).
6. D. J. Coleman, Jr. and S. M. Sze, "A low-noise metal-semiconductor-metal (MSM) microwave oscillator," *Bell Syst. Tech. J.*, **50**, 1695 (1971).
7. S. M. Sze, *Physics of semiconductor devices*, 2nd Ed., Wiley, New York, 1981.
8. S. M. Sze, *High-speed semiconductor devices*, Wiley, New York, 1990.
9. J. E. Sitch, A. Majerfeld, P. N. Robson and F. Hasegawa, "Transit-time-induced microwave negative resistance in Ga$_{1-x}$Al$_x$As–GaAs heterostructure diodes," *Electronics Lett.*, **11**, 457 (1975)
10. J. Nishizawa, "The GaAs TUNNETT diodes," in K. J. Button, Ed., *Infrared and millimeter waves*, Vol. 5, p. 215, Academic Press, 1982.
11. V. P. Kesan, D. P. Neikirk, B. G. Streetman and P. A. Blakey, "A new transit-time device using quantum-well injection," *IEEE Electron Dev. Lett.*, **EDL-8**, 129 (1987).
12. V. P. Kesan, D. P. Neikirk, P. A. Blakey. B. G. Streetman and T. D. Linton, Jr., "The influence of transit-time effects on the optimum design and maximum oscillation frequency of quantum well oscillators," *IEEE Trans. Electron Dev.*, **35**, 405 (1988).

CHAPTER
10

RESONANT-TUNNELING DIODE

10.1 HISTORY

The negative differential resistance of a resonant-tunneling diode (sometimes called double-barrier diode) was predicted by Tsu and Esaki in 1973,[1] following their pioneering work on superlattices in the late 1960s and early 1970s. The structure and characteristics of this diode were first demonstrated by Chang et al. in 1974.[2] Following the much improved results reported by Sollner et al. in 1983,[3] research interest was escalated, partially due to maturing MBE and MOCVD techniques. In 1985, room temperature negative differential resistance in this structure was reported by Shewchuk et al.,[4] and by Tsuchiya et al.[5] Meanwhile, resonant tunneling of holes instead of electrons was observed by Mendez et al.[6] For more detailed discussions on the device, the readers are referred to Refs. 7–9.

10.2 STRUCTURE

A resonant-tunneling diode requires band-edge discontinuity at the conduction band or valence band to form a quantum well and, thus, necessitates heteroepitaxy. The most popular material combination used is GaAs–AlGaAs (Fig. 10.1), followed by GaInAs–AlInAs. The middle quantum-well thickness is typically around 50 Å, and the barrier layers range from 15 to 50 Å. Symmetry of the barrier layers is not required so their thicknesses can be different. The well layer and the barrier layers are all undoped, and they are sandwiched between heavily doped, narrow energy-gap materials, which usually are the same as the well layer. Not shown in Fig. 10.1 are thin layers of undoped spacers (≈ 15 Å GaAs) adjacent to the barrier layers to ensure that dopants do not diffuse to the

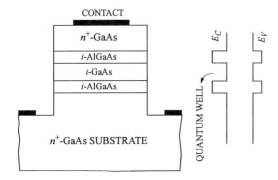

CONTACT

| n^+-GaAs |
| i-AlGaAs |
| i-GaAs |
| i-AlGaAs |

n^+-GaAs SUBSTRATE

QUANTUM WELL

E_C E_V

FIGURE 10.1
The structure of a resonant-tunneling diode using GaAs–AlGaAs hetero-structure as an example. The energy-band diagram shows the formation of a quantum well.

barrier layers. Because thin epitaxial layers and abrupt doping profiles are required, most reported studies used MBE for film deposition, but MOCVD has also been used occasionally. Device isolation is usually achieved by mesa etching, as shown in Fig. 10.1.

10.3 CHARACTERISTICS

A resonant-tunneling diode utilizes the quantization of energy states in a quantum well, as shown in Fig. 10.2(a). Quantum mechanics prescribes that in a quantum well of width W, the conduction band (or valence band) is split into discrete subbands, and the bottom of each subband is given by

$$E_n - E_C = \frac{\hbar^2 n^2}{8m^* W^2} , \qquad n = 1, 2, 3... . \qquad (10.1)$$

Notice that this equation assumes infinite barrier height, and can only serve to give a qualitative picture. In practice, the barrier (ΔE_C) lies in the range of 0.2–0.5 eV, giving an ($E_1 - E_C$) of ≈ 0.1 eV. Under bias condition, carriers can tunnel from one electrode to another via some energy states within the well. While tunneling of carriers out of the well is less constrained, tunneling of carriers into the well is the determining mechanism for the current, and this requires available empty states at the same energy level and also conservation of lateral momentum. Since the perpendicular momentum in a quantum well is zero ($k_x = 0$), the energy of carriers in each subband is given by

$$E = E_n + \frac{\hbar^2 k_\perp^2}{2m^*} \qquad (10.2)$$

where $k_\perp$ is the lateral momentum. From Eq. (10.2), it should be noted that the energy of carriers are quantized only for the bottom of the subband, but the energy

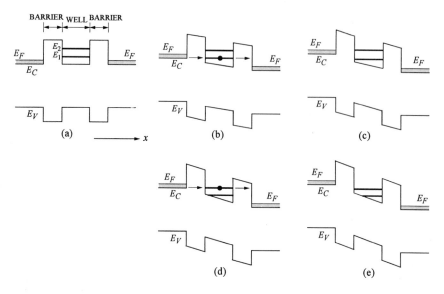

FIGURE 10.2

Energy-band diagrams of a resonant-tunneling diode under different biases. (a) Equilibrium. (b) Resonant tunneling through E_1. (c) First region of negative resistance. (d) Resonant tunneling through E_2. (e) Second region of negative resistance. Their corresponding electrical characteristics are shown in Fig. 10.3.

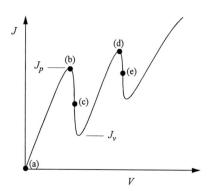

FIGURE 10.3

I-V characteristics of a resonant-tunneling diode with multiple current peaks. Labels (a)–(e) correspond to the energy-band diagrams shown in Fig. 10.2.

above E_n is continuous. The free-electron energy in the emitting electrode is, on the other hand, given by

$$E = E_C + \frac{\hbar^2 k_x^2}{2m^*} + \frac{\hbar^2 k_\perp^2}{2m^*} \ . \tag{10.3}$$

Conservation of lateral momentum requires that the last terms of Eqs. (10.2) and (10.3) are equal. This with the conservation of energy results in the relationship

$$E_C + \frac{\hbar^2 k_x^2}{2m^*} = E_n \ . \tag{10.4}$$

It can be further shown that the maximum number of carriers available for tunneling at a fixed energy occurs at $k_x = 0$.[8] This implies that for maximum tunneling current, the emitter E_C should line up with E_n ($E_C = E_n$) as shown in the bias conditions of Figs. 10.2(b) and 10.2(d). With higher bias, the emitter E_C is slightly above E_n and tunneling current is reduced, resulting in negative differential resistance. This phenomenon produces local current maxima shown in Fig. 10.3.

The ratio of local peak current (J_p) to valley current (J_v) is a critical measure of the negative differential resistance. The peak current is mainly due to tunneling which can be maximized by using material of lighter effective mass. In this respect, the material combination of GaInAs–AlInAs is advantageous over GaAs–AlGaAs. Maximum peak-current density of 3×10^5 A/cm^2 has been observed, and is quite temperature independent since it is a tunneling current. The nonzero valley current is mainly due to thermionic emission over the barriers, and it has a large temperature dependence (smaller J_v with lower temperature). Another small but conceivable contribution is due to tunneling of electrons to higher quantized levels. Even though the number of electrons available for tunneling at energy higher than E_F is very small, there is a thermal distribution tail and this number is not zero, especially when the quantized levels are close together. The maximum J_p/J_v ratio observed is about 50 at room temperature.

As discussed, each region of negative differential resistance is associated with tunneling through one particular quantized subband. The applied bias under which negative differential resistance is observed is roughly twice the value of ($E_n - E_C$)/q since only half of the bias is useful in aligning E_C to E_n (Fig. 10.2). Additional bias is also developed across the spacer layers, as well as the accumulation layer and depletion layer of the heavily doped materials next to the undoped spacers.

As an example, the characteristics shown in Fig. 10.3 have two regions of negative differential resistance for each voltage polarity. In practice, the second current peak is rarely observed, due to the small signal in a large background of thermionic-emission current. The illustration nevertheless brings out the potential advantage over a tunnel diode that is limited to only one region of negative differential resistance. This feature of multiple current peaks is especially important as a functional device, discussed further in the Applications section.

For structures with identical barriers, as in the case of Fig. 10.1, the *I-V* characteristics are symmetrical around the origin. However, the two barriers can be made different in both barrier height (material) and layer thickness, resulting in asymmetrical *I-V* characteristics.

Triple-barrier heterostructures with two successive quantum wells have also been studied, and multiple regions of negative differential resistance can be readily observed (Fig. 10.4). The first current peak is believed due to tunneling through the first quantized levels of both wells (Fig. 10.4(b)), while the second current peak can be attributed to tunneling though different quantized levels (Fig. 10.4(c)),[11] or sequential tunneling with downward transition (Fig. 10.4(d)).[12] In any case, due to an additional barrier, which acts as a filter, sharper current features (dI/dV) are possible as shown in Fig. 10.4(e). Resonant tunneling on structures with quadruple barriers (triple wells) have also been studied.[13,14]

The extreme case of multiple barriers is a compositional superlattice which consists of many alternating layers of barriers and quantum wells (see Appendix B9). Negative resistance from a compositional superlattice had been observed about the same time as from a resonant-tunneling diode.[15] The I-V characteristics with multiple current peaks and the energy-band diagrams at various bias points are shown in Fig. 10.5. One major difference in the superlattice structure is that the quantized levels are broadened into narrow subbands. The first current peak can be observed with a bias comparable to the first subband width (Fig. 10.5(a)). Up to that point, the field is uniform across the superlattice. Additional bias causes a high-field domain to develop in one of the barriers (Fig. 10.5(b)), causing a misalignment of the subbands. In Fig. 10.5(c), current rises again when the first subband is aligned to the second subband. In Figs. 10.5(d) and 10.5(e), the number of barriers with high-field domain is increased to two.

An alternate approach to achieve multiple current peaks is to connect resonant-tunneling diodes in series.[16–19] The structure can be realized with

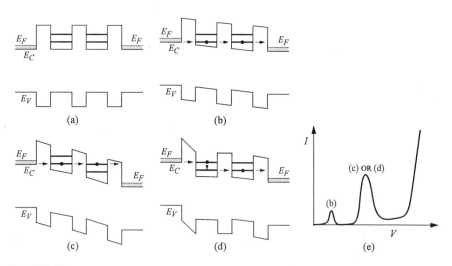

FIGURE 10.4

Tunneling in a triple-barrier heterostructure. Energy-band diagrams correspond to (a) equilibrium, (b) first peak current from tunneling through first quantized levels in both wells, (c) second current peak due to tunneling from first level to second level or (d) sequential tunneling with downward transition. (e) Its I-V characteristics.

vertically integrated double barriers, separated by heavily doped layers. This is in principle very different from the above structures of multiple quantum wells since here the resonant-tunneling diodes are only connected by relatively thick heavily doped layers, and there is no quantum mechanical communication between them. The resultant I-V characteristics in Fig. 10.6 show multiple current peaks. Another useful characteristic is that the current peaks are at approximately the same level. This is advantageous for multi-value logic applications. When a voltage V is applied across n resonant-tunneling diodes, each one absorbs approximately V/n. In practice, a minute difference in the structures would favor one to switch into the negative resistance (off-resonance) first. Since current has to be continuous through all n devices, the overall current drops initially and

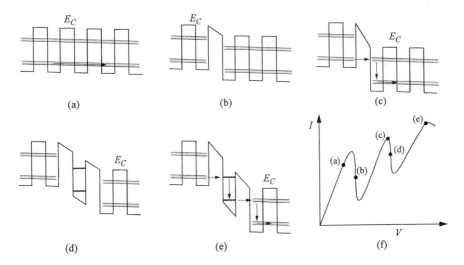

FIGURE 10.5
Tunneling in a compositional superlattice. (a)–(e) Energy-band diagrams (conduction-band edge) with increasing bias. (After Ref. 15) (f) I-V characteristics.

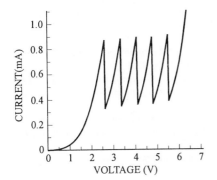

FIGURE 10.6
I-V characteristics of five resonant-tunneling diodes in series. (After Ref. 16)

follows the general shape of the individual diode. The current then rises with voltage again until another resonant-tunneling diode switches. The number of current peaks thus corresponds to the total number of resonant-tunneling diodes in series.

10.4 APPLICATIONS

Because tunneling is inherently a very fast phenomenon that is not transit-time limited, the resonant-tunneling diode is considered among the fastest devices ever made. Furthermore, it does not suffer from minority charge storage. It has been demonstrated that as a mixer it can detect radiation up to 2.5 THz, and as an oscillator it can generate 700 GHz signals. Maximum operational oscillation frequency has been projected to be over 1 THz.[20] Tunneling, on the other hand, is more difficult to supply high current and the output power of an oscillator is limited. The resonant-tunneling diode has also been used in fast pulse-forming circuits and trigger circuits.[21] Other applications that have been mentioned include the frequency multiplier, harmonic generator and parity generator.[7,10] The unique feature of multiple current peaks can result in efficient functional devices that can perform more complex functions with a single device where conventional design would take many more components. Examples are multi-value logic and memory.[22] The resonant-tunneling diode also serves as the building block for other three-terminal devices such as the resonant-tunneling bipolar transistor (Chapter 38) and the resonant-tunneling hot-electron transistor (Chapter 39). It has been incorporated in structures to study hot-electron spectroscopy.[23] For general applications of negative resistance, the readers can refer to Appendix C2.

REFERENCES

1. R. Tsu and L. Esaki, "Tunneling in a finite superlattice," *Appl. Phys. Lett.*, **22**, 562 (1973).
2. L. L. Chang, L. Esaki and R. Tsu, "Resonant tunneling in semiconductor double barriers," *Appl. Phys. Lett.*, **24**, 593 (1974).
3. T. C. L. G. Sollner, W. D. Goodhue, P. E. Tannenwald, C. D. Parker and D. D. Peck, "Resonant tunneling through quantum wells at frequencies up to 2.5 THz," *Appl. Phys. Lett.*, **43**, 588 (1983).
4. T. J. Shewchuk, P. C. Chapin and P. D. Coleman, "Resonant tunneling oscillations in a GaAs-Al$_x$Ga$_{1-x}$As heterostructure at room temperature," *Appl. Phys. Lett.*, **46**, 508 (1985).
5. M. Tsuchiya, H. Sakaki and J. Yoshino, "Room temperature observation of differential negative resistance in an AlAs/GaAs/AlAs resonant tunneling diode," *Japanese J. Appl. Phys.*, **24**, L466 (1985).
6. E. E. Mendez, W. I. Wang, B. Ricco and L. Esaki, "Resonant tunneling of holes in AlAs-GaAs-AlAs heterostructures," *Appl. Phys. Lett.*, **47**, 415 (1985).
7. T. C. L. G. Sollner, E. R. Brown, W. D. Goodhue and H. Q. Le, "Microwave and millimeter-wave resonant-tunneling devices," in F. Capasso, Ed., *Physics of quantum electron devices*, Springer-Verlag, Berlin, 1990.
8. F. Capasso, S. Sen, F. Beltram and A. Y. Cho, "Resonant tunneling and superlattice devices: Physics and circuits," in F. Capasso, Ed., *Physics of quantum electron devices*, Springer-Verlag, Berlin, 1990.
9. S. Yngvesson, *Microwave semiconductor devices*, Kluwer Academic, Boston, 1991.

10. S. Sen, F. Capasso, A. Y. Cho and D. Sivco, "Resonant tunneling device with multiple negative differential resistance: Digital and signal processing applications with reduced circuit complexity," *IEEE Trans. Electron Dev.*, **ED-34**, 2185 (1987).

11. T. Nakagawa, H. Imamoto, T. Kojima and K. Ohta, "Observation of resonant tunneling in AlGaAs/GaAs triple barrier diodes," *Appl. Phys. Lett.*, **49**, 73 (1986).

12. R. E. Nahory and N. Tabatabaie, "Resonant tunneling devices," *J. De Physique*, Colloque C5, Supp. 11, **48**, C5-585 (1987).

13. T. Tanoue, H. Mizuta and S. Takahashi, "A triple-well resonant-tunneling diode for multiple-valued logic application," *IEEE Electron Dev. Lett.*, **EDL-9**, 365 (1988).

14. H. Mizuta, T. Tanoue and S. Takahashi, "A new triple-well resonant tunneling diode with controllable double-negative resistance," *IEEE Trans. Electron Dev.*, **ED-35**, 1951 (1988).

15. L. Esaki and L. L. Chang, "New transport phenomenon in a semiconductor 'Superlattice'," *Phys. Rev. Lett.*, **33**, 495 (1974).

16. A. A. Lakhani, R. C. Potter and H. S. Hier, "Eleven-bit parity generator with a single, vertically integrated resonant tunnelling device," *Electronics Lett.*, **24**, 681 (1988).

17. A. A. Lakhani and R. C. Potter, "Combining resonant tunneling diodes for signal processing and multilevel logic," *Appl. Phys. Lett.*, **52**, 1684 (1988).

18. R. C. Potter, A. A. Lakhani, D. Beyea, H. Hier, E. Hempfling and A. Fathimulla, "Three-dimensional integration of resonant tunneling structures for signal processing and three-state logic," *Appl. Phys. Lett.*, **52**, 2163 (1988).

19. S. Sen, F. Capasso, D. Sivco and A. Y. Cho, "New resonant-tunneling devices with multiple negative resistance regions and high room-temperature peak-to-valley ratio," *IEEE Electron Dev. Lett.*, **EDL-9**, 402 (1988).

20. E. R. Brown, C. D. Parker, A. R. Calawa, M. J. Manfra, T. C. L. G. Sollner, C. L. Chen, S. W. Pang and K. M. Molvar, "High-speed resonant-tunneling diodes made from the $In_{0.53}Ga_{0.47}As/AlAs$ material system," *SPIE*, **1288**, 122 (1990).

21. E. Ozbay, D. M. Bloom and S. K. Diamond, "Looking for high frequency applications of resonant tunneling diodes: Triggering," in L. L. Chang, E. E. Mendez and C. Tejedor, Eds., *Resonant tunneling in semiconductors*, Plenum, New York, 1991.

22. A. C. Seabaugh, Y. C. Kao and H. T. Yuan, "Nine-state resonant tunneling diode memory," *IEEE Electron Dev. Lett.*, **EDL-13**, 479 (1992).

23. F. Capasso, S. Sen, A. Y. Cho and A. L. Hutchinson, "Resonant tunneling spectroscopy of hot minority electrons injected in gallium arsenide quantum wells," *Appl. Phys. Lett.*, **50**, 930 (1987).

CHAPTER

11

REAL-SPACE-TRANSFER DIODE

11.1 HISTORY

The concept of the real-space-transfer (RST) diode to obtain negative differential resistance was conceived by Gribnikov in 1972,[1] and independently by Hess et al. in 1979.[2] Analytical modeling was presented by Shichijo et al. in 1980.[3] Computer simulations using the Monte Carlo method were performed by Glisson in the same year.[4] The first experimental evidence of the negative resistance from a RST diode was shown by Keever et al. in 1981.[5] Demonstration of an RST oscillator was made by Coleman et al. in 1982.[6] This device is still under investigation and has not been produced commercially.

11.2 STRUCTURE

The requirement of a real-space-transfer diode is a heterojunction whose two materials have different mobilities. In addition, for an n-channel device, the material having lower mobility must also have a high conduction-band edge E_C. A good choice is the GaAs–AlGaAs heterostructure. Although modulation doping is not a requirement, the heavy doping in the AlGaAs further decreases its mobility and at the same time, the absence of doping in the GaAs layer increases its mobility. Modulation doping results in high mobility ratio and, thus, has been used commonly for the RST diode. An example of the structure is shown in Fig. 11.1. The thickness of the intrinsic GaAs is not important as the main channel is confined to the AlGaAs–GaAs heterointerface. Typically a GaAs thickness of ≈ 1 μm is used. The AlGaAs layer has to be much thicker than the main channel for efficient real-space transfer. In this case, since the main channel is thin

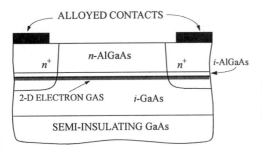

ALLOYED CONTACTS

n^+ n-AlGaAs n^+ i-AlGaAs

2-D ELECTRON GAS i-GaAs

SEMI-INSULATING GaAs

FIGURE 11.1

An example for the RST diode in which GaAs–AlGaAs heterostructure and modulation doping are employed.

($\approx$ 100 Å), the AlGaAs can be about 1000 Å. The doping in this AlGaAs layer ranges between 10^{17} to 10^{18} cm^{-3}. A thin layer of intrinsic AlGaAs ($\approx$ 50 Å) is typical for modulation doping to ensure that the heterointerface is separated from the heavily doped region to avoid impurity scattering. The n^+-regions can be formed by diffusion of the impurity from the alloyed contacts which commonly is made of AuGe.

Fine control of the layer thickness and doping profile necessitates MBE or MOCVD growth. The example shown here has only one layer of channel, but a multichannel structure can be built with repeated heterojunctions on top of one another.

11.3 CHARACTERISTICS

The real-space-transfer effect is similar to the transferred-electron effect (see Chapter 7), and it is sometimes difficult to separate them experimentally in a heterostructure. The transferred-electron effect is due to the properties of a single, homogenous material. When carriers are excited by a high applied field to a satellite band in the momentum-energy space, the mobility is decreased and the current is lowered, resulting in negative differential resistance. In the real-space-transfer effect, transfer of carriers is between two materials (in real space), rather than two energy bands (in momentum space). In low fields, electrons (in an n-channel device) are confined to the material (GaAs) with low E_C and higher mobility. The high-field energy-band diagram is shown in Fig. 11.2. Carriers near the anode acquire enough energy from the field to overcome the conduction-band discontinuity and flow to the adjacent material (AlGaAs) of lower mobility. This current can be considered as thermionic-emission current with the electron temperature replacing the room temperature. Thus, a higher field results in a smaller current, the definition of negative differential resistance. Typical I-V characteristics are shown in Fig. 11.3. The critical field for this real-space transfer has been shown to be between 1.5–3 kV/cm, while that for the transferred-electron effect is typically 3.5 kV/cm for GaAs. One has to bear in mind that these critical fields are obtained from two different types of channels (heterointerface vs. bulk), and cannot be used alone to separate the effects. Another property of the real-space transfer is that there is better control over factors such as conduction-band discontinuity, mobility ratio, and film thicknesses so that device characteristics can be varied and optimized.

The modeling of the RST diode is complicated, and there are no equations derived explicitly for the exact *I-V* characteristics. Qualitatively, the following expressions can be used to get an insight of the origin of the negative resistance. Assume that the total carrier density per unit area is N_s, distributed between the GaAs modulation-doped channel layer L_1 (n_{s1}) and AlGaAs layer L_2 (n_{s2}),

$$n_{s1} + n_{s2} = N_s \ . \tag{11.1}$$

The fraction of carriers excited to the AlGaAs layer is defined as

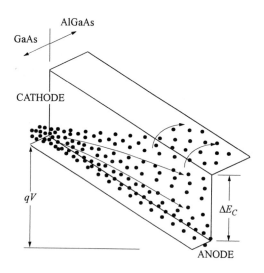

FIGURE 11.2
Energy-band diagram showing the conduction-band edge E_C of the RST diode under bias. Electrons in the main channel acquire energy from the field to overcome the barrier to spill over to the AlGaAs layer.

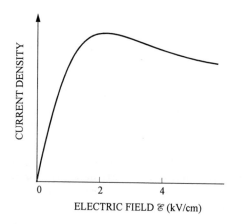

FIGURE 11.3
Typical current-voltage (field) characteristics of a RST diode.

$$R(\mathscr{E}) \equiv \frac{n_{s2}}{N_s} \tag{11.2}$$

and is a function of the applied field. It starts at zero at low field and approaches the ratio of $L_2/(L_1 + L_2)$ at high field. The total current is given by

$$\begin{aligned} I &= Aqn_{s1}\mu_1\mathscr{E} + Aqn_{s2}\mu_2\mathscr{E} \\ &= Aq\mathscr{E}N_s[\mu_1 - (\mu_1 - \mu_2)R] \end{aligned} \tag{11.3}$$

where A is the cross-section area of the channel. The differential resistance is given by

$$\frac{dI}{d\mathscr{E}} = AqN_s\left[\mu_1 - (\mu_1 - \mu_2)R - \mathscr{E}(\mu_1 - \mu_2)\frac{dR}{d\mathscr{E}}\right] \tag{11.4}$$

and it can be shown to be negative for a proper choice of μ_1, μ_2 and $dR/d\mathscr{E}$. In the GaAs–AlGaAs modulation-doped system, $\mu_1 \approx 8000$ cm^2/V-s and μ_2 is less than 500 cm^2/V-s at room temperature. Experimental data show that the current peak-to-valley ratio is not very high, with a maximum value around 1.5. Computer simulations show that a ratio of more than 2 can be achieved.

11.4 APPLICATIONS

One of the advantages of the RST diode is high-speed operation. The response time is limited by the movement of carriers across the heterointerface between the two materials, and is much faster than in a traditional diode where the transit time of carriers between the cathode and anode is the dominating factor. So far the application is demonstrated only by oscillators. The real-space-transfer effect is also applied in a three-terminal device (see Chapter 32–RST Transistor).

The general applications of negative differential resistance are listed in Appendix C2.

REFERENCES

1. Z. S. Gribnikov, "Negative differential conductivity in a multilayer heterostructure," *Soviet Phys.–Semiconductors*, **6**, 1204 (1973). Translated from *Fizika i Teknika Poluprovodnikov*, **6**, 1380 (1972).
2. K. Hess, H. Morkoc, H. Shichijo and B. G. Streetman, "Negative differential resistance through real-space electron transfer," *Appl. Phys. Lett.*, **35**, 469 (1979).
3. H. Shichijo, K. Hess and B. G. Streetman, "Real-space electron transfer by thermionic emission in GaAs-Al$_x$Ga$_{1-x}$As heterostructures: Analytical model for large layer widths," *Solid-State Electron.*, **23**, 817 (1980).
4. T. H. Glisson, J. R. Hauser, M. A. Littlejohn, K. Hess, B. G. Streetman and H. Shichijo, "Monte Carlo simulation of real-space electron transfer in GaAs-AlGaAs heterostructures," *J. Appl. Phys.*, **51**, 5445 (1980).

5. M. Keever, H. Shichijo, K. Hess, S. Banerjee, L. Witkowski, H. Morkoc and B. G. Streetman, "Measurements of hot-electron conduction and real-space transfer in GaAs-Al$_x$Ga$_{1-x}$As heterojunction layers," *Appl. Phys. Lett.*, **38**, 36 (1981).

6. P. D. Coleman, J. Freeman, H. Morkoc, K. Hess, B. Streetman and M. Keever, "Demonstration of a new oscillator based on real-space transfer in heterojunctions," *Appl. Phys. Lett.*, **40**, 493 (1982).

CHAPTER

12

RESISTOR

12.1 HISTORY

The name resistor comes from its property that resists the current flow.[1,2] The resistor is undoubtedly the oldest electrical device. The concept of resistance dated all the way back to 1826 when Ohm's law was conceived. The first resistors made before the turn of the century were of carbon composition and metal wire. Thick-film resistor, also made from carbon at the time, started around 1930. Thin-film resistor based on sputtering technology began around 1960. All these resistors were obviously discrete components until integrated-circuit technology emerged around 1970, when diffused or ion-implanted resistors were built monolithically inside the chip. Rather surprisingly, resistors in all the above forms are still in use for special requirements. This oldest electrical device is still one of the most common components in both integrated circuits and discrete circuits.

12.2 STRUCTURE

Structurally, resistors can be divided into two groups, those fabricated in integrated circuits, and those as discrete components. Integrated components can be further classified into: (1) diffused or ion-implanted resistor, (2) thin-film resistor, (3) epitaxial resistor, and (4) pinch resistor. Their structures are shown in Fig. 12.1. Most of these resistors are isolated by a *p-n* junction except for the thin-film resistor which is deposited on an insulating layer. In semiconductor resistors, *p*-type material is more common because of the higher resistance as a result of lower hole mobility. For integrated thin-film resistor, poly-Si, amorphous Si and metal alloys such as silicides are common. The pinch resistor

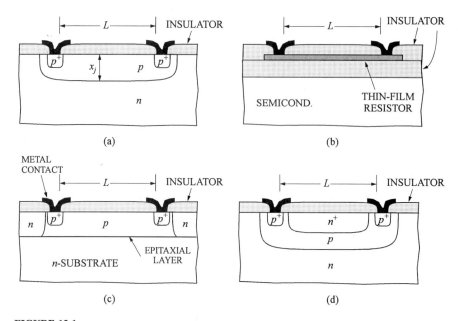

FIGURE 12.1
Resistor structures in integrated circuits. (a) Diffused or ion-implanted resistor. (b) Thin-film resistor.
(c) Epitaxial resistor. (d) Pinch resistor.

is a by-product of the bipolar technology (or JFET technology) where the base-layer resistance is "pinched" by the top emitter diffusion.

Discrete resistors can be classified into (1) thin-film resistor, (2) thick-film resistor, (3) metal wire-wound resistor and (4) bulk resistor. Discrete thin-film resistors are made from vacuum deposition, mostly sputtering, of materials such as Ta, TaN, Ni-Cr, C, and SnO_2. Common substrate materials are alumina and glass. Thick-film resistors, typically in the order of 25 μm thick, are fabricated by a different process involving coating of a resistive paste, followed by firing. Examples of materials are ruthenium and palladium alloys. Wire-wound metal resistors are mainly for high-precision applications, but they have higher inductance. Bulk resistors are made of carbon composition, cermet (the name comes from combination of ceramic and metal), and metal oxide. Film resistors often require trimming to fine-tune the resistance value. This can be done by laser trimming. An alternative is abrasive trimming for thick-film resistors, and oxidation for thin-film resistors. One special kind of discrete resistor is called the chip resistor for ease of insertion or soldering to circuit boards. These are usually film resistors, and the packages have end caps instead of open wires.

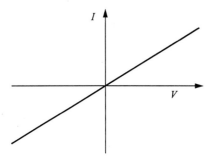

FIGURE 12.2
I-V characteristics of resistor.

12.3 CHARACTERISTICS

Ohm's law states that for a linear device, the voltage drop is proportional to the current passing through it, and the proportionality constant is the resistance,

$$V = IR \ . \tag{12.1}$$

This linear and symmetrical relationship is shown in Fig. 12.2. Except for the thin-film resistor, these structures in Figs. 12.1(a), (c), and (d) all resemble the JFET. As a result, characteristics at high voltage are nonlinear and eventually the current saturates. This is especially severe for the pinch resistor since depletion occurs at both sides (top and bottom) of the *p*-type layer.

To calculate the resistance, both the resistivity ρ of the material and the geometry have to be known, and

$$R = \frac{\rho L}{A} \tag{12.2}$$

where L is the length and A is the cross-section area perpendicular to the current flow. For semiconductors,

$$\sigma = \frac{1}{\rho} = n\mu_n q + p\mu_p q \ . \tag{12.3}$$

Equations (12.2)–(12.3) are only valid for uniform doping. For non-uniform $N(x)$ in the depth dimension, it is more convenient to define a sheet resistance $R_\square$ as

$$R_\square = \frac{1}{\displaystyle\int_0^{x_j} \frac{dx}{\rho(x)}} = \frac{1}{\displaystyle q \int_0^{x_j} N(x)\mu(x)\,dx} \tag{12.4}$$

such that

TABLE 12.1
Conventional color coding of discrete resistors.

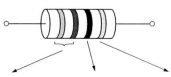

Color	1st and 2nd figures	Multiplier	Tolerance (%)
Black	0	1	–
Brown	1	10	–
Red	2	100	–
Orange	3	1k	–
Yellow	4	10k	–
Green	5	100k	–
Blue	6	1M	–
Violet	7	10M	–
Gray	8	100M	–
White	9	1G	–
Gold	–	0.1	±5
Silver	–	0.01	±10
No band	–	–	±20

$$R = R_\square \left(\frac{L}{W}\right) . \tag{12.5}$$

Here W is the width of the device. The relationship between N, ρ and μ can be found in Appendix D4.

In order to make an integrated resistor of large resistance value, the doping has to be low. However, below a critical doping level, spill-over of carriers occurs from the heavily doped diffusion regions near the contacts, and Eq. (12.3) is no longer valid. This leads to the situation discussed in the *n-i-n* structure in Section 12.5.3.

For discrete resistors, the resistance values are often coded by color bands around the cylindrical housing. The conventional code is shown in Table 12.1. In choosing a resistor, the power rating is important. The electrical power absorbed by a resistor mostly is converted into heat, which is dissipated by conduction, convection, and radiation. A resistor operated beyond the rated power level will be burned and damaged. The absorbed power is given by

$$P = VI = I^2R = \frac{V^2}{R} . \tag{12.6}$$

Another critical parameter is the temperature coefficient of resistance, given by

$$\alpha = \frac{1}{R}\frac{dR}{dT} \; .$$ (12.7)

The change of temperature could be due to the ambient or self-heating from power dissipation. The latter can lead to thermal runaway–a positive feedback of higher temperature and lower resistance.

12.4 APPLICATIONS

There are two main functions for a resistor: (1) to limit current flow or (2) to produce a voltage source from the current flow. Examples for current limiting are conversion of a voltage source to a current source (such as the base resistor controlling the base current of a bipolar transistor), control of the time constant of RC and RL circuits, impedance matching of high-speed circuits, etc. Examples of resistors as a voltage source are a voltage divider, source resistor in an ammeter, resistor load in an inverter and flip-flop, etc. Many specialized devices are also made from properties of a resistor. These include photoconductor, thermistor, and strain gauge. A resistor can also convert electrical energy into heat (resistive heating) such as an electric heater and hair dryer, and into light as an incandescent light bulb.

12.5 RELATED DEVICES

12.5.1 Varistor

The name varistor comes from variable-resistor. It differs from a mechanically controlled potentiometer by being a voltage-dependent (or voltage-sensitive) resistor. Varistor can be realized in two completely different structures: (1) ceramic varistor and (2) diode varistor. Ceramic varistors are made from compressing ceramic powders such as SiC and ZnO, and then sintering at high temperature $\approx 1200°C$. The characteristics of the ceramic varistors are shown in Fig. 12.3(a). They are described by

$$I = \pm C_1 |V|^n$$ (12.8)

and are symmetrical around the origin. For SiC, n is between 3–7 and for ZnO, the characteristics are much sharper and n is between 20–50. The conduction mechanism in these ceramics is believed to be due to thermionic emission over the barriers formed at the grain boundaries. The second kind of varistors comes from a rectifier such as p-n junction diode and Schottky-barrier diode whose characteristics are described by (Fig. 12.3(b))

$$I = I_o \left[\exp\left(\frac{qV}{kT}\right) - 1 \right] \; .$$ (12.9)

This type of varistor has asymmetrical characteristics so only the forward regime is used. The main applications of varistors are voltage-surge suppression, microwave modulation, mixing, and detection (see the end of Appendix C1).

12.5.2 Potentiometer

A potentiometer, or simply a pot, is a three-terminal device in which a wiper slides along the path of a resistor to obtain variable resistance (Fig. 12.4).[3] (It is

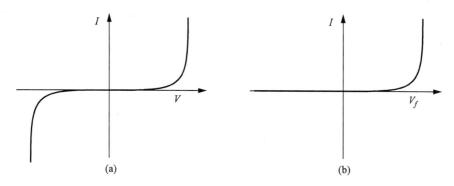

FIGURE 12.3
I-V characteristics of (a) ceramic varistors and (b) diode varistors.

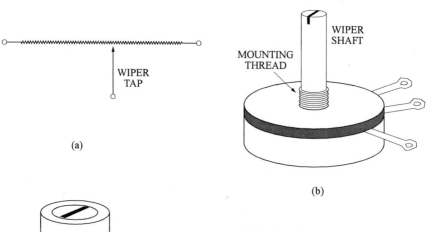

FIGURE 12.4
(a) Schematic representation of a potentiometer. Typical housing of (b) a potentiometer and (c) a trimmer pot.

confusing that a potentiometer is sometimes called a variable resistor–the name from which a varistor is derived. The author suggests that this name be reserved for the varistor only.) The position of the wiper tap is adjusted by a shaft, and the resistance between the wiper and an end could be a linear, logarithmic, or a sine function with the mechanical turn. Common materials for the potentiometer are metal wire and film, carbon composition, cermet, and conductive plastic.

There are two special potentiometers, called a rheostat and trimmer pot. A rheostat is usually wire-wound and has only two terminals, one of which being the center wiper. It is a current-limiting device for power equipment such as a motor (for speed control) and oven. A trimmer pot is designed to be mounted on circuit board for infrequent or one-time adjustment. It has a much smaller size and power rating, and is usually set with a screw driver (Fig. 12.4(c)).

12.5.3 *n-i-n* Diode

The *n-i-n* or *p-i-p* diode is sometimes called the double-junction diode. The study and understanding of this device occurred mainly in the 1980s.[4–8] The *n-i-n* diode has an intrinsic layer sandwiched between two heavily doped regions of the same type. Of particular interest is that, when the length L of the intrinsic region is small, electrons (for an *n*-type device) diffuse from the heavily doped regions to the middle of the intrinsic layer (Fig. 12.5). The electron concentration is, thus, determined by this spill-over effect. The minimum electron concentration at the center of the intrinsic layer is given by[4,5,8]

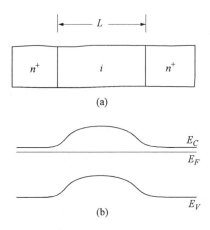

FIGURE 12.5
(a) Doping profile of an *n-i-n* diode, and (b) its energy-band diagram.

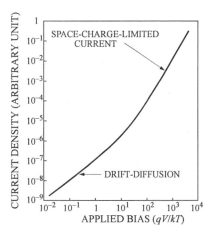

FIGURE 12.6
I-V characteristics of an *n-i-n* diode. Low bias voltage shows a linear relationship.

$$n(0) = \frac{2\pi^2 \varepsilon_s kT}{q^2 L^2} \qquad (12.10)$$

and it is independent of the low-level doping concentration. Once $n(0)$ is known, the shape of the energy band can be calculated using the Fermi statistics.

Typical I-V characteristics of the n-i-n diode are shown in Fig. 12.6.[4,5] For low biases up to $\approx 10\ kT/q$, ohmic behavior can be observed and current conduction is by drift-diffusion,[4,5,8]

$$J \approx \frac{qn(0)\mu V}{L} \qquad . \qquad (12.11)$$

For higher voltages, space-charge-limited (SCL) current dominates (see Appendix B4).

The n-i-n diode was first suggested as a current limiter in 1966.[9] However it has not been used in this application for some time. Recently it has been used as a research tool for semiconductor materials. When operated in the SCL regime, the n-i-n diode is used to study carrier transport. In particular, ballistic transport can be identified based on the voltage dependence of the SCL current.[10–12] This SCL current is also used to determine the density of bulk states in amorphous semiconductor materials.[13]

REFERENCES

1. G. W. A. Dummer, *Fixed resistors*, Pitman & Sons, London, 1956.
2. C. L. Wellard, *Resistance and resistors,* McGraw-Hill, New York, 1960.
3. C. D. Todd, *The potentiometer handbook*, McGraw-Hill, New York, 1975.
4. A. A. Grinberg and S. Luryi, "Space-charge-limited current and capacitance in double-junction diodes," *J. Appl. Phys.*, **61**, 1181 (1987).
5. S. Luryi, "Device building blocks," in S. M. Sze, Ed., *High-speed semiconductor devices*, Wiley, New York, 1990.
6. A. van der Ziel, M. S. Shur, K. Lee, T-H. Chen and K. Amberiadis, "Carrier distribution and low-filed resistance in short n^+-n^--n^+ and n^+-p^--n^+ structures," *IEEE Trans. Electron Dev.*, **ED-30**, 128 (1983).
7. P. E. Schmidt and H. K. Henisch, "Drift-diffusion theory of symmetrical double-junction diodes," *Solid-State Electron.*, **25**, 1129 (1982).
8. M. Shur, *GaAs devices and circuits*, Plenum Press, New York, 1987.
9. H. J. Boll, J. E. Iwersen and E. W. Perry, "High-speed current limiters," *IEEE Trans. Electron Dev.*, **ED-13**, 904 (1966).
10. R. Zuleeg, "Possible ballistic effects in GaAs current limiters," *IEEE Electron Dev. Lett.*, **EDL-1**, 234 (1980).
11. L. F. Eastman, S. Stall, D. Woodard, N. Dandekar, C. E. C. Wood, M. S. Shur and K. Board, "Ballistic electron motion in GaAs at room temperature," *Electronics Lett.*, **16**, 524 (1980).
12. P. E. Schmidt, M. Octavio and P. D. Esqueda, "Single-carrier space-charge controlled conduction vs. ballistic transport in GaAs devices at 77° K," *IEEE Electron Dev. Lett.*, **EDL-2**, 205 (1981).
13. W. den Boer and M. Hack, "A comparative study of single and double carrier injection in amorphous silicon alloys," *J. Non-Crystalline Solids*, **77/78**, 491 (1985).

CHAPTER
13

OHMIC CONTACT

13.1 HISTORY

An ohmic contact is a metal (or silicide) contact to a semiconductor, with a small interfacial resistance. Being ohmic implies linear I-V characteristics although in practice, a better criterion is its low resistance compared to the resistance of the semiconductor device to be contacted. The history of the ohmic contact is as early as any semiconductor device because every device must be connected to the external world. The last connection to a device is always a metallic cable or a metallic probing needle, but most often through on-chip metallic runners. Thus, for every semiconductor device, there is always a metal-semiconductor junction during testing or in use. Even though the ohmic contact has been used for a long time, its theoretical understanding was primitive until around 1970. The fundamental mechanism responsible is tunneling, and the WKB approximation is the basic tool for such analysis (see Appendix B7–Tunneling). Closed form solutions for metal-semiconductor tunneling were provided by Padovani and Stratton in 1966,[1] and by Crowell and Rideout in 1969.[2] Applications of the analytical results to calculate the specific contact resistance can be found in published papers.[3–5] Apart from the WKB approximation, numerical integration of the Schrödinger equation and the Fermi-Dirac function can also be used, with the help of a computer, to obtain more accurate results.[6]

13.2 STRUCTURE

Unlike any other device, an ohmic contact does not play an active role, but is always required by other semiconductor devices. An example is shown in

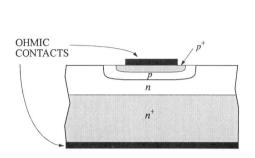

FIGURE 13.1

Example showing ohmic contacts to a *p-n* junction. Epitaxial wafer shown in this example is often used to improve the substrate contact.

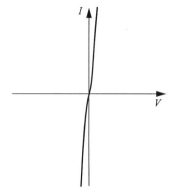

FIGURE 13.2

Typical *I-V* characteristics of an ohmic contact (between metal and the underlying n^+- or p^+-layer).

Fig. 13.1 where contacts are made for a *p-n* junction. Since tunneling requires a high electric field, the Poisson equation states that the semiconductor has to be heavily doped (degenerate), in the order of 10^{20} cm^{-3}. The most common approach to incorporate high doping concentration is ion implantation. Other methods such as diffusion, alloying, and epitaxial growth also can be used. In epitaxial wafers such as the one shown in Fig. 13.1, the degenerate substrate is obtained from the crystal growth, and the lightly doped active region is deposited subsequently by epitaxy. Before metal deposition, the semiconductor is cleaned chemically in a wet solution, or etched by back-sputtering in a vacuum. Metal can be deposited in vacuum, either by thermal evaporation or sputtering. For silicide contacts to silicon, metal is deposited and followed by heat treatment for the silicide reaction. Such contacts presumably benefit from a cleaner interface because during silicide formation, silicon is consumed so that the interface propagates away from the original silicon surface. The choice of metal for a low Schottky-barrier height is also critical for low contact resistance. Good ohmic contacts to *p*-type semiconductors are much easier to make since, in general, the barrier heights on *p*-type materials are lower than those on *n*-type. There are also additional factors that lower the contact resistance. Recombination centers can be introduced to increase the generation/recombination current. The semiconductor surface can be prepared to have textures or protrusions for increased contact area. For materials of larger energy gap, the Schottky barrier is usually high, making an ohmic contact difficult. In this case, epitaxial material with a narrower energy gap can be inserted to ensure a good metal-semiconductor contact. Ohmic contacts to compound semiconductors are also known to be less stable. Common metals for contacting various semiconductors are listed in Table 13.1.

TABLE 13.1
Common contact metals for various semiconductors.[7]

Semiconductor	Metal	Semiconductor	Metal
n-Ge	Ag-Al-Sb, Al, Al-Au-P, Au, Bi, Sb, Sn, Pb-Sn	p-Ge	Ag, Al, Au, Cu, Ga, Ga-In, In, Al-Pd, Ni, Pt, Sn
n-Si	Ag, Al, Al-Au, Ni, Sn, In, Ge-Sn, Sb, Au-Sb, Ti, TiN	p-Si	Ag, Al, Al-Au, Au, Ni, Pt, Sn, In, Pb, Ga, Ge, Ti, TiN
n-GaAs	Au(.88)Ge(.12)-Ni, Ag-Sn Ag(.95)In(.05)-Ge	p-GaAs	Au(.84)Zn(.16), Ag-In-Zn, Ag-Zn
n-GaP	Ag-Te-Ni, Al, Au-Si, Au-Sn, In-Sn	p-GaP	Au-In, Au-Zn, Ga, In-Zn, Zn, Ag-Zn
n-GaAsP	Au-Sn	p-GaAsP	Au-Zn
n-GaAlAs	Au-Ge-Ni	p-GaAlAs	Au-Zn
n-InAs	Au-Ge, Au-Sn-Ni, Sn	p-InAs	Al
n-InGaAs	Au-Ge, Ni	p-InGaAs	Au-Zn, Ni
n-InP	Au-Ge, In, Ni, Sn		
n-InSb	Au-Sn, Au-In, Ni, Sn	p-InSb	Au-Ge
n-CdS	Ag, Al, Au, Au-In, Ga, In, Ga-In		
n-CdTe	In	p-CdTe	Au, In-Ni, Indalloy 13, Pt, Rh
n-ZnSe	In, In-Ga, Pt, InHg		
n-SiC	W	p-SiC	Al-Si, Si, Ni

13.3 CHARACTERISTICS

Typical *I-V* characteristics of an ohmic contact are shown in Fig. 13.2. Linearity of these characteristics is not important as long as they provide adequate current with a small voltage drop. The definition of the specific contact resistance, R_c (Ω-cm^2), is given by

$$R_c = \left(\frac{\partial J}{\partial V}\right)^{-1}_{V \Rightarrow 0} . \qquad (13.1)$$

The current components through an ohmic contact are indicated in Fig. 13.3. In field emission (FE), carriers tunnel at an energy near the Fermi level. In thermionic-field emission, carriers tunnel at an elevated energy where the barrier becomes narrower. In thermionic emission, carriers do not tunnel, but are emitted thermally over the barrier. This mechanism is identical to a regular Schottky-barrier current conduction.

These components dominate at different regimes, determined mainly by temperature and doping concentration. When $kT \ll E_{oo}$, where E_{oo} is defined as

$$E_{oo} \equiv \frac{q\hbar}{2} \sqrt{\frac{N}{m^* \varepsilon_s}} , \qquad (13.2)$$

FE dominates, and the specific contact resistance is given by[1,2]

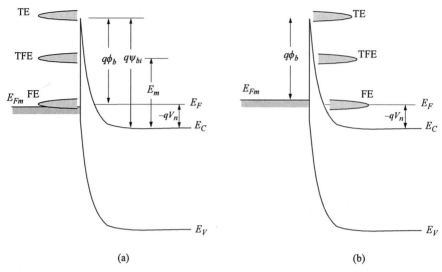

FIGURE 13.3
Energy-band diagrams showing injection of carriers (electrons in this case for contact to
n^+-semiconductor) under (a) small forward bias and (b) small reverse bias.

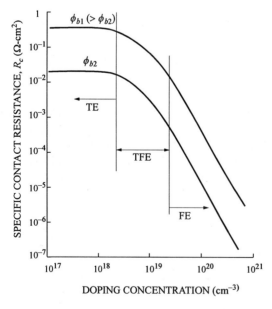

FIGURE 13.4
Dependence of specific contact
resistance on doping concentration
for different barrier heights.
Regimes of TE, TFE and FE are
indicated.

$$R_c = \frac{k \, \sin\left(\pi C_1 kT\right)}{A^* \pi q T} \exp\left(\frac{q\phi_b}{E_{oo}}\right) \, , \tag{13.3}$$

$$C_1 = \frac{1}{2E_{oo}} \ln\left(\frac{4\phi_b}{-V_n}\right) \, . \tag{13.4}$$

(V_n is negative for degenerate semiconductor.) When $kT \approx E_{oo}$, TFE dominates and R_c is given by[1,2]

$$R_c = \frac{k\sqrt{E_{oo}} \, \cosh\left(\dfrac{E_{oo}}{kT}\right) \coth\left(\dfrac{E_{oo}}{kT}\right)}{A^* Tq\sqrt{\pi q \left(\phi_b - V_n\right)}} \exp\left[\frac{q\left(\phi_b - V_n\right)}{E_{oo} \coth\left(E_{oo}/kT\right)} + \frac{qV_n}{kT}\right] \, . \tag{13.5}$$

This tunneling occurs at an energy above the conduction band of

$$E_m = q\psi_{bi}\left[\cosh\left(\frac{E_{oo}}{kT}\right)\right]^{-2} \tag{13.6}$$

where the product of carrier density and tunneling probability is at a maximum. When $kT \gg E_{oo}$, TE dominates and

$$R_c = \frac{k}{A^* Tq} \exp\left(\frac{q\phi_b}{kT}\right) \, . \tag{13.7}$$

TABLE 13.2
Dependence of specific contact resistance R_c on barrier height ϕ_b and doping concentration N. Notice that $E_{oo} \propto N^{1/2}$.

Regime	R_c
Field emission, FE, $kT \ll E_{oo}$	$\propto \exp\left(\dfrac{q\phi_b}{E_{oo}}\right)$
Thermionic-field emission, TFE, $kT \approx E_{oo}$	$\propto \exp\left(\dfrac{q\phi_b}{E_{oo} \coth\left(E_{oo}/kT\right)}\right)$
Thermionic emission, TE, $kT \gg E_{oo}$	$\propto \exp\left(\dfrac{q\phi_b}{kT}\right)$

This originates from the standard thermionic-emission current of a Schottky-barrier diode

$$J = A^* T^2 \exp\left(\frac{-q\phi_b}{kT}\right)\left[\exp\left(\frac{qV}{kT}\right) - 1\right] , \qquad (13.8)$$

in the limit of a small V.

Qualitative dependence of the specific contact resistance is shown in Fig. 13.4 for a fixed semiconductor material. The main parameters are the barrier height and the doping concentration. In TE, R_c is independent of doping concentration and dependent only on ϕ_b. In the other extreme of FE, in addition to ϕ_b, R_c has a dependence of $\propto \exp(N^{-\frac{1}{2}})$. The trend and the regimes of operation are summarized in Table 13.2. The results of calculated specific contact resistance on silicon are shown in Fig. 13.5.

It is clear that for good ohmic contacts, the barrier heights are to be minimized. There are two factors that control the barrier height, namely the metal work function and the interfacial properties. For most semiconductors, the Fermi level is pinned by interface traps to within the energy gap. For a few compound semiconductors, the Fermi level is pinned outside the energy gap. An example of n-InAs is shown in Fig. 13.6. In such a system, there is no barrier nor depletion region, but only accumulation. Such a "negative" barrier height is an ideal ohmic

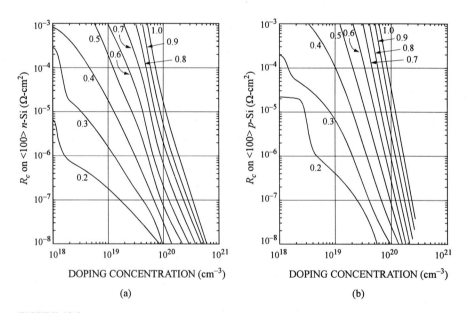

FIGURE 13.5

Calculated specific contact resistance R_c on (a) n-type and (b) p-type <100> Si surface for various barrier heights (in eV) at room temperature. (After Ref. 5)

contact and the resistance value is no longer governed by the tunneling equations above.

13.4 APPLICATIONS

An ohmic contact is inevitable for every semiconductor device. As devices are miniaturized for advanced integrated circuits, the device current density usually increases. This demands not only smaller ohmic resistance, but also contact made on a smaller area, which might present uniformity problem. The challenge for fabricating good ohmic contacts has been increasing with device miniaturization. The total contact resistance is given by

$$R = \frac{R_c}{A} \ . \tag{13.9}$$

At this point, it is timely here to mention other resistance components that are closely related. For a small round contact of radius r as shown in Fig. 13.7, in series with the ohmic contact, there is a spreading resistance given by[8]

$$R_{sp} = \frac{\rho}{2\pi r} \tan^{-1}\left(\frac{2h}{r}\right) \ . \tag{13.10}$$

This component approaches the bulk resistance of $\rho h/A$ for large r/h ratios. In cases where the contact is made on a horizontal diffusion layer (Fig. 13.8, as in the case of a MOSFET), the total resistance between point A (leading edge of the contact) and the metal contact is given by[9]

$$R = \frac{\sqrt{R_\square R_c}}{W} \coth\left(L\sqrt{\frac{R_\square}{R_c}}\right) \tag{13.11}$$

where $R_\square$ is the sheet resistance ($\Omega/\square$) of the diffusion layer. Equation (13.11) takes into account non-uniform current density through the contact (current crowding), and contributions due to the sheet resistance itself. It can also be shown that in the limit of $R_\square \Rightarrow 0$, Eq. (13.11) reduces to Eq. (13.9).

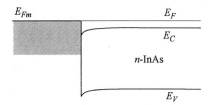

FIGURE 13.6
An ideal ohmic contact where there is no barrier for the majority carriers.

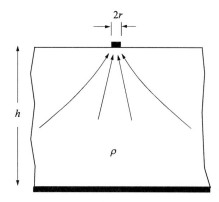

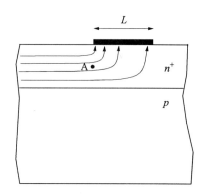

FIGURE 13.7

Current pattern for a small contact when $r \ll h$. r is the radius of the contact.

FIGURE 13.8

Current pattern for a contact to a horizontal diffusion sheet. If the sheet resistance of the diffusion layer is high, current is forced toward the leading edge of the contact.

REFERENCES

1. F. A. Padovani and R. Stratton, "Field and thermionic-field emission in Schottky barriers," *Solid-State Electron.*, **9**, 695 (1966).
2. C. R. Crowell and V. L. Rideout, "Normalized thermionic-field (T-F) emission in metal-semiconductor (Schottky) barriers," *Solid-State Electron.*, **12**, 89 (1969).
3. M. P. Lepselter and J. M. Andrews, "Ohmic contacts to silicon," in B. Schwartz, Ed., *Ohmic contacts to semiconductors*, p. 159, Electrochem. Soc., New York, 1969.
4. A. Y. C. Yu, "Electron tunneling and contact resistance of metal-silicon contact barriers," *Solid-State Electron.*, **13**, 239 (1970).
5. K. K. Ng and R. Liu, "On the calculation of specific contact resistivity on <100> Si," *IEEE Trans. Electron Dev.*, **ED-37**, 1535 (1990).
6. C. Y. Chang, Y. K. Fang and S. M. Sze, "Specific contact resistance of metal-semiconductor barriers," *Solid-State Electron.*, **14**, 541 (1971).
7. S. S. Li, *Semiconductor physical electronics*, Plenum Press, New York, 1993.
8. R. H. Cox and H. Strack, "Ohmic contacts for GaAs devices," *Solid-State Electron.*, **10**, 1213 (1967).
9. H. Murrmann and D. Widmann, "Current crowding on metal contacts to planar devices," *IEEE Trans. Electron Dev.*, **ED-16**, 1022 (1969).

14

METAL-OXIDE-SEMICONDUCTOR CAPACITOR

14.1 HISTORY

Metal-oxide-semiconductor (MOS) is a special case of the generic metal-insulator-semiconductor (MIS) structure. Because thermally grown oxide on silicon is the only high-quality oxide-semiconductor interface, MOS implies a silicon substrate with thermal silicon dioxide. Even though the name assumes a metal gate, other gate materials such as poly-silicon and silicide are also referred to by the same name.

The MOS structure was first proposed by Moll[1] and Pfann and Garrett[2] in 1959 as a varactor (voltage-dependent capacitor, see Section 1.5.4) to be a contender for the *p-n* junction varactor. The first practical MOS device was fabricated by Ligenza and Spitzer[3] in 1960 using high-pressure steam oxidation. This consequently led to the first MOSFET (Kahng and Atalla[4]) whose success critically relied on the quality of the MOS capacitor. The development of the MOS capacitor was also pushed by researchers as a powerful tool to investigate semiconductor surface and oxide properties (Terman,[5] Nicollian and Goetzberger,[6] Kuhn,[7] Snow et al.[8]), as surface passivation for junction diodes and bipolar transistors (Atalla et al.[9]), as an effective diffusion mask, and for electrical isolation (Frosch and Derick[10]). It also laid the foundation for the invention of the CCD in 1970 (Boyle and Smith[11]). For in-depth treatment of the MOS system, the readers are referred to Refs. 12–14.

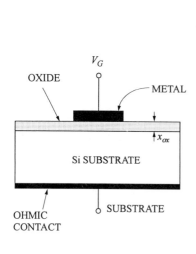

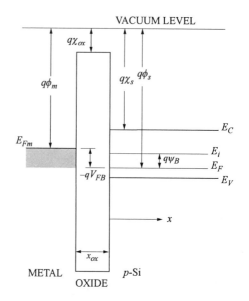

FIGURE 14.1
Cross-section of a simple MOS structure.

FIGURE 14.2
Energy-band diagram of MOS capacitor with bias V_{FB} for flat-band condition. Here the oxide and interface charges are ignored. The barrier heights at the Si–SiO$_2$ interface for electrons is 3.2 eV, and that for holes is 4.3 eV.

14.2 STRUCTURE

A simple MOS capacitor is shown in Fig. 14.1. The oxide layer is usually grown thermally for good interface and oxide quality (the oxidation rate of SiO$_2$ can be found in Appendix D8). It is common practice to introduce a trace of chlorine, such as in HCl, during oxidation to minimize sodium contamination which is a main source of mobile charge. A metal gate can be deposited in vacuum by evaporation or sputtering. A poly-Si gate is commonly used, deposited by LPCVD and subsequently doped by diffusion or ion implantation. After the gate is deposited, interface quality can be further improved by low temperature annealing ($\approx 500°C$) in a gas ambient containing hydrogen.

14.3 CHARACTERISTICS

The imperfections of an MOS capacitor due to oxide charges and interface traps are ignored for now and will be included later. The energy-band diagram at flat-band is shown in Fig. 14.2. Under this condition, the semiconductor band bending (or surface potential ψ_s) is zero, and the applied flat-band voltage V_{FB} corresponds to the difference in work functions. Under different biases, the MOS capacitor is driven into different regimes as shown in Fig. 14.3. The Fermi level remains flat under all bias conditions because of zero current flow. The main effect caused by the bias is to modulate the net carrier concentration at the semiconductor surface (the classical field effect), accompanied by a change of depletion width. At the onset of strong inversion, the depletion width reaches its maximum equilibrium value when $\psi_s = 2\psi_B$

$$
\begin{aligned}
W_{dm} &= \left[\frac{2\varepsilon_s (2\psi_B)}{qN_A} \right]^{1/2} \\
&= \left[\frac{4\varepsilon_s kT \ln (N_A/n_i)}{q^2 N_A} \right]^{1/2} .
\end{aligned}
\tag{14.1}
$$

Typical *C-V* characteristics are shown in Fig. 14.4 which contains four curves. These capacitance characteristics are obtained from a voltage source that

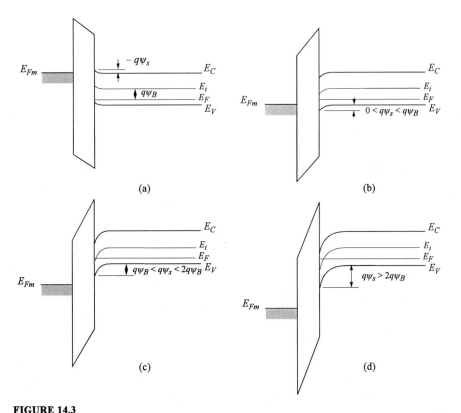

FIGURE 14.3
As a function of bias, the MOS capacitor is driven into (a) accumulation, (b) depletion, (c) weak inversion, and (d) strong inversion.

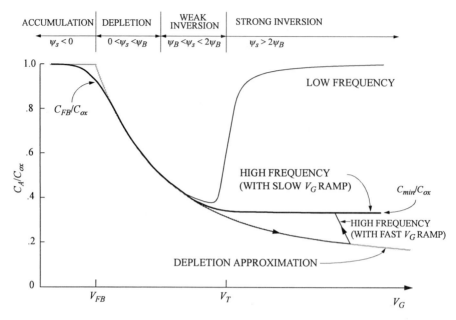

FIGURE 14.4
Typical *C-V* characteristics of an MOS capacitor at various frequencies and V_G ramping rates. Arrows on curves indicate gate voltage sweep direction. Shaded line represents deep depletion from Eq. (14.4). V_G polarity corresponds to *p*-type substrate.

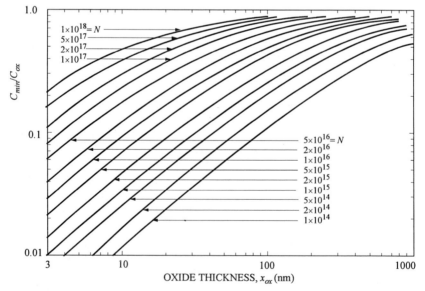

FIGURE 14.5
A plot of C_{min} from Eq. (14.7).

has a small AC signal, ranging from a few mV to ≈ 100 mV, superimposed on a V_G ramp. In the depletion approximation, the surface inversion-layer charge is ignored such that deep depletion can occur ($\psi_s > 2\psi_B$, $W_d > W_{dm}$). The capacitance is a serial combination of the oxide capacitance (C_{ox}) and the depletion-layer capacitance, with

$$C_{ox} = \frac{\varepsilon_{ox}}{x_{ox}} \tag{14.2}$$

$$C_A = \frac{1}{(x_{ox}/\varepsilon_{ox}) + (W_d/\varepsilon_s)} \ , \tag{14.3}$$

and it can be shown to be a function of gate voltage[15]

$$\frac{C_A}{C_{ox}} = \frac{1}{\left[1 + 2C_{ox}^2 (V_G - V_{FB})/(qN_A\varepsilon_s)\right]^{1/2}} \ . \tag{14.4}$$

Measurements at different frequencies display similar characteristics (again without interface traps) except in strong inversion. The flat-band capacitance before accumulation is not accurately described by Eq. (14.4) when W_d approaches the Debye length, and is given by

$$C_{FB} = \frac{1}{(1/C_{ox}) + (L_D/\varepsilon_s)} \ . \tag{14.5}$$

The different behaviors in strong inversion can be explained as follows. At high frequencies (≥ 1 kHz) with a fast V_G ramp, minority carriers are not generated fast enough to follow the AC signal or even the V_G ramp. The depletion width is thus wider than W_{dm} and characteristics similar to deep-depletion approximation are obtained. The response time to establish the inversion charge sheet resulting from a V_G ramp or pulse is called the thermal-relaxation time and is related to the minority-carrier lifetime by[16,17]

$$t \approx 10\tau \left(\frac{N}{n_i}\right) \ , \tag{14.6}$$

and it can be used to estimate τ. However this response time can be shortened by perimeter effects. With V_G ramping from the direction of strong inversion toward weak inversion, the capacitance follows another curve which is discussed below.

At high frequencies with a slow V_G ramp, minority carriers are sufficient to follow the V_G ramp (but not the AC signal) such that the depletion width saturates at W_{dm} and the minimum capacitance is given by

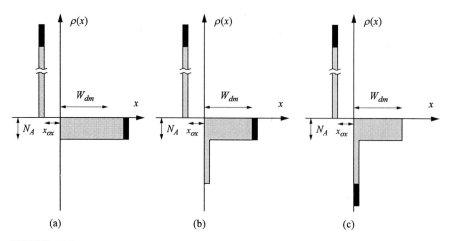

FIGURE 14.6

In strong inversion, capacitance is a function of frequency and V_G ramping rate. The small signal displacement charge (black area) is shown to demonstrate in case of (a) deep depletion resulting from high frequency with fast V_G ramp, (b) high frequency with slow V_G ramp, and (c) low frequency with slow V_G ramp.

$$C_{min} = \frac{1}{(x_{ox}/\varepsilon_{ox}) + (W_{dm}/\varepsilon_s)} \, . \tag{14.7}$$

A plot of this equation is shown in Fig. 14.5. Since C_{min} is a function of x_{ox} and doping N only, if one parameter is known, the other can be deduced from measurement. At low frequencies (≤ 10 Hz), minority carriers can follow the AC signal to modulate the inversion layer, and capacitance rises toward C_{ox}. The difference for the three sets of characteristics in strong inversion can best be explained by the placement of the AC incremental charge shown in black in Fig. 14.6.

If minority carriers are supplemented by light generation, the equilibrium high-frequency curve can be obtained even with a fast V_G ramp. If ample minority carriers are supplied by a diffused region of their type, as in the case of source/drain junctions in a MOSFET, the low-frequency curve can be obtained even with a high-frequency signal.

The imperfections of MOS structures are summarized in Table 14.1. These charges cause a parallel shift of the C-V curve in the V_G direction with the exception of Q_{it}, which changes the slope of the curve since the charge is dependent on ψ_s. Interface traps can be of the donor type or the acceptor type. Donor-type traps produce positive charge when empty (neutral when full). Acceptor-type traps produce negative charge when full (neutral when empty). Experimentally, $D_{it}(E)$ can be determined by:

1. Comparison of idealized high-frequency C-V curve with measurement.
2. Comparison of idealized low-frequency C-V curve with measurement.
3. Comparison of idealized $\psi_s(V_G)$ with measurement (by C-V or Q-V[19] method).
4. Comparison of measured low-frequency and high-frequency C-V curves.[7]
5. Conductance method.[6]

Q_m can be determined by C-V measurements before and after bias-temperature stress (≈ 1 MV/cm at $\approx 200°$C).

The flat-band voltage of an MOS capacitor is given by

$$V_{FB} = \phi_{ms} - \frac{Q_f}{C_{ox}} - \frac{Q_m}{C_{ox}} - \frac{Q_{ot}}{C_{ox}} - \frac{Q_{it}}{C_{ox}}$$

$$= \phi_{ms} - \frac{Q_f}{C_{ox}} - \frac{1}{C_{ox}} \int_0^{x_{ox}} \frac{x}{x_{ox}} \rho_m(x)\,dx - \frac{1}{C_{ox}} \int_0^{x_{ox}} \frac{x}{x_{ox}} \rho_{ot}(x)\,dx - \frac{Q_{it}}{C_{ox}} \quad (14.8)$$

and the onset of strong inversion is given by the threshold voltage

$$V_T = V_{FB} + 2\psi_B + \frac{qN_A W_{dm}}{C_{ox}} + \frac{q}{C_{ox}} \int_{E_F}^{(E_F + 2q\psi_B)} D_{it}(E)\,dE$$

$$\approx V_{FB} + 2\psi_B + \frac{qN_A W_{dm}}{C_{ox}} . \quad (14.9)$$

Qualitatively, the second term on the right is the voltage across the semiconductor, and the third term is due to voltage across the oxide layer.

14.4 APPLICATIONS

An MOS capacitor can be used as a varactor. Compared to other versions of varactors such as the p-n junction and Schottky barrier, it has much improved leakage and a wider capacitance range. It is also the "heart" of a MOSFET or

TABLE 14.1
Definitions of oxide and interface charges.[18] Units are C/cm² except for D_{it} (/cm²-eV).

Q_m	Mobile oxide charge (effective net at Si–SiO₂ interface, from bulk $\rho_m(x)$)
Q_{ot}	Oxide trapped charge (effective net at Si–SiO₂ interface, from bulk $\rho_{ot}(x)$)
Q_f	Fixed oxide charge (near Si–SiO₂ interface)
Q_{it}	Interface trapped charge (from interface traps $D_{it}(E)$, dependent on ψ_s)

CCD. As a powerful analytical tool for semiconductor surfaces and dielectrics, the following properties can be extracted[12]:

1. Semiconductor band bending and depletion width.
2. Semiconductor avalanche breakdown field.
3. Semiconductor doping profile.
4. Semiconductor minority-carrier lifetime.
5. Semiconductor dielectric constant.
6. Semiconductor surface recombination velocity.
7. Oxide thickness or oxide dielectric constant.
8. Oxide breakdown field.
9. Oxide charges.
10. Hot-carrier trapping in oxide.
11. Interface trap density distribution.
12. Interface trap capture probability.
13. Work function difference between semiconductor and gate material.
14. Tunneling in semiconductor and oxide.
15. Quantum effects in the inversion layer.

An MOS capacitor can be used as a fixed-value capacitor by doping the substrate heavily or by restricting the voltage range within the constant capacitance regime. A very important application is the storage capacitor in a DRAM cell. In this particular example, the surface area is to be maximized for large capacitance, and different approaches such as using trenches have been applied. The applications of a generic parallel-plate capacitor are discussed later.

14.5 RELATED DEVICES

14.5.1 Metal-Insulator-Semiconductor Capacitor

A metal-insulator-semiconductor (MIS) capacitor is usually referred to capacitor structures other than thermal oxide on silicon substrate. These substrates imply compound semiconductors or Ge. For these MIS capacitors, methods for fabricating the insulators are[20,21]:

1. Thermally grown oxide.
2. Anodically grown oxide, in plasma or in solution.
3. Deposited dielectrics.
4. Wide-energy-gap epitaxial undoped semiconductor (heterostructure).

Unfortunately, except the heterostructure, all methods yield unsatisfactory results. Problems are due to high conductance causing leakage, and unacceptable interface trap density.

14.5.2 Parallel-Plate Capacitor

A fixed-value parallel-plate capacitor, integrated or discrete, is one of the most common components in electronics. In the planar technology, the insulator layer can be made conveniently from thermally grown oxide or deposited dielectrics such as silicon nitride or oxide. The plates can be metal, silicide, polycrystalline semiconductor, or the substrate semiconductor that is heavily doped. Some important formulae for capacitors are:

$$C = \frac{A\varepsilon_i}{x_i} \tag{14.10}$$

$$V = \frac{1}{C} \int I dt = \frac{Q}{C} \tag{14.11}$$

$$I = C\frac{dV}{dt} \tag{14.12}$$

$$E = \frac{1}{2}CV^2 \tag{14.13}$$

$$Z = \frac{1}{j\omega C} \ . \tag{14.14}$$

The quality of a capacitor is measured by the Q (quality) factor, the dissipation factor (DF, reciprocal of Q), and the power factor (PF),

$$\frac{1}{Q} = \mathrm{DF} = \omega R_s C_s = \frac{1}{\omega R_p C_p} \tag{14.15}$$

$$\mathrm{PF} = \frac{R_s}{\sqrt{R_s^2 + [1/(\omega C_s)]^2}} = \frac{1}{\sqrt{1 + (\omega C_p R_p)^2}} \ . \tag{14.16}$$

The equivalent serial and parallel components are indicated in Fig. 14.7. The applications of a generic capacitor are listed below:

1. Isolation/coupling and filtering: Since the impedance of a capacitor is inversely proportional to frequency, a capacitor can block DC signals while being able to couple AC signals. It can be used to bypass components at high

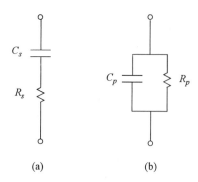

FIGURE 14.7
A non-ideal capacitor with resistance in (a) serial representation and (b) parallel representation.

(a)   (b)

frequencies when connected in parallel. It is commonly used in filters and tuned circuits.

2. Energy storage: Energy can be stored for pulsed operations such as spark plugs and pulsed lasers.

3. Regulation: The basic property of a capacitor is continuity of voltage and charge. A step voltage, for example, is not possible across a capacitor. This property is used to regulate DC voltage nodes and power supplies.

4. As a speed-up capacitor: It is used to improve the turn-on and turn-off times of a bipolar transistor when connected in parallel to the base resistor.

5. As an integrator (Eq. (14.11)): Examples of applications are analog computing and waveform generation.

6. As sensors: Since capacitance is proportional directly to the dielectric constant and inversely to the distance, it is used to detect the presence of any material. Examples are level sensor, position sensor, tactile switch, and humidity sensor. Capacitance is also used in a pressure sensor to detect displacement of a diaphragm under differential pressure.

REFERENCES

1. J. L. Moll, "Variable capacitance with large capacity charge," *Wescon Conv. Rec.,* part 3, **32** (1959).
2. W. G. Pfann and C. G. B. Garrett, "Semiconductor varactors using surface space-charge layers," *Proc. IRE,* **47,** 2011 (1959).
3. J. R. Ligenza and W. G. Spitzer, "The mechanisms for silicon oxidation in steam and oxygen," *J. Phys. Chem. Solids,* **14,** 131 (1960).
4. D. Kahng and M. M. Atalla, "Silicon-silicon dioxide field induced surface devices," in *IRE-AIEE Solid-State Device Res. Conf.* (Carnegie Inst. of Tech., Pittsburgh, PA), 1960.
5. L. M. Terman, "An investigation of surface states at a silicon–silicon oxide interface employing metal-oxide-silicon diodes," *Solid-State Electron.,* **5,** 285 (1962).
6. E. H. Nicollian and A. Goetzberger, "The Si-SiO₂ interface - Electrical properties as determined by the metal-insulator-silicon conductance technique," *Bell Syst. Tech. J.,* **46,** 1055 (1967).
7. M. Kuhn, "A quasi-static technique for MOS *C-V* and surface state measurements," *Solid-State Electron.,* **13,** 873 (1970).

8. E. H. Snow, A. S. Grove, B. E. Deal and C. T. Sah, "Ion transport phenomena in insulating films," *J. Appl. Phys.*, **36**, 1664 (1965).
9. M. M. Atalla, E. Tannenbaum and E. J. Scheibner, "Stabilization of silicon surfaces by thermally grown oxides," *Bell Syst. Tech. J.*, **38**, 749 (1959).
10. C. J. Frosch and L. Derick, "Surface protection and selective masking during diffusion in silicon," *J. Electrochem. Soc.*, **104**, 547 (1957).
11. W. S. Boyle and G. E. Smith, "Charge coupled semiconductor devices," *Bell Syst. Tech. J.*, **49**, 587 (1970).
12. E. H. Nicollian and J. R. Brews, *MOS (metal oxide semiconductor) physics and technology,* Wiley, New York, 1982.
13. S. A. Schwarz and M. J. Schulz, "Characterization of the Si-SiO$_2$ interface," in N. G. Einspruch and R. S. Bauer, Eds., *VLSI electronics: Microstructures science*, Vol. 10, p. 29, Academic, New York, 1985.
14. Y. P. Tsividis, *Operation and modeling of the MOS transistor*, McGraw-Hill, New York, 1987.
15. E. S. Yang, *Microelectronic devices*, McGraw-Hill, New York, 1988.
16. W. E. Beadle, J. C. C. Tsai and R. D. Plummer, Eds., *Quick reference manual for silicon integrated circuit technology*, Wiley, New York, 1985.
17. A. K. Sinha, "MOS (Si-gate) compatibility of RF diode and triode sputtering processes," *J. Electrochem. Soc.*, **123**, 65 (1976).
18. B. E. Deal, "Standardized terminology for oxide charges associated with thermally oxidized silicon," *IEEE Trans. Electron Dev.*, **ED-27**, 606 (1980).
19. K. Zieler and E. Klausmann, "Static technique for precise measurements of surface potential and interface state density in MOS structures," *Appl. Phys. Lett.*, **26**, 400 (1975).
20. L. G. Meiners, "Electrical properties of insulator-semiconductor interfaces on III-V compounds," in C. W. Wilmsen, Ed., *Physics and chemistry of III-V compound semiconductor interfaces*, p. 213, Plenum Press, New York, 1985.
21. H. H. Wieder, "Perspectives on III-V compound MIS structures," *J. Vac. Sci. Technol.*, **15**, 1498 (1978).

CHAPTER
15

CHARGE-COUPLED DEVICE

15.1 HISTORY

The charge-coupled device (CCD) was invented by Boyle and Smith in 1970.[1] An individual CCD, in terms of structure, is basically an MOS capacitor, a device that has been under active investigation since 1960. However, when devices are placed close together and the proper sequence of gate voltages applied, minority-carrier charges at the surface can communicate between devices and a simple shift register can be realized. Independently, the concept of an MOS bucket-brigade device (BBD) that performs similar functions was proposed by Sangster et al. around the same time.[2] CCD can be viewed as an integrated version of BBD (see Section 15.5.4). Because it is compatible with MOS technology, CCD can be made at low cost. This and other factors such as low power consumption and high packing density are the main reasons for its wide range of applications. Early development of CCD is summarized in Table 15.1. Review articles can be found in Refs. 4–8.

Both CCD and BBD are charge-transfer devices (CTDs). Under CCD, they are classified into surface-channel CCD (SCCD), buried-channel CCD (BCCD), peristaltic CCD (PCCD) and profiled-peristaltic CCD (P^2CCD). These will be discussed in Section 15.5.

15.2 STRUCTURE

Most CCDs are made from the Si MOS system because of the good interfacial properties of thermally grown SiO_2, although in some specific applications MIS structures or even Schottky barriers on other semiconductors can also be used.

TABLE 15.1
CCD chronology.[3]

1969:	(1970) Bell Labs scientists W. S. Boyle and G. E. Smith invent the CCD.
1970:	Active development of CCDs at Bell Labs and other companies.
1971:	First black-and-white CCD camera announced by Bell Labs.
1972:	First color CCD camera announced by Bell Labs.
1973:	CCD cameras marketed commercially by Fairchild Camera and Instrument Corp.
1974:	Basic CCD patent awarded to inventors Boyle and Smith.
1975:	CCD camera that meets broadcast resolution standards announced by Bell Labs.
1976:	University of Arizona astronomers use CCD imagers for astronomical research. Initial observations reveal new data about the atmosphere of the planet Uranus.
1977:	First commercially available 64-K CCD memory chips marketed by Texas Instruments.
1978:	CCD filters developed at Bell Labs for signal processing applications in "Touch-Tone" receivers.

CCDs can be operated with 2, 3, or 4 phases, depending on the design of structures. A cell or stage contains the number of CCDs that is equal to the number of phases, and charge transfer between adjacent CCDs (not cells) is considered one transfer. Some common structures are shown in Fig. 15.1. Gates are usually made of metal or polysilicon. The spacing between CCDs should be small for efficient charge transfer. For 2-phase operation, asymmetrical structures are required to define the direction of charge flow.

15.3 CHARACTERISTICS

When a large gate-voltage step is applied to an MOS capacitor (or CCD) with a polarity that inverts the surface, a large number of minority carriers are required to achieve equilibrium. The time required for sufficient carriers to be generated thermally is called thermal-relaxation time (Eq. (14.6)). A typical thermal-relaxation time for Si is quite long, in the order of seconds to minutes at room temperature. CCDs are operated in the time regime much shorter than the thermal-relaxation time so that the semiconductor is driven into deep depletion (Fig. 15.2).

The surface potential well ψ_s created by a gate voltage step is also a function of the CCD signal charge Q_{sig} (Fig. 15.2(b)). In the case of an SCCD,

$$\psi_s = V_1 + V_2 - \sqrt{V_2^2 + 2V_1 V_2} \tag{15.1}$$

where

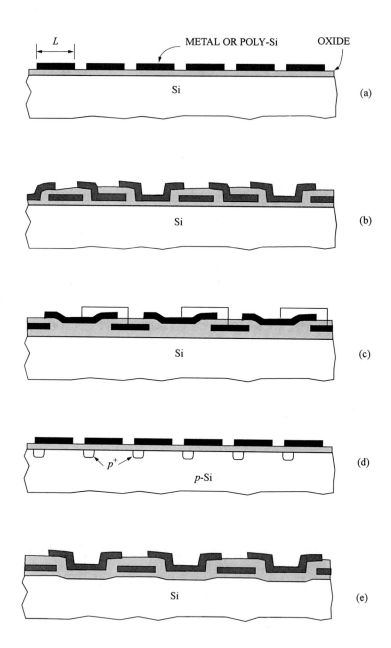

FIGURE 15.1

CCD structures using (a) 3-phase single-level gate, (b) 3-phase three-level poly-Si gate, (c) 2-phase with step oxide, (d) 2-phase with heavily doped pockets, and (e) 4-phase two-level poly-Si gate. Signal charges move from left to right in the 2-phase CCDs.

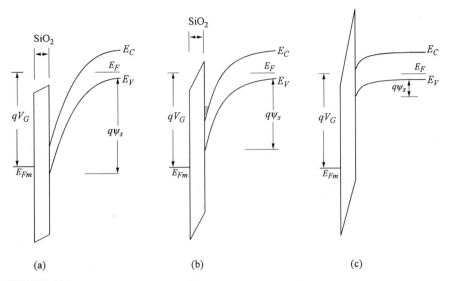

FIGURE 15.2
Energy-band diagrams of a CCD (a) immediately after a step gate voltage V_G without signal charge, (b) with signal charge, and (c) under thermal equilibrium.

$$V_1 \equiv V_G - V_{FB} - \frac{Q_{sig}}{C_{ox}} \quad , \qquad (15.2)$$

$$V_2 \equiv \frac{\varepsilon_s q N_A}{C_{ox}^2} \quad , \qquad (15.3)$$

and

$$C_{ox} = \frac{\varepsilon_{ox}}{x_{ox}} \quad . \qquad (15.4)$$

The maximum Q_{sig} that a CCD can hold is limited by

$$Q_{sig} \approx (V_G - V_T) C_{ox} \qquad (15.5)$$

where V_T is the threshold voltage for strong inversion (Eq. (14.9)). The minimum Q_{sig} for CCD operation is determined by the clock frequency because of the thermally generated minority charge as noise.

Qualitatively, the transfer of charge between CCDs is shown in Fig. 15.3 where a 3-phase operation is demonstrated. Each transfer is accomplished in two stages. The first stage is to create a potential well in the CCD where the charge is

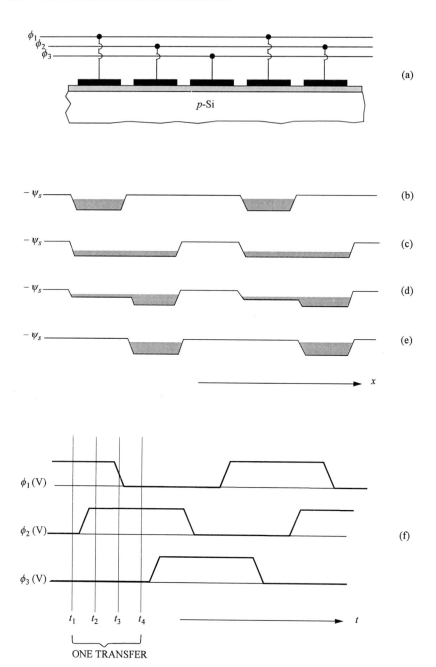

FIGURE 15.3
Illustration of charge transfer. (a) Application of 3-phase gate bias. Surface potential vs. distance at different time of (b) t_1, (c) t_2, (d) t_3, (e) t_4. Time scale is shown in (f).

to be received, followed by the stage where charge is emptied gradually from the previous CCD.

There are three driving mechanisms for the transfer of charge: (1) self-induced drift, (2) diffusion, and (3) fringing-field drift. These mechanisms are responsible for bringing the charge from the trailing edge of the electrode to the leading edge, to be ready for transfer. When the charge begins to transfer between CCDs, a lateral field results within the emptying CCD because of a gradient in charge density. This self-induced drift accounts for most of the charge transfer within a short period. The rest of the charge, in the order of 1%, is transferred either by thermal diffusion or by fringing-field drift, with much longer time constants. The time constant for thermal diffusion is given by

$$ t = \frac{4L^2}{\pi^2 D} \tag{15.6} $$

where L is the length of electrode. The time constant due to the fringing-field drift is given by[4]

$$ t = \frac{0.31L^3}{\mu V_G x_{ox}} \left(\frac{K_{ox}}{K_s} \right) . \tag{15.7} $$

This fringing field, however, is a function of distance from the surface of the semiconductor, and it maximizes at a depth of $\approx L/2$ where Eq. (15.7) applies. Because of this, BCCD can benefit much more from the fringing field than SCCD can.

The choice of the period (or frequency) of the clock signal is limited by three factors. First, it has to be long enough for reasonably complete transfer of charge. Second, it has to be much shorter than the thermal-relaxation time to minimize minority carriers generated from dark current. Especially for analog signals, the clock period has to be small enough to avoid signal loss. Third, the clock period has to be small compared to the period of the analog signal ($1/f$) to be transmitted. The frequency dependence of the output efficiency is given by[5]

$$ \frac{Q(\text{Output})}{Q(\text{Input})} = \exp\left[-n\varepsilon \left\{ 1 - \cos\left(\frac{2\pi f}{f_c} \right) \right\} \right] \tag{15.8} $$

where n is the total number of transfers, ε is the charge loss or inefficiency of each transfer, and f_c is the clock frequency. Equation (15.8) is plotted in Fig. 15.4.

There are many factors contributing to the transfer inefficiency. Among them are the nature of exponential decay of charge during transfer by diffusion and fringing-field drift, and the finite transfer time within the clock period. Efficient transfer can also be hindered by barrier hump in the gap between devices. Interface traps also contribute to charge loss because these traps capture charge rapidly but release them at a much slower rate. To avoid this effect, a background charge, called fat zero or bias charge, is used to fill these traps at all time, and this level of bias charge can be as large as 20%. The penalty is a reduced signal-to-noise ratio. Another way to get around the problem of interface traps is to use buried channel in BCCD, PCCD or P²CCD, at the expense of reduced maximum signal charge.

15.4 APPLICATIONS

1. Imaging system: The television camera, where the image is scanned and converted into electrical signal, is probably the most important application of CCD. The critical function of CCDs is to transfer the information collected from the photodetectors to a serial format in a single wire. The fact that CCDs themselves can also perform as photodetectors adds to the simplicity of fabrication, although other photodetectors such as *p-n* junctions and Schottky barriers can also be used. The usual arrangement for line- and area-sensor systems are shown in Fig. 15.5. The parallel-line format for the line sensor permits the use of a slower clock frequency. Line sensors are used for facsimile recording, aerial reconnaissance, and slow-scan television. Area sensor can use either interline transfer or frame transfer, with the latter being more common. In both systems, the transfer of columns to the main horizontal output register chain is done one bit per column simultaneously. These data are delivered via the output register with a much faster clock rate. It is important to note that the photodetectors in the frame-transfer scheme

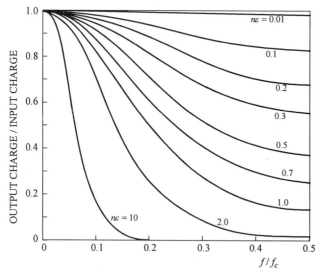

FIGURE 15.4
Frequency response of CCDs with n devices and transfer inefficiency ε.[5]

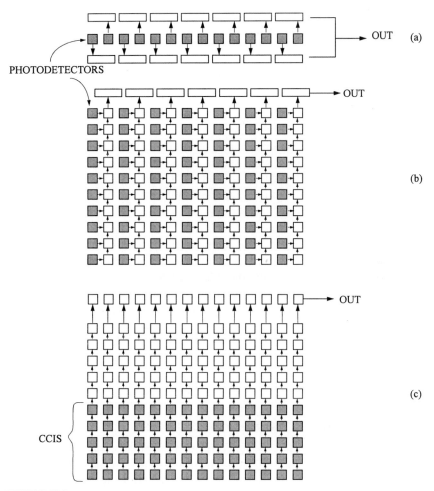

FIGURE 15.5
Arrangements of CCD imaging systems for (a) a line sensor, (b) an area sensor with interline transfer, (c) an area sensor with frame transfer. White cells are CCDs.

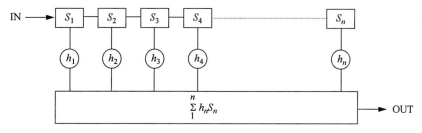

FIGURE 15.6
Block diagram for a transversal filter using CCDs. $h_1, h_2, ..., h_n$ are weighting constants.

(Fig. 15.5(c)) have to be charge-coupled image sensors (CCISs) since signals are passed through them, and they function as both sensors and shift registers. The photodetectors in Figs. 15.5(a) and (b) are not limited to CCISs.

2. Delay line: The output waveform after a chain of CCD can be delayed compared to the input. The delay is determined by the clock frequency and the total number of stages, but it is also limited by the dark current generated. A delay as long as one second can be realized.

3. Signal processing: When some stages of a shift register are tapped and used to add to or subtract from other stages, different kinds of signal processing can be performed. One specific kind is the transversal filter shown in Fig. 15.6. Signal processing is important in the fields of radar, television, communication, and instrumentation.

4. Memories: If CCDs are connected in a loop, they can be used as memories. Signal regeneration within the loop is usually required for reasonable amounts of storage time. Since CCDs are serial in nature (one dimensional), the access time is slower than other MOS memories.

5. Logic: Some simple logic circuits can be implemented with CCDs. For example, an AND gate can be formed when multiple CCDs are placed in series between an injecting diode and the output. An OR gate can be formed when they are placed in parallel between them.

15.5 RELATED DEVICES

15.5.1 Buried-Channel Charge-Coupled Device

A buried-channel charge-coupled device (BCCD) has a doped region of opposite type at the surface and is fully depleted by a DC bias, as shown in Fig. 15.7. Because the signal charge is away from the surface, it has advantages of higher mobility, less charge loss due to interface traps, and higher fringing fields for charge transfer. The penalty is less charge handling capability because the charge is further away from the gate, and thus, has less coupling.

15.5.2 Peristaltic Charge-Coupled Device

The peristaltic charge-coupled device (PCCD) is a BCCD with a relatively wide surface doped region of low doping concentration. Most of the charge is stored at the surface while a fraction is stored in the bulk. This device compromises between charge handling capability and charge loss due to interface traps.

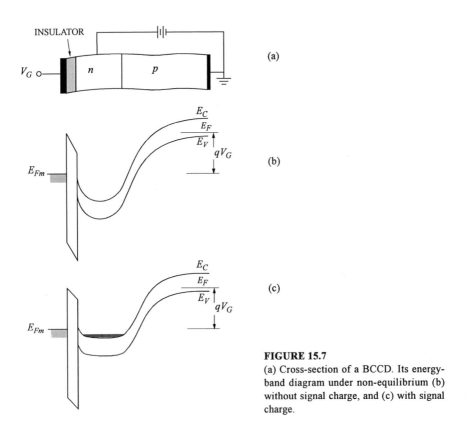

FIGURE 15.7
(a) Cross-section of a BCCD. Its energy-band diagram under non-equilibrium (b) without signal charge, and (c) with signal charge.

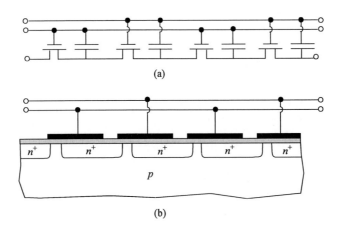

FIGURE 15.8
(a) Basic circuit for MOS BBD and (b) its implementation.

15.5.3 Profiled-Peristaltic Charge-Coupled Device

The profiled-peristaltic CCD (P^2CCD) is a special case of PCCD whose surface doped region has a two-step profile. A thin layer of highly doped region at the surface keeps the charge away from the surface by a controlled, small distance.

15.5.4 Bucket-Brigade Device

Bucket-brigade devices (BBDs) are formed by a chain of alternating switches and capacitors. MOS BBDs using MOSFETs as switches are shown in Fig. 15.8. The n^+-regions store the charges and are referred to as "buckets." BBDs are inherently 2-phase systems, and they are less effective in terms of integration density and transfer efficiency compared to CCDs.

REFERENCES

1. W. S. Boyle and G. E. Smith, "Charge coupled semiconductor devices," *Bell Syst. Tech. J.*, **49**, 587 (1970).
2. F. L. J. Sangster, "Integrated MOS and bipolar analog delay lines using bucket-brigade capacitor storage," *Proc. IEEE Int. Solid-State Circuits Conf.*, 74 (1970).
3. "A versatile electronic device comes of age," *Industrial Research/Development*, 192 (Feb. 1980).
4. G. S. Hobson, "Charge-coupled devices," *Proc. IEE,* **124**, 925 (1977).
5. M. F. Tompsett, "Charge transfer devices," *J. Vac. Sci. Technol.*, **9**, 1166 (1972).
6. W. S. Boyle and G. E. Smith, "The inception of charge-coupled devices," *IEEE Trans. Electron Dev.*, **23**, 661 (1976).
7. L. J. M. Esser and F. L. J. Sangster, "Charge transfer devices," in C. Hilsum, Vol. Ed., T. S. Moss, Ser. Ed., *Handbook on semiconductors*, Vol. 4, p. 335, North-Holland, Amsterdam, 1981.
8. W. F. Kosonocky and J. E. Carnes, "Basic concepts of charge-coupled devices," *RCA Review*, **36**, 566 (1975).

CHAPTER 16

METAL-INSULATOR-SEMICONDUCTOR SWITCH

16.1 HISTORY

The MISS (metal-insulator-semiconductor switch, MIS switch) was discovered by Yamamoto and Morimoto in 1972, using silicon dioxide as the insulator.[1] A subsequent report was made by Kroger and Wegener in 1973, using another insulator–silicon nitride.[2] Further understanding of the device was not advanced until 1977, and most analytical studies, as well as more experimental results, were presented between 1977 to 1980. These include the works by Simmons and El-Badry,[3,4] Kroger and Wegener,[5] Habib and Simmons,[6,7] Sarrabayrouse et al.,[8] and Zolomy.[9]

16.2 STRUCTURE

The MISS structure depicted in Fig. 16.1 is basically an MIS tunnel diode in series with a p-n junction. Almost all reported structures used silicon material with silicon dioxide being the tunneling insulator. This thin oxide has to be in the range of 20–50 Å, and is usually thermally grown at relatively low temperature around 700°C. In the example shown, an n-type epitaxial layer of 2–10 μm thick is grown on a p^+-substrate. The conjugate structure of metal, oxide on p-layer on n^+-substrate has also been reported in the literature.

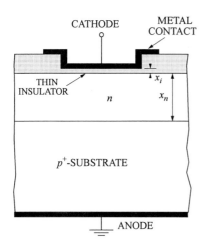

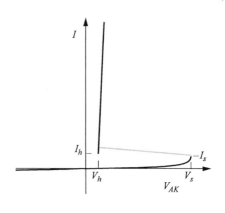

FIGURE 16.1
Cross-section of the MISS structure. The thicker insulator, usually an oxide layer, is used to eliminate edge effects of the metal contact.

FIGURE 16.2
I-V characteristics of an MISS. V_s, I_s, V_h, I_h are switching voltage, switching current, holding voltage and holding current respectively.

16.3 CHARACTERISTICS

The MISS is characterized by having bistable states: a high-impedance, low-current off-state and a low-impedance, high-current on-state. The *I-V* characteristics shown in Fig. 16.2 can be explained qualitatively with the energy-band diagrams shown in Fig. 16.3. With negative anode-to-cathode voltage ($- V_{AK}$), the MIS tunnel diode is under forward bias and the *p-n* junction under reverse bias. The current is dominated by that of generation within the depletion region (W_d) of the *p-n* junction, given by

$$J_{ge} = \frac{q n_i W_d}{2\tau} \approx \frac{n_i}{\tau} \sqrt{\frac{q\varepsilon_s (|V_{AK}| + \psi_{bi})}{2N_D}} \quad . \tag{16.1}$$

In this bias direction, no switching occurs.

　　With positive V_{AK}, the MIS tunnel diode is under reverse bias and the *p-n* junction under forward bias (Fig. 16.3(c)). In the low-current off-state, current is dominated by generation in the surface depletion region, given by the same expression except that ψ_{bi} is related, in this case, to the barrier height ϕ_b at equilibrium. The thermally generated electrons approach the *p-n* junction and recombine with holes in the depletion region of the forward biased *p-n* junction. This implies that the current through the *p-n* junction is via recombination, rather than diffusion, due to the low current level passing through it (see Eq. (1.13) and comments below it). It will be shown that the current gain of hole current to

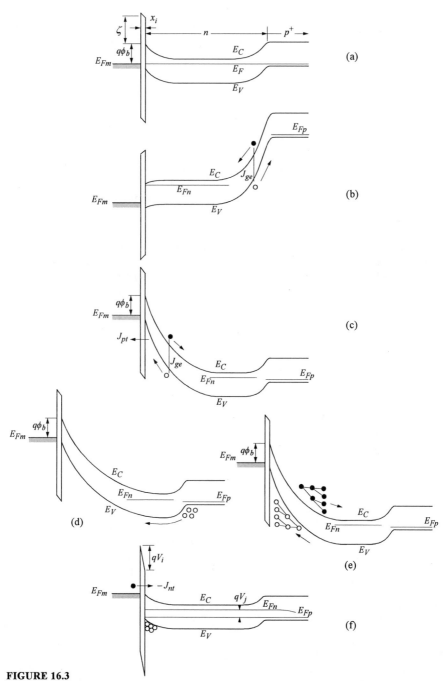

FIGURE 16.3
Energy-band diagrams of the MISS under different biases. (a) Equilibrium. (b) Negative V_{AK}. (c) Positive V_{AK}, off-state. (d) Onset of punch-through. (e) Onset of avalanche multiplication. (f) High-current on-state.

electron current associated with diffusion in the *p-n* junction is needed for switching. The electrons tunneling from metal to semiconductor is the reverse current of an MIS tunnel diode. It is negligible in the off-state and is given by (see Section 3.5.2)

$$J_{nt} = A^* T^2 \exp(-\sqrt{\zeta}x_i) \exp\left(-\frac{q\phi_b}{kT}\right) \tag{16.2}$$

where ζ is the average tunneling barrier over the insulator. This current will be shown later to be the dominant current in the on-state.

The switching criterion of the MISS depends critically on the supply of holes toward the tunneling insulator. When this hole current is small, it is semiconductor-limited. In this condition, the semiconductor surface is in deep depletion, and an inversion layer of holes at the surface is not formed. If an additional supply of hole current from other sources is available, the tunneling current is not sufficient to drain the hole current and it becomes tunneling-limited, and a hole inversion layer appears. The collapse of the surface potential (surface band bending) increases the voltage across the insulator V_i, and increases the J_{nt} in two respects. First, the barrier height ϕ_b is reduced, and second, ζ is also reduced. The latter is equivalent to a higher electric field across the insulator. The large J_{nt} passes through the *p-n* junction and the current mechanism in the *p-n* junction changes from recombination to diffusion. An electron current J_n can inject a much larger hole current since $N_A \gg N_D$, by a factor of $\approx 1/(1-\gamma)$ where γ is the injection efficiency of the *p-n* junction (ratio of hole current to total current). The total hole current tunneling through the insulator becomes

$$J_{pt} = J_n\left(\frac{1}{1-\gamma}\right) . \tag{16.3}$$

The MIS tunnel diode and the *p-n* junction pair creates a regenerative feedback and results in negative differential resistance.

The regenerative feedback can also be viewed as a result of two current gains: a gain of electron current from hole current in an MIS tunnel diode, as originally proposed by Green and Shewchun,[10] and a gain of hole current from electron current in the p^+-*n* junction. To achieve the current gain in an MIS tunnel diode, the precise insulator thickness is critical, and it has to lie in the range of 20–50 Å for the case of silicon dioxide. Oxides thinner than 20 Å cannot confine holes at the surface to support an inversion layer and to decrease ϕ_b, and current is always semiconductor-limited. Oxides thicker than 50 Å do not allow deep depletion, and current is always tunneling-limited.

In practice, the current initiated by generation is not large enough to trigger switching. The two most common, additional sources are from punch-through and avalanche. In the punch-through condition shown in Fig. 16.3(d), the depletion region of the MIS diode merges with that of the *p-n* junction. The potential barrier for holes is reduced and a large hole current is injected. The switching voltage in this punch-through mode is given by

$$V_s = \frac{qN_D(x_n - W_d)^2}{2\varepsilon_s} \tag{16.4}$$

where W_d is the depletion region of the p-n junction.

In the absence of punch-through conditions, if the electric field near the surface is high enough, avalanche multiplication occurs and also gives rise to a large hole current toward the surface (Fig. 16.3(e)). The switching voltage in this mode is the same as the avalanche breakdown voltage of a p-n junction. For silicon it can be approximated by[11]

$$V_s = 5.34 \times 10^{13} (N_D)^{-0.75} . \tag{16.5}$$

The avalanche-mode switching dominates in structures with high doping concentrations in the epitaxial layer, usually higher than 10^{17} cm^{-3}.

The energy-band diagram in Fig. 16.3(f) shows an MISS after it is switched to the high-current on-state. Notice that neither punch-through nor avalanche continues. The conduction-band edge at the surface is below E_{Fm} ($\phi_b = 0$), and J_{nt} controls the on-current. The holding voltage can be approximated by

$$V_h \approx V_i + V_j . \tag{16.6}$$

V_i is the voltage across the insulator, and is approximately equal to the original barrier height ϕ_b at equilibrium (≈ 0.5–0.9 V). The forward bias on the p-n junction V_j is around 0.7 V, giving a holding voltage of ≈ 1.5 V.

Besides the aforementioned punch-through and avalanche, two other sources of hole current are also possible. One is by a third terminal contact and another by optically generated current. The three-terminal MISS is sometimes called an MIS thyristor (MIST),[12] and variations of the structure are shown in Fig. 16.4. With either a minority-carrier injector or a majority-carrier injector, the function is the same–to increase the hole current flowing toward the insulator. While the minority-carrier injector injects holes directly, the majority-carrier injector controls the potential of the n-layer, and hole current is injected from the p^+-substrate. In either structure, with a positive gate current flowing into the device, a lower switching voltage results, as shown in Fig. 16.4(c). When the MISS is exposed to a light source, J_p is generated optically and the switching voltage is reduced. Similar characteristics to those in Fig. 16.4(c) are observed as a function of light intensity. For a fixed V_{AK}, light can induce turn-on and the device becomes a light-triggered switch.

16.4 APPLICATIONS

The MISS offers the potential of high-speed switching. Turn-on time and turnoff time have been shown to be 1–2 ns. The MISS can be applied in digital logic and a shift register has been demonstrated.[13] Other applications include memories such as SRAM,[14] microwave generation when incorporated in a relaxation oscillator circuit, and as a light-triggered switch for alarm system. For general applications of the negative resistance, the readers are referred to Appendix C2. The limitation of the MISS is its relatively high holding voltage, and the difficulty in reproducing a uniformly thin tunneling insulator.

16.5 RELATED DEVICES

16.5.1 Metal-Insulator-Semiconductor-Metal Switch

When the *p-n* junction of an MISS is replaced by a Schottky barrier, an MISM (metal-insulator-semiconductor-metal) switch is formed (Fig. 16.5).[15] The

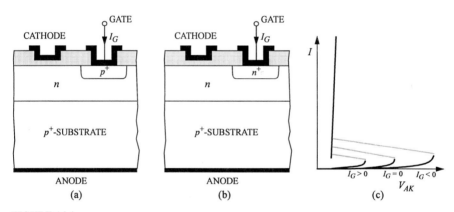

FIGURE 16.4
Three-terminal MISS (MIS thyristor) using (a) a minority-carrier injector and (b) a majority-carrier injector. The switching characteristics, as a function of gate current, are shown in (c).

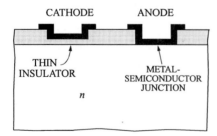

FIGURE 16.5
Structure of the MISM switch.

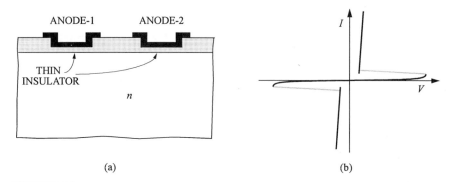

FIGURE 16.6
(a) Structure of an MISIM switch and (b) its bidirectional switching characteristics.

metal-semiconductor contact has to be formed at the surface rather than at the bottom of the substrate so that it can be close to the MIS tunnel diode. The hole injector is now a Schottky barrier instead of a *p-n* junction, and the injection efficiency is much lower. Therefore, a much higher switching current I_s results. The shape of its *I-V* characteristics resembles that of Fig. 16.2. A three-terminal MISM switch to control the switching voltage has been reported.

16.5.2 Metal-Insulator-Semiconductor-Insulator-Metal Switch

The MISIM (metal-insulator-semiconductor-insulator-metal) switch has an MIS tunnel diode as the injector and the structure simply consists of two identical MIS tunnel diodes adjacent to each other (Fig. 16.6(a)).[16] Because of its symmetry, it features bidirectional switching as shown in Fig. 16.6(b). The switching current is even higher than that of an MISM switch, due to the insulator added to the injector, in spite of the MISIM's higher injection efficiency. A third terminal has also been explored to control the switching voltage.

REFERENCES

1. T. Yamamoto and M. Morimoto, "Thin-MIS-structures Si negative-resistance diode," *Appl. Phys. Lett.*, **20**, 269 (1972).
2. H. Kroger and H. A. R. Wegener, "Bistable impedance states in MIS structures through controlled inversion," *Appl. Phys. Lett.*, **23**, 397 (1973).
3. J. G. Simmons and A. El-Badry, "Theory of switching phenomena in metal/semi-insulator/*n-p*⁺ silicon devices," *Solid-State Electron.*, **20**, 955 (1977).
4. A. El-Badry and J. G. Simmons, "Experimental studies of switching in metal semi-insulating *n-p*⁺ silicon devices," *Solid-State Electron.*, **20**, 963 (1977).
5. H. Kroger and H. A. R. Wegener, "Steady-state characteristics of two terminal inversion-controlled switches," *Solid-State Electron.*, **21**, 643 (1978).
6. S. E. D. Habib and J. G. Simmons, "Theory of switching in *p-n*-insulator (tunnel)-metal devices. Part I: Punchthrough mode," *Solid-State Electron.*, **22**, 181 (1979).

7. S. E. D. Habib and J. G. Simmons, "Theory of switching in *p-n*-insulator (tunnel)-metal devices –II: Avalanche mode," *Solid-State Electron.*, **23**, 497 (1980).

8. G. Sarrabayrouse, J. Buxo, A. E. Owen, A. M. Yague and J. P. Sabaa, "Inversion-controlled switching mechanism of M.I.S.S. devices," *IEE Proc., Pt. I*, **127**, 119 (1980).

9. I. Zolomy, "Modified theory of MISS, MIST and OMIST devices," *Solid-State Electron.*, **26**, 643 (1983).

10. M. A. Green and J. Shewchun, "Current multiplication in metal-insulator-semiconductor (MIS) tunnel diodes," *Solid-State Electron.*, **17**, 349 (1974).

11. S. M. Sze and G. Gibbons, "Avalanche breakdown voltages of abrupt and linearly graded *p-n* junctions in Ge, Si, GaAs, and GaP," *Appl. Phys. Lett.*, **8**, 111 (1966).

12. S. E. D. Habib and J. G. Simmons, "Theory of the metal-insulator-semiconductor thyristor," *IEE Proc., Pt. I*, **127**, 176 (1980).

13. T. Yamamoto, K. Kawamura and H. Shimizu, "Silicon *p-n* insulator-metal (*p-n-I-M*) devices," *Solid-State Electron.*, **19**, 701 (1976).

14. J. G. Simmons and A. A. El-Badry, "Switching phenomena in metal-insulator-n/p^+ structures: Theory, experiment and applications," *Radio & Electron. Eng.*, **48**, 215 (1978).

15. M. Darwish and K. Board, "Switching in m.i.s.m. structures," *IEE Proc., Pt. I*, **127**, 317 (1980).

16. M. Darwish and K. Board, "Theory of switching in MISIM structures," *IEE Proc., Pt. I*, **128**, 165 (1981).

PLANAR-DOPED-BARRIER SWITCH

17.1 HISTORY

The planar-doped-barrier (PDB) switch is also called a triangular-barrier switch. This device is an extension of the planar-doped-barrier diode that was developed in 1980. The PDB switch was first proposed and demonstrated by Board et al. in 1981,[1] and shortly after by Wood et al.[2] and Najjar et al.[3] in 1982. Theoretical analysis of the device was presented by Najjar et al.,[3] Board and Darwish,[4] and Habib and Board.[5]

17.2 STRUCTURE

The two-terminal PDB switch consists of a PDB diode in series with a p-n junction, as shown in Fig. 17.1. The planar-doped p^+-layer has a thickness of ≈ 100 Å, and is doped to a concentration larger than 10^{18} cm^{-3}. This layer yields a fully depleted charge sheet of $\approx 2\times10^{12}$ q/cm^2. This thin charge sheet necessitates a well-controlled epitaxial growth process such as MBE or MOCVD. Notice that the two intrinsic layers are not equal in thickness, with $x_2 \gg x_1$. This becomes apparent in Fig. 17.2(b) when in the off-state, the barrier ϕ_b is weakly dependent on the bias. The doping concentrations for the n-regions are in the 10^{17} cm^{-3} range. Most devices reported were made in GaAs although there is no fundamental limit to other materials.

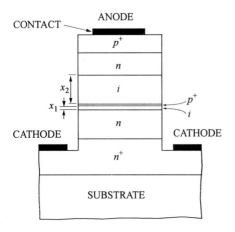

FIGURE 17.1
Cross-section of the planar-doped-barrier switch structure.

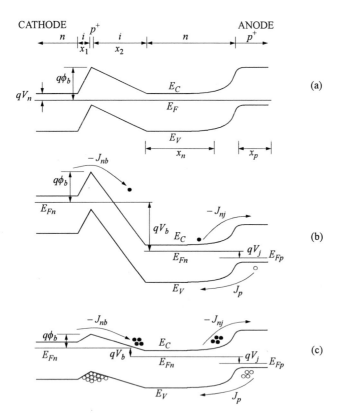

FIGURE 17.2
Energy-band diagrams of the planar-doped-barrier switch (a) under thermal equilibrium, (b) in forward bias, high-impedance off-state, and (c) low-impedance on-state.

17.3 CHARACTERISTICS

The operation of the planar-doped-barrier switch can be explained with the energy-band diagrams shown in Fig. 17.2. With a positive anode-to-cathode voltage V_{AK}, the p-n junction is under forward bias and the planar-doped barrier under reverse bias (since $x_2 \gg x_1$). Before the device switches to the low-impedance on-state (Fig. 17.2(b)), most of the applied voltage is developed across the planar-doped barrier (as V_b), and the barrier height is the controlling factor for the currents. With increasing V_{AK}, the electron current over the barrier J_{nb} increases. This increased J_{nb} (same as the electron current across the p-n junction J_{nj}) also induces a larger hole current J_p since the ratio of electron current to hole current is fixed in a p-n junction (injection efficiency). On their way to the cathode, some of the holes get trapped at the barrier peak, lower the barrier height ϕ_b, and enhance the J_{nb} further. This regenerative feedback is responsible for switching. The I-V characteristics are shown in Fig. 17.3. After switching to the on-state, the barrier ϕ_b collapses to a small value, and the I-V characteristics resemble those of a p-n junction under forward bias.

This qualitative picture can be expressed analytically. In the off-state, current is controlled by J_{nb} which is a thermionic-emission current over the planar-doped barrier (see Chapter 4), given by

$$J_{nb} = A^* T^2 \exp\left(-\frac{q\phi_b}{kT}\right) \ . \tag{17.1}$$

The barrier height is controlled by[3]

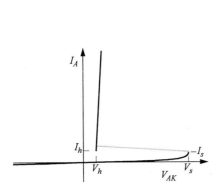

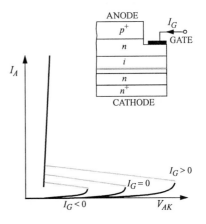

FIGURE 17.3
I-V characteristics of a planar-doped-barrier switch. V_s, I_s, V_h, I_h are switching voltage, switching current, holding voltage, and holding current respectively.

FIGURE 17.4
Forward I-V characteristics of a gated planar-doped-barrier switch.

$$\phi_b = \frac{x_1 x_2 (Q_A - \tau J_p)}{(x_1 + x_2)\varepsilon_s} + V_n - \frac{x_1 V_b}{x_1 + x_2} \quad . \tag{17.2}$$

Here Q_A is the fully depleted charge sheet (C/cm^2) in the p^+-layer, and τ is the average lifetime of holes in the energy maximum of the valence band. When J_p is zero, ϕ_b is the same as in a PDB diode. With increasing J_p, holes, trapped at the barrier peak, neutralize part of the charge sheet, and the net charge is reduced to $Q_A - \tau J_p$. The subsequent decrease of ϕ_b with J_p is the basis for switching.

The electron and hole diffusion currents J_{nj} and J_p at the p-n junction are given by

$$J_{nj} = \frac{q D_n n_i^2}{N_A x_p} \exp\left(\frac{q V_j}{kT}\right) = J_{no} \exp\left(\frac{q V_j}{kT}\right) \quad , \tag{17.3}$$

$$J_p = \frac{q D_p n_i^2}{N_D x_n} \exp\left(\frac{q V_j}{kT}\right) = J_{po} \exp\left(\frac{q V_j}{kT}\right) \quad . \tag{17.4}$$

V_j is the applied voltage across the p-n junction. These equations assume that x_p and x_n are shorter than the diffusion lengths L_n and L_p, respectively. It can be seen here that since $N_A \gg N_D$, $J_p \gg J_{nj}$ and it is one of the current gains responsible for switching. Another current gain is J_{nb} over J_p from the lowering of ϕ_b.

The switching condition can be calculated with $dV/dJ = 0$ where V is the total voltage,

$$V = V_b + V_j \tag{17.5}$$

and J is the total current

$$J = (J_{no} + J_{po}) \exp\left(\frac{q V_j}{kT}\right) \quad . \tag{17.6}$$

V_j and V_b can be expressed in terms of J by rearranging Eqs. (17.6) and (17.1), with the following substitution

$$J_{nb} = J_{nj} = \left(\frac{J_{no}}{J_{no} + J_{po}}\right) J \quad . \tag{17.7}$$

The switching current J_s can be shown to be equal to[3]

$$J_s = \frac{\varepsilon_s kT (2x_1 + x_2)(J_{no} + J_{po})}{\tau x_1 x_2 q J_{po}} \quad . \tag{17.8}$$

Another mode of switching can be triggered by punch-through when the depletion layer of the planar-doped barrier completely consumes the middle n-layer and merges with the depletion region of the p-n junction. This occurs in structures with lower n-layer doping, and is less common since the previous mode usually occurs first.

With negative V_{AK}, latching does not occur. In this case, the p-n junction is under reverse bias and the planar-doped barrier under forward bias. Current is controlled by diffusion current of the p-n junction and there is no regenerative feedback.

A third terminal, making contact to the n-region of the p-n junction, is sometimes used to control the switching voltage (Fig. 17.4). With a gate current I_G flowing into the device, electrons are drawn out of the gate, and J_{nj} and J_p are both reduced. This suppresses regenerative feedback and the switching voltage is increased. An alternate explanation is that positive I_G implies a higher gate potential, which suppresses the hole diffusion current J_p. As an alternative to adding a third terminal, exposing the device to a light source can generate added J_p, reduce the switching voltage and trigger turn-on. In this mode, the device becomes a light-triggered switch.

17.4 APPLICATIONS

The PDB switch offers certain advantages over the MISS. One advantage is that it avoids the problems associated with having to grow a uniform, thin tunnel oxide, but only at the expense of requiring a costly epitaxial step such as MBE or MOCVD. This is one of the main reasons why this device has not been produced commercially. The PDB switch can be used to perform high-speed logic, or to generate microwave. It can be used as a light-triggered switch. The readers can refer to Appendix C2 for general applications of the negative resistance.

17.5 RELATED DEVICES

17.5.1 Polysilicon-n-p Switch

A polysilicon-n-p switch is formed by depositing polysilicon (≈ 0.1–1 μm) onto a single-crystal silicon substrate that has an n-layer over the p-substrate (Fig. 17.5).[6] This device takes advantage of the polysilicon property of having a large negative fixed charge at the grain boundaries. This natural charge sheet is equivalent to the planar-doped layer and it forms a triangular barrier. One difference in this device is that it has multiple grain boundaries and, thus, multiple barriers. Otherwise the switching mechanism is similar to the single-barrier, single-crystal PDB switch.

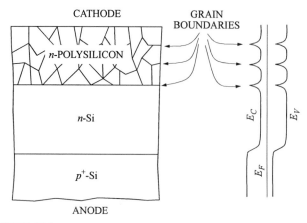

FIGURE 17.5
Structure of a polysilicon-*n-p* switch and its energy-band diagram from anode to cathode, under thermal equilibrium.

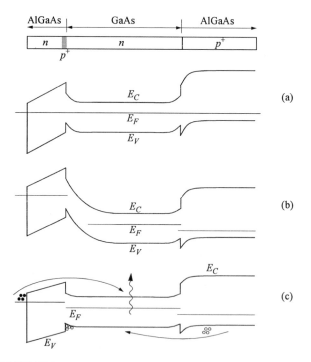

FIGURE 17.6
Energy-band diagrams of a DOES, using the AlGaAs–GaAs system as an example. (a) Under thermal equilibrium. (b) Forward biased in the high-impedance off-state, no light output. (c) In the low-impedance on-state, with light output.

17.5.2 Double-Heterostructure Optoelectronic Switch

A DOES (double-heterostructure optoelectronic switch) incorporates heterojunctions in the PDB switch, with the narrow-energy-gap material placed in the middle (Fig. 17.6).[7] Another minor difference is that more heavily doped n-layers ($\approx 10^{17}$ cm^{-3}) replace the intrinsic layers. Due to carrier confinement within the middle n-layer by the heterostructure, light is produced in the on-state from electron-hole recombination. The DOES, in addition to electrical switching similar to that shown in Fig. 17.3, also has a bistable optical output: no light output in the high-impedance off-state, and light output in the low-impedance on-state. Another interesting property of the DOES is its sensitivity to light, which can lower the switching voltage and trigger turn-on. As a result, the DOES can be used as an optical amplifier, which is triggered by a weak light input to produce a larger light output. Such a device is useful for optical logics or optical computing.

A third terminal contacting the middle n-layer has been shown to control the light output.[8] Such a three-terminal device is a controllable LED and is called a ledistor by the inventors. By properly designing the structural surfaces and dimensions, stimulated emission, as opposed to spontaneous emission, is also feasible.[9] The device becomes a controllable laser and is called a lasistor by the inventors.

REFERENCES

1. K. Board, K. Singer, R. Malik, C. E. C. Wood and L. F. Eastman, "A planar-doped barrier switching device," *Proc. 8th Biennial Cornell Microwave Conf.*, 115 (1981).
2. C. E. C. Wood, L. F. Eastman, K. Board, K. Singer and R. Malik, "Regenerative switching device using MBE-grown gallium arsenide," *Electronics Lett.*, **18**, 676 (1982).
3. F. E. Najjar, J. A. Barnard, S. C. Palmateer and L. F. Eastman, "The triangular barrier switch," *Tech. Digest IEEE IEDM*, 177 (1982).
4. K. Board and M. Darwish, "A new form of two-state switching device, using a bulk semiconductor barrier," *Solid-State Electron.*, **25**, 571 (1982).
5. S. E. D. Habib and K. Board, "Theory of the triangular-barrier switch," *IEE Proc., Pt. I*, **130**, 292 (1983).
6. M. Darwish and K. Board, "Theory of switching in polysilicon n-p^+ structures," *Solid-State Electron.*, **27**, 775 (1984).
7. G. W. Taylor, J. G. Simmons, A. Y. Cho and R. S. Mand, "A new double heterostructure optoelectronic switching device using molecular beam epitaxy," *J. Appl. Phys.*, **59**, 596 (1986).
8. D. L. Crawford, G. W. Taylor and J. G. Simmons, "Optoelectronic transient response of an n-channel double heterostructure optoelectronic switch," *Appl. Phys. Lett.*, **52**, 863 (1988).
9. G. W. Taylor and P. Cooke, "Double-heterostructure optoelectronic switch as a single quantum well laser," *Appl. Phys. Lett.*, **56**, 1308 (1990).

CHAPTER
18

AMORPHOUS THRESHOLD SWITCH

18.1 HISTORY

The amorphous threshold switch is also known as the ovonic threshold switch, named after the inventor S. R. Ovshinsky whose landmark paper in 1968 sparked a new field of research in the 1970s and 1980s.[1] Amorphous semiconductors can be divided into two major forms: chalcogenide semiconductors (chalcogenide glasses) which contain chalcogenide elements in Group VI of the periodic table such as sulfur S, selenium Se or tellurium Te, and tetrahedrally bound semiconductors such as silicon and germanium, or simply amorphous Si or Ge. Ovshinsky's original paper, as well as most of the studies on the device, were based on chalcogenide semiconductors. Amorphous silicon was first used by Feldman and Moorjani in 1970, prepared by vacuum evaporation.[2,3] It was not until 1982 that other deposition techniques of amorphous Si such as sputtering and glow discharge were pursued by Gabriel and Adler,[4] Owen et al.,[5] and den Boer.[6] For reviews of this device, the readers can refer to Refs. 7–10.

Ever since the conception of the device, there has been much controversy over its fundamental operation and potential applications. Over the past few years, the number of reports on this subject has decreased. Up to now, the device has not been as commercially successful as once thought.

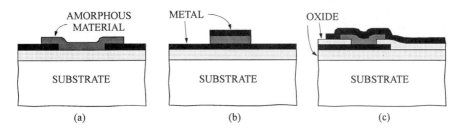

FIGURE 18.1
Structures of an amorphous threshold switch. (a) Coplanar structure. (b) Mesa geometry sandwich structure and (c) channel geometry sandwich structure.

18.2 STRUCTURE

The amorphous threshold switch is a thin film device and its different structures are shown in Fig. 18.1. It can have current conduction along the film in a coplanar structure, and perpendicular through the film in a sandwich structure. Chalcogenide semiconductors are usually deposited by sputtering. A popular material used is SiGeTeAs. Amorphous Si can be deposited by evaporation, sputtering, or glow discharge. Glow discharge is another name for plasma-enhanced chemical vapor deposition (PECVD), and amorphous Si is deposited by decomposition of silane SiH_4. For both sputtering and glow discharge depositions of chalcogenide glass and amorphous Si, the addition of hydrogen is known to improve the film quality by neutralizing dangling bonds. The resulting films are called hydrogenated chalcogenide glass and hydrogenated amorphous Si (a-Si:H or α-Si:H). These amorphous films typically lie in the range of 0.2–1 µm. Molybdenum is the most common metal electrode, followed by titanium and chromium. The substrate provides mechanical support, and can be silicate glass, stainless steel, or a single-crystal silicon wafer.

18.3 CHARACTERISTICS

As the name implies, the amorphous threshold switch changes from a high-impedance state to a low-impedance stage as the applied voltage is raised above a threshold level. The *I-V* characteristics are shown in Fig. 18.2, and they are symmetric around the origin. Typical resistance in the high-impedance state (off-state) is in the order of 1 MΩ, and that in the low-impedance state (on-state) is 1 kΩ or below. The threshold voltage is in the 10–100 V range, and the holding voltage is between 1–2 V.

Due to the disordered nature of the material, there have been numerous debates on the origin of the switching mechanism.[9] There are three schools of thought on the theory: (1) thermal, (2) electronic, and (3) electrothermal. One commonality among them is that the on-state conduction is not a bulk phenomenon, but is through a small filament connecting between the two

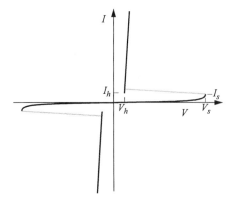

FIGURE 18.2
Switching characteristics of an amorphous threshold switch. V_s, I_s, V_h, I_h are switching voltage, switching current, holding voltage and holding current respectively.

electrodes. In the thermal model, current causes Joule heating that raises the temperature and increases the conductivity of the material. This, in turn, further increases the current. This positive feedback is also called thermal runaway. The conductance G is related to the temperature by an activation energy E_a

$$G = G_o \exp\left(\frac{-E_a}{kT}\right) . \tag{18.1}$$

Within the electronic model, there are also a few possibilities. These include tunneling, injection from electrodes, impact ionization, and bulk traps. In the electronic model involving bulk traps, it is believed that once the traps are filled with carriers, the carrier mobility is much enhanced, leading to a low-impedance state.[11] Finally, the electrothermal model claims that both thermal and electronic properties are needed and are coupled together.[12,13] Some suggest that switching is initiated by a thermal process, but the on-state is sustained by an electronic process. Most publications in recent years favor the electronic or electrothermal model, claiming that a pure thermal effect is unlikely.

There are some undesirable effects associated with the amorphous threshold switch. First of all, when it switches from the off-state to the on-state, there is a delay between the applied bias and the actual switching. This delay is typically in the range of 10–50 µs. The actual switching process itself is found to be very fast, less than 1 µs. Some claim that it is even below 0.1 ns. Another peculiarity is the forming process during the first switch, the so-called "first-fire." It is common that the threshold voltage for the first-fire is higher than the subsequent events. Lastly, the switch suffers from a limit on the number of switching. A typical reported lifetime is 10^9 cycles.

18.4 APPLICATIONS

Since the amorphous threshold switch is a thin-film device, it is inexpensive to make, and can be deposited on a large substrate, unlike that for single-crystal semiconductor processing. It can be used as switching devices in a flat-panel display, and for transient suppression (ESD protection) of integrated circuits. For general applications of negative resistance, the readers can refer to Appendix C2.

It has been more than 25 years since the conception, but this device has not been widely accepted in commercial circuits. This can be attributed to numerous factors such as reproducibility and reliability, limited switching lifetime, slow delay, etc.

18.5 RELATED DEVICE

18.5.1 Amorphous Memory Switch

In an amorphous memory switch[9] (or ovonic memory switch), the on-state characteristics have no holding voltage or holding current, and they pass through the origin as shown in Fig. 18.3. This implies that the on-state is permanent, and is nonvolatile such that the on-state can be maintained without any power. It is believed that the low-impedance state is due to permanent phase transformation of local regions, leading to a filament of crystallites whose conductance is much higher than the surrounding amorphous material. To achieve this, a current pulse of 1–10 mA is applied for a few ms. To transform the crystallites back to amorphous material, a current pulse of slightly higher current is used but for a much shorter time, in the order of a few μs. Such a fast temperature drop quenches the transformation and does not allow adequate time for crystallization.

In both device structure and material, the amorphous memory switch is similar to the amorphous threshold switch. Very often the same device can be

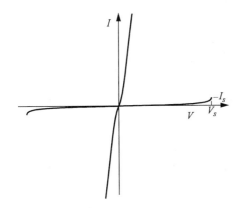

FIGURE 18.3
Switching characteristics of an amorphous memory switch.

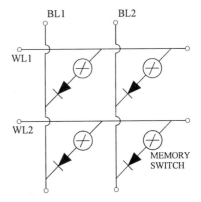

FIGURE 18.4
A nonvolatile memory array using amorphous memory switches. BL and WL represent bit line and word line, respectively.

operated in both regimes, controlled by the amplitude and duration of the bias pulse. Most materials used for this memory device are chalcogenides, and the most common is GeTeSbS. The choice of material for this device is based on its tendency to crystallize, which is to be avoided in a threshold switch. As for amorphous silicon material, results were presented briefly using evaporated Si,[2] and more recently on a doped junction of *p-n-i* structure, prepared by glow discharge.[5,10]

The amorphous memory switch naturally can be applied in a nonvolatile memory, or specifically an EEPROM. As shown in Fig. 18.4, each cell consists of a memory switch and a diode in series. Again, the commercial market for this device is very limited.

REFERENCES

1. S. R. Ovshinsky, "Reversible electrical switching phenomena in disordered structures," *Phys. Rev. Lett.*, **21**, 1450 (1968).
2. C. Feldman and K. Moorjani, "Switching in elemental amorphous semiconductors," *J. Non-Cryst. Solids*, **2**, 82 (1970).
3. K. Moorjani and C. Feldman, "Electrical conduction in amorphous boron and silicon," *J. Non-Cryst. Solids*, **4**, 248 (1970).
4. M. C. Gabriel and D. Adler, "Switching in hydrogenated amorphous silicon," *J. Non-Cryst. Solids*, **48**, 297 (1982).
5. A. E. Owen, P. G. LeComber, G. Sarrabayrouse and W. E. Spear, "New amorphous-silicon electrically programmable nonvolatile switching device," *IEE Proc.*, **129**, Pt. I, 51 (1982).
6. W. den Boer, "Threshold switching in hydrogenated amorphous silicon," *Appl. Phys. Lett.*, **40**, 812 (1982).
7. D. Adler, "Amorphous-semiconductor devices," *Sci. Am.*, **236**, 36 (1977).
8. C. F. Drake, "A decade of the metal-insulator-metal device," *Thin Solid Films*, **50**, 125 (1978).
9. A. Madan and M. P. Shaw, *The physics and applications of amorphous semiconductors,* Academic Press, New York, 1988.
10. P. G. LeComber, A. E. Owen, W. E. Spear, J. Hajto and W. K. Choi, "Electronic switching in amorphous silicon junction devices," in J. I. Pankove, Ed., *Semiconductors and semimetals*, **21**, Part D, 275 (1984).
11. D. Adler, M. S. Shur, S. Silver and S. R. Ovshinsky, "Threshold switching in chalcogenide-glass thin films," *J. Appl. Phys.*, **51**, 3289 (1980).
12. A. E. Owen, J. M. Robertson and C. Main, "The threshold characteristics of chalcogenide-glass memory switches," *J. Non-Cryst. Solids*, **32**, 29 (1979).
13. M. P. Shaw and K. F. Subhani, "An electrothermal model for threshold switching in thin amorphous chalcogenide films," *Solid-State Electron.*, **24**, 233 (1981).

CHAPTER
19

METAL-OXIDE-SEMICONDUCTOR
FIELD-EFFECT
TRANSISTOR

19.1 HISTORY

The metal-oxide-semiconductor (sometimes called metal-oxide-silicon) field-effect transistor is more commonly known as the MOSFET. It is also simply called MOST for metal-oxide-semiconductor transistor. It belongs to a general group of devices, called IGFET (insulated-gate field-effect transistor) or MISFET (metal-insulator-semiconductor field-effect transistor), that have a gate isolated electrically from the semiconductor by a dielectric layer. A MOSFET has oxide as the insulator, and thus it is commonly referred to silicon devices because of the near ideal oxide–semiconductor interface that is grown thermally. A MISFET, on the other hand, implies an IGFET made on a compound semiconductor (see Section 19.5.6).

The idea of field effect can be traced back to Lilienfeld in 1926[1-3] and to Heil in 1935.[4] During the late 1940s, experiments were focused on making field-effect devices. In fact, it was in the course of such activities that the bipolar transistor was discovered experimentally in 1947. The first experimental FET was shown by Shockley and Pearson in 1948.[5] Up to that point, field effect was only used to modulate majority-carrier conduction near the surface in bulk material. Ross in 1955 proposed using the field effect on minority carriers in the surface inversion layer,[6] and the Si–SiO$_2$ system was first proposed in 1960 by Atalla.[7] After the invention of the bipolar transistor, most activities were shifted toward that area. Another road block was the unavailability of a good oxide–semiconductor system without excessive leakage, oxide charges, and interface

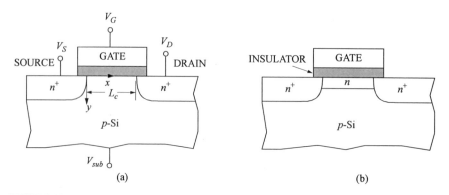

FIGURE 19.1

Cross-sections showing MOSFETs of (a) n-channel enhancement mode, and (b) depletion mode. Source and drain are reversible.

traps. The pioneering work by Ligenza and Spitzer[8] on oxides grown in steam at high pressure was instrumental in the development of the first MOSFET reported by Kahng and Atalla in 1960.[9] Since then, the popularity of the MOSFET has been rising. Early MOSFETs were dominated by p-channel devices because of the inability to realize enhancement mode for n-channel devices due to positive oxide charges. When oxide quality improved, n-channel devices provided improved performance due to higher electron mobility. Most circuits now utilize complementary MOS devices (CMOS) that include both channel types. The MOSFET is the most common transistor found in commercial ICs because of its simplicity, low cost, small size, and low power. Historical development of the MOSFET was documented in Refs. 10–11.

Device modeling on MOSFET characteristics was developed around 1963 by Ihantola and Moll,[12] Sha,[13] Hofstein and Heiman.[14] Detailed studies on the device can be found in Refs. 15–17.

19.2 STRUCTURE

The cross-section of a MOSFET is shown in Fig. 19.1. For an n-channel device, the current is conducted by electrons and the source and drain are formed by n^+-regions (in the order of 10^{20} cm^{-3}) for good contacts to the channel. The source and drain are formed by ion implantation after the gate structure is defined so that they are self-aligned to the gate. The gate-to-source and -drain overlap is critical for the formation of a continuous channel. The device is symmetrical so that the source and drain can be interchanged. The distance between the metallurgical junctions is the effective channel length L_c. The substrate is of an opposite type to ensure source and drain isolation. The oxide is grown thermally for good interfacial properties. The most common gate material is polysilicon, but metals and silicides can also be used. In the latter cases, refractory metals and silicides are necessary for compatibility with high-temperature processing. For a channel length of 0.3 μm, typical parameters are: oxide thickness $\approx$ 10 nm, substrate doping $\approx 3 \times 10^{17}$ cm^{-3}, source and drain junction depth $\approx$ 0.2 μm. An optimized MOSFET usually has nonuniform substrate doping in the y-direction and has a bell-shape profile which peaks at about 0.2 μm in depth. The higher bulk concentration serves to prevent punch-through between the source and drain, and the low doping at the surface maintains a low threshold voltage, and minimizes mobility degradation due to a high surface field.

For each type of channel, the threshold gate voltage to turn on the channel can be adjusted. If the channel is off at zero gate voltage (normally off), it is called an enhancement device because gate voltage is required to "enhance" a channel. If the channel is already on at zero gate voltage (normally on), it is called a depletion device because gate voltage is required to "deplete" the channel. A common way to achieve a depletion-mode device is to incorporate a buried channel as shown in Figs. 19.1(c) and (d). This buried channel is formed by ion implantation.

19.3 CHARACTERISTICS

For the discussion of the rest of the chapter, an n-channel enhancement device is assumed with source and substrate voltages equal to zero (unless stated otherwise). A critical parameter for a MOSFET is the threshold voltage, given by

$$V_T = V_{FB} + 2\psi_B + \frac{\sqrt{2\varepsilon_s qN(2\psi_B)}}{C_{ox}} \tag{19.1}$$

where

$$C_{ox} = \frac{\varepsilon_{ox}}{x_{ox}} . \tag{19.2}$$

The flat-band voltage, V_{FB}, ignoring oxide and interface charges, is simply the work function difference between the gate and the semiconductor substrate (Fig. 19.2). Beyond the flat-band condition, the threshold voltage is the sum of voltages across the oxide and the semiconductor. To turn on the channel, strong inversion requires a surface bending ψ_s of $2\psi_B$. The last term in Eq. (19.1) is simply the voltage across the oxide layer, given by the charge in the depletion layer divided by the oxide capacitance.

In the presence of a negative substrate bias, V_T is increased. The amount can be calculated by changing the surface potential from $2\psi_B$ to $(2\psi_B + |V_{sub}|)$ in Eq. (19.1). This dependence of V_T on substrate bias is called the body effect, and is undesirable for circuits that encounter a substrate bias.

When the drain is biased, the channel potential $V_c(x)$ changes from drain to source. According to Figs. 19.2 and 19.3, $V_c(x)$ is the semiconductor potential ψ

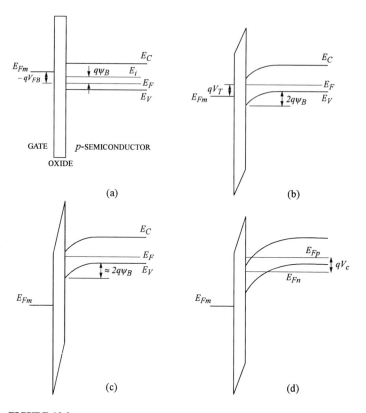

FIGURE 19.2

Energy-band diagram as a function of y at (a) flat-band condition, (b) onset of threshold. Beyond threshold voltage, the band bending (c) at source and (d) along the channel.

or $-E_i/q$ at the surface, with respect to the source. $V_c(x)$ is also close to $(E_{Fp} - E_{Fn}(x))/q$. At gate voltage above threshold, the inversion-layer charge density Q_i as a function of x is given by

$$Q_i(x) = C_{ox}[V_G - V_T - V_c(x)] \tag{19.3}$$

where the gradual-channel approximation is applied. The gradual-channel approximation requires that the longitudinal field be much smaller than the transverse field. This implies that $V_c(x)$ is a slow-varying function such that a simple one-dimensional approximation of Eq. (19.3) can be used.

Using the drift equation, the MOSFET current is given by

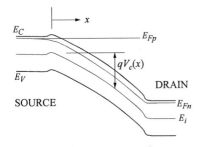

FIGURE 19.3

Energy-band diagram at the semiconductor surface from source to drain, above threshold with drain bias. The channel potential V_c can be visualized here. Notice that E_{Fn} is nearly pinned to $(E_i + q\psi_B)$.

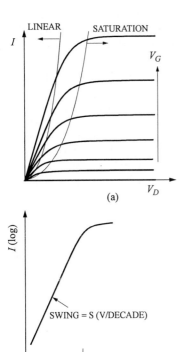

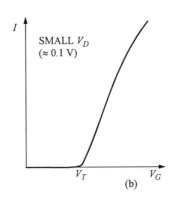

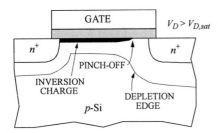

FIGURE 19.4

Common I-V plots for a MOSFET. (a) Output characteristics. (b) Linear characteristics where V_T and μ can be measured. (c) Subthreshold characteristics.

FIGURE 19.5

In the saturation regime $V_D > (V_G - V_T)$, the pinch-off point ($Q_i = 0$) moves away from the drain.

$$I = W\mu Q_i \mathscr{E}_x$$

$$= W\mu C_{ox} [V_G - V_T - V_c(x)] \frac{dV_c(x)}{dx} \quad .$$

(19.4)

Integrating Eq. (19.4) from $x = 0$ to L_c yields

$$I = \frac{\mu C_{ox} W}{L_c} \left[(V_G - V_T) V_D - \frac{V_D^2}{2} \right] \quad .$$

(19.5)

The output characteristics of a MOSFET is shown in Fig. 19.4(a). Note that Eq. (19.5) only describes the non-saturating region because current would be negative at infinite V_D. These curves show that for a fixed V_G, the current increases with V_D until $V_{D,sat}$ beyond which the current saturates to a value I_{sat}. This onset of saturation corresponds to the condition that Q_i at the drain approaching zero. Substituting $V_{D,sat}$ for V_c, and $Q_i = 0$, Eq. (19.3) gives

$$V_{D,sat} = V_G - V_T \quad .$$

(19.6)

Beyond that drain value, the "pinch-off" point where $Q_i = 0$ moves toward the source as shown in Fig. 19.5. Qualitatively, the current becomes independent of V_D because at the pinch-off point, the channel potential remains at $V_{D,sat}$, so that the bias across the strong inversion region remains constant. Substituting $V_{D,sat}$ into Eq. (19.5) gives

$$I_{sat} = \frac{\mu C_{ox} W}{2L_c} (V_G - V_T)^2 \quad .$$

(19.7)

The transconductance in the saturation regime is given by

$$g_{m,sat} \equiv \frac{dI_{sat}}{dV_G} = \frac{\mu C_{ox} W (V_G - V_T)}{L_c}$$

(19.8)

and it increases with V_G.

Two other common I-V plots are shown in Fig. 19.4. In the linear regime with small V_D (≈ 0.1 V), the current increases linearly with V_G,

$$I_{lin} = \frac{\mu C_{ox} W (V_G - V_T) V_D}{L_c}$$

(19.9)

giving a transconductance of

$$g_{m,lin} \equiv \frac{dI_{lin}}{dV_G} = \frac{\mu C_{ox} W V_D}{L_c}$$

(19.10)

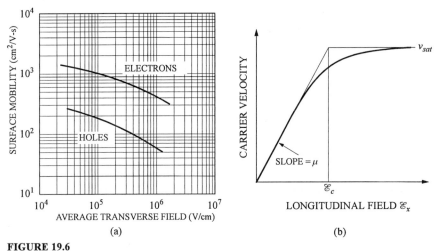

FIGURE 19.6
(a) Low-field surface mobility for Si as a function of average transverse field. (After Ref. 18) (b) Carrier velocity as a function of longitudinal field. At high fields beyond $\mathscr{E}_c$, velocity saturates to v_{sat}. Piecewise linear approximation is indicated.

A decrease of slope at higher V_G is due to a decrease in surface mobility μ. Studies have shown that the surface mobility is a strong function of the field perpendicular to the surface, induced by V_G (Fig. 19.6(a)), presumably due to increased surface scattering effects. This I-V plot (Fig. 19.4(b)) is also commonly used to extrapolate V_T from measurements. Similar to bulk mobilities, the surface mobility of electrons is usually higher than that of holes, by a factor of ≈ 4. This is the reason for the better performance of n-channel devices. The surface mobilities are much smaller than the bulk values, about half or less. Discussion so far has been based on the mobility regime in which the carrier velocity is proportional to the longitudinal field. It will be shown later that for devices with a channel length less than ≈ 1 μm, the field becomes so high that carriers will reach a constant saturated velocity (Fig. 19.6(b)). This has drastic effects on the saturation regime of the characteristics and will be discussed later.

The off-current at $V_G = 0$, as shown in the linear plot of Fig. 19.4(a), is very small. However, for a very large circuit, the exact value is important for low power. This minute off-current can be measured in the subthreshold region on a logarithmic scale (Fig. 19.4(c)). MOS theory indicates that for V_G above threshold, the inversion charge varies linearly with the channel potential (Eq. (19.3)). However, when V_G is below V_T, the minority-carrier concentration at the surface changes exponentially with ψ_s. Under a drain bias, there exists at the surface a large gradient of minority carriers from source to drain, giving rise to a domination of diffusion current over drift current. The subthreshold diffusion current is given by

$$
I = -qAD_n\frac{dn}{dx} \approx qWx_{ac}D_n\frac{n(0) - n(L_c)}{L_c}
$$

$$
\approx \frac{qWx_{ac}D_n n_{po}}{L_c}\left[\exp\left(\frac{q\psi_s(0)}{kT}\right)\right]\left[1 - \exp\left(\frac{-qV_D}{kT}\right)\right]
$$

$$
\approx \frac{qWx_{ac}D_n n_{po}}{L_c}\exp\left(\frac{q\psi_s(0)}{kT}\right)
$$

$$(19.11)$$

where A is the cross-section area of the surface channel, and $\psi_s(0)$ is the surface potential (band bending in y-direction) at the source end. x_{ac} is the thickness of the channel and it can be approximated by

$$
x_{ac} \approx \frac{kT}{q\mathscr{E}_y(0)}
$$

$$(19.12)$$

where $\mathscr{E}_y(0)$ is the transverse field at the surface,

$$
\mathscr{E}_y(0) = \sqrt{\frac{2qN\psi_s}{\varepsilon_s}}.
$$

$$(19.13)$$

x_{ac} is typically in the range of 3–10 nm.

Equation (19.11) indicates two interesting features. First, if V_D exceeds a few kT, the current is independent of V_D. Second, the current rises exponentially with ψ_s, and since V_G changes quite linearly with ψ_s, the current changes exponentially with V_G. The subthreshold swing S, expressed in gate voltage for a change of one decade of current (V/decade), can be shown to be[16]

$$
S \approx \frac{kT}{q}(\ln 10)\left(1 + \frac{C_d}{C_{ox}}\right)
$$

$$(19.14)$$

where C_d is the depletion-layer capacitance given by

$$
C_d = \frac{\varepsilon_s}{W_d} = \sqrt{\frac{qN\varepsilon_s}{2\psi_s}}.
$$

$$(19.15)$$

The subthreshold swing, according to Eq. (19.11), is based on the control of ψ_s by V_G. In the presence of large interface trap density, this control is weakened as part of the induced charge becomes a trapped charge, which is immobile. The subthreshold swing is increased to

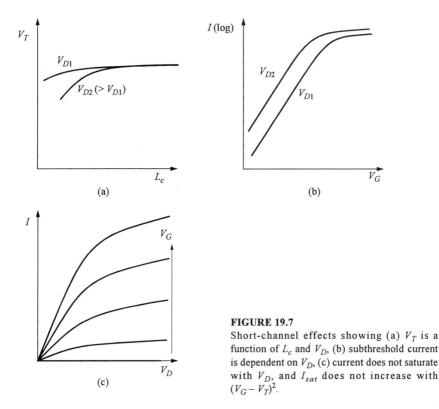

FIGURE 19.7
Short-channel effects showing (a) V_T is a function of L_c and V_D, (b) subthreshold current is dependent on V_D, (c) current does not saturate with V_D, and I_{sat} does not increase with $(V_G - V_T)^2$.

$$\frac{S(\text{with } D_{it})}{S(\text{without } D_{it})} = \frac{[1 + (C_d/C_{ox})] + (C_{it}/C_{ox})}{1 + (C_d/C_{ox})} \qquad (19.16)$$

where

$$C_{it} = q^2 D_{it} \qquad (19.17)$$

is the capacitance associated with interface traps.

The considerations so far are applicable only to a long-channel device where the channel length is large compared to the source and drain depletion width. When the channel length is shorter than ≈ 1 μm, some equations have to be modified to account for "short-channel" effects. Major short-channel effects are shown in Fig. 19.7 where one notices that (a) the V_T is a function of L_c and V_D, (b) current in the subthreshold and saturation regions are dependent on V_D, and (c) current is a linear function of V_G in the saturation region. These effects will be discussed next.

The threshold voltage can be viewed as the gate voltage required to induce charge in the maximum depletion width ($\psi_s = 2\psi_B$) before a strong-inversion charge starts to form. One common approach to explain some of the short-channel effects is charge sharing due to geometrical effect. Figure 19.8(a) shows that charge induced by the gate in the depletion layer has a trapezoidal shape. The rest of the depletion charge is compensated by the n^+-side of the p-n junction. The last term of Eq. (19.1) is thus reduced from a box-shape approximation. It can also be realized in this argument that the short-channel effects are reduced if the junction depth is reduced, as the trapezoid approaches a rectangle.

Figure 19.8(b) also shows that the charge in the trapezoid being controlled by the gate is reduced further by the drain bias. This also means that there is a dependence of V_T on V_D. Apart from the V_T variation, this figure shows that the effective channel length is reduced with drain bias. Therefore, a more accurate description of the channel length is the spacing between the depletion edges of the source and drain, rather than the metallurgical junctions. The combined effects of V_T and L_c reductions account for the non-saturating currents in both the subthreshold region (Fig. 19.7(b)) and the saturation region (Fig. 19.7(c)).

The third short-channel effect comes from velocity saturation of carriers, determined by $\mathscr{E}_c$ and v_{sat} of Fig. 19.6(b). If the drain bias is below $V_{D,sat}$ but the field already reaches velocity saturation, i.e., $V_D \approx \mathscr{E}_c L_c < (V_G - V_T)$, the current saturates prematurely to a value of

$$
\begin{aligned}
I_{sat} &= W Q_i v_{sat} \\
&= W C_{ox} (V_G - V_T) v_{sat}
\end{aligned}
\tag{19.18}
$$

at a new $V_{D,sat}$ of $\approx \mathscr{E}_c L_c$. Notice that the current is now independent of the channel length, and is a linear function of V_G rather than the square function given in Eq. (19.7). The transconductance becomes

$$
g_{m,sat} \equiv \frac{dI_{sat}}{dV_G} = W C_{ox} v_{sat}
\tag{19.19}
$$

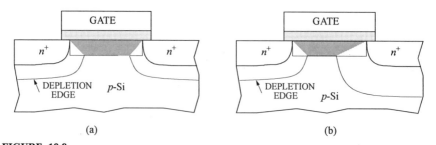

FIGURE. 19.8
Charge-sharing effect for short-channel devices. Trapezoidal area is the depletion charge induced by the gate. (a) With small drain bias. (b) With large drain bias.

and is independent of V_G, rather than proportional to $(V_G - V_T)$. For silicon, $\mathscr{E}_c \approx 1$–2×10^4 V/cm and $v_{sat} \approx 1\times10^7$ cm/s.

The cutoff frequency f_T of a MOSFET gives an indication of the upper limit on circuit speed. It is the unity current gain of the equivalent circuit, given by

$$f_T = \frac{g_{m,sat}}{2\pi \, (WL_c C_{ox} + C_{par})} \qquad (19.20)$$

where the relevant $g_{m,sat}$ should be used. C_{par} is the input parasitic capacitance. The theoretical cutoff frequency for a 0.1 μm MOSFET (the shortest channel length projected) is about 150 GHz but it is expected to operate at about 20 GHz in practical circuits.

Different versions of the source and drain structures have been shown to solve specific problems. For submicron-length MOSFETs, reliability caused by hot electrons posts a serious long-term degradation problem. This arises because hot carriers acquire enough energy to overcome the Si–SiO$_2$ barrier, and create trapped charges at the interface. To reduce the internal field near the drain, a lightly doped region is introduced. One approach is the LDD (lightly doped drain) structure, usually fabricated by two implantations, before and after a spacer on the edge of the gate (Fig. 19.9(a)). Another approach is to use a DDD (doubly diffused drain) structure where two doping species are used and one diffuses faster than the other (Fig. 19.9(b)). The disadvantage of these approaches to improve device lifetime is an increase in series resistance.

Schottky barriers have also been used as source/drain alternatives (Fig. 19.9(c)). The advantages are reduced latch-up phenomenon in CMOS circuits, reduced short-channel effects (zero junction depth), and simplicity in

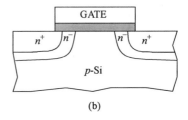

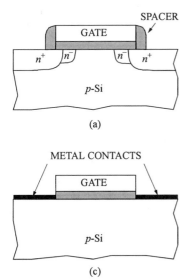

FIGURE 19.9
MOSFETs with different source and drain structures. (a) LDD (lightly doped drain). (b) DDD (doubly diffused drain). (c) Schottky drain.

fabrication. The disadvantage is an insufficient supply of minority carriers, leading to much increased series resistance.

19.4 APPLICATIONS

A MOSFET enjoys a wide range of applications in the electronic industry and it is now the most common transistor in commercial ICs. In terms of performance, it has high-speed capability, extremely high input resistance, and relatively constant input capacitance. It is inexpensive to produce and relatively easy to get high yield. It occupies a small area and has low power consumption. These features enable MOSFETs to be used in both high-performance circuits and high-density circuits. Examples of high-performance circuits are the laser driver and multiplexer. For high-density circuits, MOSFETs are almost exclusively used for SRAMs and DRAMs. MOSFETs are also used in conjunction with bipolar transistors, which have higher current drive capability, in BiCMOS (bipolar-CMOS) circuits. MOSFET is also used for specialized device applications. Examples are nonvolatile memories, chemical sensors and bucket brigade devices.

The popularity of the MOSFET as a power device has been increasing. Compared to the bipolar transistor, it is more reliable and more robust, and has a better temperature stability. It also has better switching speed due to the absence of storage time, and higher gain at high current levels. Specific examples are switching power supplies, radio-frequency generators, and motor drivers.

The general applications of a transistor are listed in Appendix C3.

19.5 RELATED DEVICES

19.5.1 Double-Diffused Metal-Oxide-Semiconductor (DMOS) Transistor

The performance of a MOSFET improves with decreased channel length, which is determined by lithography on the gate structure. A DMOS transistor achieves very short channel length using diffusion properties (Figs. 19.10(a) and (b)). The substrate in this structure has the same doping type as the source/drain and serves as part of the drain. The channel length is defined by out-diffusion of dopants of the opposite type from the source region. The DMOS transistors are used only as power MOSFETs.

19.5.2 Hexagonal Field-Effect Transistor (HEXFET)

The HEXFET incorporates vertical DMOS transistors in a three-dimensional structure as shown in Fig. 19.10(c). The hexagonal shape of the source and the mesh gate structures further maximizes the surface area for power applications.

19.5.3 V-Groove (or Vertical) Metal-Oxide-Semiconductor (VMOS) Transistor

A VMOS structure is shown in Fig. 19.10(d). The V-groove is etched by a solution that etches semiconductor preferentially according to the crystal orientation. When the Si surface is on a <100> plane, the resulting V-groove is on <111> planes since they have a very slow etching rate. This structure also provides short channel length without depending on lithography capability. The vertical current flow also maximizes the total current for a given surface area. This structure is used only for power applications.

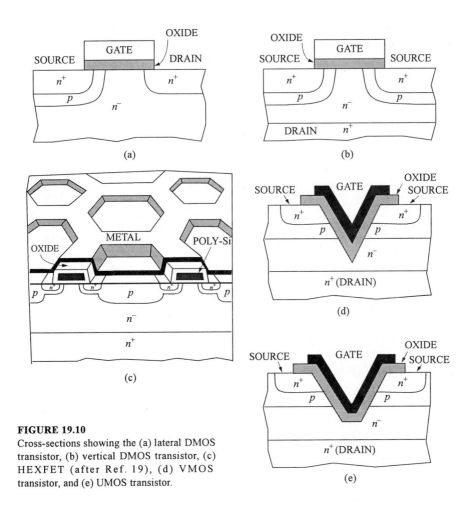

FIGURE 19.10
Cross-sections showing the (a) lateral DMOS transistor, (b) vertical DMOS transistor, (c) HEXFET (after Ref. 19), (d) VMOS transistor, and (e) UMOS transistor.

19.5.4 U-Groove Metal-Oxide-Semiconductor (UMOS) Transistor

The UMOS transistor is similar to the VMOS transistor except for a flat region that is left at the bottom of the groove (Fig. 19.10(e)). The operation is identical to a VMOS transistor.

19.5.5 Thin-Film Transistor (TFT)

A TFT is an IGFET whose active layer is a deposited film on an insulator substrate or layer. Since the thin film is non-crystal, the device performance is inferior to that of the bulk device. The current drive is much smaller and the speed is lower. The advantages are their ease and flexibility in fabrication. The structure of a TFT is shown in Fig. 19.11. Unlike a bulk IGFET, a TFT can have the gate above or below the active layer. Such flexibility can sometimes benefit the layout of a circuit. The gate insulator can be either thermal oxide or a deposited dielectric. A typical application is a flat-panel display where each TFT controls a display element (Fig. 19.11(c)). Since the display panel is usually big, such as a TV screen, TFTs are much more attractive than discrete devices. Another example is the load device for an SRAM cell. If the load MOSFETs are made from TFTs, they

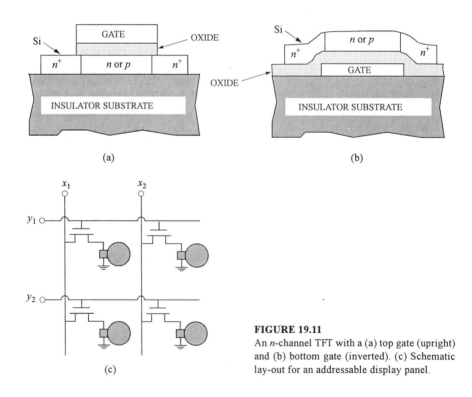

(a)

(b)

(c)

FIGURE 19.11
An n-channel TFT with a (a) top gate (upright) and (b) bottom gate (inverted). (c) Schematic lay-out for an addressable display panel.

can be deposited on top of the bulk transistors such that the cell area is much reduced.

19.5.6 Metal-Insulator-Semiconductor Field-Effect Transistor (MISFET)

As mentioned before a MISFET is generally referred to as an IGFET fabricated on a compound semiconductor or Ge. A quality insulator–semiconductor interface still cannot be achieved easily on compound semiconductors. An oxide can be grown by thermal oxidation, or anodization in a solution or a plasma. Alternatively, a dielectric can be deposited by LPCVD or by sputtering.

19.5.7 Pressure-Sensitive Field-Effect Transistor (PRESSFET)

The pressure-sensitive field-effect transistor, as shown in Fig. 19.12, has a suspended gate such that when pressure is applied, the gate moves closer to the channel. This results in a higher gate capacitance, lower V_T, and higher MOSFET current. As a pressure sensor, the sensitivity can be shown to improve with larger applied gate voltage. In real applications, such large gate bias is not practical and is alleviated by adding a polarized layer called an electret. Another option is to use a piezoelectric material as the gate dielectric, and to eliminate the air gap. The piezoelectric material has a property of generating a gate voltage under pressure.

19.5.8 Gate-Controlled Diode

The gate-controlled diode, or gated diode, has the structure of one side of a MOSFET as shown in Fig. 19.13. It is a p-n junction with part of the surface of the metallurgical junction placed under the gate. Depending on the gate voltage, the area under the gate can be turned into n-type or p-type. The I-V and C-V characteristics of the p-n junction can then be a function of the gate bias. This

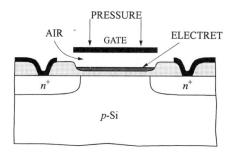

FIGURE 19.12
Structure of a PRESSFET.

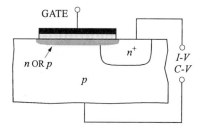

FIGURE 19.13
Structure of a gate-controlled diode.

structure is useful only as a characterization technique for interface properties. The reverse breakdown as a function of the gate voltage had been considered for transistor action by Grove.[20]

REFERENCES

1. J. E. Lilienfeld, "Method and apparatus for controlling electric currents," U.S. Patent 1,745,175. Filed 1926. Granted 1930.
2. J. E. Lilienfeld, "Amplifier for electric currents," U.S. Patent 1,877,140. Filed 1928. Granted 1932.
3. J. E. Lilienfeld, "Device for controlling electric current," U.S. Patent 1,900,018. Filed 1928. Granted 1933.
4. O. Heil, "Improvements in or relating to electrical amplifiers and other control arrangements and devices," British Patent 439,457. Filed 1935. Granted 1935.
5. W. Shockley and G. L. Pearson, "Modulation of conductance of thin films of semiconductors by surface charges," *Phys. Rev.*, **74**, 232 (1948).
6. I. M. Ross, U.S. Patent 2,791,760. Filed 1955. Granted 1957.
7. M. M. Atalla. "Semiconductor devices having dielectric coatings," U.S. Patent 3,206,670. Filed 1960. Granted 1965.
8. J. R. Ligenza and W. G. Spitzer, "The mechanisms for silicon oxidation in steam and oxygen," *J. Phys. Chem. Solids*, **14**, 131 (1960).
9. D. Kahng and M. M. Atalla, "Silicon-silicon dioxide field induced surface devices," in *IRE-AIEE Solid-State Device Res. Conf.* (Carnegie Inst. of Tech., Pittsburgh, PA), 1960.
10. D. Kahng, "A historical perspective on the development of MOS transistors and related devices," *IEEE Trans. Electron Devices*, **ED-23**, 655 (1976).
11. C-T. Sah, "Evolution of the MOS transistor - From conception to VLSI," *Proc. IEEE*, **76**, 1280 (1988).
12. H. K. J. Ihantola and J. L. Moll, "Design theory of a surface field-effect transistor," *Solid-State Electron.*, **7**, 423 (1964).
13. C. T. Sha, "Characteristics of the metal-oxide-semiconductor transistors," *IEEE Trans. Electron Devices*, **ED-11**, 324 (1964).
14. S. R. Hofstein and F. P. Heiman, "The silicon insulated-gate field-effect transistor," *Proc. IEEE*, **51**, 1190 (1963).
15. Y. P. Tsividis, *Operation and modeling of the MOS transistor*, McGraw-Hill, New York, 1987.
16. S. M. Sze, *Physics of semiconductor devices*, 2nd Ed., Wiley, New York, 1981.
17. M. Shur, *Physics of semiconductor devices*, Prentice Hall, Englewood Cliffs, 1990.
18. K. Yamaguchi, "Field-dependent mobility model for two-dimensional numerical analysis of MOSFET's," *IEEE Trans. Electron Dev.*, **ED-26**, 1068 (1979).
19. P. Rossel, "Power M.O.S. devices," *Microelectron. Reliab.*, **24**, 339 (1984).
20. A. S. Grove, *Physics and technology of semiconductor devices*, Wiley, New York, 1967.

CHAPTER

20

JUNCTION
FIELD-EFFECT
TRANSISTOR

20.1 HISTORY

The junction field-effect transistor (JFET) or junction-gate FET was originally proposed by Shockley in 1952.[1] The first JFET was realized by Dacey and Ross in 1953.[2,3] During the 1950s, major activities were concentrated on the bipolar transistor invented in 1948. The 1960s, on the other hand, saw rapid development of the MOSFET, which was started in 1960. The advancement of JFET technology was made mainly in the 1970s, especially when the enhancement-mode device was made practical around 1977. The JFET is similar to IGFET and MESFET, and it serves as an alternative to these devices. For more details on the JFET, the readers are referred to Refs. 4 and 5.

20.2 STRUCTURE

The structures for an n-channel JFET are shown in Fig. 20.1. For p-channel devices, the dopant types are simply the opposite. In Si JFETs, the heavily doped substrate usually serves as the bottom gate. The active layer of n-region can be grown epitaxially (Fig. 20.1(a)), or formed by ion implantation or diffusion (Fig. 20.1(b)). For GaAs devices, an intrinsic semi-insulating substrate is usually used, and a bottom gate is absent. In all cases, the top gate defines the channel length L. The distance between the top gate and the source or drain should be kept small to minimize the series resistance of the device.

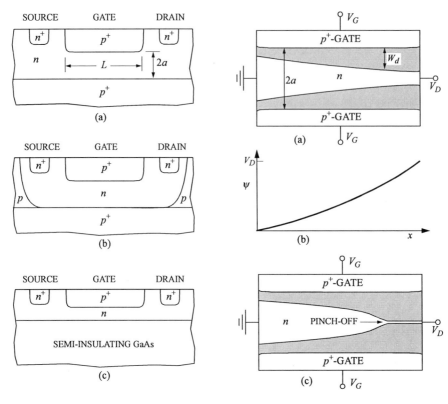

FIGURE 20.1
Cross-sections of the JFET. (a) Channel grown epitaxially. (b) Diffused channel. (c) For GaAs, the structure is usually built on semi-insulating substrate.

FIGURE 20.2
(a) Under gate and drain biases, the channel opening is controlled by the gate depletion region. (b) Semiconductor potential along the channel (mid-point between gates) with respect to the source. (c) Channel opening beyond pinch-off.

20.3 CHARACTERISTICS

The operation of a JFET is based on the modulation of the junction depletion width by the gate bias to control the net channel opening. In the following analysis, the gate bias is applied to both the top and the bottom gates. For operation with a single gate, the analysis has to be modified slightly. The details of the channel opening under gate and drain biases are shown in Fig. 20.2. The transistor current I is between the source and the drain. The semiconductor potential ψ is taken at the midpoint between the two gates along the channel. The depletion width W_d is a function of x because of the semiconductor potential variation due to the applied drain bias. In the gradual-channel approximation, this potential variation, or electric field, along the channel is small compared to the component perpendicular to the channel (equivalently $L \gg a$), and the analysis can be simplified to a one-dimensional solution. The depletion width is controlled by

$$W_d = \sqrt{\frac{2\varepsilon_s (\psi_{bi} + \psi - V_G)}{qN_D}} \, .$$ (20.1)

The built-in potential ψ_{bi} is a function of the doping concentrations in both sides of the junction,

$$\psi_{bi} = \frac{kT}{q} \ln \left(\frac{N_D N_A}{n_i^2} \right) \, .$$ (20.2)

The incremental resistance of the channel is controlled by the channel cross-sectional area A,

$$dR = \frac{\rho}{A(x)} dx$$

$$= \frac{dx}{2q\mu_n N_D W [a - W_d(x)]} \, .$$ (20.3)

The potential variation in Fig. 20.2(b) is given by

$$d\psi = I \, dR$$

$$= \frac{I \, dx}{2q\mu_n N_D W [a - W_d(x)]} \, .$$ (20.4)

Integrating Eq. (20.4) from the source to the drain yields the expression for the current

$$I = G_o \left\{ V_D - \frac{2}{3\sqrt{V_P}} \left[(V_D + \psi_{bi} - V_G)^{3/2} - (\psi_{bi} - V_G)^{3/2} \right] \right\}$$ (20.5)

where G_o is the maximum channel conductance when $W_d = 0$,

$$G_o = \frac{2q\mu_n N_D aW}{L}$$ (20.6)

and

$$V_P = \frac{qN_D a^2}{2\varepsilon_s} \, .$$ (20.7)

Typical I-V characteristics as a function of V_D for various V_G are shown in Fig. 20.3. For a fixed V_G, current increases with V_D until saturation. According to Fig. 20.2(a), W_d at the drain increases with V_D and when it becomes equal to a, the channel opening is reduced to zero and pinch-off is said to occur. Beyond this value of $V_{D,sat}$, the current remains constant and the pinch-off point starts to move toward the source. The total potential difference ($\psi_{bi} - V_G + \psi$) across the gate junction that causes pinch-off is called the pinch-off voltage V_P (Eq. (20.7)). The drain voltage for the onset of pinch-off is $V_{D,sat}$, given by

$$V_{D,\,sat} = V_P - \psi_{bi} + V_G = V_G - V_T \; . \qquad (20.8)$$

The threshold voltage V_T will be defined later in Eq. (20.23). The reason for the current saturation is that when V_D is above $V_{D,sat}$, the potential at the pinch-off point remains at a maximum value of $V_{D,sat}$ (Fig. 20.2(c)). The drift region between the source and the pinch-off point has an electric field that is weakly dependent on V_D. In practice, current beyond $V_{D,sat}$ still rises gradually due to the reduction of the effective channel length, measured by the distance between the source and the pinch-off point.

In the characteristics shown in Fig. 20.3, there are two regimes of special interest, one corresponds to a very small V_D (linear region) and the other to a very large V_D (saturation region). In the linear region, Eq. (20.5) can be reduced to

$$I_{lin} = G_o\left(1 - \sqrt{\frac{\psi_{bi} - V_G}{V_P}}\right)V_D \qquad (20.9)$$

where ohmic characteristics are observed. The transconductance in this linear region is given by

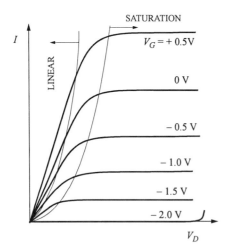

SATURATION

$V_G = +0.5\text{V}$

0 V

-0.5 V

-1.0 V

-1.5 V

-2.0 V

V_D

FIGURE 20.3
I-V characteristics of a JFET (depletion mode) as a function of V_D for various V_G.

$$g_{m,\,lin} \equiv \frac{dI_{lin}}{dV_G}$$

$$= \frac{G_o V_D}{2\sqrt{V_P(\psi_{bi} - V_G)}} \quad . \tag{20.10}$$

Equation (20.9) can be reduced to a familiar FET format by Taylor's expansion around $V_G = V_T$,

$$I_{lin} \approx \frac{G_o}{2V_P}(V_G - V_T)\,V_D \quad . \tag{20.11}$$

In the saturation region, when Eq. (20.8) is substituted into Eq. (20.5), the saturation current becomes

$$I_{sat} = G_o\left[\frac{V_P}{3} - (\psi_{bi} - V_G)\left(1 - \frac{2}{3}\sqrt{\frac{\psi_{bi} - V_G}{V_P}}\right)\right] \tag{20.12}$$

and

$$g_{m,\,sat} \equiv \frac{d\,I_{sat}}{dV_G}$$

$$= G_o\left(1 - \sqrt{\frac{\psi_{bi} - V_G}{V_P}}\right) \quad . \tag{20.13}$$

Alternately, using the Taylor's series expansion around $V_G = V_T$, Eq. (20.12) can also be approximated by

$$I_{sat} \approx \frac{G_o}{4V_P}(V_G - V_T)^2 \quad . \tag{20.14}$$

For depletion-mode devices, Eq. (20.12) is often expressed by another equation

$$I_{sat} \approx I_{ss}\left(1 + \frac{V_G}{V_P}\right)^2 \tag{20.15}$$

and is quite adequate. I_{ss} is I_{sat} of Eq. (20.12) with $V_G = 0$,

$$I_{ss} \equiv G_o\left[\frac{V_P}{3} - \psi_{bi}\left(1 - \frac{2}{3}\sqrt{\frac{\psi_{bi}}{V_P}}\right)\right] \quad . \tag{20.16}$$

In devices of shorter channel lengths (less than $\approx 1~\mu m$), current saturation comes from carrier velocity saturation before pinch-off occurs. The velocity-field relationship for electrons is shown in Fig. 20.4. At high fields, carrier velocity saturates to a fixed value and, thus, current does not increase with V_D. For some materials such as GaAs, there is an additional feature of negative mobility where velocity decreases with field. This phenomenon is complicated and will not be discussed here. The carrier velocity for Si can be characterized by a critical field $\mathscr{E}_c$ and v_{sat}. The modified saturation region for short-channel devices, thus, have a lower $V_{D,sat}$, given by

$$V_{D,\,sat} \approx \mathscr{E}_c L \qquad (20.17)$$

and

$$I_{sat} \approx 2qv_{sat}WN_D a\left(1 - \sqrt{\frac{\psi_{bi} - V_G}{V_P}}\right). \qquad (20.18)$$

The corresponding transconductance is given by

$$g_{m,\,sat} \approx \frac{qv_{sat}WaN_D}{\sqrt{V_P(\psi_{bi} - V_G)}}. \qquad (20.19)$$

The intrinsic speed of a JFET can be estimated by the cutoff frequency

$$f_T = \frac{g_{m,\,sat}}{2\pi(C_G + C_{par})} \qquad (20.20)$$

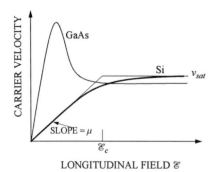

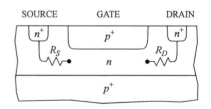

FIGURE 20.4
Electron velocity under an applied electric field for Si and GaAs.

FIGURE 20.5
Schematic representation of source resistance (R_S) and drain resistance (R_D).

where C_{par} is the input parasitic capacitance. In the long-channel model, the gate capacitance C_G at pinch-off is given by

$$C_G = \frac{4WL\varepsilon_s}{a} .$$ (20.21)

The factor of 4 originates from a factor 2 due to the double gates, and another factor of 2 due to higher capacitance (smaller W_d) near the source. In the short-channel velocity-saturation model, there is no pinch-off and the gate capacitance is given by

$$C_G = \frac{2WL\varepsilon_s}{W_d} = \frac{2WL\varepsilon_s}{a\sqrt{(\psi_{bi} - V_G)/V_P}} .$$ (20.22)

It can be shown that $g_{m,sat}/C_G$ reduces to the reciprocal of the transit time of the device (v_{sat}/L).

Figure 20.3 also shows that the transistor is on when there is no gate bias, and negative V_G is required to turn the transistor off. This kind of device is called a normally on or depletion device. From Eq. (20.9) or (20.12), the V_G required to turn the transistor off, called the threshold voltage, is given by

$$V_T = \psi_{bi} - V_P .$$ (20.23)

Since V_P is determined mainly by a and N_D, it can be designed to be smaller than ψ_{bi} to give a positive V_T, resulting in a normally off or enhancement device. In order to turn this transistor on, positive V_G is required. The enhancement-mode device, unfortunately, requires a gate voltage that puts the gate junction into forward bias, resulting in a much higher input current. This limits the maximum input voltage to less than the built-in potential before excessive current results.

In a JFET structure, the gap between the gate and the source or the drain creates source series resistance R_S or drain series resistance R_D (Fig. 20.5). These undesirable resistances reduce the net biases from the applied gate bias V^*_G and the applied drain bias V^*_D to

$$V_G = V^*_G - IR_S ,$$ (20.24)

$$V_D = V^*_D - I(R_S + R_D) .$$ (20.25)

Substitution of these equations into the current equations gives the net current as a function of applied biases implicitly. In particular, the $g_{m,sat}$ can be shown by small-signal analysis to be reduced to

$$g_{m,sat}(\text{With R}) = \frac{g_{m,sat}(\text{No R})}{1 + R_S g_{m,sat}(\text{No R})} .$$ (20.26)

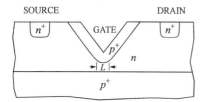

FIGURE 20.6
In a V-groove FET, the channel length is controlled by the bottle-neck of the channel at the bottom of the V-groove.

In the saturation region, R_D is not a factor because current is independent of V_D.

The breakdown of a JFET at high drain voltage occurs in the gate-to-channel p-n junction near the drain. This breakdown is the same as a junction avalanche breakdown described in Appendix B3. The breakdown voltage is limited by the potential difference between the gate and the drain.

20.4 APPLICATIONS

The performance of a JFET is not competitive compared to a MOSFET, and the JFET is, therefore, much less popular. It finds its applications for materials that do not grow the high-quality dielectric required for an IGFET. In comparison to a MESFET, which has a metal Schottky gate, it offers some advantages. The built-in potential in the gate junction is higher so that higher input bias in the forward direction can be applied. This is important for enhancement devices. Using MESFETs, there is difficulty in the formation of complementary circuits (n-channel and p-channel) because of the limitations of Schottky barriers on p-type materials. This can be avoided in a JFET. JFET technology is more compatible with the bipolar transistor and a merged bipolar-JFET (BiFET) logic can be used. The high input impedance of the JFET compared to a bipolar transistor can be advantageous. Unlike a bipolar transistor, a JFET inherently has negative temperature coefficient so that thermal runaway is not a problem. The channel length of a JFET, however, is harder to control than that of an IGFET and MESFET, due to the gate diffusion. This puts a lower limit on the channel length.

The JFET is often used as power transistor due to its robustness. It can also be used as a current limiter when the gate is shorted to the source.[6] This two-terminal device has characteristics in Fig. 20.3 with $V_G = 0$, and is sometimes called a field-effect diode.

The general applications of a transistor are listed in Appendix C3.

20.5 RELATED DEVICE

20.5.1 V-Groove Field-Effect Transistor (VFET)

There are a few versions of the V-groove field-effect transistor.[7] The main feature is shown in Fig. 20.6. The objective is to obtain short-channel devices for high-frequency or high-power operations without the limitation of lithography. The V-groove is formed by wet-chemical anisotropic etching on a <100> Si surface. It is a result of the exposed <111> crystal surface on which the etching rate is preferentially much slower. The figure shown with p^+-gate is a JFET. If the p^+-gate is replaced by a metal gate, it becomes a MESFET version of the VFET.

REFERENCES

1. W. Shockley, "A unipolar field-effect transistor," *Proc. IRE*, **40**, 1365 (1952).
2. G. C. Dacey and I. M. Ross, "Unipolar field-effect transistor," *Proc. IRE*, **41**, 970 (1953).
3. G. C. Dacey and I. M. Ross, "The field-effect transistor," *Bell Syst. Tech. J.*, **34**, 1149 (1955).
4. S. M. Sze, *Physics of semiconductor devices*, 2nd Ed., Wiley, New York, 1981.
5. E. S. Yang, *Microelectronic devices*, McGraw-Hill, New York, 1988.
6. H. Lawrence, "A diffused field effect current limiter," *IEEE Trans. Electron Dev.*, **ED-9**, 82 (1962).
7. D. P. Lecrosnier and G. P. Pelous, "Ion-implanted FET for power applications," *IEEE Trans. Electron Dev.*, **ED-21**, 113 (1974).

CHAPTER

21

METAL-SEMICONDUCTOR FIELD-EFFECT TRANSISTOR

21.1 HISTORY

MESFET is the acronym for the metal-semiconductor field-effect transistor. Practical field-effect transistors were made in the forms of the JFET in 1953 and the MOSFET in 1960. Only silicon material is used in the MOSFET because of its unique, near-ideal native-oxide quality. GaAs, on the other hand, provides some important features such as high carrier mobility and low capacitance due to the semi-insulating substrate. A MESFET is more suitable for compound semiconductors, predominantly made from GaAs. Compared to a JFET, it offers advantages in the fabrication procedure. The first MESFET was reported by Mead in 1966.[1] The microwave capability of the MESFET was demonstrated shortly thereafter by Hooper and Lehrer in 1967.[2] Currently, the MESFET is the dominant device for high-speed and microwave circuits. For more detailed discussions on the device, readers are referred to Refs. 3–5.

21.2 STRUCTURE

The MESFET structures are shown in Fig. 21.1, featuring gates formed by metal-semiconductor (Schottky-barrier) junctions. The semiconductor material used, as discussed before, is usually GaAs. The substrate is intrinsic and semi-insulating for low parasitic capacitance, and the active layer is deposited epitaxially. The channel doping is around 10^{17} cm^{-3}, with a thickness less than 0.2 μm. A nonuniform channel-doping profile, in the direction perpendicular to

188

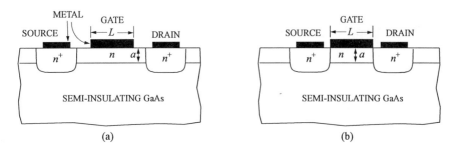

FIGURE 21.1
MESFET structures for (a) non-self-aligned source and drain and (b) self-aligned source and drain to the gate.

the gate, that offers advantages such as good linearity and low noise has been considered.[6] This leads to the extreme case of the planar-doped FET (see Chapter 25). n-type channel is preferred for high-speed operations due to its higher electron mobility compared to holes. The source and drain regions are formed by ion implantation, with concentrations in the order of 10^{18} cm^{-3}. Common source and drain contacts for GaAs are AuGe alloys. Popular gate materials for n-channel devices include Al, Ti-Pt-Au layered structure, Pt, W, and WSi$_2$. It is desirable to have high barrier height to reduce the leakage current from the gate, especially for enhancement-mode devices, which require a forward-biased gate junction. The source and drain contacts and the gate metallization are often defined by lift-off technique in which photoresist is defined, followed by metal deposition and resist removal. The ratio of channel length to channel depth L/a is kept around four as a trade-off for speed, short-channel effects, and parasitics. In the non-self-aligned structure (Fig. 21.1(a)), the source and drain contacts are usually formed before the gate because of the high-temperature alloy step ($\approx 450°C$). The spacing between the source or drain to the gate should be minimized to reduce source and drain resistances. This can be improved by the self-aligned structure shown in Fig. 21.1(b). In this case, the gate is formed before the source and drain ion implantation. Refractory materials, which can withstand the subsequent annealing and alloying heat treatments in forming the source and drain, are preferred.

21.3 CHARACTERISTICS

A MESFET is similar to a JFET with the distinctions that (1) it has a single gate and (2) the gate is formed by a metal-semiconductor junction. The transistor current I between the source and drain is controlled mainly by the gate. The gate bias modulates the depletion width under the gate such that the channel opening is varied (Fig. 21.2). Analytically, if the potential variation along the channel is much smaller than that perpendicular to the channel (equivalently $L \gg a$), the

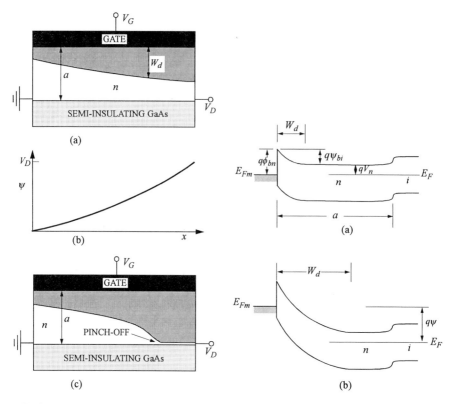

FIGURE 21.2
(a) Channel opening as a function of position under drain bias. (b) Channel potential ψ with respect to source (grounded) along channel. (c) Pinch-off condition when $V_D > V_{D,sat}$.

FIGURE 21.3
Energy-band diagrams showing depletion width W_d as a function of ψ due to V_D. In this example $V_G = 0$. (a) At the source. (b) Near the drain.

gradual-channel approximation is used in which a one-dimensional solution can be applied. The depletion width under the gate, shown in Fig. 21.3, is given by

$$W_d(x) = \sqrt{\frac{2\varepsilon_s [\psi_{bi} + \psi(x) - V_G]}{qN_D}} \qquad (21.1)$$

where ψ is the semiconductor channel potential with respect to the source (at ground), and ψ_{bi} is given by

$$\psi_{bi} = \phi_{bn} - V_n = \phi_{bn} - \phi_T \ln\left(\frac{N_C}{N_D}\right) \qquad (21.2)$$

where ϕ_{bn} is the Schottky-barrier height. The incremental resistance along the channel is controlled by the channel opening or the cross-sectional area A, given by

$$dR = \frac{\rho}{A(x)} dx$$

$$= \frac{dx}{q\mu_n N_D W [a - W_d(x)]} \quad . \tag{21.3}$$

The potential variation along the channel is proportional to the current

$$d\psi = I \, dR$$

$$= \frac{I \, dx}{q\mu_n N_D W [a - W_d(x)]} \quad . \tag{21.4}$$

Integration of Eq. (21.4) from source to drain gives the transistor current

$$I = G_i \left\{ V_D - \frac{2}{3\sqrt{V_P}} \left[(V_D + \psi_{bi} - V_G)^{3/2} - (\psi_{bi} - V_G)^{3/2} \right] \right\} \tag{21.5}$$

where

$$G_i = \frac{q\mu_n N_D a W}{L} \tag{21.6}$$

is the full channel conductance when $W_d = 0$. V_P is called the pinch-off voltage, given by

$$V_P = \frac{q N_D a^2}{2\varepsilon_s} \quad . \tag{21.7}$$

It is the net value of potential difference $(\psi + \psi_{bi} - V_G)$ across the gate junction corresponding to pinch-off condition when $W_d = a$.

The output characteristics of a MESFET are shown in Fig. 21.4. Equation (21.5) describes these characteristics only from small drain bias up to saturation after which the current, in first order, remains constant. In the linear region, $V_D \ll (V_G - V_T)$ and Eq. (21.5) is reduced to

$$I_{lin} = G_i \left(1 - \sqrt{\frac{\psi_{bi} - V_G}{V_P}} \right) V_D \tag{21.8}$$

where ohmic characteristics are observed. The transconductance in the linear region is given by

$$g_{m,lin} \equiv \frac{dI_{lin}}{dV_G}$$

$$= \frac{G_i V_D}{2\sqrt{V_P(\psi_{bi} - V_G)}} \ . \tag{21.9}$$

Equation (21.8) can be simplified by Taylor's expansion around $V_G = V_T$ to

$$I_{lin} \approx \frac{G_i}{2V_P} (V_G - V_T) V_D \tag{21.10}$$

with

$$V_T = \psi_{bi} - V_P \ . \tag{21.11}$$

V_T is the gate threshold voltage around which the transistor is turned on and off.

When the drain bias continues to increase, the transistor current becomes nonlinear, but continues to be described by Eq. (21.5). When V_D reaches a value such that the channel opening closes at the drain end, pinch-off is said to occur. This value can be shown to be

$$V_{D,sat} = V_P - \psi_{bi} + V_G = V_G - V_T \ . \tag{21.12}$$

The current in the saturation region can be found by substituting $V_{D,sat}$ into Eq. (21.5)

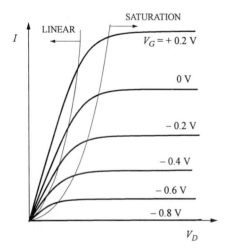

FIGURE 21.4
I-V characteristics of a depletion-mode (normally on) MESFET.

$$I_{sat} = G_i \left[\frac{V_P}{3} - (\psi_{bi} - V_G) \left(1 - \frac{2}{3} \sqrt{\frac{\psi_{bi} - V_G}{V_P}} \right) \right]$$ (21.13)

and

$$g_{m,sat} \equiv \frac{d\,I_{sat}}{dV_G}$$

$$= G_i \left(1 - \sqrt{\frac{\psi_{bi} - V_G}{V_P}} \right) .$$ (21.14)

Qualitatively, for drain bias higher than $V_{D,sat}$, the pinch-off point starts to migrate toward the source (Fig. 21.2(c)). However, the potential at the pinch-off point remains $V_{D,sat}$, independent of V_D. The field within the drift region, thus, remains fairly constant, giving rise to current saturation. Practical devices show that I_{sat} does not completely saturate with V_D. This is due to the reduction of the effective channel length, which is measured between the source and the pinch-off point. Equation (21.13) can also be simplified using Taylor's expansion around $V_G = V_T$

$$I_{sat} \approx \frac{G_i}{4V_P} (V_G - V_T)^2 .$$ (21.15)

Analysis up to this point is based on Eq. (21.3) where the mobility regime is assumed. In short-channel devices ($L < 1$ μm), the channel longitudinal field is high enough to drive carriers into velocity saturation. The velocity-field relationship can be characterized by a critical field $\mathscr{E}_c$ and the saturation velocity v_{sat} as shown in Fig. 21.5. In this case, current saturates with V_D even before pinch-off, with a new $V_{D,sat}$[7]

$$V_{D,sat} \approx \mathscr{E}_c L$$ (21.16)

and

$$I_{sat} \approx q v_{sat} W N_D a \left(1 - \sqrt{\frac{\psi_{bi} - V_G}{V_P}} \right) .$$ (21.17)

The transconductance is given by

$$G_{m,sat} \approx \frac{q v_{sat} W a N_D}{2\sqrt{V_P (\psi_{bi} - V_G)}} .$$ (21.18)

Compared to the mobility regime, $V_{D,sat}$, I_{sat} and $g_{m,sat}$ are all degraded by velocity saturation.

The speed of an FET is measured by the cutoff frequency

$$f_T = \frac{g_{m,sat}}{2\pi\,(C_G + C_{par})} \tag{21.19}$$

where C_{par} is the input parasitic capacitance. The gate capacitance C_G beyond pinch-off is given by

$$C_G = \frac{2WL\varepsilon_s}{a} \;. \tag{21.20}$$

The factor of 2 comes from averaging the depletion widths at the drain end and the source end where the depletion width is much smaller than a. In the velocity-saturation regime, pinch-off does not occur and

$$C_G = \frac{WL\varepsilon_s}{W_d} = \frac{WL\varepsilon_s}{a\sqrt{(\psi_{bi} - V_G)/V_P}} \;. \tag{21.21}$$

It can be shown that $g_{m,sat}/C_G$ reduces to v/L, or the reciprocal of carrier transit time across the device. In practical devices, parasitic capacitance is added to the gate capacitance, slowing down the device from the theoretical limit. Experimental cutoff frequency in excess of 100 GHz has been reported.

The example shown in Fig. 21.4 has current conduction without a gate bias, and a negative V_G is required to turn off the transistor. This kind of FET is called

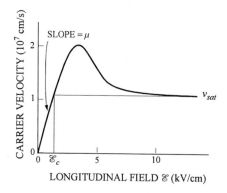

LONGITUDINAL FIELD $\mathscr{E}$ (kV/cm)

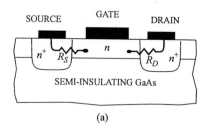

(a)

FIGURE 21.5
Electron velocity-field relationship for GaAs. Approximation is made by the critical field $\mathscr{E}_c$ and saturation velocity v_{sat}.

FIGURE 21.6
Representation of source resistance (R_S) and drain resistance (R_D) for a non-self-aligned MESFET.

depletion-mode or normally on device. Mathematically, V_T in Eq. (21.11) is negative when V_P is larger than ψ_{bi}. One can also design an enhancement-mode or normally off device with small a or low N_D such that V_P is smaller and V_T is positive. The disadvantage of this mode is that positive gate bias is required that puts the Schottky-gate junction into forward bias, resulting in excessive gate current. In practice, V_T can be designed to be around 0.2 V, and the highest operating voltage limited to about 0.6 V.

The series resistance of the MESFET, especially in the non-self-aligned structure, severely affects the device performance. With the source and drain resistances indicated in Fig. 21.6, the net internal drain and gate biases are reduced from the externally applied values V^*_D, V^*_G to

$$V_G = V^*_G - IR_S \ , \tag{21.22}$$

$$V_D = V^*_D - I(R_S + R_D) \ . \tag{21.23}$$

Substitutions of these into the current equations do not give explicit expressions for the current. An explicit form can be obtained for $g_{m,sat}$

$$g_{m,sat}(\text{With R}) = \frac{g_{m,sat}(\text{No R})}{1 + R_S g_{m,sat}(\text{No R})} \ . \tag{21.24}$$

Since, in general, R_D does not affect the characteristics in the saturation region, R_S is shown to be much more critical.

21.4 APPLICATIONS

The MESFET structure makes GaAs FETs practical. This device offers speed advantage due to higher carrier mobility and, because of the semi-insulating substrate, lower capacitance. It dominates in high-performance circuits of communication, computer, and military systems. Specific functions for MESFETs include microwave power amplifiers, oscillators, switches, and mixers. Commercial microwave amplifiers up to 40 GHz are already available, with the potential of going up to 100 GHz for 0.25 μm channel-length devices.

Compared to a bipolar transistor, a MESFET has higher input impedance. Another advantage is the negative temperature coefficient which inhibits thermal runaway. Compared to a Si MOSFET, it does not have problems related to oxide traps, arising from hot-electron or radiation effect. A MESFET has better channel-length control than the JFET, which requires diffusion to form the gate. The low resistance of the metal gate sometimes is advantageous to the design of high-speed circuits. Although, in general, GaAs technology is less mature than Si, the MESFET is still relatively easy to fabricate for commercial products.

The MESFET is also used as microwave power device to which a voltage of around 10 V can be applied. An ungated FET, or saturated resistor, is sometimes used as the load device in MESFET logic. This two-terminal current limiter has characteristics similar to those shown in Fig. 21.4 with $V_G = 0$ (actually positive V_G for flat-band condition so that the whole channel is conducting), and current saturation usually comes from velocity saturation.

The general applications of a transistor are listed in Appendix C3.

REFERENCES

1. C. A. Mead, "Schottky barrier gate field effect transistor," *Proc. IEEE*, **54**, 307 (1966).
2. W. W. Hooper and W. I. Lehrer, "An epitaxial GaAs field-effect transistor," *Proc. IEEE*, **55**, 1237 (1967).
3. M. Shur, "Modeling of GaAs and AlGaAs/GaAs field effect transistors," in C. T. Wang, Ed., *Introduction to semiconductor technology*, Wiley, New York, 1990.
4. B. Turner, "GaAs MESFETs," in M. J. Howes and D. V. Morgan, Eds., *Gallium arsenide: Materials, devices, and circuits*, Wiley, New York, 1985.
5. M. A. Hollis and R. A. Murphy, "Homogenous field-effect transistors," in S. M. Sze, Ed., *High-speed semiconductor devices*, Wiley, New York, 1990.
6. R. E. Williams and D. W. Shaw, "Graded channel FET's: Improved linearity and noise figure," *IEEE Trans. Electron Dev.*, **ED-25**, 600 (1978).
7. M. S. Shur, "Analytical model of GaAs MESFET's," *IEEE Trans. Electron Dev.*, **ED-25**, 612 (1978).

CHAPTER

22

MODULATION-DOPED
FIELD-EFFECT
TRANSISTOR

22.1 HISTORY

The modulation-doped field-effect transistor (MODFET) is also known as the high-electron-mobility transistor (HEMT), two-dimensional electron-gas field-effect transistor (TEGFET), and selectively doped heterojunction transistor (SDHT). Frequently, it is referred to by a general name HFET (heterojunction field-effect transistor). The unique feature of the MODFET is the heterostructure in which the wide-energy-gap material is doped and carriers diffuse to the undoped narrow-energy-gap material where the channel is formed. The net result of this modulation doping is that carriers in the undoped heterointerface are spatially separated from the doped region and have extremely high mobilities because there is no impurity scattering. Carrier transport parallel to the layers of a superlattice was first considered by Esaki and Tsu in 1969.[1] The development of MBE and MOCVD technologies in the 1970s made heterostructures, quantum wells, and superlattices practical. Dingle et al. first demonstrated the enhanced mobility in the AlGaAs–GaAs modulation-doped superlattice in 1978.[2] Stormer et al. subsequently reported a similar effect using a single AlGaAs–GaAs heterojunction in 1979.[3] This effect was applied to field-effect transistors by Mimura et al. in 1980,[4] and later by Delagebeaudeuf et al. in the same year.[5] Since then, the MODFET has been the subject of major research activities, and promises to be an alternative to MESFETs in high-speed circuits. For in-depth treatment of the MODFET, readers are referred to Refs. 6–10.

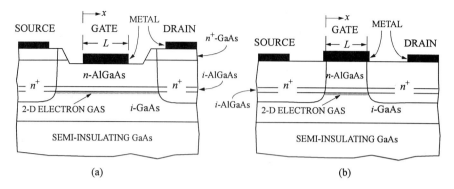

FIGURE 22.1
Structures for MODFETs using (a) recess-gate technology and (b) self-aligned ion-implantation technology.

22.2 STRUCTURE

The most common heterojunctions for the MODFETs are the AlGaAs–GaAs and InP-based heterointerfaces. In the literature there are two different schemes to fabricate the MODFET. The recess-gate and the self-aligned, ion-implanted MODFET structures are shown in Fig. 22.1. In both of these, an intrinsic layer of GaAs about 1 μm thick is first deposited on a semi-insulating substrate, followed by a buffer layer of 30–60 Å of intrinsic AlGaAs. This layer ensures the separation of the heterointerface from the doped AlGaAs region and is critical for high carrier mobility. The doped AlGaAs layer is around 500 Å thick, and has a concentration of $\approx 2 \times 10^{18}$ cm^{-3}. Since precise control of the film thicknesses is critical, MBE is the common approach although MOCVD has also been shown to be feasible. In the recess-gate structure (Fig. 22.1(a)), another film of n^+-GaAs (≈ 500 Å) is deposited for better source and drain ohmic contacts. Then, the n^+-GaAs and n-AlGaAs films in the gate area are etched. The etching has to be controlled since the threshold voltage of the MODFET is determined by the total doped material thickness under the gate. One special case is when the gate is deposited on the unetched n^+-GaAs layer to obtain a depletion-mode device. The source and drain contacts are made from alloys containing Ge, such as AuGe. During the alloying step at around 450°C, Ge is believed to diffuse to the heterointerface to form the n^+-source and drain. The gate materials include Ti, Mo, WSi, W or Al. In the self-aligned structure (Fig. 22.1(b)), the source and drain implantation of $\approx 10^{18}$ cm^{-3} is made after the gate is defined. Since high-temperature anneal (> 800°C) is needed to activate the dopants, refractory gate material is required. Most MODFETs reported are n-channel devices for high electron mobility.

22.3 CHARACTERISTICS

Like any other field-effect transistor, the most important parameter is the threshold voltage, the gate bias at which the channel starts to form between the source and drain. According to the energy-band diagram of Fig. 22.2, a first-order approximation shows that this occurs when E_F at the GaAs surface coincides with E_C. Figure 22.2(b) shows that

$$V_T = \phi_{bn} - V_P - \frac{\Delta E_C}{q} \tag{22.1}$$

where V_P is the pinch-off voltage for the AlGaAs layer, given by

$$V_P = \frac{q}{\varepsilon_s} \int_0^{x_d} N_D(y)\, y \; dy = \frac{q N_D x_d^2}{2\varepsilon_s} \tag{22.2}$$

for a uniformly doped layer. It can be seen here that by adjusting x_d, V_T can be varied, between positive and negative values. The example shown in Fig. 22.2 has a positive V_T, and the transistor is called an enhancement-mode device (normally off), as opposed to a depletion-mode device (normally on).

With gate voltage larger than the threshold, the charge sheet induced by the gate is capacitively coupled, and is given by

$$n_s(x) = \frac{C_o[V_G - V_T - \psi(x)]}{q} . \tag{22.3}$$

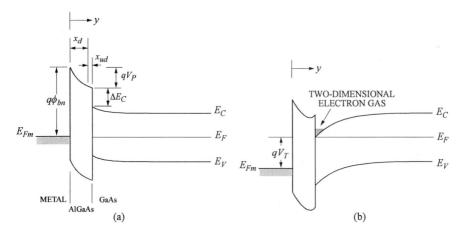

FIGURE 22.2
Energy-band diagrams for an enhancement-mode MODFET at (a) equilibrium, (b) onset of threshold. x_d and x_{ud} are doped and undoped regions, respectively.

where

$$C_o = \frac{\varepsilon_s}{x_d + x_{ud} + \Delta d} \ . \tag{22.4}$$

x_d and x_{ud} are the doped and undoped AlGaAs thicknesses, and Δd is the channel thickness of the two-dimensional electron gas, estimated to be ≈ 80 Å. ψ is the channel potential with respect to the source. It varies along the channel from 0 to the drain bias V_D. The drift current at any point along the channel is given by

$$
\begin{aligned}
I &= W\mu_n q n_s \mathscr{E}_x \\
&= W\mu_n C_o [V_G - V_T - \psi(x)] \frac{d\psi(x)}{dx} \ .
\end{aligned}
\tag{22.5}
$$

Since the current is constant along the channel, integrating this equation from source to drain gives

$$I = \frac{W\mu_n C_o}{L} \left[(V_G - V_T) V_D - \frac{V_D^2}{2} \right] \ . \tag{22.6}$$

The output characteristics for an enhancement-mode MODFET are shown in Fig. 22.3. In the linear region where $V_D \ll (V_G - V_T)$, Eq. (22.6) is reduced to an ohmic equation

$$I_{lin} = \frac{\mu_n C_o W (V_G - V_T) V_D}{L} \tag{22.7}$$

and the transconductance is given by

$$g_{m,lin} \equiv \frac{dI_{lin}}{dV_G} = \frac{\mu_n C_o W V_D}{L} \ . \tag{22.8}$$

At high V_D, n_s at the drain is reduced to zero (Eq. (22.3)), corresponding to the pinch-off condition, and current saturates with V_D. It can be shown from Eq. (22.3) that

$$V_{D,sat} = V_G - V_T \tag{22.9}$$

and

$$I_{sat} = \frac{\mu_n C_o W}{2L} (V_G - V_T)^2 \ , \tag{22.10}$$

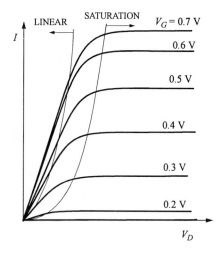

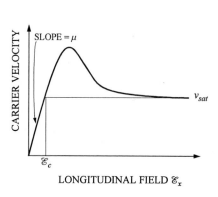

FIGURE 22.3
Output characteristics of an enhancement-mode MODFET.

FIGURE 22.4
Velocity-field relationship for the two-dimensional electron gas. Linear piecewise approximation is indicated.

$$g_{m,sat} \equiv \frac{dI_{sat}}{dV_G} = \frac{\mu_n C_o W (V_G - V_T)}{L} \quad . \tag{22.11}$$

In most practical devices, current becomes saturated with V_D before the pinch-off condition occurs, due to carrier velocity saturation. This is directly related to the high mobilities obtained from modulation doping. Figure 22.4 shows the electron velocity-field relationship where a piecewise approximation is made with a critical field $\mathscr{E}_c$. Electron mobilities reported for the AlGaAs–GaAs heterointerface are $\approx 10^4$ cm²/V-s at 300 K, $\approx 2 \times 10^5$ cm²/V-s at 77 K, and $\approx 2 \times 10^6$ cm²/V-s at 4 K. The mobility enhancement at low temperatures in a MODFET is very pronounced since impurity scattering dominates in that regime. But the improvement of v_{sat} at low temperatures is much less, ranging from 30% to 100%. High mobility also implies low $\mathscr{E}_c$, and the drain bias needed to drive the device into velocity saturation is reduced, given by

$$V_{D,sat} \approx \mathscr{E}_c L \tag{22.12}$$

and the saturation current in this velocity-saturation regime becomes

$$\begin{aligned} I_{sat} &= Wqn_s v_{sat} \\ &= WC_o (V_G - V_T) v_{sat} \quad . \end{aligned} \tag{20.13}$$

The transconductance becomes

$$g_{m,sat} \equiv \frac{dI_{sat}}{dV_G} = WC_o v_{sat} \ . \tag{20.14}$$

Notice that I_{sat} is independent of L and $g_{m,sat}$ is independent of L and V_G. However the reduction of gate length is still desirable to obtain velocity overshoot that gives higher saturation current.

At large V_G, $g_{m,sat}$ shown in Fig. 22.3 starts to decrease. The AlGaAs–GaAs heterointerface can confine a maximum n_s of $\approx 1 \times 10^{12}$ cm^{-2}. Above this V_G ($1 \times 10^{12} q/C_o \approx 0.8$ V), charge is induced within the AlGaAs layer whose mobility is much lower. This parallel current path is analogous to that in a MESFET.

The speed of the MODFET can be measured by the cutoff frequency

$$f_T = \frac{g_{m,sat}}{2\pi (WLC_o + C_{par})} \tag{22.15}$$

where C_{par} is the input parasitic capacitance. f_T as high as 100 GHz has been reported for 0.25 μm devices, and is expected to be higher than 150 GHz for 0.10 μm devices.

22.4 APPLICATIONS

The MODFET was originally developed mainly for high-speed applications due to its high transconductance. It was later found, somewhat surprisingly, that it also gives superior noise performance to other FETs. This improved noise property is related to the nature of the two-dimensional electron gas, but the exact mechanism is not known. The speed of MODFET circuits is about three times as fast as that of MESFETs. Commercially available MODFETs already operate at frequencies higher than 60 GHz, with channel lengths ranging between 0.25 μm and 0.5 μm. An ultimate speed up to 100 GHz is expected in the future. Some examples of analog applications are low-noise small-signal amplifiers, power amplifiers, oscillators, and mixers. For digital circuits, high-speed logic and RAM will be useful for high-speed computers.

Compared to the MESFET, the MODFET can tolerate higher gate bias due to the higher barrier of the AlGaAs. Another advantage is the much reduced short-channel effects, partially from low-voltage operation because of the low $\mathscr{E}_c$ needed to drive the device to saturation. One drawback of the MODFET is the limit of charge-sheet density of $\approx 1 \times 10^{12}$ cm^{-2} at the AlGaAs–GaAs heterointerface that limits the maximum current drive.

For general applications of a transistor, the readers are referred to Appendix C3.

22.5 RELATED DEVICES

22.5.1 Inverted Heterojunction Field-Effect Transistor

The structure of the inverted HFET (or inverted MODFET) is shown in Fig. 22.5(a). The top layer of GaAs provides a more stable surface on which to form the Schottky-barrier gate.

22.5.2 Planar-Doped Heterojunction Field-Effect Transistor

The doping in the AlGaAs layer of the planar-doped (delta-doped, pulse-doped) HFET is incorporated into an atomic monolayer as shown in Fig. 22.5(b). This monolayer (≈ 5 Å) produces a doping density of $n_{sh} \approx 5 \times 10^{12}$ cm^{-2}. To obtain the threshold voltage, V_P in Eq. (22.1) is given instead by

$$V_P = \frac{q n_{sh} x_{pd}}{\varepsilon_s} \tag{22.16}$$

where x_{pd} is the distance of the planar-doped layer from the gate. The advantage here, compared to the uniformly doped AlGaAs layer, is the reduction of traps that are believed to be responsible for the anomalous behavior of current collapse at low temperature. The close proximity of dopants to the channel also gives a lower threshold voltage.

22.5.3 Single-Quantum-Well Heterojunction Field-Effect Transistor

The single-quantum-well HFET, sometimes called a double-heterojunction FET (DHFET), is shown in Fig. 22.5(c). Because there are two parallel heterointerfaces, the maximum charge sheet and current is doubled. Multiple quantum-well FETs have been fabricated based on this principle.

22.5.4 Superlattice Heterojunction Field-Effect Transistor

In the superlattice HFET, doping is incorporated into the superlattice (Fig. 22.5(d)). Within the superlattice, the narrow-energy-gap layers are doped while the wider-energy-gap layers are undoped. This structure eliminates traps in the AlGaAs layer, and also in the parallel MESFET conduction path within the doped AlGaAs layer.

22.5.5 Pseudomorphic Heterojunction Field-Effect Transistor

In the pseudomorphic HFET structure (Fig. 22.5(e)), a narrower-energy-gap material such as InGaAs is used for the channel for better carrier confinement. Even though InGaAs has a lattice mismatch to GaAs, a strained, thin layer of

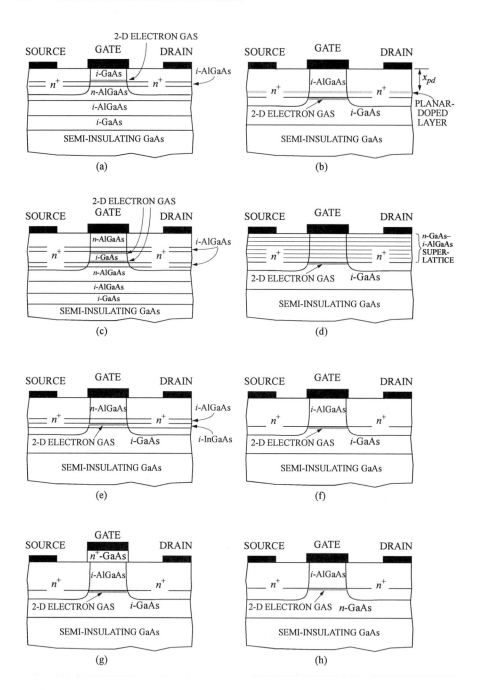

FIGURE 22.5
Structures for MODFET-related devices. (a) Inverted HFET. (b) Planar-doped HFET. (c) Single-quantum-well HFET. (d) Superlattice HFET. (e) Pseudomorphic HFET. (f) HIGFET. (g) SISFET. (h) Doped-channel HFET.

100–200 Å can still result in good crystal and interface quality (pseudomorphic layer). This InGaAs layer yields even higher mobility and saturation velocity than GaAs. It also has better noise performance.

22.5.6 Heterojunction Insulated-Gate Field-Effect Transistor

A heterojunction insulated-gate field-effect transistor (HIGFET) differs from a MODFET in that the wide-energy-gap material as well as the narrow-energy-gap material are undoped (Fig. 22.5(f)). The advantage is better V_T control for complementary circuits in which n-channel and p-channel devices are fabricated simultaneously.

22.5.7 Semiconductor-Insulator-Semiconductor Field-Effect Transistor

A semiconductor-insulator-semiconductor field-effect transistor (SISFET) is similar to a HIGFET except that the gate material contacting the wide-energy-gap material is another semiconductor that is usually the same as the channel layer, and is heavily doped (Fig. 22.5(g)).

22.5.8 Doped-Channel Heterojunction Field-Effect Transistor

The doped-channel HFET is similar to a HIGFET except that the narrow-energy-gap semiconductor is doped (Fig. 22.5(h)). The structure loses the mobility enhancement due to modulation doping and the operation is similar to a MISFET (see Section 19.5.6).

REFERENCES

1. L. Esaki and R. Tsu, "Superlattice and negative conductivity in semiconductors," *IBM Research*, RC 2418, March 1969.
2. R. Dingle, H. L. Stormer, A. C. Gossard and W. Wiegmann, "Electron mobilities in modulation-doped semiconductor heterojunction superlattices," *Appl. Phys. Lett.*, **33**, 665 (1978).
3. H. L. Stormer, R. Dingle, A. C. Gossard, W. Wiegmann and M. D. Sturge, "Two-dimensional electron gas at a semiconductor-semiconductor interface," *Solid State Commun.* **29**, 705 (1979).
4. T. Mimura, S. Hiyamizu, T. Fujii and K. Nanbu, "A new field-effect transistor with selectively doped GaAs/n-$Al_xGa_{1-x}As$ Heterojunctions," *Jap. J. Appl. Phys.*, **19**, L225 (1980).
5. D. Delagebeaudeuf, P. Delescluse, P. Etienne, M. Laviron, J. Chaplart and N. T. Linh, "Two-dimensional electron gas M.E.S.F.E.T. structure," *Electron. Lett.*, **16**, 667 (1980).
6. M. Shur, *GaAs devices and circuits*, Plenum Press, New York, 1987.
7. S. S. Pei and N. J. Shah, "Heterostructure field effect transistors," in C. T. Wang, Ed., *Introduction to semiconductor technology*, Wiley, New York, 1990.
8. H. Morkoc, H. Unlu and G. Ji, *Principles and technology of MODFETs*, Vol. 1 and 2, Wiley, New York, 1991.
9. F. Ali and A. Gupta, Eds., *HEMTs & HBTs: Devices, fabrication, and circuits*, Artech House, Boston, 1991.
10. J. M. Golio, Ed., *Microwave MESFETs & HEMTs*, Artech House, Boston, 1991.

CHAPTER

23

PERMEABLE-BASE TRANSISTOR

23.1 HISTORY

The name permeable-base transistor was initiated by Bozler et al. when they presented results on GaAs material with tungsten grids in 1979.[1,2] Structures on Si with $CoSi_2$ grids were reported by Rosencher et al. in 1986.[3] These two structures have well-defined metal grids, patterned by lithography, that are completely embedded in the semiconductors. Slightly different structures can be found in literature earlier. Lindmayer in 1960 used a thin metal film of molybdenum and utilized the small, natural pinholes as channel openings.[4] He called this device a metal-gate transistor. This technique was also examined more recently, using epitaxial $CoSi_2$ for Si devices[5,6] and tungsten for GaAs devices.[7] To avoid epitaxial overgrowth of semiconductor on metal, Wright in 1960 mentioned a trenched semiconductor structure where the subsequently deposited metal grids were not completely embedded in the semiconductor.[8] This structure has been reported and analyzed more vigorously by Rathman.[9] Up to now, the permeable-base transistor remains a subject for research and is not produced commercially.

23.2 STRUCTURE

The permeable-base transistor is basically a vertical MESFET with a very short channel length. The structure shown in Fig. 23.1(a) has completely embedded metal grids that are defined by lithography and etching. The line and space currently achievable are in the order of 0.2 μm. The channel doping is around 10^{16} cm^{-3} and is usually designed for an enhancement device such that the

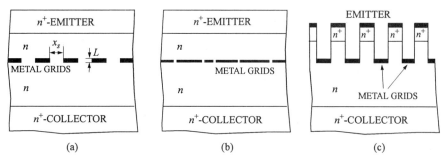

FIGURE 23.1
Structures of a permeable-base transistor. (a) Embedded metal grids which are defined by lithography. (b) Embedded thin metal grids with random pinholes. (c) Exposed grids deposited on semiconductor trenches. Metal grids are connected together in a different plane.

depletion width surrounding the metal grids at zero base voltage is larger than half the spacing between the metal strips,

$$\sqrt{\frac{2\varepsilon_s \psi_{bi}}{q N_D}} > \frac{x_s}{2} \ . \tag{23.1}$$

The metal thickness becomes the channel length and thicknesses of a few hundred Angstroms have been used. The metal should be chosen to yield high Schottky-barrier height to minimize forward-bias leakage, and it should be a refractory metal or silicide that can withstand high temperature during subsequent epitaxial growth. For n-channel GaAs devices, tungsten has been used, and for Si devices, both $CoSi_2$ and molybdenum have been used. The technology for epitaxial overgrowth of semiconductor on metal is not trivial. The mechanism is first by vertical growth of the semiconductor over the window, followed by lateral growth over the metal. The control of the doping level in the area directly over the metal is sometimes a practical problem. The epitaxial film thicknesses for the n-type emitter and collector layers are in the order of 0.2 μm and 1.0 μm, respectively. In the structure shown in Fig. 23.1(b), the metal grids are not defined, but are natural random pinholes ($\approx$ 100 Å) that exist in a very thin metal or silicide film whose thickness is less than 100 Å. The channel openings, in this case, are much narrower and the device operation regime will be different, as discussed later. The third structure shown in Fig. 23.1(c) eliminates the need for epitaxial overgrowth of a semiconductor on metal. The semiconductor trench is created by lithography and anisotropic etching. The depth of the trench is typically around 0.5 μm.

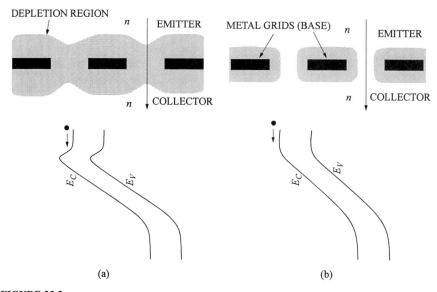

FIGURE 23.2
Depletion regions (grey area) surrounding the metal base when the transistor is (a) off, and (b) on. The energy-band diagrams show that a potential barrier for electrons exists only when depletion regions merge.

23.3 CHARACTERISTICS

The terminals of a permeable-base transistor have been given the nomenclatures of a potential-effect transistor (emitter, base, collector) because of its close structural resemblance to a metal-base transistor. Under normal operation, the transistor behaves like a MESFET with very short channel length. The emitter, base, and collector terminals can be described more accurately as the source, gate, and drain, respectively, of an FET. The channels are the vertical gaps between the metal grids, and the effective channel width is controlled by the depletion width around the metal base. Figure 23.2 shows that when the depletion regions are merged together, the channel is cut off. When the depletion width is reduced by a forward base bias, a neutral region or channel opening exists and the transistor is considered to be on. The corresponding energy-band diagrams in the middle of the channel are also shown. The off-state is caused by the potential barrier near the emitter. The threshold voltage for the base (with the emitter grounded) to eliminate this barrier potential is given by

$$V_T = \psi_{bi} - V_P \qquad (23.2)$$

where V_P is the pinch-off voltage

$$V_P = \frac{qN_D(x_s/2)^2}{2\varepsilon_s} \ .$$ (23.3)

ψ_{bi} is the built-in potential with zero base bias,

$$\psi_{bi} = \phi_{bn} - \phi_T \ln\left(\frac{N_C}{N_D}\right) \ .$$ (23.4)

One recognizes that an enhancement device means positive V_T, and Eq. (23.1) has the same criterion. The output characteristics are shown in Fig. 23.3. Current in each channel opening in the linear region is described by

$$I_{lin} \approx \frac{G_o}{2V_P}(V_B - V_T)V_C$$ (23.5)

where

$$G_o \equiv \frac{q\mu_n N_D x_s W}{L} \ .$$ (23.6)

Saturation is always driven by velocity saturation rather than channel pinch-off, due to the extremely short channel length. Saturation starts with

$$V_{C,sat} \approx L\left(\frac{v_{sat}}{\mu_n}\right) \ ,$$ (23.7)

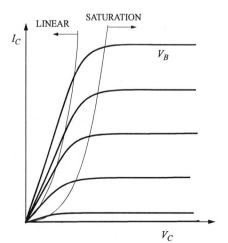

FIGURE 23.3
Output characteristics of a permeable-base transistor for different base voltages (emitter grounded).

and saturation current in each channel opening is given by

$$I_{sat} \approx q v_{sat} W N_D x_s \left(1 - \sqrt{\frac{\psi_{bi} - V_B}{V_P}} \right) . \tag{23.8}$$

The ultra-short channel length can potentially result in ballistic transport with an overshoot velocity higher than the v_{sat} (see Appendix B1).

Below threshold, the current is limited mainly by thermionic emission over the barrier (Fig. 23.2(a)), and it rises exponentially with the base voltage. Devices reported in the structural form of Fig. 23.1(b) have very small channel openings such that the condition of a neutral region (Fig. 23.2(b)) cannot be met. These devices operate only in the subthreshold regime. The input to the base is more meaningful as a current source rather than a voltage source, and current gain becomes a more conventional parameter. Modeling of current conduction in this mode has been analyzed rigorously by Pfister et al.[10] and by Hensel.[11]

23.4 APPLICATIONS

The main advantages of a permeable-base transistor is that it provides a means to achieve ultra-short channel length without suffering from the limitation of lithography. The device is predicted to be capable of high-speed operation up to a f_T of $\approx$ 200 GHz. Microwave measurements of f_{max} = 220 GHz and f_T = 50 GHz have been demonstrated.[12] Another advantage is the low base resistance. The vertical current flow also provides efficient area usage for maximum current density, which is beneficial in power applications. The potential applications of the permeable-base transistor in logic circuits are discussed in Ref. 13. This device is still under development and is not found in any commercial circuit.

For general applications of a transistor, readers are referred to Appendix C3.

REFERENCES

1. C. O. Bozler, G. D. Alley, R. A. Murphy, D. C. Flanders and W. T. Lindley, "Fabrication and microwave performance of the permeable base transistor," *Tech. Digest IEDM*, 384 (1979).
2. C. O. Bozler and G. D. Alley, "Fabrication and numerical simulation of the permeable base transistor," *IEEE Trans. Electron Dev.*, **ED-27**, 1128 (1980).
3. E. Rosencher, G. Glastre, G. Vincent, A. Vareille and F. A. D'Avitaya, "Si/CoSi₂/Si permeable base transistor obtained by silicon molecular beam epitaxy over a CoSi₂ grating," *Electronics Lett.*, **22**, 699 (1986).
4. J. Lindmayer, "The metal-gate transistor," *Proc. IEEE*, **52**, 1751 (1964).
5. J. C. Hensel, A. F. J. Levi, R. T. Tung and J. M. Gibson, "Transistor action in Si/CoSi₂/Si heterostructures," *Appl. Phys. Lett.*, **47**, 151 (1985).
6. R. T. Tung, A. F. J. Levi and J. M. Gibson, "Control of a natural permeable CoSi₂ base transistor," *Appl. Phys. Lett.*, **48**, 635 (1986).
7. G. E. Derkits, Jr., J. P. Harbison, J. Levkoff and D. M. Hwang, "Transistor action in novel GaAs/W/GaAs structures," *Appl. Phys. Lett.*, **48**, 1220 (1986).

8. G. T. Wright, "A proposed space-charge-limited dielectric triode," *J. Brit. I. R. E.*, 337 (1960).

9. D. D. Rathman, "Optimization of the doping profile in Si permeable base transistors for high-frequency, high-voltage operation," *IEEE Trans. Electron Dev.*, **ED-37**, 2090 (1990).

10. J. C. Pfister, E. Rosencher, K. Belhaddad and A. Poncet, "Electrical influence of pinholes in metal-base transistors," *Solid-State Electron.*, **29**, 907 (1986).

11. J. C. Hensel, "Operation of the $Si/CoSi_2/Si$ heterostructure transistor," *Appl. Phys. Lett.*, **49**, 522 (1986).

12. M. A. Hollis, K. B. Nichols, R. A. Murphy and C. O. Bozler, "Advances in the technology for the permeable base transistor," *SPIE.*, **797**, 335 (1987).

13. C. O. Bozler and G. D. Alley, "The permeable base transistor and its application to logic circuits," *Proc. IEEE*, **70**, 46 (1982).

24

STATIC-INDUCTION TRANSISTOR

24.1 HISTORY

The static-induction transistor (SIT) was introduced by Nishizawa et al. in 1972.[1,2] Subsequently in 1975, more studies were reported by Ogawa et al.[3] and Yamaguchi et al.[4] The transistor features non-saturating I-V characteristics with increasing drain voltage because the barrier for carriers is lowered by "electrostatic induction" from the drain. Early development of the device was performed mostly by Japanese researchers. Theoretical treatment of the SIT can be found in Refs. 2, 5–9, and computer simulations are reported in Refs. 10–13. Review articles can be found in Refs. 14–18. The static-induction transistor began to be produced in the commercial market in the mid-1980s as power devices.

Structures similar, if not identical, to the SIT can be found in literature earlier than 1975, although the operations from these devices are slightly different. Shockley, in 1952, proposed the analog transistor whose current is limited by space-charge-limited (SCL) current.[19] He used the name "analog" because of the analogy to vacuum-tube triode operation. The general characteristics of the SCL current are similar to those of the static-induction current. They both display triode-like (non-saturating) behavior in the I_D-V_D plot as opposed to pentode-like (saturating) behavior as in a conventional FET. The SCL current is known to have a power-law dependence on drain bias, while the static-induction current has an exponential dependence. The difference will be further clarified. Realization of a vertical structure was proposed by Roosild et al. in 1963.[20] Experimental results of what will be described as bipolar-mode SIT were reported by Buchanan et al. in 1964.[21] Other devices include the gridistor,

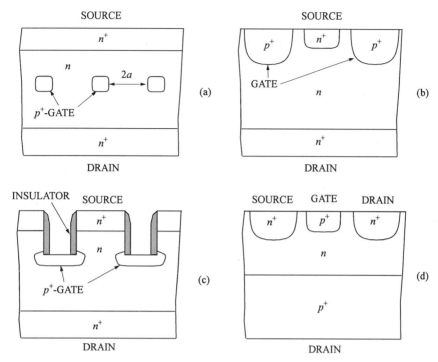

FIGURE 24.1
Different schemes for the structure of SIT. (a) Buried gate. (b) Planar gate. (c) Recessed gate. (d)
Planar gate with lateral current flow.

proposed by Teszner and Gicquel,[22] and the multi-channel FET proposed by
Zuleeg and Hinkle,[23,24] both in 1964.

24.2 STRUCTURE

Different structures for the static-induction transistor are shown in Fig. 24.1. All
but Fig. 24.1(d) have vertical current flow. The buried-gate structure is the
originally proposed scheme while the planar-gate structure in Fig. 24.1(b) is
probably the most common today. The most critical parameters in an SIT are the
spacing between gates ($2a$) and the channel doping level (N_D). Since most SITs
are designed normally-on, the doping is chosen such that the depletion regions
from the gates do not merge and there exists a narrow, neutral channel opening
with zero gate bias. Typical gaps between gates are a few microns, with channel
doping levels around 10^{15} cm^{-3} range. The structures also show that the gates are
formed by p-n junctions, but the SIT operations can be generalized to include
metal (Schottky) gates,[25] or even MIS gates. In the case of metal gates, the device
will be similar to a permeable-base transistor. The main difference then will be

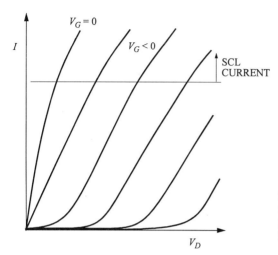

FIGURE 24.2
Output characteristics of an SIT. At higher current levels, space-charge-limited current dominates.

the device operation regime, not the structure. Most SITs reported are made on a Si substrate, with GaAs being the next choice of material for higher-speed operations.

24.3 CHARACTERISTICS

The static-induction transistor is basically a JFET or MESFET with super-short channel length, and with multiple channels connected in parallel. One major difference in structure is that the gates in the SIT do not extend close to the source or drain. As a result of the short channel (gate) length, punch-through occurs with high drain bias even if the transistor is turned off (static induction is equivalent to punch-through). The output characteristics of an SIT are shown in Fig. 24.2. At zero gate bias, the depletion regions around the gates do not pinch-off the gap completely and this condition corresponds to

$$\sqrt{\frac{2\varepsilon_s \psi_{bi}}{qN_D}} < a \tag{24.1}$$

where ψ_{bi} is the built-in potential of the *p-n* junction from the gate,

$$\psi_{bi} = \phi_T \ln\left(\frac{N_A N_D}{n_i^2}\right) . \tag{24.2}$$

A neutral region between the gates with zero gate bias provides a current path for a depletion-mode device (normally-on). The current conduction is drift in nature and is similar to an FET. With negative gate bias, the depletion regions widen,

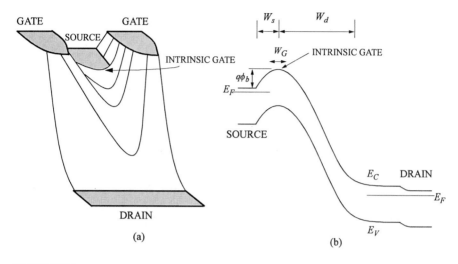

FIGURE 24.3
(a) Two-dimensional energy profile (conduction-band edge) of the SIT. (After Ref. 15) (b)
Energy-band diagram from source to drain in the middle of the channel between gates.

pinch-off the channel, and electrons from the source start to see a potential barrier
(Fig. 24.3). This begins when the gate voltage is more negative than

$$V_T = \psi_{bi} - V_P \tag{24.3}$$

and the pinch-off voltage V_P is given by

$$V_P = \frac{qN_D a^2}{2\varepsilon_s} . \tag{24.4}$$

Once a barrier is formed, the current is controlled by diffusion, and the barrier
height ϕ_b is the controlling factor for the supply of carriers. This barrier height
can be influenced by the gate voltage as well as the drain voltage. As shown in
Fig. 24.4, negative gate voltage raises the barrier and positive drain voltage
lowers the barrier. The efficiency by which the terminal voltages affect the barrier
is indicated by η and θ, with

$$\Delta\phi_b = -\eta\Delta V_G \tag{24.5}$$

and

$$\Delta\phi_b = -\theta\Delta V_D . \tag{24.6}$$

The change of barrier by the drain bias (Eq. (24.6)) is the concept behind static induction. The factors η and θ are geometry dependent, and thus different for different structures in Fig. 24.1. To use the structure in Fig. 24.1(a) as an example,[16]

$$\eta \approx \frac{W_s}{a + W_s} \quad , \tag{24.7}$$

$$\theta \approx \frac{W_s}{W_s + W_d} \tag{24.8}$$

where W_s and W_d are the depletion widths of the intrinsic gate toward the source and the drain as indicated in Fig. 24.3(b).

The current of an SIT when the channel is pinched off is given by the form

$$J = qN_D^+ \left(\frac{D_n}{W_G}\right) \exp\left(\frac{-q\phi_b}{kT}\right) \tag{24.9}$$

where N_D^+ is the doping concentration in the source. The term D_n/W_G is the carrier diffusion velocity. When W_G (effective thickness of the barrier, shown in Fig. 24.3(b)) becomes small, carriers are limited by the thermal velocity, giving a current of [2]

$$J = qN_D^+ \sqrt{\frac{kT}{2\pi m^*}} \exp\left(\frac{-q\phi_b}{kT}\right) \quad . \tag{24.10}$$

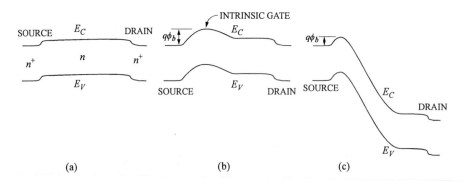

FIGURE 24.4
Energy-band diagrams in the middle of the channel with biases (a) $V_G = 0$, $V_D = 0$, (b) $V_G < 0$, $V_D = 0$, barrier ϕ_b increased, (c) $V_G < 0$, $V_D > 0$, barrier ϕ_b decreased.

In either Eq. (24.9) or Eq. (24.10), the barrier height ϕ_b at the intrinsic gate is given by[9]

$$\phi_b = \phi_T \ln \left(\frac{N_D^+}{N_D} \right) - \eta \left[V_G - (\psi_{bi} - V_P) \right] - \theta V_D \quad , \quad V_G < (\psi_{bi} - V_P) \quad (24.11)$$

The first term on the right is the built-in potential of the n^+–n junction, and the second and third terms are contributions from the gate and drain, respectively. The last term gives rise to the non-saturating characteristics with drain bias, and, thus, the static-induction effect. The channel width, as pictured in Fig. 24.3(a), is only a small fraction of the gap between gates. Since the diffusion current is exponential with ϕ_b, the effective channel width is in the order of a few Debye lengths. Such insight can be provided by computer simulations. Overall, the current can be put in the form

$$J = J_o \exp \left[\frac{q \, (\eta V_G + \theta V_D)}{kT} \right] . \quad (24.12)$$

At high current levels, the injected electrons are comparable to the doping level N_D. The injected carriers, thus, modify the field distribution and the current is controlled by the SCL current (see Appendix B4). The *I-V* characteristics have the forms

$$J = \frac{9 \varepsilon_s \mu_n V_D^2}{8 L^3} \quad , \quad (24.13)$$

$$J = \frac{2 \varepsilon_s v_{sat} V_D}{L^2} \quad , \quad (24.14)$$

$$J = \frac{4 \varepsilon_s}{9 L^2} \left(\frac{2q}{m^*} \right)^{1/2} V_D^{3/2} \quad , \quad (24.15)$$

when carriers are in the mobility regime, velocity saturation regime, or ballistic regime, respectively. These equations assume that there is negligible barrier limiting the injection of carriers. In the case of an SIT, the barrier created by the gate bias controls the onset of the SCL current. In other words, SCL current starts when the ϕ_b is lowered by V_D to approximately zero. Because of this, V_D in Eqs. (24.13) to (24.15) has a threshold value and should be replaced by $(V_D + \alpha V_G)$ where α is another constant similar in nature to η and θ.[26] With this substitution, the SCL current becomes a function of V_G. Also, comparing Eq. (24.13) to Eq. (24.12), one can now see more clearly the fundamental difference between an analog transistor and an SIT. As discussed by Nishizawa, in an analog transistor, the SCL current does not have an exponential dependence.[2] When I_D is plotted against V_D in a log-log scale, the static-induction current can have a slope higher than two, and can be distinguished from the SCL current.

Another mode of operation in the SIT family is the bipolar-mode SIT (BSIT) when the gate is forward biased to further achieve lower on-resistance.[27,28] It also has been referred to as a depleted-base transistor. In this device design the gap (a) is smaller and/or the doping in the channel is lower such that

$$\sqrt{\frac{2\varepsilon_s \psi_{bi}}{qN_D}} > a \quad . \tag{24.16}$$

This corresponds to pinch-off condition with zero gate bias and the device is normally-off (enhancement). With forward gate bias (positive), the barrier is lowered since the built-in potential is reduced. Furthermore, the p^+-gates, being forward biased, inject holes to the channel. The holes get collected at a potential minimum (energy maximum) at the intrinsic gate, raise the potential, and enhance the electron supply from the source. This mode of operation is similar to a bipolar transistor except here the intrinsic gate is a virtual base whose potential is accessed by the p^+-gate (or base in the bipolar terminology) indirectly. At this point, the electron concentration is much higher than the background doping level, so the current is larger than a conventional JFET. The output characteristics of a BSIT are shown in Fig. 24.5(a). They are drastically different from an SIT in

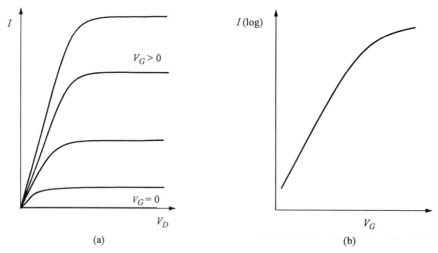

(a) (b)

FIGURE 24.5
(a) Output characteristics of a BSIT. (b) For a fixed V_D, the current rises exponentially with V_G, similar to the base-emitter bias of a bipolar transistor, until the diode is too strongly biased, ≈ 0.7 V.

that the currents are saturating with V_D (pentode-like rather than triode-like). The general characteristics resemble those of a bipolar transistor.

24.4 APPLICATIONS

The main attractiveness of an SIT is the combination of high-voltage and high-speed capability. The low doping brings about high breakdown voltage up to a few hundred volts. For a buried-gate structure, the frequency of operation is limited to only 2–5 MHz due to excessive parasitic capacitance. Using structures with exposed gates, the frequency can be increased above 2 GHz. Most applications of the SIT are in the power area. As an audio power amplifier, the SIT has low noise, low distortion and low output impedance. It can be used in high-power oscillator of microwave equipments such as communication broadcasting transmitters and microwave ovens. Other specific applications mentioned in literature include logics,[29] dynamic memory circuit,[30] image sensor and phototransistor,[31] and SIT thyristor (see Chapter 46).

For general applications of a transistor, the readers are referred to Appendix C3.

REFERENCES

1. J. Nishizawa, "A low impedance field effect transistor," *Tech. Digest IEEE IEDM*, 144 (1972).
2. J. I. Nishizawa, T. Terasaki and J. Shibata, "Field-effect transistor versus analog transistor (static induction transistor)," *IEEE Trans. Electron Dev.*, **ED-22**, 185 (1975).
3. H. Ogawa, A. Abe, T. Nakajima and T. Kajiwara, "Direct observation of the depletion layer in a multichannel vertical J.F.E.T. (M.J.F.E.T.)," *Electronics Lett.*, **11**, 223 (1975).
4. K. Yamaguchi, T. Toyabe and H. Kodera, "Two-dimensional analysis of triode-like operation of junction gate FET's," *IEEE Trans. Electron Dev.*, **ED-22**, 1047 (1975).
5. Y. Mochida, J. I. Nishizawa, T. Ohmi and R. K. Gupta, "Characteristics of static induction transistors: Effects of series resistance," *IEEE Trans. Electron Dev.*, **ED-25**, 761 (1978).
6. R. K. Gupta, "Mechanism of operation of field-effect devices," *Solid-State Electron.*, **23**, 1011 (1980).
7. P. Plotka and B. Wilamowski, "Interpretation of exponential type drain characteristics of the static induction transistor," *Solid-State Electron.*, **23**, 693 (1980).
8. R. K. Gupta, "Static *I-V* characteristics of static induction transistors," *J. Appl. Phys.*, **53**, 1754 (1982).
9. C. Bulucea and A. Rusu, "A first-order theory of the static induction transistor," *Solid-State Electron.*, **30**, 1227 (1987).
10. K. Yamaguchi, T. Toyabe and H. Kodera, "Two-dimensional analysis of vertical junction gate FET's," *Japanese J. Appl. Phys., Suppl.*, **15**, 163 (1976).
11. J. L. Morenza and D. Esteve, "Entirely diffused vertical channel JFET: Theory and experiment," *Solid-State Electron.*, **21**, 739 (1978).
12. T. Ohmi, "Punching through device and its integration – Static induction transistor," *IEEE Trans. Electron Dev.*, **ED-27**, 536 (1980).
13. T. Yamamoto, K. Matsumoto and A. Yusa, "Analysis of SIT *I-V* characteristics by two-dimensional simulation," *Solid-State Electron.*, **30**, 549 (1987).
14. J. I. Nishizawa, "Recent progress and potential of SIT," *Jap. J. Appl. Phys.*, **19** (Suppl. 19-1), 3 (1980).

15. J. I. Nishizawa and K. Yamamoto, "High-frequency high-power static induction transistor," *IEEE Trans. Electron Dev.*, **ED-25**, 314 (1978).

16. J. I. Nishizawa, "Junction field-effect devices," *Proc. Brown Boveri Symp.*, 241 (1982).

17. J. I. Nishizawa, M. Tatsuta and T. Tamamushi, "Recent development of the power static induction transistors in Japan," *Proc. PCI*, 118 (1987).

18. R. J. Regan, S. J. Butler, C. A. Armiento and F. C. Rock, "Static induction transistors: HF to X band," *Microwave J.*, 175 (1987).

19. W. Shockley, "Transistor electronics: Imperfections, unipolar and analog transistors," *Proc. IRE*, **40**, 1289 (1952).

20. S. A. Roosild and R. P. Dolan, Jr. and D. O'Neil, "A unipolar structure applying lateral diffusion," *Proc. IEEE*, **51**, 1059 (1963).

21. B. Buchanan, S. Roosild and R. Dolan, "Silicon current amplifier for microampere current levels," *Proc. IEEE*, **52**, 1364 (1964).

22. S. Teszner and R. Gicquel, "Gridistor – A new field-effect device," *Proc. IEEE*, **52**, 1502 (1964).

23. R. Zuleeg and V. O. Hinkle, "A multichannel field-effect transistor," *Proc. IEEE*, **52**, 1245 (1964).

24. R. Zuleeg, "Multi-channel field-effect transistor theory and experiment," *Solid-State Electron.*, **10**, 559 (1967).

25. P. M. Campbell, W. Garwacki, A. R. Sears, P. Menditto and B. J. Baliga, "Trapezoidal-groove Schottky-gate vertical channel GaAs FET (GaAs static induction transistor)," *Tech. Digest IEDM*, 186 (1984).

26. O. Ozawa and K. Aoki, "A multi-channel FET with a new diffusion type structure," *Japanese J. Appl. Phys., Suppl.*, **15**, 171 (1976).

27. J. I. Nishizawa, T. Ohmi and H. L. Chen, "Analysis of static characteristics of a bipolar-mode SIT (BSIT)," *IEEE Trans. Electron Dev.*, **ED-29**, 1233 (1982).

28. T. Tamama, M. Sakaue and Y. Mizushima, "'Bipolar-mode' transistors on a voltage-controlled scheme," *IEEE Trans. Electron Dev.*, **ED-28**, 777 (1981).

29. J. I. Nishizawa, E. Iwanami, S. Arai, M. Shimbo, K. Tanaka and A. Watanabe, "Low-power SITL IC," *IEEE J. Solid-State Circuits*, **SC-17**, 919 (1982).

30. J. I. Nishizawa, T. Tamamushi, Y. Mochida and T. Nonaka, "High speed and high density static induction transistor memory," *IEEE J. Solid-State Circuits*, **SC-13**, 622 (1978).

31. A. Yusa, J. I. Nishizawa, M. Imai, H. Yamada, J. I. Nakamura, T. Mizoguchi, Y. Ohta and M. Takayama, "SIT image sensor: Design considerations and characteristics," *IEEE Trans. Electron Dev.*, **ED-33**, 735 (1986).

CHAPTER
25

PLANAR-DOPED FIELD-EFFECT TRANSISTOR

25.1 HISTORY

The planar-doped field-effect transistor is also called delta-doped (δ-doped) FET or pulse-doped FET. It originated from the MESFET when variations of the doping profile in the direction perpendicular to the channel were considered, and is a special case in which the channel doping is incorporated in a ultra-thin layer. The transistor's operation was first considered theoretically by Board et al. in 1981.[1] Schubert and Ploog reported the first result on a depletion-mode device in 1985 using MBE on GaAs.[2] An enhancement-mode device was demonstrated by Schubert et al. in 1986.[3] Theoretical analysis of the quantum well resulting from the planar-doped layer was presented on GaAs[4] and Si[5] substrates. This relatively new device is not produced commercially and is still under investigation.

25.2 STRUCTURE

The structure for the planar-doped FET is shown in Fig. 25.1. The semiconductor material used is usually GaAs, although experimental results on Si have been reported.[6] The planar-doped layer typically contains an area doping density of $\approx 5 \times 10^{12}$ cm^{-2}. It has been shown that for densities higher than $\approx 10^{13}$ cm^{-2}, carriers are not confined to the potential well. Ideally, this doping plane is incorporated in an atomic monolayer (≈ 5 Å) with a density of $\approx 10^{20}$ cm^{-3}. Electron carrier profiles obtained from C-V measurements show approximately that the planar-doped layer is between 50–100 Å, with a peak concentration

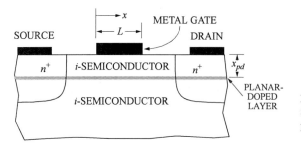

FIGURE 25.1
Structure of an n-channel planar-doped FET.

around 5×10^{18} cm^{-3}. This is consistent with the calculated width of the quantum well. Because of the stringent requirement of the abrupt doping profile, MBE or MOCVD is used to grow the layers. The intrinsic layer (x_{pd}) above the planar-doped layer reportedly ranges from less than 100 Å to a few thousand Å.[7] The subsequent processing temperature has to be carefully controlled to avoid diffusion of the dopants. The gate is formed by a metal Schottky junction, similar to that in a MESFET. The n^+-source and drain are formed by either ion implantation or diffusion from the alloyed contacts.

25.3 CHARACTERISTICS

The energy-band diagram of a depletion-mode planar-doped FET is shown in Fig. 25.2. From Fig. 25.2(b), it can be seen that the negative gate voltage required to turn the channel off is given by

$$V_T = \phi_{bn} - V_P - V_n \tag{25.1}$$

where

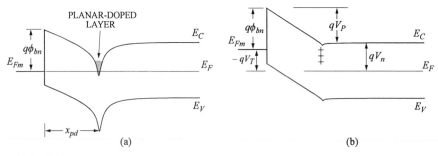

FIGURE 25.2
Energy-band diagrams for a depletion-mode planar-doped FET at (a) equilibrium, and (b) onset of threshold (negative V_T for depletion device).

$$V_P = \frac{qx_{pd}N_s}{\varepsilon_s} \tag{25.2}$$

and N_s is the planar-doped-layer density (cm^{-2}). Equation (25.1) is applicable for both enhancement-mode and depletion-mode devices, with a positive V_T value and a negative V_T value, respectively.

The net charge density controlled by the gate along the channel is given by

$$qn_s = C_G[V_G - V_T - \psi(x)] \tag{25.3}$$

where

$$C_G = \frac{\varepsilon_s}{x_{pd}} \tag{25.4}$$

and ψ is the channel potential with respect to the source. The drift current along the channel is given by

$$\begin{aligned} I &= W\mu qn_s \mathscr{E}_x \\ &= W\mu C_G[V_G - V_T - \psi(x)]\frac{d\psi(x)}{dx} \quad . \end{aligned} \tag{25.5}$$

Integrating Eq. (25.5) from source to drain gives a common FET equation

$$I = \frac{\mu C_G W}{L}\left[(V_G - V_T)V_D - \frac{V_D^2}{2}\right] \quad . \tag{25.6}$$

The output characteristics are shown in Fig. 25.3(a). In the linear region of small V_D, Eq. (25.6) is reduced to an ohmic equation

$$I_{lin} = \frac{\mu C_G W(V_G - V_T)V_D}{L} \tag{25.7}$$

and the transconductance is given by

$$g_{m,lin} \equiv \frac{dI_{lin}}{dV_G} = \frac{\mu C_G W V_D}{L} \quad . \tag{25.8}$$

The saturation region corresponds to the pinch-off condition when n_s in Eq. (25.3) becomes zero at the drain end. This saturation starts with

$$V_{D,sat} = V_G - V_T \quad , \tag{25.9}$$

and

$$I_{sat} = \frac{\mu C_G W}{2L} (V_G - V_T)^2 \quad, \tag{25.10}$$

$$g_{m,sat} \equiv \frac{dI_{sat}}{dV_G} = \frac{\mu C_G W (V_G - V_T)}{L} \quad. \tag{25.11}$$

In short-channel devices ($L < 1$ μm), the electric field is high enough to drive the carriers into velocity saturation ($\mathscr{E} > \mathscr{E}_c$ in Fig. 25.3(b)). In this case, saturation occurs before the pinch-off condition, with a reduced $V_{D,sat} \approx \mathscr{E}_c L$, giving a saturation current of

$$
\begin{aligned}
I_{sat} &= W q n_s v_{sat} \\
&= W C_G (V_G - V_T) v_{sat}
\end{aligned}
\tag{25.12}
$$

and

$$g_{m,sat} \equiv \frac{dI_{sat}}{dV_G} = W C_G v_{sat} \quad. \tag{25.13}$$

The cutoff frequency f_T is given by

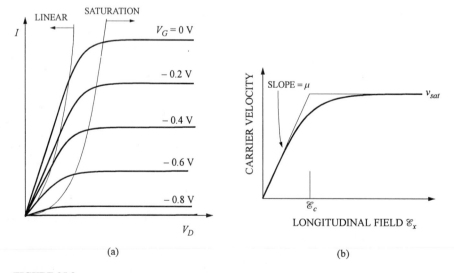

(a)   (b)

FIGURE 25.3
(a) Output characteristics for a depletion-mode planar-doped FET. (b) Linear piecewise approximation for carrier velocity-field relationship.

$$f_T = \frac{g_{m,sat}}{2\pi \, (WLC_G + C_{par})} \qquad (25.14)$$

where C_{par} is the input parasitic capacitance.

An improvement in carrier mobility has been discussed in this planar-doped channel.[4] Since the effective channel width is actually wider than the planar-doped layer, most carriers are outside the heavily doped region and impurity scattering is reduced. Measurements show that the mobility is enhanced by a factor of ≈ 3, compared to a material doped homogeneously with an equivalent level of $\approx 10^{18}$ cm^{-3}. This effect is similar to the modulation doping in a heterostructure.

25.4 APPLICATIONS

The planar-doped FET offers certain advantages over other devices. It has higher channel carrier density ($\approx 5\times10^{12}$ cm^{-2}) compared to a MODFET, which is limited to about 1×10^{12} cm^{-2}. It also has higher breakdown voltage because the field between the gate and the channel is constant. In the MESFET and MODFET, the material directly underneath the gate is doped, and the electric field is quadratic with distance from the surface. Therefore for a fixed gate bias, the local maximum field in these devices is much higher. Compared to a MESFET, the planar-doped FET potentially has a higher transconductance due to the proximity of the gate to the channel. This advantage is brought about by a fixed gate-to-channel distance independent of the gate voltage. The planar-doped FET is attractive for linear circuits because its g_m is less dependent on V_G that in conventional MESFETs.

The planar-doped FET is still under development and has no specific applications. The general applications of a transistor are listed in Appendix C3.

REFERENCES

1. K. Board, A. Chandra, C. E. C. Wood, S. Judaprawira and L. F. Eastman, "Characteristics of planar doped FET structures," *IEEE Trans. Electron Dev.*, **ED-28**, 505 (1981).
2. E. F. Schubert and K. Ploog, "The δ-doped field-effect transistor," *Jap. J. Appl. Phys.*, **24**, L608 (1985).
3. E. F. Schubert, J. E. Cunningham and W. T. Tsang, "Self-aligned enhancement-mode and depletion-mode GaAs field-effect transistors employing the δ-doping technique," *Appl. Phys. Lett.*, **49**, 1729 (1986).
4. E. F. Schubert, A. Fischer and K. Ploog, "The delta-doped field-effect transistor (δFET)," *IEEE Trans. Electron Dev.*, **ED-33**, 625 (1986).
5. Q. Chen and M. Willander, "Analysis of charge control in Si delta-doped field-effect transistor," *J. Appl. Phys.*, **69**, 8233 (1991).
6. H. P. Zeindl, B. Bullemer and I. Eisele, "Delta-doped MESFET with MBE-grown Si," *J. Electrochem. Soc.*, **136**, 1129 (1989).
7. A. Ishibashi, K. Funato and Y. Mori, "Ultra-thin-channelled GaAs MESFET with double-δ-doped layers," *Electron. Lett.*, **24**, 1034 (1988).

26

LATERAL RESONANT-TUNNELING FIELD-EFFECT TRANSISTOR

26.1 HISTORY

The lateral resonant-tunneling field-effect transistor (LRTFET) is unique among resonant-tunneling devices in that it is the only device that has resonant tunneling in the direction parallel to the heterointerface, and the quantum wells are induced by the gates, rather than from heterojunctions. Early studies focused on structures with multiple quantum wells in series, resulting in the so-called surface lateral-superlattice. Sakaki et al. in 1976 first pointed out that a superlattice can result from a corrugated thin film, and negative differential resistance can occur in such a 2-terminal device.[1] The concept of using field effect from a third terminal to induce such a superlattice was introduced by Bate in 1977,[2] and discussed by Stiles in 1978.[3] The lateral-superlattice was demonstrated in 1985 by Warren et al. using a MOSFET channel,[4] and also by Ismail et al. in 1988 using a MODFET channel.[5,6] The reduction of multiple quantum wells to a single quantum well to simulate a transistor action was proposed by Chou et al. in 1988,[7,8] and subsequently shown by Chou et al.[9] and Ismail et al.[10] More detailed discussions on the device can be found in Refs. 11 and 12.

26.2 STRUCTURE

In terms of structure, the LRTFET is an FET with discontinuous but closely spaced grating gates. Most structures reported are built on a GaAs–AlGaAs

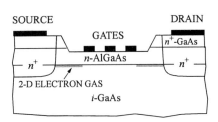

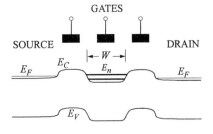

FIGURE 26.1

Structure of the LRTFET using a GaAs–AlGaAs MODFET as an example.

FIGURE 26.2

Energy-band diagram of the LRTFET along the MODFET channel (top GaAs surface) showing the quantum well induced by the gate potentials.

MODFET channel as shown in Fig. 26.1, but other FET channels such as a MOSFET can be used. The LRTFET can be generalized to include a single quantum well or serial multiple quantum wells. The example shown in Fig. 26.1 has a single quantum well which is controlled by three gates. The two outer gates control the barriers while the middle gate controls the well potential. In some cases, the middle gate can be omitted. The metal gates can be made of a Ti-Au or Ti-Pt stack. The gate size and the spacing are critical for quantum-mechanical resonant-tunneling phenomenon. The smallest dimensions achievable so far are around 50 nm, for either the gate or the space, obtained by X-ray lithography or electron-beam lithography, together with dry etching. The GaAs–AlGaAs heterostructures are grown by MBE or MOCVD. The n-doped AlGaAs layer, typically, is around 40 nm, with an additional intrinsic spacer layer of ≈ 7 nm adjacent to the GaAs channel.

26.3 CHARACTERISTICS

In the LRTFET, the current between the source and drain is due to resonant-tunneling via quantized levels in the quantum well, which is field-induced by the gates. The energy-band diagram along the FET channel (top GaAs surface) is shown in Fig. 26.2. In this example, a single quantum well is used. Qualitatively, the barriers are controlled by the outer gates, the well depth is controlled by the middle gate, and the substrate bias (all relative to the source) has an influence on the source/drain Fermi levels. The energy levels within the quantum well are quantized into subbands, and their discrete bottom values above E_C are given by

$$E_n \approx \frac{h^2 n^2}{8m^* W^2} \ , \qquad n = 1, 2, 3... \tag{26.1}$$

where W is the width of the well. According to Fig. 26.2, W is approximately one period of the gate grating (line-width plus space). Equation (26.1) is only an approximation since it assumes infinite barrier height with an abrupt step-like potential transition. More realistically the shape of the well is parabolic, and this leads to near uniform subband energy spacing, rather than the square relation indicated by Eq. (26.1). Resonant-tunneling current peaks when E_C in the source is aligned to one of the quantized levels in the well.

The general characteristics of the LRTFET are shown in Fig. 26.3. For a fixed drain-to-source voltage V_{DS}, when the outer-gate voltage (to source) V_{GS} is varied, it changes W and the barrier height. Both of these shift the quantized levels in relation to the E_C in the source. Since larger current flows whenever one of the quantized levels is aligned to the E_C in the source, negative transconductance results as shown in Fig. 26.3(a). In these measurements, V_{DS} has to be small, typically a few mV, otherwise it masks or inhibits the negative transconductance signature. Another aspect of the transistor action is shown in Fig. 26.3(b) where V_{DS} is varied while V_{GS} is fixed. This mode of operation is very similar to that in a two-terminal resonant-tunneling diode (see Chapter 10), and results in negative differential resistance.

It can be seen here that the LRTFET provides a continuously tunable quantum well that is flexible and is useful for studying resonant-tunneling phenomenon. Another advantage is the insulated gate, which limits the gate current and, thus, has low power dissipation. On the other hand, for any quantum device, small dimension is critical. In this device the lateral dimension is dictated by lithography and etching capabilities. This currently sets a limit of about 50 nm, which is much larger than a vertical quantum well grown by heteroepitaxy whose quantum-well size W can be as small as 5 nm. Another drawback is that the potential profile in a field-induced quantum well is not nearly as sharp as in a

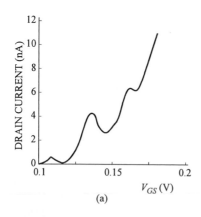

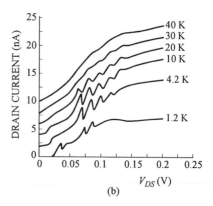

FIGURE 26.3

I-V characteristics of an LRTFET. (a) Drain current as a function of gate bias, $V_{DS} = 0.2$ mV. (After Ref. 12) (b) Drain current as a function of drain bias at different temperatures. (After Ref. 13)

heterostructure quantum well. The barriers are also much lower. A quick calculation shows that E_n is in the order of 0.5 meV, and is much smaller than that obtained from vertical quantum wells. Because of this, low temperature operation is required since thermal energy must not smear the quantization effects $(kT < E_n)$. This point is demonstrated in Fig. 26.3(b).

26.4 APPLICATIONS

The potential of LRTFET in circuit applications is not obvious at this point. The limitations are low-temperature operation (< 10 K), low current, stringent demand on lithography and etching, etc. It is interesting as a research tool to study resonant tunneling and to explore new device concepts since it provides a tunable quantum well. For general applications of negative resistance, the readers can refer to Appendix C2.

REFERENCES

1. H. Sakaki, K. Wagatsuma, J. Hamasaki and S. Saito, "Possible applications of surface corrugated quantum thin films to negative-resistance devices," *Thin Solid Films*, **36**, 497 (1976).
2. R. T. Bate, "Electrically controllable superlattice," *Bull. Amer. Phys. Soc.*, **22**, 407 (1977).
3. P. J. Stiles, "The artificial superlattice in a two-dimensional system," *Surface Sci.*, **73**, 252 (1978).
4. A. C. Warren, D. A. Antoniadis, H. I. Smith and J. Melngailis, "Surface superlattice formation in silicon inversion layers using 0.2-μm period grating-gate electrodes," *IEEE Electron Dev. Lett.*, **EDL-6**, 294 (1985).
5. K. Ismail, W. Chu, D. A. Antoniadis and H. I. Smith, "Surface-superlattice effects in a grating-gate GaAs/GaAlAs modulation doped field-effect transistor," *Appl. Phys. Lett.*, **52**, 1071 (1988).
6. K. Ismail, W. Chu, A. Yen, D. A. Antoniadis and H. I. Smith, "Negative transconductance and negative differential resistance in a grid-gate modulation-doped field-effect transistor," *Appl. Phys. Lett.*, **54**, 460 (1989).
7. S. Y. Chou, J. S. Harris, Jr. and R. F. W. Pease, "Lateral resonant tunneling field-effect transistor," *Appl. Phys. Lett.*, **52**, 1982 (1988).
8. S. Y. Chou, E. Wolak, J. S. Harris, Jr. and R. F. W. Pease, "A lateral resonant tunneling FET," *Superlattices and Microstructures*, **4**, 181 (1988).
9. S. Y. Chou, D. R. Allee, R. F. W. Pease and J. S. Harris, Jr., "Observation of electron resonant tunneling in a lateral dual-gate resonant tunneling field-effect transistor," *Appl. Phys. Lett.*, **55**, 176 (1989).
10. K. Ismail, D. A. Antoniadis and H. I. Smith, "Lateral resonant tunneling in a double-barrier field-effect transistor," *Appl. Phys. Lett.*, **55**, 589 (1989).
11. S. Y. Chou, D. R. Allee, R. F. Pease and J. S. Harris, Jr., "Lateral resonant tunneling transistors employing field-induced quantum wells and barriers," *Proc. IEEE*, **79**, 1131 (1991).
12. K. E. Ismail, P. F. Bagwell, T. P. Orlando, D. A. Antoniadis and H. I. Smith, "Quantum phenomena in field-effect-controlled semiconductor nanostructures," *Proc. IEEE*, **79**, 1106 (1991).
13. A. C. Seabaugh, J. N. Randall, Y. C. Kao, J. H. Luscombe and A. M. Bouchard, "$In_{0.52}Al_{0.48}As/In_{0.53}Ga_{0.47}As$ lateral resonant tunneling transistor," *Electronics Lett.*, **27**, 1832 (1991).

CHAPTER
27

STARK-EFFECT TRANSISTOR

27.1 HISTORY

The Stark-effect transistor has a unique configuration. The base, which is not situated between the emitter and the collector, is behind the collector away from the emitter. It is also isolated by a large energy-gap semiconductor layer, similar to an IGFET. For these reasons, this base terminal is often referred to as the gate. The current between the emitter and the collector is through a tunneling junction. As it was originally proposed by Bonnefoi et al. in 1985, the tunneling junction can consist of a single barrier or double barriers.[1] Experimental demonstration of a structure with a singe-barrier tunneling junction was presented by Beltram et al. in 1988,[2] and that with a double-barrier tunneling junction was reported by Yang et al. in 1989.[3,4] Modeling of the latter device was also presented by Chen et al.[5] The Stark-effect transistor, as shown by the small number of publications, is still under preliminary investigation.

27.2 STRUCTURE

The structures with both single barrier and double barriers between the emitter and the collector are shown in Fig. 27.1. The barriers are created by the larger energy gap of AlAs compared to GaAs. It is interesting and important to note that the collector layer is a quantum well itself with a thickness of $\approx 100\text{--}200$ Å. For the tunneling junction between the emitter and the collector, the barrier layers and the quantum-well thicknesses are in the order of 50 Å. The gate insulator layer can range from 1000 Å to a few thousand Å. Contacts to the collector and the gate are made on the exposed layers of the etched mesa steps, although the gate connection

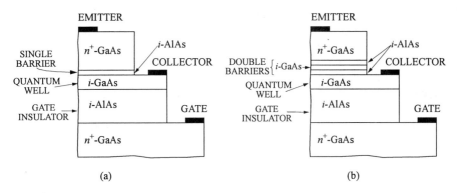

FIGURE 27.1
Structures of the Start-effect transistor with, between the emitter and collector, (a) single-barrier tunneling junction, and (b) double-barrier tunneling junction.

can be made by the bottom ohmic contact. The heterostructure is deposited by MBE because of the thin barrier layers and quantum-well layers required.

27.3 CHARACTERISTICS

One important feature of the Stark-effect transistor is that the collector layer is a quantum well. First-order quantum-mechanical approximation states that the bottom of the quantized subbands in a quantum well is given by

$$E_n - E_C \approx \frac{h^2 n^2}{8m^* W^2} , \qquad n = 1, 2, 3 \ldots \qquad (27.1)$$

where W is the collector quantum-well thickness. This equation, however, does not take into account the height of the confining barriers, their shapes, and the field within the quantum well. All these factors have an impact on shifting the subband levels away from those in Eq. (27.1). When a gate voltage is applied, the energy-band diagrams in Fig. 27.2 show that the shape of the barriers, especially the one between the collector and the gate, and the shape of the well are drastically changed, inducing a shift of the subbands within the collector quantum well. This phenomenon in the change of the energy-band structure by an external field is called Stark effect, and is responsible for the transistor action. When the collector subbands are scanned up and down, the resonant-tunneling current changes accordingly. This current peaks when one of the collector quantized subbands is aligned to the conduction-band edge E_C in the emitter. In the case of the double-barrier tunneling junction, the quantized level in the quantum well between the collector and emitter has to be aligned also. The alignment of these levels is a requirement for conservation of energy and lateral momentum in tunneling (see Chapter 10–Resonant-tunneling diode). Beyond the current peak, a further increase in gate voltage pulls the subband below the emitter E_C, reduces the resonant-tunneling current, and results in negative transconductance. The characteristics are shown in Fig. 27.3(a).

Apart form the Stark effect, the gate bias can also modulate the subbands by having the electric field penetrate beyond the collector quantum well to reach the emitter. Because of inter-electrode capacitance, the charge on the gate is balanced partly by the charge in the collector quantum well, and partly by the charge induced in the emitter terminal. The field developed across the

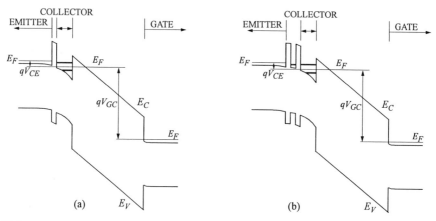

FIGURE 27.2
Energy-band diagrams of the Stark-effect transistor under positive gate-to-collector bias V_{GC} and collector-to-emitter bias V_{CE}. (a) Structure with single-barrier tunneling junction. (b) With double-barrier tunneling junction.

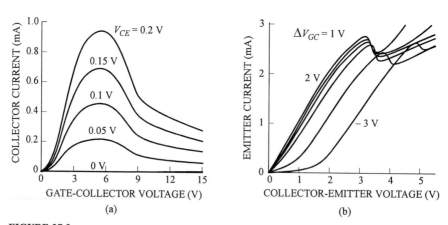

FIGURE 27.3
Characteristics of a Stark-effect transistor. (a) Collector current as a function of gate bias for fixed V_{CE}. (After Ref. 4) (b) Common-collector output characteristics for fixed V_{GC}. (After Ref. 2)

emitter-to-collector tunneling junction can change the collector well potential with respect to the emitter potential, together with its subbands. It has been estimated that this control factor of dE_n/dV_G is $\approx 1/50$.[2] The contribution from the Stark effect is also $\approx 1/50$, giving a net dE_n/dV_G of $\approx 1/25$.

The collector bias also has more direct impact on the collector quantum-well potential. The common-collector characteristics in Fig. 27.3(b) show negative differential resistance as the collector subbands are scanned in and out of alignment with the emitter E_C. It can be seen here that at high gate biases, the shift of current peak for every volt in gate bias is around 40 mV, agreeing with the above estimation (1/25). The occurrence of current peak at such a high V_{CE} is attributed to the high series resistance of the extrinsic collector layer. The Stark-effect transistor has both negative resistance as well as negative transconductance.

It should be noted that since the collector layer is contacted laterally as shown in Fig. 27.1, it must have a reasonable sheet conductivity to alleviate excessive series resistance. For this reason, the first subband level in the collector quantum well is always below the collector Fermi level so that it is filled with electrons to provide the desired conductivity. Resonant tunneling is, thus, through the second and upper subband levels.

Finally, it has been pointed out that when two or more resonant-tunneling diodes are connected through a common substrate, three-terminal transistor action can be observed which could be confused with the Stark-effect transistor.[6]

27.4 APPLICATIONS

The Stark-effect transistor is potentially an ultra-high-speed device because the main transistor current is via tunneling which is a fast phenomenon. Similar to an IGFET, it has low gate leakage for low-power operation. Its major drawback is the critical dimensions it requires and it is a very difficult issue for epitaxial growth. The shift in energy levels that is sensitive to the dimensions, for example, makes it difficult for circuit-level implementation. Because the device is still under investigation, there has been no demonstration or specific mention of circuit applications. The readers can refer to Appendix C2 for general applications of negative resistance.

REFERENCES

1. A. R. Bonnefoi, D. H. Chow and T. C. McGill, "Inverted base-collector tunnel transistors," *Appl. Phys. Lett.*, **47**, 888 (1985).
2. F. Beltram, F. Capasso, S. Luryi, S. G. Chu, A. Y. Cho and D. L. Sivco, "Negative transconductance via gating of the quantum well subbands in a resonant tunneling transistor," *Appl. Phys. Lett.*, **53**, 219 (1988).
3. C. H. Yang, Y. C. Kao and H. D. Shih, "New field-effect resonant tunneling transistor: Observation of oscillatory transconductance," *Appl. Phys. Lett.*, **55**, 2742 (1989).

4. C. H. Yang, "Realization of a field-effect resonant tunneling transistor at room temperature: Observation of negative transconductance due to quantum tunneling," *Appl. Phys. Lett.*, **60**, 1250 (1992).

5. J. Chen, C. H. Yang and R. A. Wilson, "Modeling of a new field-effect resonant tunneling transistor," *J. Appl. Phys.*, **71**, 1537 (1992).

6. C. H. Yang and H. D. Shih, "Integration of resonant tunneling diodes: an N-terminal device," *Inst. Phys. Conf. Ser.*, **96**, 611 (1989).

CHAPTER 28

VELOCITY-MODULATION TRANSISTOR

28.1 HISTORY

The velocity-modulation transistor (VMT) was proposed by Sakaki in 1982 as a very-high-speed device.[1] Although it has not been demonstrated experimentally as a transistor, the VMT represents a new class of field-effect transistors in which the transistor current is not modulated by the amount of carriers or charge induced by the gate. Rather, the modulation of current is due to a change in carrier velocity, with the unique feature that the total number of carriers remains constant. Experimentally, it was shown by Hirakawa et al. in 1985 that the mobility of a two-dimensional electron gas in a single heterointerface could be changed by $\approx 50\%$, controlled by a front gate and a back gate.[2] The ratio of mobilities in two adjacent heterointerfaces can be as high as 1000, according to the Monte Carlo simulations performed by Bhobe et al.[3] The speed advantage of the VMT was also examined by computer simulations by Bhobe et al.[3] and Kizilyalli and Hess.[4]

28.2 STRUCTURE

The original scheme of the velocity-modulation transistor proposed by Sakaki has dual channels and dual gates in a modulation-doped AlGaAs–GaAs quantum well (Fig. 28.1). Since the mobility in one channel compared to the other has to be much reduced, compensating impurities of opposite types can be incorporated locally in one half of the GaAs layer to introduce impurity scattering. The film thicknesses for the GaAs and AlGaAs are in the order of 500 Å. This particular example resembles a MODFET.

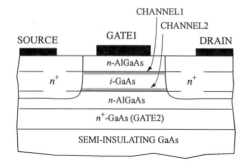

FIGURE 28.1

An example of the VMT with dual channels and dual gates, using the two heterointerfaces of a quantum well. Channels are created by modulation doping.

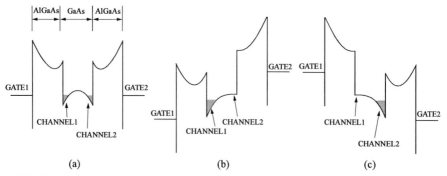

(a) (b) (c)

FIGURE 28.2

Energy-band diagrams (conduction-band edge) showing the shifting of carriers between two channels. (a) Equilibrium. (b) Voltage on gate1 is positive with respect to gate2. (c) Voltage on gate2 is positive with respect to gate1.

28.3 CHARACTERISTICS

The principle of the VMT is based on the change in carrier mobility or velocity in different space, and the carrier location is controlled by the gate bias. In the case of dual channels with dual gates, the change in mobility is obtained by shifting the carriers between the two channels. This is depicted in a quantum well in Fig. 28.2 where the carriers are controlled by the relative voltage between gate1 and gate2. The total drift current for the device is given by

$$I = qW(n_{s1}v_1 + n_{s2}v_2) \tag{28.1}$$

where n_s is the carrier density per unit area in each channel, and the total density

$$n_o = n_{s1} + n_{s2} \tag{28.2}$$

remains constant. The conductance at low field (low V_D) as a function of the relative gate bias is shown in Fig. 28.3(a). Assuming that $\mu_1 \gg \mu_2$, the maximum and minimum channel conductance are given by

$$G_{max} = n_o q \mu_1 \left(\frac{W}{L}\right) \ ,$$
(28.3)

$$G_{min} = n_o q \mu_2 \left(\frac{W}{L}\right) \ .$$
(28.4)

The expected output characteristics for the VMT are shown in Fig. 28.3(b).

The main advantage of the velocity-modulation transistor is the intrinsic device speed. For a conventional FET, when a gate bias is abruptly applied to turn the transistor on, the charge induced by the gate comes from the source. By the same token, the off-state requires the charge to dissipate through the drain. The intrinsic speed of a standard FET is thus limited by the transit time between the source and the drain. In the VMT, the change of state is accomplished by transferring charges between two channels that can be much closer (< 500 Å) than the channel length between source and drain. Computer simulations show that the response time can be as short as 0.2 ps.[4]

To take full advantage of the VMT, the gate voltage has to be within a range such that the total charge in the channels is conserved. This is not trivial to demonstrate experimentally because output characteristics similar to Fig. 28.3(b) can be achieved by conventional FET action where higher gate voltage induces an

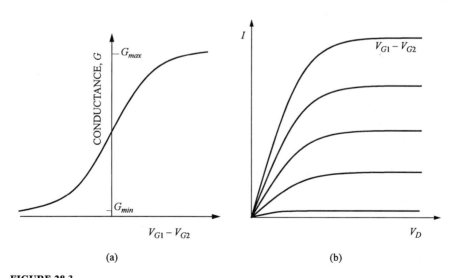

(a)

(b)

FIGURE 28.3
Channel conductance of a VMT as a function of the relative gate voltage. (b) Expected output characteristics.

extra channel charge. Independent measurements, such as Hall measurement, are required to confirm a VMT.

In the above example, the VMT requires a simultaneous change of voltages to both gate1 and gate2. Any out-of-phase bias will reduce the speed of the device and defeats the main purpose. While it is not practical to do so, variations of the original scheme have been envisaged. For example, the device can be designed such that at zero top-gate bias, carriers reside completely in one channel. The bottom-gate potential can be fixed and so a voltage change in one gate only is required. Ideally, the bottom gate can be eliminated. The channels can also be in the bulk materials instead of heterointerfaces.[5] It has been suggested that the source and drain only contact one channel so that the carriers in the second channel do not contribute to the transistor current at all.[6] Alternatively, a VMT can be made with a single channel where the gate voltage directly affects the mobility. For a channel next to a heterointerface, the mobility can be adjusted by the front and back gate biases to control the proximity of the channel to the heterointerface.[2] For channels in some bulk materials, e.g., GaSb, the gate bias can change the effective mass, which also affects the mobility.[1]

It should be pointed out that for short-channel devices, the carrier velocity is no longer proportional to the longitudinal field, and it approaches a saturation velocity at high fields (see Appendix B1). In this operation regime, the difference in mobility is less meaningful than the difference in the saturation velocity of the two channels. This difference in saturation velocity, in practice, is usually less than that in mobility.

28.4 APPLICATIONS

Due to the potential high speed of the VMT, the main applications are for high-speed circuits. However, to realize high-speed performance, extreme care must be taken to reduce parasitic capacitance and resistance, which can easily inhibit the intrinsic device advantage. Up to now, neither the transistor nor any specific circuit has been experimentally demonstrated. For general applications of a transistor, the readers can refer to Appendix C3.

REFERENCES

1. H. Sakaki, "Velocity-modulation transistor (VMT) – A new field-effect transistor concept," *Japanese J. Appl. Phys.*, **21**, L381 (1982).
2. K. Hirakawa, H. Sakaki and J. Yoshino, "Mobility modulation of the two-dimensional electron gas via controlled deformation of the electron wave function in selectively doped AlGaAs-GaAs heterojunctions," *Phys. Rev. Lett.*, **54**, 1279 (1985).
3. S. Bhobe, W. Porod, S. Bandyopadhyay and D. J. Kirkner, "Modulated interfacial disorder scattering in quantum wells and its device applications," *Surface and Interface Analysis*, **14**, 590 (1989).
4. I. C. Kizilyalli and K. Hess, "Ensemble Monte Carlo simulation of a velocity-modulation field effect transistor (VMT)," *Japanese J. Appl. Phys.*, **26**, 1519 (1987).

5. K. Maezawa, T. Mizutani and S. Yamada, "A GaAs(T)/AlAs(X) double-channel structure for velocity modulation transistors," *Inst. Phys. Conf. Ser.*, **No. 112**, Ch. 7, 515 (1990).
6. C. Hamaguchi, K. Miyatsuji and H. Hihara, "A proposal of single quantum well transistor (SQWT) - Self-consistent calculations of 2D electrons in a quantum well with external voltage," *Japanese J. Appl. Phys.*, **23**, L132 (1984).

CHAPTER
29

BIPOLAR
TRANSISTOR

29.1 HISTORY

The name bipolar is used because in this transistor both types of carriers are critical, as opposed to a field-effect transistor which is considered unipolar (see discussion in Introduction). The bipolar transistor is often called the junction transistor because its structure has two *p-n* junctions back-to-back. Not only was it the first transistor ever realized in practice, more important, its invention sparked rapid advancement of semiconductor fundamentals that revolutionized the electronics industry worldwide.

In December 1947, in the course of searching for a field-effect transistor, the point-contact transistor was discovered by Bardeen and Brattain of, then, Bell Telephone Laboratories.[1,2] The point-contact transistor, shown in Fig. 29.1(a), had two metal contacts (cat's whiskers) pressed onto a piece of Ge. It was observed that the reverse current of one contact to the substrate was dependent on the forward current of the other contact that was close by. Within two months of that historical event, the junction transistor using *p-n* junctions was conceived by Shockley of the same group in early 1948.[3] Demonstration of the junction transistor was made in 1950, using junctions grown from molten Ge. Bipolar transistors produced in the 1950s were typically made with alloyed junctions as shown in Fig. 29.1(b). The planar technology developed around 1960 started to favor silicon as the semiconductor material. Today, bipolar transistors enjoy a large market share, but they have been challenged by MOSFETs because of factors such as cost, yield, power, etc. Nevertheless, the bipolar transistor maintains a place in high-performance circuits because of its high transconductance.

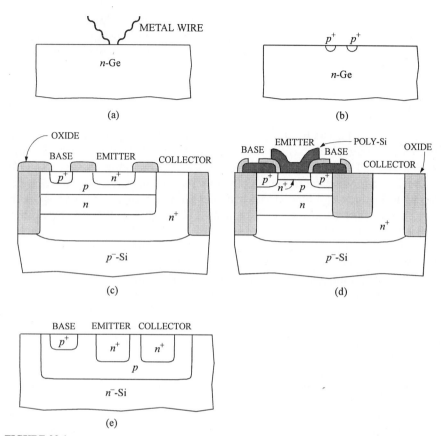

FIGURE 29.1

Different structures of bipolar transistor. (a) The original point-contact transistor. (b) Early transistor with alloyed junctions. (c) Vertical *n-p-n* structure in planar technology. (d) Advanced structure with self-aligned base contact and poly-emitter. (e) Lateral structure.

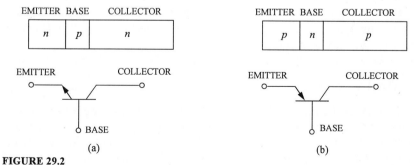

FIGURE 29.2

Bipolar transistor can be of an (a) *n-p-n* or (b) *p-n-p* structure. Circuit symbols are also shown.

The historical events surrounding the invention of the bipolar transistor are described by Shockley.[4] In 1953, Bardeen, Brattain and Shockley were awarded the Nobel Prize in physics for their seminal work. For additional information on the bipolar transistor, readers are referred to Refs. 5–8.

29.2 STRUCTURE

A bipolar transistor can be an *n-p-n* or *p-n-p* structure as shown schematically in Fig. 29.2. It is critical that the middle layer (base) be thin (« 1 μm) for high current gain. (The name "base" was obtained from the point-contact transistor where Ge was equivalent to the middle layer and served as the mechanical base.) The main features of a bipolar transistor are shown in Fig. 29.1(c). Most of the bipolar transistors have vertical current flow although a lateral structure can be realized as shown in Fig. 29.1(e). A more advanced bipolar structure is shown in Fig. 29.1(d), which includes a self-aligned base contact for reduced base resistance and a poly-emitter contact for improved current gain.

A typical doping profile for an *n-p-n* transistor is shown in Fig. 29.3(b). The emitter doping is generally higher than the base doping for high injection efficiency, and the collector doping is lower than the base doping so that the neutral base x_B is a weak function of the collector-base voltage. A common approach to form the emitter and base regions is by a double-diffused technique in which the base is diffused first, followed by a shallower, heavier-doping diffusion of the emitter. The integrated doping in the base (neutral region excluding depletion) is defined as the Gummel number

$$G_N \equiv \int N_A dx$$
$$\approx N_A x_B$$

(29.1)

and it usually lies between 10^{12} and 10^{13} cm^{-2} for Si. It will be shown that a small Gummel number is critical for current gain, but the lower limit is set by punch-through between the collector and the emitter. Most commercial bipolar transistors are made from Si because it has a more mature technology. For microwave applications the *n-p-n* structure is preferred for its higher electron mobility. Although GaAs offers potential benefits in performance, its technology is more difficult for manufacturing.

29.3 CHARACTERISTICS

A bipolar transistor can be operated in different regimes that are determined by the biases of the two junctions. The four modes of operations are summarized in Table. 29.1. The most important regime is the active (normal) mode where the emitter-base junction is forward biased and the collector-base junction is reverse biased. It is in this mode that current gain is realized. Figure 29.4 shows the *I-V*

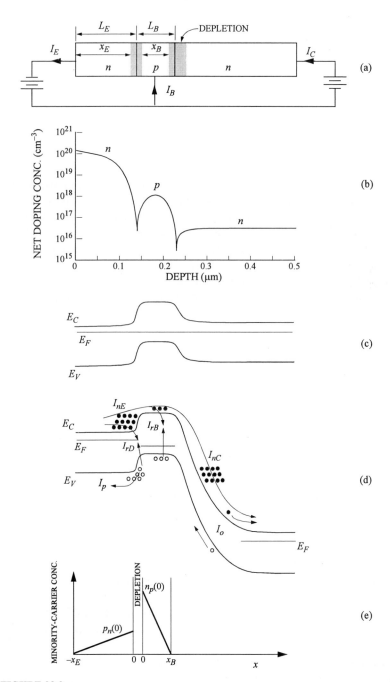

FIGURE 29.3
(a) An *n-p-n* bipolar transistor biased in the normal mode. (b) Typical doping profile for a Si device.
(c) Energy-band diagram under equilibrium. (d) Energy-band diagram in the normal mode. Current
components are indicated. (e) Minority-carrier concentrations in the neutral base and emitter.

TABLE 29.1

Operation modes of a bipolar transistor.

Operation Mode	Emitter-base junction	Collector-base junction
Active, normal	Forward	Reverse
Cutoff	Reverse	Reverse
Saturation	Forward	Forward
Inverse	Reverse	Forward

characteristics in the common-base and common-emitter configurations. The different modes of operations are indicated in these characteristics. In the saturation mode, the collector current I_C is a weak function of I_E or I_B. In the cutoff mode, set by I_E or $I_B = 0$, the transistor is off and I_C is close to zero. In the following, we first analyze the active mode to establish the basic mechanisms for current gain in analog applications. Switching between the saturation mode and cutoff mode for digital applications will follow.

The energy-band diagram of an *n-p-n* structure in the active mode is shown in Fig. 29.3(d), which also includes the major current components. In the emitter-base junction, the forward current consists of electron and hole diffusion

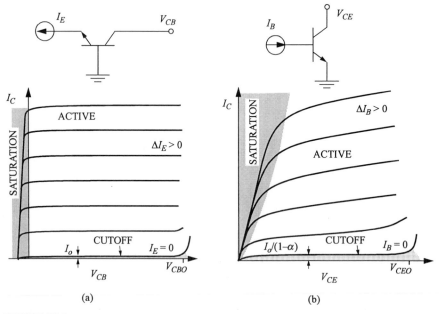

(a)   (b)

FIGURE 29.4

Typical output characteristics of a bipolar transistor in the (a) common-base configuration, (b) common-emitter configuration.

currents, I_{nE} and I_p, as well as the recombination currents in the depletion region I_{rD} (see Appendix B2) and in the base I_{rB}. These current components are given by, assuming uniform dopings,

$$I_{nE} = \frac{qAD_n n_i^2}{N_A x_B} \exp\left(\frac{qV_{BE}}{kT}\right) , \qquad (29.2)$$

$$I_p = \frac{qAD_p n_i^2}{N_{DE} x_E} \exp\left(\frac{qV_{BE}}{kT}\right) , \qquad (29.3)$$

$$I_{rD} = I_r \exp\left(\frac{qV_{BE}}{2kT}\right) . \qquad (29.4)$$

Here N_{DE} is the donor concentration in the emitter, x_B and x_E and the neutral base and emitter (smaller than the total length L_B and L_E). I_{nE} and I_p are standard p-n junction diffusion currents, with x_B replacing L_n and x_E replacing L_p when these dimensions are smaller than the corresponding diffusion lengths. These conditions define the minority-carrier concentration profiles which can be approximated by linear functions (Fig. 29.3(e)). The injected electron concentration in the base is given by

$$n_p(x) = \left[n_{po}\exp\left(\frac{qV_{BE}}{kT}\right)\right]\left(1 - \frac{x}{x_B}\right) . \qquad (29.5)$$

I_{rB} is the recombination current in the base and is given by

$$I_{rB} = \frac{Q_B}{\tau_n} = \frac{Aqx_B n_{po}}{2\tau_n} \exp\left(\frac{qV_{BE}}{kT}\right) , \qquad (29.6)$$

since Q_B is the excess charge in the base

$$Q_B = Aq \int_0^{x_B} [n_p(x) - n_{po}]\, dx$$

$$= \frac{Aqx_B n_{po}}{2} \exp\left(\frac{qV_{BE}}{kT}\right) . \qquad (29.7)$$

I_{nC} can also be estimated from the carrier profile in Fig. 29.3(e),

TABLE 29.2
Important parameters for a bipolar transistor.

Emitter injection efficiency	$\gamma \equiv I_{nE}/I_E$
Base transport factor	$\alpha_T \equiv I_{nC}/I_{nE}$
Common-base current gain	$\alpha \equiv \partial I_C/\partial I_E = \gamma\alpha_T = I_{nC}/I_E \approx I_C/I_E$
Common-emitter current gain, h_{FE}	$\beta \equiv \partial I_C/\partial I_B = \alpha/(1-\alpha) \approx I_C/I_B$

$$I_{nC} = qAD_n \frac{dn_p}{dx} = \frac{qAD_n n_p(0)}{x_B}$$

$$= \frac{2D_n Q_B}{x_B^2}$$

(29.8)

and is shown to be proportional to the stored charge in the base. I_o is the reverse saturation current of the collector-base junction and it consists of diffusion and generation currents.

It can be seen from Fig. 29.3 that

$$I_E = I_C + I_B$$
$$= I_{nE} + I_{rD} + I_p \quad,$$

(29.9)

$$I_B = I_p + I_{rD} + I_{rB} - I_o \quad,$$

(29.10)

$$I_C = I_{nC} + I_o \quad,$$

(29.11)

and

$$I_{nC} = I_{nE} - I_{rB} \quad.$$

(29.12)

Important parameters for a bipolar transistor are listed in Table 29.2. From the previous expressions, it can be shown that

$$\gamma \equiv \frac{I_{nE}}{I_E} = \frac{I_{nE}}{I_{nE} + I_p + I_{rD}}$$

$$= \left[1 + \frac{D_p N_A x_B}{D_n N_{DE} x_E} + \frac{I_r N_A x_B}{qAD_n n_i^2}\exp\left(\frac{-qV_{BE}}{2kT}\right)\right]^{-1} \quad,$$

(29.13)

$$\alpha_T \equiv \frac{I_{nC}}{I_{nE}} = \frac{1}{\cosh\left(x_B / L_n\right)} \approx 1 - \frac{x_B^2}{2L_n^2} \,. \tag{29.14}$$

α is a product of γ and α_T, and its value is slightly less than unity, giving a large value for β since

$$\beta = \frac{\alpha}{1 - \alpha} \,. \tag{29.15}$$

β can also be calculated directly from the current components

$$\beta = \frac{\alpha}{1 - \alpha} = \frac{I_{nC}}{I_B + I_o} \approx \frac{I_{nE}}{I_p + I_{rB} + I_{rD}}$$

$$\approx \left[\frac{N_A x_B D_p}{N_{DE} x_E D_n} + \frac{x_B^2}{2L_n^2} + \frac{I_r N_A x_B}{q A D_n n_i^2} \exp\left(\frac{-q V_{BE}}{2kT}\right) \right]^{-1} \,. \tag{29.16}$$

The advantage of a small Gummel number $N_A x_B$ as well as a small base width is apparent here. A typical curve for β as a function of bias is shown in Fig. 29.5. At low V_{BE} or I_C, the current component I_{rD}, which does not benefit the transistor action, takes up most of I_B and β is degraded. As I_C is increased, β reaches a maximum value. Typical values of β for a Si device range from ≈ 50 to a few hundred. At higher I_C, β starts to decrease because of high-level injection into the lightly doped collector.

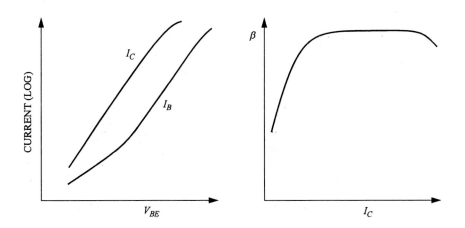

FIGURE 29.5
(a) Typical collector and base currents as a function of base-emitter bias. Also known as the Gummel plot. (b) β ($\partial I_C / \partial I_B$) as a function of I_C.

Going back to the output characteristics shown in Fig. 29.4, in the common-base configuration, the collector current can be shown to be

$$I_C = \alpha I_E + I_o \tag{29.17}$$

and in the common-emitter configuration,

$$I_C = \beta I_B + \frac{I_o}{1 - \alpha} \ . \tag{29.18}$$

The emitter current can also be related to the base current by

$$I_E = \frac{I_B + I_o}{1 - \alpha} \ . \tag{29.19}$$

The breakdown voltage V_{CBO} in the common-base configuration is similar to the collector-base p-n junction breakdown. Another mechanism that can cause breakdown is when x_B approaches zero so that punch-through occurs between the collector and the emitter. This also puts a lower limit on the Gummel number. In practice, the junction breakdown occurs before the punch-through condition. The breakdown voltage V_{CEO} in the common-emitter configuration can be calculated from the following. Near the collector junction breakdown, the multiplication M can be approximated empirically by

$$M = \frac{1}{1 - (V/V_{CBO})^n} \ . \tag{29.20}$$

For Si, n has a value between 2 and 6. In the common-base configuration, the collector current is multiplied to

$$I_C = (\alpha I_E + I_o) M \ . \tag{29.21}$$

To obtain V_{CEO} in the common-emitter configuration, setting $I_B = 0$ and $I_C = I_E$ gives

$$I_C = \frac{I_o M}{1 - \alpha M} \ . \tag{29.22}$$

V_{CEO} is then calculated by setting $\alpha M = 1$, giving

$$V_{CEO} = V_{CBO} (1 - \alpha)^{1/n}$$
$$\approx V_{CBO} \beta^{-1/n} \ . \tag{29.23}$$

It can be seen that in the common-emitter configuration, the breakdown voltage is lower and the residual off-current is higher. Another feature in Fig. 29.4(b) is that I_C is not constant with V_{CE} in the active region. This is due to the dependence of x_B on V_{CE} from the growth of the depletion width. This non-saturating characteristic of I_C with V_{CE} is called the Early effect, and the currents can be extrapolated to the V_{CE} axis to arrive at an Early voltage which is approximately equal to

$$V_A \approx \frac{q N_A L_B^2}{\varepsilon_s} \ . \tag{29.24}$$

The figure of merit for the frequency response of a bipolar transistor is given by the cutoff frequency f_T where the short-circuit current gain becomes unity. The f_T is limited by the charging times for the emitter τ_E and the collector τ_C, and by the transit times in the base τ_B and the collector-base depletion region τ_{dC},

$$\frac{1}{2\pi f_T} = \tau_E + \tau_B + \tau_{dC} + \tau_C$$

$$= \frac{\phi_T(C_E + C_C)}{I_E} + \frac{L_B^2}{2D_n} + \frac{W_{dC}}{2v_{sat}} + R_C C_C \ . \tag{29.25}$$

C_E and C_C are the emitter and collector capacitances, W_{dC} is the collector-base depletion width, and R_C is the collector series resistance. A plot of f_T as a function of I_C is shown in Fig. 29.6. The f_T increases with I_C (or I_E) until high-level injection occurs. For Si devices, an f_T of over 70 GHz has been achieved.

In digital applications, the response of the bipolar transistor has additional constraints when switching in and out of saturation (Fig. 29.7). In the active region, the stored charge in the base Q_B is given by Eq. (29.7). In saturation, Q_B rises above that value without increasing I_C. It is the change of Q_B that gives rise to the transient response shown in Fig. 29.7(d). After the transistor is turned on by a base current ($I_B \approx V_{BE}/R_B$), Q_B approaches a steady state value of $I_B \tau_n$ according to

$$Q_B = I_B \tau_n \left[1 - \exp\left(\frac{-t}{\tau_n}\right) \right] \ . \tag{29.26}$$

t_{on} is the time it takes Q_B to increase to its saturation value Q_s. The criterion for saturation is given by (Eq. (29.8))

$$Q_s = \frac{I_C x_B^2}{2D_n} \tag{29.27}$$

and I_C is given by $\approx V_{DD}/R_C$. The turn-on time is therefore given by

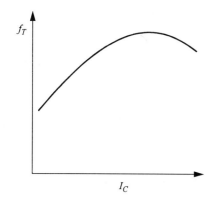

FIGURE 29.6
Cutoff frequency as a function of collector current.

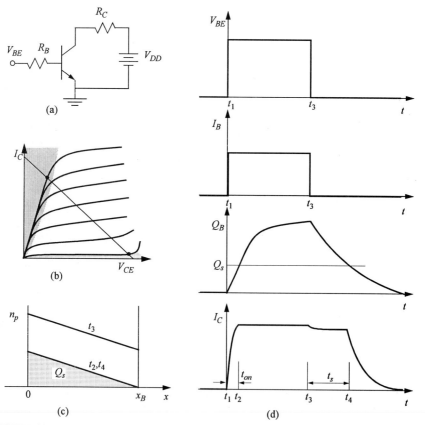

FIGURE 29.7
(a) A bipolar circuit to define the steady-state operating points in (b). (c) Minority-carrier profile in the base. (d) Response of Q_B and I_C to a square base input.

$$t_{on} = \tau_n \ln\left[\frac{1}{1 - (Q_s/I_B\tau_n)}\right]. \tag{29.28}$$

After t_3, Q_B decays exponentially with a time constant τ_n. The storage time t_s is the time interval for Q_B to decay from $I_B\tau_n$ to Q_s,

$$t_s = \tau_n \ln\left(\frac{I_B\tau_n}{Q_s}\right). \tag{29.29}$$

After t_4, I_C also decreases exponentially with the time constant τ_n.

The storage time severely limits the switching speed in digital circuits, and it is caused by excess charge injected from the collector to the base under forward bias. One way to reduce this minority-carrier injection is to add a Schottky barrier clamp in parallel to the collector-base junction (Fig. 29.8). This Schottky diode absorbs the forward current between the base and the collector. Being a majority-carrier device, the Schottky diode has negligible minority-carrier injection.

The transconductance g_m of a bipolar transistor is given by

$$g_m \equiv \left.\frac{\partial I_C}{\partial V_{BE}}\right|_{V_{CE}} = \frac{I_C}{\phi_T} \tag{29.30}$$

and is proportional to the collector current. High g_m enables a bipolar transistor to have high-current drive for high-speed circuits, especially when the load capacitance is large.

To achieve high β, the injection efficiency has to be maximized. To do so, I_p must be minimized. Experiments show that a poly-emitter in contact with the single-crystal emitter is quite effective. The exact mechanisms for such an improvement are not certain. Possible effects can be due to a thin oxide at the poly-Si/single-crystal-Si interface, and the reduced mobility within the poly-Si. Technologically, better control of the emitter can be obtained when it is formed by out-diffusion of dopants from the poly-Si.

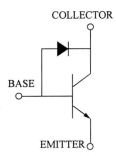

FIGURE 29.8
A bipolar transistor with a Schottky clamp to reduce minority-carrier injection from the collector to the base in saturation.

Looking back to the first point-contact transistor, an ideal Schottky diode as the emitter would have provided negligible minority-carrier injection for transistor action. The observation of transistor action must mean that the point-contact Schottky emitter had non-ideal Schottky behavior such that minority-carrier injection was increased. This could arise in the presence of a thin dielectric layer between the metal wire and the semiconductor.[9] A Schottky diode under large forward bias is also known to increase the minority-carrier injection. Most likely, these contacts were created by a forming process (by a current pulse) in which diffusion of impurities occurred and local *p-n* junctions were formed.

29.4 APPLICATIONS

The bipolar transistor along with the MOSFET are the most popular transistors in the commercial electronic market. While MOSFETs are more common in high-density circuits, bipolar transistors enable high-speed circuits because of their high transconductance. A good example is the BiCMOS circuit where MOSFETs provide the density and bipolar transistors provide the current drive for large capacitive loads. Another advantage of the bipolar transistor is that the threshold for turn-on is less sensitive to process variation. In bipolar memory applications, soft-error from α-particle is more tolerable. Bipolar transistors are also used in power applications where high voltage (≈ 400 V) and high current density are required. The limitations of a bipolar transistor compared to a MOSFET are intrinsic speed constraints due to charge storage, low input impedance, high power dissipation, more complex processing, and large area. For example, in bipolar memory circuits, the chip size is typically 16 times that of MOS technology for the same memory count.

A bipolar transistor can be used as a temperature sensor. It is an improvement over a *p-n* diode temperature sensor because in a diode, other current components such as recombination current are less predictable and have different temperature dependence. In a bipolar transistor, the collector current is a pure diffusion current from the base-emitter junction while the recombination current only goes to the base. With a constant I_C, V_{BE} is monitored, being

$$V_{BE} = \frac{kT}{q} \ln \left(\frac{I_C}{I_s} \right) \tag{29.31}$$

and is fairly linear with temperature. I_s is the pre-exponential term of the diffusion current in the base-emitter junction.

The general applications of a transistor are listed in Appendix C3.

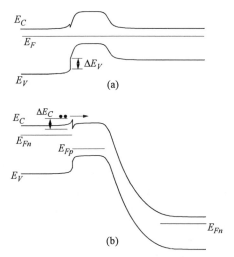

(a)

(b)

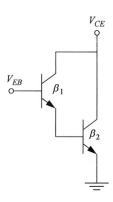

FIGURE 29.9
(a) Energy-band diagram of a HBT in equilibrium. ΔE_V suppresses hole diffusion from the base to the emitter. (b) ΔE_C helps to inject hot electrons for ballistic transport.

FIGURE 29.10
Circuit symbol and connection for a Darlington amplifier.

29.5 RELATED DEVICES

29.5.1 Heterojunction Bipolar Transistor

To improve injection efficiency, the emitter of a bipolar transistor needs to have a very high doping level. Beyond a critical doping level, the emitter energy gap decreases and, as a result, the injection efficiency drops. The heterojunction bipolar transistor (HBT) was proposed by Shockley in 1951,[10] and was analyzed in more detail by Kroemer in 1957.[11] Practical HBTs started to be built in the mid-1970s with the emergence of LPCVD, MBE and MOCVD technologies. They incorporate a heterojunction in the emitter-base junction, with the emitter having a larger energy gap (Fig. 29.9). The reduction of I_p by ΔE_V improves the overall β by

$$\beta_{\text{HBT}} = \beta \exp\left(\frac{\Delta E_V}{kT}\right) . \tag{29.32}$$

With much improved β, other parameters can benefit from the HBT design with a trade-off from β. The base region can be doped more heavily to reduce the base resistance. The emitter can also be doped more lightly to reduce the emitter capacitance. The existence of ΔE_C is sometimes used to obtain a hot-electron transistor. Figure 29.9(b) shows that the injected electrons have higher energy and

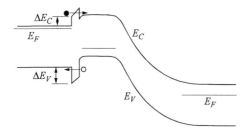

FIGURE 29.11
Energy-band diagram of a tunneling-emitter bipolar transistor under bias.

higher velocity to reduce the base transit time, resulting in an intrinsically faster device. An additional heterojunction at the collector, in a sometimes called double-heterojunction bipolar transistor (DHBT), minimizes minority carriers injected into the base from the collector in the saturation mode. HBTs are usually realized in compound semiconductors due to the availability of heterojunctions of minimal lattice mismatch. HBT on Si bipolar has been studied using SIPOS (semi-insulating polycrystalline-Si) as the emitter.[12]

29.5.2 Darlington Amplifier

A Darlington amplifier consists of two cascaded bipolar transistors connected as shown in Fig. 29.10. The emitter of one transistor is fed to the base of the other transistor. As a result, the overall β is much higher, and is the product of the individual βs. The drawback of a Darlington amplifier is that a larger voltage V_{CE} is required for the output.

29.5.3 Tunneling-Emitter Bipolar Transistor

The emitter injection inefficiency can be improved in a tunneling-emitter bipolar transistor by inserting a tunneling barrier near the emitter-base junction.[13] As shown in the energy-band diagram of Fig. 29.11, ΔE_C impedes the electron current and ΔE_V impedes the hole current. Since tunneling is related to the product of the effective mass and the barrier height, if $m^*_p \Delta E_V > m^*_n \Delta E_C$, the injection efficiency is improved.

REFERENCES

1. J. Bardeen and W. H. Brattain, "The transistor, a semi-conductor triode," *Phys. Rev.*, **74**, 230 (1948).
2. J. Bardeen and W. H. Brattain, "Physical principles involved in transistor action," *Phys. Rev.*, **75**, 1208 (1949).
3. W. Shockley, "The theory of *p-n* junctions in semiconductors and *p-n* junction transistors," *Bell Syst. Tech. J.*, **28**, 435 (1949).
4. W. Shockley, "The path to the conception of the junction transistor," *IEEE Trans. Electron Dev.*, **ED-23**, 597 (1976).
5. P. A. H. Hart, "Bipolar transistors and integrated circuits," in C. Hilsum, Vol. Ed., T. S. Moss, Ser. Ed., *Handbook on semiconductors*, Vol. 4, p. 87, North-Holland, Amsterdam, 1981.

6. S. M. Sze, *Physics of semiconductor devices*, 2nd Ed., Wiley, New York, 1981.

7. M. Shur, *Physics of semiconductor devices*, Prentice Hall, Englewood Cliffs, 1990.

8. E. S. Yang, *Microelectronic devices*, McGraw-Hill, New York, 1988.

9. M. A. Green and R. B. Godfrey, "Super-gain silicon MIS heterojunction emitter transistors," *IEEE Electron Dev. Lett.*, **EDL-4**, 225 (1983).

10. W. Shockley, "Circuit element utilizing semiconductive material," U.S. Patent 2,569,347 (1951).

11. H. Kroemer, "Theory of a wide-gap emitter for transistors," *Proc. IRE*, **45**, 1535 (1957).

12. T. Matsushita, N. Oh-uchi, H. Hayashi and H. Yamoto, "A silicon heterojunction transistor," *Appl. Phys. Lett.*, **35**, 549 (1979).

13. F. E. Najjar, D. C. Radulescu, Y. K. Chen, G. W. Wicks, P. J. Tasker and L. F. Eastman, "dc characteristics of the AlGaAs/GaAs tunneling emitter bipolar transistor," *Appl. Phys. Lett.*, **50**, 1915 (1987).

CHAPTER
30

TUNNELING HOT-ELECTRON-TRANSFER AMPLIFIER

30.1 HISTORY

The THETA (tunneling hot-electron-transfer amplifier) represents a class of hot-electron transistors whose emitter injection current is via tunneling through a thin barrier. These devices differ from the tunnel-emitter transistor by having a base composed of metal or heavily doped semiconductor, as opposed to an induced inversion layer (see Chapter 34). The first THETA was reported by Mead in 1960, using an MOMOM (metal-oxide-metal-oxide-metal) structure, sometimes called an MIMIM (metal-insulator-metal-insulator-metal) structure.[1,2] In these structures both the emitter and collector barriers are formed by the oxide. A slight variation of the structure is formed when the collector barrier is replaced by a metal-semiconductor junction, resulting in an MOMS (metal-oxide-metal-semiconductor), or an MIMS (metal-insulator-metal-semiconductor) structure, described by Spratt et al. in 1961.[3] Still another variation is to use a *p-n* junction in the collector. Kisaki reported results on an MO*p-n* (or MI*p-n)* structure in 1973.[4] He used a semiconductor (Si) as the base, with the emitter barrier formed by a thermal SiO_2. Since all these structures use the same emitter injection mechanism of tunneling, they suffer from the same problem of low current gain. This is translated to a technological problem because a good transfer ratio calls for an ultra-thin oxide layer of ≈ 15 Å.[5] At the present time it is unattainable to grow such a thin oxide film without pinholes. There has been a renewed interest in the THETA since Heiblum suggested, in 1981, using a wide-energy-gap semiconductor as the tunneling barrier, and a degenerately doped narrow-energy-gap semiconductor as the emitter, base and collector.[5] This idea was especially timely after the rapid development of epitaxial techniques such as MBE and MOCVD in the 1970s. The first heterojunction THETA was reported by Yokoyama et al. in 1984,[6,7] followed by Heiblum et al.[8] and Hase et al. in 1985.[9] A good review on the THETA can be found in Refs. 5 and 10.

30.2 STRUCTURE

Different THETA structures are shown in Fig. 30.1, along with their energy-band diagrams under operating conditions. In the MOMOM and MOMS structures, the metal base was aluminum, typically between 100–300 Å thick, and the emitter barrier was Al_2O_3, formed by anodization to a thickness of 50–100 Å. The oxide in the collector barrier was deposited SiO_2 to a thickness of several hundred Angstroms. For the MOp-n structure, the oxide was thermally grown and was, thus, more controllable. For the heterojunction structure (Fig. 30.1(d)), the AlGaAs–GaAs system is the most common, but other materials such as InGaAs–InAlAs, InGaAs–InP, InAs–AlGaAsSb, and InGaAs–InAlGaAs have been reported. The narrow-energy-gap material for the emitter, base, and collector are typically doped to 5×10^{17}–2×10^{18} cm^{-3} while the wide-energy-gap layers are undoped. The barrier layer thickness for the tunneling emitter is in the range of 7.5–50 nm, while the barrier layer for the collector is much thicker, ranging from 100–250 nm. The base width ranges from 10 nm to 100 nm. A thin base improves the transfer ratio, but is harder to make contact to it without shorting to the collector layer. The collector-base junction is often graded in composition to reduce quantum-mechanical reflection. The examples used throughout this chapter are based on electron tunneling current, but THETAs using hole tunneling current have also been demonstrated.

30.3 CHARACTERISTICS

For this discussion of the working principle, the heterojunction THETA is assumed since it is of the greatest interest. Under normal operating conditions, the emitter is negatively biased (for the doping type shown) with respect to the base, and the collector is positively biased (Fig. 30.2). Since the barrier created by the heterojunction is low, typically in the 0.2–0.4 eV range, it is necessary to operate the THETA at low temperatures to reduce the thermionic-emission current over the barrier. Elections are injected from the emitter to the n^+-base, making the THETA a majority-carrier device. The emitter-base current is a tunneling current through the barrier, either by direct tunneling or by Fowler-Nordheim tunneling (see Appendix B7). The injected electrons at the base have a maximum kinetic energy of

$$E = q\,(V_{BE} - V_n) \tag{30.1}$$

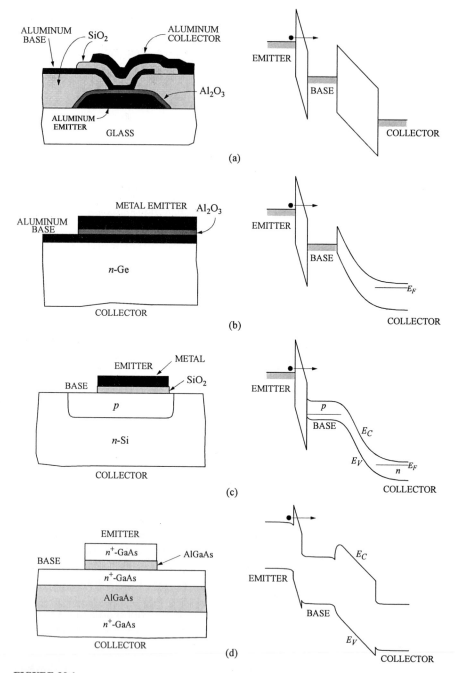

FIGURE 30.1
Different structures of the THETA, and their energy-band diagrams under operating conditions. (a) MOMOM. (After Ref. 2) (b) MOMS. (c) MO*p-n*. (d) Heterojunction THETA.

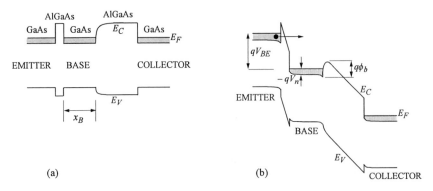

FIGURE 30.2
Energy-band diagram of the heterojunction THETA (a) at equilibrium and (b) under operation as a transistor.

(V_n is negative for a degenerate semiconductor). As electrons traverse through the base, energy is lost through some scattering events. At the base-collector junction, carriers with energy above the barrier $q\phi_b$ will result in collector current, while the rest will contribute to undesirable base current. The base transport factor α_T can be broken down into different components as

$$I_C = \alpha_T I_E$$
$$= \alpha_B \alpha_{BC} \alpha_C I_E \ . \tag{30.2}$$

α_B, due to scattering in the base layer, is given by

$$\alpha_B = \exp\left(-\frac{x_B}{l_m}\right) \tag{30.3}$$

where l_m is the mean free path in the base. Reported values for l_m range from 70 nm to 280 nm. l_m is also known to be dependent on the electron energy. When the energy is too high, l_m starts to decrease. In the case of an MOM emitter, because the oxide barrier is much higher, a large V_{BE} is required to inject a specific current level. A higher V_{BE}, unfortunately, increases the electron energy and reduces l_m. This is the factor that requires the oxide thickness in the MOM barrier to be small (≈ 15 Å).[5] To improve α_B, the base thickness must be minimized, but this results in excessive base resistance. It has been suggested to use an induced base or modulation doping for the base layer such that it can be thin (≈ 100 Å) and yet conductive. The second factor α_{BC} is due to quantum-mechanical reflection at the base-collector junction band-edge discontinuity. For an abrupt junction, it is given by[11]

$$\alpha_{BC} \approx 1 - \left[\frac{1 - \sqrt{1 - \dfrac{q\phi_b}{E}}}{1 + \sqrt{1 - \dfrac{q\phi_b}{E}}} \right]^2 .$$ (30.4)

Composition grading for the collector barrier would improve the reflection loss. α_C is the collector efficiency due to scattering in the wide-energy-gap material.

To have a high β (common-emitter current gain) value, α_T should be close to unity since

$$\beta \approx \frac{\alpha_T}{1 - \alpha_T} .$$ (30.5)

The best β value reported is 40.[12] An example for the output characteristics of a THETA is shown in Fig. 30.3.

30.4 APPLICATIONS

The THETA has gone through rapid development in the past few years but is still far away from being used in commercial applications. The most attractive structure, the heterojunction THETA, requires MBE or MOCVD for epitaxial growth, which are both too costly for manufacturing. The requirement for low temperature operation also limits the application. The THETA offers potential for high-speed operation due to ballistic transport through the base, and the absence of minority-carrier storage. For general applications of a transistor, readers are referred to Appendix C3.

The THETA has been used as a research tool to study properties of hot carriers. A specific function is a spectrometer to measure the energy spectrum of the tunneled hot electrons in the base. In this operation, the collector is biased

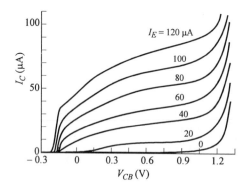

FIGURE 30.3

Example showing the common-base output characteristics of a THETA. (After Ref. 13)

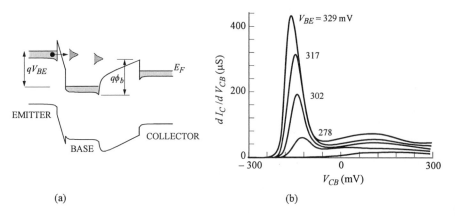

(a)   (b)

FIGURE 30.4
(a) Energy-band diagram of the THETA used as a spectrometer. The collector voltage is negative with respect to the base to vary the effective collector barrier height. (b) Hot-electron energy spectrum. (After Ref. 13)

positively with respect to the base to vary the effective collector barrier (Fig. 30.4(a)). When the incremental collector current is plotted against the effective collector barrier height, the energy spectrum of the hot electrons is obtained. It can be seen from Fig. 30.4(b) that for each V_{BE}, the energy (related to V_{CB}) at the peak of the distribution increases with V_{BE}.

REFERENCES

1. C. A. Mead, "The tunnel-emission amplifier," *Proc. IRE*, **48**, 359 (1960).
2. C. A. Mead, "Operation of tunnel-emission devices," *J. Appl. Phys.*, **32**, 646 (1961).
3. J. P. Spratt, R. F. Schwarz and W. M. Kane, "Hot electrons in metal films: Injection and collection," *Phys. Rev. Lett.*, **6**, 341 (1961).
4. H. Kisaki, "Tunnel transistor," *Proc. IEEE*, **61**, 1053 (1973).
5. M. Heiblum, "Tunneling hot electron transfer amplifiers (THETA): Amplifiers operating up to the infrared," *Solid-State Electron.*, **24**, 343 (1981).
6. N. Yokoyama, K. Imamura, T. Ohshima, H. Nishi, S. Muto, K. Kondo and S. Hiyamizu, "Tunneling hot electron transistor using GaAs/AlGaAs heterojunctions," *Japanese J. Appl. Phys.*, **23**, L311 (1984).
7. N. Yokoyama, K. Imamura, T. Ohshima, H. Nishi, S. Muto, K. Kondo and S. Hiyamizu, "Characteristics of double heterojunction GaAs/AlGaAs hot electron transistors," *IEEE IEDM Tech. Digest*, 532 (1984).
8. M. Heiblum, D. C. Thomas, C. M. Knoedler and M. I. Nathan, "Tunneling hot-electron transfer amplifier: A hot-electron GaAs device with current gain," *Appl. Phys. Lett.*, **47**, 1105 (1985).
9. I. Hase, H. Kawai, S. Imanaga, K. Kaneko and N. Watanabe, "MOCVD-grown AlGaAs/GaAs hot-electron transistor with a base width of 30 nm," *Electron. Lett.*, **21**, 757 (1985).
10. M. Heiblum and M. V. Fischetti, "Ballistic electron transport in hot electron transistors," in F. Capasso, Ed., *Physics of quantum electron devices*, Springer-Verlag, New York, 1990.

11. S. Luryi, "Hot-electron injection and resonant-tunneling heterojunction devices," in F. Capasso and G. Margaritondo, Eds., *Heterojunction band discontinuities: Physics and device applications*, Elsevier Science, New York, 1987.

12. K. Seo, M. Heiblum, C. M. Knoedler, J. E. Oh, J. Pamulapati and P. Bhattacharya, "High-gain pseudomorphic InGaAs base ballistic hot-electron device," *IEEE Electron Dev. Lett.*, **10**, 73 (1989).

13. M. Heiblum, M. I. Nathan, D. C. Thomas and C. M. Knoedler, "Direct observation of ballistic transport in GaAs," *Phys. Rev. Lett.*, **55**, 2200 (1985).

CHAPTER
31

METAL-BASE
TRANSISTOR

31.1 HISTORY

The metal-base transistor is often referred to as semiconductor-metal-semiconductor (SMS) transistor. While the first hot-electron transistor, conceived in 1960, used tunneling current for the emitter injection, the metal-base transistor has a Schottky-barrier emitter-base junction and the associated thermionic-emission current provides a higher current drive. The metal-base transistor was proposed and demonstrated by Atalla and Kahng,[1] and Geppert[2] in 1962. Since an epitaxial semiconductor could not be grown on metal at that time, early structures were of the point-contact kind. Following the development of an epitaxial silicide technique,[3] $Si–CoSi_2–Si$ monolithic structures were subsequently reported in the mid-1980s. Most notable are the works from Rosencher et al. since 1984,[4,5] and of Hensel et al.[6] Even though the history of the metal-base transistor is more than thirty years, the device has not matured enough to be commercially useful. Partially, this is due to the technological difficulty of growing epitaxial semiconductors on metal or silicide. More importantly, the fundamental limitation of low current gain due to quantum-mechanical reflection puts a serious doubt on the potential of the device.[7,8]

31.2 STRUCTURE

An early point-contact structure for the metal-base transistor is shown in Fig. 31.1(a). The thin metal film of ≈ 10 nm is either vacuum deposited or electroplated onto a semiconductor surface. Another piece of semiconductor is shaped to a fine point, and is pressed gently onto the metal film. Around 1984, the

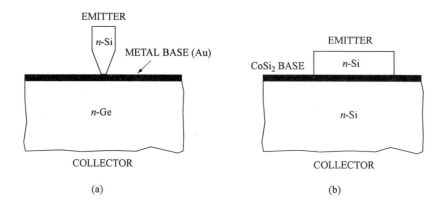

FIGURE 31.1
Structures of a metal-base transistor. (a) An early structure consisted of point-contact of semiconductor onto a thin metal film which has been deposited on another semiconductor surface. (b) A monolithic structure using epitaxial CoSi$_2$ and silicon.

discovery of a technique to grow epitaxial silicides on Si (CoSi$_2$ and NiSi$_2$) generated renewed interest on growing monolithic structures,[3] shown in Fig. 31.1(b). Epitaxial silicide is grown by deposition of a thin metal film in ultrahigh vacuum, followed by annealing around 650°C. The CoSi$_2$ base ranges between 5–30 nm. Thicker films are known to produce morphology that is rough and discontinuous. Thinner films, on the other hand, are more prone to pinholes, which provide parallel current conduction as in a permeable-base transistor. The top epitaxial semiconductor layer is grown by MBE to a thickness of ≈ 0.2–0.8 μm. Both the semiconductor emitter and collector are doped to the same type, to a level of ≈ 10^{16} cm^{-3}.

31.3 CHARACTERISTICS

Under normal operation, the emitter-base junction is forward biased while the collector-base junction is reverse biased (Fig. 31.2). The forward current of a Schottky-barrier diode is due to thermionic emission of majority carriers and is given by

$$J = A^* T^2 \exp\left(-\frac{q\phi_{bE}}{kT}\right)\left[\exp\left(\frac{qV_{BE}}{nkT}\right) - 1\right] . \tag{31.1}$$

The minority-carrier current J_{pE} is a diffusion current and is negligibly small. Before the injected electrons arrive at the collector, they go through numerous loss mechanisms represented by the equation

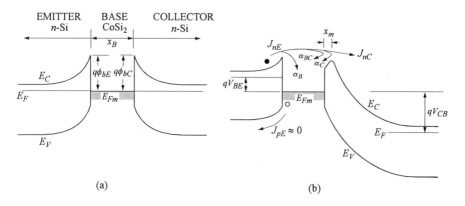

FIGURE 31.2
The energy-band diagram of a metal-base transistor (a) under thermal equilibrium and (b) under normal biases. x_m is the field reversal region from image-force lowering. The loss of hot electrons to the base are indicated by α_B, α_{BC}, and α_C.

$$J_{nC} = \alpha_T J_{nE}$$
$$= \alpha_B \alpha_{BC} \alpha_C J_{nE} \quad . \tag{31.2}$$

α_T is the base transport factor of hot electrons. The loss of uncollected hot electrons contributes to an undesirable base current. α_B is due to electron scattering in the metal base, given by

$$\alpha_B = \exp\left(-\frac{x_B}{l_{mB}}\right) \tag{31.3}$$

where l_{mB} is the carrier mean free path in the metal base. Typical l_{mB} is 10 nm at room temperature and 30 nm at 77 K. α_{BC} is due to quantum-mechanical reflection at the base-collector interface,[9]

$$\alpha_{BC} \approx 1 - \left[\frac{1 - \sqrt{1 - \dfrac{q\phi_{bC}}{E}}}{1 + \sqrt{1 - \dfrac{q\phi_{bC}}{E}}}\right]^2 \quad . \tag{31.4}$$

E is the electron energy with respect to the metal Fermi level and is, to the first order, equal to the emitter-base barrier height $q\phi_{bE}$. It can be seen from Eq. (31.4) that for a symmetrical device, $E \approx q\phi_{bE} \approx q\phi_{bC}$, and α_{BC} approaches zero. It is therefore desirable for an asymmetrical device with $q\phi_{bE} > q\phi_{bC}$ to improve α_{BC}.

The collector efficiency α_C is due to back-scattering of electrons within the distance x_m of the image-force lowering (see Appendix B6), and is given by[10]

$$\alpha_C = \exp\left(-\frac{x_m}{l_{mC}}\right) \tag{31.5}$$

where l_{mC} is the mean free path in the collector. Experimental results of common-base output characteristics are shown in Fig. 31.3.

To have reasonable common-emitter current gain (β), α_T should be made close to unity since

$$\beta \approx \frac{\alpha_T}{1 - \alpha_T} \;. \tag{31.6}$$

To maximize α_B, the metal film thickness (base) has to be minimized. The lower limit is bound by technological problems when pinholes start to form. The current path through these pinholes is that of a permeable-base transistor (see Chapter 23), and the higher current gain obtained might be misleading. When that happens, in spite of a larger current gain, the ultimate advantages of a hot-electron transistor are lost. It is, therefore, important to check for pinholes in the metal film of a metal-base transistor. Optically, it is difficult to rule out pinholes since a small number of them would be sufficient to shunt out a large area. Two electrical measurement techniques have been applied to distinguish between these transistor actions.[5] One is measuring the dependence of I_E on V_{BC}, and the other by observing the difference in I-V characteristics when the emitter and collector terminals are interchanged.

It has been pointed out that even for zero metal thickness, the effects of α_{BC} and α_C are already putting a severe constraint on the transfer ratio that is

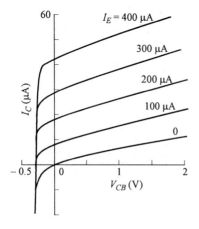

FIGURE 31.3
Common-base output characteristics of a metal-base transistor. (After Ref. 5)

calculated to be less than 0.5 for realistic device designs.[7,8] With more optimized device parameters, the results can be improved but not drastically. All experimental data seem to subscribe to the above conclusion.

31.4 APPLICATIONS

The metal-base transistor has no commercial value but it has been used as a tool to study fundamental properties of hot electrons in metals and silicides. A major factor that prevents it from being a practical device is the low current gain due to quantum-mechanical reflection. The metal-base transistor offers certain potential advantages such as low base resistance and high-speed operation due to ballistic transport in the base and the absence of minority-carrier storage. It had been accessed to be capable of higher-frequency operation than the bipolar transistor and other hot-electron transistors.[11,12]

General applications of a transistor are listed in Appendix C3.

REFERENCES

1. M. Atalla and D. Kahng, "A new 'hot electron' triode structure with semiconductor-metal emitter," *1962 IEEE Device Res. Conf., IEEE Trans. Electron Dev.*, **ED-9**, 507 (1962).
2. D. V. Geppert, "A metal-base transistor," *Proc. IRE*, **50**, 1527 (1962).
3. R. Tung, "Schottky barrier formation at single crystal metal-semiconductor interfaces," *Phys. Rev. Lett.*, **52**, 461 (1984).
4. E. Rosencher, S. Delage, Y. Campidelli and F. A. d'Avitaya, "Transistor effect in monolithic $Si/CoSi_2/Si$ epitaxial structures," *Electronics Lett.*, **20**, 762 (1984).
5. E. Rosencher, P. A. Badoz, J. C. Pfister, F. A. d'Avitaya, G. Vincent and S. Delage, "Study of ballistic transport in Si-$CoSi_2$-Si metal base transistors," *Appl. Phys. Lett.*, **49**, 271 (1986).
6. J. C. Hensel, A. F. J. Levi, R. T. Tung and J. M. Gibson, "Transistor action in $Si/CoSi_2/Si$ heterostructures," *Appl. Phys. Lett.*, **47**, 151 (1985).
7. C. R. Crowell and S. M. Sze, "Quantum-mechanical reflection of electrons at metal-semiconductor barriers: Electron transport in semiconductor-metal-semiconductor structures," *J. Appl. Phys.*, **37**, 2683 (1966).
8. S. M. Sze and H. K. Gummel, "Appraisal of semiconductor-metal-semiconductor transistor," *Solid-State Electron.*, **9**, 751 (1966).
9. S. Luryi, "Hot-electron injection and resonant-tunneling heterojunction devices," in F. Capasso and G. Margaritondo, Eds., *Heterojunction band discontinuities: Physics and device applications*, Elsevier Science, New York, 1987.
10. E. Rosencher, F. A. d'Avitaya, P. A. Badoz, C. d'Anterroches, G. Glastre, G. Vincent and J. C. Pfister, "The physics of metal base transistors," *Proc. Mat. Res. Soc. Symp.*, **91**, 415 (1987).
11. J. L. Moll, "Comparison of hot electron and related amplifiers," *IEEE Trans. Electron Dev.*, **ED-10**, 299 (1963).
12. M. M. Atalla and R. W. Soshea, "Hot-carrier triodes with thin-film metal base," *Solid-State Electron.*, **6**, 245 (1963).

CHAPTER
32

REAL-SPACE-TRANSFER TRANSISTOR

32.1 HISTORY

The real-space-transfer (RST) transistor is based on the real-space transfer of carriers between two materials. This real-space-transfer effect was first applied to a two-terminal device to obtain negative differential resistance (see Chapter 11–RST diode). In the RST diode, whose development was started in 1980, the material with the higher conduction-band edge E_C (for electrons as carriers) should have minimum mobility. Under a high field, electrons are excited to this material of reduced mobility, resulting in a reduced current, and thus, negative differential resistance. In an RST transistor, a third terminal contacts this material to extract the emitted carriers and to control the transverse field for efficient carrier transfer.

The RST transistor was first proposed as a negative-resistance field-effect transistor (NERFET) by Kastalsky and Luryi in 1983,[1] and was subsequently realized in a GaAs–AlGaAs modulation-doped heterostructure by Kastalsky et al. in 1984.[2] Its microwave capability as an oscillator was demonstrated by Kastalsky et al. later that year.[3] An analytical solution for NERFET operation was presented by Grinberg et al. in 1987,[4] and computer simulation using the Monte Carlo approach was performed by Kizilyalli and Hess in 1989.[5] For detailed discussions on the device, readers are referred to Refs. 6 and 7. The charge-injection transistor (CHINT) as a hot-electron transistor was proposed and demonstrated by Luryi et al. in 1984.[8] The structure as well as the device physics are identical to the NERFET except for the bias conditions. Both device operations will be discussed later.

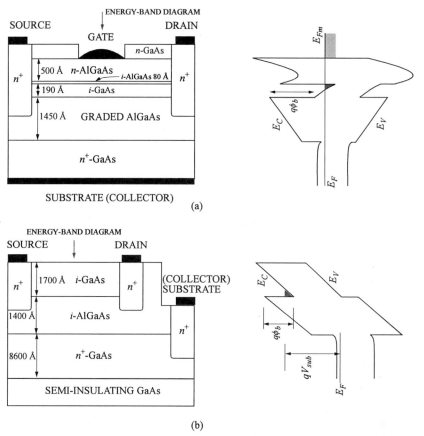

FIGURE 32.1
Structures and energy-band diagrams of real-space-transfer transistors. (a) Early devices used modulation doping and graded barrier. (b) Later devices eliminate modulation doping and the channel is induced by a substrate bias.

32.2 STRUCTURE

As mentioned above, the RST effect requires a heterojunction in which the material with higher E_C (for electrons) has much reduced mobility. The GaAs–AlGaAs system has largely been used so far for the RST transistor. In early structures, shown in Fig. 32.1(a), modulation doping is incorporated with the top AlGaAs layer doped to $\approx 10^{18}$ cm^{-3}. The barrier to the substrate is another AlGaAs layer but with graded composition. This provides a built-in field to extract electrons in this layer. The gate contact can control the channel carrier density. In later structures, the gate, the modulation doping, and the grading in the barrier are all eliminated, and the channel is created by a substrate bias that also provides a field to extract the hot electrons. This structure is found to yield better

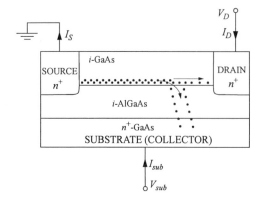

FIGURE 32.2
Schematic diagram showing carrier transfer (electrons) and terminal currents.

isolation between the substrate and the source/drain. Typical film thickness for both structures are indicated in the figures, and MBE or MOCVD has been used for precise thickness and doping control. The source and drain are formed by GeAu-based alloys. The n^+-diffusion depth has to be controlled such that it connects the channel layer without shorting to the substrate n^+-GaAs layer.

32.3 CHARACTERISTICS

We first discuss the operation of the NERFET, followed by that of the CHINT. The terminal currents of a NERFET are indicated schematically in Fig. 32.2. The current between source and drain is similar to the channel current of an FET such as a MOSFET or a MESFET. The substrate is analogous to the gate, with the additional function of depleting the channel carriers after they are emitted over the barrier. The *I-V* characteristics for a fixed large V_{sub} are shown in Fig. 32.3(a). The source current is a standard current for an FET, including the linear region and the saturation region. The substrate current is a hot-electron current, and it increases with the longitudinal field, or V_D. This current usually occurs in the saturation region in which the field is non-uniform and has a higher local peak near the drain. Kirchhoff's current law requires that

$$I_S = I_D + I_{sub} \quad .$$ (32.1)

The drain current has to drop when I_{sub} rises, giving a negative differential resistance dV_D/dI_D. A maximum peak-to-valley ratio of the drain current of 160 has been observed.

This change of I_D is related to the substrate current, given by

$$\frac{dI_D}{W dx} = -J_{sub} \quad .$$ (32.2)

The substrate current is due to thermionic emission of hot-electrons. A simple analysis is to assume that the hot-carriers have a Maxwellian distribution, with a mean electron temperature T_e that is higher than the room or lattice temperature. This thermionic-emission current is given by

$$J_{sub} = qnv \exp\left(-\frac{q\phi_b}{kT_e}\right) \tag{32.3}$$

with electron velocity

$$v = \sqrt{\frac{kT_e}{2\pi m^*}} . \tag{32.4}$$

The symbol ϕ_b is the barrier height due to the conduction-band discontinuity shown in Fig. 32.1. The electron temperature is related directly to the high field near the drain, and it has been shown empirically to be proportional to the square of drain bias.[6] Since the drain current is a drift current,

$$I_D = Wn\Delta qv_{sat} \tag{32.5}$$

where Δ is the channel thickness, solving the differential equations of Eqs. (32.2), (32.3), and (32.5) shows that the electron concentration n, assuming a uniform field, decays exponentially from source to drain.

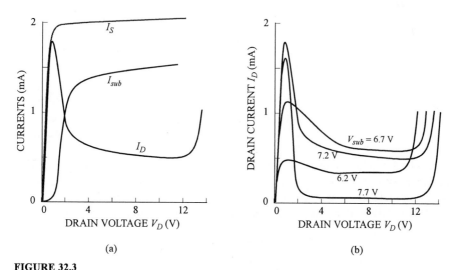

(a)

(b)

FIGURE 32.3
Terminal currents of a NERFET. (a) Source, drain, and subtract currents for a fixed V_{sub}. (b) Drain current for various V_{sub}. (After Ref. 6)

Complete output characteristics for various values of V_{sub} are shown in Fig. 32.3(b). The increase of V_{sub} has the following effects on the device: (1) channel carriers are increased, (2) the field within AlGaAs for efficient collection of emitted carriers is increased, and (3) T_e is decreased due to a redistribution of a more uniform field in the channel (at lower V_{sub} the field in the drain-source direction is more concentrated near the drain end, and higher local field gives rise to higher T_e). These effects have important and sometimes opposite impacts on the hot-electron current. Figure 32.3(b) shows three distinct regions according to different values of V_D. At low V_D, carriers do not have enough energy from the longitudinal field to surmount the barrier. The channel is modulated by the substrate and characteristics are similar to the linear region of an FET. The most interesting region is with medium V_D corresponding to the saturation region of an FET. However, negative differential resistance can be observed only for high values of V_{sub}. At low V_{sub}, the transverse field is not high enough for an efficient collection of the carriers within the AlGaAs layer. This is compounded by the space-charge effect, which further reduces the field. The voltage built-up by the space-charge effect in the barrier film is given by

$$\Delta V = \frac{J_{sub} l^2}{2 \varepsilon_s v_{sat}} \tag{32.6}$$

where l is the AlGaAs thickness. A quick estimate shows that $\Delta \times V$ can be as high as 2 V.[7] Another interesting feature in this region is that both positive and negative transconductance (dI_D/dV_{sub}) coexist. Positive transconductance is due to the increase of channel carriers, and also the decrease of T_e and I_{sub} with V_{sub}. Negative transconductance is due to the increase of transverse field and I_{sub} with V_{sub}. Finally, the third region is at high V_D where leakage starts to occur between the drain and the substrate.

The intrinsic speed of a NERFET is limited by two time constants, the energy relaxation time to establish T_e and the time-of-flight within the high-field domain near the drain. The latter is transit time over a very short distance, unlike in an FET where the total distance is from source to drain. Both of these time constants are around 1 ps. Consequently the NERFET is proposed to be a very fast device with an ultimate speed, for a well-scaled device, around 100 GHz. A cutoff frequency higher than 30 GHz has been demonstrated.

The RST effect produces I-V characteristics very similar to that of the transferred-electron effect in which electrons are excited to a satellite band in the energy-momentum space, as opposed to a different material in real space. To achieve an efficient NERFET, a proper choice of heterojunction with optimum band-edge discontinuity, together with a high satellite valley to avoid the transferred-electron effect (or the absence of a satellite valley) are desired.

The main difference of a CHINT from a NERFET is that the substrate is used as the output and the drain as the input, while the structures can be identical. The I_{sub} becomes the main transistor current. Since the I_{sub} is limited by

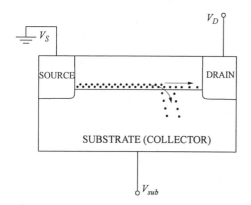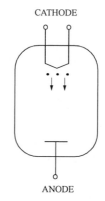

FIGURE 32.4
Comparison of a CHINT to a vacuum tube diode.

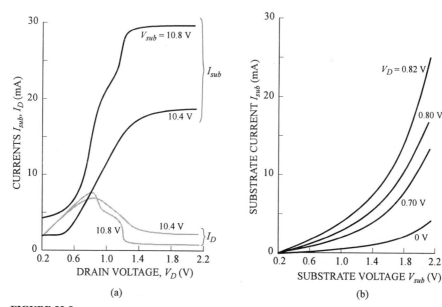

FIGURE 32.5
Characteristics of a CHINT. (a) I_{sub} and I_D as a function of input voltage V_D. (b) Output (common-emitter) characteristics. (After Ref. 9)

thermionic emission over a barrier, its operation is closer to a potential-effect transistor than an FET. For this reason, the following analogy to a bipolar transistor can be drawn; source ≡ emitter, drain ≡ base, and substrate ≡ collector.

The transistor current I_{sub} is determined by the electron temperature T_e created by V_D. The operation of a CHINT can be compared to a vacuum diode whose cathode filament is heated resistively by a current (Fig. 32.4).[8] The CHINT input and output currents are shown in Fig. 32.5(a) as a function of input voltage V_D. It can be seen that the transconductance g_m (dI_{sub}/dV_D) is at a maximum before negative differential resistance starts. The operation of the CHINT is thus confined to a small V_D (≈ 0.8 V) and negative resistance is not utilized. A maximum g_m of ≈ 1000 mS/mm has been obtained which is comparable to a bipolar transistor. The common-emitter characteristics are shown in Fig. 32.5(b).

32.4 APPLICATIONS

Compared to a two-terminal RST diode, the added third terminal in a NERFET has at least three advantages: (1) control of negative differential resistance, (2) higher-speed operation since emitted carriers are drained away and will not return to the main channel (this is the limit of response in a RST diode), and (3) higher peak-to-valley current ratio. The peak-to-valley ratio is expected also to be higher than a transfer-electron device. A NERFET can be used as a controllable microwave amplifier and generator. It has also been demonstrated that if the

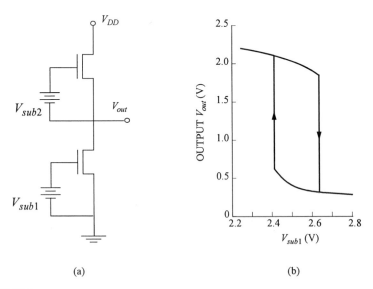

(a)   (b)

FIGURE 32.6
(a) Connection and (b) transfer characteristics for an inverter formed by two NERFETs. $V_{DD} = 2.5$ V.
(After Ref. 6)

substrate terminal is left to float, the stored charge in this layer can be maintained and the device can be utilized as a memory element.[6] Two NERFETs connected back-to-back can also be used as an inverter or a bistable switch (Fig. 32.6). The drawback of the NERFET is excessive input current I_{sub}. For general applications of negative differential resistance, readers can refer to Appendix C2.

The CHINT has been demonstrated to have high speed and high g_m.[10] The general applications of a transistor can be found in Appendix C3. In addition, the CHINT also has the potential of being a functional device (single device capable of performing functions) as well as a light-emitting device.[11,12]

REFERENCES

1. A. Kastalsky and S. Luryi, "Novel real-space hot-electron transfer devices," *IEEE Electron Dev. Lett.*, **EDL-4**, 334 (1983).
2. A. Kastalsky, S. Luryi, A. C. Gossard and R. Hendel, "A field-effect transistor with a negative differential resistance," *IEEE Electron Dev. Lett.*, **EDL-5**, 57 (1984).
3. A. Kastalsky, R. A. Kiehl, S. Luryi, A. C. Gossard and R. Hendel, "Microwave generation in NERFET," *IEEE Electron Dev. Lett.*, **EDL-5**, 321 (1984).
4. A. A. Grinberg, A. Kastalsky and S. Luryi, "Theory of hot-electron injection in CHINT/NERFET devices," *IEEE Trans. Electron Dev.*, **ED-34**, 409 (1987).
5. I. C. Kizilyalli and K. Hess, "Physics of real-space transfer transistors," *J. Appl. Phys.*, **65**, 2005 (1989).
6. S. Luryi, "Hot-electron transistors," in S. M. Sze, Ed., *High-speed semiconductor devices*, Wiley, New York, 1990.
7. S. Luryi and A. Kastalsky, "Hot electron injection devices," *Superlattices and Microstructures*, **1**, 389 (1985).
8. S. Luryi, A. Kastalsky, A. C. Gossard and R. H. Hendel, "Charge injection transistor based on real-space hot-electron transfer," *IEEE Trans. Electron Dev.*, **ED-31**, 832 (1984).
9. A. Kastalsky, J. H. Abeles, R. Bhat, W. K. Chan and M. A. Koza, "High frequency amplification and generation in charge injection devices," *Appl. Phys. Lett.*, **48**, 71 (1986).
10. G. L. Belenky, P. A. Garbinski, P. R. Smith, S. Luryi, A. Y. Cho, R. Hamm and D. L. Sivco, "Microwave studies of self-aligned top-collector charge injection transistors," *Tech. Digest IEEE IEDM*, 423 (1993).
11. S. Luryi, P. M. Mensz, M. R. Pinto, P. A. Garbinski, A. Y. Cho and D. L. Sivco, "Charge injection logic," *Appl. Phys. Lett.*, **57**, 1787 (1990).
12. M. Mastrapasqua, S. Luryi, G. L. Belenky, P. A. Garbinski, A. Y. Cho and D. L. Sivco, "Multiterminal light-emitting logic device electrically reprogrammable between OR and NAND functions," *IEEE Trans. Electron Dev.*, **40**, 1371 (1993).

33

BIPOLAR INVERSION-CHANNEL FIELD-EFFECT TRANSISTOR

33.1 HISTORY

The BICFET (bipolar inversion-channel field-effect transistor) was proposed by Taylor and Simmons in 1985.[1] The first experimental demonstration was made with an AlGaAs–GaAs heterostructure by Taylor et al. in 1988.[2] Later that year, a device made with the InAlAs–InGaAs system was reported by Lebby et al.[3] Devices with much improved current gains were subsequently reported by Taft et al. in 1988 using Si–SiGe,[4,5] and by Kiely et al. in 1989 using the InAlGaAs–InGaAs system.[6] Large-signal and small-signal analysis of the BICFET can be found in the introductory articles by Taylor and Simmons.[1,7,8] Computer simulations were performed by Meyyappan et al.[9,10] This relatively new device is still under investigation and has not been employed in any commercial circuit.

33.2 STRUCTURE

The BICFET requires a heterojunction and an example using the AlGaAs–GaAs system for a p-channel device is shown in Fig. 33.1. Another requirement is a thin-layer charge sheet near the heterointerface. This charge sheet can be incorporated in either the narrow-energy-gap material or, preferably, the wide-energy-gap material. It is fully depleted, thus forbidding a neutral base region. This charge sheet has a thickness of 10–30 Å and a doping of

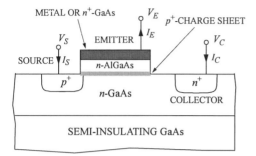

FIGURE 33.1
A p-channel BICFET using the AlGaAs–GaAs heterostructure.

10^{18}–10^{19} cm^{-3}, giving a charge-sheet density (N_s) of 10^{11} to 10^{12} cm^{-2}. The source terminal feeding the heterointerface requires self-alignment for reduced series resistance. The collector layer is on the order of 1 μm, and is doped to 10^{17} to 10^{18} cm^{-3}. The wide-energy-gap material, typically, has a thickness of ≈ 300 Å and is doped to ≈ 10^{18} cm^{-3} so that the whole layer is also fully depleted. The emitter material can be metal or heavily doped narrow-energy-gap material. Due to the stringent requirements of the planar-doped charge sheet and the thin wide-energy-gap layer, MBE is used for the film growth. For the doping types shown in Fig. 33.1, even though the collector current is carried by electrons, the inventors chose to call it a p-channel device because of the similarity of the source current (holes) to an FET current.

33.3 CHARACTERISTICS

The special feature of a BICFET is the absence of a neutral base. The establishment of a base is helped by the fully depleted charge sheet, and induced electrostatically by the collector bias. This induced base is an ultra-thin channel (≈ 100 Å) at the heterointerface. Because it does not have a neutral base, the device does not suffer from conventional problems of bipolar transistors or HBTs such as charge storage, recombination, impurity scattering, base transit delay, and large base-input capacitance. The BICFET is predicted to be capable of a f_T of ≈ 600 GHz, a high current gain of ≈ 10^5, and a high current density of 10^6 A/cm^2.

The energy-band diagram for an AlGaAs–GaAs heterojunction without a charge sheet layer is shown in Fig. 33.2(a). The GaAs surface is naturally accumulated, rather than inverted. Inversion is obtained by the introduction of a charge sheet as shown in Fig. 33.2(b). Under high collector bias, a base is established, as indicated by the layer of holes in Fig. 33.2(c), and the barrier for electrons ($\phi_{bn} + \Psi_i$) is controlled by the source voltage or current.

Defining Ψ_i and Ψ_s as the band bending in the wide-energy-gap material (insulator) and collector, respectively, and p_o as the hole concentration at the heterointerface, the equilibrium values (indicated by *) can be solved simultaneously by the following equations,[1,7]

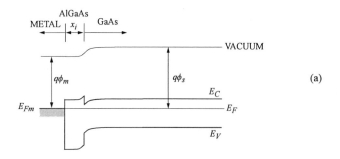

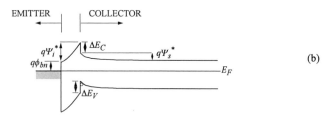

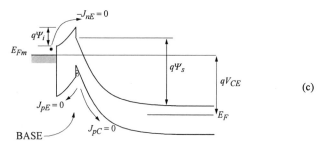

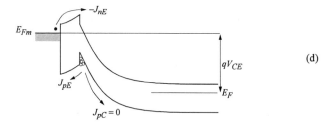

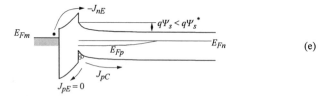

FIGURE 33.2

Energy-band diagrams of the BICFET. (a) Equilibrium, without charge sheet. (b) Equilibrium, with p^+-charge sheet. (c) Large V_{CE}, $V_S = 0$. (d) Large V_{CE}, $V_S > 0$. (e) Small V_{CE}, $V_S > 0$.

$$\phi_s - \phi_m = \Psi_i^* - \Psi_s^* \tag{33.1}$$

$$\Psi_i^* = \frac{1}{C_i}\left[qN_s - \sqrt{(2\varepsilon_s kT)\,(p_o^* + \beta_T \Psi_s^* N_D)}\right] \tag{33.2}$$

$$C_i = \frac{\varepsilon_{si}}{x_i} \tag{33.3}$$

$$p_o^* = \frac{n_i^2}{N_D}\exp\,(\beta_T \Psi_s^*) \tag{33.4}$$

where ε_{si} and ε_s are permittivities in the wide-energy-gap and narrow-energy-gap materials, respectively, and N_D is the collector doping level. The space charge in the wide-energy-gap material has been ignored because it is so thin and of moderate doping that its effect is small. Under collector and source biases, the non-equilibrium values of Ψ_i, Ψ_s, and p_o needed to calculate the currents can be solved by the next group of equations (emitter grounded),

$$V_C = \Delta\Psi_s - \Delta\Psi_i \tag{33.5}$$

$$V_S = -\Delta\Psi_i + \phi_T \ln\left(\frac{p_o}{p_o^*}\right) \tag{33.6}$$

$$\Psi_i = \frac{1}{C_i}\left[qN_s - \sqrt{(2\varepsilon_s kT)\,(p_o + \beta_T \Psi_s N_D)}\right]\,. \tag{33.7}$$

It is understood that $\Delta\Psi_i$ and $\Delta\Psi_s$ are deviations from their equilibrium values. Once Ψ_i, Ψ_s, and p_o are known, the current components shown in Fig. 33.2 can be calculated,

$$J_{nE} = qv_n N_C \exp\left[-\beta_T(\phi_{bn} + \Psi_i^*)\right]\left[\exp\,(-\beta_T \Delta\Psi_i) - 1\right] \tag{33.8}$$

$$J_{pE} = qv_p p_o \exp\left(\frac{-\Delta E_V - q\Psi_i^*}{kT}\right)\left[\exp\,(-\beta_T \Delta\Psi_i) - 1\right] \tag{33.9}$$

$$J_{pC} = \frac{qD_p}{L_p}\left[p_o \exp\,(-\beta_T \Psi_s) - \frac{n_i^2}{N_D}\right] \qquad \Psi_s < \Psi_s^*$$

$$= 0 \qquad\qquad\qquad\qquad\qquad \Psi_s > \Psi_s^* \tag{33.10}$$

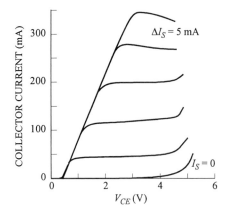

FIGURE 33.3

Common-emitter characteristics of a BICFET. (After Ref. 2)

v_n and v_p are the effective velocities of electrons and holes that combine thermionic-emission current and diffusion current.[1] At room temperature, the main current J_{nE} is dominated by thermionic-emission current in most reports. The terminal currents are

$$J_C = J_{nE} - J_{pC} \tag{33.11}$$

$$J_E = J_{pE} + J_{nE} \tag{33.12}$$

$$J_S = J_{pE} + J_{pC} \ . \tag{33.13}$$

The common-emitter output characteristics are shown in Fig. 33.3. At high V_{CE}, $J_{pC} = 0$ and the current gain, assuming $v_n \approx v_p$, is given by

$$G = \frac{I_C}{I_S} = \frac{I_{nE}}{I_{pE}} = \frac{N_C}{P_o} \exp\left(\frac{\Delta E_V - q\phi_{bn}}{kT}\right) \ . \tag{33.14}$$

It is clear that to obtain high gain, ϕ_{bn} should be minimized and ΔE_V should be maximized. The high ΔE_V preference shares the same argument as in a HBT. At low V_{CE}, the base-collector junction is forward biased (Fig. 33.2(e)). The hole current finds it easier to go to the collector rather than the emitter ($J_{pE} \approx 0$), and it contributes to negative I_C. The cut-in V_{CE} when I_C changes sign is around 0.2 V. This effect gets worse with larger ΔE_V and, thus, there is a trade-off between the cut-in V_{CE} and current gain. This drawback can be eliminated by energy-gap grading at the collector depletion region.[1] When V_{CE} is increased, J_{pC} and Ψ_i decrease, which in turn causes J_{nE} to rise. J_{nE} eventually saturates when Ψ_i is pinned to a fixed value, and further increases of V_{CE} are absorbed by $\Delta\Psi_s$.

33.4 APPLICATIONS

The BICFET is still under investigation and is not used in any commercial circuit. Because of its potential high-speed, high-gain, and high-current capability, it will be useful for high-performance circuits. However, the high cost of fabrication which requires MBE bars the technology from low-cost, high-volume products.

For general applications of a transistor, readers are referred to Appendix C3.

33.5 RELATED DEVICE

33.5.1 Bulk-Barrier Transistor

The bulk-barrier transistor, sometimes called bulk unipolar transistor, also uses a planar-doped charge sheet to create a barrier, but the heterojunction is eliminated. Notice that without the heterojunction, the bulk-barrier transistor is not a hot-electron transistor. This device was discussed by Habib and Board in 1983,[11] and a structure using a camel diode was first reported by Mader et al. (Fig. 33.4(a)).[12] A similar structure using a planar-doped-barrier diode (n-i-p^+-i-n) was reported by Chang et al. in 1985 (Fig. 33.4(b)).[13] The energy-band diagrams for the latter structure under different biases are shown in Fig. 33.5, which shows that the barrier height ϕ_b is controlled by both the collector voltage and the base voltage. The collector current is also due to thermionic emission, given by[13]

$$J_C = A^* T^2 \exp\left[-\beta_T(\phi_{bo} - k_1 V_{BE})\right] \left[\exp\left(k_2 \beta_T V_{CE}\right) - 1\right] \quad . \quad (33.15)$$

(See also Chapter 4–Planar-Doped-Barrier Diode.) The barrier height at equilibrium is determined by

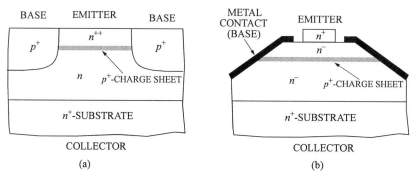

FIGURE 33.4
Bulk-barrier transistor using (a) a camel diode[12] and (b) a planar-doped-barrier diode.[13]

$$\phi_{bo} = \frac{d_1 d_2}{d_1 + d_2} \left(\frac{q N_s}{\varepsilon_s} \right) + V_n \, .$$ (33.16)

The constant k_2 is given by

$$k_2 \approx \frac{d_1}{d_1 + d_2} \, .$$ (33.17)

k_1 is a more complicated constant determined by the device geometry and the base resistance. The output characteristics of a bulk-barrier transistor are shown in

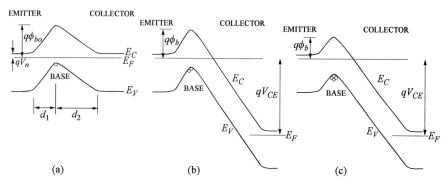

FIGURE 33.5
Energy-band diagrams of a bulk-barrier transistor using a planar-doped barrier. (a) Equilibrium. (b) $V_C > 0$. (c) With both $V_B > 0$ and $V_C > 0$.

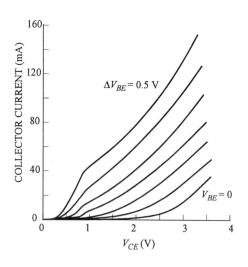

FIGURE 33.6
Common-emitter output characteristics of a bulk-barrier transistor. (After Ref. 13)

Fig. 33.6. A unified model for different versions of the bulk-barrier transistor has been presented by Al-Bustani.[14]

REFERENCES

1. G. W. Taylor and J. G. Simmons, "The bipolar inversion channel field-effect transistor (BICFET)–A new field-effect solid-state device: Theory and structures," *IEEE Trans. Electron Dev.*, **ED-32**, 2345 (1985).
2. G. W. Taylor, M. S. Lebby, A. Izabelle, B. Tell, K. Brown-Goebeler, T. Y. Chang and J. G. Simmons, "Demonstration of a *P*-channel GaAs/AlGaAs BICFET," *IEEE Electron Dev. Lett.*, **EDL-9**, 84 (1988).
3. M. S. Lebby, G. W. Taylor, A. Izabelle, B. Tell, K. Brown-Goebeler, T. Y. Chang and J. G. Simmons, "A *p*-channel BICFET in the InGaAs/InAlAs material system," *IEEE Electron Dev. Lett.*, **EDL-9**, 278 (1988).
4. R. C. Taft, J. D. Plummer and S. S. Iyer, "Fabrication of a *p*-channel BICFET in the Ge_xSi_{1-x}/Si system," *Tech. Digest IEEE IEDM*, 570 (1988).
5. R. C. Taft, J. D. Plummer and S. S. Iyer, "Advanced heterojunction Ge_xSi_{1-x}/Si bipolar devices," *Tech. Digest IEEE IEDM*, 655 (1989).
6. P. A. Kiely, G. W. Taylor, A. Izabelle, M. S. Lebby, B. Tell, K. F. Brown-Goebeler and T. Y. Chang, "An *n*-channel BICFET in the InGaAs/InAlGaAs/InAlAs material system," *IEEE Electron Dev. Lett.*, **EDL-10**, 304 (1989).
7. J. G. Simmons and G. W. Taylor, "A new ultra-high-speed heterojunction transistor," *J. Inst. Elect. Radio Eng.* (Suppl), **57**, S13 (1987).
8. G. W. Taylor And J. G. Simmons, "Small-signal model and high-frequency performance of the BICFET," *IEEE Trans. Electron Dev.*, **ED-32**, 2368 (1985).
9. M. Meyyappan, J. P. Kreskovsky and H. L. Grubin, "Numerical simulation of an AlGaAs/GaAs bipolar inversion channel field effect transistor," *Solid-State Electron.*, **31**, 1023 (1988).
10. J. G. Simmons and G. W. Taylor, "Response to 'Numerical simulation of an AlGaAs/GaAs bipolar inversion channel field effect transistor,'" *Solid-State Electron.*, **31**, 1467 (1988).
11. S. E. D. Habib and K. Board, "Theory of triangular-barrier bulk unipolar diodes including minority-carrier effects," *IEEE Trans. Electron Dev.*, **ED-30**, 90 (1983).
12. H. Mader, R. Muller and W. Beinvogl, "Bulk-barrier transistor," *IEEE Trans. Electron Dev.*, **ED-30**, 1380 (1983).
13. C. Y. Chang, Y. H. Wang, W. C. Liu and S. A. Liao, "MBE grown n^+-i-$\delta(p^+)$-i-n^+ GaAs V-groove barrier transistor," *IEEE Electron Dev. Lett.*, **EDL-6**, 123 (1985).
14. A. Al-Bustani, "Bulk unipolar transistors in the limit of nonpunch-through," *IEE Proc.*, **134**, Pt. I, 116 (1987).

CHAPTER
34

TUNNEL-EMITTER
TRANSISTOR

34.1 HISTORY

The first transistor to use the non-equilibrium properties of a thin tunneling insulator to achieve current gain was reported by Shewchun and Clarke as a surface-oxide transistor in 1973 (see Section 34.5.1).[1] This device simply consists of two MIS tunnel diode placed adjacent to each other with the semiconductor substrate as the transistor base. In 1986, much improved devices using an induced base were reported independently by three different groups. Simmons and Taylor discussed the working principle of the new device concept which they called a tunnel-emitter transistor (TETRAN), and presented limited preliminary results.[2] Moravvej-Farshi and Green showed much improved characteristics on a similar MIS structure using the same ultra-thin silicon dioxide as the tunneling insulator.[3] Their idea evolved from another device called BICFET, and they classified their device by the same name, which might have caused confusion. A different device structure but based on the same principle was reported by Matsumoto et al.[4] They used a wide-energy-gap material of a heterostructure as the insulator, and called their device an inversion-base bipolar transistor. In this chapter, the name TETRAN is adopted for both the MIS structure and the heterostructure because it is more descriptive of the device operation. More detailed analysis on the device can be found in the articles by Simmons and Taylor,[2] and by Chu and Pulfrey.[5] Computer simulation has been performed by Meyyappan and Grubin.[6]

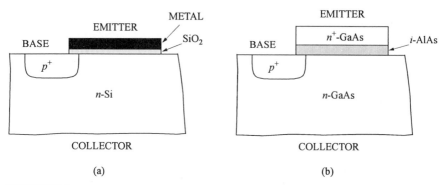

FIGURE 34.1
Structures for (a) MIS TETRAN and (b) heterostructure TETRAN.

34.2 STRUCTURE

The structures for the MIS TETRAN and heterostructure TETRAN are shown in Fig. 34.1. The commonality between them is the absence of a neutral base under the emitter. The p^+-base is self-aligned to the emitter mesa such that it connects to a base that is induced by bias. In the heterostructure TETRAN, the AlAs–GaAs and AlGaAs–GaAs systems have been employed. The wide-energy-gap material is around 100 Å thick and is undoped. This precise thickness control requires MBE or MOCVD growth. In the MIS TETRAN structure, the oxide thickness is in the range of 15–20 Å, and is grown by thermal oxidation. Controlling the growth of such a thin oxide is difficult in a production environment. The requirement for a much thinner film in this case than the heterostructure is due to a higher barrier height in the SiO_2–Si system such that it gives a comparable tunneling current. The collector doping level for both structures is not critical. Values reported range from 10^{16} cm^{-3} down to intrinsic level.

34.3 CHARACTERISTICS

The working principle of a TETRAN can best be demonstrated by the energy-band diagrams in Fig. 34.2, using the MIS TETRAN as an example. It can be seen in Fig. 34.2(a) that under equilibrium, the semiconductor surface is depleted and there is no base region. With a high collector-emitter bias V_{CE} but no base-emitter bias V_{BE}, the semiconductor is driven into deep depletion, with little change in the oxide field. Not shown in Fig. 34.2(b) is the p^+-base region which is unbiased relative to the emitter. Ignoring the work function difference between the metal and the semiconductor, the collector-emitter bias is shared between the oxide layer and the semiconductor surface,

$$V_{CE} \approx \Psi_{ox} + \Psi_s \ .$$

$$(34.1)$$

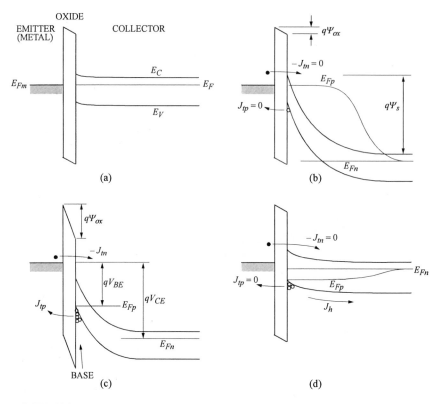

FIGURE 34.2

Energy-band diagrams of the MIS TETRAN under different bias conditions. (a) Equilibrium. (b) Large V_{CE}, V_{BE} (or I_B) = 0. (c) Large V_{CE} with $V_{BE} \neq 0$. A base is formed as an inversion layer. (d) Small V_{CE} with $V_{BE} \neq 0$.

The hole tunneling current J_{tp} in this condition is near zero since there is no net supply of holes. The electron tunneling current J_{tn} is also negligible since the oxide field is not significantly increased while Ψ_s absorbs most of the applied V_{CE}. In Fig. 34.2(c), a base-emitter bias V_{BE} increases the supply of holes and reduces the semiconductor band bending Ψ_s, and thereby increases the oxide field and, consequently, the electron tunneling current. In addition to the higher field, another factor that increases the J_{tn} is the larger range of energy in which electrons can tunnel, since as shown in Fig. 34.2(b), electrons cannot tunnel into the forbidden gap. The hole tunneling current is also increased by the same V_{BE}, but the current level is much lower. Among other reasons, the available holes for tunneling are less abundant and the barrier height for holes is larger. The ratio of J_{tn} (or collector current), increased by V_{BE}, to J_{tp} (base current), increased by the same V_{BE}, contributes to the common-emitter current gain. A gain of 120 has been reported.[3] One difference in the heterostructure TETRAN operation is that J_{nt}

could be caused by Fowler-Nordheim tunneling rather than direct tunneling due to the thicker tunneling layer and lower barrier height.

The common-emitter output characteristics for an MIS TETRAN are shown in Fig. 34.3. The current gain at high V_{CE} has been discussed above. At low V_{CE}, there are some peculiarities compared to a bipolar transistor. There exists a cut-in V_{CE} voltage below which the collector current is negative. This cut-in voltage is around 0.6–0.9 V. The source of this anomaly can be understood with the energy-band diagram of Fig. 34.2(d). In addition to the hole tunneling current to the emitter, there is another hole current I_h between the base and the collector. When V_{BC} is negative, I_h is a generation current (reverse direction) which could be ignored. For small V_{CE}, V_{BC} could be positive, and I_h is a forward-bias diffusion current, given by

$$J_h = \frac{q D_p n_i^2}{L_p N_D} \left[\exp\left(\frac{q V_{BC}}{kT}\right) - 1 \right] . \tag{34.2}$$

When $J_h > J_{tn}$, negative collector current results. With increasing V_{CE}, J_h is reduced and J_{tp} is increased, which results in a sharp rise in J_{tn} and collector current I_C. I_C eventually saturates with V_{CE} when any additional bias is absorbed by the semiconductor Ψ_s and J_{tp} is constant.

Another drawback of the TETRAN is a large V_{BE} threshold to establish a base.[4,6,7] This voltage can be estimated from Figs. 34.2(b) and 34.2(c) to be a large fraction of the energy gap. This threshold can be as large as 1.8 V for a AlAs–GaAs structure.[7] The large V_{BE} threshold is the fundamental cause of the cut-in V_{CE}.

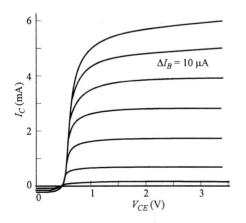

FIGURE 34.3
Common-emitter output characteristics of an MIS TETRAN. (After Ref. 3)

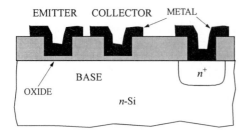

FIGURE 34.4
Structure of a surface-oxide transistor.

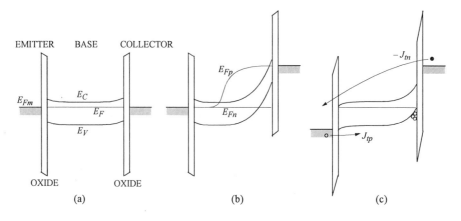

FIGURE 34.5
Energy-band diagrams of a surface-oxide transistor under different biases. (a) Equilibrium. (b) Large V_{BC}, no hole injection from emitter. (c) Large V_{BC}, with hole injection.

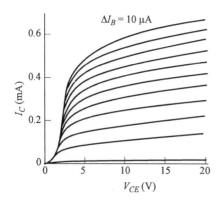

FIGURE 34.6
Common-emitter output characteristics of a surface-oxide transistor. (After Ref. 9)

34.4 APPLICATIONS

The TETRAN has not been used in any commercial circuit or even demonstrated in any circuit configuration. Heterostructure TETRAN processing has been shown to be compatible with that of a SISFET so that integration of these devices is possible.[8] Nevertheless, the potential application of the device seems to be rather limited. Although the transit time through the thin induced base is very short, the cut-off frequency of the MIS TETRAN has been analyzed to be only ≈ 1 GHz due to the large capacitance of the ultra-thin insulator.[5] The heterostructure TETRAN would probably be faster, but it requires low-temperature operation due to its large thermionic emission current over the low barrier. In general, tunneling current is too low to drive parasitic capacitance to operate real circuits at reasonable speed. Besides, the technology for the MIS TETRAN is not easily controlled while that for the heterostructure TETRAN is too expensive to justify its medium performance.

For general applications of a transistor, the readers can refer to Appendix C3.

34.5 RELATED DEVICE

34.5.1 Surface-Oxide Transistor

The surface-oxide transistor was first demonstrated by Shewchun and Clarke in 1973,[1] and more recently by Ruzyllo et al. in 1980.[9,10] The structure is shown in Fig. 34.4 where two identical MIS tunnel diode structures (may be of different area) are placed close together. The transistor action is based on the non-equilibrium properties of the MIS tunnel diode under reverse bias.[11,12] By non-equilibrium it is meant that electron and hole quasi-Fermi levels spilt such that $E_{Fn} \neq E_{Fp}$. As shown in Fig. 34.5(b), under a high V_{BC}, the oxide is too thin to confine a large hole concentration at the surface, and the semiconductor is driven into deep depletion. With the injection of holes from the emitter, excess holes accumulate at the Si surface under the collector and help to maintain equilibrium. In doing so, Si band bending is reduced, and the oxide field is increased for a much enhanced electron tunneling current. The large increase of J_{tn} due to a change in J_{tp} is accountable for the current gain. Most of J_{tp} originated from the emitter becomes the base current. The common-emitter characteristics are shown in Fig. 34.6.

REFERENCES

1. J. Shewchun and R. A. Clarke, "The surface oxide transistor (SOT)," *Solid-State Electron.*, **16**, 213 (1973).
2. J. G. Simmons and G. W. Taylor, "Concepts of gain at an oxide-semiconductor interface and their application to the TETRAN – A tunnel emitter transistor – and to the MIS switching device," *Solid-State Electron.*, **29**, 287 (1986).

3. M. K. Moravvej-Farshi and M. A. Green, "Operational silicon bipolar inversion-channel field-effect transistor (BICFET)," *IEEE Electron Dev. Lett.*, **EDL-7**, 513 (1986).

4. K. Matsumoto, Y. Hayashi, N. Hashizume, T. Yao, M. Kato, T. Miyashita, N. Fukuhara, H. Hirashima and T. Kinosada, "GaAs inversion-base bipolar transistor (GaAs IBT)," *IEEE Electron Dev. Lett.*, **EDL-7**, 627 (1986).

5. K. M. Chu and D. L. Pulfrey, "An analysis of the DC and small-signal AC performance of the tunnel emitter transistor," *IEEE Trans. Electron Dev.*, **ED-35**, 188 (1988).

6. M. Meyyappan and H. L. Grubin, "Modeling of an inversion base bipolar transistor," *IEEE Trans. Electron Dev.*, **ED-36**, 1 (1989).

7. C. I. Huang, M. E. Cheney, M. J. Paulus, J. E. Scheihing, J. O. Crist, M. E. Sopko, C. A. Bozada, C. E. Stutz, R. L. Jones and K. R. Evans, "A study of GaAs inversion-base bipolar transistor," *Proc. IEEE/Cornell Conf. on Advanced Concepts in High Speed Semicond. Dev. and Circuits*, 293 (1987).

8. K. Matsumoto, Y. Hayashi, T. Kojima, T. Nagata and T. Yoshimoto, "Integration of a GaAs SISFET and GaAs inversion-base bipolar transistor," *Japanese J. Appl. Phys.*, **27**, L2427 (1988).

9. J. Ruzyllo, "Lateral MIS tunnel transistor," *IEEE Electron Dev. Lett.*, **EDL-1**, 197 (1980).

10. J. Ruzyllo, K. Kucharski and A. Jakubowski, "Effect of minority carrier injection on lateral current in MIS tunnel structures," *Solid-State Electron.*, **23**, 1041 (1980).

11. R. A. Clarke and J. Shewchun, "Non-equilibrium effects on metal-oxide-semiconductor tunnel currents," *Solid-State Electron.*, **14**, 957 (1971).

12. M. A. Green and J. Shewchun, "Current multiplication in metal-insulator-semiconductor (MIS) tunnel diodes," *Solid-State Electron.*, **17**, 349 (1974).

CHAPTER
35

PLANAR-DOPED-BARRIER
TRANSISTOR

35.1 HISTORY

Starting in 1979, Shannon et al. presented different versions of a new hot-electron transistor they called the camel transistor.[1-5] These camel transistors (discussed in more detail in Section 35.5.1) all use a camel diode to form the barrier between the collector and the base while the emitter-base junction is formed either by a Schottky barrier or another camel diode. Similar to a camel diode, a planar-doped-barrier diode, developed around 1980 (see Chapter 4), uses a fully depleted space-charge layer to form the potential barrier. When two planar-doped-barrier diodes are stacked, a planar-doped-barrier transistor is formed. The first planar-doped-barrier transistor was reported by Malik et al. in 1981,[6,7] followed by Hollis et al. in 1983.[8] This device, so far, has not been used in any commercial product and is used mainly as a research tool to study the properties of hot electrons.

35.2 STRUCTURE

The structure of a planar-doped-barrier transistor is shown in Fig. 35.1. The middle n^+-layer connects two planar-doped-barrier diodes together and serves as the base. It reportedly has thickness in the range of 600–2000 Å and a doping range of 4×10^{17}–1×10^{18} cm^{-3}. The p^+-planar-doped layers must be fully depleted, so they must be thin, around 100 Å, with a doping level $\approx 1 \times 10^{18}$ cm^{-3}. The intrinsic-layer thickness typically is below 2500 Å. Due to the stringent requirement of the planar-doped layers, MBE or MOCVD is required to grow the structure. Even though there is no special requirement on the semiconductor

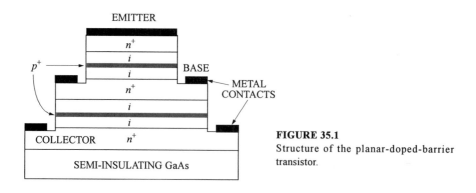

FIGURE 35.1
Structure of the planar-doped-barrier transistor.

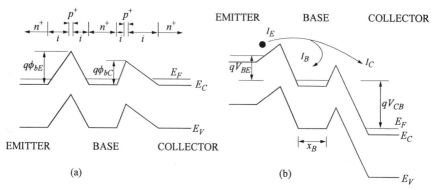

FIGURE 35.2
Energy-band diagrams of the planar-doped-barrier transistor (a) under thermal equilibrium and (b) under operation.

material, most reported structures use GaAs because of its relatively advanced MBE technology.

35.3 CHARACTERISTICS

The energy-band diagram of the planar-doped-barrier transistor is shown in Fig. 35.2. Under normal transistor operation, hot electrons are injected from the emitter to the base by thermionic emission. The formation of the barrier and the *I-V* characteristics of a planar-doped-barrier diode are discussed in Chapter 4 and will not be repeated here. If these hot electrons do not lose a significant amount of energy traversing the base, they can surmount the collector barrier and be collected as collector current. The fraction of hot electrons unable to reach the collector results in a base current. The common-base current gain is nearly equal to the base transfer ratio which is given by

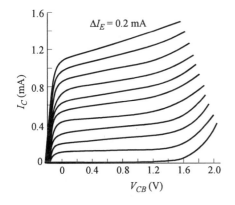

FIGURE 35.3
Common-base output characteristics of a planar-doped-barrier transistor at 77 K. (After Ref. 8)

$$\alpha_T = \frac{I_C}{I_E}$$

$$\approx \exp\left(-\frac{x_B}{l_m}\right) \ .$$

(35.1)

It has been pointed out that the mean free path l_m in the base is a strong function of the base doping level.[8]

The barrier height near the collector ϕ_{bC} is designed to be slightly lower than the one near the emitter ϕ_{bE}. This is to minimize the loss of hot electrons to the base. To minimize the change in ϕ_{bC} with the collector-base bias, the intrinsic layer next to the base facing the collector is made much thinner than the other intrinsic layers. However, too abrupt a potential profile will result in excessive quantum-mechanical reflection, which is a major drawback for the metal-base transistor. A good compromise for this intrinsic layer thickness is calculated to be 200–300 Å.[9]

A set of common-base output characteristics are shown in Fig. 35.3. Usually the transistor must operate in a low temperature ambient because of the large thermionic emission in the collector-base junction at room temperature.

35.4 APPLICATIONS

The planar-doped-barrier transistor up to now has not be applied in any circuit configuration and has no commercial value. Its advantage is high-speed operation due to ballistic transport through the base for reduced base transit time, the absence of minority carrier storage, and small capacitance. It is expected to have an f_T higher than 100 GHz.[2] For general applications of a transistor, the readers are referred to Appendix C3.

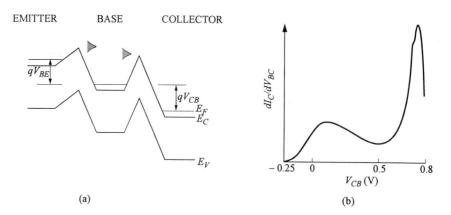

FIGURE 35.4

Using a planar-doped-barrier transistor as a hot-electron spectrometer. (a) Energy-band diagram. (b) Energy spectrum of hot electrons. (After Ref. 10) Energy (barrier) is largest with small V_{CB}. Peak at low V_{CB} indicates ballistic hot electrons.

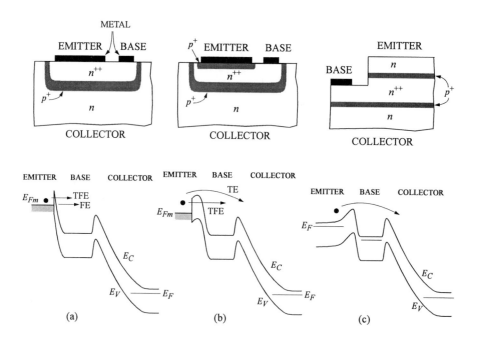

FIGURE 35.5

Different versions of camel transistor, with their energy-band diagrams under operation. The difference is the emitter structure using (a) a Schottky barrier, (b) a Schottky diode with barrier enhancement, and (c) a camel diode.

One application of the planar-doped-barrier transistor is in a hot-electron spectrometer to study the energy spectrum of hot carriers. As shown by the energy-band diagram of this specialized structure (Fig. 35.4(a)), the collector barrier is designed to be larger than the emitter barrier, and it is varied by a collector-base voltage. When this barrier is scanned, the differential collector current follows the energy distribution of hot electrons in the base (Fig. 35.4(b)).

35.5 RELATED DEVICES

35.5.1 Camel Transistor

The first version of the camel transistor, demonstrated by Shannon in 1979,[1] has a camel diode as the collector-base junction, and a Schottky barrier on degenerate semiconductor as the emitter (Fig. 35.5(a)). The injection mechanism is via field emission (FE) and thermionic-field emission (TFE). A slightly different structure, reported by Shannon and Gill in 1981,[3] has an additional ion implantation at the surface to enhance the barrier height (Fig. 35.5(b)). The injection is by thermionic-field emission and thermionic emission (TE). The third structure incorporates another camel diode for the emitter-base junction, and the injection is pure thermionic emission over the barrier (Fig. 35.5(c)). This structure was proposed by Shannon in 1981,[2] and experimentally demonstrated by Woodcock et al. in 1985.[4,5] The structures in Figs. 35.5(a) and 35.5(b) can be formed by ion implantation to tailor the doping profile near the surface, while the structure in Fig. 35.5(c) requires well-controlled epitaxial growth such as MBE and MOCVD.

35.5.2 Field-Effect Hot-Electron Transistor

The field-effect hot-electron transistor (name given by the author since the one used by the few publications–vertical FET is confusing with other devices such as the permeable-base transistor and other vertical FETs) has only one planar-doped barrier between the source and the drain (Fig. 35.6).[11] The

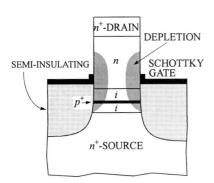

FIGURE 35.6
Schematic structure of a field-effect hot-electron transistor using a planar-doped barrier as a hot-electron launcher.

modulation of the current is controlled by the net channel opening that is pinched by the depletion regions under the gates, similar to a JFET. The advantage of this transistor compared to other FETs is the ballistic transport in the channel, leading to high transconductance and high intrinsic speed.

REFERENCES

1. J. M. Shannon, "Hot-electron camel transistor," *Solid-State and Electron Dev.*, **3**, 142 (1979).
2. J. M. Shannon, "Calculated performance of monolithic hot-electron transistors," *IEE Proc.*, **128**, 134 (1981).
3. J. M. Shannon and A. Gill, "High current gain in monolithic hot-electron transistors," *Electronics Lett.*, **17**, 620 (1981).
4. J. M. Woodcock, J. J. Harris and J. M. Shannon, "Monolithic hot electron transistors in GaAs with high current gain," *Physica*, **134B**, 111 (1985).
5. J. M. Woodcock, J. J. Harris and J. M. Shannon, "Controlled growth of GaAs layers for monolithic hot electron transistors," *J. Vac. Sci. Technol.*, **B4**, 609 (1986).
6. R. J. Malik, M. A. Hollis, L. F. Eastman, D. W. Woodard, C. E. C. Wood and T. R. AuCoin, "GaAs planar doped barrier transistors," *1981 IEEE Device Res. Conf., IEEE Trans. Electron Dev.*, **ED-28**, 1246 (1981).
7. R. J. Malik, M. A. Hollis, L. F. Eastman, D. W. Woodard, C. E. C. Wood and T. R. AuCoin, "GaAs planar-doped barrier transistors grown by molecular beam epitaxy," *Proc. 8th Biennial Cornell Conf. Active Microwave Semicond. Dev. & Circuits*, 87 (1981).
8. M. A. Hollis, S. C. Palmateer, L. F. Eastman, N. V. Dandekar and P. M. Smith, "Importance of electron scattering with coupled plasmon-optical phonon modes in GaAs planar-doped barrier transistors," *IEEE Electron Dev. Lett.*, **EDL-4**, 440 (1983).
9. A. Chandra and L. F. Eastman, "Quantum mechanical reflection at triangular 'planar-doped' potential barriers for transistors," *J. Appl. Phys.*, **53**, 9165 (1982).
10. J. R. Hayes and A. F. J. Levi, "Dynamics of extreme nonequilibrium electron transport in GaAs," *IEEE J. Quan. Electron.*, **QE-22**, 1744 (1986).
11. Y. H. Won, K. Yamasaki, T. Daniels-Race, P. J. Tasker, W. J. Schaff and L. F. Eastman, "A high voltage-gain GaAs vertical field-effect transistor with an InGaAs/GaAs planar-doped barrier launcher," *IEEE Electron Dev. Lett.*, **11**, 376 (1990).

CHAPTER
36

HETEROJUNCTION
HOT-ELECTRON
TRANSISTOR

36.1 HISTORY

The heterojunction hot-electron transistor has an emitter-base junction that is formed by an abrupt heterostructure or by graded composition, and emitter injection is by thermionic emission. An injector with a graded-composition barrier was first studied in a hot-electron spectrometer by Long et al. in 1986,[1,2] as an alternative to a tunneling injector or a planar-doped-barrier injector. The abrupt heterojunction used as hot-electron emitter in a hot-electron transistor was first reported by Levi and Chiu in 1987,[3,4] and later by Taira et al.[5] and Kawai et al.[6] The heterojunction hot-electron transistor was analyzed theoretically by Ershov et al.[7] This device is still in its infancy and limited literature is available.

36.2 STRUCTURE

For a heterojunction with graded composition, the $Al_xGa_{1-x}As$–GaAs system has been examined. The structure is shown in Fig. 36.1(a). The base, in this case, is heavily doped n-GaAs. For the abrupt heterojunction, the AlSbAs–InAs–GaSb (asymmetrical) and GaSb–InAs–GaSb (symmetrical) systems have been studied. Example of the former structure is shown in Fig. 36.1(b). The thin base (≈ 100 Å InAs) is modulation doped from the adjacent emitter and collector layers, and has a carrier density of $\approx 2\times10^{12}$ cm^{-2}. This is the main difference from an induced-base transistor whose base conductivity has to be induced by a collector-base bias.

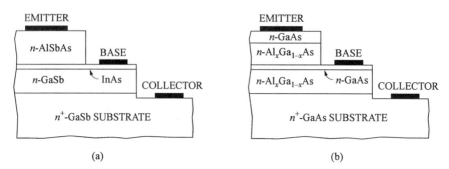

FIGURE 36.1
Structures of heterojunction hot-electron transistor using (a) abrupt heterojunctions and (b) graded-composition junctions.

36.3 CHARACTERISTICS

The energy-band diagrams for the heterojunction hot-electron transistor are shown in Fig. 36.2. Notice that at the InAs–GaSb interface, the E_C of InAs is below the E_V of GaSb, but this property is not critical for the device operation. The emitter injection of hot carriers is by thermionic emission. An example of the transistor characteristics, of a device using abrupt heterojunctions, is shown in Fig. 36.3. A common-emitter current gain β of larger than 10 has been obtained at room temperature. To minimize quantum-mechanical reflection at the base-collector interface, unequal barrier heights for emitter and collector are critical. Minimum reflection is met by[3]

$$\frac{m^*_B}{m^*_C} = \frac{\phi_E}{\phi_E - \phi_C} \tag{36.1}$$

where m^*_B and m^*_C are the effective masses in the base and collector, respectively. The quantum-mechanical reflection can also be minimized by a graded base-collector heterointerface.

Figure 36.3 also shows an offset of V_{CE} (≈ 0.5 V). This offset comes from the fact that ϕ_E is larger than ϕ_C, a condition to minimize the quantum-mechanical reflection. Ideally, for a low V_{CE} offset, ϕ_C should be larger than ϕ_E so that at low V_{CE} near the origin, the base current goes to the emitter instead of the collector. Otherwise, the base current prefers to go to the collector, and negative collector current is the cause of this V_{CE} offset. Additionally, this offset is worsened by structures having a base-collector junction area much larger than that of the base-emitter junction.

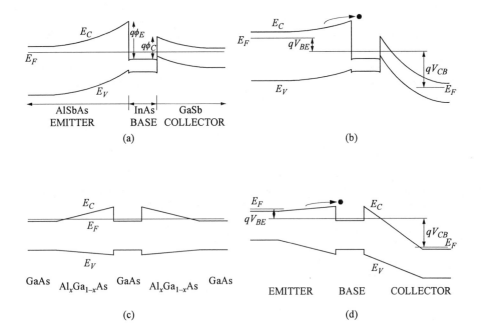

FIGURE 36.2
Energy-band diagrams of heterojunction hot-electron transistors. (a) Abrupt heterostructure, without bias and (b) with bias. (c) Graded-composition heterostructure, without bias and (d) with bias.

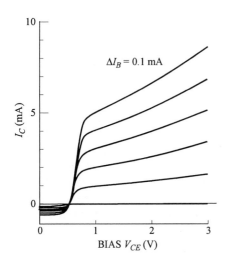

FIGURE 36.3
Common-emitter characteristics of a heterojunction hot-electron transistor. (After Ref. 3)

36.4 APPLICATIONS

The heterojunction hot-electron transistor is still under investigation and has no commercial significance currently. The limitations are low β, an offset in V_{CE}, and complicated processing. This device can be used in fundamental study such as hot-electron spectroscopy. For general applications of a transistor, the readers are referred to Appendix C3.

REFERENCES

1. A. P. Long, P. H. Beton, M. J. Kelly and T. M. Kerr, "Hot-electron injection by graded $Al_xGa_{1-x}As$," *Electronics Lett.*, **22**, 130 (1986).
2. A. P. Long, P. H. Beton and M. J. Kelly, "Hot-electron transport in heavily doped GaAs," *Semicond. Sci. Technol.*, **1**, 63 (1986).
3. A. F. J. Levi and T. H. Chiu, "Room-temperature operation of hot-electron transistors," *Appl. Phys. Lett.*, **51**, 984 (1987).
4. A. F. J. Levi and T. H. Chiu, "Unipolar hot electron transistors," *Physica Scripta.* **123**, 227 (1988).
5. K. Taira, F. Nakamura, I. Hase, H. Kawai and Y. Mori, "InAs/GaSb hot electron transistors grown by low-pressure metalorganic chemical vapor deposition," *Japanese J. Appl. Phys.*, **29**, L2414 (1990).
6. H. Kawai, K. Funato, K. Taira and F. Nakamura, "Two DEG-base GaSb/InAs hot electron transistors," *Microelectronic Eng.*, **15**, 95 (1991).
7. M. Y. Ershov, A. A. Zakharova and V. I. Ryzhil, "Theory of hot electron transport in heterostructure transistors," *Sov. Phys. Semicond.*, **24**, 796 (1990).

CHAPTER 37

INDUCED-BASE
TRANSISTOR

37.1 HISTORY

The induced-base transistor was proposed by Luryi in 1985.[1,2] It resembles an older device, the metal-base transistor, with the metal base replaced by a two-dimensional electron gas. The new device concept was first demonstrated in a GaAs–AlGaAs heterostructure by Chang et al. in the following year.[3,4] Up to now very few papers have reported on this device.

37.2 STRUCTURE

The device structure is shown in Fig. 37.1. The transistor base consists of a quantum well formed by heterojunctions. The emitter-base junction is a triangular barrier formed by a graded-energy-gap layer, and the collector-base junction is a rectangular barrier formed by abrupt heterojunctions. The thickness of the quantum well can be as small as 10 nm, and the emitter barrier and collector barrier layers range from 50 to 200 nm. All the middle layers are undoped, and the emitter and collector outer layers are heavily doped. Due to the small dimension of the quantum well, MBE or MOCVD is required for the epitaxial growth. To contact the base within the quantum well, Au-Ge is deposited on the exposed V-grooves that are formed by orientation-dependent wet chemical etching.

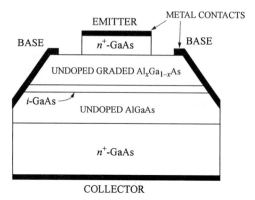

FIGURE 37.1
Structure of an induced-base transistor. In this example, the emitter junction is formed by a graded-energy-gap layer. (After Ref. 3)

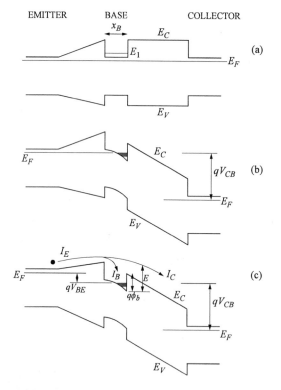

FIGURE 37.2
Energy-band diagrams of an induced-base transistor under different biases. (a) Equilibrium. E_1 is the lowest quantized subband. (b) With V_{CB} only. (c) With V_{CB} and V_{BE}.

37.3 CHARACTERISTICS

The main feature of an induced-base transistor is the way its base is electrostatically formed. As shown in Fig. 37.2(a), under thermal equilibrium, the base has very high sheet resistance in the direction perpendicular to the heterointerface, since the quantum well is undoped. Within the quantum well, the lowest quantized subband E_1 is indicated. Since this E_1 is above the Fermi level, it is not populated with electrons under equilibrium. Once there is a collector-base bias V_{CB}, Fig. 37.2(b) shows that E_1 is pulled below the Fermi level, and a two-dimensional electron gas is induced. It has been estimated that the maximum carrier density that can be induced in a GaAs–AlGaAs system is around 2×10^{12} cm^{-2}, limited only by breakdown.[1,2] Since the quantum well is undoped, its carrier mobility is high, and the charge sheet is calculated to give a sheet resistance of ≈ 400 $\Omega/\square$ at room temperature. Experimentally, a slightly lower value has been demonstrated.[3,4]

Figure 37.2(c) shows the injection of electrons from the emitter by a base-emitter bias, via thermionic emission. This current is the forward current of a graded-composition barrier (see Section 5.5.1). The base transport factor α_T is limited mainly by two mechanisms,

$$I_C = \alpha_T I_E$$
$$= \alpha_B \alpha_{BC} I_E \ . \tag{37.1}$$

α_B is the loss of hot electrons to the base through scattering, given by

$$\alpha_B = \exp\left(\frac{-x_B}{l_m}\right) \ . \tag{37.2}$$

This factor is estimated to be close to unity since x_B is small, and the mean free path l_m in an undoped semiconductor is large. Another argument is that the time spent by hot electrons in traversing the base is only in the order of 0.01 ps which is too short for significant scattering.[1] α_{BC} is due to the quantum-mechanical reflection at the base-collector interface, given by[5]

$$\alpha_{BC} \approx 1 - \left[\frac{1 - \sqrt{1 - \dfrac{q\phi_b}{E}}}{1 + \sqrt{1 - \dfrac{q\phi_b}{E}}} \right]^2 \ . \tag{37.3}$$

Unlike in a metal-base transistor, the hot-electron energy E in Fig. 37.2(c) is much larger than the barrier $q\phi_b$, and α_{BC} is estimated to be high, ≈ 0.97.[1,2] Experimentally, an overall α_T of 0.96 has been reported.[3,4] The common-emitter output characteristics of an induced-base transistor are shown in Fig. 37.3.

It has been suggested that other variations of the emitter barrier can be incorporated. Figure 37.4 shows the energy-band diagram of a structure under operation using a planar-doped barrier in the emitter.[2] The two planar-doped p^+- and n^+-layers are fully depleted.

37.4 APPLICATIONS

The induced-base transistor so far is limited only to research interest and has no commercial value. It offers some advantages over other hot-electron transistors. In transistors with doped semiconductor base such as the THETA or the planar-doped-barrier transistor, a thinner base enhances the transfer ratio but the base resistance becomes too large. In the induced-base transistor, the conductance is provided by a two-dimensional charge sheet and is independent of the quantum well thickness, at least down to ≈ 10 nm. Compared to a metal-base transistor which has very low base resistance, it has much reduced quantum-mechanical reflection at the base-collector interface, and is easier to fabricate without suffering from pinholes since it is an all-semiconductor structure.

For general applications of a transistor, the readers are referred to Appendix C3.

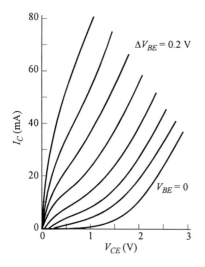

FIGURE 37.3
Common-base output characteristics of an induced-base transistor. (After Ref. 3)

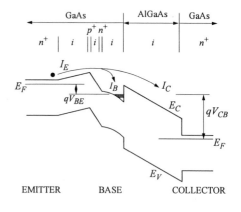

FIGURE 37.4
Energy-band diagram of an induced-base transistor using a planar-doped barrier in the emitter.

REFERENCES

1. S. Luryi, "An induced base hot-electron transistor," *IEEE Electron Dev. Lett.*, **EDL-6**, 178 (1985).
2. S. Luryi, "Induced base transistor," *Physica*, **134B**, 466 (1985).
3. C. Y. Chang, W. C. Liu, M. S. Jame, Y. H. Wang, S. Luryi and S. M. Sze, "Induced base transistor fabricated by molecular beam epitaxy," *IEEE Electron Dev. Lett.*, **EDL-7**, 497 (1986).
4. C. Y. Chang, W. C. Liu, M. S. Jame and Y. H. Wang, "The new high speed device: The TEG-base transistor," *Extended Abstracts 18th (1986 Int.) Conf. Solid State Dev. and Materials,* 355 (1986).
5. S. Luryi, "Hot-electron injection and resonant-tunneling heterojunction devices," in F. Capasso and G. Margaritondo, Eds., *Heterojunction band discontinuities: Physics and device applications*, Elsevier Science, New York, 1987.

CHAPTER
38

RESONANT-TUNNELING BIPOLAR TRANSISTOR

38.1 HISTORY

A resonant-tunneling bipolar transistor (RTBT or RBT) incorporates a double-barrier quantum well in a bipolar transistor. The two-terminal resonant-tunneling diode, whose current flows across a double-barrier quantum well, had undergone basic development in the early 1970s (see Chapter 10). The RTBT in its original form, as proposed by Capasso and Kiehl in 1985, placed the quantum well in the base region.[1] The device was subsequently demonstrated by Capasso et al. in 1986.[2] Other variations of the structures were also presented shortly after. Futatsugi et al. studied structures with the quantum well placed in the emitter-base junction,[3] and also within the emitter region.[4] The first transistor using resonant tunneling with multiple negative-resistance regions (multiple current peaks) was demonstrated by Capasso et al. in 1988, using serial quantum wells in the emitter.[5] A review of the RTBT can be found in Ref. 6.

38.2 STRUCTURE

Structures of different variations of the RTBTs, depending on the placement of the double-barrier quantum well, are shown in Fig. 38.1. The examples shown use GaAs–AlGaAs heterostructures but the GaInAs–AlInAs system has been shown to yield better transistor performance. Contact to the base is made by the mesa structure where the base is exposed. The base layer thickness ranges between 2000 Å and 3000 Å, while those for the emitter and collector are slightly larger.

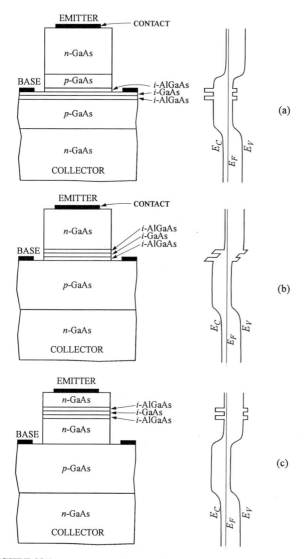

FIGURE 38.1
Variations of the RTBT structures and their energy-band diagrams at equilibrium. The placement of the double-barrier quantum well is (a) in the base region, (b) at the base-emitter junction, and (c) in the emitter region.

The quantum-well layer has a typical thickness of ≈ 50 Å, surrounded by two barrier layers which lie in the range of 20–50 Å. All three layers that form the quantum well are undoped. Intrinsic GaAs spacer layers of ≈ 15 Å outside the barrier layers are usually used to avoid diffusion of dopants to the barrier layers.

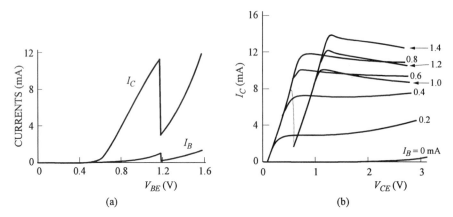

FIGURE 38.2

Characteristics of an RTBT. (a) Collect and base currents as a function of V_{BE}, for a fixed V_{CE} of 2 V. (b) Common-emitter output characteristics. (After Ref. 7)

Like other quantum-well devices, the RTBTs are grown with MBE to ensure sharp composition and doping interface.

Besides those shown in Fig. 38.1, other variations of RTBTs have been proposed or demonstrated. For example, the emitter-base *p-n* junction of Fig. 38.1(a) can be modified with an anisotype heterojunction, or with additional tunneling barriers. Nevertheless, the characteristics discussed below should be, for the most part, applicable to all structures.

38.3 CHARACTERISTICS

The general characteristics of an RTBT are shown in Fig. 38.2. In Fig. 38.2(a), the terminal currents all show a negative differential transconductance as a function of base-to-emitter voltage V_{BE}. This can be explained by the energy-band diagrams shown in Fig. 38.3 using, as an example, a structure that has the quantum well residing in the emitter region (Fig. 38.1(c)). Inside the quantum well, the energy subbands are quantized, and the bottom of each subband can be approximated by

$$E_n - E_C = \frac{h^2 n^2}{8m^* W^2} \ , \qquad n = 1, 2, 3... \qquad (38.1)$$

where W is the quantum-well thickness. Since resonant tunneling requires the conservation of carrier energy and lateral momentum, maximum tunneling occurs when the conduction-band edge E_C in the outer emitter layer aligns to the quantized level, as shown in Fig. 38.3(b) (see Chapter 10–Resonant-Tunneling Diode). Beyond that V_{BE} bias, the number of electrons satisfying energy and momentum requirements decreases, and the tunneling current starts to decrease, giving rise to negative transconductance. With further increase in V_{BE}, the current goes through a valley point and then rises again. This second rise of current could be due to resonant tunneling through the second quantized level, inelastic tunneling, or thermionic emission over the barriers. The best reported value for the peak-to-valley current ratio is about 6 at room temperature, and 20 at 77 K.

The common-emitter output characteristics shown in Fig. 38.2(b) also display negative differential resistance as a function of collector-to-emitter bias V_{CE}. For small base currents I_B, the negative resistance in the V_{BE} direction in Fig. 38.2(a) is not reached, and the transistor behaves more or less like a regular bipolar transistor. With higher I_B, the collector current goes through a peak, followed by a region of negative differential resistance. The mechanism for this can be explained as follows. When V_{CE} is increased, V_{BE} increases. The relationship between V_{CE} and V_{BE}, for a fixed I_B, is depicted in Fig. 38.4. When V_{CE} increases, electrons traversing the base are extracted by the collector more

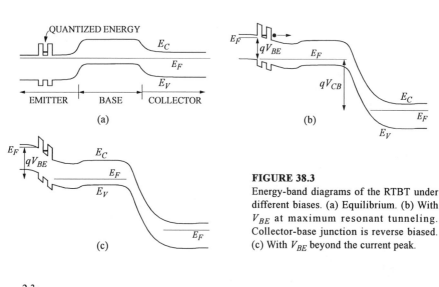

(a)

(b)

(c)

FIGURE 38.3
Energy-band diagrams of the RTBT under different biases. (a) Equilibrium. (b) With V_{BE} at maximum resonant tunneling. Collector-base junction is reverse biased. (c) With V_{BE} beyond the current peak.

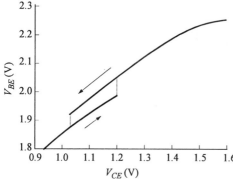

FIGURE 38.4
Change of V_{BE} as a function of V_{CE}, for a fixed I_B. (After Ref. 8)

efficiently. This reduces the electron recombination in the base. To maintain the same I_B, V_{BE} has to increase. A jump in V_{BE} corresponds to the quenching of resonant-tunneling current. The increase of V_{BE} has two effects. First it increases the component of hole current, and degrades the injection efficiency (and electron current). Second, the collector-to-base voltage is decreased and it degrades the base transport factor. Both of these factors contribute to the decrease of I_C with increase of V_{CE}. It can be seen also in Fig. 38.2(b) that for higher V_{CE}, I_C increases and then decreases with I_B, indicating a region of negative current gain. The maximum DC current gain I_C/I_B (β) observed is around 60 at room temperature, and 150 at 77 K. The RTBT has been measured to give a cutoff frequency f_T of 24 GHz. A maximum current density close to 10^5 A/cm^2 has been shown.

For the RTBT to perform efficiently as a functional device (a single device capable of performing more complex functions), multiple regions of negative resistance/transconductance or multiple current peaks are preferable. This has been achieved with multiple quantum wells in the emitter layer.[5,9]

It would be interesting to compare the difference between an RTBT and an RHET (see Chapter 39). The RTBT does not have a barrier in the collector-base junction, and so the carrier energy in the case is not very critical in order for the electrons to be collected by the collector. The collector-base isolation here is by a *p-n* junction which has very low leakage. On the other hand, a higher hole current might arise between the base and the emitter and degrade the emitter injection efficiency.

38.4 APPLICATIONS

Being a three-terminal device, the RTBT has a tunable negative differential resistance as well as a negative differential transconductance, and more importantly, it provides isolation between the input and output circuits. Possessing characteristics of multiple current peaks is an important factor for an efficient functional device. Examples of applications are analog-to-digital converter, frequency multiplier, parity generator, multi-value logic and multi-value memory.[6] The RTBT requires precise control of the layer thicknesses and thus necessitates expensive epitaxial techniques such as MBE. It is limited only to research interest now and has no commercial value yet.

For general applications of negative resistance, the readers are referred to Appendix C2.

REFERENCES

1. F. Capasso and R. A. Kiehl, "Resonant tunneling transistor with quantum well base and high-energy injection: A new negative differential resistance device," *J. Appl. Phys.*, **58**, 1366 (1985).

2. F. Capasso, S. Sen, A. C. Gossard, A. L. Hutchinson and J. H. English, "Quantum-well resonant tunneling bipolar transistor operating at room temperature," *IEEE Electron Dev. Lett.*, **EDL-7**, 573 (1986).
3. T. Futatsugi, Y. Yamaguchi, K. Imamura, S. Muto, N. Yokoyama and A. Shibatomi, "A resonant-tunneling bipolar transistor (RBT) – A new functional device with high current gain," *Japanese J. Appl. Phys.*, **26**, L131 (1987).
4. T. Futatsugi, Y. Yamaguchi, S. Muto, N. Yokoyama and A. Shibatomi, "InAlAs/InGaAs resonant tunneling bipolar transistors (RBTs) operating at room temperature with high current gains," *Tech. Digest IEEE IEDM*, 877 (1987).
5. F. Capasso, S. Sen, A. Y. Cho and D. L. Sivco, "Multiple negative transconductance and differential conductance in a bipolar transistor by sequential quenching of resonant tunneling," *Appl. Phys. Lett.*, **53**, 1056 (1988).
6. F. Capasso, S. Sen and F. Beltram, "Quantum-effect devices," in S. M. Sze, Ed., *High-speed semiconductor devices*, Wiley, New York, 1990.
7. T. Futatsugi, Y. Yamaguchi, S. Muto, N. Yokoyama and A. Shibatomi, "Resonant tunneling bipolar transistors using InAlAs/InGaAs heterostructures," *J. Appl. Phys.*, **65**, 1771 (1989).
8. J. S. Wu, C. Y. Chang, C. P. Lee, K. H. Chang, D. G. Liu and D. C. Liou, "Characterization of improved AlGaAs/GaAs resonant tunneling heterostructure bipolar transistors," *Japanese J. Appl. Phys.*, **30**, L160 (1991).
9. S. Sen, F. Capasso, A. Y. Cho and D. L. Sivco, "Multiple-state resonant-tunneling bipolar transistor operating at room temperature and its application as a frequency multiplier," *IEEE Electron Dev. Lett.*, **EDL-9**, 533 (1988).

CHAPTER
39

RESONANT-TUNNELING HOT-ELECTRON TRANSISTOR

39.1 HISTORY

The resonant-tunneling hot-electron transistor (RHET) is the first three-terminal device that makes use of the resonant-tunneling phenomenon, and is based on the fundamental research on the two-terminal resonant-tunneling diode started in the 1970s (see Chapter 10). The RHET was first proposed and demonstrated by Yokoyama et al. in 1985, using GaAs–AlGaAs heterostructures.[1,2] Improved device performance from GaInAs–AlInAs materials was reported by Imamura et al. in 1987.[3] Satisfactory device characteristics at room temperature were demonstrated by Mori et al. in 1988[4] and by Seabaugh et al. in 1990.[5] Device modeling was presented by Ohnishi et al.[6,7] A review of the RHET can be found in Ref. 8.

39.2 STRUCTURE

Early structures of the RHET were made from the GaAs–AlGaAs system which is shown in Fig. 39.1. Alternatively, the GaInAs–AlInAs heterostructures have been used and have advantages that will be discussed later. The junction between the emitter and the base is equivalent to a resonant-tunneling diode. The quantum-well layer is typically between 20–60 Å, sandwiched between two barrier layers that are also around 20–60 Å thick. The two barrier layers are not necessarily identical in either thickness or composition. These three layers, plus the barrier layer in the collector, are all undoped while the rest of the structure is

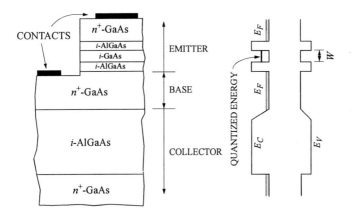

FIGURE 39.1
Structure of an RHET using GaAs–AlGaAs heterostructure as an example, and its energy-band diagram at equilibrium.

heavily doped with n-type impurities (for devices with electron current). There is also an intrinsic GaAs spacer layer (≈ 15 Å), inserted between the quantum-well barrier layer (i-AlGaAs) and the n^+-GaAs emitter or base, to avoid dopant diffusion to the barrier layers. The degenerate base layer has a thickness in the range of 100–1000 Å. The collector usually has a transition layer (≈ 50 Å) of graded composition to reduce quantum mechanical reflection arising from a sharp potential interface. The barrier layer within the collector is relatively thick, ranging from 2000 Å to 3000 Å, to ensure a high breakdown voltage between the collector and the base. Because the quantum well requires ultra-thin layers, MBE is usually used for film deposition.

39.3 CHARACTERISTICS

The operation of the RHET is demonstrated by the energy-band diagrams in Fig. 39.2. The injection current from the emitter is a resonant-tunneling current through quantized energy subbands in a quantum well. The bottom of these quantized subband levels can be approximated by

$$E_n - E_C \approx \frac{h^2 n^2}{8 m^* W^2} \ , \qquad n = 1, 2, 3... \tag{39.1}$$

where W is the well thickness. The barrier in the collector serves to prevent leakage between the base and the outer collector, both of which are heavily doped and of the same type. Figure 39.2(b) shows that with increasing base-to-emitter voltage V_{BE}, the conduction-band edge E_C in the emitter approaches the quantized level in the well. Since resonant tunneling requires the conservation of energy and

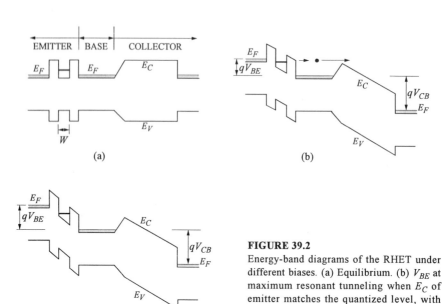

FIGURE 39.2

Energy-band diagrams of the RHET under different biases. (a) Equilibrium. (b) V_{BE} at maximum resonant tunneling when E_C of emitter matches the quantized level, with $V_{CB} > 0$. (c) V_{BE} beyond current peak.

lateral momentum, maximum current injection occurs when E_C in the emitter matches the quantized level (see Chapter 10–Resonant-Tunneling Diode). A further increase in V_{BE} decreases the resonant-tunneling current when the emitter E_C is above E_n. This condition is shown in Fig. 39.2(c), and is the basis for the negative differential resistance/transconductance. The collector-to-base voltage V_{CB} is applied to attract the emitted electrons efficiently.

The general characteristics of an RHET are shown in Fig. 39.3. In Fig. 39.3(a), the emitter current is similar to that of a resonant-tunneling diode, showing a characteristic negative differential resistance/transconductance. The

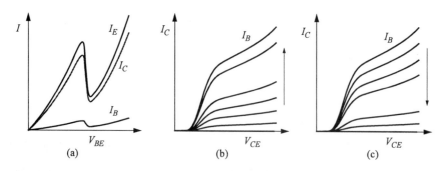

FIGURE 39.3

General characteristics of an RHET. (a) Terminal currents as a function of V_{BE}, for a fixed V_{CB}. (b) Common-emitter characteristics with increasing I_B steps, and (c) with decreasing I_B steps.

current peak should correspond to $V_{BE} \approx 2(E_n - E_C)/q$ since only half of the bias is effective in aligning the emitter E_C to the quantized level, and the other half is developed across the second barrier adjacent to the base. Experimentally, a higher V_{BE} is required due to the voltage across the spacer layers and the series resistance of the emitter and the base. The rise in current beyond the valley current is due either to resonant tunneling through a second quantized level, or thermionic emission over the barriers. The collector current reflects the transfer ratio α_T, and is given by

$$I_C = \alpha_T I_E + I_o \qquad (39.2)$$

where I_o is the leakage current between the collector and the base. α_T is a function of both V_{BE} and V_{CE}. As an example, in the extreme case when V_{BE} is small such that the electron energy traversing the base is smaller than the collector barrier, α_T would be zero. The collector peak-to-valley current ratio is an important measure of the negative differential resistance, and values around 20 have been observed at room temperature. Also, for practical applications, a high collector current is critical, and thin barrier layers are important. It has been shown that a barrier thickness of less than 30 Å is required to give a collector current density of 2×10^5 cm^{-2}. The ratio I_C/I_B is the common-emitter current gain (β), and a value of ≈ 10 has been observed at room temperature (25 at 77 K).

The common-emitter characteristics in Figs. 39.3(b) and 39.3(c) show an interesting dependence on the stepping direction of I_B.[9] When I_B is stepped upward, I_C displays a sudden jump. This occurs when I_B is increased beyond the current peak, and V_{BE} is increased suddenly to maintain the current I_B, inducing a sudden change in α_T. By the same token, when I_B is stepped downward, a sudden change in V_{BE} is experienced below the valley current.

It has been shown that if a carrier acquires enough energy to transfer to an upper valley in the momentum space, a lose in α_T can result from inter-valley scattering in both the base and the collector regions. One advantage in the GaInAs–AlInAs system is an increased valley-to-valley separation (≈ 0.55 eV) compared to the GaAs–AlGaAs system (≈ 0.30 eV). Another advantage is the smaller effective mass, leading to higher tunneling current.

39.4 APPLICATIONS

Compared to a two-terminal resonant-tunneling diode, the third terminal of an RHET makes the negative differential resistance/transconductance tunable. It isolates the input and output circuits, which is especially important for the RHET to perform efficiently as a functional device (a single device capable of more complex functions). Another unique feature of resonant tunneling is multiple negative-resistance regions (multiple current peaks), which are beneficial to a logic device. Examples of applications are analog-to-digital converters, frequency multipliers, and logic functions such as exclusive-NOR,[10,11] parity generator, and memory.[12] Combining resonant tunneling with hot-electron ballistic transport in the base, the RHET is a super-high-speed device. An extrapolated current gain cutoff frequency of ≈ 70 GHz has been demonstrated at room temperature[5] (120 GHz at 77 K[13]).

For general applications of the negative resistance, the readers can refer to Appendix C2.

REFERENCES

1. N. Yokoyama, K. Imamura, S. Muto, S. Hiyamizu and H. Nishi, "A new functional, resonant-tunneling hot electron transistor (RHET)," *Japanese J. Appl. Phys.*, **24**, L853 (1985).
2. N. Yokoyama, K. Imamura, S. Muto, S. Hiyamizu and H. Nishi, "A resonant-tunneling hot electron transistor (RHET)," *Inst. Phys. Conf. Ser. No. 79*, Ch. 13, 739 (1986). (Int. Symp. GaAs and Related Compounds, Japan, Sept. 1985)
3. K. Imamura, S. Muto, H. Ohnishi, T. Fujii and N. Yokoyama, "Resonant-tunnelling hot-electron transistor (RHET) using a GaInAs/(AlGa)InAs heterostructure," *Electronics Lett.*, **23**, 870 (1987).
4. T. Mori, K. Imamura, H. Ohnishi, Y. Minami, S. Muto and N. Yokoyama, "Microwave analysis of resonant-tunneling hot electron transistors at room temperature," *Extended Abstracts 20th (1988 Int.) Conf. Solid State Devices and Materials*, 507 (1988).
5. A. Seabaugh, Y. C. Kao, J. Randall, W. Frensley and A. Khatibzadeh, "Room temperature resonant-tunneling hot electron transistors with dc and microwave gain," *Extended Abstracts 22nd (1990 Int.) Conf. Solid State Devices & Materials*, 15 (1990)
6. H. Ohnishi, N. Yokoyama and A. Shibatomi, "Modeling electron transport in InGaAs-based resonant-tunneling hot-electron transistors," *IEEE Trans. Electron Dev.*, **ED-36**, 2335 (1989).
7. H. Ohnishi, N. Yokoyama and A. Shibatomi, "Transport analysis of a resonant-tunneling hot electron transistor (RHET)," *Electron. and Commun. in Japan*, **71**, Pt. 2, 50 (1988).
8. N. Yokoyama, S. Muto, H. Ohnishi, K. Imamura, T. Mori and T. Inata, "Resonant-tunnelling hot electron transistors (RHET)," in F. Capasso, Ed., *Physics of quantum electron devices*, Springer-Verlag, Berlin, 1990.
9. N. Yokoyama and K. Imamura, "Flip-flop circuit using a resonant-tunneling hot electron transistor (RHET)," *Electronics Lett.*, **22**, 1228 (1986).
10. M. Takatsu, K. Imamura, H. Ohnishi, T. Mori, T. Adachihara, S. Muto and N. Yokoyama, "Logic circuits using resonant-tunneling hot-electron transistors (RHET's)," *IEEE J. Solid-State Circuits*, **27**, 1428 (1992).
11. T. S. Moise, A. C. Seabaugh, E. A. Beam, III and J. N. Randall, "Room-temperature operation of a resonant-tunneling hot-electron transistor based integrated circuit," *IEEE Electron Dev. Lett.*, **14**, 441 (1993).
12. T. Mori, S. Muto, H. Tamura and N. Yokoyama, "An SRAM cell using a double-emitter RHET for gigabit-plus memory applications," *Extended Abstracts 1993 Int. Conf. Solid State Devices & Materials*, 1074 (1993).
13. T. Mori, T. Adachihara, M. Takatsu, H. Ohnishi, K. Imamura, S. Muto and N. Yokoyama, "121 GHz resonant-tunneling hot electron transistors having new collector barrier structure," *Electronics Lett.*, **27**, 1523 (1991).

CHAPTER

40

QUANTUM-WELL-BASE RESONANT-TUNNELING TRANSISTOR

40.1 HISTORY

The device covered in this chapter has been reported only sparsely, and under different device names that are not very specific. The author prefers to call it a quantum-well-base resonant-tunneling transistor (QWBRTT). This new device is basically a resonant-tunneling diode (see Chapter 10) with a third terminal contacting the quantum well which is used as a base to control its potential. The quantum-well base can be doped with either the same type as the emitter and collector, or with the opposite type. The former is often referred to as a unipolar device and the latter as bipolar. Devices reported have electron tunneling so that both emitter and collector are doped with an n-type impurity. QWBRTT with p-type base was first suggested by Ricco and Solomon in 1984,[1] and studied experimentally by Seabaugh et al. in 1988,[2,3] by Reed et al. in 1989[4] (see also patent by Frensley and Reed[5]) and by Waho et al. in 1991.[6] Devices with an n-type base was proposed by Schulman and Waldner in 1988,[7] and independently by Haddad et al. in 1989.[8] Experimental data were presented subsequently by Reddy et al.,[9] and by Haddad et al.[10] Calculations to model the resonant tunneling current in a general transistor structure has been presented by Jogai and Wang in 1985.[11] The QWBRTT is still in its infancy and many predicted characteristics have not yet been observed.

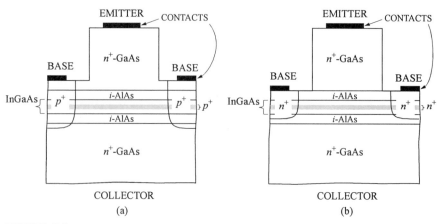

FIGURE 40.1
Structures showing the two embodiments of the QWBRTT. (a) Bipolar device with *p*-type base. (b) Unipolar device with *n*-type base.

40.2 STRUCTURE

Unlike the resonant-tunneling diode, the QWBRTT needs a heterostructure made from layers with three different energy gaps. The barrier layers should have the highest energy gap, and the base layer must have a smaller energy gap than the emitter and collector to reduce leakage current from the base. An example is the GaAs–AlAs–InGaAs system as shown in Fig. 40.1. The base layer, typically, ranges from 60 Å to 150 Å, although bipolar QWBRTTs have been demonstrated with base widths as wide as 1200 Å. The base doping is incorporated at the center of the layer. The barrier layers are in the range of 10 Å to 50 Å. Contact to the base requires a mesa structure, but for the structure shown in Fig. 40.1(a), a precise etch stop at the barrier layer or well layer is not critical. The heterostructures are deposited by MBE because of the small vertical dimensions.

40.3 CHARACTERISTICS

The operation principle of the QWBRTT is based on resonant tunneling between the emitter and the collector through quantized subbands in the quantum well. For the case of a rectangular quantum-well base, the quantized subband levels above the conduction band E_C, assuming infinite barrier heights, are determined by

$$E_n \approx \frac{h^2 n^2}{8 m^* W^2} \quad , \quad n = 1, 2, 3... \quad (40.1)$$

where W is the well thickness. Since the quantum well is contacted by the base terminal, its potential and the quantized energy levels can be shifted by this third terminal, resulting in a transistor action. According to the structures shown in Fig. 40.1, the well is contacted laterally, and it should be doped to yield reasonably low sheet resistance. The energy-band diagrams in Fig. 40.2 show both p-type and n-type bases. For a p-type base (well), holes provide the conductivity in the base, and a valance-band discontinuity ΔE_V between the emitter and the base is desirable for a small base current. In the case of the n-type base, the Fermi level in equilibrium is above the first quantized level so that this filled level provides the base conductivity parallel to the heterointerface. The carrier density in this quantized level is calculated to be $\approx 2 \times 10^{12}$ cm^{-2} which is lower than that achievable in a doped p-type base. It is also critical that there be a large conduction-band discontinuity ΔE_C between the well and the emitter/collector such that this first, filled quantized level is bound by barriers on both sides. In this structure, resonant tunneling between the emitter and collector is via the second and higher quantized levels. Since ΔE_V is needed for the p-type

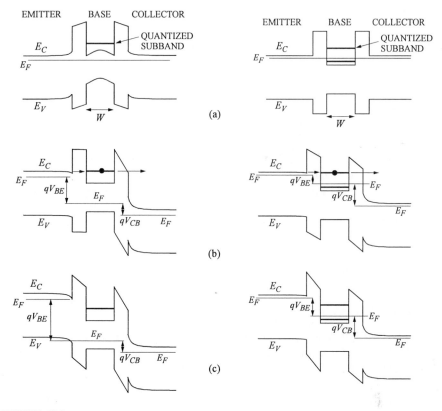

FIGURE 40.2
Energy-band diagrams of the QWBRTTs under different biases. Those at left correspond to structure with p-type base and those at right with n-type base. (a) Equilibrium. (b) At V_{BE} for maximum resonant tunneling, with collector-to-base bias V_{CB}. (c) Higher V_{BE} beyond the current peak.

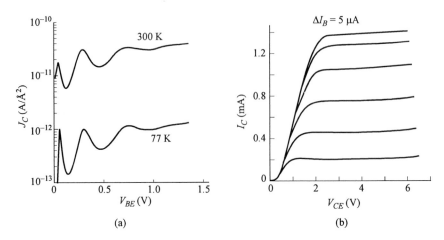

FIGURE 40.3

Electrical characteristics of a QWBRTT. (a) Calculated I_C as a function of V_{BE} for a fixed V_{CB}. (After Ref. 11) (b) Experimental common-emitter output characteristics, with I_B steps. (After Ref. 4)

base and ΔE_C needed for the n-type base, both structures in practice require a well layer with smaller energy gap than the emitter and collector layers.

Figure 40.2 shows the energy-band diagrams of the QWBRTTs under different biases. In Fig. 40.2(b), the base is biased for maximum resonant tunneling when the conduction band in the emitter matches a quantized level in the well. With a larger base-to-emitter voltage V_{BE}, the conduction-band edge exceeds the quantized level and resonant tunneling is reduced (Fig. 40.2(c)), giving rise to negative differential resistance as shown in Fig. 40.3(a). It should be noted that from Fig. 40.2(b), the V_{BE} at current peak for the p-type base is much larger than that for the n-type base. The common-emitter output characteristics are shown in Fig. 40.3(b). The highest current gain ($I_C/I_B = \beta$) reported is around 50. When these characteristics are plotted with V_{BE} steps instead of I_B steps, the collector current I_C first increases with V_{BE}, and then decreases due to the negative resistance characteristics shown in Fig. 40.3(a).

40.4 APPLICATIONS

The QWBRTT is potentially an ultra-fast device since carrier conduction from emitter to collector is via tunneling. Its negative resistance characteristics can be utilized to construct logic and memory circuits. (For general applications of negative resistance, the readers can refer to Appendix C2.) Being a three-terminal device, isolation is provided between the input and output, and logic functions can be efficiently implemented. An example of the device as an adder circuit is discussed in Ref. 13. The resonant-tunneling phenomenon can provide multiple current peaks which enable the QWBRTT to be a functional device. General applications of a transistor are summarized in Appendix C3.

REFERENCES

1. B. Ricco and P. M. Solomon, "Tunable resonant tunnelling semiconductor emitter structure," *IBM Tech. Disc. Bull.*, **27**, 3053 (1984).
2. A. C. Seabaugh, M. A. Reed, W. R. Frensley, J. N. Randall and R. J. Matyi, "Realization of pseudomorphic and superlattice bipolar resonant tunneling transistors," *Tech. Digest IEEE IEDM*, 900 (1988).
3. A. C. Seabaugh, W. R. Frensley, J. N. Randall, M. A. Reed, D. L. Farrington and R. J. Matyi, "Pseudomorphic bipolar quantum resonant-tunneling transistor," *IEEE Trans. Electron Dev.*, **ED-36**, 2328 (1989).
4. M. A. Reed, W. R. Frensley, R. J. Matyi, J. N. Randall and A. C. Seabaugh, "Realization of a three-terminal resonant tunneling device: The bipolar quantum resonant tunneling transistor," *Appl. Phys. Lett.*, **54**, 1034 (1989).
5. W. R. Frensley and M. A. Reed, "Three terminal tunneling device and method," U.S. patent 4,959,696, granted Sept. 1990.
6. T. Waho, K. Maezawa and T. Mizutani, "Resonant tunneling in a novel coupled-quantum-well base transistor," *Japanese J. Appl. Phys.*, **30**, L2018 (1991).
7. J. N. Schulman and M. Waldner, "Analysis of second level resonant tunneling diodes and transistors," *J. Appl. Phys.*, **63**, 2859 (1988).
8. G. I. Haddad, R. K. Mains, U. K. Reddy and J. R. East, "A proposed narrow-band-gap base transistor structure," *Superlattices and Microstructures*, **5**, 437 (1989).
9. U. K. Reddy, I. Mehdi, R. K. Mains and G. I. Haddad, "Design, fabrication and operation of a hot electron resonant tunnelling transistor," *Solid-State Electron.*, **32**, 1377 (1989).
10. G. I. Haddad, U. K. Reddy, J. P. Sun and R. K. Mains, "The bound-state resonant tunneling transistor (BSRTT): Fabrication, D. C. I-V characteristics and high-frequency properties," *Superlattices and Microstructures*, **7**, 369 (1990).
11. B. Jogai and K. L. Wang, "Dependent of tunneling current on structural variations of superlattice devices," *Appl. Phys. Lett.*, **46**, 167 (1985).
12. A. C. Seabaugh, Y. C. Kao, W. R. Frensley, J. N. Randall and M. A. Reed, "Resonant transmission in the base/collector junction of a bipolar quantum-well resonant-tunneling transistor," *Appl. Phys. Lett.*, **59**, 3413 (1991).
13. S. Mohan, P. Mazumder, R. K. Mains, J. P. Sun and G. I. Haddad, "Ultrafast pipeline adders using RTTs," *Electronics Lett.*, **27**, 830 (1991).

CHAPTER

41

FLOATING-GATE AVALANCHE-INJECTION METAL-OXIDE-SEMICONDUCTOR TRANSISTOR

41.1 HISTORY

The first floating-gate transistor to be used for nonvolatile memory was suggested and demonstrated by Kahng and Sze in 1967.[1] The charge transfer to the floating gate was via tunneling through thin oxides. To avoid leakage associated with nonuniform thin oxides, Frohman-Bentchkowsky in 1971 started using avalanche injection over the barrier, as opposed to tunneling, so that thicker oxide can be used.[2–4] This idea developed into a FAMOS (floating-gate avalanche-injection metal-oxide-semiconductor) transistor. Erasing the injected charge by incorporating a second control gate was examined by Tarui et al. in 1972,[5] and by Card and Worrall in 1973.[6] The development of the FAMOS transistor has been chronicled by Chang.[7] Pioneering papers have been collected in an edited book by Hu.[8] The FAMOS transistor has been enjoying a very successful market in nonvolatile memories as it is the main component for the EPROM circuits.

41.2 STRUCTURE

Early FAMOS transistors started with only a floating gate as shown in Fig. 41.1. The additional control gate situated directly over the floating gate can serve as the select gate in a memory array so that a separate select transistor for programming is not needed. It is also important for some erase schemes that are performed electrically rather than using radiation. Unlike most of the current devices, early

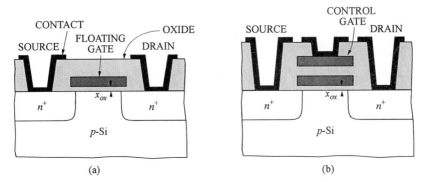

FIGURE 41.1
Structures of the FAMOS transistors (a) without a control gate and (b) with a control gate.

devices used p-channel configuration due to the ease of electron injection by junction avalanche. As will be discussed later, in recent n-channel devices, hot carriers arise from the channel rather than from the junction avalanche. The gate oxide thickness under the floating gate is between 150–350 Å, and that under the control gate is between 300–500 Å. The gates are usually made of LPCVD poly-silicon, and a silicon substrate is used exclusively since FAMOS is based on the mature silicon MOS technology.

41.3 CHARACTERISTICS

Since the FAMOS transistor is mainly used as a nonvolatile memory which is digital in nature, one can view it as having two states; a more conductive state and a more resistive state between the source and the drain terminals. This is ultimately related to the threshold voltage of the transistor which is defined as the voltage on the gate (or floating gate) required to turn the transistor on. For an n-channel device, when this threshold voltage is high, the transistor is in a highly resistive state, and when it is low or negative, the transistor is in a more conductive state. The change of threshold voltage is accomplished by the injection of hot electrons to the floating gate, called programming, and the reverse process of discharge is called erase. These two operations will be discussed below.

During the programming operation, the drain and the control gate are biased with a positive voltage, as shown in Fig. 41.2. The channel electrons acquire energy from the lateral field (from source to drain) and, without significant scattering, can emit over the Si–SiO$_2$ barrier to the floating gate. This hot-electron effect is different from tunneling through the barrier as shown in Fig. 41.3. The control gate bias V_{CG} is usually higher than the drain's, and it helps to turn on the channel and to attract electrons. The programming time is typically in the order of 10 μs. A requirement for a nonvolatile memory is that the injected charge

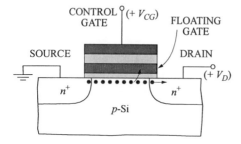

FIGURE 41.2
Programming of the FAMOS transistor. Hot electrons from the n-type inversion channel are emitted over the Si–SiO$_2$ barrier to the floating gate.

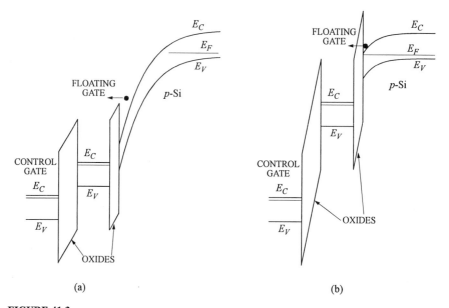

(a)   (b)

FIGURE 41.3
Energy-band diagrams showing electron injection mechanisms in floating-gate transistors. (a) Hot-electron injection over the Si–SiO$_2$ barrier. (b) Fowler-Nordheim tunneling through the barrier.

remains in the floating gate for at least ten years without any power or bias to the device.

It can be seen here that these hot electrons are not produced by the junction avalanche as originally proposed for p-channel devices. If junction avalanche is used, the drain in a p-channel device is under negative bias which favors electron injection toward the gate. The positive drain bias in an n-channel device favors hot-hole injection but it is much less efficient, partly due to larger Si–SiO$_2$ barrier for holes than for electrons. Because of the shorter channel in present-day devices, the use of hot electrons emitted from the inversion channel is a much more viable approach. Even though these devices do not exactly use avalanche injection, the name FAMOS is still applied.

To erase the stored negative charge in the floating gate, different schemes can be used. The most popular is by exposure to ultra-violet light or X-ray. These high-energy radiations can excite electrons in the floating gate, emitting them to both the silicon substrate and the control gate. The erase process takes several minutes to complete. The disadvantages of this erase approach are that, often, the chip has to be removed from the system, and that the whole chip is erased without byte selectivity. Another way to erase is electrical, which involves tunneling between the floating gate and the source/drain, or between the floating gate and the control gate. This tunneling is the reverse of the process shown in Fig. 41.3(b).

The electrical characteristics after erase and programming are shown in Fig. 41.4. The threshold voltage for the floating gate in an n-channel device is given by

$$V_T = V_{FB} + 2\psi_B + \frac{\sqrt{4\varepsilon_s q N \psi_B}}{C_{ox}} - \frac{Q_{FG}}{C_{ox}} \tag{41.1}$$

where

$$C_{ox} = \frac{\varepsilon_{ox}}{x_{ox}} . \tag{41.2}$$

Equation (41.1) differs from a conventional MOSFET by the charge density in the floating gate Q_{FG} (C/cm^2), and a negative charge increases the threshold voltage. The floating-gate voltage V_{FG} is capacitively coupled to the control-gate bias V_{CG}, as well as the drain bias V_D. With the equivalent circuit shown in Fig. 41.5, V_{FG} is given by[9]

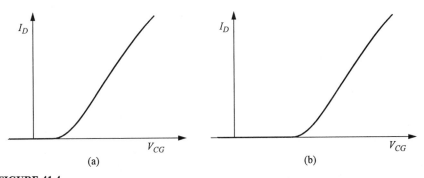

FIGURE 41.4
The drain current I_D characteristics (vs. V_{CG} for a fixed V_D) of a FAMOS transistor showing the change of threshold voltage after (a) erase and (b) program.

$$V_{FG} \approx \frac{C_{GD}V_D}{C_{GD} + C_{GS} + C_{FG} + C_{CG}} + \frac{C_{CG}V_{CG}}{C_{GD} + C_{GS} + C_{FG} + C_{CG}} \quad . \quad (41.3)$$

The definitions for the capacitance terms are explained in the caption of the figure. It should be pointed out that this equation is only qualitative and is an approximation. The channel capacitance C_{FG} between the floating gate and the substrate is complicated and is a function of bias. Nevertheless, the threshold voltage for the floating gate is reflected in the V_{CG} as shown in Fig. 41.4. The FAMOS transistor has to withstand many program and erase operations, and a typical specification is 10^4 cycles. After that, the threshold voltage window (difference after erase and program) decreases due to the deterioration of the oxide quality in terms of interface traps, injection efficiency, and leakage.

41.4 APPLICATIONS

The FAMOS transistor is used exclusively for nonvolatile memories. For a summary of memory types and their general applications, the readers can refer to Appendix C6. Specifically, the FAMOS transistor is most common in EPROM, followed by flash EEPROM. The difference in these applications is the erase mechanism, as shown in Table 41.1. Since the EPROM is the most popular among all nonvolatile memories, the FAMOS transistor is of significant commercial value. It also makes possible a flash EEPROM whose one-transistor cell is much smaller than a full-featured EEPROM cell. The latter needs a select transistor and results in a two-transistor cell. The flash EEPROM also enables electrical erase, a feature that is advantageous over the EPROM, and, thus, it is a good compromise between an EPROM and an EEPROM.

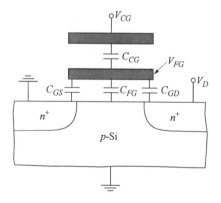

FIGURE 41.5
Equivalent circuit used to calculate the floating-gate voltage due to capacitive coupling from the control-gate voltage and the drain voltage. C_{FG} = capacitance between floating gate and substrate. C_{CG} = capacitance between control gate and floating gate. C_{GD} and C_{GS} are overlap capacitances of the floating gate to the drain and source, respectively.

TABLE 41.1
A summary of the nonvolatile memory devices, their programming and erasing mechanisms, and their memory circuits.

Device	Program	Erase	Memory
FAMOS	Avalanche	UV/X-ray	EPROM
FAMOS	Avalanche	Tunneling	Flash EEPROM
FLOTOX	Tunneling	Tunneling	EEPROM
MNOS	Tunneling	Tunneling	EEPROM

41.5 RELATED DEVICE

41.5.1 Floating-Gate Tunnel-Oxide Transistor

The FLOTOX (floating-gate tunnel-oxide) transistor was introduced in 1980 and is now currently the industrial standard for EEPROM.[10,11] As shown in Table 41.1, the injection and erase mechanisms are both due to Fowler-Nordheim tunneling, thus, it is closer to the original scheme proposed by Kahng and Sze.[1] The difference in the FLOTOX transistor is that a thin tunneling oxide (≈ 100 Å) is present only locally over the drain area while the gate oxide over the channel area is much thicker (Fig. 41.6). Programming is performed by applying a positive voltage to the control gate, with the source and drain grounded, giving rise to a net negative charge in the floating gate. Erasing is performed by applying a positive voltage to the drain, with the control gate grounded and the source floating. After erase, a net positive charge results in the floating gate. Note that only a positive voltage is needed for both programming and erasing while opposite-polarity voltages are required for an MNOS transistor.

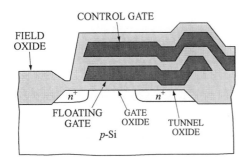

FIGURE 41.6
Structure of the FLOTOX transistor.
(After Ref. 11)

REFERENCES

1. D. Kahng and S. M. Sze, "A floating gate and its application to memory devices," *Bell Syst. Tech. J.*, **46**, 1288 (1967).
2. D. Frohman-Bentchkowsky, "Memory behavior in a floating-gate avalanche-injection MOS (FAMOS) structure," *Appl. Phys. Lett.*, **18**, 332 (1971).
3. D. Frohman-Bentchkowsky, "A fully decoded 2048-bit electrically programmable FAMOS read-only memory," *IEEE J. Solid-State Circuits*, **SC-6**, 301 (1971).
4. D. Frohman-Bentchkowsky, "FAMOS – A new semiconductor charge storage device," *Solid-State Electron.*, **17**, 517 (1974).
5. Y. Tarui, Y. Hayashi and K. Nagai, "Electrically reprogrammable nonvolatile semiconductor memory," *IEEE J. Solid-State Circuits*, **SC-7**, 369 (1972).
6. H. C. Card and A. G. Worrall, "Electrically alterable avalanche-injection memory," *Electronics Lett.*, **9**, 14 (1973).
7. J. J. Chang, "Nonvolatile semiconductor memory devices," *Proc. IEEE*, **64**, 1039 (1976).
8. C. Hu, Ed., *Nonvolatile semiconductor memories. Technologies, design, and applications*, IEEE Press, New York, 1991.
9. S. T. Wang, "On the *I-V* characteristics of floating-gate MOS transistors," *IEEE Trans. Electron Dev.*, **ED-26**, 1292 (1979).
10. W. S. Johnson, G. Perlegos, A. Renninger, G. Kuhn and T. R. Ranganath, "A 16Kb electrically erasable nonvolatile memory," *IEEE ISSCC Dig. Tech. Pap.*, 152 (1980).
11. S. K. Lai and V. K. Dham, "VLSI electrically erasable programmable read only memory," in N. G. Einspruch, Ed., *VLSI handbook*, Academic Press, Orlando, 1985.

CHAPTER 42

METAL-NITRIDE-OXIDE-SEMICONDUCTOR TRANSISTOR

42.1 HISTORY

The MNOS (metal-nitride-oxide-semiconductor or metal-nitride-oxide-silicon) transistor belongs to a group of MIOS (metal-insulator-oxide-semiconductor) structures having a special feature of dual gate dielectrics–insulator on oxide. With nitride being the most popular, other insulators include alumina (MAOS), tantalum oxide, and titanium oxide. The MNOS transistor used as nonvolatile memory was first proposed and demonstrated by Wegener et al. in 1967.[1] Memory effect in an MNOS capacitor was studied by Pao and O'Connell the following year.[2] More detailed studies on the MNOS transistor were presented in 1969 by Frohman-Bentchkowsky and Lenzlinger,[3,4] Wallmark and Scott,[5] and Ross and Wallmark.[6] Dill and Toombs also studied injection by hot carriers over the Si–SiO$_2$ barrier, as opposed to tunneling.[7] The first MNOS nonvolatile memory circuit was present by Frohman-Bentchkowsky.[8] The development of the MNOS transistor has been reviewed by Chang,[9] Pepper,[10] and Hu.[11]

42.2 STRUCTURE

The structure of an MNOS transistor, as shown in Fig. 42.1, is similar to a MOSFET except that the gate insulator consists of dual dielectrics. The oxide layer is in the range of 20–50 Å thick, and is thermally grown on the silicon substrate. The purpose of this oxide film is to provide a good interface to the semiconductor, and to prevent back-tunneling of the injected charge for better

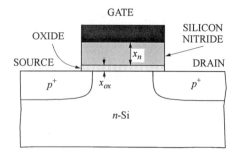

FIGURE 42.1
Structure of the MNOS transistor.

charge retention. Typically, the deposited nitride layer ranges from 200 Å to 600 Å thick. The thickness has to be balanced between programming voltage and charge retention: not so thick that it causes excessive programming voltage, and not so thin that the stored charge leaks to the gate. Both channel types have been used but p-channel devices are more common. As in a MOSFET, the gate is usually composed of polysilicon, and a silicon substrate has been used exclusively.

42.3 CHARACTERISTICS

The memory effect of an MNOS transistor is due to the charge trapped in the nitride layer. In fact, nitride is chosen because of its high trapping density. On passage of an electron current from the gate to substrate (electrons from Si substrate to gate), some electrons are trapped in the nitride layer near the oxide–nitride interface, giving rise to a negative charge sheet (Q_n in C/cm^2) that is uniformly distributed above the channel. The negative charge sheet changes the threshold voltage of the MNOS transistor. This charging process is called programming. By sensing the threshold voltage, memory can be read. The reverse process or discharge is called erase, which returns the threshold voltage to its original value.

The threshold voltage for a p-channel device is given by

$$V_T = V_{FB} - 2\psi_B - \frac{\sqrt{4\varepsilon_s q N_D \psi_B}}{C_G} - \frac{Q_n}{C_n}.$$

(42.1)

The total gate capacitance C_G is equal to the serial combination of the nitride capacitance C_n and oxide capacitance C_{ox}, given by

$$C_G = \frac{1}{(1/C_n) + (1/C_{ox})} = \frac{C_{ox}C_n}{C_{ox} + C_n},$$

(42.2)

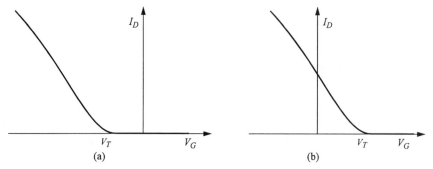

FIGURE 42.2

The drain current I_D characteristics (vs. V_G for a fixed V_D) of a p-channel MNOS transistor, showing the change of threshold voltage after (a) erase and (b) program.

$$C_n = \frac{\varepsilon_n}{x_n} , \qquad (42.3)$$

$$C_{ox} = \frac{\varepsilon_{ox}}{x_{ox}} , \qquad (42.4)$$

where ε_n and ε_{ox} are the permittivities of nitride and oxide, respectively. After programming, the negative charge sheet increases the threshold voltage (less negative), often to a positive value so that the transistor becomes a depletion-mode device (normally-on). The drain current characteristics after programming and erase are shown in Fig. 42.2.

In the programming process, a large positive bias is applied to the gate. Current conduction is known to be due to electrons, which are emitted from the substrate to the gate, as shown in Fig. 42.3. The conduction mechanisms in the two dielectric layers are very different, and have to be considered in series. The current through the oxide J_{ox} is by tunneling. Notice that electrons tunnel through the trapezoidal oxide barrier, followed by a triangular barrier in the nitride. This form of tunneling has been identified as modified Fowler-Nordheim tunneling, as opposed to Fowler-Nordheim tunneling through a single triangular barrier, which has the following form

$$J_{ox} = C_1 \mathscr{E}_{ox}^2 \exp\left(-\frac{C_2}{\mathscr{E}_{ox}}\right) , \qquad (42.5)$$

where $\mathscr{E}_{ox}$ is the field in the oxide layer. The theory for modified Fowler-Nordheim tunneling is much more complicated and will not be elaborated further. The current through the nitride layer J_n is controlled by Frenkel-Poole transport which has the following form

$$J_n = C_3 \mathscr{E}_n \exp\left(\frac{-\phi_B + \sqrt{q\mathscr{E}_n/\pi\varepsilon_n}}{\phi_T}\right)$$ (42.6)

where $\mathscr{E}_n$ is the electric field in nitride, ϕ_B is the trap level below the conduction band (≈ 1.3 V), and $C_3 = 3\times10^{-9}$ $(\Omega\text{-cm})^{-1}$. The charging process of the traps is governed by

$$-\frac{dQ_n}{dt} = J_{ox} - J_n \ ,$$ (42.7)

$$\varepsilon_{ox}\mathscr{E}_{ox} = \varepsilon_n\mathscr{E}_n + Q_n \ ,$$ (42.8)

$$x_{ox}\mathscr{E}_{ox} + x_n\mathscr{E}_n = V_p$$ (42.9)

where V_p is the programming gate voltage. It is known that at the beginning of the programming process, the modified Fowler-Nordheim tunneling is capable of a higher current and conduction is limited by Frenkel-Poole transport through the nitride layer. When the negative charge starts to build up, the oxide field decreases and the modified Fowler-Nordheim tunneling starts to limit the current. The threshold voltage as a function of programming pulse width is shown in Fig. 42.4. Initially, the threshold voltage changes linearly with time, followed by a

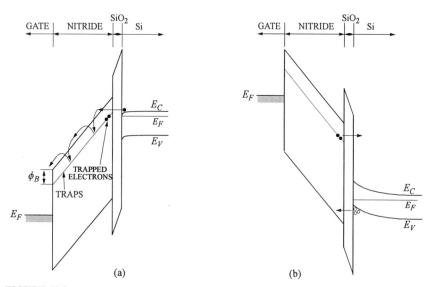

(a)   (b)

FIGURE 42.3
Energy-band diagrams showing the current transport, trapping, and detrapping of electrons. (a) Programming with a positive gate voltage. (b) Erasing with a negative gate voltage. Metal gate is assumed.

logarithmic dependence, and finally, it tends to saturate. A rough estimate of the maximum V_T shift can be obtained by setting $\mathscr{E}_{ox} = 0$ in Eqs. (42.8) and (42.9), giving

$$Q_n \approx -V_p C_n \quad , \tag{42.10}$$

$$\Delta V_T \approx -\frac{Q_n}{C_n} \approx V_p \quad . \tag{42.11}$$

In practical circuit applications, the saturated V_T is never reached, and the programming pulse width varies from 10 µs to 1 ms. This programming speed is largely affected by the choice of the oxide thickness, and a thinner oxide allows a shorter programming time. Programming speed has to be balanced with charge retention since too thin an oxide will allow the trapped charge to tunnel back to the silicon substrate. Typical threshold shift is 5–10 V, with a programming gate voltage between 15 V and 30 V. The high programming voltage is a disadvantage for the MNOS transistor, and efforts to decrease it have been made using the MONOS transistor which is discussed in Section 42.5.1.[13,14]

Once the traps are filled with electrons, the resultant negative charge has to remain trapped for at least ten years, to satisfy the requirement of a nonvolatile memory, with a long interruption of the power supply. This trapped charge has been shown to lie within $\approx$ 200 Å of the oxide–nitride interface, and for practical purpose, can be considered to be at the interface. The major reliability problem of the MNOS transistor is the continuous loss of charge through the thin oxide. This is the main reason why the MNOS transistor is not very successful commercially.

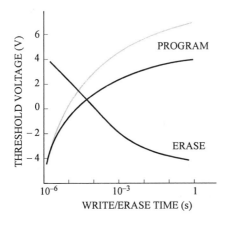

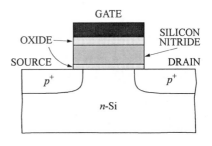

FIGURE 42.4

Shift of threshold voltage as a function of program and erase pulse width. Solid lines, $V_G = \pm 15$ V. Dotted line, $V_G = + 25$ V. (After Ref. 12)

FIGURE 42.5

Structure of an MONOS/SONOS transistor. The difference from an MNOS is the additional blocking oxide between the gate and the nitride layer.

It should be pointed out that unlike a FAMOS transistor, the programming current passes through the whole channel region so that the trapped charge is distributed uniformly throughout the channel. In a FAMOS transistor, the injected charge to the floating gate can redistribute within the gate material, but injection can take place locally near the drain.

In the erase process, a large negative bias is applied to the gate. The energy-band diagram, under negative bias, is shown in Fig. 42.3(b). Traditionally, the discharge process is believed due to the tunneling of trapped electrons back to the silicon substrate. New evidence shows that the major process is due to tunneling of holes from the substrate to neutralize the trapped electrons.[15,16] The discharge process as a function of pulse width is also shown in Fig. 42.4.

The MNOS transistor has to endure many programming and erasing cycles, and a typical specification is 10^4 cycles. The passage of tunneling current gradually increases the interface trap density at the semiconductor surface, and also causes a loss of trapping efficiency due to leakage or tunneling of trapped electrons back to the substrate. These result in a narrowing threshold voltage window after many cycles of program and erase.

42.4 APPLICATIONS

The MNOS transistor is used mainly in nonvolatile memory, specifically an EEPROM. For a summary of the memory types and their applications, the readers can refer to Appendix C6. The MNOS transistor is the oldest technology for EEPROM, but it has been surpassed by the FLOTOX transistor developed in the 1980s. Advantages of the MNOS transistor include reasonable speed for program and erase so that it is a candidate for nonvolatile RAM circuits. It also has superior radiation hardness due to a minimal oxide thickness. The drawbacks of the MNOS transistor are large programming and erasing voltages, and non-uniform threshold voltage from device to device.

42.5 RELATED DEVICES

42.5.1 Metal-Oxide-Nitride-Oxide-Semiconductor Transistor

The MONOS (metal-oxide-nitride-oxide-semiconductor) transistor is sometimes called the SONOS ((poly)silicon-oxide-nitride-oxide-semiconductor) transistor. It is similar to an MNOS transistor except it has an additional blocking oxide layer placed between the gate and the nitride layer, as shown in Fig. 42.5. This layer is usually thicker than the bottom oxide layer. The function of the blocking oxide is to prevent electron injection from the metal to the nitride layer during erase. As a result, a thinner nitride layer can be used, leading to a lower programming voltage, as well as better charge retention.[13,14]

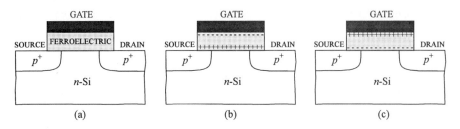

FIGURE 42.6
(a) Structure of an FEFET. After polarization with (b) a positive gate voltage, (c) a negative gate voltage.

42.5.2 Ferroelectric Field-Effect Transistor

An FEFET (ferroelectric field-effect transistor) is an IGFET that uses ferroelectric material as the gate dielectric, as shown in Fig. 42.6.[17] Examples of materials used are lead zirconate titanate, lithium niobate and bismuth titanate. These ferroelectrics can be polarized by a high gate voltage (field), resulting in an equivalent charge sheet located near the semiconductor interface, and inducing a shift of the threshold voltage. The device offers certain advantages such as high-speed programming and erasing, between 1–10 ns, and high endurance, up to 10^{12} cycles. The high dielectric constant, typically over 1000, also provides high gate capacitance, and thus high transconductance. The device, however, has poor polarization retention compared to the charge retention of other nonvolatile memory devices. To improve polarization retention, adding a thin dielectric between the ferroelectric and the silicon substrate has been considered, but due to the large difference in dielectric constants, the programming and erasing voltages are raised significantly.

REFERENCES

1. H. A. R. Wegener, A. J. Lincoln, H. C. Pao, M. R. O'Connell and R. E. Oleksiak, "The variable threshold transistor, a new electrically-alterable, non-destructive read-only storage device," *Tech. Digest IEEE IEDM*, 70 (1967).
2. H. C. Pao and M. O'Connell, "Memory behavior of an MNS capacitor," *Appl. Phys. Lett.*, **12**, 260 (1968).
3. D. Frohman-Bentchkowsky and M. Lenzlinger, "Charge transport and storage in metal-nitride-oxide-silicon (MNOS) structures," *J. Appl. Phys.*, **40**, 3307 (1969).
4. D. Frohman-Bentchkowsky, "The metal-nitride-oxide-silicon (MNOS) transistor – Characteristics and applications," *Proc. IEEE*, **58**, 1207 (1970).
5. J. T. Wallmark and J. H. Scott, "Switching and storage characteristics of MIS memory transistors," *RCA Review*, **30**, 335 (1969).
6. E. C. Ross and J. T. Wallmark, "Theory of the switching behavior of MIS memory transistors," *RCA Review*, **30**, 366 (1969).
7. H. G. Dill and T. N. Toombs, "A new MNOS charge storage effect," *Solid-State Electron.*, **12**, 981 (1969).

8. D. Frohman-Bentchkowsky, "An integrated metal-nitride-oxide-silicon (MNOS) memory," *Proc. IEEE*, **57**, 1190 (1969).

9. J. J. Chang, "Nonvolatile semiconductor memory devices," *Proc. IEEE*, **64**, 1039 (1976).

10. M. Pepper, "MNOS memory transistors," *Inst. Phys. Conf. Ser., No. 50*, Chapter 3, 193 (1980).

11. C. Hu, Ed., *Nonvolatile semiconductor memories. Technologies, design, and applications*, IEEE Press, New York, 1991.

12. Y. Yatsuda, S. Nabetani, K. Uchida, S. I. Minami, M. Terasawa, T. Hagiwara, H. Katto and T. Yasui, "Hi-MNOS II technology for a 64-kbit byte-erasable 5-V-only EEPROM," *IEEE J. Solid-State Circuits*, **SC-20**, 144 (1985).

13. E. Suzuki, H. Hiraishi, K. Ishii and Y. Hayashi, "A low-voltage alterable EEPROM with metal-oxide-nitride-oxide-semiconductor (MONOS) structures," *IEEE Trans. Electron Dev.*, **ED-30**, 122 (1983).

14. C. C. Chao and M. H. White, "Characterization of charge injection and trapping in scaled SONOS/MONOS memory devices," *Solid-State Electron.*, **30**, 307 (1987).

15. A. K. Agarwal and M. H. White, "New results on electron injection, hole injection, and trapping in MONOS nonvolatile memory devices," *IEEE Trans. Electron Dev.*, **ED-32**, 941 (1985).

16. G. L. Heyns and H. E. Maes, "A new model for the discharge behavior of metal-nitride-oxide-silicon (MNOS) non-volatile memory devices," *Appl. Surf. Science*, **30**, 153 (1987).

17. D. Bondurant and F. Gnadinger, "Ferroelectrics for nonvolatile RAMs," *IEEE Spectrum*, 30 (July 1989).

CHAPTER

43

SILICON-CONTROLLED RECTIFIER

43.1 HISTORY

The SCR (silicon-controlled rectifier or semiconductor-controlled rectifier) is the parent and still the main member of the thyristor family. It is the workhorse of high-power electronics and is sometimes simply referred to as a thyristor. (A thyristor is loosely defined as a device having a four-layer *p-n-p-n* structure, leading to bistable behavior.) The first *p-n-p-n* structure was described as a bipolar transistor with a *p-n* hook-collector by Shockley in 1950.[1,2] The current-gain mechanism of this hook-collector transistor was further analyzed by Ebers in 1952.[3] The switching characteristics of a two-terminal *p-n-p-n* structure was first explored by Moll et al. in 1956.[4] Subsequently, the control of switching using a third terminal was examined by Mackintosh,[5] and by Aldrich and Holonyak[6] in 1958. For an overview of the SCR, the readers are referred to Refs. 7–10.

Since the 1960s, the SCR has significant commercial value in the power electronic industry. The SCR is the basis for many specialized but closely related devices that will be described in Section 43.5.

43.2 STRUCTURE

An SCR has a four-layer *p-n-p-n* structure as shown in Fig. 43.1(a). The outermost *n*- and *p*-terminals are called cathode and anode, respectively, and the contact to the *p*-base is the gate (or cathode gate). The top view of the device usually has a circular shape, with the gate located at the center. A typical doping profile between the cathode and the anode is shown in Fig. 43.1(b). Notice that

337

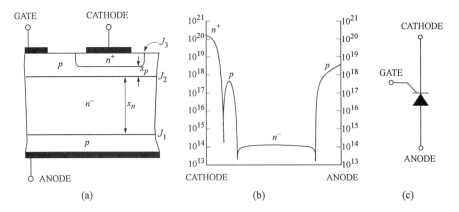

FIGURE 43.1
(a) The structure of an SCR. J_1–J_3 represent the three junctions. (b) Doping profile (cm^{-3}) between cathode and anode. (c) Circuit symbol.

the n-base layer is much thicker, from a few microns to a few hundred microns, has a much lower doping density ($\approx 10^{13}$–10^{15} cm^{-3}), and is designed to support a large blocking voltage. The impurities usually are incorporated by diffusion into lightly doped starting material, and the two p-regions ($\approx 5 \times 10^{18}$ cm^{-3}) can be diffused at the same time. SCRs with high-power capability are discrete devices. They are mounted on pedestals with a good heat sink to dissipate generated heat. The anode is usually bonded onto the package since the gate terminal is near the cathode and needs to be connected separately. As the name implies, SCRs are made of silicon because of its good thermal conductivity, high-voltage and high-current capability, and more-mature technology.

43.3 CHARACTERISTICS

An SCR has two distinct states in the forward direction (anode voltage positive with respect to cathode V_{AK}): a low-current, high-voltage off-state and a high-current, low-voltage on-state. The I-V characteristics of a typical SCR are shown in Fig. 43.2. In the forward blocking mode, there is a breakover voltage for V_{AK} above which the SCR is switched to the on-state. This breakover voltage V_{BO} is a function of the gate current. With high gate current (into the device), V_{BO} is very low and the forward characteristics resemble that of a p-n junction. In practical circuits, when the SCR is off, it is biased at some fixed voltage below V_{BO}, and triggered by a gate current (I_G) to switch to the on-state. After the SCR has been switched on, the gate loses control and a continuous I_G is not required to maintain the on-state. The on-current has to be limited by an external load, otherwise a large current will burn out the device. The forward voltage drop V_{on} to carry a certain value of current is another critical parameter. Sometimes, this is measured by the on-resistance, which is the slope of that portion of the I-V curve.

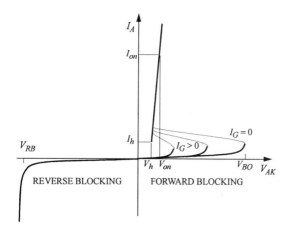

FIGURE 43.2
Static I-V characteristics of an SCR.

A negative I_G is not an effective approach to turn off the SCR (except for the special gate-turn-off thyristor to be discussed in Section 43.5.2). To turn the device off, it is necessary to change the applied V_{AK} to a value below the holding voltage V_h. In practice, often a reverse V_{AK} is applied to speed up the turn-off process, and this is called forced commutation.

In the reverse blocking mode, junctions J_1 and J_3 are reverse biased, but most of the voltage drop is supported by the n-base depletion region. The breakdown in this mode can be due to (1) depletion of the whole n-base region (punch-through) or (2) avalanche breakdown of the junction J_1. The punch-through voltage V_{pt} for the first mechanism can be estimated by a step-junction depletion approximation to be

$$V_{pt} = \frac{qN_D x_n^2}{2\varepsilon_s} \quad . \tag{43.1}$$

The avalanche breakdown voltage for an isolated p^+-n step junction in Si can be approximated by[11]

$$V_B = 5.34 \times 10^{13} (N_D \text{ in cm}^{-3})^{-3/4} \quad \text{V} \quad . \tag{43.2}$$

The reverse breakdown voltage based on these two limits are shown in Fig. 43.3. For low doping concentrations, punch-through is the limiting factor while for high concentrations, avalanche breakdown sets the limit. In a more vigorous analysis, the avalanche breakdown voltage should be reduced since it resembles an open-base p-n-p bipolar transistor breakdown. The breakdown condition is given by

$$M\alpha_{pnp} = 1 \tag{43.3}$$

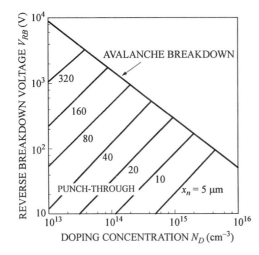

FIGURE 43.3
The reverse breakdown voltage V_{RB} of an SCR as a function of the n-base thickness and doping concentration. In avalanche breakdown, only junction breakdown is considered. This breakdown voltage will be lowered by an open base, bipolar transistor feedback. (After Ref. 7)

where α is the common-base current gain and M is the avalanche multiplication factor, approximated by

$$M = \frac{1}{1 - (V/V_B)^m} \ . \tag{43.4}$$

m is a constant and is equal to 6 for a Si p^+-n junction. Combining the above two equations, the breakdown voltage in Eq. (43.2) should be modified to

$$V^*_B = V_B(1 - \alpha_{pnp})^{1/m} \ . \tag{43.5}$$

In the forward blocking mode, the switching mechanism can best be explained by the two-transistor model shown in Fig. 43.4. The four-layer structure can be bisected into a p-n-p and an n-p-n bipolar transistor, with each base connected to the other's collector. Qualitatively, an initial small base current I_{B2} produces a larger collector current I_{C2}. This I_{C2} is a base current for the p-n-p transistor, and it is further amplified to give a still larger collector current I_{C1}. This I_{C1} adds to I_G and becomes the original base current I_{B2}. This regenerative feedback gives rise to switching. Mathematically, with both transistors biased in the active region (see Chapter 29–Bipolar Transistor),

$$I_{C2} = \alpha_{npn} I_K + I_{o2} \ , \tag{43.6}$$

$$I_{B1} = (1 - \alpha_{pnp}) I_A - I_{o1} \ . \tag{43.7}$$

I_{o1} and I_{o2} are the leakage currents due to the reverse-biased collector-base junctions of the two transistors. Equating these two equations, and using

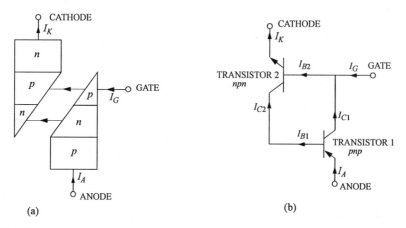

FIGURE 43.4
(a) Schematic structure of the two-transistor model and (b) its equivalent circuit.

$$I_K = I_A + I_G \; , \tag{43.8}$$

one obtains

$$I_A = \frac{\alpha_{npn} I_G + (I_{o1} + I_{o2})}{1 - (\alpha_{pnp} + \alpha_{npn})} \; . \tag{43.9}$$

Switching corresponds to the condition of $(\alpha_{pnp} + \alpha_{npn}) = 1$. The α of a bipolar transistor here is largely determined by the emitter injection efficiency γ, given by

$$\gamma \approx \frac{I_{dif}}{I_{dif} + I_{rec}}$$

$$\approx \frac{I_d \exp{(qV/kT)}}{I_d \exp{(qV/kT)} + I_r \exp{(qV/2kT)}} \; . \tag{43.10}$$

The degradation of γ is due mainly to the recombination current (I_{rec}). Since the junction diffusion current (I_{dif}) increases faster with voltage than does I_{rec}, γ improves with base current. Also if $(\alpha_{pnp} + \alpha_{npn})$ increases with current (or voltage), it is necessary to have $(\alpha_{pnp} + \alpha_{npn}) < 1$ at low bias before switching. As seen in Eq. (43.9), the main function of I_G for triggering is not to increase the numerator, but to increase $(\alpha_{pnp} + \alpha_{npn})$ to meet the condition of $(\alpha_{pnp} + \alpha_{npn}) = 1$.

In the reverse blocking mode, J_1 and J_3 are reverse biased and only J_2 is forward biased. There is no switching in this mode. The difference in this situation from Fig. 43.4(b) is that the internal nodes become the emitters, rather

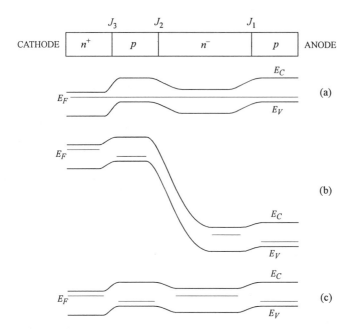

FIGURE 43.5
Energy-band diagrams of an SCR (a) in equilibrium, (b) in forward blocking mode, and (c) after switching to the on-state.

than collectors, of the two bipolar transistors. It can be shown by similar current equations that regenerative feedback does not occur.

The energy-band diagrams before and after switching are shown in Fig. 43.5. When the SCR is turned on, all three junctions are forward biased. The V_{on} is the sum of one forward junction bias plus the V_{CE} of a bipolar transistor in saturation. These values are approximately 0.7 V and 0.2 V, respectively, leading to a V_{on} of ≈ 0.9 V.

In the forward blocking mode, the breakover voltage in the presence of avalanche multiplication can be analyzed as being similar to the reverse breakdown voltage. Now with two transistors in action, the breakdown condition becomes

$$M(\alpha_{pnp} + \alpha_{npn}) = 1 \; . \tag{43.11}$$

This is similar to the previous condition of $(\alpha_{pnp} + \alpha_{npn}) = 1$, but with the additional multiplication factor included. Combining this with Eq. (43.4) leads to a breakover voltage of

$$V_{BO} = V_B(1 - \alpha_{npn} - \alpha_{pnp})^{1/m} \; . \tag{43.12}$$

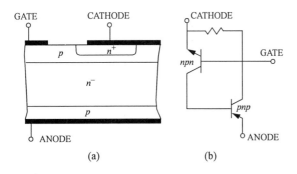

FIGURE 43.6
(a) An SCR with a cathode short, and (b) its equivalent circuit.

To improve V_{BO}, α_{npn} must be minimized. Comparing Eq. (43.12) to Eq. (43.5), the maximum V_{BO} becomes the same as the reverse breakdown voltage. Notice that breakdown here is from junction J_2 now instead of J_1. Also if the SCR is triggered by a gate current, avalanche is not a factor. In that case M is equal to one for Eq. (43.11) and Eq. (43.12) is not applicable.

One approach to reduce α_{npn} is to incorporate a cathode short between the cathode and the gate, as shown in Fig. 43.6. This shunt resistance reduces the injection efficiency of the n-p-n transistor at low I_G levels, decreases α_{npn} and increases the V_{BO}. Another benefit of the reduced α_{npn} from a cathode short is to satisfy the requirement of $(\alpha_{pnp} + \alpha_{npn}) < 1$ before switching. An alternative is to deteriorate both α_{pnp} and α_{npn} by introducing recombination centers to shorten the minority-carrier lifetimes. But the penalty is a higher V_{on} and the cathode short is a better approach. One more benefit of the cathode short is to improve the transient response. When an abrupt V_{AK} is applied to the SCR, even with a value below V_{BO}, it can still turn on the SCR. The origin of this dV/dt triggering is a displacement current from the capacitance of the reverse-biased junction J_2. This displacement current passes through the emitter-base junctions of the two bipolar transistors, and increases α_{pnp} and α_{npn} to trigger the switching. In effect, this displacement current plays the role of the gate current. The cathode short bypasses this displacement current through the n-p-n transistor and improves the dV/dt tolerance.

The frequency response of an SCR is related to the turn-on time and turn-off time. The turn-on time is defined from the start of the gate current pulse, to the time for the anode current to rise to 90% of the steady state value (Fig. 43.7(a)). It has been shown to be approximately equal to the geometric mean of the transit times through the two base layers[7]

$$t_{on} = \sqrt{\left(\frac{x^2_n}{2D_p}\right)\left(\frac{x^2_p}{2D_n}\right)} \, . \tag{43.13}$$

Typical t_{on} values are 0.1–1 μs for a low-power SCR, and 10–30 μs for a high-power SCR. The turn-off time is usually longer, and is defined as the time

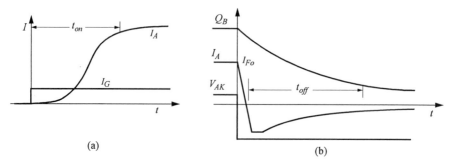

FIGURE 43.7
Waveforms showing (a) the turn-on process and (b) the turn-off process. The definitions of t_{on} and t_{off} are indicated.

interval between $I_A = 0$ (before reversing direction) and the time that, if a high positive V_{AK} (but below V_{BO}) is reapplied, the SCR does not lose the off-state (Fig. 43.7(b)). During the turn-off process, the charge in the base of the *p-n-p* transistor decays exponentially, with[9]

$$Q_B = \tau_p \alpha_{pnp} I_{Fo} \exp\left(\frac{-t}{\tau_p}\right).$$
(43.14)

At any time in this interval, if a positive V_{AK} is reapplied, the immediate forward current is proportional to Q_B, given by

$$I_F \propto Q_B$$
$$= I_{Fo} \exp\left(\frac{-t}{\tau_p}\right).$$
(43.15)

To maintain the off-state, Q_B has to decay to a value such that the I_F does not exceed the holding current I_h. The turn-off time is then calculated to be

$$t_{off} = \tau_p \ln\left(\frac{I_{Fo}}{I_h}\right).$$
(43.16)

Typical frequency response of an SCR is limited to below 50 kHz.

43.4 APPLICATIONS

An SCR is basically used as a switch to turn on and off the power to a load. A refined technique can also control variable power fed to the load. Another important application is to convert a power source from one waveform to another. The gate terminal is the control where a small gate-current pulse controls a much

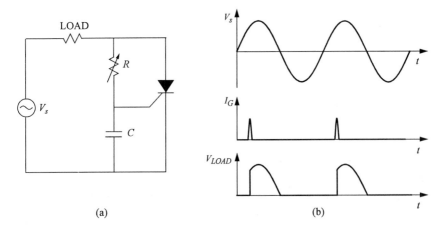

FIGURE 43.8
(a) A phase-control circuit to limit partial power delivered to the load. (b) Waveforms for voltage source, gate trigger current and voltage seen by the load.

larger power flow. In comparison to other three-terminal power switches such as the bipolar transistor and the MOSFET, a continuous voltage or current source to the gate to maintain the on-state is not necessary. It can also handle much larger current, and has a lower V_{on}. The disadvantage of an SCR is the low-speed operation, typically below 10 kHz–50 kHz, depending on the power level.

It is probably safe to say that the SCR is the most widely used power device. It is capable of carrying thousands of amperes and supporting thousands of volts. The majority of the applications can be classified into the following functions:

1. Static switch: An SCR replaces the electromechanical relay. Typical examples are automobile ignition switch, gas-appliance ignition system, battery charger, and alarm system.

2. Power control: In AC operations, the SCR controls the amount of power delivered to the load. Examples are light dimmer, variable-speed motor, heater control, etc. The phase-control circuit is shown in Fig. 43.8. The setting of the variable resistor determines the phase-lag of the gate pulse with respect to the source. Once the SCR is turned on, it remains to be on until it is turned off by the negative cycle. The waveform seen by the load is shown in Fig. 43.8(b). The average power received by the load is related to the area under this V_{LOAD} curve.

3. Power conversion: The SCR is used in power conversion and regulation circuits. These include conversion of power source from AC to AC, DC to AC, AC to DC, and DC to DC.

4. Surge protection: The characteristics of an SCR are suitable for a protection device for ICs and discrete components. When a voltage rises beyond a

critical value, the SCR is turned on to dissipate the charge or voltage quickly. An example is protection of telephone equipment when the telephone line is exposed to lightning.

43.5 RELATED DEVICES

43.5.1 Gate-Assisted-Turn-Off Thyristor

To speed up the turn-off process of an SCR, a negative gate voltage is sometimes applied, in addition to reducing or reversing V_{AK}. This gate bias helps to drain the minority carriers stored in the n-base, and to ensure that the gate-cathode junction J_3 is not forward biased. The structure of a gate-assisted-turn-off thyristor (GATT) is similar to an SCR except narrow cathode strips are often used so that the gate has more control because it is closer to the center of the cathode. Interdigitated gate–cathode structures are also used for large-area devices.

43.5.2 Gate-Turn-Off Thyristor

The gate-turn-off (GTO) thyristor is sometimes called a gate-turn-off switch. In this device, the negative gate current alone is able to turn off the SCR, without changing the V_{AK} (forced commutation). In order to have more efficient gate-controlled turn-off, during the on-state I_{B2} and I_{C1} in Fig. 43.4(b) have to be minimized. This demands that $\alpha_{npn} \gg \alpha_{pnp}$. The GTO thyristor structure either has a thicker n-base layer, or it incorporates an anode short (anode to n-base short) to reduce α_{pnp}. Another difference in structure from a regular SCR is that a cathode short is not feasible. Similar to that of the GATT, the cathode terminal is made of narrow strips, often interdigitated with the gate strips. The main advantage of the GTO thyristor is the elimination of external circuitry for forced commutation. Another advantage is a smaller turn-off time (≈ 1 μs) and the capability of higher-speed operation. The disadvantage is a larger I_G required for turn-on.

43.5.3 Asymmetric Thyristor

In certain applications, the SCR does not see a reverse V_{AK} and thus the reverse blocking capability is not needed. The structure of a typical asymmetric thyristor (asymmetric SCR or ASCR) is shown in Fig. 43.9(a) where both cathode short and anode short are incorporated. These shorts would produce a large leakage for negative V_{AK} (Fig. 43.9(b)), but provide much improvement in the forward blocking mode, such as larger breakover voltage. Without having to operate in the reverse blocking mode, J_2 is never reverse biased, and the n-base layer can be made much thinner. A reduced n-base layer leads to a reduced V_{on}, and it also improves the turn-on time and turn-off time.

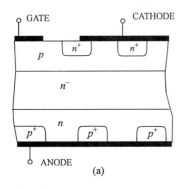
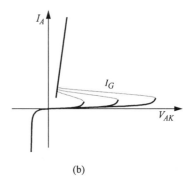

FIGURE 43.9
(a) Structure of an asymmetric thyristor and (b) its I-V characteristics.

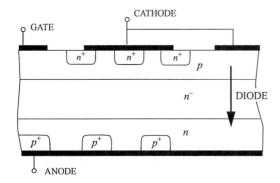

FIGURE 43.10
Structure of a reverse-conducting thyristor.

43.5.4 Reverse-Conducting Thyristor

In some circuit applications, it is necessary to connect a diode in parallel to the asymmetric SCR to clamp V_{AK} in the reverse direction. The reverse-conducting thyristor (RCT) is simply an ASCR with a large built-in diode to replace the external diode. The structure is shown in Fig. 43.10 and the I-V characteristics are similar to that of the ASCR. The advantage is to reduce the stray inductance in the external diode connection, and also to provide a less expensive package. The structure, however, needs good isolation between the diode and the SCR. The minority charge stored in the diode when it is in forward bias (with negative V_{AK}) can diffuse to the SCR region and affects the off-state.

43.5.5 Breakover Diode

The breakover diode is also known as Shockley diode, four-layer diode and p-n-p-n diode. It is a two-terminal device without the gate connection, and the I-V characteristics are the same as an SCR with an open gate, or $I_G = 0$ (Fig. 43.11).

In this device, the trigger is performed by a large V_{AK} exceeding the V_{BO}, or by dV/dt transient. The device is often used as a trigger switch for another SCR. This trigger switch is connected to the gate of a regular SCR to provide a much sharper gate pulse for a more timely turn-on.

43.5.6 Diode AC Switch

A DIAC (diode AC switch) is a bilateral switch that can be turned on in both the forward and reverse polarities. The device can be a three-layer structure (*n-p-n* or *p-n-p*) or a five-layer structure as shown in Fig. 43.12. In the three-layer structure, switching occurs when the reverse-biased junction experiences avalanche breakdown. When that happens, the large current increases the α of the bipolar transistor, and decreases the voltage drop across the device. This, in turn, produces negative resistance (Fig. 43.13). Notice that for a three-layer device, the *I-V* characteristics do not "latch," as in the case of the five-layer structure. The five-layer DIAC can be considered as two breakover diodes connected in antiparallel. The DIAC is often used as a trigger switch for SCR or TRIAC which is to be discussed next.

43.5.7 Triode AC Switch

The TRIAC (triode AC switch) is a DIAC with a gate contact to control the switching voltage. As shown in Fig. 43.14(a), the gate contact is made to the *p*-base, with an additional *n*-type diffusion layer underneath the gate. The switching characteristics of a TRIAC are shown in Fig. 43.14(c). The operation of a TRIAC is quite complicated. It has a special property that both positive and negative gate voltage lower the V_{BO} and can trigger switching. For positive V_G, it controls the *p*-base potential and acts as a regular gate. For negative V_G, the

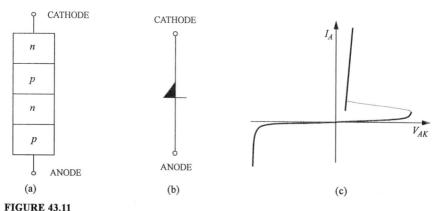

FIGURE 43.11
(a) Schematic structure of a breakover diode. (b) Circuit symbol. (c) *I-V* characteristics.

n-pocket injects electrons into the central *n*-base and triggers the switching. The TRIAC is more common for AC operation.

43.5.8 Light-Activated Thyristor

In a light-activated thyristor (light-activated SCR, LASCR or light-triggered thyristor), the gate current to trigger switching is provided by internally generated electron-hole pairs upon exposure to light. The structure and its *I-V* characteristics are shown in Fig. 43.15. Most LASCRs incorporate a cathode short to improve the *dV/dt* tolerance, but it also raises the light power required to trigger the device. Light is mostly absorbed in the depletion region of the central n^--layer. The holes generated are attracted to the cathode short around the *n*-diffusion, and produce an *IR* drop to forward bias the cathode emitter junction J_3. The electrons

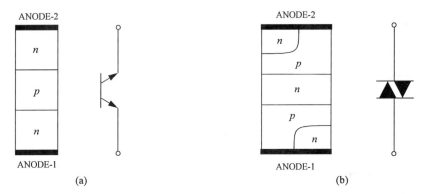

FIGURE 43.12
A DIAC and its circuit symbol with (a) a 3-layer structure and (b) a 5-layer structure.

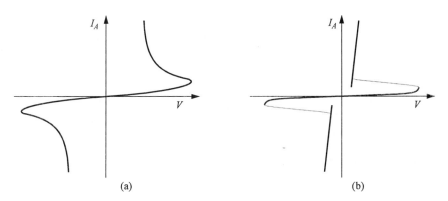

FIGURE 43.13
I-V characteristics of a DIAC with (a) a 3-layer structure and (b) a 5-layer structure.

generated remain in the n^--layer, and supply the base current of the p-n-p transistor. The light power required for switching is in the order of mW. After switching to the on-state, elimination of light does not turn off the device and force commutation is required. The advantages of the LASCR include complete electrical isolation from the trigger circuit, and a more compact and inexpensive integration of a photodetector and an SCR. The turn-on is also faster than a regular SCR since the internally generated gate current is more evenly distributed within the device. Typical examples for LASCR applications are switches for street lamps and card readers.

43.5.9 Programmable Unijunction Transistor

A programmable unijunction transistor (PUT) is very different in structure and working principle from a unijunction transistor (see Chapter 45), although the electrical characteristics and applications are similar. The structure shown in

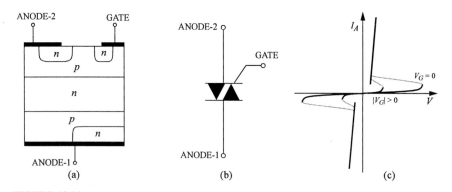

FIGURE 43.14
(a) Structure of a TRIAC. (b) Circuit symbol. (c) I-V characteristics.

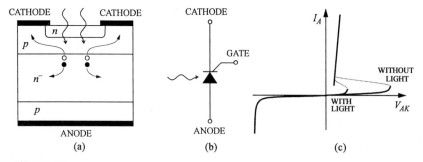

FIGURE 43.15
(a) Structure of a light-activated thyristor. (b) Its circuit symbol and (c) I-V characteristics.

Fig. 43.16(a) is similar to a regular SCR but has a gate contact to the n-base. Since this gate contact is made to the n-region instead of the p-base, a negative gate current switches the device on. This occurs when the anode potential is slightly (≈ 0.7 V) higher than V_G. Unlike in an SCR, the breakover voltage increases with the gate voltage (Fig. 43.16(c)). In a practical biasing circuit shown in Fig. 43.17, the gate voltage is programmed by external components R_1, R_2, and V_o to control the breakover voltage V_{BO}, hence the name programmable unijunction transistor. Compared to a unijunction transistor, the PUT is a more reliable device, less expensive to make, and it often replaces the former. An example for the PUT application is a relaxation oscillator shown in Fig. 43.18.

43.5.10 Silicon-Controlled Switch

A silicon-controlled switch (SCS) has both an anode gate and a cathode gate connection (Fig. 43.19(a)). The device can thus be switched on by a positive voltage to the cathode gate or a negative voltage to the anode gate. In a low-power SCS, the device is often designed to be capable of gate-controlled turn-off without

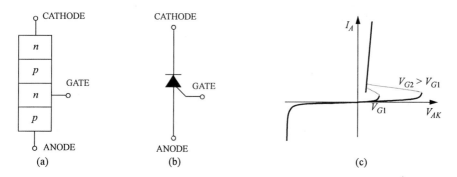

FIGURE 43.16

(a) Structure of a programmable unijunction transistor. (b) Circuit symbol and (c) I-V characteristics.

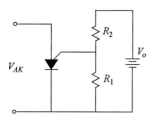

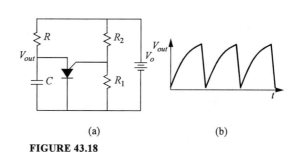

FIGURE 43.17

Biasing circuit for a programmable unijunction transistor.

FIGURE 43.18

(a) A relaxation oscillator using the programmable unijunction transistor. (b) Output waveform.

forced commutation. To trigger turn-off, a negative voltage can be applied to the cathode gate or a positive voltage to the anode gate. The combination of multiple gates with turn-on and turn-off capability yields greater flexibility in designing thyristor circuits.

43.5.11 Silicon Unilateral Switch

In a silicon unilateral switch (SUS), the gate terminal is connected to the n-base, and a cathode short is usually incorporated (Fig. 43.20(a)). The switching in this device is initiated by avalanche breakdown between the anode gate and the p-base (J_2). The characteristics are similar to that of the SCR (Fig. 43.2) where a more positive gate voltage induces a lower breakover voltage and switching to the on-state. The SUS is a more stable device since the avalanche process is less temperature dependent, and it requires lower voltage to trigger. It is usually used only in low-power applications.

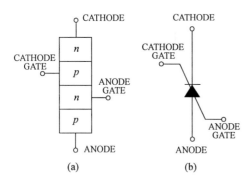

FIGURE 43.19
(a) Structure of a silicon-controlled switch. (b) Its circuit symbol.

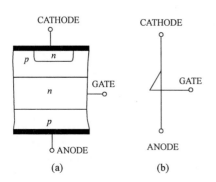

FIGURE 43.20
(a) Structure of a silicon unilateral switch and (b) its circuit symbol.

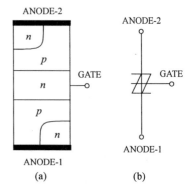

FIGURE 43.21
(a) Structure of a silicon bilateral switch and (b) its circuit symbol.

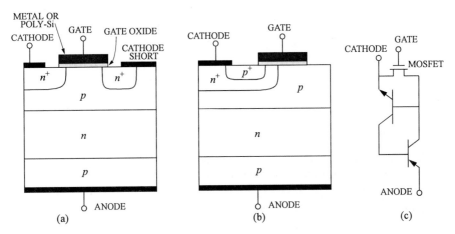

FIGURE 43.22
Structures of an MOS-controlled thyristor, of (a) *n*-channel type and (b) *p*-channel type. (c) Their equivalent circuit.

43.5.12 Silicon Bilateral Switch

The silicon bilateral switch (SBS) has a structure equivalent to two SUSs connected in antiparallel (Fig. 43.21(a)). The *I-V* characteristics are similar to that of a TRIAC. The SBS is often used as a trigger switch for a TRIAC.

43.5.13 MOS-Controlled Thyristor

As discussed previously, a cathode short in an SCR improves the off-state characteristics such as dV/dt tolerance and larger breakover voltage. The penalty is that the turn-on process requires longer t_{on} and higher triggering I_G. The V_{on} is also larger after switched on. The MOS-controlled thyristor is an SCR with a cathode short that can be connected or disconnected by a MOSFET, whenever desired. With a positive gate voltage applied to the structure in Fig. 43.22(a), an *n*-channel is formed under the gate and the cathode short is put in place electrically. Negative gate voltage for the structure in Fig. 43.22(b) will perform the same function. Another benefit is the gate-controlled turn-off capability. Connecting the cathode short decreases α_{npn}, and can induce turn-off. For these reasons, optimum performance can be achieved with the cathode short connected during turn-off and in the off-state, and disconnected during turn-on and in the on-state. The MOS-controlled thyristor has extremely high input impedance to the gate. It is a candidate to replace the GTO thyristor. Notice that in this structure, the MOSFET connects between the cathode and the *p*-base, which is different from an insulated-gate bipolar transistor (see Chapter 44) where the MOSFET connects the cathode to the *n*-base.

REFERENCES

1. W. Shockley, *Electrons and holes in semiconductor*, Van Nostrand, Toronto, 1950.
2. W. Shockley, M. Sparks and G. K. Teal, "*p-n* junction transistors," *Phys. Rev.*, **83**, 151 (1951).
3. J. J. Ebers, "Four-terminal *P-N-P-N* transistors," *Proc. IRE*, **40**, 1361 (1952).
4. J. L. Moll, M. Tanenbaum, J. M. Goldey and N. Holonyak, "*P-N-P-N* transistor switches," *Proc. IRE*, **44**, 1174 (1956).
5. I. M. Mackintosh, "The electrical characteristics of silicon *P-N-P-N* triodes," *Proc. IRE*, **46**, 1229 (1958).
6. R. W. Aldrich and N. Holonyak, Jr., "Multiterminal *P-N-P-N* switches," *Proc. IRE*, **46**, 1236 (1958).
7. S. M. Sze, *Physics of semiconductor devices*, 2nd Ed., Wiley, New York, 1981.
8. S. K. Ghandhi, *Semiconductor power devices*, Wiley, New York, 1977.
9. A. Blicher, *Thyristor physics*, Springer-Verlag, New York, 1976.
10. P. D. Taylor, *Thyristor design and realization*, Wiley, New York, 1987.
11. S. M. Sze and G. Gibbons, "Avalanche breakdown voltages of abrupt and linearly graded *p-n* junctions in Ge, Si, GaAs, and GaP," *Appl. Phys. Lett.*, **8**, 111 (1966).

44

INSULATED-GATE BIPOLAR TRANSISTOR

44.1 HISTORY

The name insulated-gate bipolar transistor (IGBT) comes from its operation based on an internal interaction between an insulated-gate FET (IGFET) and a bipolar transistor. It has also been called by different authors as IGT (insulated-gate transistor), IGR (insulated-gate rectifier), COMFET (conductivity-modulated field-effect transistor), GEMFET (gain-enhanced MOSFET), BiFET (bipolar FET), and injector FET. The device was first demonstrated by Baliga in 1979,[1] and in 1980 by Plummer and Scharf,[2] Leipold et al.,[3] and Tihanyi.[4] A more detailed account on the device's advantages was presented in 1982 by Becke and Wheatley[5] and Baliga et al.[6] In the following year, more work was published by Russel et al.[7] Chang et al.[8] and Goodman et al.[9] Ever since the device's conception, there has been active studies on the IGBT, with improving understanding and performance. The device has been used commercially since the late 1980s, and still is gaining popularity. For more insight into the device physics, the readers are referred to Refs. 10–13.

44.2 STRUCTURE

The structure for an IGBT is shown in Fig. 44.1. It can be viewed as an SCR with a MOSFET (or more specifically a DMOS transistor, see Section 19.5.1) connecting the cathode (n^+-region) to the n-base (n^--region). This device should not be confused with the MOS-controlled thyristor where the MOSFET connects

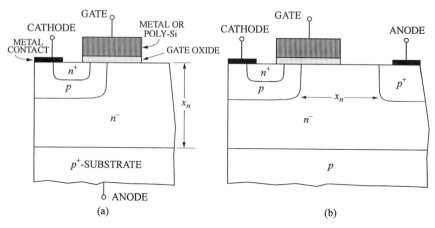

FIGURE 44.1
(a) Vertical structure and (b) lateral structure (LIGT) of an n-channel IGBT.

the cathode to the p-base (see Section 43.5.13). The structure can also be viewed as a DMOS transistor with an additional p-n junction within the drain region. In the vertical structure (Fig. 44.1(a)), the p^+-anode is the low-resistivity substrate material, and the n^--layer is an epitaxial layer about 50 μm thick, with a doping concentration below 10^{14} cm^{-3}. In this structure, isolation between devices is difficult and devices are diced as discrete components. In the lateral structure (LIGT as the lateral insulated-gate transistor) shown in Fig. 44.1(b), the anode is incorporated at the surface, and isolation to the substrate is achieved by the p-type material. Like the SCR, an IGBT is made with silicon material because of its good thermal conductivity and high breakdown voltage. The examples shown in Fig. 44.1 have an n-channel DMOS transistor and are called an n-channel IGBT. A complimentary device, the p-channel IGBT is also possible with opposite doping types, and operated with reverse voltage polarities. The terminologies of anode/cathode/gate are adopted from an SCR, but some authors have used terms such as drain/source/gate and collector/emitter/gate.

44.3 CHARACTERISTICS

The bulk of the device is the n^--layer which is the drain of the DMOS transistor, as well as the base of the p-n-p bipolar transistor. It is lightly doped and is wide in order to support a large blocking voltage. In the on-state, conductivity in this region is enhanced by excess electrons injected from the n^+-cathode via the DMOS transistor surface channel, and by excess holes from the p^+-anode. This conductivity modulation is the reason for the name COMFET.

With a zero gate bias, the channel of the DMOS transistor is not formed. The structure is equivalent to a breakover diode (p-n-p-n structure) with a cathode

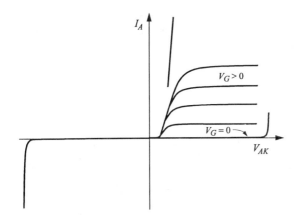

FIGURE 44.2
Output characteristics of an n-channel IGBT.

short (metal contact between cathode and p-base). The anode (or cathode) current I_A is minimal until breakdown in both polarities (Fig. 44.2). For forward V_{AK}, the breakdown is initiated by avalanche breakdown of the n^--p junction and for reverse V_{AK}, the same process of the n^--p^+ junction. With a large positive gate voltage V_G, an n-type channel is induced underneath the gate, connecting the two n-type regions. Depending on the value of V_{AK}, three different modes of operation can be observed. With a small V_{AK} up to ≈ 0.7 V, the equivalent circuit is a DMOS transistor in series with a p-i-n diode (Fig. 44.3(a)). With negligible voltage across the DMOS transistor, the p-i-n diode is under forward bias, and the current conduction is via recombination of excess electrons and holes in the n^--region. To maintain charge neutrality, these excess electrons and holes are equal in number, being supplied from the cathode and anode, respectively. The current equation in this mode is similar to that of a p-i-n diode under forward bias (see Chapter 2),

$$ I_A \approx \frac{4Aqn_i D_a}{x_n} \exp\left(\frac{qV_{AK}}{2kT}\right) . \qquad (44.1) $$

D_a is the ambipolar diffusion coefficient,

$$ D_a \approx \frac{2D_p D_n}{D_p + D_n} . \qquad (44.2) $$

The factor of 2 within the exponential term is a characteristic of recombination current. This exponential rise of current with V_{AK} shows up as an offset voltage in the linear scale of Fig. 44.2. The current is also independent of V_G since the voltage drop across the DMOS transistor is already negligible.

The second regime starts with $V_{AK} > 0.7$ V where the characteristics resemble those of a MOSFET. Under such high V_{AK}, the excess holes injected from the anode cannot be totally absorbed by recombination. They spill over to the middle p-region and contribute to a p-n-p bipolar current. The equivalent circuit is indicated in Fig. 44.3(b). The MOSFET current I_{MOS} becomes the base current of the bipolar transistor, and the anode current is the emitter current, given by

$$I_A = (1 + \beta_{pnp}) I_{MOS} . \tag{44.3}$$

It can be seen in Fig. 44.2 that the anode current duplicates the general shape of the MOSFET characteristics, except amplified by a current gain. The bipolar current gain β_{pnp} is small due to the large base dimension of the n^--layer. With

$$\beta = \frac{\alpha}{1 - \alpha} \tag{44.4}$$

and

$$\alpha \approx \alpha_T \approx \frac{1}{\cosh(x_{nn}/L_n)} , \tag{44.5}$$

(α_T is the base transport factor and x_{nn} is the neutral base) β_{pnp} is around one, meaning that electron and hole currents are comparable in magnitude.

In the third mode, if the current exceeds a critical level, the characteristics latch onto a low-impedance state, similar to the on-state of an SCR. This is due to the internal interaction of the p-n-p-n structure. In spite of the low on-resistance, this state is not desirable because once latching occurs, the gate looses control in

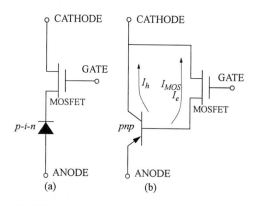

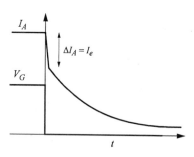

FIGURE 44.3
Equivalent circuits of an IGBT for (a) low V_{AK}, below the offset voltage, (b) high V_{AK}, above the offset voltage.

FIGURE 44.4
Waveform of the anode–cathode current during turn-off.

turning off the device. The gate-controlled turn-off is critical and is precisely the advantage over an SCR. The cathode short between the n^+- and p-regions helps to suppress latching by decreasing the current gain of the n-p-n bipolar transistor. Special design with higher p-region concentration near the cathode has also been examined.

Besides the possibility of latching, another drawback of the IGBT is a slow turnoff process due to charge storage in the n^--region. Typical anode current waveform during turnoff is shown in Fig. 44.4. The decay of I_A takes place in two stages. There is first a sudden drop (ΔI_A), followed by a slow exponential decay. The initial current drop, for first-order approximation, is due to the starvation of the electron current I_e supplied by the DMOS transistor.[14] Since the current components can be separated into electron current I_e and hole current I_h,

$$I_e = (1 - \alpha) I_A \qquad (44.6)$$

$$I_h = \alpha I_A \ , \qquad (44.7)$$

the current drop ΔI_A can be estimated. The current I_h decays exponentially with a characteristic minority-carrier lifetime for holes. This turnoff process takes typically 10–50 μs, and limits the IGBT to operations below 10 kHz. One technique to speed up the turnoff is to degrade the carrier lifetime by electron irradiation, but at the expense of a higher forward-voltage drop.

44.4 APPLICATIONS

The IGBT combines the salient features of a MOSFET and a bipolar transistor. In common with a MOSFET, it has high input resistance and low input capacitance. Similar to a bipolar transistor or an SCR, it has low on-resistance (or low forward voltage drop) and high-current capability. A more important feature is the gate-controlled turn-off capability. In an SCR, the gate alone cannot turn off the device, and forced commutation is needed to change the V_{AK}. Such commutation circuit adds extra cost and inflexibility.

A power semiconductor device has two main functions: (1) to control power fed to a load and (2) to change a power source from one waveform to another. An IGBT is especially suitable for controlling motor drives. A specific example of its use in power supply circuits is the DC to AC converter.

REFERENCES

1. B. J. Baliga, "Enhancement- and depletion-mode vertical-channel M.O.S. gated thyristors," *Electronics Lett.*, **15**, 645 (1979).
2. J. D. Plummer and B. W. Scharf, "Insulated-gate planar thyristors: I – Structure and basic operation," *IEEE Trans. Electron Dev.*, **ED-27**, 380 (1980).
3. L. Leipold, W. Baumgartner, W. Ladenhauf and J. P. Stengl, "A FET-controlled thyristor in SIPMOS technology," *Tech. Digest IEEE IEDM*, 79 (1980).

4. J. Tihanyi, "Functional integration of power MOS and bipolar devices," *Tech. Digest IEEE IEDM*, 75 (1980).

5. H. W. Becke and C. F. Wheatley, Jr., "Power MOSFET with an anode region," U.S. Patent 4,364,073 (1982).

6. B. J. Baliga, M. S. Adler, P. V. Gray, R. P. Love and N. Zommer, "The insulated gate rectifier (IGR): A new power switching device," *Tech. Digest IEEE IEDM*, 264 (1982).

7. J. P. Russel, A. M. Goodman, L. A. Goodman and J. M. Neilson, "The COMFET – A new high conductance MOS-gated device," *IEEE Electron Dev. Lett.*, **EDL-4**, 63 (1983).

8. M. F. Chang, G. C. Pifer, B. J. Baliga, M. S. Adler and P. V. Gray, "25 amp, 500 volt insulated gate transistors," *Tech. Digest IEEE IEDM*, 83 (1983).

9. A. M. Goodman, J. P. Russell, L. A. Goodman, C. J. Nuese and J. M. Neilson, "Improved COMFETs with fast switching speed and high-current capability," *Tech. Digest IEEE IEDM*, 79 (1983).

10. A. R. Hefner, Jr. and D. L. Blackburn, "An analytical model for the steady-state and transient characteristics of the power insulated-gate bipolar transistor," *Solid-State Electron.*, **31**, 1513 (1988).

11. B. J. Baliga, "Temperature behavior of insulated gate transistor characteristics," *Solid-State Electron.*, **28**, 289 (1985).

12. D. S. Kuo, C. Hu and S. P. Sapp, "An analytical model for the power bipolar-MOS transistor," *Solid-State Electron.*, **29**, 1229 (1986).

13. H. Yilmaz, W. Ron Van Dell, K. Owyang and M. F. Chang, "Insulated gate transistor physics: Modeling and optimization of the on-state characteristics," *IEEE Trans. Electron Dev.*, **ED-32**, 2812 (1985).

14. B. J. Baliga, "Analysis of insulated gate transistor turn-off characteristics," *IEEE Electron Dev. Lett.*, **EDL-6**, 74 (1985).

CHAPTER 45

UNIJUNCTION
TRANSISTOR

45.1 HISTORY

The unijunction transistor bears its name because its structure has only a single *p-n* junction, in light of the bipolar transistor which has two *p-n* junctions. It was called a filamentary transistor by Shockley et al. in their original work in 1949.[1,2] It was also referred to as a double-base diode in the 1950s when experimental work was reported by Lesk and Mathis[3] and Aldrich and Lesk,[4] and a theoretical analysis by Suran.[5,6] The current name has been used since the 1960s.[7,8] Even though the device structure does not contain *p-n-p-n* layers, it is generally accepted as part of the thyristor family.

45.2 STRUCTURE

Different versions of the unijunction transistor structures are shown in Fig. 45.1. The device in all three forms consists of two ohmic contacts to the bulk of the structure, with a *p-n* junction somewhere in between. The two ohmic contacts are labeled as bases (base-1 and base-2), and the *p-n* junction is the emitter. Most unijunction transistor structures are made on *n*-type material although complementary devices on *p*-type material are also possible. Early in its development, germanium substrates were explored but more recent devices are made of Si. The resistivity of the material is in the order of 100 Ω-cm (doping $\approx 10^{14}$ cm^{-3}) and the resistance between the two base contacts, without current injection from the emitter, is typically between 5–10 kΩ. The structure looks somewhat similar to a JFET. The difference here is that under all operational

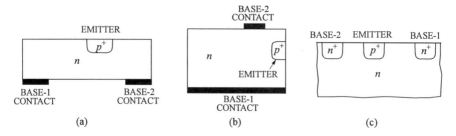

FIGURE 45.1
Different versions of the unijunction transistor. (a) Bar structure. (b) Cube structure. (c) Planar structure.

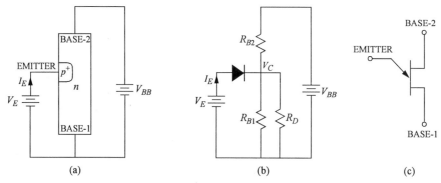

FIGURE 45.2
Schematic diagrams showing (a) the structure with bias, (b) the equivalent circuit and (c) the circuit symbol.

voltages, the depletion layer of the emitter junction does not reach the opposite side to cut off the channel between the two bases.

45.3 CHARACTERISTICS

The structure and the equivalent circuit of a unijunction transistor are shown schematically in Fig. 45.2. R_{B1} and R_{B2} are simply the body resistance of the n-type material, and their values depend on the location of the emitter junction in relation to the two bases. Conventionally the grounded base terminal is called base-1. The intrinsic stand-off ratio is defined as

$$\eta \equiv \frac{R_{B1}}{R_{B1} + R_{B2}} \tag{45.1}$$

and it usually has a value between 0.5 and 0.85. The shunt resistor R_D arises from carrier injection when the emitter junction is under high forward bias, and it plays a critical role in the resultant characteristics. When the emitter junction is unbiased, R_D is infinite. When this junction is under strong forward bias, holes are injected into the bulk material, and drift toward base-1 by the field applied between base-2 and base-1. When this hole concentration is higher than the background doping concentration, a high-level injection is said to occur. These excess holes also draw an equal number of excess electrons from base-1 to maintain charge neutrality. This conductivity modulation due to excess electrons and holes gives rise to the shunt resistor R_D.

With the above phenomenon in mind, the emitter/base-1 *I-V* characteristics shown in Fig. 45.3 can be readily explained. With the interbase voltage V_{BB} equal to zero, the characteristics are simply the same as a regular *p-n* junction under forward bias. Consider the middle solid curve with a positive fixed V_{BB}, the voltage at the cathode side of the *p-n* diode, indicated by V_C, has a value of ηV_{BB}. If the emitter voltage V_E is below this value, the diode is under reverse bias and the emitter current is negative. Increasing V_E above ηV_{BB} starts to change I_E to positive. Before substantial carrier injection occurs, this operational range is called the cutoff region. The negative differential resistance region starts with a V_E equal to

$$V_p \approx \eta V_{BB} + \frac{kT}{q} \ln\left(\frac{I_p}{I_o}\right)$$

$$\approx \eta V_{BB} + V_f$$

(45.2)

where I_o is the saturation current of the emitter *p-n* junction and V_f is close to the built-in potential, ≈ 0.7 V. Under this condition, a high level of carrier injection induces a drop in R_D which decreases V_C. A smaller V_C puts the diode into even higher bias and higher carrier injection. This positive feedback accounts for the decreases of V_C (or V_E) with I_E, and, thus, negative differential resistance. After

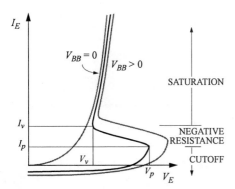

FIGURE 45.3

Characteristics of the unijunction transistor. V_p, I_p, V_v, I_v are called peak voltage, peak current, valley voltage, and valley current, respectively.

the V_E drops to a valley voltage of V_v, the characteristics fall back to that of a regular diode in forward bias, called the saturation region. It is also shown in Fig. 45.3 that V_p, I_p as well as V_v, I_v increase with the interbase bias V_{BB}.

45.4 APPLICATIONS

The unijunction transistor has a low α (common-base current gain) value and is not used for voltage or current amplification as in the case of a conventional transistor. A common application is the relaxation oscillator to generate sawtooth waveform, as shown in Fig. 45.4. The output voltage V_{out} charges up exponentially until it reaches V_p and the unijunction transistor switches out of the cutoff region to a more conductive state. It gets discharged through the transistor to a value below V_v to turn it off, and the cycle repeats itself. The period is close to the charge-up time

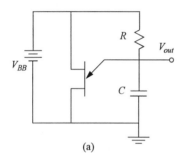
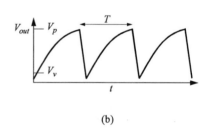

(a)   (b)

FIGURE 45.4
(a) A relaxation oscillator circuit and (b) its output waveform.

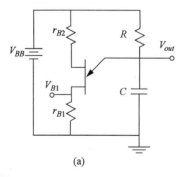
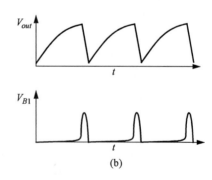

(a)   (b)

FIGURE 45.5
(a) A pulse generator using additional small resistors r_{B1} and r_{B2} to the relaxation oscillator and (b) the output waveforms.

$$T \approx RC \ln \left(\frac{1}{1 - \eta} \right) \quad . \tag{45.3}$$

The resistor value R has to be small to provide enough current to turn on the unijunction transistor, and large enough to limit the current below I_v to turn it off. Equivalently, R has to fall in the range of

$$\frac{V_{BB} - V_p}{I_p} > R > \frac{V_{BB} - V_v}{I_v} \quad . \tag{45.4}$$

A closely related circuit is a pulse generator shown in Fig. 45.5. The voltage pulse occurs during the short time period when the transistor is highly conductive. This pulse waveform can be used to trigger an SCR.

For other general applications of negative resistance, the readers can refer to Appendix C2.

One disadvantage of a unijunction transistor is the long turn-off time and turn-on time, in the order of a few μs. This limits the operation to ≈ 100 kHz. Another limitation is the strong temperature dependence of the characteristics. The unijunction transistor is no longer very active in the commercial market.

REFERENCES

1. W. Shockley, G. L. Pearson and J. R. Haynes, "Hole injection in germanium–Quantitative studies and filamentary transistors," *Bell Syst. Tech. J.*, **28**, 344 (1949).
2. W. Shockley, *Electrons and holes in semiconductor*, Van Nostrand, Toronto, 1950.
3. I. A. Lesk and V. P. Mathis, "The double-base diode: A new semiconductor device," *IRE Convention Record*, Part 6, 2 (1953).
4. R. W. Aldrich and I. A. Lesk, "The double-base diode: A semiconductor thyratron analog," *IRE Trans. Electron Dev.*, **ED-1**, 24 (1954).
5. J. J. Suran, "Low-frequency circuit theory of the double-base diode," *IRE Trans. Electron Dev.*, **ED-2**, 40 (1955).
6. J. J. Suran, "Small-signal wave effects in the double-base diode," *IRE Trans. Electron Dev.*, **ED-4**, 34 (1957).
7. F. N. Trofimenkoff and G. J. Huff, "D. C. theory of the unijunction transistor," *Int. J. Electronics*, **20**, 217 (1966).
8. L. Clark, "Now, new unijunction geometries," *Electronics*, 93 (June 1965).

CHAPTER
46

STATIC-INDUCTION THYRISTOR

46.1 HISTORY

The static-inductor thyristor (SIThy) is also called a field-controlled thyristor. Over a large portion of the operation regime, the device is similar to the static-induction transistor (SIT, Chapter 28) which was conceived around the same time. The static-induction thyristor was presented in part of a paper by Nishizawa et al.,[1] and was described in more details by Houston et al.,[2] both in 1975. More work followed from Houston et al.,[3] Barandon and Laurenceau,[4] and Nishizawa and Nakamura[5] in 1976. For more information on the device, the readers can refer to Refs. 6 and 7.

46.2 STRUCTURE

The structure of the static-induction thyristor, as shown in Fig. 46.1, is a *p-i-n* diode with part of the channel surrounded by closely spaced junction grids or gates. It is also similar to the SIT with the p^+-anode replacing the n^+-drain. The structure can be made in the form of a planar grid or a buried grid. The advantage of the planar grid is a lower grid resistance since a metal contact can be deposited directly over it. This results in a smaller gate debiasing effect during turnoff when there is a substantial current going through the gate. The advantages of the buried grid are a more efficient use of cathode area, and more effective gate control of the current, resulting in a higher forward-blocking voltage gain, to be discussed later. The double-gate SIThy has been shown to be capable of higher speed and lower voltage drop than the single-gate structures.[8] The thickness of the n^--layer ranges widely, from ≈ 50 μm to a few hundred μm, depending on the requirement

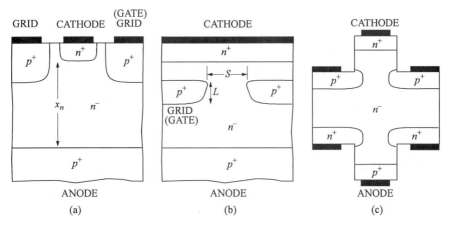

FIGURE 46.1
Structures of the static-inductor thyristor with (a) planar gates (grids), (b) buried gates, and (c) double gates.

of the blocking voltage. For a thinner n^--layer, an epitaxial layer is deposited onto a p^+-substrate. For a thicker n^--layer, the layer corresponds to the bulk material, and diffusion is used to incorporate the p^+-anode and the n^+-cathode on the two surfaces of the wafer. The doping level of the n^--layer is typically below 10^{14} cm^{-3}. The gate junctions have length or depth, (L) in the order of 10–20 μm, and the horizontal spacing between them (S) has slightly smaller dimension. For normally off devices, this dimension S is smaller than 5 μm. Most SIThys reported were made with silicon material.

46.3 CHARACTERISTICS

In a static-induction thyristor, the gate controls the current in two distinct ways. Using the structure in Fig. 46.1(b) as an example, before pinch-off (Fig. 46.2(a)), the depletion regions of the two gates do not merge, and the gate voltage controls the effective area of the *p-i-n* diode between the anode and the cathode. For large negative (reverse) gate voltage, the junctions are under reverse bias and the depletion regions widen, and eventually meet (Fig. 46.2(b)). Under this pinch-off condition, a barrier for electrons is formed, and it controls the current flow.

The gate voltage corresponding to pinch-off can be approximated by a simple one-dimensional depletion theory

$$V_G = \psi_{bi} - \frac{qN_D (S/2)^2}{2\varepsilon_s} \qquad (46.1)$$

where ψ_{bi} is the built-in potential of the gate junction,

$$\psi_{bi} = \frac{kT}{q} \ln \left(\frac{N_A N_D}{n_i^2} \right) .$$ (46.2)

By adjusting S, one can design a device to be normally on or normally off. In a normally on SIThy, pinch-off does not occur with zero gate voltage, and a high current can flow. In a normally off SIThy, S is smaller (or N_D in the n^--layer is lower) such that pinch-off occurs with zero gate bias. In order to turn on the device, the gate has to be forward biased to reduce the depletion regions to open up a channel. The normally off device is less common, due to the larger gate current under forward bias, although for only a very short moment for triggering.

The output characteristics for a normally on SIThy are shown in Fig. 46.3. Before pinch-off, the current conduction is that of a p-i-n diode, given by

$$I_A = \frac{4AqD_a n_i}{x_n} \exp \left(\frac{qV_{AK}}{2kT} \right)$$ (46.3)

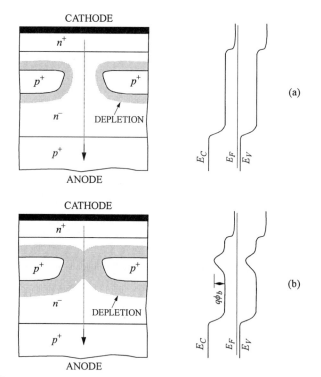

FIGURE 46.2
Schematic diagrams showing the effects of depletion width on the channel, and their energy-band diagrams at zero V_{AK}. (a) Before pinch-off. (b) After pinch-off. Energy-band diagram is along the middle of the channel shown by the dotted line.

which is a recombination current of excess electrons and holes in the n^--region (see Chapter 2). D_a is the ambipolar diffusion coefficient given by

$$D_a \approx \frac{2D_p D_n}{D_p + D_n} \; . \tag{46.4}$$

Under forward bias V_{AK}, electrons are injected from the cathode and holes from the anode, and they are equal in number to maintain charge neutrality. These excess electrons and holes increase the conductivity of the n^--layer. This phenomenon is called conductivity modulation. Note that although the output characteristics are similar in shape to those of the SIT, the p^+-anode can inject holes and enable conductivity modulation, resulting in a lower forward-voltage drop or lower on-resistance.

With a larger reverse gate bias, pinch-off is introduced, and a barrier for electrons is formed (Fig. 46.2(b)). This barrier limits the electron supply and becomes the controlling factor for the overall current. Without an ample electron supply, the hole current reduces to the diffusion current and becomes insignificant. The barrier height ϕ_b not only is controlled by the gate voltage, it can also be lowered by a large V_{AK}. This dependence of ϕ_b on V_{AK} is called static induction, and is the main current conduction mechanism in a static-induction transistor. Static-induction current is basically a punch-through current due to the thin barrier in the direction of the current flow. It is a diffusion current with the barrier controlling the supply of carriers, given in the form

$$I_A \propto \exp\left(\frac{-q\phi_b}{kT}\right)$$

$$= I_o \exp\left[\frac{q(\eta V_G + \theta V_{AK})}{kT}\right] \; . \tag{46.5}$$

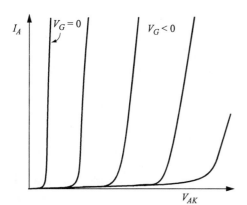

FIGURE 46.3
Output characteristics of a normally on static-induction thyristor. For a normally off device, similar curves are obtained with forward gate voltages.

η and θ indicate the control of V_G and V_{AK} on the barrier height.

One useful parameter for the SIThy is the forward-blocking voltage gain μ which is defined as the change of V_{AK} induced by the change of V_G for the same anode current. According to the previous expression, it is equal to

$$\mu = -\left.\frac{\partial V_{AK}}{\partial V_G}\right|_{I_A} = \frac{\eta}{\theta} \quad . \tag{46.6}$$

It has been shown experimentally that[7]

$$\mu \approx \frac{LW_d}{S^2} \tag{46.7}$$

where W_d is the depletion width of the gate junction in the direction toward the anode.

One of the advantages of the SIThy is higher-speed operation compared to an SCR, due to a faster turnoff process. During turnoff, the reverse gate bias can extract the excess minority carriers (holes) quickly. The excess electrons, being majority carriers in the n^--layer, can be swept off quickly by the drift process. The hole current contributes to an instantaneously large gate current, and a small gate resistance is critical to avoid gate debiasing. An alternate technique to reduce the turnoff time is to reduce the minority-carrier lifetime by proton or electron irradiation. The penalty for using this technique is a larger forward voltage drop.

It has also been proposed to use light to trigger or quench a SIThy.[9] When a SIThy is off, either as a normally off device or turned off by a gate bias, light-generated holes get trapped at the barrier (Fig. 46.2(b)). These positive charges decrease the barrier height for electrons and trigger turn-on. For a normally on SIThy, the gate is connected to a negative voltage source via a phototransistor. Light can activate the phototransistor, and the negative voltage source is applied to the gate to turn off the SIThy.

46.4 APPLICATIONS

The static-induction thyristor offers certain advantages over other thyristors. Due to the faster turn-off, an operating frequency up to 100 kHz is possible. Because the turn-on process does not depend on regenerative feedback as in an SCR, it has more stable operation at higher temperatures, and in dI/dt, dV/dt transients. It has low forward-voltage drop, high blocking-voltage gain up to ≈ 700, and gate-controlled turn-off capability (an SCR after latching cannot be turned off by simply removing the gate bias). The SIThy has been applied mainly in power source conversion such as AC to DC converters, DC to AC converters, and chopper circuits.[10] AC to DC converters and DC to AC converters are used in high-voltage DC transmission line systems. A DC to AC converter also provides variable frequency for speed control of AC motors. Another application is pulse generation, for induction heating, lighting of fluorescent lamp, and driving pulsed lasers.

REFERENCES

1. J. Nishizawa, T. Terasaki and J. Shibata, "Field-effect transistor versus analog transistor (static induction transistor)," *IEEE Trans. Electron Dev.*, **ED-22**, 185 (1975).
2. D. E. Houston, S. Krishna, D. Piccone, R. J. Finke and Y. S. Sun, "Field controlled thyristor (FCT) – A new electronic component," *Tech. Digest IEEE IEDM*, 379 (1975).
3. D. E. Houston, S. Krishna, D. E. Piccone, R. J. Finke and Y. S. Sun, "A field terminated diode," *IEEE Trans. Electron Dev.*, **ED-23**, 905 (1976).
4. R. Barandon and P. Laurenceau, "Power bipolar gridistor," *Electronics Lett.*, **12**, 486 (1976).
5. J. Nishizawa and K. Nakamura, "Characteristics of new thyristor," *Proc. 8th Conf. Solid State Devices, Tokyo, 1976., Japanese J. Appl. Phys.*, **16** (Supp.16-1), 541 (1977).
6. P. D. Taylor, *Thyristor design and realization*, Wiley, New York, 1987.
7. J. Nishizawa, K. Muraoka, T. Tamamushi and Y. Kawamura, "Low-loss high-speed switching devices, 2300-V 150-A static induction thyristor," *IEEE Trans. Electron Dev.*, **ED-32**, 822 (1985).
8. J. Nishizawa, Y. Yukimoto, H. Kondou, M. Harada and H. Pan, "A double-gate-type static-induction thyristor," *IEEE Trans. Electron Dev.*, **ED-34**, 1396 (1987).
9. J. Nishizawa, T. Tamamushi and K. Nonaka, "Totally light controlled static induction thyristor," *Physica*, **129B**, 346 (1985).
10. J. Nishizawa, "Application of the power static induction (SI) devices," *Proc. PCIM*, 1 (1988).

CHAPTER
47

LIGHT-EMITTING DIODE

47.1 HISTORY

The light-emitting diode, commonly known as the LED, is a popular electronic light source based on electroluminescence. Electroluminescence is a process that changes an electrical input to a light output, the opposite of the photovoltaic effect. It was first discovered by Round as early as 1907 in a contact to a SiC substrate, but was reported only in a short note.[1] More detailed experiments were presented by Lossev whose work spanned from the 1920s to the 1930s.[2,3] After the development of the *p-n* junction in 1949, LED production changed from using point contacts to *p-n* junctions. The mechanism of LED operation was studied by Lehovec et al.[4,5] and Roosbroeck and Shockley.[6] Other semiconductor materials besides SiC were subsequently studied. Haynes and Briggs studied Ge and Si LEDs.[7] Since these semiconductors have indirect energy gap, their efficiencies were very limited. A very high quantum efficiency was reported for direct-energy-gap GaAs in 1962 by Keyes and Quist,[8] and by Pankove and associates.[9,10] These studies quickly led to the realization of the semiconductor laser later the same year. Up to that point, it was considered imperative to use direct-energy-gap material for efficient electroluminescence. Significant advancement was made on indirect-energy-gap material during 1964 and 1965 by introducing isoelectronic impurities. These studies were presented by Grimmeiss and Scholz,[11] Eten and Haanstra,[12] and Thomas et al.[13] The studies had a profound impact on the current commercial LEDs made from indirect-energy-gap $GaAs_{1-x}P_x$.

Details of the historical development of the LED are provided by Ref. 14. For a more in-depth study of the device, the readers can refer to Refs. 15–17.

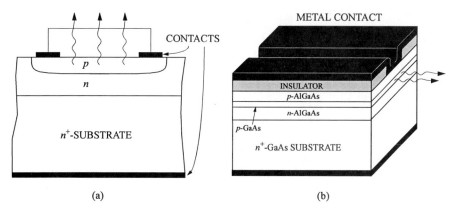

FIGURE 47.1
Two basic structures of the LED. (a) Surface-emitting LED. (b) Edge-emitting LED.

47.2 STRUCTURE

LEDs are special *p-n* junction diodes that are designed for optimum electroluminescence. There are two basic configurations, surface-emitting and edge-emitting (Fig. 47.1). In the surface-emitting structure, light radiates perpendicular to the plane of the *p-n* junction. In the edge-emitting structure, light is confined to a plane and radiates parallel to the junction. In this configuration, a heterostructure is usually utilized for both optical confinement (as waveguide) and carrier confinement. Light output is much more directional. Another advantage of a heterojunction, applicable to both configurations, is improved injection efficiency.

Common semiconductor materials, mostly III-V compounds, are shown in Fig. 47.2, with their range of emitted wavelengths and the sensitivity of the human eye to these wavelengths. Even though most II–VI compound semiconductors have direct energy gap and an expected more-efficient electroluminescence, unfortunately, they usually have a technical problem of impurity doping in forming *p-n* junctions, making these compounds impractical for LEDs. The active films are usually grown epitaxially by liquid-phase epitaxy or vapor-phase epitaxy, on substrates that have a close lattice match to the active layers. Common substrates are GaAs, GaP and InP. The *p-n* junction can be formed by impurity diffusion, ion implantation, or incorporated during epitaxial growth. Commercial LEDs exist as single elements and as monolithic arrays. It should be mentioned that just like the original devices, Schottky contacts or MIS structures are also possible instead of *p-n* junctions, but they are usually less efficient and are used only in cases where a *p-n* junction is difficult to form.

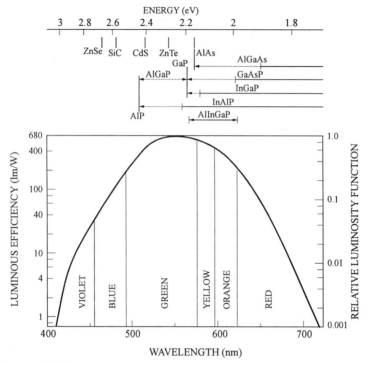

FIGURE 47.2
Common LED materials with respect to their emitted wavelength (after Ref. 15), and the luminous efficiency of the human eye. Dashed lines represent compositions that have an indirect energy gap.

47.3 CHARACTERISTICS

To produce light output, an LED must be operated in the forward-bias regime. A detailed derivation of the electrical characteristics can be found in Chapter 1–*p-n* Junction Diode. The energy-band diagram in Fig. 47.3(a) shows that there are three major current components: (1) electron diffusion current, (2) hole diffusion current, and (3) space-charge recombination current. Mathematically, they are given by

$$
J = J_n + J_p + J_{re}
$$

$$
= \frac{qD_n n_i^2}{L_n N_A}\left[\exp\left(\frac{qV_f}{kT}\right) - 1\right] + \frac{qD_p n_i^2}{L_p N_D}\left[\exp\left(\frac{qV_f}{kT}\right) - 1\right]
$$

$$
+ \frac{qn_i W_d}{2\tau_{nr}}\left[\exp\left(\frac{qV_f}{2kT}\right) - 1\right] .
$$

$$(47.1)$$

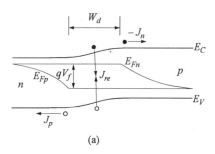
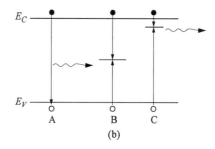

FIGURE 47.3
(a) Energy-band diagram of a *p-n* junction under forward bias, showing the electron and hole diffusion currents, and recombination current in the space-charge region. (b) Major recombination processes outside the space-charge region. A = band-to-band radiative recombination. B = nonradiative recombination through deep-level traps. C = recombination through isoelectronic traps that can be radiative or nonradiative.

Due to the $2kT$ term, the space-charge recombination current is more pronounced at low bias and at low temperature. The origin of this current is recombination via deep-level traps and is nonradiative. The injected minority carriers in both sides of the junction create an excess of minority carriers, which then recombine with the majority carriers. This recombination process, which occurs mostly within a diffusion length of the junction, produces light with a wavelength whose energy equals the energy gap,

$$hv = E_g \tag{47.2}$$

or

$$\lambda \, (\mu m) = \frac{1.24}{E_g \, (eV)} \, . \tag{47.3}$$

In practice, it is more efficient, for homostructures, to design devices with light generated solely from the *p*-side of the junction. There are two main reasons. First, the injection efficiency is higher for electrons than for holes due to greater electron mobility. Second, the energy-gap-narrowing effect from high-level doping is more pronounced in *p*-type material than in *n*-type. This means that light originated in the *p*-region has an energy smaller than the energy gap in the *n*-region, and is not easily absorbed in the latter. For these reasons, the useful current component is only the electron diffusion current J_n, and the injection efficiency is given by

$$\eta_{inj} = \frac{J_n}{J_n + J_p + J_{re}} \, . \tag{47.4}$$

Furthermore, J_n is not 100% radiative. The major recombination processes outside the space-charge region are shown in Fig. 47.3(b). Process A is the direct band-to-band recombination, which is radiative. For low-level injection, the radiative recombination R_r is proportional to both electron and hole populations,

$$R_r = B_r np$$
$$= B_r \Delta n N_A .$$

(47.5)

B_r is the recombination coefficient and is a function of the temperature and the band structure. In electroluminescence, for conversion of electron-hole pairs to light, both conservation of energy and momentum must be obeyed. The conservation of energy is described by Eq. (47.2). Since the momentum of light ($h\nu/c$) is very small, the electron and hole, before recombination, should have the same momentum. This implies that the conduction-band minimum should be at the same momentum space as the valence-band maximum in the E-k relationship, which is a definition of direct energy gap. This band-to-band recombination (Process A) can be characterized by a radiative lifetime τ_r, given by

$$\tau_r = \frac{\Delta n}{R_r}$$
$$= \frac{1}{B_r N_A} .$$

(47.6)

Process B is recombination through deep-level traps, and is nonradiative. This process is discussed in more detail in Appendix B2. The nonradiative lifetime associated with these traps is given by

$$\tau_{nr} = \frac{1}{\sigma v_{th} N_t} .$$

(47.7)

The recombination Process C in Fig. 47.3(b) is for indirect-energy-gap materials only and will be discussed later. The competition between Process A and Process B determines the so-called radiative efficiency η_{rad}, given by

$$\eta_{rad} = \frac{R_r}{R_r + R_{nr}}$$
$$= \frac{\tau_{nr}}{\tau_{nr} + \tau_r}$$
$$= \frac{\tau}{\tau_r} .$$

(47.8)

The total lifetime is given by

$$\frac{1}{\tau} = \frac{1}{\tau_r} + \frac{1}{\tau_{nr}} \ . \tag{47.9}$$

For indirect-energy-gap semiconductors, a phonon has to be involved to help conserving momentum. The radiative band-to-band recombination is much less probable, resulting in a much smaller B_r value. ($B_r \approx 10^{-10}$ cm^3/s for direct-energy-gap materials, and $\approx 10^{-15}$ cm^3/s for indirect-energy-gap materials.) To improve the radiative recombination in LEDs made with indirect-energy-gap semiconductors, isoelectronic impurities are introduced. These impurities replace one element of the compound, and are neutral dopants. Examples are N and ZnO in GaP. The function of an isoelectronic trap is to capture an electron. Subsequently, the charged center captures a hole and the annihilation of the electron-hole pair releases a photon. Conservation of momentum is not violated here without a phonon because the isoelectronic trap is highly localized in space, and because of the Uncertainty principle, has a wide spectrum in the momentum space. Such a system can be visualized in the E-k relationship shown in Fig. 47.4. Recombinations through the isoelectronic traps are still not all radiative. For analytical purpose, these extrinsic recombinations can be classified into radiative and nonradiative lifetimes such that Eq. (47.8) is still applicable.

For heterostructures, the energy gap can be engineered and additional factors come into play. In these devices, low-energy-gap "active" material is sandwiched between larger-energy-gap confining layers. Injection of carriers from the confining layers produces light in the active layer.

The internal quantum efficiency of an LED is given by the product

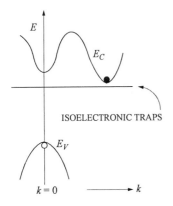

FIGURE 47.4
E-k relationship of an indirect-energy-gap material with iso-electronic traps.

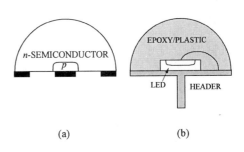

(a) (b)

FIGURE 47.5
LED geometries to improve optical efficiency. (a) Dome-shape semiconductor body. (b) A discrete component with epoxy/plastic coating.

$$\eta_{int} = \frac{\text{\# of photons produced internally}}{\text{\# of carriers across junction}}$$

$$= \eta_{inj}\eta_{rad} \ . \tag{47.10}$$

Light generated near the p-n junction experiences optical losses leaving the junction. These losses can be attributed to the following factors: (a) absorption by the semiconductor material, (b) partial reflection at the semiconductor-ambient interface when light is nearly perpendicular to the interface, and (c) total reflection when the incident light has a larger angle than the critical angle determined from Snell's law. Considering all these factors, the optical efficiency η_{opt} can be estimated by

$$\eta_{opt} = \frac{1}{1 + \dfrac{4\alpha V}{A T_{av}}} \ . \tag{47.11}$$

V is the volume of the semiconductor body and A is the surface area. T_{av} is the average transmission through the semiconductor–ambient interface, given by

$$T_{av} \approx \left(\frac{n_a^2}{n_s^2}\right)\left[1 - \left(\frac{n_s - n_a}{n_s + n_a}\right)^2\right] \tag{47.12}$$

where n_s and n_a are the refractive indexes of the semiconductor and the ambient, respectively. Figure 47.5 shows two structures that optimize η_{opt}. The dome-shape semiconductor body ensures that light is always perpendicular to the semiconductor–ambient interface. This configuration is expensive to make and is not commercially practical. A more common approach is to add a coating of epoxy with a refractive index whose value lies between that of the semiconductor and the ambient.

The overall external quantum efficient is given by

$$\eta_{ext} = \frac{\text{\# of photons emitted externally}}{\text{\# of carriers across junction}}$$

$$= \eta_{int}\eta_{opt}$$

$$= \eta_{inj}\eta_{rad}\eta_{opt} \ . \tag{47.13}$$

Practical η_{int} larger than 50% can be achieved, while η_{ext} typically lies in the range of 0.1–10%.

Another term to quantify the LED is the brightness. Because the human eye has different sensitivity to different colors, the LED should be designed for optimum visibility–especially important for display applications. The luminous efficiency of the human eye is shown in Fig. 47.2. Maximum efficiency of

680 lm/W occurs at a wavelength of 555 nm, the middle of the green spectrum. The brightness is calculated by

$$B = 1150 \left(\frac{A_j}{A_s}\right) \frac{L\eta_{ext}J}{\lambda} \qquad \text{ft-l} \qquad (47.14)$$

where A_j and A_s are the junction area and the exposed emitting surface area, respectively, L is the luminous efficiency (lm/W), J is in A/cm^2, and λ is the wavelength in μm.

This equation also implies that, for normal operation, the brightness is proportional to the applied current. Typically, an LED is biased with a voltage slightly below its energy gap (E_g/q), and the current is in the order of 1 mA. The light output has a spectral width of $\approx 2kT$–$3kT$, or between 20–50 nm. The cutoff frequency is given by

$$f_T \approx \frac{1}{2\pi\tau} \ . \qquad (47.15)$$

At that speed of current modulation, the light output is diminished to about half of its value at DC. A maximum speed of $\approx$ 1 Gb/s has been demonstrated.

47.4 APPLICATIONS

An LED is a practical light source in modern electronics. Reportedly 20 billion visible LEDs are produced each year.[18] The on/off state is usually controlled by a transistor, with the LED connected to the collector or drain. Compared to an incandescent light, it is more reliable and has lower power consumption. Compared to a laser, it is easier to make, less expensive, and more reliable. It has longer operating lifetime, simpler driving circuit, less temperature sensitivity, and better analog modulation. The LEDs can be made surface-emitting without much difficulty compared to a laser, and they can be more easily integrated in a monolithic array. The main disadvantage compared to a laser is lower speed and the less directional light emission.

The major applications of an LED can be classified into three categories:

1. Display: LEDs have been popular as numeric and alphabetic displays in watches, calculators, audio and video equipments, etc. Some common configurations are shown in Fig. 47.6. A serious contender in this application is the LCD (see Appendix A4) which has even lower power consumption, but it cannot be seen in total darkness. An LED is also used as a signal display such as an on/off switch or pilot light for instrument panels. A potential use of LEDs is for large-area display such as a TV monitor.

2. Fiber-optics communication: An LED can be the light source in optical-fiber communication. The structure for a surface-emitting LED is shown in Fig. 47.7. Edge-emitting LED can also be used in this application. For

ultra-high-speed operation above 1 Gb/s over km spans of fiber, a laser is required. However, an LED may be more suitable for analog transmission.

3. As a light source in source-detector package: There are many applications that need a light source and detector combination. Figure 47.8 shows an opto-isolator (or opto-coupler) which, using light as a link, electrically isolates the input from the output. Other applications are in proximity detectors. Examples are smoke detectors and tachometers.

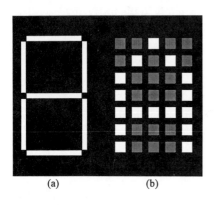

FIGURE 47.6
Typical arrays for (a) numerical display (seven-segment) and (b) alphabetical display (5x7 array).

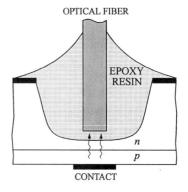

FIGURE 47.7
A package showing the interfacing of the optical fiber and the LED.

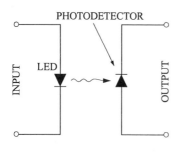

FIGURE 47.8
An opto-isolator provides electrical isolation between input and output.

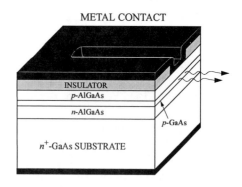

FIGURE 47.9
In a superluminescent diode, the metal contact to the semiconductor does not extend to both ends, avoiding optical feedback and lasing.

47.5 RELATED DEVICE

47.5.1 Superluminescent Diode

A superluminescent diode, also known as superradiant LED, is a special case of an edge-emitting LED designed for higher light power. It is biased with a higher current until stimulated emission and optical gain occur (see Chapter 48 –Injection Laser). Lasing is suppressed intentionally by eliminating the Fabry-Perot cavity for reflection and optical feedback. The optical gain therefore comes from only a single optical pass. The structure in Fig. 47.9 shows that the metal contact and, thus, injection is not uniform across the device. This ensures some optical loss in one end and avoids oscillation. The optical bandwidth of the light output is narrower than the LED, between 10 to 15 nm, but is still much wider than the laser.

REFERENCES

1. H. J. Round, "A note on carborundum," *Electrical World*, **49**, 309 (1907).
2. O. V. Lossev, *Wireless World and Radio Rev.*, **271**, 93 (1924).
3. O. V. Lossev, "Luminous carborundum detector and detection effect and oscillations with crystals," *Phil. Mag.*, **6**, 1024 (1928).
4. K. Lehovec, C. A. Accardo and E. Jamgochian, "Injected light emission of silicon carbide crystals," *Phys. Rev.*, **83**, 603 (1951).
5. K. Lehovec, "New photoelectric devices utilizing carrier injection," *Proc. IRE*, **40**, 1407 (1952).
6. W. van Roosbroeck and W. Shockley, "Photo-radiative recombination of electrons and holes in germanium," *Phys. Rev.*, **94**, 1558 (1954).
7. J. R. Haynes and H. B. Briggs, "Radiation produced in germanium and silicon by electron-hole recombination," *Bull. Am. Phys. Soc.*, **27**, 14 (1952).
8. R. J. Keyes and T. M. Quist, "Recombination radiation emitted by gallium arsenide," *Proc. IRE*, **50**, 1822 (1962).
9. J. I. Pankove and J. E. Berkeyheiser, "A light source modulated at microwave frequencies," *Proc. IRE*, **50**, 1976 (1962).
10. J. I. Pankove and M. J. Massoulie, "Injection luminescence from gallium arsenide," *Bull. Am. Phys. Soc.*, **7**, 88 (1962).
11. H. G. Grimmeiss and H. Scholz, "Efficiency of recombination radiation in GaP," *Phys. Lett.*, **8**, 233 (1964).
12. A. C. Eten and J. H. Haanstra, "Electroluminescence in tellurium-doped cadmium sulphide," *Phys. Lett.*, **11**, 97 (1964).
13. D. G. Thomas, J. J. Hopfield and C. J. Frosch, "Isoelectronic traps due to nitrogen in gallium phosphide," *Phys. Rev. Lett.*, **15**, 857 (1965).
14. E. E. Loebner, "Subhistories of the light emitting diode," *IEEE Trans. Electron Dev.*, **ED-23**, 675 (1976).
15. M. H. Pilkuhn, "Light emitting diodes," in C. Hilsum, Ed., T. S. Moss, Ed., *Handbook on semiconductors*, Vol. 4, North-Holland, Amsterdam, 1981.
16. R. H. Saul, T. P. Lee and C. A. Burrus, "Light-emitting-diode device design," in W. T. Tsang, Ed., *Semiconductors and semimetals*, Vol. 22, Pt. C, Academic Press, New York, 1985.
17. A. A. Bergh and P. J. Dean, "Light-emitting diodes," *Proc. IEEE*, **60**, 156 (1972).
18. M. G. Craford, "LEDs challenge the incandescents," *IEEE Circuits and Devices*, **8**(5), 24 (1992).

CHAPTER
48

INJECTION
LASER

48.1 HISTORY

The name laser comes from the acronym for *l*ight *a*mplification by *s*timulated *e*mission of *r*adiation. Laser is the descendant of the maser which stands for *m*icrowave *a*mplification by *s*timulated *e*mission of *r*adiation. The difference between them is in the range of output frequencies. Laser and maser are both based on the phenomenon of stimulated emission, which was postulated by Einstein in the 1910s. The laser medium can be gas, liquid, amorphous solid, or semiconductor. The semiconductor laser is also called injection laser, junction laser, or laser diode. Maser action was first realized by Townes and his students,[1] and by Basov and Prokhorov,[2] both in 1954, using ammonia gas. For their pioneering work on optical amplification, Townes, Basov, and Prokhorov received the Nobel prize in physics in 1964. Laser action was obtained first on solid ruby (non-semiconductor) in 1960, and then on helium-neon gas in 1961. The analysis of laser conditions in semiconductor was made by Bernard and Duraffourg,[3] and Dumke.[4] In 1962, four papers reported the injection laser almost simultaneously. These include the works of Hall et al.,[5] Nathan et al.[6] and Quist et al.[7] on GaAs while Holonyak and Bevacqua studied GaAsP material.[8] Improvement from heterostructures was suggested by Kroemer,[9] and by Alferov and Kazarinov[10] in 1963. Eventually Hayashi et al. in 1970 achieved CW operation at room temperature using a double-heterojunction laser.[11] The historical development of the laser, from maser to heterojunction laser, can be found collectively in Refs. 12–14. The laser, a very important device in modern optoelectronics among other applications, is the subject of many texts and reference books.

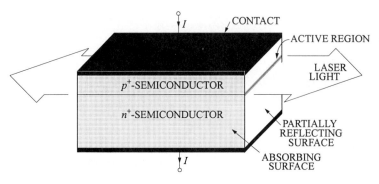

FIGURE 48.1

A broad-area laser showing the main laser structure.

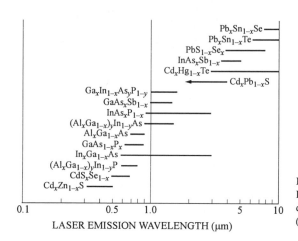

LASER EMISSION WAVELENGTH (μm)

FIGURE 48.2

Laser emission wavelengths for different semiconductor alloys. (After Ref. 15)

48.2 STRUCTURE

The main features of a laser are represented in Fig. 48.1 showing a broad-area laser. It can be seen that a laser is basically a vertical *p-n* junction with special design for optical reflection from vertical walls. It is necessary, however, for both *n*-type and *p*-type regions to be doped to degeneracy to achieve population inversion, to be discussed later. It is usually started with an n^+-substrate on which an epitaxial layer is grown. Liquid-phase epitaxy, vapor-phase epitaxy, MBE, and MOCVD have all been used, with LPE being the most common technique in commercial types. The top, heavily doped region can be incorporated by diffusion, ion implantation, or deposited during epitaxy. It is also necessary that the semiconductor have a direct energy gap for efficient light emission to achieve lasing, unlike an LED where isoelectronic impurity can be added to semiconductors of indirect energy gap. Common materials for lasers are shown in Fig. 48.2, with their emission wavelengths. Common starting substrates for

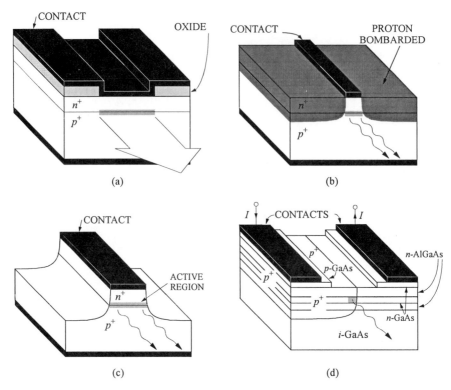

FIGURE 48.3

Examples of stripe-geometry lasers using (a) oxide isolation, (b) proton bombardment, and (c) mesa etching. (d) A transverse-junction stripe laser.

epitaxial growth are GaAs and InP. Most laser materials, especially common ones in practice, are III–V compounds. This is because most II–VI compound semiconductors are difficult to dope to both n- and p-type.

Another unique structural requirement for a laser is an optical resonator, called Fabry-Perot etalon, in the direction of the laser light output. This means that the two vertical walls that form the resonator should be perfectly perpendicular to the junction, and have mirror-like smoothness with optimum reflectivity. This can be achieved by etching, polishing, or most commonly, by cleaving. A typical length L is between 200–500 μm, but a precise dimension is not required since L is much larger than the wavelength of emission. For this reason, practical lasers are discrete components. One of the Fabry-Perot mirrors can be totally reflecting so light comes out from only one side. The mirror walls parallel to the laser output are roughened to be highly absorbing to prevent lasing in the transverse direction. To confine light output in the lateral direction, stripe geometries are used. A few examples are shown in Fig. 48.3.

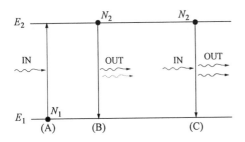

FIGURE 48.4
Principle optical processes in a two-level system. (A) Absorption. (B) Spontaneous emission. (C) Stimulated emission.

48.3 CHARACTERISTICS

We first consider the optical processes of a two-level system, not necessarily restricted to semiconductors, with energies E_1 and E_2, and electron concentrations N_1 and N_2 (Fig. 48.4). The three main processes are absorption (A), spontaneous emission (B), and stimulated emission (C). Absorption is characterized by the absorption coefficient (α) and is the principle process in photodetectors and solar cells. In spontaneous emission, light produced is random in space and time, shown by the dashed electromagnetic wave. It is the predominant mechanism in an LED. In stimulated emission, a photon input is required to stimulate an electron transition to yield another photon of identical wavelength and phase (coherent). Stimulated emission is the main mechanism for lasing. From this simple picture, the concept of optical gain can be derived. The net change of light intensity (or number of photons Nhv) is given by

$$\frac{d(Nhv)}{dt} = \text{stimulated emission} + \text{spontaneous emission} - \text{absorption}$$

$$= B_{21}(Nhv)N_2 + A_{21}N_2 - B_{12}(Nhv)N_1 \quad . \tag{48.1}$$

Since spontaneous emission is negligible in lasing, and it can be proven that $B_{21} = B_{12}$, optical gain requires $N_2 > N_1$, or population inversion. The state of population inversion does not occur naturally because of the relationship

$$\frac{N_2}{N_1} = \exp\left[-\frac{(E_2 - E_1)}{kT}\right] . \tag{48.2}$$

To acquire population inversion, pumping from external sources such as light can be used. In the case of an injection laser, forward bias to the p-n junction provides carrier injection, as shown in the energy-band diagram in Fig. 48.5(b). In each side of the junction, minority carriers are injected to recombine with the majority carriers to produce light. In practical devices, the p-region is more effective in light emission due to higher electron injection (higher mobility). To be consistent with the picture depicted in Fig. 48.4, the concept of holes is neglected for now, and the region near the junction is shown in Fig. 48.6. For the sake of simplicity, at low temperature, states below the Fermi levels are completely filled and those

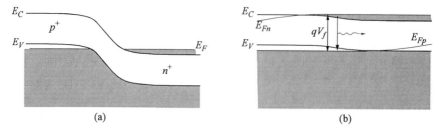

FIGURE 48.5
Energy-band diagrams of a laser (a) in equilibrium and (b) under bias.

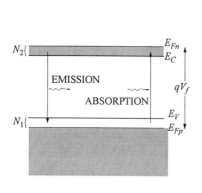

FIGURE 48.6
Energy-band diagram to show population inversion in the semiconductor, under injection, and $N_2 \gg N_1$.

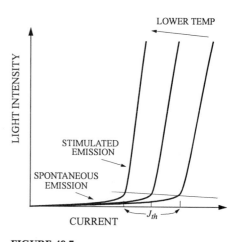

FIGURE 48.7
Laser light intensity as a function of pumping current. Threshold currents are indicated.

above are completely empty. Each level of E_1 and E_2 is now broadened into bands, namely E_C to E_{Fn} and E_{Fp} to E_V. N_1 and N_2 are integrated electron densities within these bands. Therefore, N_2 equals n and N_1 equals 0. The state of population inversion should not be confused with the non-equilibrium condition $pn > n_i^2$. The former is required for lasing (or optical gain) and the latter for net recombination. Figure 48.6 also demonstrates that the emitted wavelength should be within the range of

$$E_g < hv < (E_{Fn} - E_{Fp}) \tag{48.3}$$

or equivalently

$$E_g < hv < qV_f . \tag{48.4}$$

The *I-V* characteristics of a laser is similar to the conventional *p-n* junction diode and will not be discussed here (see Chapter 1). Even though both sides of the junction are degenerate, the transition region is less abrupt compared to a tunnel diode so that there is no negative differential resistance under forward bias. The light output intensity as a function of forward current is shown in Fig. 48.7. There is a characteristic knee in each curve at which the current level is called the threshold current J_{th} for lasing. Below J_{th}, spontaneous emission dominates, and the device behaves like an LED. Above J_{th}, lasing occurs and light intensity increases more rapidly with current. The threshold current is a function of the optical gain g, which has to overcome the loss of absorption and reflections

$$R_1 R_2 \exp\left[2\left(g-\alpha\right)L\right] > 1 \quad . \tag{48.5}$$

R_1 and R_2 are refections at the two surfaces of the optical cavity. The optical gain can be related to the current by

$$g = \frac{C_1 J}{d} - C_2 \tag{48.6}$$

where d is the vertical length of the active region near the junction where light is produced. At threshold, Eq. (48.5) is set to unity and the threshold current is calculated

$$J_{th} = \frac{d}{C_1}\left[C_2 + \alpha + \frac{1}{2L}\ln\left(\frac{1}{R_1 R_2}\right)\right] \quad . \tag{48.7}$$

J_{th} is proportional to d and as will be discussed later in double-heterojunction (DH) lasers (Section 48.5.1), d is reduced by structural confinement to lower J_{th}. As shown in Fig. 48.7, J_{th} is also a function of temperature. Empirically, it can be fitted to

$$J_{th} \propto \exp\left(\frac{T}{T_o}\right) \tag{48.8}$$

where T is in °C and T_o is 110–165°C for DH lasers.

The output spectrum of a laser is shown in Fig. 48.8, for different current pumping level. Below J_{th}, similar to an LED, the spectrum produced by spontaneous emission has a bandwidth of 200–500 Å. For a current slightly higher than J_{th}, discrete narrow lines appear, with a much reduced width of a few Å. These multiple modes occur because to build up the coherent light, repeatedly reflected light has to be in phase with the rest of the light in the cavity. This condition is satisfied whenever L is a multiple of the half wavelength, or

$$N_i\left(\frac{\lambda'}{2}\right) = L \quad . \tag{48.9}$$

λ' and λ are wavelengths in and out of the semiconductor medium with a refractive index n_r. The separations of these modes in wavelength and frequency are given by

$$\Delta\lambda = \frac{\lambda^2}{2Ln_r} \tag{48.10}$$

$$\Delta\nu = \frac{c}{2Ln_r} . \tag{48.11}$$

The multiple oscillation lines are called longitudinal modes because they are determined by the longitudinal length L parallel to the light output. At still higher current, the number of longitudinal modes is reduced as shown in Fig. 48.8(c). It is often a challenge to make lasers oscillate with only a single mode.

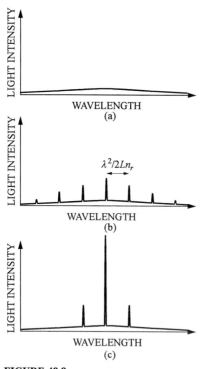

FIGURE 48.8
Laser-light spectrum at different current levels. (a) $J < J_{th}$. (b) $J > J_{th}$. (c) $J \gg J_{th}$.

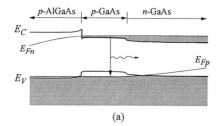

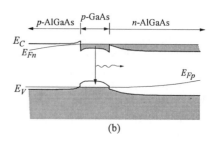

FIGURE 48.9
Energy-band diagrams of (a) a single-heterojunction laser and (b) a double-heterojunction laser, under forward bias.

48.4 APPLICATIONS

The main features of a laser beam are (1) high directionality, (2) narrow spectrum (monochromatic), (3) coherence, (4) high power density, and (5) high switching speed. A laser is attractive for its small size, high efficiency, and low-voltage operation. It can be operated in CW mode for low-power applications and in pulse mode for high-power applications. The laser is indispensable as the light source for advanced optical-fiber communication whose main advantage is large bandwidth (see Figs. C4.1 and C4.2). The optimum choice of wavelength is between 1.3–1.5 μm for this purpose. A modulation rate of higher than 20 Gb/s has been demonstrated. Another related application is direct-beam communication, e.g., between satellites. A laser is also useful in laser radar systems, in range-finders for terrain profile, in military navigation, tracking and guidance systems, and in intrusion alarm systems. It is important for holography where three-dimensional images can be stored and retrieved. The highly directional beam is useful for precision alignment, and with extremely high power density it can be used for cutting metal, drilling (also for wood and ceramics), and welding. The metal interconnections in ICs that serve as fuses can be burnt off by a laser beam. Lasers are also used in the medical field for surgeries, such as retina repair and in cancer research. It is a good analytical tool in chemical-emission spectroscopy such as exhaust and pollution analysis, and for meteorology. In more common commercial applications, it is used in compact disc (CD) audio and video players, copy machines, and printers. One shortcoming of lasers is that they cannot be easily fabricated in an integrated circuit for monolithic optoelectronics.

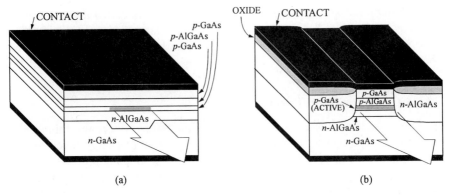

FIGURE 48.10
Structures for (a) channeled-substrate planar laser, and (b) buried-heterojunction laser.

48.5 RELATED DEVICES

48.5.1 Heterojunction Laser

In a single-heterojunction laser, an isotype heterojunction is used. The energy-band diagram is shown in Fig. 48.9(a). The function of the band-edge discontinuity is to confine carriers and to reduce d of Eq. (48.7) for lower J_{th}. In this example GaAs also has a higher index of refraction so that light is more confined as in a waveguide.

A double-heterojunction (DH) laser (Fig. 48.9(b)) not only gives better optical and carrier confinement, but the anisotype p-n heterojunction also provides improved injection efficiency for electrons.

Taking advantage of the heterostructure as a waveguide, there are many stripe-geometry lasers for better lateral beam confinement. Two examples, shown in Fig. 48.10, are the channeled-substrate planar laser and the buried-heterojunction laser.

48.5.2 Large-Optical-Cavity Laser

In a standard DH laser, optical intensity in the waveguide layer is very high and it sometimes causes catastrophic failure at the reflecting surfaces. In a large-optical-cavity (LOC) laser (Fig. 48.11(a)), the middle layer is thickened and it contains the p-n junction. In this structure, the optical cavity is much wider than the recombination region where light originates.

48.5.3 Separate-Confinement Heterojunction Laser

The separate-confinement heterojunction (SCH) laser has four heterojunctions (Fig. 48.11(b)). The inner two define the region of recombination, and the outer two define the optical cavity. This structure combines the advantages of DH laser and LOC laser. A refinement of this structure, using graded composition for the outer heterojunctions, is shown in Fig. 48.11(c) and is called a graded-index separate-confinement heterojunction (GRIN-SCH) laser. This structure is often used in quantum-well lasers where the middle layer is too thin for optical confinement.

48.5.4 Quantum-Well Laser

In the extreme case, when the middle layer of the DH laser becomes thinner than the de Broglie wavelength ($h/p < 500$ Å), quantization of energy levels start to appear as shown in Fig. 48.12(a). The advantages of a quantum-well laser are further reduction in J_{th}, less temperature sensitivity in J_{th}, greater frequency tuning range, and higher quantum efficiency. The problem it introduces is optical confinement in a very thin layer. To alleviate this, there are several approaches.

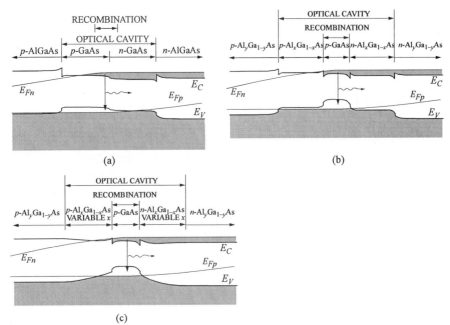

FIGURE 48.11
Energy-band diagrams of (a) large-optical-cavity laser, (b) separate-confinement heterojunction laser, and (c) graded-index separate-confinement heterojunction laser. In these structures, the optical cavity is much larger than the region of recombination.

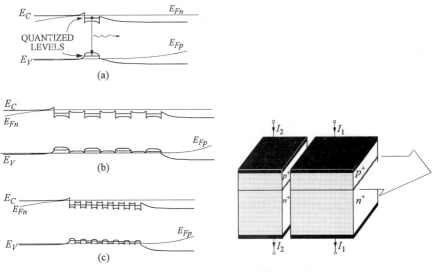

FIGURE 48.12
Energy-band diagrams of (a) quantum-well laser, (b) multiple-quantum-well laser, and (c) superlattice laser, all under forward bias.

FIGURE 48.13
The cleaved-coupled-cavity (C^3) laser consists of two segments coupled optically to each other.

One is to use a GRIN-SCH structure (Fig. 48.11(c)). Multiple quantum wells can also be used to enlarge the optical cavity (Fig. 48.12(b)). With this structure, when the dimensions of the barriers and wells are further reduced to be smaller than the carrier mean free path, a superlattice laser is formed (Fig. 48.12(c)).

48.5.5 Cleaved-Coupled-Cavity Laser

The cleaved-coupled-cavity (C^3) laser consists of two segments, with a gap of ≈ 5 µm between them (Fig. 48.13). The two Fabry-Perot etalons are coupled optically to each other for single-mode lasing, since it is more discriminating for a common wavelength that can satisfy Eq. (48.9) for both segments. The two segments are usually driven at two different current levels. One of them can be used to tune the wavelength because the injected carriers affect the index of refraction, and hence the effective resonator length.

48.5.6 Distributed-Feedback Laser

Another approach to single-mode lasing is to use a distributed-feedback laser. The structure (Fig. 48.14(a)) has a grating adjacent to the active layer. These corrugations determine the coherent wavelength by Bragg scattering, and

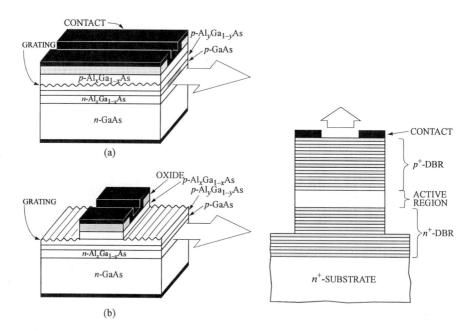

FIGURE 48.14
Structures of (a) a distributed-feedback laser and (b) a distributed-Bragg-reflector laser.

FIGURE 48.15
Structure of a vertical-cavity surface-emitting laser.

de-emphasize the role of the Fabry-Perot mirrors. Another advantage is that there is less temperature dependence in the lasing wavelength. A similar structure is the distributed-Bragg-reflector laser (Fig. 48.14(b)) in which the gratings are only incorporated outside the region of recombination.

48.5.7 Vertical-Cavity Surface-Emitting Laser

The vertical-cavity surface-emitting laser (VCSEL) is a quantum-well laser with a cavity defined vertically by multiple-quantum-well structures, called distributed-Bragg reflectors (DBRs) (Fig. 48.15). The active region often contains multiple quantum wells also. The advantages of the VCSELs are the realization of 2-D laser arrays, and compatibility with IC processing so that they can be integrated with the circuitry on the same chip.

REFERENCES

1. J. P. Gordon, H. J. Zeiger and C. H. Townes, "Molecular microwave oscillator and new hyperfine structure in the microwave spectrum of NH_3," *Phys. Rev.*, **95**, 282 (1954).
2. N. G. Basov and A. M. Prokhorov, "Application of molecular beams to the radio spectroscopic study of the rotation spectra of molecules," *Zh. Eksp. Theo. Fiz.*, **27**, 431 (1954).
3. M. G. A. Bernard and G. Duraffourg, "Laser conditions in semiconductors," *Phys. Status Solidi*, **1**, 699 (1961).
4. W. P. Dumke, "Interband transitions and maser action," *Phys. Rev.*, **127**, 1559 (1962).
5. R. N. Hall, G. E. Fenner, J. D. Kingsley, T. J. Soltys and R. O. Carlson, "Coherent light emission from GaAs junctions," *Phys. Rev. Lett.*, **9**, 366 (1962).
6. M. I. Nathan, W. P. Dumke, G. Burns, F. H. Dill, Jr. and G. Lasher, "Stimulated emission of radiation from GaAs *p-n* junctions," *Appl. Phys. Lett.*, **1**, 62 (1962).
7. T. M. Quist, R. H. Rediker, R. J. Keyes, W. E. Krag, B. Lax, A. L. McWhorter and H. J. Zeigler, "Semiconductor maser of GaAs," *Appl. Phys. Lett.*, **1**, 91 (1962).
8. N. Holonyak, Jr. and S. F. Bevacqua, "Coherent (visible) light emission from $Ga(As_{1-x}P_x)$ junctions," *Appl. Phys. Lett.*, **1**, 82 (1962).
9. H. Kroemer, "A proposed class of heterojunction injection lasers," *Proc. IEEE*, **51**, 1782 (1963).
10. Z. I. Alferov and R. F. Kazarinov, U. S. S. R. patent 181,737 (Applied 1963, approved 1965).
11. I. Hayashi, M. B. Panish, P. W. Foy and S. Sumski, "Junction lasers which operate continuously at room temperature," *Appl. Phys. Lett.*, **17**, 109 (1970).
12. R. N. Hall, "Injection lasers," *IEEE Trans. Electron Dev.*, **ED-23**, 700 (1976).
13. A. L. Schawlow, "Masers and lasers," *IEEE Trans. Electron Dev.*, **ED-23**, 773 (1976).
14. I. Hayashi, "Heterostructure lasers," *IEEE Trans. Electron Dev.*, **ED-31**, 1630 (1984).
15. S. M. Sze, *Physics of semiconductor devices*, 2nd Ed., Wiley, New York, 1981.

CHAPTER

49

PHOTOCONDUCTOR

49.1 HISTORY

The photoconductor has been called a photoresistor, photoconductive cell or, simply, a photocell. It was the first of the quantum photodetectors developed after a long period of having only thermal photodetectors. Photoconductivity was discovered by Smith in 1873 in selenium.[1] A photoconductor involving excitation of carriers from the valence band to the conduction band is called intrinsic, and that between an impurity level and the valence band or the conduction band is called extrinsic. The first intrinsic photoconductor was demonstrated by Case using TlS in 1920.[2] PbS, PbSe, and PbTe devices were studied in the 1930s and the 1940s. Another milestone was set by the realization of extrinsic photoconductors in Si and Ge, by Rollin and Simmons in 1952,[3,4] and by Burstein el al. in 1953.[5] The photoconductor, being a simple device, enjoys a wide spectrum of usage, from photodetector to optoelectronic switch. Review articles for the device can be found in Refs. 6–8.

49.2 STRUCTURE

The photoconductor is a light-sensitive resistor whose horizontal body, between the two contacts, is exposed to light, as shown in Fig. 49.1(a). In this structure the active semiconductor layer, usually lightly doped, is deposited onto a semi-insulating substrate, forming an epitaxial heterostructure. In some practical devices, especially those designed as discrete components, the metal contacts have interdigitated patterns as shown in Fig. 49.1(b). This maximizes the exposed area with a large W, and enhances the gain with a small L. The active film can also be polycrystalline so it can simply be deposited onto an inexpensive substrate

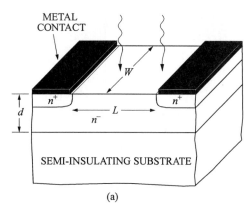 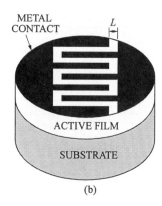

(a)   (b)

FIGURE 49.1
Different structures of photoconductors.

such as ceramic. Since the resistance is the main measurement, the contact resistance of the metal has to be minimized. This can be achieved by introducing a heavily doped region at the metal contact. Common semiconductors used for photoconductors are CdSe, CdS, CdTe, InSb, InP, PbS, PbSe, Ge, Si, GaAs, and GaP.

49.3 CHARACTERISTICS

Photoconductivity is due to the generation of mobile carriers when photons are absorbed in a semiconductor. These absorption processes are shown in the energy-band diagram of Fig. 49.2. In an intrinsic photoconductor, the dominant mechanism is direct transition from the valence band to the conductor band. An extrinsic photoconductor requires shallow impurity dopants that are not ionized in the absence of light. Since the transition energy has to be equal to the photon energy,

$$E = h\nu = \frac{hc}{\lambda} \ , \tag{49.1}$$

extrinsic photoconductors are designed for long wavelengths–infrared light. To avoid thermal generation, the extrinsic photoconductor has to be operated at a low enough temperature, $kT \ll h\nu$. Infrared detectors are cooled below room temperature for this restriction.

The electrical characteristics of a photoconductor with and without light are shown in Fig. 49.3. Taking an n-type device as an example, the dark I-V curve is given by

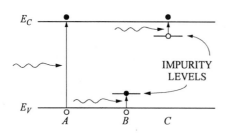

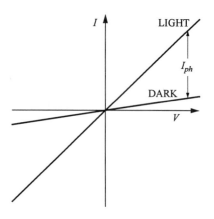

FIGURE 49.2
Generation of excess carriers by photon. In an intrinsic photoconductor, process A is direct transition from valence band to conduction band. For extrinsic photoconductors, process B creates excess holes from acceptor impurities, and process C creates excess electrons from donor impurities.

FIGURE 49.3
I-V characteristics of a photoconductor with and without light. The difference in current is called photocurrent.

$$I = \frac{qN_D\mu_n WdV}{L} \ .$$ (49.2)

The increase in current with light is called photocurrent (I_{ph}), and it is due to excess carriers. In the case of an intrinsic photoconductor,

$$\Delta n = \Delta p = G_{op}\tau_p = \frac{\eta F_{ph}\tau_p}{d}$$ (49.3)

where η is the internal quantum efficiency, and F_{ph} is the photon flux. Equation (49.3) assumes that photons are totally and uniformly absorbed within the active layer. Some deviation from this assumption will be addressed later but it does not affect the following analysis.

The I_{ph} in an intrinsic photoconductor is a result of both excess electrons and holes,

$$\begin{aligned}
I_{ph} &= \frac{q\,(\Delta n\mu_n + \Delta p\mu_p)\,WdV}{L} \\
&= \frac{q\,(\mu_n + \mu_p)\,\eta F_{ph}\tau_p WV}{L} \ .
\end{aligned}$$ (49.4)

In an extrinsic photoconductor, the I_{ph} is due to one type of excess carrier only, and

$$I_{ph} = \frac{q\Delta n\mu_n W d V}{L}$$

$$= \frac{q\mu_n \eta F_{ph}\tau_n W V}{L} \ .$$

(49.5)

It can be seen here that in both Eqs. (49.4) and (49.5), the I_{ph} is a function of applied bias. This means that at large V, even for a given F_{ph}, I_{ph} can be very large. This phenomenon requires the concept of optical gain (G) which is generally defined for all detectors as

$$I_{ph} = Aq\eta F_{ph}G \ .$$

(49.6)

A is the area receiving the photon flux F_{ph}, and, in this case, is equal to WL. It can be shown that for an intrinsic photoconductor,

$$G = \frac{(\mu_n + \mu_p)\tau_p V}{L^2}$$

(49.7)

and for an extrinsic photoconductor,

$$G = \frac{\mu_n \tau_n V}{L^2} \ .$$

(49.8)

Both are for an n-type device.

The existence of gain in a photoconductor is not obvious and somewhat surprising. One observation is that in other photodetectors such as p-i-n photodiode or phototransistor, the exact location of the light exposure is not critical, as long as photons are absorbed in the high-field region with high internal quantum efficiency. In a photoconductor, since the principle is to change the conductivity of the electrical path, the area of exposure has to connect the two contacts. In this respect, the light is always perpendicular to the current flow. It is based on this assumption that all equations here are derived. The gain here can be interpreted as the ratio of carrier lifetime to the transit time across L,

$$G = \frac{\tau}{L/v} = \frac{\tau\mu V}{L^2} \ .$$

(49.9)

It can also be interpreted as the ratio of the flow of carriers to the total generation rate

$$G = \frac{\Delta n v W d}{\eta F_{ph}LW} = \frac{\tau\mu V}{L^2} \ .$$

(49.10)

The gain in either interpretation is shown to increase with τ, μ, V, and $1/L^2$. In practical devices, a gain of ≈ 1000 can readily be obtained. To maximize gain, the bias should be high, often limited by breakdown mechanisms and the space-charge effect. Operating voltage can vary from a few volts to a few hundred volts. The carrier lifetime τ should be long, but this degrades the turnoff speed of the device. In applications where speed is important, the lifetime is intentionally shortened by the introduction of recombination centers, at the expense of gain and sensitivity. Ultra-fast photoconductors with a response time of ≈ 1 ps has been reported.

In practical applications, the light source is not monochromatic and absorption is not uniform in the semiconductor as a function of depth from the surface. The photon flux F_{ph} in the previous equations can be viewed as an average value and can be obtained from the power density $P(\lambda)$

$$
\begin{aligned}
F_{ph} &= \int_0^{hc/E} \frac{P(\lambda)\,(1-R)\,[1-\exp(-\alpha d)]}{h\nu}\,d\lambda \\
&= \frac{1}{hc} \int_0^{hc/E} P(\lambda)\lambda\,(1-R)\,[1-\exp(-\alpha d)]\,d\lambda
\end{aligned}
\tag{49.11}
$$

where R is the reflection, E is the energy gap for an intrinsic photoconductor and the impurity level from the band edge for an extrinsic photoconductor. The exponential term considers not only non-uniform absorption, but also incomplete absorption for a thin sample. It should be mentioned that in extrinsic photoconductors, the absorption coefficient is much lower, and a device with thicker d is desirable.

49.4 APPLICATIONS

The photoconductor is attractive for its simple structure, low cost, and rugged features. For these reasons, it is quite widely used in applications such as photographic meters, flame/smoke/burglar detectors, card readers, lighting controls for street lamps, etc. Extrinsic photoconductors can extend the long-wavelength limit without using materials of very narrow energy gap, and they are used as popular infrared photodetectors. The general applications of a photodetector are summarized in Appendix C4. A photoconductor is also used to detect nuclear radiation (see Section 50.5.2). Besides being a photodetector, it has another useful application as an electrical switch controlled by light. A schematic setup is shown in Fig. 49.4 where a very short light pulse, such as that from a laser, can generate sharp voltage-pulse waveforms. This technique is useful in high-speed optoelectronics, such as sampling in analog-to-digital conversion, and generating high-voltage pulses to drive another laser. Another potential use of a photoconductor is to provide variable resistance in a circuit.

49.5 RELATED DEVICES

49.5.1 Photoelectromagnetic Detector

The photoelectromagnetic (PEM) detector is based on the PEM effect. When electrons and holes are generated by light near the front surface (Fig. 49.5), they diffuse toward the back surface. In the presence of a magnetic field, these carriers are deflected in opposite directions due to their opposite charges, and subsequently a voltage between the two terminals is developed. It can be seen that the structure is similar, if not identical, to a photoconductor. Since charges of opposite polarities are needed, only band-to-band transitions are applicable. The PEM detector is not as sensitive as other photodetectors, and is seldom used for this purpose. It is used primarily as a tool to study surface effects such as the surface recombination velocity.

49.5.2 Free-Carrier Photoconductor

The free-carrier photoconductor is also called a hot-electron photoconductor or a hot-electron bolometer. In this device, free carriers are excited to a higher energy state within the band (Fig. 49.6), and the mobility is increased with light intensity. The increase of current in response to light is due to the change in mobility, but the number of carriers remains the same. The hot-electron effect is often characterized by an equivalent hot-electron temperature which is not to be confused with the physical temperature of the device. A standard bolometer is based on the change of its physical temperature (see Section 63.5.2–Thermistor Bolometer).

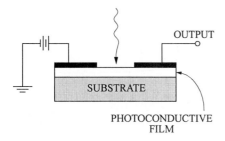

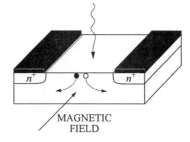

FIGURE 49.4
A photoconductor as an optoelectronic switch, using light as a control.

FIGURE 49.5
In a photoelectromagnetic detector, electrons and holes generated near the front surface diffuse towards the back surface, and are deflected by the magnetic field in opposite directions.

49.5.3 Putley Detector

In a Putley detector,[9] the semiconductor is put in a magnetic field. Quantization of energy within the continuum conduction band or the valence band leads to discrete Landau levels, and transitional energy between these closely separated levels is called cyclotron resonance energy. Since carrier mobility is different for different Landau levels, a change of conductivity is the signal of light.

49.5.4 Dember-Effect Detector

The Dember effect requires two conditions: (1) inhomogeneous electron and hole generation such that a concentration gradient exists, and (2) a large difference in mobility (or diffusion coefficient) between electrons and holes.[10] Condition (1) is satisfied when light is irradiated onto a semiconductor surface, as shown in Fig. 49.7. The optical generation rate per unit volume decays exponentially as a function of distance, with a characteristic absorption length ($1/\alpha$). The difference in mobility is also common in semiconductors where μ_n is usually larger than μ_p.

The carrier profiles immediately after light generation are shown in Fig. 49.7(b). If $\mu_n \gg \mu_p$, excess electrons diffuse quickly toward the back surface, while excess holes remain behind. This separation of charge develops a voltage

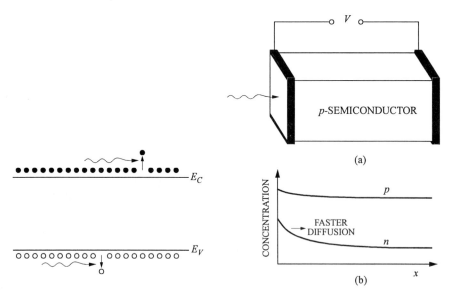

FIGURE 49.6
In a free-carrier photoconductor, electrons or holes are excited to higher energy but within the band.

FIGURE 49.7
(a) Structure of a Dember-effect detector. (b) Carrier profiles immediately after the exposure of light. Surface recombination is neglected.

difference between the front surface and the back surface. It is interesting to note that a Dember-effect detector structurally can be the same as a photon-drag detector (Chapter 58).

REFERENCES

1. W. Smith, "The action of light on selenium," *J. Soc. Tel. Engrs.*, **2**, 31 (1873).
2. T. W. Case, "'Thalofide cell'–A new photo-electric substrate," *Phys. Rev.*, **15**, 289 (1920).
3. B. V. Rollin and E. L. Simmons, "Long wavelength infra-red photoconductivity of silicon at low temperatures," *Proc. Phys. Soc.*, **B65**, 995 (1952).
4. B. V. Rollin and E. L. Simmons, "Long wavelength infra red photoconductivity of silicon at low temperatures," *Proc. Phys. Soc.*, **B66**, 162 (1953).
5. E. Burstein, J. J. Oberly and J. W. Davisson, "Infrared photoconductivity due to neutral impurities in silicon," *Phys. Rev.*, **89**, 311 (1953).
6. R. K. Willardson and A. C. Beer, Eds., *Semiconductors and semimetals*, Vol. 12, Academic Press, New York, 1977.
7. F. Stockmann, "Photoconductivity–A centennial," *Phys. Stat. Sol. A*, **15**, 381 (1973).
8. D. Long, "Photovoltaic and photoconductive infrared detectors," in R. J. Keyes, *Optical and infrared detectors*, Springer-Verlag, Berlin, 1980.
9. E. H. Putley, "Indium antimonide submillimeter photoconductive detectors," *Appl. Opt.*, **4**, 649 (1965).
10. T. Niedziela and J. Piotrowski, "Ultimate parameters of middle and long wavelength infrared detectors (Cd, Hg)Te based on the Dember effect," *J. Tech. Phys.*, **28**, 173 (1987).

CHAPTER
50

p-i-n PHOTODIODE

50.1 HISTORY

The *p-i-n* photodiode is one of the most common photodetectors, and is sometimes referred to simply as a photodiode. The *p-n* junction, developed in the late 1940s, was used for many photonic devices such as photodiodes, solar cells, and LEDs in the 1950s. The *p-i-n* photodiode, developed in the late 1950s, is an improvement over the *p-n* photodiode. The importance of light absorption in a wide depletion region of a *p-i-n* structure was first addressed by Gartner in 1959.[1] Further analysis of the performance as a photodetector was made by Riesz, and the *p-i-n* photodiode was demonstrated with Ge in 1962.[2] For more detailed study on this device, the readers are referred to Refs. 3 and 4.

50.2 STRUCTURE

The special feature of the *p-i-n* photodiode is the thick intrinsic layer inserted at a *p-n* junction, as shown in Fig. 50.1(a). The doping level of this layer is usually less than 10^{15} cm^{-3}, and is generally of the same doping type as the substrate heavily doped region. To ensure complete absorption of light within this high-field region, its thickness should be larger than the absorption length ($1/\alpha$), but not significantly larger because of speed considerations. The intrinsic layer can either be an epitaxial film deposited on heavily doped substrate, or simply the entire thickness of the wafer, with high-level diffusion from the bottom of the wafer. The structure of a heterojunction *p-i-n* photodiode is shown in Fig. 50.1(b). This structure has the added flexibility of receiving light from the substrate, which has larger energy gap, and, thus, is transparent to the incoming light. The

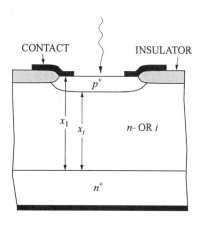
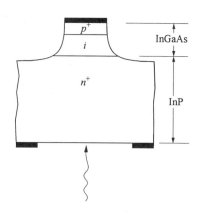

FIGURE 50.1

(a) Structure of a *p-i-n* photodiode. (b) In a heterojunction *p-i-n* photodiode, light can be coupled from the substrate.

advantage of this inverted configuration is that it avoids the loss of exposure area due to the metal contacts. Minimization of the junction area is important to reduce the junction capacitance for speed considerations, and the mesa structure helps to achieve this goal. The path of the light, alternatively, can be parallel to the junction, coming from the side of the detector. This has the potential of reduced intrinsic layer thickness, shorter transit time and, thus, higher speed, but at the expense of reduced quantum efficiency.

50.3 CHARACTERISTICS

The main advantages of the thick intrinsic layer are twofold: (1) to collect photo-generated carriers efficiently and (2) to reduce junction capacitance. The second point is trivial since

$$C = \frac{\varepsilon_s A}{W_d} = \frac{\varepsilon_s A}{x_i} \ . \tag{50.1}$$

In operation, the *p-i-n* photodiode is under a moderate reverse bias to ensure that the entire intrinsic layer is fully depleted. The speed limitation due to RC delay, R being the load resistance, is thus minimized.

Going back to the first point, the intrinsic layer provides a thick region of uniform high field. It is critical to have light absorbed in a region of high field for two reasons: speed and quantum efficiency. If light is absorbed outside the

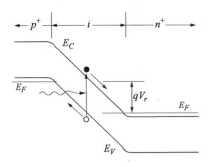

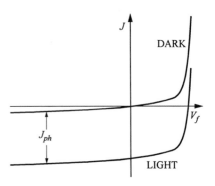

FIGURE 50.2
Energy-band diagram showing the electron-hole pair generation in the intrinsic region.

FIGURE 50.3
I-V characteristics of a *p-i-n* photodiode with and without light.

depletion layer, carriers are collected by a diffusion process, and the time required for carriers to diffuse a distance x is known to be

$$t \approx \frac{x^2}{4D} \quad . \tag{50.2}$$

On the other hand, the time required for a high-field drift process is given by

$$t_t \approx \frac{x}{v_{sat}} \quad . \tag{50.3}$$

A quick estimate with $x_i = 10$ μm, $D = 50$ cm²/s, $v_{sat} = 10^7$ cm/s shows that diffusion takes about 5 ns while a drift process only requires 0.1 ns. The overall speed of the *p-i-n* photodetector is limited by the transit time or the *RC* time constant. In practice, the transit time (Eq. (50.3)) across the intrinsic layer is the limiting factor. For this reason, the intrinsic layer should be larger than the absorption length for complete absorption, but not so thick as to slow down the response. On quantum efficiency, carriers generated within the high-field depletion region are separated rapidly by the field, and have little chance for recombination (Fig. 50.2). Quantum efficiency is close to 100% in this region. Carriers generated outside the depletion region in the neutral layer have quantum efficiency of only (see Section 50.5.1 below)

$$\eta = \frac{\alpha L_p}{1 + \alpha L_p} \quad . \tag{50.4}$$

The overall internal quantum efficiency for the structure in Fig. 50.1(a) is given by

$$\eta = 1 - \left(1 - \frac{\alpha L_p}{1 + \alpha L_p}\right) \exp\left(-\alpha x_1\right)$$

$$= 1 - \frac{\exp\left(-\alpha x_1\right)}{1 + \alpha L_p} \quad . \tag{50.5}$$

The exponential term is due to reduced light reaching the neutral region. It is also assumed that light absorbed within the thin p^+-region has 100% efficiency. Between Eqs. (50.3) and (50.5), the intrinsic layer thickness has to be optimized between speed and efficiency.

The *I-V* characteristics with and without light are shown in Fig. 50.3. The dark current is the total of the diffusion current and the recombination/generation current within the intrinsic layer. These components are given by

$$J = \left(\frac{qD_p n_i^2}{L_p N_D} + \frac{qD_n n_i^2}{L_n N_A}\right)\left[\exp\left(\frac{qV_f}{kT}\right) - 1\right] + \frac{qx_i n_i}{2\tau}\left[\exp\left(\frac{qV_f}{2kT}\right) - 1\right] . \tag{50.6}$$

Since the p^+- and n^+-layers sandwiching the intrinsic layer are heavily doped, N_A and N_D are high and the diffusion current is usually negligible. For a more detailed discussion of the recombination/generation current in a *p-i-n* structure, the readers can refer to Section 2.3. In response to light, a photocurrent J_{ph} shifts the dark current by an amount equal to

$$J_{ph} = (1 - R) F_{ph} q \eta \tag{50.7}$$

where R is the surface reflection and F_{ph} is the photon flux (per area per unit time) whose energy is larger than the energy gap of the semiconductor material. As seen from the above equation, the *p-i-n* photodiode has no gain (gain = 1).

50.4 APPLICATIONS

Even though a *p-i-n* photodiode does not have gain, compared to high-gain photodetectors such as avalanche photodiode and phototransistor, it has better linearity with light intensity, and higher quantum efficiency. It is attractive for its low cost, simple and rugged structure, high speed, low voltage, and simplicity of the bias circuit. Operational frequency of higher than 30 GHz has been reported. Common use for the *p-i-n* photodiode is in audio and video compact disc players, and in fiber-optics communication systems. For general applications of a photodetector, the readers are referred to Appendix C4.

50.5 RELATED DEVICES

50.5.1 *p-n* Photodiode

In a *p-n* photodiode, the intrinsic layer is absent and the depletion region terminates in a region of higher doping concentration (Fig. 50.4). The depletion width in this case is determined by the standard equation

$$W_d = \sqrt{\frac{2\varepsilon_s (V_r + \psi_{bi})}{qN_D}} \quad . \tag{50.8}$$

One can arbitrarily choose a very low doping for a large depletion width, but the series resistance in the substrate becomes large, and also the field is non-uniform.

Since in this device a larger portion of the light is absorbed outside the depletion region, it is of interest here to derive the quantum efficiency when carriers are generated in the neutral region. Changing the *x*-coordinate starting from the depletion edge as shown in Fig. 50.5, the generation rate is given by

$$G_{op}(x) = F'_{ph}\alpha \exp(-\alpha x) \quad . \tag{50.9}$$

Substituting this into the continuity equation at steady state

$$D_p \frac{\partial^2 p_n}{\partial x^2} - \frac{p_n - p_{no}}{\tau_p} + G_{op}(x) = 0 \quad , \tag{50.10}$$

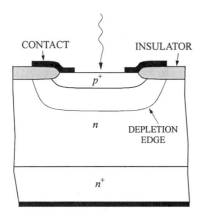

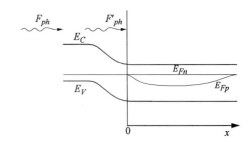

FIGURE 50.5

Energy-band diagram of a *p-n* photodiode, showing the boundary conditions for excess hole concentration, related to E_{Fp}, used to derive the quantum efficiency outside the depletion region.

FIGURE 50.4

In a *p-n* photodiode, the intrinsic layer is omitted and the depletion layer terminates within the *n*-layer.

one obtains the general solution of

$$
p_n = p_{no} + C_1 \exp\left(\frac{x}{L_p}\right) + C_2 \exp\left(\frac{-x}{L_p}\right) + \frac{\alpha F'_{ph} \tau_p \exp(-\alpha x)}{1 - \alpha^2 L_p^2} \quad . \tag{50.11}
$$

Under short-circuit, the boundary condition at $x = 0$ is $p_n = p_{no}$ because the high field in the depletion region sweeps away excess carriers effectively. The boundary condition at $x = \infty$ is also $p_n = p_{no}$ assuming that the sample thickness is much larger than $1/\alpha$. With these assumptions, Eq. (50.11) is reduced to

$$
p_n = p_{no} + \frac{\alpha F'_{ph} \tau_p}{\alpha^2 L_p^2 - 1}\left[\exp\left(\frac{-x}{L_p}\right) - \exp(-\alpha x)\right] \quad . \tag{50.12}
$$

The photocurrent is given by

$$
J_{ph} = -qD_p \frac{\partial p_n}{\partial x}\bigg|_{x=0}
$$

$$
= -qF'_{ph}\left(\frac{\alpha L_p}{1 + \alpha L_p}\right) \quad , \tag{50.13}
$$

thus implying a quantum efficiency of

$$
\eta = \frac{\alpha L_p}{1 + \alpha L_p} \quad . \tag{50.14}
$$

When a heterostructure is applied in a *p-n* photodiode, the top heavily doped layer can have a wider energy gap so that light is not absorbed in that region. The advantage is that there is no restriction on the thickness of this layer.

50.5.2 Nuclear-Radiation Detector

The *p-i-n* structure is the most common detector for nuclear radiation, among others like *p-n* photodiode, CCIS, Schottky-barrier photodiode, and photoconductor. Nuclear radiation can be due to high-energy charged or uncharged particles, or electromagnetic radiation. A detector for these is also called a radiation detector, particle detector, or nuclear detector. Most common materials used are Si and Ge, followed by CdTe and HgI_2. The energy of each particle or photon falls in the range of ≈ 100 eV to ≈ 100 MeV. The interaction of high-energy particles with the detector crystal differs with their energy, but the end result is the same–ionization of carriers, leading to the generation of electron-hole pairs. Also, since the ionization energy is only ≈ 3 eV, about one tenth compared to a gaseous detector, many electron-hole pairs can be generated by a single high-energy particle or photon. The response is thus a function of their energy. Because nuclear radiation is very penetrating, a very large and pure intrinsic layer is demanded. For example, to completely deplete the standard wafer thickness of ≈ 500 μm, a low doping level of $< 10^{12}$ cm^{-3} is required. A common approach to achieve high-purity intrinsic material is the lithium-drift process. If lithium is let to diffuse into p-type Si or Ge, since lithium is an n-type dopant, a field is built up wherever there is under- or over-compensation, and it controls the diffusion automatically. Detectors from this process are called lithium-drifted Si (or Ge) detectors.

REFERENCES

1. W. W. Gartner, "Depletion-layer photoeffects in semiconductors," *Phys. Rev.*, **116**, 84 (1959).
2. R. P. Riesz, "High speed semiconductor photodiodes," *Rev. Sci. Inst.*, **33**, 994 (1962).
3. V. Svoboda, "Silicon *p-i-n* photodetectors," *AWA Tech. Rev.*, **16**, 27 (1975).
4. S. M. Sze, *Physics of semiconductor devices*, 2nd Ed., Wiley, New York, 1981.

CHAPTER 51

SCHOTTKY-BARRIER
PHOTODIODE

51.1 HISTORY

The Schottky-barrier photodiode is also called a metal-semiconductor photodiode. It is a unique photodetector in that it can operate in two detection modes: (1) electron-hole pair generation from band-to-band (energy-gap) excitation in the semiconductor, and (2) emission of carriers from metal to the semiconductor over the Schottky barrier. The latter process is often referred to as internal photoemission. While the general photo-response of Schottky barriers had been mentioned earlier,[1–3] point-contact photodiodes using energy-gap excitation were studied by Kibler in 1962,[4] and by Sharpless in 1964.[5] Schottky-barrier photodiodes with evaporated metal films were presented by Ahlstrom and Gartner in 1962[6] and by Schneider in 1966.[7] A Schottky-barrier photodiode based on internal photoemission was first studied by Peters in 1967.[8] This effect was modeled by different authors in 1970–1971, namely Williams,[9] Dalal,[10,11] and Vickers.[12] In 1973, Shepherd and Yang suggested and demonstrated the use of internal photoemission for infrared imaging arrays.[13] This work generated much interest in development and eventually resulted in successful commercial Schottky-barrier focal-plane arrays. For further information on the Schottky-barrier photodiode, the readers can refer to Refs. 14 and 15.

51.2 STRUCTURE

Different variations of the Schottky-barrier photodiodes are shown in Fig. 51.1. In the general structure of Fig. 51.1(a), the metal layer forming the Schottky

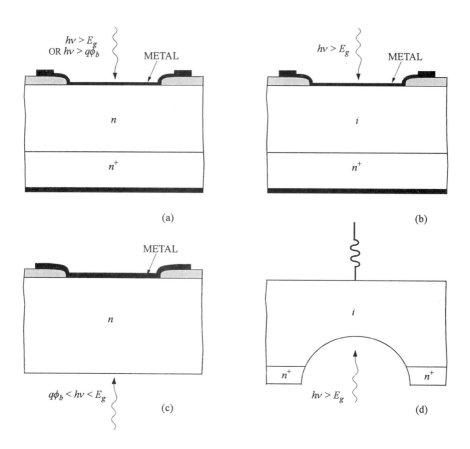

FIGURE 51.1
Different versions of Schottky-barrier photodiodes. (a) General structure. (b) Metal-*i-n* structure. (c) Schottky-barrier photodiode with back illumination. (c) Point-contact photodiode. Note that the wavelength of interest is slightly different for each structure.

barrier is very thin, under ≈ 150 Å, to let sufficient light reach the interface (for internal photoemission) or the semiconductor (for energy-gap excitation). Shown in Fig. 51.1(b) is a metal-*i-n* structure, also called a Mott barrier, whose operation and advantages are similar to those of a *p-i-n* photodiode. This structure is mainly advantageous for energy-gap excitation. The long intrinsic layer is fully depleted by a moderate reverse bias, and provides a long region of uniform high field in which photo-generated carriers are collected efficiently. For detectors with internal photoemission, it is more efficient to direct light through the substrate as shown in Fig. 51.1(c). Since the barrier height is always smaller than the energy gap, light with $q\phi_b < h\nu < E_g$ is not absorbed in the semiconductor, and intensity is not reduced at the metal-semiconductor interface. The metal layer in this structure can be thicker for easier thickness control and to minimize series

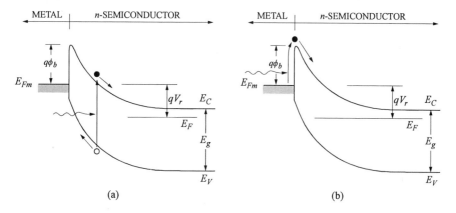

FIGURE 51.2

Absorption of photons by (a) band-to-band excitation and (b) internal photoemission.

resistance. Another version is the point-contact photodiode shown in Fig. 51.1(d). This device has minimum junction area, small junction capacitance and very-high-speed capability.

The semiconductor layer is usually *n*-type for visible-wavelength detection since in practice it is easier to obtain a higher barrier height. In applications requiring long-wavelength detection, internal photoemission with a small barrier height is desirable, and a *p*-type semiconductor is more common. For Si devices, additional options are available using silicides in place of the metal. A silicide usually has a more reproducible interface since it is formed by reacting metal with Si so that the new interface is never exposed. Common silicides used for this purpose are PtSi, Pd$_2$Si, and IrSi. Another advantage of a Schottky-barrier diode is that high-temperature processing for diffusion or implantation anneal is not required. Omitted in Fig. 51.1 are antireflection coatings on the metal films to reduce reflection.

51.3 CHARACTERISTICS

The two modes of photon absorption in a Schottky-barrier photodiode are depicted in Fig. 51.2. In the band-to-band excitation (Fig. 51.2(a)), a photon is absorbed inside the semiconductor and produces an electron-hole pair. Carriers generated in the depletion region are separated rapidly by the large field, and the internal quantum efficiency is near 100%. Outside the depletion region in the neutral semiconductor, photo-generated carriers are collected only by diffusion and the internal quantum efficiency is reduced (see Section 50.5.1),

$$\eta = \frac{\alpha L_p}{1 + \alpha L_p} \tag{51.1}$$

where α is the optical absorption coefficient. The overall internal quantum efficiency is similar to that in a p-i-n photodiode

$$\eta = 1 - \left(1 - \frac{\alpha L_p}{1 + \alpha L_p}\right) \exp\left(-\alpha W_d\right)$$

$$= 1 - \frac{\exp\left(-\alpha W_d\right)}{1 + \alpha L_p} . \tag{51.2}$$

Diffusion is a much slower process than drift, and for both speed and efficiency, a metal-i-n structure shown in Fig. 51.1(b) is advantageous since the whole intrinsic layer becomes the depletion region. However, this intrinsic layer should not be excessively large because the transit time across this layer can place another limit on speed.

For internal photoemission, the photon is absorbed in the metal and a carrier is excited to a higher energy. These hot carriers have momentum in random directions, and those having excess energy larger than the barrier height and momentum toward the semiconductor contribute to the photocurrent. Unlike the energy-gap excitation, the internal photoemission process is very energy dependent, and the quantum efficiency is given by

$$\eta = C_1 \frac{(h\nu - q\phi_b)^2}{h\nu} , \tag{51.3}$$

where C_1 is the Fowler emission coefficient. This phenomenon is often applied to measure the barrier height as shown in Fig. 51.3(a). When a Schottky-barrier photodiode is scanned with light of variable wavelength, Fig. 51.3(b) shows that the quantum efficiency has a threshold of $q\phi_b$, and it increases with the photon energy. When the photon energy reaches the energy-gap value, the quantum efficiency jumps to a much higher value and it is relatively energy independent. In practical applications, the internal photoemission has typical quantum efficiencies of only less than 1%.

In either mode of operation, the photocurrent is given by

$$J_{ph} = (1 - R) q F_{ph} \eta \tag{51.4}$$

where R is due to losses from reflection and absorption by the metal film. The I-V characteristics with and without light are shown in Fig. 51.4. The dark current is given by (see Chapter 3–Schottky-barrier diode)

$$J = A^* \, T^2 \exp\left(-\frac{q\phi_b}{kT}\right)\left[\exp\left(\frac{qV_f}{nkT}\right) - 1\right] . \qquad (51.5)$$

This dark current is known to be due to thermionic emission of majority carriers and it does not suffer from charge storage of minority diffusion current, which limits the speed capability. Ultra-fast Schottky-barrier photodiodes operating beyond 100 GHz has been reported. It can be seen in Fig. 51.4 that the dark current does not completely saturate with reverse bias, and part of the contributions is from barrier lowering due to image force (see Appendix B6). This effect is sometimes used to extend the long-wavelength detection limit.

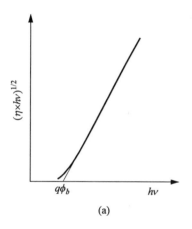
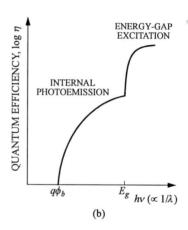

FIGURE 51.3
(a) Using the photo-response to deduce the Schottky-barrier height. (b) Quantum efficiency as a function of wavelength.

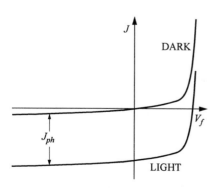

FIGURE 51.4
I-V characteristics of the Schottky-barrier photodiode with and without light.

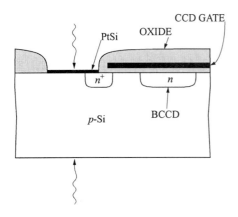

FIGURE 51.5
Integration of a Schottky-barrier photodiode with a buried-channel CCD in a sensor array.

51.4 APPLICATIONS

The main advantages of the Schottky-barrier photodiode are high speed and long-wavelength detection capability. Because of the compatibility with the mature silicon and silicide technology, these photodetectors can be integrated with excellent uniformity as staring-mode sensor arrays for cameras. A structure of the photodetector with a CCD transfer gate is shown in Fig. 51.5. The CCDs are convenient shift registers to carry signals from 2-D arrays, and they are also compatible with the Si technology. For these reasons, Schottky-barrier photodiodes constitute the most successful infrared focal-plane arrays in the market. (A focal-plane array is a photodetector array integrated with circuits right on the focal plane. These circuits perform certain signal processing tasks such as delay and multiplexing to reduce significantly the number of signal leads leaving the array.) The disadvantages of the Schottky-barrier photodiodes are low temperature operation for IR light due to the relatively large thermionic-emission current, and also low quantum efficiency for internal photoemission.

For general applications of a photodetector, the readers can refer to Appendix C4. A Schottky-barrier or metal-*i-n* structure can also be used as nuclear-radiation detector (see Section 50.5.2)

REFERENCES

1. See for example, S. Benzer, "The photo-diode and photo-peak characteristics in germanium," *Phys. Rev.*, **70**, 105 (1946).
2. See for example, R. Bray and K. Lark-Horovitz, "Photo- and thermo-effects in *p*-type germanium rectifiers," *Phys. Rev.*, **71**, 141 (1947).
3. See for example, J. I. Pantchechnikoff, "A large area germanium photocell," *Rev. Sci. Instr.*, **23**, 135 (1952).
4. L. U. Kibler, "A high-speed point contact photodiode," *Proc. IRE*, **50**, 1834 (1962).
5. W. M. Sharpless, "Cartridge-type point-contact photodiode," *Proc. IEEE*, **52**, 207 (1964).
6. E. Ahlstrom and W. W. Gartner, "Silicon surface-barrier photocells," *J. Appl. Phys.*, **33**, 2602 (1962).

7. M. V. Schneider, "Schottky barrier photodiodes with antireflection coating," *Bell Syst. Tech. J.*, **45**, 1611 (1966).
8. D. W. Peters, "An infrared detector utilizing internal photoemission," *Proc. IEEE*, **55**, 704 (1967).
9. R. Williams, "Injection by internal photoemission," in R. K. Willardson, Ed., A. C. Beer, Ed., *Semiconductors and semimetals*, Vol. 6, Academic Press, New York, 1970.
10. V. L. Dalal, "Simple model for internal photoemission," *J. Appl. Phys.*, **42**, 2274 (1971).
11. V. L. Dalal, "Analysis of photoemissive Schottky barrier photodetectors," *J. Appl. Phys.*, **42**, 2280 (1971).
12. V. E. Vickers, "Model of Schottky barrier hot-electron-mode photodetection," *Appl. Optics*, **10**, 2190 (1971).
13. F. D. Shepherd, Jr. and A. C. Yang, "Silicon Schottky retinas for infrared imaging," *Tech. Digest IEEE IEDM*, 310 (1973).
14. W. F. Kosonocky, "Review of Schottky-barrier imager technology," *SPIE*, **1308**, 2 (1990).
15. J. I. Pankove, *Optical processes in semiconductors*, Dover, New York, 1971.

CHAPTER

52

CHARGE-COUPLED IMAGE SENSOR

52.1 HISTORY

The charge-coupled image sensor (CCIS) can also be called a charge-transfer image sensor (CTIS). It is a specialized photodetector version of the parent charge-coupled device (CCD) or charge-transfer device (CTD), and is sometimes simply referred by these generic names. Due to its structure, the CCIS is also called an MOS (metal-oxide-semiconductor) photodetector or an MIS (metal-insulator-semiconductor) photodetector. When the concept of CCD was introduced by Boyle and Smith in 1970, the possibility of using it as an imaging device was briefly mentioned in their seminal paper.[1] This idea sparked intensive research activities immediately in both CCD and CCIS. The CCIS as a linear scanning system was first demonstrated by Tompsett et al. in 1970.[2,3] This was later extended to an area scanning system, presented by Bertram et al. in 1972.[4] To extend the wavelength beyond that detectable by Si devices, compound semiconductors started to be examined in 1973.[5,6] Since the 1970s, the CCIS has developed into a mature technology for two-dimensional imaging systems such as those used in cameras. More in-depth treatment on this device can be found in Refs. 7 and 8.

52.2 STRUCTURE

The structures of the CCIS are similar to the CCD, with the exception that the gates are semitransparent to let light passing through (Fig. 52.1). A common

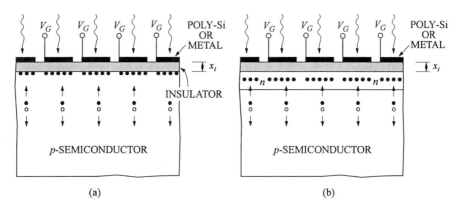

FIGURE 52.1
Structures of (a) surface-channel CCIS and (b) buried-channel CCIS.

material for the gates is polysilicon. Alternatively, the CCIS can be illuminated from the back of the substrate to avoid light absorption by the gate. In this configuration, the semiconductor has to be thinned down so that most of the light can be absorbed within the depletion region at the top surface, and that spatial resolution is not lost since each pixel typically is only about 10 μm on the side. Unlike other photodetectors, CCISs are usually closely spaced to one another in a chain. This is due to the unique feature that besides being photodetectors, they can function as shift registers like regular CCDs. Figure 52.1(b) shows a buried-channel CCIS with a layer of opposite type at the surface. This thin layer (≈ 0.2–0.3 μm) is fully depleted and the photo-generated charge is kept away from the surface (Fig. 52.2(b)). This structure has the advantages of higher transfer efficiency and lower dark current, from reduced surface recombination. The penalty is smaller charge capacity, by a factor of 2–3 compared to the surface-channel type. The most common semiconductor used for CCISs is Si. The insulator for Si devices is usually thermally grown oxide, and for compound semiconductors they are deposited films. Examples are ZnS for HgCdTe devices and deposited SiO_2 for InSb devices. The gates can be made of metal, polysilicon, or silicide.

52.3 CHARACTERISTICS

The CCIS is a unique photodetector in that there is no external DC photocurrent during light exposure. The photo-generated carriers are integrated during light exposure, and the signal is stored in the form of a charge, to be detected later. This is somewhat similar to a photodiode (p-i-n or Schottky) operated under an open-circuit condition. Since each CCIS is basically an MIS capacitor, it has to be operated in a non-equilibrium condition under a large gate pulse. If the

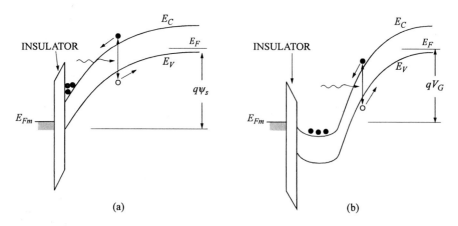

FIGURE 52.2

Energy-band diagrams of (a) a surface-channel CCIS and (b) a buried-channel CCIS, under non-equilibrium condition of a high gate pulse. For p-type substrate, a positive gate bias is applied to drive the semiconductor into deep depletion.

semiconductor is allowed to recover from deep depletion, the collection of the photo-generated charge would not be efficient.

For the sake of simplicity, we will limit our discussion to surface-channel devices. The energy-band diagram immediately after applying a large gate pulse is shown in Fig. 52.2(a). The gate bias has the polarity that drives the semiconductor to deep depletion. The semiconductor band bending, or surface potential ψ_s, at a non-equilibrium condition is given by

$$\psi_s = V_G - V_{FB} + \frac{qN_A\varepsilon_s}{C_i^2} - \frac{1}{C_i}\sqrt{2qN_A\varepsilon_s\left(V_G - V_{FB}\right) + \left(\frac{qN_A\varepsilon_s}{C_i}\right)^2} \qquad (52.1)$$

where C_i is the insulator capacitance

$$C_i = \frac{\varepsilon_i}{x_i} . \qquad (52.2)$$

This large surface potential creates a potential well for the photo-generated electrons while the photo-generated holes diffuse to the substrate and are lost to the external circuit. Similar to that in a photodiode, the internal quantum efficiency η within the depletion region is close to 100%, and the overall η with frontal illumination is given by

$$\eta = 1 - \frac{\exp(-\alpha W_d)}{1 + \alpha L_n} \tag{52.3}$$

where

$$W_d = \sqrt{\frac{2\varepsilon_s \psi_s}{q N_A}} \ . \tag{52.4}$$

The total charge is, thus, proportional to the light intensity and the total exposure time. As the electrons start to accumulate at the semiconductor surface, the field across the insulator starts to increase, and the surface potential and the depletion width begin to shrink, given by

$$\psi_s = V_G - V_{FB} + \frac{q N_A \varepsilon_s}{C_i^2} - \frac{Q_A}{C_i}$$
$$- \frac{1}{C_i} \sqrt{2 q N_A \varepsilon_s \left(V_G - V_{FB} - \frac{Q_A}{C_i} \right) + \left(\frac{q N_A \varepsilon_s}{C_i} \right)^2} \tag{52.5}$$

where Q_A is the signal charge density. It can be shown that the maximum signal can be collected is

$$Q_{max} \approx C_i V_G \ . \tag{52.6}$$

With this maximum charge density, the surface potential collapses to the value corresponding to thermal equilibrium of

$$\psi_s = \frac{2kT}{q} \ln \left(\frac{N_A}{n_i} \right) \tag{52.7}$$

which is to be avoided. Practical devices have maximum charge density of $\approx 10^{11}$ carriers /cm^2. A device 10 µm square thus can hold 10^5 carriers, and with a minimum detectable signal of ≈ 20 carriers, a dynamic range of $\approx 10^4$ can be achieved.

In addition to light generation, various sources for generation of dark current also supply charge to the surface and act as background noise. The total supply of charge density is given by the sum of dark current and the photocurrent,

$$\frac{dQ_A}{dt} = J_{dark} + J_{ph}$$

$$= \frac{qn_i W_d}{2\tau} + \frac{qn_i S_o}{2} + \frac{qn_i^2 L_D}{N_A \tau} + \eta q F_{ph} \quad .$$

$$(52.8)$$

Here the first three terms represent, in order, generation in the depletion region, generation at the surface, and generation in the neutral bulk. The dark current also limits the maximum integration time to

$$t = \frac{Q_{max}}{J_{dark}} \qquad (52.9)$$

before it drives the system to thermal equilibrium. Typical exposure time is in the range of 100 μs to 100 ms. For detection of very weak signals, cooling is often required to minimize the dark current so that a longer integration time can be used.

After the exposure period, the charge is transported to an amplifier by way of conventional CCD operation as a shift register. Such a mechanism is discussed in detail in Chapter 15. A CCIS thus has dual functions, as a photodetector and as a shift register.

52.4 APPLICATIONS

Because the CCIS can also be used as a shift register, there is great benefit to use this photodetector in an imaging-array system since the signals can be brought out sequentially to a single node, without complicated x-y addressing to each pixel. This is the main advantage of a focal-plane array which the CCISs are very successful in. The detection mode of integrating charge over long period of time enables detection of weaker signals. This is an important feature for astronomy imaging. Besides these, the CCISs have advantages of low dark current, low-noise and low-voltage operation, good linearity and good dynamic range. The structure is simple and compact, stable and robust, and is compatible with MOS/MIS technology. These factors contribute to high yield which enables the CCISs to be feasible in consumer products. The CCISs can be used in cameras for personal camcorders, broadcasting systems, robot vision, image analysis, astronomy, surveillance, and military aiming, guidance and tracking systems.

Different readout mechanisms for the line imager and the area imagers are shown in Fig. 52.3. A line imager with dual output registers has improved readout speed. Most common area imagers use either interline-transfer (Fig. 52.3(b)) or frame-transfer (Fig. 52.3(c)) readout architecture. In the former, signals are transferred to the neighboring pixels, and they are subsequently passed along to the output register chain while the light sensitive pixels start to collect charge for the next data. In the frame-transfer scheme, signals are shifted to a storage area

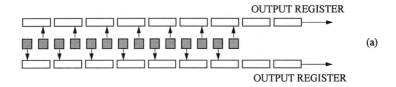

(a)

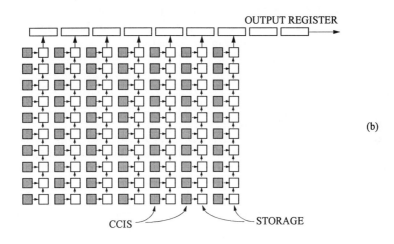

(b)

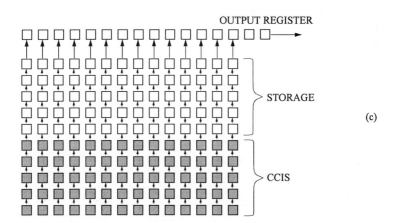

(c)

FIGURE 52.3
Schematic layouts showing the readout mechanisms of (a) a line imager with dual output registers,
(b) an area imager with interline transfer, and (c) with frame transfer. Grey pixels represent CCISs as
photodetectors. The output register is usually clocked at a higher frequency than the internal transfer.

away from the sensing area. The advantage of this compared to the interline transfer is more efficient light sensing area, but there is more image smear since CCISs continue to receive light as signal charges are passed through them. For both the interline transfer and frame transfer, all columns advance their charge signals to the horizontal output register simultaneously, and the output register carries these signals out at a much higher clocking rate.

The CCIS can also be used as nuclear-radiation detector (see Section 50.5.2). One disadvantage of a CCIS is potential damage from light, especially of high-energy radiation. This is a common concern for MOS/MIS devices. Radiation damage is a result of generation of interface traps at the Si–insulator interface and fixed charge in the insulator.

52.5 RELATED DEVICE

52.5.1 Charge-Injection Device

The charge-injection device (CID) does not necessarily imply a different structure from a CCIS. The difference lies in the readout mode. Instead of transferring the accumulated charge laterally, the charge-injection device releases the charge to the substrate by lowering the gate voltage. In an area-imaging system, x-y addressing of this photodetector is accomplished by implementing a two-well unit cell as shown in Fig. 52.4. With two closely spaced gates, the photo-generated charge can be shifted between the wells, controlled by the gate voltages. The charge is injected to the substrate only when both gate potentials are lowered and the semiconductor surface is driven into accumulation.

There are two readout mechanisms for the CIDs: sequential injection and parallel injection.[9] In the sequential-injection scheme, a pixel is selected when both gate potentials are left to float, and as the charge is injected into the substrate, a displacement current can be sensed either at the substrate terminal or at the gate (Fig. 52.5(a)). In the parallel injection scheme, a whole row is selected and all columns are read at the same time (Fig. 52.5(b)). A signal is detected when charge

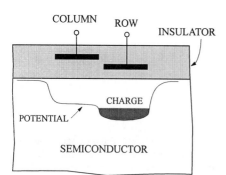

FIGURE 52.4

Structure of a charge-injection device with dual gates controlling two adjacent potential wells. Charge can be shifted between the wells, or released to the substrate.

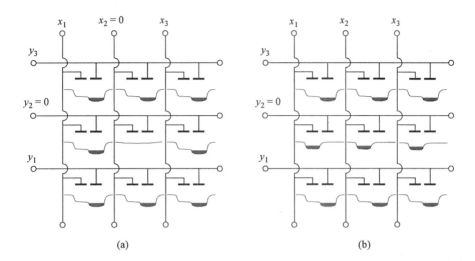

FIGURE 52.5

Readout mechanisms in area charge-injection device arrays. (a) Sequential injection. (b) Parallel injection. In (a), $(x,y) = (2,2)$ is selected. In (b), the whole row of y_2 is selected.

is transferred from one well (which has higher gate voltage and/or thinner gate dielectric) to another within the unit cell. In such a readout as a displacement current in the gate, the charge is preserved.

The CID area arrays have advantage of random access capability. Transfer between cells is not necessary and therefore transfer efficiency is not critical. The trade-off is higher power dissipation which can be improved by an epitaxial substrate, larger noise due to large capacitance of the whole column, and necessity of better sensing amplifier due to weaker signals.

REFERENCES

1. W. S. Boyle and G. E. Smith, "Charge coupled semiconductor devices," *Bell Syst. Tech. J.*, **49**, 587 (1970).
2. M. F. Tompsett, G. F. Amelio and G. E. Smith, "Charge coupled 8-bit shift register," *Appl. Phys. Lett.*, **17**, 111 (1970).
3. M. F. Tompsett, G. F. Amelio, W. J. Bertram, Jr., R. R. Buckley, W. J. McNamara, J. C. Mikkelsen, Jr. and D. A. Sealer, "Charge-coupled imaging devices: Experimental results," *IEEE Trans. Electron Dev.*, **ED-18**, 992 (1971).
4. W. J. Bertram, D. A. Sealer, C. H. Sequin, M. F. Tompsett and R. R. Buckley, "Recent advances in charge coupled imaging devices," *INTERCON Digest*, 292 (1972).
5. T. F. Tao J. R. Ellis, L. Kost and A. Doshier, "Feasibility study of PbTe and $Pb_{0.76}Sn_{0.24}Te$ infrared charge coupled imager," *Proc. Int. Conf. Tech. Appl. Charge Coupled Devices*, 259 (1973).
6. J. C. Kim, "InSb MIS structures for infrared imaging devices," *Tech. Digest IEEE IEDM*, 419 (1973).
7. D. F. Barbe, "Imaging devices using the charge-coupled concept," *Proc. IEEE*, **63**, 38 (1975).

8. Special issues on solid-state image sensors, *IEEE Trans. Electron Dev.*, **ED-32**, Aug. 1985 and **ED-38**, May 1991.

9. H. K. Burke and G. J. Michon, "Charge-injection imaging: Operating techniques and performances characteristics," *IEEE Trans. Electron Dev.*, **ED-23**, 189 (1976).

CHAPTER
53

AVALANCHE PHOTODIODE

53.1 HISTORY

Avalanche multiplication in semiconductor was first addressed by McKay and McAfee in 1953.[1,2] This high-field phenomenon is the source of the gain in the avalanche photodiode (APD) which is the solid-state counterpart of the photomultiplier tube. The silicon avalanche photodiode was first studied by Haitz el al.[3] and Goetzberger et al.[4] in 1963, and later by Johnson[5] and Anderson et al.[6] in 1965. Lucovsky and Emmons presented results on InAs in the same year,[7] and Melchior and Lynch studied Ge devices in the following year.[8] The first Schottky-barrier avalanche photodiode, as opposed to the *p-n* junction type, was made by Lindley et al. in 1969 with GaAs.[9] The gain distribution with its associated noise problem in an APD was modeled by McIntyre,[10,11] Personick,[12,13] and Tager,[14] and the response speed was modeled by Emmons.[15] In-depth treatment of the avalanche photodiode can be found in Refs. 16 and 17.

53.2 STRUCTURE

The structure of an avalanche photodiode is similar to a *p-i-n* or a *p-n* photodiode (Fig. 53.1). Alternatively, a metal-semiconductor junction (Schottky barrier) can be used but is less common. Since an avalanche photodiode is operated under a large reverse bias, it is critical to incorporate a guard ring at the perimeter of the junction to prevent surface breakdown mechanisms. Common materials are Si, Ge and III–V compound semiconductors. The majority of commercial avalanche photodiodes are made of Si. As discussed later, for minimum noise, a large difference in ionization coefficients for electrons (α_n) and holes (α_p) is critical.

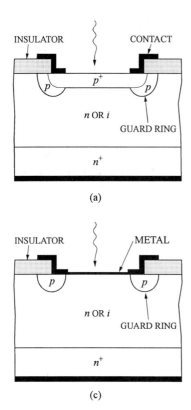

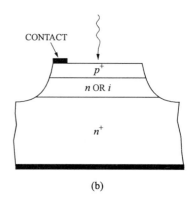

FIGURE 53.1
Different structures of the avalanche
photodiode. (a) A general planar *p-i-n* or *p-n*
structure. (b) A mesa structure. (c) A
Schottky-barrier structure.

Silicon has a large α_n/α_p ratio of 50, while Ge and III–V compounds have ratios
less than ≈ 2. Despite higher noise, the latter materials are used for longer
wavelengths that require smaller energy gap.

53.3 CHARACTERISTICS

The mechanism for gain in an avalanche photodiode is avalanche multiplication,
which is a consequence of impact ionization, usually repeated many times (see
Appendix B3). An impact ionization event can occur when a carrier is injected
into a high-field region. The carrier acquires excess kinetic energy from the field.
If it has enough energy for ionization when it collides with the lattice, an
electron-hole pair is generated. This ionization energy is related to the energy gap
and is always larger than E_g. This process can be repeated by the primary carrier
and the secondary carriers, and carriers are said to multiply. A system with
electron injection, assuming $\alpha_n/\alpha_p \gg 1$, is shown in Fig. 53.2. The multiplication
gain, M_n in this case, is given by

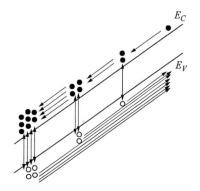

FIGURE 53.2
Multiplication of carriers by impact ionization. Here electrons are used as the primary current, and $\alpha_n \gg \alpha_p$.

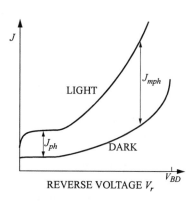

FIGURE 53.3
Reverse characteristics of an avalanche photodiode in dark and under light.

$$M_n = \cfrac{1}{1 - \displaystyle\int_0^L \alpha_n \exp\left[-\int_x^L (\alpha_n - \alpha_p)\, dx'\right] dx} \tag{53.1}$$

where L is the total length of the multiplication region. Some special cases are:

$$M_n = \exp \int_0^L \alpha_n\, dx \quad , \quad \alpha_n \gg \alpha_p \quad , \tag{53.2}$$

$$M = \cfrac{1}{1 - \displaystyle\int_0^L \alpha\, dx} \quad , \quad \alpha_n = \alpha_p = \alpha \quad . \tag{53.3}$$

The ionization coefficients are a strong function of the electric field (see Appendix B3). In practical devices, gains of a few hundred can readily be obtained.

The *I-V* characteristics of an avalanche photodiode are shown in Fig. 53.3. At low voltages, the behavior is similar to that of a *p-i-n* photodiode or a Schottky-barrier photodiode. At higher voltages, both dark current and photocurrent are amplified. The quantum efficiency of photons generating the primary photocurrent J_{ph} depends on the depletion width (except in the case of internal photoemission over the barrier in a Schottky-barrier detector)

$$\eta = 1 - \frac{\exp(-\alpha W_d)}{1 + \alpha L_p} \quad . \tag{53.4}$$

α in this equation is the absorption coefficient. Usually η is above 50%. From these, J_{ph} can be calculated. The multiplied photocurrent J_{mph} is simply given by

$$J_{mph} = MJ_{ph} \; . \tag{53.5}$$

Unfortunately, multiplication also applies to the dark current. The dark current in a p-n junction is composed of the standard diffusion current and generation current in the depletion region. In a Schottky-barrier junction, the diffusion current is replaced by the thermionic-emission current, which is many orders of magnitude larger. Another component is current generated at the perimeter near the guard ring due to higher field and higher number of defects at the semiconductor surface. This perimeter component, however, gets multiplied by a different factor than the photocurrent.

   Examination of Eqs. (53.1) and (53.3) reveals that with increased bias, the denominators approach zero, and the gain becomes infinite. This condition corresponds to breakdown at a breakdown voltage V_{BD}. Before this breakdown condition, the gain can be estimated by an empirical equation

$$M = \cfrac{1}{1 - \left(\cfrac{V_r - IR}{V_{BD}}\right)^n} \; . \tag{53.6}$$

The value of n depends on the materials, and it is in the range of 3–6. In practice, when the bias approaches V_{BD}, the gain is found to be limited by the series resistance R, and the maximum gain can be shown to be[8]

$$M_{max} = \sqrt{\frac{V_{BD}}{nAJ_{ph}R}} \; . \tag{53.7}$$

This means that at high biases, the multiplied photocurrent increases only with the square root of the primary current J_{ph}.

   The main drawback of the avalanche photodiode is excessive noise. Avalanche multiplication is statistical in nature, and this random process does not lead to the same multiplication for every injected carrier. The noise attributed to the variation in gain is measured by the excess noise factor F, which is the ratio of the mean square of the gain to the square of the mean gain[10]

$$F = \frac{\langle M^2 \rangle}{\langle M \rangle^2} = M\left[1 - (1 - k)\left(\frac{M-1}{M}\right)^2\right]$$
$$\approx kM + 2(1 - k) \; , \tag{53.8}$$

where k is α_p/α_n for electron injection/multiplication and α_n/α_p for hole injection/multiplication. From this equation, k should be minimized (large α ratio) to reduce noise. Qualitatively, $k \approx 1$ means equal ionization by electrons and holes. Ionized holes in Fig. 53.2 can also produce electron-hole pairs, and such positive feedback only reinforces the fluctuation noise.

The response time of an avalanche photodiode is limited by the avalanche build-up. This is in addition to the transit time across the device, and, thus, an avalanche photodiode is slower than a p-i-n photodiode or a Schottky-barrier photodiode. The response time is related to an effective transit time within the avalanche region ($t_t = L/v_{sat}$),[15]

$$t = MN(k)t_t \ . \tag{53.9}$$

$N(k)$ is a weak function of k and is in the range of 1/3 to 2 as k varies from 1 to 10^{-3}. Frequency operation beyond 10 GHz has been reported. Equation (53.9) also shows that the response time goes up linearly with gain, and the gain-bandwidth product remains constant. A gain-bandwidth product of higher than 100 GHz can be reached.

It is clear from the noise consideration that not only the ratio of ionization coefficients needs to be large, the primary photocurrent should also have the larger coefficient. A more optimized structure, called the p-i-p-i-n reach-through structure, is shown in Fig. 53.4(a) with its energy-band diagram. The wide low-field region ensures a more complete absorption of the light, giving a higher quantum efficiency according to Eq. (53.4). The electron current is then fed to the narrower high-field avalanche region. This approach of separating the absorption region and the multiplication region guarantees that the primary photocurrent travels the entire avalanche region. A narrower avalanche region also gives lower noise. A simpler structure to fabricate without the thin, deeply buried, and fully depleted p^+-region is shown by the energy-band diagram in Fig. 53.4(b).

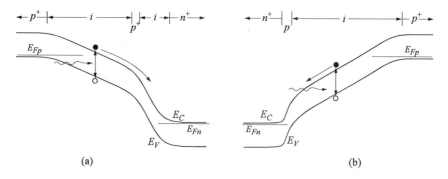

FIGURE 53.4

Energy-band diagrams of more optimized reach-through structures for avalanche photodiode. (a) A p-i-p-i-n (lo-hi-lo) structure. (b) An n-p-i-p (hi-lo) structure. Both use electrons as primary photocurrent.

53.4 APPLICATIONS

The avalanche photodiode has very high gain and is particularly suitable for detecting weak optical signals. Because it also has reasonable speed, it is often used in combination with a laser source. An example is a fiber-optics communication system. The disadvantages of avalanche photodiodes are large noise, high-bias requirements (exceeding 50 V to a few hundred V), and the need for a very stable voltage source and temperature environment since the avalanche process is very sensitive to these factors.

The general applications of a photodetector are listed in Appendix C4.

53.5 RELATED DEVICES

53.5.1 Separate-Absorption-Multiplication Avalanche Photodiode

For long-wavelength detection, the energy gap of the semiconductor must be small. This presents a problem for an avalanche photodiode since at high fields, tunneling is more pronounced for these materials. The separate-absorption-multiplication avalanche photodiode (SAM-APD) is designed to lower the tunneling current by having the high-field avalanche process in a separate region with larger E_g (Fig. 53.5).[18] This device differs from those of Fig. 53.4 by being a heterostructure, and it has additional benefits. In InP, α_p is larger than α_n, and holes are used as the primary photocurrent. It has been found that due to the discontinuity ΔE_V in the valence-band edge, the response is delayed by the accumulation of holes at this discontinuity. An improvement is realized by a graded heterojunction, resulting in a separate-absorption-graded-multiplication avalanche photodiode (SAGM-APD).[19]

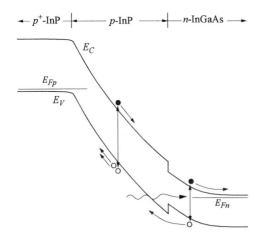

FIGURE 53.5
Energy-band diagram of a separate-avalanche-multiplication avalanche photodiode using InP–InGaAs heterostructure. The primary photocurrent is due to holes.

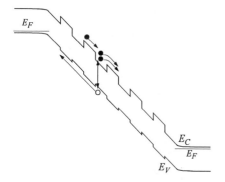

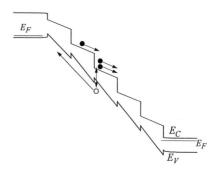

FIGURE 53.6

Energy-band diagram of a superlattice avalanche photodiode.

FIGURE 53.7

Energy-band diagram of a staircase avalanche photodiode.

53.5.2 Superlattice Avalanche Photodiode

The benefit of the superlattice avalanche photodiode is that the noise level can be reduced by tailoring very different ionization coefficients for electrons and holes.[20] In the example shown in Fig. 53.6, the effective α_n is enhanced by excess energy acquired at the conduction-band discontinuity ΔE_C. The α_p is not affected as much due to smaller ΔE_V. Another advantage in this structure is that multiplication is much more localized, giving rise to still lower noise. The individual layer thicknesses are in the range of 100–500 Å.

53.5.3 Staircase Avalanche Photodiode

The staircase avalanche photodiode is a superlattice with a graded composition.[21] The advantage is reduced noise that results from a large difference in ionization coefficients for electrons and holes. Figure 53.7 shows that α_n is enhanced by extra energy gained at ΔE_C, while α_p is impeded by ΔE_V.

REFERENCES

1. K. G. McKay and K. B. McAfee, "Electron multiplication in silicon and germanium," *Phys. Rev.*, **91**, 1079 (1953).
2. K. G. McKay, "Avalanche breakdown in silicon," *Phys. Rev.*, **94**, 877 (1954).
3. R. H. Haitz, A. Goetzberger, R. M. Scarlett and W. Shockley, "Avalanche effects in silicon *p-n* junctions. I. Localized photomultiplication studies on microplasmas," *J. Appl. Phys.*, **34**, 1581 (1963).
4. A. Goetzberger, B. McDonald, R. H. Haitz and R. M. Scarlett, "Avalanche effects in silicon *p-n* junctions. II. Structurally perfect junctions," *J. Appl. Phys.*, **34**, 1591 (1963).
5. K. M. Johnson, "High-speed photodiode signal enhancement at avalanche breakdown voltage," *IEEE Trans. Electron Dev.*, **ED-12**, 55 (1965).

6. L. K. Anderson, P. G. McGullin, L. A. D'Asaro and A. Goetzberger, "Microwave photodiodes exhibiting microplasma-free carrier multiplication," *Appl. Phys. Lett.*, **6**, 62 (1965).

7. G. Lucovsky and R. B. Emmons, "Avalanche multiplication in InAs photodiodes," *Proc. IEEE*, **53**, 180 (1965).

8. H. Melchior and W. T. Lynch, "Signal and noise response of high speed germanium avalanche photodiodes," *IEEE Trans. Electron Dev.*, **ED-13**, 829 (1966).

9. W. T. Lindley, R. J. Phelan, Jr., C. M. Wolfe and A. G. Foyt, "GaAs Schottky barrier avalanche photodiodes," *Appl. Phys. Lett.*, **14**, 197 (1969).

10. R. J. McIntyre, "Multiplication noise in uniform avalanche diodes," *IEEE Trans. Electron Dev.*, **ED-13**, 164 (1966).

11. R. J. McIntyre, "The distribution of gains in uniformly multiplying avalanche photodiodes: Theory," *IEEE Trans. Electron Dev.*, **ED-19**, 703 (1972).

12. S. D. Personick, "New results on avalanche multiplication statistics with applications to optical detection," *Bell Syst. Tech. J.*, **50**, 167 (1971).

13. S. D. Personick, "Statistics of a general class of avalanche detectors with applications to optical communication," *Bell Syst. Tech. J.*, **50**, 3075 (1971).

14. A. S. Tager, "Current fluctuations in a semiconductor (dielectric) under the conditions of impact ionization and avalanche breakdown," *Sov. Phys.–Solid St.*, **6**, 1919 (1965).

15. R. B. Emmons, "Avalanche-photodiode frequency response," *J. Appl. Phys.*, **38**, 3705 (1967).

16. P. P. Webb, R. J. McIntyre and J. Conradi, "Properties of avalanche photodiodes," *RCA Review*, **35**, 234 (1974).

17. G. E. Stillman and C. M. Wolfe, "Avalanche photodiodes," in R. K. Willardson, Ser. Ed., A. C. Beer, Vol. Ed., *Semiconductors and semimetals*, Vol. 12, Academic Press, New York, 1977.

18. K. Nishida, K. Taguchi and Y. Matsumoto, "InGaAsP heterostructure avalanche photodiodes with high avalanche gain," *Appl. Phys. Lett.*, **35**, 251 (1979).

19. J. C. Campbell, A. G. Dentai, W. S. Holden and B. L. Kasper, "High-performance avalanche photodiode with separate absorption, 'grading', and multiplication regions," *Electronics Lett.*, **19**, 818 (1983).

20. F. Capasso, W. T. Tsang, A. L. Hutchinson and G. F. Williams, "Enhancement of electron impact ionization in a superlattice: A new avalanche photodiode with a large ionization rate ratio," *Appl. Phys. Lett.*, **40**, 38 (1982).

21. F. Capasso, W-T. Tsang and G. F. Williams, "Staircase solid-state photomultipliers and avalanche photodiodes with enhanced ionization rates ratio," *IEEE Trans. Electron Dev.*, **ED-30**, 381 (1983).

CHAPTER
54

PHOTOTRANSISTOR

54.1 HISTORY

The phototransistor is a bipolar junction transistor that amplifies the photocurrent collected by the built-in photodiodes. The phototransistor was proposed by Shockley et al. in 1951 soon after the establishment of the bipolar transistor in the late 1940s.[1] It was first demonstrated by Shive in an *n-p-n* Ge structure in 1953.[2] In-depth treatment of the phototransistor can be found in Ref. 3.

54.2 STRUCTURE

A common phototransistor differs from a standard bipolar transistor (*n-p-n* or *p-n-p*) by omitting the base contact, and by having much larger base and collector areas compared to the emitter (Fig. 54.1(a)). Advantages can be gained by the heterojunction phototransistor whose emitter has a larger energy gap than the base. One example is shown in Fig. 54.1(b). An emitter with a wider energy gap has higher injection efficiency leading to higher gain, and it allows the base to be more heavily doped for lower base resistance. Also it can be transparent to the incoming light so that light is more efficiently absorbed in the base and the collector. A metal-semiconductor (Schottky) junction can be used in place of the *p-n* junction for the collector, but it is much less common. Early phototransistors were made from Si and Ge. More recent devices include III–V compound semiconductors, especially for heterojunction phototransistors. Heterostructures studied include AlGaAs–GaAs, InP–InGaAs, CdS–Si, Cu_2Se–Si, and PbS–Si. Most commercial phototransistors are made on Si. Homostructure devices are made from diffusion or ion implantation, while those of heterostructures are made from epitaxial growth of lattice-matched materials, followed by mesa isolation.

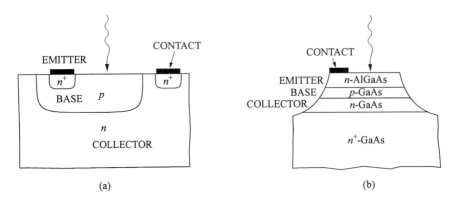

FIGURE 54.1
Structures of phototransistors. (a) A homojunction planar structure. (b) A heterojunction mesa structure, using AlGaAs–GaAs as an example.

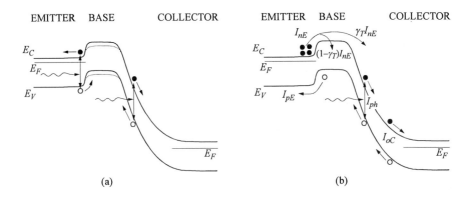

FIGURE 54.2
Energy-band diagrams of a phototransistor showing (a) the change of base potential (dashed line) caused by the accumulation of photo-generated holes, and (b) different current components.

54.3 CHARACTERISTICS

The phototransistor is biased in the active regime. For a floating base, that simply means positive bias to the collector with respect to the emitter for an *n-p-n* structure. A qualitative energy-band diagram illustrating the response to light is shown in Fig. 54.2(a). Photo-generated holes, more or less independent of the location of excitation, flow to the energy maximum and they are trapped in the base. This accumulation of holes or positive charges lowers the base energy (raises the potential), and allows a large flow of electrons from the emitter to the collector. The result of a much larger electron current caused by a small hole

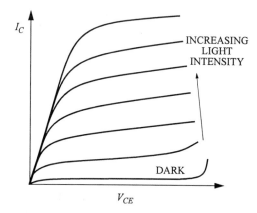

FIGURE 54.3
I-V characteristics of a phototransistor under different light intensities.

current is the consequence of emitter injection efficiency γ, and is the dominant gain mechanism that is common for both the bipolar transistor and the phototransistor, provided that the electron transit time through the base is much shorter than the minority carrier lifetime. The photo-generated electrons, depending on the location of origin, can flow to the emitter or to the collector. Strictly speaking, they can reduce the emitter current or enhance the collector current, but only by a very small amount since the gain is large and the total collector current or emitter current is much larger than the photocurrent. For simplicity, the following analysis assumes that light is absorbed near the base-collector junction as shown in Fig. 54.2(b).

From Fig. 54.2(b), and using the conventional bipolar transistor parameters summarized in Table 29.2, the total collector current is given by

$$I_C = I_{ph} + I_{oC} + \gamma_T I_{nE} \tag{54.1}$$

where I_{ph} is the photocurrent and I_{oC} is the reverse leakage current of the collector-base junction. Since the base is open, the net base current is zero and

$$I_{pE} + (1 - \gamma_T) I_{nE} = I_{ph} + I_{oC} \ . \tag{54.2}$$

From Eqs. (54.1) and (54.2) and the definition of emitter injection efficiency

$$I_{nE} = \gamma I_E \ , \tag{54.3}$$

it can be shown that

$$I_C = (I_{ph} + I_{oC})(\beta + 1) \ . \tag{54.4}$$

The *I-V* characteristics of a phototransistor under different light intensities are shown in Fig. 54.3. These are similar to a conventional bipolar transistor with the base current replaced by photocurrent. Equation (54.4) indicates a photocurrent gain of $(\beta + 1)$. Unfortunately the dark current is also amplified by the same factor. In practical homojunction phototransistors, gains vary from 50 to a few hundred. For heterojunction phototransistors, gains up to 10 k can be obtained. One drawback of the phototransistor is that the gain is not constant with light intensity since the latter affects the base potential (see Fig. 54.2(a)).

The speed of a phototransistor is limited by the charging times of the emitter and the collector,

$$\tau = \tau_E + \tau_C$$
$$= \beta \left[\frac{kT}{qI_C} (C_{EB} + C_{CB}) + R_L C_{CB} \right] .$$

(54.5)

In practical homojunction devices, the response time is very long, usually in the range of 1–10 μs, limiting the operational frequency to ≈ 200 kHz. The frequency of heterojunction phototransistors can go beyond 2 GHz. Several observations can be made from Eq. (54.5). First, the speed goes down when the light signal (or I_C) is smaller. In applications where speed is critical, the device is made with a base contact, and an applied DC bias increases the DC collector current. The trade-off is reduced photocurrent gain. Second, the speed is inversely proportional to the gain. For this reason, a gain-bandwidth product is a better measure of the performance.

54.4 APPLICATIONS

The advantages of the phototransistor are low cost, high gain, and compatibility with integrated circuit technology. However, due to its low speed and nonlinearity, it is most commonly used as a light-sensitive switch in less-demanding systems. Heterojunction phototransistors have improved speed and higher gain, but, currently, they are too costly to be commercially feasible. Common applications of phototransistors are object and position detection. Examples are intrusion alarm systems, tachometers for servomotors, card and tape readers, etc. Other applications are photoflash control, indoor/outdoor lighting control, and opto-isolator. For general applications of photodetectors, the readers are referred to Appendix C4.

54.5 RELATED DEVICES

54.5.1 Darlington Phototransistor

The Darlington phototransistor is often called a photo-Darlington. It is simply a cascaded pair of bipolar transistors (Fig. 54.4). One of the transistors serves as a phototransistor, with the emitter current fed to the base of the other transistor which acts as an additional amplifier. The combined gain is much larger than a single phototransistor, but the response time is even longer, around 50–100 μs.

54.5.2 Avalanche Phototransistor

In an avalanche phototransistor, the collector-base junction is biased to a very high field and avalanche multiplication occurs in this region.[4] The gain can be shown to increase to

$$\text{GAIN} = \frac{M(\beta + 1)}{1 - (M - 1)\beta} \tag{54.6}$$

where M is the multiplication factor which is discussed in more detail in Appendix B3.

54.5.3 Photosensitive Field-Effect Transistor

The photosensitive field-effect transistor (photo-FET) covers a class of FETs that combine high-impedance amplifiers with built-in photodetectors. The photo-FETs studied include JFET, MESFET, and MOSFET. Different modes of operation have been reported and discussed. The simplest mode is based on photoconductivity. Photo-generated excess carriers increase the conductivity of the channel and the conduction principle is similar to that in a photoconductor. Another mode is specific to a JFET or a MESFET where the gate is not insulated. The gate-to-channel junction can be viewed as a photodiode, and a gate current can flow when the device is exposed to light. If the gate is connected to an external resistor R_G, an IR drop raises the gate voltage and a larger channel current results. The gain can be shown to equal to $\approx R_G g_m$.[5] For a MOSFET, the gate is insulated and different modes of operation have been suggested. First, photo-generated carriers can be trapped at the surface of the semiconductor. These charges change the surface potential and induce a change in the channel current.[6] Another approach is to incorporate deep-level impurities within the depletion

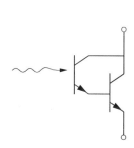

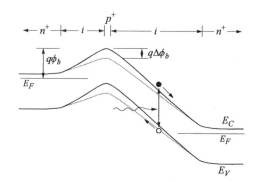

FIGURE 54.4
Schematic diagram of a Darlington phototransistor.

FIGURE 54.5
Energy-band diagram of a bulk barrier phototransistor, showing the change of barrier when the device is exposed to light.

region near the channel. When exposed to light, these impurities are ionized, and the effective doping level increases. This results in a higher threshold voltage and, for fixed drain and gate biases, the channel current is reduced with light. Since the ionization energy for impurities is much smaller than the energy gap, light of longer wavelength can be detected.[7]

54.5.4 Bulk-Barrier Phototransistor

The bulk-barrier phototransistor is also called planar-doped-barrier photodiode, triangular-barrier photodiode, and modulated-barrier photodiode.[8] There are two main differences from a conventional phototransistor. Structurally, the base is very thin and fully depleted, and the depleted base is surrounded by intrinsic layers. Electrically, the emitter-to-collector current is governed by thermionic emission, rather than diffusion (see Chapter 4). The energy-band diagram with and without light is shown in Fig. 54.5. Similar to a phototransistor, the photo-generated holes accumulate at the valence-band peak, and cause a barrier lowering of $\Delta\phi_b$. Since the thermionic-emission current is determined by the barrier height

$$J_n = A^* T^2 \exp\left(\frac{-q\phi_b}{kT}\right) \ , \tag{54.7}$$

the total change in current is given by

$$\Delta J_n = J_{dark}\left[\exp\left(\frac{q\Delta\phi_b}{kT}\right) - 1\right] \ . \tag{54.8}$$

Similar operation can be obtained from a camel diode where one of the intrinsic layer thickness approaches zero.[9]

54.5.5 Static-Induction Phototransistor

In a static-induction phototransistor, the depletion regions around the gates pinch off the channel between the source and drain (Fig. 54.6).[10] The structure differs from a JFET by having a very short channel length. The gates are analogous to the base of a bipolar phototransistor and are left floating. Photo-generated holes accumulate at the intrinsic gate and lower the barrier. The current between the source and drain is given by

$$J_n = qN_D^+\left(\frac{D_n}{W_G}\right)\exp\left(\frac{-q\phi_b}{kT}\right) \tag{54.9}$$

where N_D^+ is the source doping and W_G is the barrier width (see Chapter 24). The photo-induced current is also given by the form of Eq. (54.8).

54.5.6 Tunnel-Emitter Phototransistor

In a tunnel-emitter phototransistor, the tunneling layer is very thin such that the bulk semiconductor is driven into deep depletion under large reverse bias (see Chapter 34). In response to light, photo-generated holes accumulate at the semiconductor surface, and voltage is redistributed between the layers as shown in Fig. 54.7. The electron tunneling current is largely increased due to (1) the field across the tunneling layer is increased and (2) the barrier thickness is reduced since E_C at the surface is below E_{Fm}. This tunneling layer can be made of a dielectric[11] or a heterostructure.

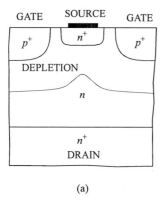

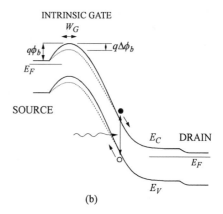

(a)   (b)

FIGURE 54.6
(a) Structure and (b) energy-band diagram of the static induction phototransistor. Dashed lines indicate the lowering of barrier when exposed to light.

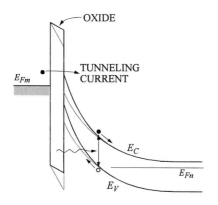

FIGURE 54.7
Energy-band diagram of the tunnel emitter phototransistor, using an MIS structure as an example. Dashed lines indicate the response to light.

REFERENCES

1. W. Shockley, M. Sparks and G. K. Teal, "*p-n* junction transistors," *Phys. Rev.*, **83**, 151 (1951).
2. J. N. Shive, "The properties of germanium phototransistors," *J. Opt. Soc. Am.*, **43**, 239 (1953).
3. J. C. Campbell, "Phototransistors for lightwave communications," in W. T. Tsang, Ed., *Semiconductors and semimetals*, Vol. 22, Part D, Academic Press, New York, 1985.
4. C. W. Chen and T. K. Gustafson, "Characteristics of an avalanche phototransistor fabricated on a Si surface," *Appl. Phys. Lett.*, **39**, 161 (1981).
5. T. Sugeta and Y. Mizushima, "High speed photoresponse mechanism of a GaAs-MESFET," *Japanese J. Appl. Phys.*, **19**, L27 (1980).
6. K. Matsumoto, I. Takayanagi, T. Nakamura and R. Ohta, "The operation mechanism of a charge modulation device (CMD) image sensor," *IEEE Trans. Electron Dev.*, **38**, 989 (1991).
7. L. Forbes, L. L. Wittmer and K. W. Lok, "Characteristics of the indium-doped infrared sensing MOSFET (IRFET)," *IEEE Trans. Electron Dev.*, **ED-23**, 1272 (1976).
8. C. Y. Chen, "Theory of a modulated barrier photodiode," *Appl. Phys. Lett.*, **39**, 979 (1981).
9. N. Georgoulas, "The camel diode as photodetector with high internal gain," *IEEE Electron Dev. Lett.*, **EDL-3**, 61 (1982).
10. J. Nishizawa and K. Nonaka, "Current amplification in nonhomogeneous-base structure and static induction transistor structure," *J. Appl. Phys.*, **57**, 4783 (1985).
11. M. A. Green and J. Shewchun, "Current multiplication in metal-insulator-semiconductor (MIS) tunnel diodes," *Solid-State Electron.*, **17**, 349 (1974).

CHAPTER
55

METAL-SEMICONDUCTOR-METAL PHOTODETECTOR

55.1 HISTORY

The metal-semiconductor-metal (MSM) photodetector was proposed and demonstrated by Sugeta et al. in 1979.[1,2] It was then reported by Slayman and Figueroa[3,4] and by Wei et al.[5] in 1981. Since it was introduced in 1988, the concept of adding a thin barrier-enhancement layer to reduce the dark current has received increased interest,[6-8] especially for the wavelength range of 1.3–1.5 μm for high-speed optical-fiber communication applications. For a more detailed discussion of the MSM photodetector, the readers can refer to Ref. 9.

55.2 STRUCTURE

The structure of the MSM photodetector, as shown in Fig. 55.1, is basically two Schottky barriers connected back-to-back. Light is received at the gap between the two metal contacts, and the MSM photodetector avoids absorption of light by the metal layer as in a conventional Schottky-barrier photodiode. For compound semiconductors, the light absorption layer is usually deposited on a semi-insulating substrate. InGaAs received the most attention for applications in the 1.3–1.5 μm range, which has the optimum performance for optical fibers. For more complete light absorption, the active layer has a thickness slightly larger than the absorption length ($1/\alpha \approx 1$ μm), and has low doping of $\approx 1 \times 10^{15}$ cm^{-3}. The barrier-enhancement layer, at a similar doping level, is not an absolute requirement but it can drastically reduce the dark current of a narrow-energy-gap semiconductor such as InGaAs. By inserting this layer of wider energy gap, the barrier height becomes much larger. This layer has been made of AlInAs, GaAs,

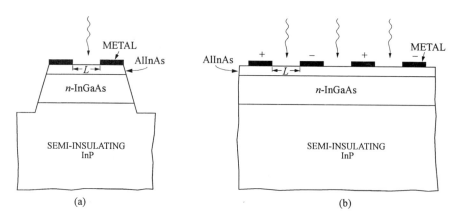

FIGURE 55.1
MSM photodetectors in the form of (a) a mesa structure, and (b) a planar interdigitated structure.

AlGaAs and InP, and its thickness ranges from 30 nm to 100 nm. This barrier-enhancement layer can be compositionally graded to avoid carrier trapping at the band-edge discontinuity (see Fig. 55.2(d) near the cathode). The spacing of the metal contacts should be minimized for improved speed, and it is limited by lithography and etching to about 0.5 μm in the early 1990s. The metal contacts usually have the shape of interdigitated strips.

55.3 CHARACTERISTICS

Since the MSM photodetector has two Schottky barriers connected back-to-back, bias of any polarity will put one Schottky barrier in the reverse direction and the other in the forward direction. The energy-band diagrams between the two metal contacts through the active layer are shown in Fig. 55.2. We first discuss the characteristics of the dark current. Two forms of dark *I-V* curves have been observed. The one shown in Fig. 55.3 has current saturation starting at a low voltage and is typical of thermionic-emission current. Unlike a single Schottky junction, both electron and hole current components have to be considered, and the saturation current has the general expression,[11]

$$J = A_n^* T^2 \exp\left(\frac{-q\phi_{bn}}{kT}\right) + A_p^* T^2 \exp\left(\frac{-q\phi_{bp}}{kT}\right) . \tag{55.1}$$

In another form, the current rises exponentially with bias and can arise from thermionic emission or tunneling. A non-saturating current in thermionic emission can be due to image-force lowering that modifies the barrier heights.

Typical photocurrent characteristics are shown in Fig. 55.3. The photocurrent is shown first to rise with voltage, and then becomes saturated. The

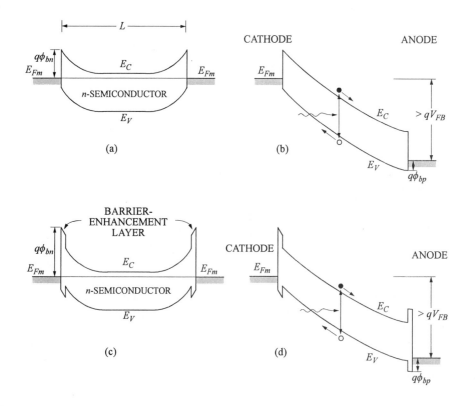

FIGURE 55.2
Energy-band diagrams of MSM photodetectors at equilibrium and under bias beyond flat-band. (a), (b) Without and (c), (d) with the barrier-enhancement layer.

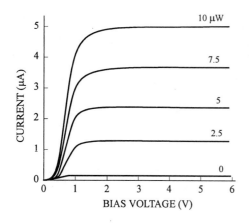

FIGURE 55.3
I-V characteristics of an MSM photodetector under different light powers. (After Ref. 10)

increase of photocurrent at low bias is due to the expansion of the depletion region in the reverse-biased Schottky junction and the internal quantum efficiency is improved. The voltage at which the photocurrent saturates corresponds to the flat-band condition in which the electric field at the anode becomes zero (Figs. 55.2(b) and 55.2(d)).[11] This can be estimated by a one-dimensional depletion equation

$$V_{FB} \approx \left(\frac{qN}{2\varepsilon_s}\right)L^2 \ .$$

(55.2)

Operation beyond punch-through also has the advantage of minimum capacitance. (Punch-through is before flat-band, and it occurs when the two depletion widths consume the whole length L.)

Internal photocurrent gain is sometimes observed in the MSM photodetector but the exact mechanism is not well known. One theory to explain the gain is that when photo-generated holes are accumulated at the valence-band peak near the cathode, these positive charges increase the field across the wide-energy-gap barrier-enhancement layer, and induce a larger electron tunneling current. Similar effect can be said of electrons accumulated near the anode and the hole tunneling current is enhanced. This mechanism is somewhat similar to a phototransistor, especially to a tunnel-emitter phototransistor (Section 54.5.6). Another explanation of the gain is photoconductivity caused by long-lifetime traps, located either within the barrier-enhancement layer or at the heterointerface. In any case, there has been an effort to eliminate this gain because the gain mechanism slows the response time of the photodetector, especially the turnoff process.

The MSM photodetector is attractive in that it has very low capacitance because of the two-dimensional effect, and that it can be made on a semi-insulating substrate. Compared to a p-i-n photodiode or a Schottky-barrier photodiode of similar quantum efficiency, its capacitance is reduced to about half. With such a small capacitance, the RC charging time is not a limiting factor to speed. Speed is determined by the transit time, which is directly proportional to the gap dimension. A bandwidth of ≈ 100 GHz has been reported.[12]

55.4 APPLICATIONS

The MSM photodetector has main advantages of high speed and compatibility with FET technology. Its simple, planar structure is easy to integrate with FETs in a single chip. One potential application is an integrated receiver for fiber-optics communication. For general applications of a photodetector, the readers are referred to Appendix C4.

REFERENCES

1. T. Sugeta, T. Urisu, S. Sakata and Y. Mizushima, "Metal-semiconductor-metal photodetector for high-speed optoelectronic circuits," *Proc. 11th Conf. (1979 Int.) Solid State Devices,* Tokyo, 1979. *Japanese J. Appl. Phys.*, Supp. **19-1**, 459 (1980).
2. T. Sugeta and T. Urisu, "High-gain metal-semiconductor-metal photodetectors for high-speed optoelectronics circuits," *Proc. IEEE Dev. Research Conf.*, 1979. Also in *IEEE Trans. Electron Dev.*, **ED-26**, 1855 (1979).
3. C. W. Slayman and L. Figueroa, "Frequency and pulse response of a novel high speed interdigital surface photoconductor (IDPC)," *IEEE Electron Dev. Lett.*, **EDL-2**, 112 (1981).
4. L. Figueroa and C. W. Slayman, "A novel heterostructure interdigital photodetector (HIP) with picosecond optical response," *IEEE Electron Dev. Lett.*, **EDL-2**, 208 (1981).
5. C. J. Wei, H. J. Klein and H. Beneking, "Symmetrical Mott barrier as a fast photodetector," *Electronics Lett.*, **17**, 688 (1981).
6. D. L. Rogers, J. M. Woodall, G. D. Pettit and D. McInturff, "High-speed 1.3-μm GaInAs detectors fabricated on GaAs substrates," *IEEE Electron Dev. Lett.*, **EDL-9**, 515 (1988).
7. H. Schumacher, H. P. Leblanc, J. Soole and R. Bhat, "An investigation of the optoelectronic response of GaAs/InGaAs MSM photodetectors," *IEEE Electron Dev. Lett.*, **EDL-9**, 607 (1988).
8. J. B. D. Soole, H. Schumacher, R. Esagui and R. Bhat, "Waveguide integrated MSM photodetector for the 1.3μm-1.6μm wavelength range," *Tech. Digest IEEE IEDM*, 483 (1988).
9. J. B. D. Soole and H. Schumacher, "InGaAs metal-semiconductor-metal photodetectors for long wavelength optical communications," *IEEE J. Quan. Elect.*, **27**, 737 (1991).
10. C. Shi, D. Grutzmacher, M. Stollenwerk, Q. Wang and K. Heime, "High-performance undoped InP/n-In$_{0.53}$Ga$_{0.47}$As MSM photodetectors grown by LP-MOVPE," *IEEE Trans. Electron Dev.*, **39**, 1028 (1992).
11. S. M. Sze, D. J. Coleman, Jr. and A. Loya, "Current transport in metal-semiconductor-metal (MSM) structures," *Solid-State Electron.*, **14**, 1209 (1971).
12. B. J. van Zeghbroeck, W. Patrick, J. Halbout and P. Vettiger, "105-GHz bandwidth metal-semiconductor-metal photodiode," *IEEE Electron Dev. Lett.*, **9**, 527 (1988).

CHAPTER
56

QUANTUM-WELL INFRARED PHOTODETECTOR

56.1 HISTORY

Infrared absorption within the conduction band or the valence band, instead of band-to-band, in a quantum well was first studied during 1983–1985 by Chiu et al.,[1] Smith et al.,[2] and West and Eglash.[3] The first functional quantum-well infrared photodetector (QWIP), based on bound-to-bound intersubband transition in a GaAs–AlGaAs heterostructure, was realized by Levine et al. in 1987.[4,5] The same group also presented improved detector results on bound-to-continuum transition in 1988.[6] Subsequently, they also studied QWIP using InGaAs–InAlAs multiple quantum wells.[7] Another type of transition, bound-to-miniband, had been presented by Yu and Li in 1991.[8] Because all of these photodetectors do not respond to light that is normal to the heterointerface, Yang and Pan proposed using SiGe–Si for QWIPs.[9] This device was realized by Karunasiri et al. in 1990.[10] Recently, an order of magnitude enhancement in normal-incidence optical coupling has been achieved.[11] The photoconductive gain of the QWIP was modeled by Liu in 1992.[12] For a more comprehensive review of quantum-well and superlattice photodetectors, the readers can refer to Refs. 13–14.

56.2 STRUCTURE

The structure of a QWIP using GaAs–AlGaAs heterostructure is shown in Fig. 56.1. The quantum-well layers, in this case GaAs, have a thickness of about 50 Å, and are usually doped to n-type around 1×10^{18} cm^{-3}. The barrier layers are

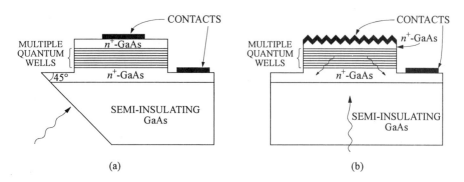

FIGURE 56.1

Structures of GaAs–AlGaAs QWIPs showing approaches to couple light to the detector. (a) Light is incident normal to a polished facet making a 45° angle to the quantum well. (b) A grating is used to refract light coming from the substrate.

undoped and have a thickness in the range of 300–500 Å. A typical number of periods is from 20 to 50. These multiple quantum wells are sandwiched between the n^+-GaAs layers that are used for contacts. Because thin films are required, MBE or MOCVD is used for epitaxial deposition.

For quantum wells formed by direct-energy-gap materials, incident light normal to the surface has zero absorption because intersubband transitions require that the electric field of the electromagnetic wave has components normal to the quantum-well plane. This polarization selection rule demands other approaches to couple light to the detector and two popular schemes are shown in Fig. 56.1. In Fig. 56.1(a), a polished 45° facet is made at the edge adjacent to the detector. Notice that the wavelength of interest is transparent to the substrate. In Fig. 56.1(b), a grating on the top surface refracts light back to the detector. Alternatively, a grating can be made on the substrate surface to scatter the incoming light. This selection rule, however, does not apply to p-type quantum wells or wells formed by indirect-energy-gap materials such as SiGe–Si and AlAs–AlGaAs heterostructures.

56.3 CHARACTERISTICS

The QWIP is based on photoconductivity due to intersubband excitation. The three types of transitions are depicted in Fig. 56.2. In the bound-to-bound transition, both quantized energy states are confined and below the barrier energy. A photon excites an electron from the ground state to the first bound state and the electron subsequently tunnels out of the well. In the bound-to-continuum (or bound-to-extended) excitation, the first state above the ground state is over the barrier and excited electrons can escape the well more easily. This bound-to-continuum excitation is more promising in that it has higher absorption, broader wavelength response, lower dark current, higher detectivity, and it

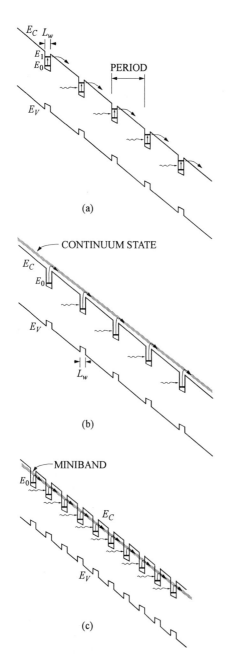

(a)

(b)

(c)

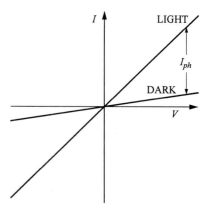

FIGURE 56.2
Energy-band diagrams of QWIPs under bias showing (a) bound-to-bound intersubband transition, (b) bound-to-continuum transition, and (c) bound-to-miniband transition (superlattice).

FIGURE 56.3
Qualitative I-V characteristics of a QWIP.

requires lower voltage. In the bound-to-miniband transition, a miniband is present because of the superlattice structure. QWIPs based on this have shown great promise for focal-plane array imaging sensor system applications.[8]

The first-order QWIP *I-V* characteristics are similar to those of a regular photoconductor (Fig. 56.3). Asymmetric characteristics might occur due to band bending arising from dopant-migration effect in the quantum wells. The photocurrent is given by the same general expression used for photoconductors

$$I_{ph} = q\phi_{ph}\eta G \tag{56.1}$$

where ϕ_{ph} is the total photon arrival rate (/s). The quantum efficiency η is different from a photoconductor since in the QWIP, light absorption and carrier generation occur only in the quantum wells but not homogeneously throughout the structure. It is given by

$$\eta = (1 - R) [1 - \exp(-N_p \alpha N_i L_w)] E_p P \tag{56.2}$$

where R is the reflection, N_p is the number of optical passes, and N_i is the number of quantum wells, each of length L_w. The escape probability E_p is a function of bias which extracts the excited carriers out of the quantum wells.[15] P is the polarization correction factor. For GaAs, it is 0.5 for n-type quantum wells, and unity for p-type quantum wells. The absorption coefficient α is a function of the incident angle and it is proportional to $\sin^2\theta$ where θ is the angle between light propagation and the normal of the quantum-well plane.

The photoconductive gain has been derived to be[12,13]

$$G = \frac{1}{N_i C_p} \tag{56.3}$$

where C_p is the capture probability in the well, given by

$$C_p = \frac{t_p}{\tau} = \frac{t_t}{N_i \tau} . \tag{56.4}$$

t_p is the transit time across a single period of the structure and t_t is the transit time across the entire QWIP active length l (wells and barriers). Combining Eqs. (56.3) and (56.4) yields

$$G = \frac{\tau}{t_t} \tag{56.5}$$

and it is similar to the gain of a standard photoconductor. For carriers in the mobility regime (without velocity saturation),

$$t_t = \frac{l}{v_d} = \frac{l^2}{\mu V} \tag{56.6}$$

where a uniform field is assumed across the whole length l, giving

$$G = \frac{\tau \mu V}{l^2} \ . \tag{56.7}$$

The dark current of a QWIP is due to thermionic emission over the quantum-well barriers and thermionic-field emission (thermally assisted tunneling) near the barrier peaks. Since this photodetector aims at wavelengths from ≈ 3 μm to about 20 μm, the barriers forming the wells have to be small, around 0.2 eV. In order to limit the dark current, the QWIP has to be operated at low temperature, in the range of 4–77 K.

For the sake of completeness, we will discuss another class of transition–interband with type-II offset. The type of heterostructure shown in the energy-band diagrams of Fig. 56.2 where electrons and holes are confined in the same layers is called having type-I offset. For heterostructure with type-II offset (Fig. 56.4), electrons and holes are confined in different layers. The interesting result is that the transition energy of this heterostructure can be smaller than either of the individual energy gaps. Photoconductors and *p-i-n* photodiodes using this transition in InSb–InAsSb multiple quantum wells and superlattices have been demonstrated.[16,17] Another advantage of photoconductors using this type of multiple quantum wells is that since electrons and holes are separated in space, the carrier lifetime is very long, giving rise to much higher photoconductive gains.

56.4 APPLICATIONS

The QWIP is an attractive alternative for long-wavelength photodetectors that use HgCdTe material, which has problems of excessive tunneling dark current and reproducibility in precise composition to give the exact energy gap. It is compatible with GaAs technology and circuits for monolithic integration. The

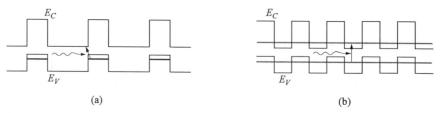

(a)   (b)

FIGURE 56.4
Interband photo-excitation with type-II offset in (a) multiple quantum wells and (b) a superlattice.

detection wavelength range is also tunable by the quantum-well thickness. Long-wavelength capability close to 20 µm has been demonstrated.[15] The QWIP can be applied in focal-plane arrays for two-dimensional imaging. Examples are thermal and terrestrial imaging. One difficulty with the QWIP, at least for n-type GaAs wells, is detecting normal-incidence light.

The general applications of a photodetector are summarized in Appendix C4.

REFERENCES

1. L. C. Chiu, J. S. Smith, S. Margalit, A. Yariv and A. Y. Cho, "Application of internal photoemission from quantum-well and heterojunction superlattices to infrared photodetectors," *Infrared Phys.*, **23**, 93 (1983).
2. J. S. Smith, L. C. Chiu, S. Margalit, A. Yariv and A. Y. Cho, "A new infrared detector using electron emission from multiple quantum wells," *J. Vac. Sci. Technol.*, **B 1**, 376 (1983).
3. L. C. West and S. J. Eglash, "First observation of an extremely large-dipole infrared transition within the conduction band of a GaAs quantum well," *Appl. Phys. Lett.*, **46**, 1156 (1985).
4. B. F. Levine, K. K. Choi, C. G. Bethea, J. Walker and R. J. Malik, "New 10 µm infrared detector using intersubband absorption in resonant tunneling GaAlAs superlattices," *Appl. Phys. Lett.*, **50**, 1092 (1987).
5. K. K. Choi, B. F. Levine, C. G. Bethea, J. Walker and R. J. Malik, "Multiple quantum well 10 µm GaAs/Al$_x$Ga$_{1-x}$As infrared detector with improved responsivity," *Appl. Phys. Lett.*, **50**, 1814 (1987).
6. B. F. Levine, C. G. Bethea, G. Hasnain, J. Walker and R. J. Malik, "High-detectivity $D^* = 1.0 \times 10^{10}$ cm Hz$^{0.5}$/W GaAs/AlGaAs multiquantum well $\lambda = 8.3$ µm infrared detector," *Appl. Phys. Lett.*, **53**, 296 (1988).
7. B. F. Levine, A. Y. Cho, J. Walker, R. J. Malik, D. A. Kleinman and D. L. Sivco, "InGaAs/InAlAs multiquantum well intersubband absorption at a wavelength of $\lambda = 4.4$ µm," *Appl. Phys. Lett.*, **52**, 1481 (1988).
8. L. S. Yu and S. S. Li, "A metal grating coupled bound-to-miniband transition GaAs multiquantum well/superlattice infrared detector," *Appl. Phys. Lett.*, **59**, 1332 (1991).
9. C. Yang and D. Pan, "Intersubband absorption of silicon-based quantum wells for infrared imaging," *J. Appl. Phys.*, **64**, 1573 (1988).
10. R. P. G. Karunasiri, J. S. Park, Y. J. Mii and K. L. Wang, "Intersubband absorption in Si$_{1-x}$Ge$_x$/Si multiple quantum wells," *Appl. Phys. Lett.*, **57**, 2585 (1990).
11. G. Sarusi, B. F. Levine, S. J. Pearton, K. M. S. V. Bandara and R. E. Leibenguth, "Improved performance of quantum well infrared photodetectors using random scattering optical coupling," to be published.
12. H. C. Liu, "Photoconductive gain mechanism of quantum-well intersubband infrared detectors," *Appl. Phys. Lett.*, **60**, 1507 (1992).
13. B. F. Levine, "Quantum-well infrared photodetectors," *J. Appl. Phys.*, **74**, R1 (1993).
14. M. O. Manasreh, Ed., *Semiconductor quantum wells and superlattices for long-wavelength infrared detectors*, Artech House, Boston, 1993.
15. B. F. Levine, A. Zussman, J. M. Kuo and J. de Jong, "19 µm cutoff long-wavelength GaAs/Al$_x$Ga$_{1-x}$As quantum-well infrared photodetectors," *J. Appl. Phys.*, **71**, 5130 (1992).
16. S. R. Kurtz, L. R. Dawson, R. M. Biefeld, T. E. Zipperian and I. J. Fritz, "Prototype InAsSb strained-layer superlattice photovoltaic and photoconductive infrared detectors," *Tech. Digest IEEE IEDM*, 479 (1988).
17. S. R. Kurtz, L. R. Dawson, R. M. Biefeld, I. J. Fritz and T. E. Zipperian, "Long-wavelength InAsSb strained-layer superlattice photovoltaic infrared detectors," *IEEE Electron Dev. Lett.*, **10**, 150 (1989).

CHAPTER

57

NEGATIVE-ELECTRON-AFFINITY PHOTOCATHODE

57.1 HISTORY

A photocathode, among all photodetectors, has a unique process of photoemission in which a photo-excited electron is emitted into vacuum from the near surface of the material. Photoemission from metals has been studied since the turn of the century, highlighted by Einstein's theory of the photoelectric effect in 1905. The negative-electron-affinity (NEA) photocathode or NEA photoemitter, as opposed to classical photocathodes, was predicted in 1958 by Spicer.[1–3] The first experimental NEA photocathode was made by Scheer and van Laar in 1965 on GaAs.[4] Reports on other materials were presented by Williams and Simon on GaP in 1967,[5] by Bell and Uebbing on InP in 1968,[6] by Uebbing and Bell on InGaAs,[7] and by Martinelli on Si in 1970.[8] For detailed discussion of the device, the readers are referred to Refs. 9–11.

57.2 STRUCTURE

Since the NEA photocathode is structurally a sheet of semiconductor with only one terminal, it can hardly be called a device. To complete the circuit, another terminal, an anode, is placed near the NEA photocathode in a vacuum as shown in Fig. 57.1, resulting in a photocathode tube, also called a photoemissive tube or a vacuum photodiode. The semiconductor photoemitter layer is typically doped p-type, with acceptor levels in the range of 3×10^{18}–3×10^{19} cm^{-3}. Nearly degenerate doping levels are required in order to give a small surface depletion width comparable to or smaller than the electron mean free path. On the other hand, too high a doping degrades the minority-carrier lifetime which reduces the

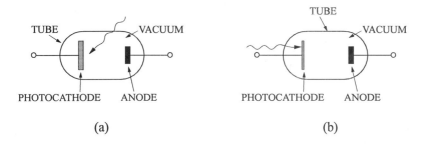

FIGURE 57.1
Structures of (a) a reflection-mode photocathode tube and (b) a transmission-mode photocathode tube.

diffusion length and hence the escape depth for electrons. The transmission NEA photocathode shown in Fig. 57.1(b) has the important advantage of photoelectron imaging at very low light levels. For the photo-generated electrons to be emitted from the opposite surface, the semitransparent NEA photoemissive layer has to be on the order of the minority-carrier diffusion length and the absorption length $(1/\alpha)$. Thin photocathodes are typically prepared by selective chemical etching of epitaxial layers and subsequent bonding of the thin photocathode structure to glass. Alternatively, certain epitaxial films can be grown on substrates with wider energy gap so that the substrate is transparent to the light of interest. Examples of substrates are GaAs, GaP, and InP. Materials studied for NEA photocathodes include GaAs, InGaAs, InGaAsP, GaP, GaAsP, and Si. The photoemissive yield (# of electrons emitted/# of incident photons) improves by orders of magnitude with thin layers, usually under 10 Å, of Cs and O_2 alternatively deposited on the vacuum-cleaned emitting surface. The metal anode is biased with positive voltage with respect to the photocathode to collect the emitted electrons. This bias ranges from a few volts to a few hundred volts.

57.3 CHARACTERISTICS

Photoemission from a photocathode surface consists of three sequential steps: (1) generation of electron-hole pairs by incident photons, (2) transport of the photo-generated electrons to the surface, and (3) escape of electrons to the vacuum. The difference between NEA photocathodes and classical photocathodes is best explained by the energy-band diagrams of Fig. 57.2. For a metal photoemitter, the threshold photon energy is the work function,

$$hv = q\phi \ .$$
(57.1)

In a classical semiconductor photocathode (Fig. 57.2(b)), assuming that there is no band bending in the semiconductor, the minimum photon energy for photoemission is

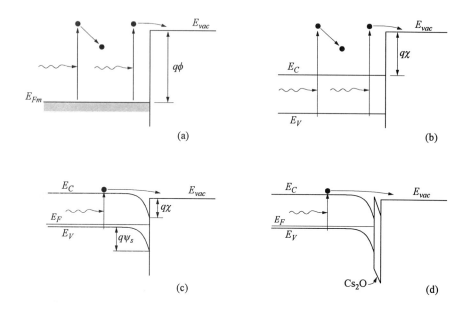

FIGURE 57.2

Energy-band diagrams to show the threshold photon energy for photoemission. (a) A classical metal photocathode. (b) A classical semiconductor photocathode. (c) An NEA photocathode. (d) An NEA photocathode including a Cs_2O layer.

$$hv = E_g + q\chi \quad .$$

(57.2)

Ideally, if electrons can be excited from the conduction band instead of the valence band, the photon energy required drops to the value of electron affinity. In practice, even with a degenerate n-type semiconductor, excitation from the conduction band is much less probable since the overall electron population is still much higher in the valence band. For an NEA photocathode, the p-type surface naturally gets pinned to some interface-trap energy level lying well within the energy gap. The depletion layer and the associated field has a band bending downward toward the surface. It can be seen in Fig. 57.2(c) that if $\psi_s > \chi$, the vacuum level is below the E_C in the bulk, so that the "effective" electron affinity is negative, hence the name negative electron affinity. Notice that the fundamental electron affinity is defined as $E_{vac} - E_C$ at the same location and is unchanged by ψ_s. In this system, the threshold photon energy for photoemission is reduced to a minimum of

$$hv = E_g \quad .$$

(57.3)

The advantages of NEA photocathodes over the classical photocathodes are clear now. First, the photon energy for photoemission is minimized to the energy-gap value, extending the capability for long-wavelength detection. Second, the quantum efficiency is much improved. In the classical photocathode, electrons emitted to the vacuum level are hot carriers, i.e., their energy is much above E_C or E_F. They quickly lose their kinetic energy in scattering events. This means that only electrons generated within a mean free path of the surface are useful, and the escape depth (or emission depth) becomes the mean free path. In the NEA photocathode, excited electrons are cold, i.e., they rest on E_C. These electrons migrate to the surface by diffusion, and the escape depth becomes the diffusion length which is much longer than the mean free path. The mean free path in a semiconductor is also much longer than that in the metal. The only requirement in the NEA photocathode is that the depletion width (≈ 100 Å) has to be smaller than the mean free path to avoid scattering in that region, and this is the reason for high doping since

$$W_d = \sqrt{\frac{2\varepsilon_s \psi_s}{qN_A}} \ . \tag{57.4}$$

Another advantage of a semiconductor photocathode over a metal photocathode is reduced optical reflection from the semiconductor surface. The yield of a reflection-mode photocathode is given by

$$\text{YIELD} = \frac{P(1-R)}{1 + (1/\alpha L_n)} \ . \tag{57.5}$$

Here P is the electron escape probability and R is the optical reflection. Experimental yields on classical photocathodes are in the order of 0.1% while those on NEA photocathodes are as high as 30%.

The *I-V* characteristics of an NEA photocathode are displayed qualitatively in Fig. 57.3. The saturated photocurrent increases linearly with the light intensity. The dark current is due to thermionic emission from the surface. The frequency response of the photocurrent is in the order of 100 MHz.

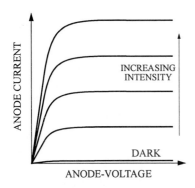

FIGURE 57.3
Qualitative characteristics of an NEA photocathode under light of different intensities.

57.4 APPLICATIONS

The most important application of the NEA photocathode is in large-area imaging tubes, either as an image intensifier tube or as an image converter tube. The general arrangements for both applications are shown in Fig. 57.4. Light first strikes the transmission photocathode and the emitted electrons are accelerated by the high voltage of the anode. The image is reproduced when electrons bombard the luminescent screen which is part of the anode. In an image intensifier tube, the image brightness in the phosphor-type luminescent screen depends on the energy of the impinging electrons, and optical gain is achieved by the high anode potential in the order of kV. The number of electrons can also be multiplied by inserting a microchannel plate (see Section 57.5.1) in front of the luminescent screen. The image intensifier tubes are useful in detecting images of low intensity or of short duration. Areas of applications are in astronomical observation and nuclear physics experiments in association with a scintillator to trace nuclear particles. In an image converter tube, the NEA photocathode responds to light outside the visible spectrum, and the image is reproduced in the screen within the visible spectrum. One such application is in night-vision devices.

One can see the advantage for area imaging; only one large-area photocathode tube is needed instead of an array of photodetectors. Another application of the NEA photocathode is as the photocathode or dynodes for the photomultipliers. The drawbacks of the NEA photocathodes are the need for a vacuum, its structural complexity, generally high cost, and limited robustness to environmental and optoelectronic overstress.

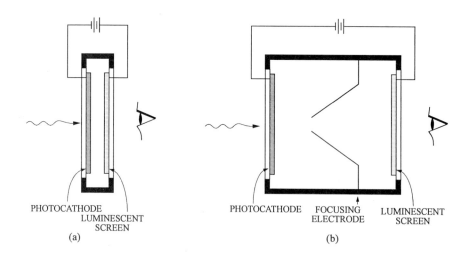

PHOTOCATHODE   PHOTOCATHODE   FOCUSING   LUMINESCENT
        LUMINESCENT   ELECTRODE   SCREEN
          SCREEN
        (a)   (b)

FIGURE 57.4

General arrangements of photocathode imaging tubes. (a) In the proximity tube, the screen is very close (≈ 5 mm) to the photocathode. (b) Electrostatically focused tube.

57.5 RELATED DEVICES

57.5.1 Photomultiplier

A photomultiplier consists of a photocathode and an anode, with dynodes between, all contained in a vacuum tube (Fig. 57.5). The nearly noise-free gain mechanism is from secondary emission of electrons from the dynodes which are made of materials with good secondary-emission coefficients. Secondary emission is the process in which a primary electron of high kinetic energy strikes a surface and multiple electrons are emitted. Typical gain for each stage (g) is between 3–6, and the number of dynodes (N) ranges from 5–16. The overall gain is given simply by

$$\text{Gain} = g^N \ . \tag{57.6}$$

Typical gains are between 10^6 and 10^8. The biasing of the dynodes is arranged such that there is a differential voltage of 100–200 V between successive stages.

The photosensitive electrode can be made of a classical photocathode or an NEA photocathode if longer-wavelength detection is required. Most popular materials for the dynodes are classical emitters such as CsSb, AgMgO, and CuBeO. Most NEA photocathode materials can also be used because they have excellent secondary-emission coefficients. Cs_2O-coated GaP is most often used in practice, however. Common arrangements for the dynodes are shown in Fig. 57.6, including the systems of venetian blind, box and grid, linear focused and circular-cage focused. An alternate arrangement, called a channel electron multiplier, eliminates complicated biasing circuit (Fig. 57.7). The channel is formed inside a hollow tube whose wall is coated with a continuous film of secondary emissive material. The resistivity of the film is very high such that a large bias can be applied between the two ends, resulting in a natural potential

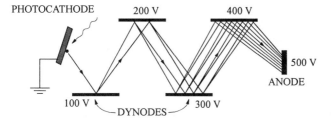

FIGURE 57.5
Schematic diagram of a photomultiplier showing the arrangement of the electrodes and the electron multiplication. A gain of two for each stage is assumed.

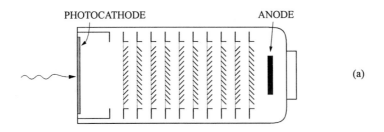

(a)

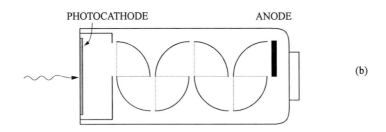

(b)

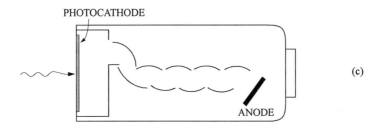

(c)

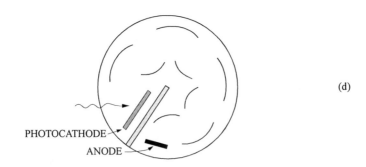

(d)

FIGURE 57.6
Common photomultiplier tube constructions. (a) Venetian blind. (b) Box and grid. (c) Linear focused.
(d) Circular-cage focused.

PHOTOCATHODE   ANODE

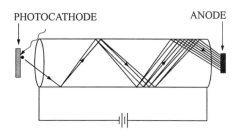

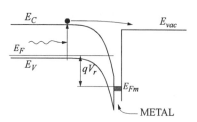

FIGURE 57.7
Electron multiplication in a channel electron multiplier.

FIGURE 57.8
Energy-band diagram of a transferred-electron photocathode under bias.

gradient along the channel. When many of these channels are grouped together in an array for area imaging, a microchannel plate is formed.

The extremely high gain of the photomultiplier is best used to detect light of extremely low intensity, and also short pulses of radiation. The gain can be so high that an overexposure of the incident light can result in damage to the multiplier. Examples of applications are photon-counting experiments, heterodyne detection, nuclear-physics experiments with scintillators, astronomy, and image intensifier tubes.

57.5.2 Transferred-Electron Photocathode

In a transferred-electron photocathode, a thin metal is deposited on the p-type semiconductor surface. In operation, the metal-semiconductor (Schottky) junction is under a large reverse bias to increase the surface band bending to obtain negative electron affinity (Fig. 57.8). The metal film has to be thinner than the mean free path to avoid interruption of the ballistic electrons. This field-assisted photoemission process can result in the transferred-electron effect (Gunn effect) in which a high fraction of the photo-generated electrons are lifted to the next higher satellite valley before they are emitted to vacuum. The transferred-electron photocathode has not been commercialized to date.

REFERENCES

1. W. E. Spicer, "Photoemissive, photoconductive, and optical absorption studies of alkali-antimony compounds," *Phys. Rev.*, **112**, 114 (1958).
2. W. E. Spicer, "The influence of defect levels on photoemission," *RCA Rev.*, **19**, 555 (1958).
3. W. E. Spicer, "Photoemission and related properties of the alkali-antimonides," *J. Appl. Phys.*, **31**, 2077 (1960).
4. J. J. Scheer and J. van Laar, "GaAs-Cs: A new type of photoemitter," *Solid State Comm.*, **3**, 189 (1965).
5. B. F. Williams and R. E. Simon, "Direct measurement of hot electron-phonon interactions in GaP," *Phys. Rev. Lett.*, **18**, 485 (1967).

6. R. L. Bell and J. J. Uebbing, "Photoemission from InP-Cs-O," *Appl. Phys. Lett.*, **12**, 76 (1968).

7. J. J. Uebbing and R. L. Bell, "Improved photoemitters using GaAs and InGaAs," *Proc. IEEE*, **56**, 1624 (1968).

8. R. U. Martinelli, "Infrared photoemission from silicon," *Appl. Phys. Lett.*, **16**, 261 (1970).

9. P. N. J. Dennis, *Photodetectors*, Plenum Press, New York, 1986.

10. H. R. Zwicker, "Photoemissive detectors," in R. J. Keyes, Ed., *Optical and infrared detectors,* Springer-Verlag, Berlin, 1980.

11. J. S. Escher, "NEA semiconductor photoemitters," in R. K. Willardson, Ser. Ed., A. C. Beer, Vol. Ed., *Semiconductors and semimetals*, Vol. 15, Academic Press, New York, 1981.

CHAPTER 58

PHOTON-DRAG
DETECTOR

58.1 HISTORY

The photon-drag effect, in the case of interband optical transition, was first observed in 1970 independently by Danishevskii et al.[1] and Gibson et al.[2] The theory of the effect was developed by Grinberg in the same year.[3] For the classical range of the electromagnetic-wave frequencies ($\hbar\omega \ll kT$), the effect had been considered earlier by Barlow in 1958.[4] The microscopic theory of the classical photon-drag effect was developed by Gurevich and Rumyantsev in 1967.[5] A photon-drag effect on quantum-well structures, arising from intersubband transition rather than interband transition, was suggested by Luryi and Grinberg in 1987–1988.[6,7] For more discussion on the photon-drag detector, the readers are referred to Ref. 8.

58.2 STRUCTURE

The photon-drag detector consists simply of a bar of semiconductor with a contact ring at each end, as shown in Fig. 58.1. The shape of the cross-section is not critical. It can be rectangular, square, or circular. Typical lengths L are 1–5 cm, and cross-sectional areas 0.2–1 cm^2. Materials studied include Ge, Si, InSb, GaP, GaAs, Te, and CdTe. p-type Ge doped to ≈ 10 Ω-cm is the most common material.

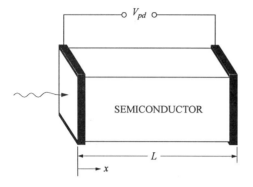

FIGURE 58.1
Structure of a photon-drag detector.

58.3 CHARACTERISTICS

When light is absorbed by a carrier in a semiconductor, both energy and momentum have to be conserved. The transfer of momentum from a photon to a free carrier gives rise to the photon-drag effect. Conceptually, light pushes carriers away from the exposed surface. This radiation pressure builds up a voltage difference between the front surface and the back surface.

In the classical limit when energy of the photon satisfies $\hbar\omega \ll kT$ and light absorption is determined by free carriers, a simple estimate of the photon-drag voltage can be made by considering the momentum (p) possessed by each photon,

$$p = \frac{E}{c} \ . \tag{58.1}$$

Since light is not absorbed uniformly within the semiconductor, the rate of change of momentum per unit volume is given by

$$\frac{dp(x)}{dt} = \frac{n_r P \alpha \exp(-\alpha x)}{Ac} \ . \tag{58.2}$$

Here P is the power of the light beam which falls on the cross-sectional area A, and the division by A gives an average value such that Eq. (58.2) becomes one-dimensional. Furthermore, in an open-circuit condition, the average rate of change of momentum to each carrier must be balanced by an EMF acting on the carrier (taking n-type as an example),

$$q\mathscr{E}(x) = \frac{n_r P \alpha \exp(-\alpha x)}{Acn} \ . \tag{58.3}$$

The photon-drag voltage V_{pd} is from the integration of this longitudinal field over the whole length,

$$V_{pd} = \frac{n_r P \left[1 - \exp\left(-\alpha L\right) \right]}{qAcn} \ . \tag{58.4}$$

A typical V_{pd} signal is in the range of 1–40 μV/W. Signal linearity with power is good up to a power density of ≈ 50 MW/cm^2 where the signal becomes saturated. Permanent damage to the detector starts to occur around 100 MW/cm^2. The response time of the photon-drag detector is very short, less than 1 ns.

Responsivity is found to obey Eq. (58.4) only for wavelengths longer than a few hundred μm. The criterion is set by $2\pi f\tau_m \ll 1$ where τ_m is the scattering mean free time, which is a function of both the doping level and temperature. For shorter wavelengths, responsivity is wavelength dependent and its output voltage is less than that given by Eq. (58.4). The controlling mechanism becomes very complicated, especially in the case when light absorption is determined by interband optical transitions. In this case the lattice participates in the momentum conservation law and as a result, the drag of the carriers can be opposite to the light propagation direction. The sign of the photon-drag voltage changes with wavelength in the 1–10 μm range.

58.4 APPLICATIONS

The advantages of the photon-drag detector include low cost, rugged structure, unbiased and room-temperature operation, long-wavelength capability, high speed, and, of most practical importance, high power tolerance. A photon-drag detector is used routinely to calibrate high-power CO_2 pulse lasers. The disadvantage of this detector is low responsivity compared to other photodetectors.

REFERENCES

1. A. M. Danishevskii, A. A. Kastalskii, S. M. Ryvkin and I. D. Yaroshetskii, "Dragging of free carriers by photons in direct interband transitions," *Sov. Phys. –JETP*, **31**, 292 (1970).
2. A. F. Gibson, M. F. Kimmitt and A. C. Walker, "Photon drag in germanium," *Appl. Phys. Lett.*, **17**, 75 (1970).
3. A. A. Grinberg, "Theory of the photoelectric and photomagnetic effects produced by light pressure," *Sov. Phys. –JETP*, **31**, 531 (1970).
4. H. M. Barlow, "The Hall effect and its application to microwave power measurement," *Proc. IRE*, **46**, 1411 (1958).
5. L. E. Gurevich and A. A. Rumyantsev, "Theory of the photoelectric effect in finite crystals at high frequencies and in the presence of an external magnetic field," *Sov. Phys. –Solid State*, **9**, 55 (1967).
6. S. Luryi, "Photon-drag effect in intersubband absorption by a two-dimensional electron gas," *Phys. Rev. Lett.*, **58**, 2263 (1987).
7. A. A. Grinberg and S. Luryi, "Theory of the photon-drag effect in a two-dimensional electron gas," *Phys. Rev. B*, **38**, 87 (1988).
8. A. F. Gibson and M. F. Kimmitt, "Photon drag detection," in K. J. Button, Ed., *Infrared and millimeter waves*, Vol. 3, Academic Press, New York, 1980.

CHAPTER
59

SELF-ELECTROOPTIC-EFFECT DEVICE

59.1 HISTORY

The self-electrooptic-effect device (SEED) is one of the few bistable optical devices that has bistable light output states with light as an input. It is an all-optical device (light in and light out) and has potential for optical computing. The SEED is based on the electroabsorption effect in quantum wells, the so-called quantum-confined Stark effect. This effect was first observed in 1983, and led to the realization of the quantum-well electroabsorption modulator in 1984. The SEED was first proposed and demonstrated by Miller et al. in 1984.[1] Being such a new device, it is still being investigated but with increasing interest. More in-depth theoretical treatment can be found in Refs. 2–4.

59.2 STRUCTURE

The structure of a SEED is shown in Fig. 59.1. It can be seen that it is identical to a quantum-well electroabsorption modulator (see Chapter 62). The only difference lies in the range of input wavelength. For a SEED, the optical absorption coefficient (α) increases with the internal field, while for a quantum-well electroabsorption modulator, α decreases with the field. The structure is a p-i-n diode with multiple quantum wells inserted in the intrinsic layer. The quantum wells have typical well and barrier thicknesses of ≈ 100 Å. Consequently, MBE or MOCVD is required for precise epitaxial growth. The bulk of the substrate is removed by wet chemical etching to prevent excessive absorption in the substrate. Heterostructures studied include GaAs–AlGaAs, InGaAs–InP, InGaAs–InAlAs, and GaSb–GaAlSb.

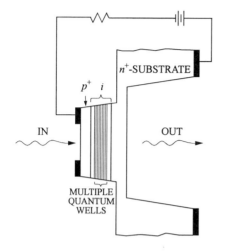

FIGURE 59.1
Schematic diagram for the structure and operation of a SEED.

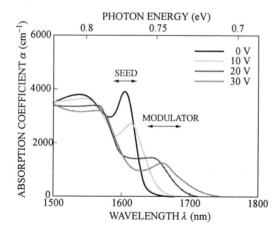

FIGURE 59.2
Absorption coefficient as a function of wavelength at different biases for a quantum well. The region of interest for the SEED is indicated. (After Ref. 5)

59.3 CHARACTERISTICS

Since the electroabsorption effect in a quantum well is instrumental for the operation of SEED, it is discussed first. Experimental data for the absorption coefficient as a function of applied voltage are shown in Fig. 59.2. This influence of α by the field in a quantum well has been referred to as the quantum-confined Stark effect. At zero bias, an absorption edge is clearly observed, and in this example it occurs at a wavelength (λ) of ≈ 1650 nm. Below this wavelength, there are local absorption peaks that are referred to as exciton peaks. With increased reverse bias to the *p-i-n* diode, the absorption spectrum is changed. Notice that for wavelength longer than the original absorption edge ($\lambda > 1650$ nm), α increases with the field. This is the operational range for a quantum-well electroabsorption modulator. For wavelength below the original absorption edge (higher optical energy), α decreases with the field. This is especially pronounced at the first exciton peak from the original absorption edge, and this range of wavelength is most suitable for the SEED input.

The optical characteristics of a SEED are shown in Fig. 59.3. There are two important features. First, at some input power level, the output power changes abruptly (switching). Second, this abrupt change occurs at two different input levels, and it depends on whether the input level is increasing or decreasing. This leads to a hysteresis loop so that within a range of input power, the output has two states (bistable).

The switch in output power can be explained by a positive feedback between the dual properties of a photodetector and an electroabsorption modulator. As the light input power increases, the photo-generated current is increased. The increased current develops an IR drop across the external resistor (or any parasitic series resistance), and the effective field for the quantum wells is reduced. This increases α and thus the photocurrent. The increase in photocurrent decreases the internal field further and a positive feedback begins. During this feedback loop, α increases rapidly, resulting in a drop of transmitted output power. Similar argument can be made for the switching at decreasing light input.

The hysteresis loop can be explained by a different picture. The I-V characteristics for three different input powers are shown in Fig. 59.4. For each input power, the curve displays negative differential resistance similar to that in a tunnel diode, but of different origin. The initial rise of current with applied bias is due to improved internal quantum efficiency. The following drop in

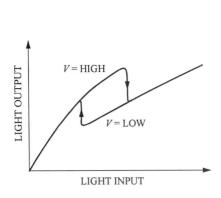

FIGURE 59.3
Optical characteristics of a SEED. The internal voltage V across the quantum wells is also indicated.

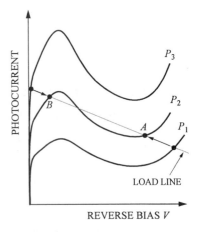

FIGURE 59.4
Electrical characteristics of a SEED under different light input powers, $P_3 > P_2 > P_1$.

photocurrent is from the electroabsorption effect of decreasing α with field. The final rise is, presumably, due to high-field avalanche effect. The load line is shown to intersect the middle curve at two stable points, A and B. Point A has higher voltage, lower α, and higher output power. At input intensities P_1 and P_3, only one state is possible. It can be seen that with increasing input power it is locked to A or higher output state, while with decreasing input power, it is locked to B or lower output state.

Operation with a constant current bias, rather than a constant voltage bias, is also possible. The possible feedback mechanism is the same, resulting in similar optical characteristics.

59.4 APPLICATIONS

For optical computing, the SEED can provide the required optical bistability. The applications of a bistable optical device are summarized in Appendix C5. The low optical switching power of a bistable optical device has been demonstrated in the SEED to be ≈ 10 fJ/μm^2. The high-speed capability, on the other hand, has not been demonstrated. The switching time so far reported is not limited by intrinsic mechanism, but is RC limited to above 30 ns. The advantages of the SEED are room-temperature operation, technology compatibility with other photonic devices, and compared to the bistable etalon, a Fabry-Perot cavity is not needed.

REFERENCES

1. D. A. B. Miller, D. S. Chemla, T. C. Damen, A. C. Gossard, W. Wiegmann, T. H. Wood and C. A. Burrus, "Novel hybrid optically bistable switch: The quantum well self-electro-optic effect device," *Appl. Phys. Lett.*, **45**, 13 (1984).
2. D. A. B. Miller, D. S. Chemla, T. C. Damen, T. H. Wood, C. A. Burrus, Jr., A. C. Gossard and W. Wiegmann," *IEEE J. Quantum Electron.*, **QE-21**, 1462 (1985).
3. D. A. B. Miller, "Quantum-well self-electro-optic effect devices," *Optical Quantum Electron.*, **22**, S61 (1990).
4. P. J. Mares and S. L. Chuang, "Comparison between theory and experiment for InGaAs/InP self-electro-optic effect devices," *Appl. Phys. Lett.*, **61**, 1924 (1992).
5. I. Bar-Joseph, C. Klingshirn, D. A. B. Miller, D. S. Chemla, U. Koren and B. I. Miller, "Quantum-confined Stark effect in InGaAs/InP quantum wells grown by organometallic vapor phase epitaxy," *Appl. Phys. Lett.*, **50**, 1010 (1987).

CHAPTER
60

BISTABLE
ETALON

60.1 HISTORY

The bistable etalon has also been called other names such as the nonlinear (or bistable) Fabry-Perot resonator (or interferometer). While optical bistability was first studied in lasers in 1964–5, "passive" optical bistability was predicted by Szoke et al. in 1969,[1] and by Seidel independently.[2] The first bistable etalon was made with sodium vapor as the nonlinear material in 1975,[3,4] followed by that made with ruby in 1977. The first semiconductor bistable etalon was reported by Gibbs et al. in 1979, using GaAs.[5] Later that year, results on InSb were also presented by Miller et al.[6] Considerable advancement of the bistable etalon was made during the 1980s, both theoretically and experimentally. This is partly due to the push for optical computing, and partly to the availability of quantum-well growth technology which adds device performance. More detailed discussions on this device can be found in Refs. 7–10.

60.2 STRUCTURE

The bistable etalon, as the name implies, is structurally a Fabry-Perot resonator, with specific designs for the cavity length L and the reflectivity of the surfaces (Fig. 60.1). A Fabry-Perot resonator, also called an etalon or an interferometer, by definition has parallel smooth mirror surfaces perpendicular to the direction of light propagation. In a bistable etalon, these surfaces have high reflectivity of around 0.9, and sometimes they are coated to achieve these values. The other two surfaces parallel to the optical path are not critical and can be made totally absorbing. The etalon can be in the form of a slab, with cleaved surfaces as shown

468

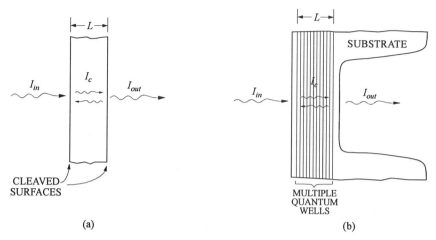

FIGURE 60.1
Structures of the bistable etalon in the form of (a) a slab with cleaved surfaces, typical for bulk semiconductors, and (b) a chemically thinned-down sample, typical for quantum-well devices.

in Fig. 60.1(a), or chemically thinned down as in the case of a quantum-well structure in Fig. 60.1(b). It can also be a platelet or a thin-film structure deposited onto a transparent substrate. To design the proper L, the etalon has to be detuned from resonance at low input power, meaning $n_r L \neq N\lambda/2$. In order to have better control, L should be limited to a few wavelengths of the input light. The nonlinear semiconductors studied include GaAs, InSb, ZnS, ZnSe, CuCl, InAs, CdS, and HgCdTe, with GaAs being the most successful. Bistable etalons with multiple quantum wells have improved performance, and can adjust the absorption edge to permit a design for a chosen input wavelength. Such heterostructures include GaAs–AlGaAs, InGaAs–InP, and InGaAs–InAlAs.

60.3 CHARACTERISTICS

The operating principle of the bistable etalon is based on positive feedback. Two mechanisms are involved: (1) the refraction index is a function of light intensity, and (2) the light intensity is a function of the optical length ($n_r L$) which depends on the refractive index. The first mechanism requires a nonlinear optical material. The second mechanism is a property of a Fabry-Perot etalon.

In a semiconductor with a nonlinear refractive index, the n_r can be changed by the cavity intensity (I_c) of the light in two ways. First, it can be affected by the light intensity directly through the optical Kerr effect. The optical Kerr effect is a change of optical properties due to an increased electron-hole plasma. This effect can be expressed by

$$n_r = n_{ro} + C_1 I_c \; . \tag{60.1}$$

Notice that in this approximation, the n_r is linearly dependent on I_c. This is not to be confused with the term "nonlinear" as in nonlinear material which is defined simply as a material of variable n_r with light intensity. The proportionality constant C_1 lies in the range of 0.1–3 cm^2/kW. Optical bistability due to the optical Kerr effect is called dispersive. The second phenomenon is called dissipative optical bistability. For input light with a wavelength whose energy is slightly below the energy gap, the absorption coefficient α decreases with light intensity, and the n_r is affected indirectly by the change of α, through the Kramers-Kronig relationship. This saturable absorption is expressed by

$$\alpha = \frac{\alpha_o}{1 + C_2 I_c} \tag{60.2}$$

where C_2 is another constant. The origin of the decrease of α with light is different for bulk semiconductors and quantum wells. In bulk semiconductors, at high intensity, electrons fill the bottom portion of the conduction band and holes fill the top portion of the valence band. The effective energy gap for further electron-hole generation is thus increased, and this band-filling effect leads to the decrease of α. In a quantum well, the so-called exciton absorption is reduced, caused by state filling and screening of the Coulomb interaction by excess carriers. The Coulomb interaction is responsible for a large binding energy of the exciton, which originally increases the absorption coefficient. In either case of dispersive nonlinearity or dissipative nonlinearity, the net effect is the same–the change of n_r or optical length with light intensity.

We now proceed with the optical properties of a Fabry-Perot etalon. The transmission T of an etalon is expressed by the Airy function as a function of the optical length by

$$T = \frac{I_{out}}{I_{in}} = \left\{ 1 + C_3 \sin^2 \left[\frac{\pi n_r L}{(\lambda/2)} \right] \right\}^{-1} \; . \tag{60.3}$$

This function is plotted in Fig. 60.2(a). Due to the wave nature of coherent light, the light intensity in the cavity I_c varies with the optical length. When the optical length is exactly equal to a multiple of half-wavelengths, or

$$n_r L = N_i \left(\frac{\lambda}{2} \right) \; , \tag{60.4}$$

constructive interference occurs. At this resonance, the I_c builds up to ≈ 10 times the input power I_{in}, and the transmission I_{out}/I_{in} becomes unity. In off-resonance when $n_r L \neq N_i \lambda/2$, destructive interference occurs and the transmission is low. By controlling the n_r, the output power switches between the high state and the low state, leading to optical bistability. (In an etalon, the finesse is defined as the ratio of the resonance width at half peak to the resonance period.)

The optical characteristics of a bistable etalon are shown in Fig. 60.2(b). The two main features of these are: (1) at some critical I_{in}, the I_{out} switches rapidly with a small change in I_{in}, and (2) this switching occurs at two different I_{in} levels, depending on whether I_{in} is increasing or decreasing. The latter also results in a hysteresis loop. At low I_{in}, the etalon is at off-resonance such that T, I_c, and I_{out} are all at low level. With I_{in} increasing to a critical level (C in Fig. 60.2(b)), I_c and n_r build up rapidly through positive feedback, and I_{out} switches to a high level. Beyond that level, I_{in} is pushed beyond optical resonance (E), the transmission is decreased and I_{out} no longer continues to rise with I_{in}. This is a result of negative feedback. With decreasing I_{in}, T switches at a lower I_{in} value than with increasing I_{in}. In this case, high transmission is easier to maintain since I_c is already built up in the cavity.

The optical characteristics of Fig. 60.2(b) can also be obtained graphically from the Airy function of Fig. 60.2(a). Since the optical length is proportional to the refractive index, it is linearly dependent on I_c. Also, I_{out} is known to be proportional to I_c, related by the reflectivities of the two etalon surfaces, so $T = I_{out}/I_{in} \propto I_c/I_{in}$. Therefore, for every fixed I_{in}, there is a linear relationship between T and the optical length, indicated by the straight lines in Fig. 60.2(a). Lines with lower slopes correspond to higher I_{in}. It can be seen that some of the lines have multiple intersections, and they form the basis for bistability and the hysteresis loop.

The response of I_{out} to a rapidly changing I_{in} of an all-optical device is inherently very fast. In the bistable etalon, the turn-on time can be as short as a

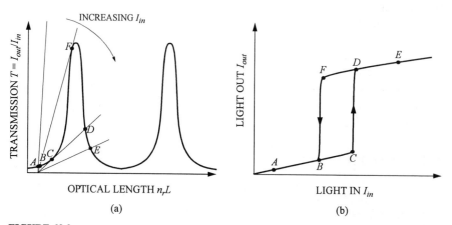

FIGURE 60.2

(a) The Airy function for an etalon, showing the transmission I_{out}/I_{in} as a function of the optical length. The straight lines intersecting the Airy function are from different I_{in} levels. (b) Optical characteristics of a bistable etalon.

few ps. The turn-off time, however, is limited by carrier recombination in the semiconductor, and it can be longer than 10 ns. This slow turn off can be improved by surface recombination, or by introducing recombination centers from proton bombardment. It should be added that using the reflected light as output, as opposed to transmitted light, can also result in optical bistability.

60.4 APPLICATIONS

The bistable etalon is one of few bistable optical devices available for future optical computing. The general applications of a bistable optical device are discussed in more detail in Appendix C5. The bistable etalon has extremely low switching power, in the order of fJ. The advantage of the bistable etalon compared to the SEED is the absence of electrical bias. The disadvantages are the necessity of using a Fabry-Perot structure which is difficult to manufacture, and the restriction of requiring coherent-light input.

60.5 RELATED DEVICE

60.5.1 Interference Filter

The interference filter has optical characteristics similar to that shown in Fig. 60.2(b). The first semiconductor interference filter was made by Karpushko and Sinitsyn on ZnS in 1978,[11] slightly earlier than the semiconductor bistable etalon. The nonlinearity in refractive index is thermal in nature,[7,12] given by

$$n_r = n_{ro} + C_4 \Delta T \ . \tag{60.5}$$

This thermo-optical effect is from heating of the etalon by the light in the cavity. The proportionality constant C_4 has a value in the order of 10^{-4} K^{-1}. The positive feedback between the n_r and the light intensity is similar to that in the bistable etalon. Structurally, the interference filter is usually a thin-film device deposited onto a substrate with good thermal isolation. The disadvantages of the interference filter are higher switching power, with a lowest limit of ≈ 10 μW, and also slower switching speed. Nevertheless, switching speed can be still under 1 ns. The advantage of this device is its structural simplicity.

REFERENCES

1. A. Szoke, V. Daneu, J. Goldhar and N. A. Kurnit, "Bistable optical element and its applications," *Appl. Phys. Lett.*, **15**, 376 (1969).
2. H. Seidel, "Bistable optical circuit using saturable absorber within a resonant cavity," U. S. patent, 3,610,731, 1971.
3. S. L. McCall, H. M. Gibbs, G. G. Churchill and T. N. C. Venkatesan, "Optical transistor and bistability," *Bull. Am. Phys. Soc.*, **20**, 636 (1975).

4. H. M. Gibbs, S. L. McCall and T. N. C. Venkatesan, "Differential gain and bistability using a sodium-filled Fabry-Perot interferometer," *Phys. Rev. Lett.*, **36**, 1135 (1976).

5. H. M. Gibbs, S. L. McCall, T. N. C. Venkatesan, A. C. Gossard, A. Passner and W. Wiegmann, "Optical bistability in semiconductors," *Appl. Phys. Lett.*, **35**, 451 (1979).

6. D. A. B. Miller, S. D. Smith and A. Johnston, "Optical bistability and signal amplification in a semiconductor crystal: applications of new low-power nonlinear effects in InSb," *Appl. Phys. Lett.*, **35**, 658 (1979).

7. H. M. Gibbs, *Optical bistability: Controlling light with light*, Academic Press, Orlando, 1985.

8. E. Abraham, C. T. Seaton and S. D. Smith, "The optical computer," *Scien. Am.*, **248(2)**, 85 (1983).

9. P. W. Smith and W. J. Tomlinson, "Bistable optical devices promise subpicosecond switching," *IEEE Spectrum*, June Issue, 26 (1981).

10. D. A. B. Miller, "Bistable optical devices: Physics and operating characteristics," *Laser Focus*, April Issue, 79 (1982).

11. F. V. Karpushko and G. V. Sinitsyn, "An optical logic element for integrated optics in a nonlinear semiconductor interferometer," *J. Appl. Spectrosc. USSR*, **29**, 1323 (1978).

12. B. S. Wherrett, D. C. Hutchings, F. A. P. Tooley, Y. T. Chow and A. D. Lloyd, "Optical computing architectures based on nonlinear interference filter technology," *SPIE*, **881**, 2 (1988).

CHAPTER
61

SOLAR CELL

61.1 HISTORY

The photovoltaic effect, the generation of voltage when a device is exposed to light, was first discovered by Becquerel back in 1839, in a junction formed between an electrode and an electrolyte.[1] Similar effects on selenium were observed by Adams and Day in 1876,[2] and by Lange in 1930,[3] and on cuprous oxide by Schottky in 1930,[4] and by Grondahl in 1933.[5] Photovoltaic effect on Ge was reported by Benzer in 1946,[6] and by Pantchechnikoff in 1952.[7] It was not until 1954 that the solar cell received increased interest, initiated by the works of Chapin et al. on single-crystal silicon cells,[8] and of Reynolds et al. on cadmium sulfide cells.[9] For other materials, Gremmelmaier presented results on GaAs in 1955,[10] and Carlson and Wronski generated much interest in amorphous silicon in 1976.[11] Analytical studies had been performed by Cummerow,[12,13] Rittner,[14] Prince[15] and Loferski.[16] For a more detailed account on the historical development of solar cells, the readers can refer to Refs. 17–19. More in-depth treatment on the device can be found in Refs. 19–24.

61.2 STRUCTURE

A solar cell can be made of a *p-n* junction or a Schottky barrier, as shown in Fig. 61.1. The *p-n* junction version (*p* on *n* or *n* on *p*) is more common because it has better reliability and higher open-circuit voltage. The metallurgical junction is usually shallow, typically 0.5–1 µm deep. Too shallow a junction will increase the sheet resistance of the top layer, and also increase the dark current (see comments below Eq. (1.12)). A deep junction is not efficient in collecting carriers

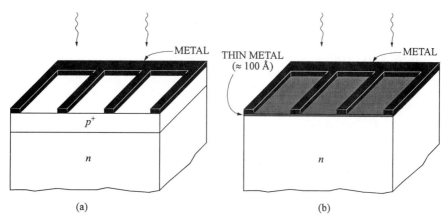

FIGURE 61.1
Structures of solar cells using (a) a *p-n* junction and (b) a Schottky-barrier junction. Antireflection coating on the top surface and the bottom ohmic contact are not shown.

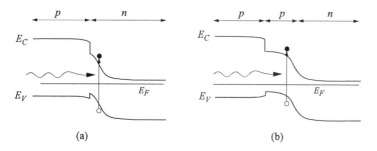

FIGURE 61.2
Energy-band diagrams of (a) a heterojunction solar cell and (b) a heteroface solar cell, under short-circuit condition.

excited near the surface, especially from light of shorter wavelength which has high absorption coefficient. Another possible structure is the heterojunction solar cell whose energy-band diagram is shown in Fig. 61.2(a). It has a material of higher energy gap at the surface so little light is absorbed in that layer. When this layer is heavily doped, it has the combination of low sheet resistance, low dark current and good short-wavelength response. A similar structure is the heteroface solar cell shown in Fig. 61.2(b) where an isotype heterojunction is incorporated. The Schottky-barrier version offers certain advantages because no high-temperature processing is needed. This, for example, avoids enhanced diffusion along grain boundaries in poly-crystal materials. Another advantage is that the junction is at the surface for better short-wavelength response. An inherent disadvantage of the Schottky-barrier cell is a larger dark current. This

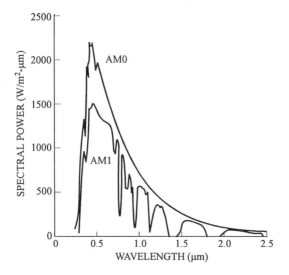

FIGURE 61.3
Power spectrum of the sun's irradiation at AM0 and AM1.

can be improved somewhat by introducing a thin tunneling oxide layer of 10–20 Å between the metal and the semiconductor, resulting in an MIS solar cell (see Section 3.5.2).[25] The right choice of oxide thickness can decrease the dark current without affecting the light-generated current. The benefit of a low dark current will be shown later.

Since the solar cell is used as a power-generating source, series resistance is a critical factor, unlike the case of photodetectors. Figure 61.1 shows that a metal grid structure is used to form ohmic contact. To design the shape of the grid, a compromise is struck between series resistance and area lost to exposure to light. Transparent conducting films such as InSn oxide (ITO) have been explored. Another film of antireflection coating is usually deposited to minimize overall reflection. Cells with texturized surface have also been made so that some of the reflected light can be reabsorbed.

More common materials for single-crystal cells are Si, GaAs, InP, and CdTe. Deposited thin-film solar cells offer low cost and large-area capability, but they are limited to low efficiency. These materials include polycrystal and amorphous Si, GaAs, and CdS (Cu_2S–CdS heterostructure). The thickness of the solar-cell body needs to be only a few absorption lengths in order to absorb most of the power since the penetration of light decreases with distance as

$$P(x) = P(0) \exp(-\alpha x) \quad . \tag{61.1}$$

61.3 CHARACTERISTICS

The power spectrum ($P(\lambda)$) of the sun's irradiation is shown in Fig. 61.3. The intensity of the irradiation at sea level is indicated by the "air mass" number. Its

AM value is equal to the secant of the angle between the sun and the zenith. At AM1, the sun is directly overhead, and the total power density is ≈ 1 kW/m^2, assuming a clear sky. The solar power outside the earth's atmosphere is about 1.35 kW/m^2 and it is designated as AM0. For photoelectric effect, the irradiation has to be thought as a beam of photons, each with energy $h\nu$. If this energy exceeds the energy gap, an electron-hole pair is generated as shown in Fig. 61.4. Whether the solar cell is a *p-n* junction or a Schottky barrier, the built-in field separates these carriers and results in an external current. The main steps of photovoltaic power generation are light absorption to produce excess carriers, followed by separation of these carriers. It should be pointed out that in a Schottky-barrier solar cell, a photon with an energy larger than the barrier height (but smaller than the energy gap) is sufficient to excite carriers from the metal as well, but this process is very localized and inefficient so it can be ignored.

When a solar cell is under irradiation, the terminal voltage is determined by the load it is driving. For maximum current, the load is of zero resistance, and the current is called short-circuit current J_{sc}. This occurs because the built-in field is at its maximum. This J_{sc} can be calculated from the photon flux $F_{ph}(\lambda)$ whose energies are larger than E_g,

$$
\begin{aligned}
J_{sc} &= q \int_0^{\lambda \ (\text{at } h\nu = E_g)} \eta F_{ph}(\lambda)\, d\lambda \\
&= q \int_0^{\lambda \ (\text{at } h\nu = E_g)} \frac{\eta P(\lambda)}{h\nu}\, d\lambda \ .
\end{aligned}
$$

$$(61.2)$$

Notice that for shorter wavelengths, since each photon has larger energy, the number of photons available is reduced. Theoretical J_{sc}, assuming unity quantum efficiency η, as a function of E_g is plotted in Fig. 61.5(a). As a reference, the total number of photons at AM1 is 5×10^{17}/cm^2-s, giving an upper J_{sc} limit of 80 mA/cm^2. This figure shows that a cell of typical E_g collects $\approx$ 20–60% of the total photons under short-circuit condition. The above assumption of unity

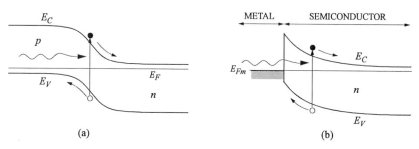

FIGURE 61.4
Energy-band diagrams showing the generation of electron-hole pairs in (a) a *p-n* junction solar cell and (b) a Schottky-barrier solar cell, under short-circuit condition.

quantum efficiency is only justified for electron-hole pairs generated within the depletion width where the field is high. In the neutral region, the driving force for the separation of generated carriers is diffusion. It is a slower process and there is more time for recombination. A vigorous derivation shows that for light absorbed in the neutral region, the collection efficiency is reduced to (see Section 50.5.1)

$$\eta_{ne} = \frac{\alpha L_p}{1 + \alpha L_p} \ . \tag{61.3}$$

From this it is important to have light absorbed within a diffusion length in the neutral region from the depletion edge. The overall collection efficiency is thus given by

$$\begin{aligned} \eta &= 1 - \left(1 - \frac{\alpha L_p}{1 + \alpha L_p}\right) \exp\left(-\alpha W_d\right) \\ &= 1 - \frac{\exp\left(-\alpha W_d\right)}{1 + \alpha L_p} \end{aligned} \tag{61.4}$$

where W_d is the depletion layer edge from the surface of the semiconductor. This equation neglects the efficiency loss near the surface.

For the solar cell to deliver maximum power, the entire I-V curve up to the open-circuit voltage, shown in Fig. 61.6, has to be considered. The electrical

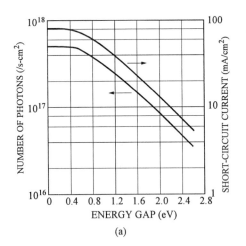

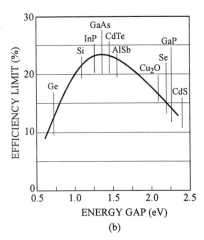

(a) (b)

FIGURE 61.5

As a function of E_g, (a) the theoretical short-circuit current decreases monotonically while (b) the theoretical efficiency has a local peak. (After Ref. 26)

characteristics under irradiation can be analyzed by using the superposition principle on the dark current and the light current,

$$J = J_o \left[\exp\left(\frac{qV}{nkT} \right) - 1 \right] - J_{sc} \quad . \tag{61.5}$$

The pre-exponential term J_o depends on the type of cell. It is a diffusion current for a *p-n* junction cell (see Chapter 1) or a thermionic-emission current for a Schottky-barrier cell (see Chapter 3). n is the ideality factor of the diode, which is affected by recombination and it has a value between 1 and 2. Recombination also increases J_o from its ideal value. The open-circuit voltage V_{oc} can be solved by setting Eq. (61.5) to zero,

$$V_{oc} = \frac{nkT}{q} \ln\left(\frac{J_{sc}}{J_o} + 1 \right) \quad . \tag{61.6}$$

It can be seen that in order to get larger V_{oc}, J_o has to be minimized, and this can be related to the benefit of large E_g. Using E_g as a variable, there is a trade-off between J_{sc} and V_{oc}, and the power output or conversion efficiency is plotted in Fig. 61.5(b). Optimum E_g is found to be around 1.5 eV.

The maximum power in Fig. 61.6 is given by $P_m = V_m I_m$. This condition is obtained by solving for $d(VI)/dV = 0$, giving

$$V_m = \frac{nkT}{q} \ln\left[\frac{(J_{sc}/J_o) + 1}{(qV_m/nkT) + 1} \right] \quad . \tag{61.7}$$

For high P_m, it is important to have a sharp *I-V* curve which is measured by the fill factor defined as

$$FF = \frac{V_m J_m}{V_{oc} J_{sc}} \quad . \tag{61.8}$$

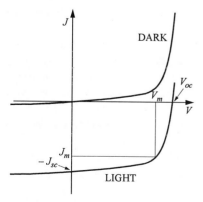

FIGURE 61.6
I-V characteristics of a solar cell in the dark and under irradiation. V_m and J_m are at maximum power output.

The overall conversion efficiency of a solar cell under input power density P_{in} is given by

$$\eta = \frac{V_m J_m}{P_{in}}$$

$$= \frac{FF.V_{oc}J_{sc}}{P_{in}} .$$

(61.9)

Practical solar cells have fill factors of 0.6–0.8, V_{oc} of 0.5–1.0 V, J_{sc} of 10–40 mA/cm², and conversion efficiencies of 5–25%. Qualitatively, the loss of conversion efficiency is due to the following factors:

1. Optical losses due to reflection and shadowing by the metal contact.
2. Loss of generated electron-hole pairs due to carrier recombination in the bulk and at the surface (quantum efficiency less than unity).
3. Unused portion of spectrum $h\nu < E_g$.
4. Waste of excess energy $h\nu > E_g$.

61.4 APPLICATIONS

Solar-energy conversion is attractive because it is inexhaustible and non-polluting. The main drawbacks are high cost and large area needed to collect enough solar power to make an impact on our daily total power demand.[24] Nevertheless, a few solar power stations have been tried around the world to minimize the consumption of fossil fuels. Solar cells currently find unique applications in two particular areas. The first is for generating power for remote and rural areas. The extreme case is for space vehicles and satellites. Other examples are marine navigation lights, remote weather stations, telecommunication links, water pumps for irrigation, etc. Another area of applications is to replace low-power, high-cost batteries in consumer electronic products such as watches, calculators, exposure meters in photographic equipment, etc. It is also more convenient not having to change batteries periodically.

In applications where higher voltages are needed, solar cells can be connected in series. Similarly, they can be connected in parallel to supply larger currents. One approach to reduce the cost of the solar cell is to use a concentrator to focus light onto a smaller area. Actually the overall efficiency can increase with concentrated light intensity up to the equivalent of 100 suns. This is so because J_{sc} increases linearly with light intensity (before excessive heating), and the logarithmic increase of V_{oc} also in turn improves the fill factor.

REFERENCES

1. E. Becquerel, "On electric effects under the influence of solar radiation," *Compt. Rend.*, **9**, 561 (1839).
2. W. G. Adams and R. E. Day, "The action of light on selenium," *Proc. Roy. Soc. London Ser. A*, **25**, 113 (1876).
3. B. Lange, "New photoelectric cell," *Zeit. Phys.*, **31**, 139 (1930).
4. W. Schottky, "Cuprous oxide photoelectric cells," *Zeit. Phys.*, **31**, 913 (1930).
5. L. O. Grondahl, "The copper-cuprous-oxide rectifier and photoelectric cell," *Rev. Mod. Phys.*, **5**, 141 (1933).
6. S. Benzer, "Excess-defect germanium contacts," *Phys. Rev.*, **72**, 1267 (1947).
7. J. I. Pantchechnikoff, "A large area germanium photocell," *Rev. Sci. Instr.*, **23**, 135 (1952).
8. D. M. Chapin, C. S. Fuller and G. L. Pearson, "A new silicon *p-n* junction photocell for converting solar radiation into electrical power," *J. Appl. Phys.*, **25**, 676 (1954).
9. D. C. Reynolds, G. Leies, L. L. Antes and R. E. Marburger, "Photovoltaic effect in cadmium sulfide," *Phys. Rev.*, **96**, 533 (1954).
10. R. Gremmelmaier, "GaAs-photoelement," *Z. Naturforschg*, **10a**, 501 (1955).
11. D. E. Carlson and C. R. Wronski, "Amorphous silicon solar cell," *Appl. Phys. Lett.*, **28**, 671 (1976).
12. R. L. Cummerow, "Photovoltaic effect in *p-n* junctions," *Phys. Rev.*, **95**, 16 (1954).
13. R. L. Cummerow, "Use of silicon *p-n* junctions for converting solar energy to electrical energy," *Phys. Rev.*, **95**, 561 (1954).
14. E. S. Rittner, "Use of *p-n* junctions for solar energy conversion," *Phys. Rev.*, **96**, 1708 (1954).
15. M. B. Prince, "Silicon solar energy converters," *J. Appl. Phys.*, **26**, 534 (1955).
16. J. J. Loferski, "Theoretical considerations governing the choice of the optimum semiconductor for photovoltaic solar energy conversion," *J. Appl. Phys.*, **27**, 777 (1956).
17. F. M. Smits, "History of silicon solar cells," *IEEE Trans. Electron Dev.*, **ED-23**, 640 (1976).
18. E. S. Rittner, "Comments on "History of silicon solar cells"," *IEEE Trans. Electron Dev.*, **ED-24**, 1130 (1977).
19. F. C. Treble, "Solar cells," *IEE Proc.*, **127**, Pt. A, 505 (1980)
20. H. J. Hovel, "Solar cells," in R. K. Willardson and A. C. Beer, Eds., *Semiconductors and semimetals*, Vol. 11, Academic Press, Orlando, 1975.
21. M. A. Green, *Solar cells: Operating principles, technology, and system applications*, Prentice Hall, Englewood Cliffs, 1982.
22. A. L. Fahrenbruch and R. H. Bube, *Fundamentals of solar cells: Photovoltaic solar energy conversion*, Academic Press, New York, 1983.
23. R. H. Bube, "Solar cells," in C. Hilsum, Vol. Ed., T. S. Moss, Ser. Ed., *Handbook on semiconductors*, Vol. 4, North-Holland, Amsterdam, 1981.
24. Z. I. Alferov, "Photovoltaic solar energy conversion," in V. M. Tuchkevich and V. Y. Frenkel, Eds., *Semiconductor physics*, Consultants Bureau, New York, 1986.
25. M. Y. Doghish and F. D. Ho, "A comprehensive analytical model for metal-insulator-semiconductor (MIS) devices: A solar cell application," *IEEE Trans. Electron Dev.*, **40**, 1446 (1993).
26. M. Wolf, "Limitations and possibilities for improvement of photovoltaic solar energy converters. Part I: Considerations for earth's surface operation," *Proc. IRE*, **48**, 1246 (1960).

CHAPTER
62

ELECTROABSORPTION MODULATOR

62.1 HISTORY

There are many types of optical modulators. Some use electrooptical effects in which the polarization or phase of light is changed with an electrical input. One type is based on the electroabsorption effect in which the absorption coefficient is enhanced with an applied field. Only this phenomenon requires semiconductor properties, and it is responsible for the realization of an electroabsorption modulator.

The electroabsorption effect in bulk semiconductors was identified by Franz[1] and Keldysh[2] in 1958, and is known as the Franz-Keldysh effect. It was further analyzed by Tharmalingam[3] and Callaway[4,5] in 1963. The electroabsorption effect in semiconductor bulk material was exploited as an optical modulator by Stillman et al. in 1976.[6] Later, it was discovered that the electroabsorption effect in quantum wells is much more pronounced, by a factor as large as 50. This effect was first studied by Chemla et al. in 1983.[7] The quantum-well electroabsorption modulator was first reported by Wood et al. in 1984.[8] Review articles on the subject can be found in Refs. 9–12.

62.2 STRUCTURE

Whether it is a bulk or quantum-well electroabsorption modulator, the basic form is a *p-i-n* structure as shown in Fig. 62.1. When this *p-i-n* diode is under reverse bias, a large field is developed across the intrinsic layer, without a large leakage current. The active layer can also be sandwiched between Schottky barriers in place of the *p-n* junction. For the case of a quantum-well device, multiple

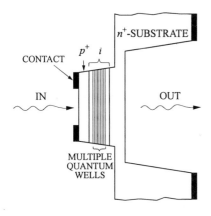

FIGURE 62.1

Schematic structure of an electroabsorption modulator, using multiple quantum wells.

quantum wells are incorporated within the intrinsic layer, each has a typical well dimension of ≈ 100 Å. This small dimension requires MBE or MOCVD growth, on a heavily doped substrate. If the substrate is opaque at the operating wavelength, its majority is then removed by chemical etching to form an optical window, leaving only the thin active layer a few microns thick. To obtain a longer optical path for more effective modulation, light can be passed along the plane of the quantum-well layer, resulting in a waveguide type of optical modulator. Another approach, but less common, is to deposit the active layer onto a reflecting dielectric layer so that the reflected light passes through the active layer twice. The semiconductor material should have direct energy gap for more efficient absorption. Heterostructures studied include GaAs–AlGaAs, InGaAs–InGaAlAs, InGaAs–InAlAs, InGaAs–GaAs, InGaAs–InP, InGaAs–InGaAsP, and GaSb–AlGaSb.

62.3 CHARACTERISTICS

The principle of an electroabsorption modulator is that when light of energy slightly below the absorption edge ($\approx E_g$) is passed through the modulator, absorption is negligible and transmission is high. With an applied field, the absorption edge is reduced, resulting in high absorption and low transmission. This modulation of absorption and transmission by an electrical signal is the electroabsorption effect. This electroabsorption effect in bulk semiconductor is attributed to the Franz-Keldysh effect which is a band-edge broadening phenomenon in the presence of a large electric field, and results in a narrower energy gap. It is often interpreted as photon-assisted tunneling. Consideration including the exciton is in general called the Stark effect. For a quantum well, the absorption edge is given by

$$hv = E_g + E_{e1} + E_{h1} - E_B \qquad (62.1)$$

where E_{e1} and E_{h1} are the first-level subband energies, which are measured from the band edges, and E_B is the exciton binding energy. With increased applied field perpendicular to the plane of the heterointerface, not only E_g changes, but also E_{e1}, E_{h1}, and E_B. These additional shifts that change the absorption edge have been called quantum-confined Stark effect. Of the four terms in Eq. (62.1), the dominant shifts are from E_{e1} and E_{h1}. The absorption-edge shift is shown in the energy-band diagrams of Fig. 62.2. If, however, the applied field is in the direction of the plane of the quantum well, the electroabsorption effect becomes similar to that in a bulk material, and the benefit of the quantum-confined Stark effect is lost.

The transmitted light intensity of an electroabsorption modulator as a function of applied bias is shown qualitatively in Fig. 62.3. For a proper choice of wavelength, a change in absorption coefficient $\Delta\alpha$ modulates the transmitted intensity by a ratio

$$R = \exp(\Delta\alpha L) \quad . \tag{62.2}$$

L is the critical optical path. For light perpendicular to the plane of the quantum wells as shown in Fig. 62.1, L is the summation of the well thicknesses. In most reports L is smaller than 1 μm and the modulation ratios are only around 2. It has been shown that for a much thicker L ($\approx$ 5 μm), modulation of 10 is achievable.[13] For light parallel to the quantum-well plane in the waveguide type of modulator, L becomes the length of the sample, and can be hundreds of microns.[14,15]

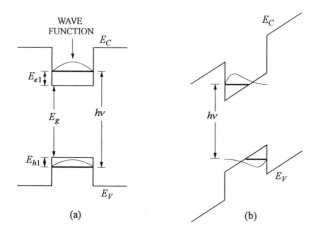

FIGURE 62.2
Energy-band diagrams of a quantum well under (a) zero field and (b) high transverse field. The absorption edge is indicated by the photon energy $h\nu$. The shapes of the wave functions are also skewed by the field.

The electroabsorption effect is inherently a very fast phenomenon. The practical operating speed is limited by the charging of the parasitic and device capacitances. Modulation frequency up to 40 GHz has been realized. There is a trade-off in L between high-frequency limit and the driving voltage. A large L increases the frequency by reducing the device capacitance, but raises the voltage required to obtain an equivalent field.

62.4 APPLICATIONS

An electroabsorption modulator is used primarily to generate light pulses or other light waveforms from a CW light source such as a CW laser. Its advantages are small size, low power, and room-temperature operation. Its technology is compatible with other photonic devices such as LED and laser, so that integration with these on a monolithic chip is possible. The electroabsorption modulator has reasonable high-frequency capability, only slightly below that of a laser. On the other hand, it does not suffer from chirping, which shifts and broadens the output spectrum of a laser at high modulation frequencies. The electroabsorption modulator can also be used as a wavelength-tunable photodetector. The combination of its modulator and detector properties leads to the realization of the self-electrooptic-effect device (SEED, see Chapter 59).

62.5 RELATED DEVICE

62.5.1 Optical Waveguide

An optical waveguide provides optical confinement to a small cross-sectional area such that light can propagate efficiently without losing intensity in the radial directions. This is accomplished by having nonuniform index of refraction in the lateral dimensions. In general the core of the waveguide has material of higher index of refraction, and is surrounded by cladding materials of lower indexes. The most common optical waveguide is the optical fiber, shown in Fig. 62.4(a). For a

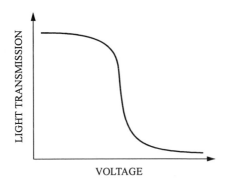

FIGURE 62.3
General characteristics of an electro-absorption modulator, showing the modulation of light transmission by a bias.

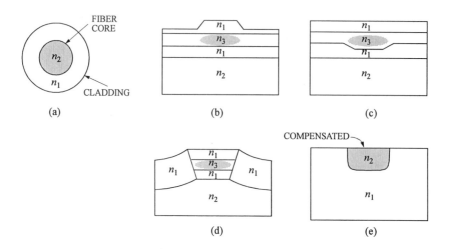

FIGURE 62.4

Cross-sections showing different forms of optical waveguides including (a) optical fiber and (b) – (e) semiconductor waveguides. (b) Ridge structure. (c) Inverted ridge structure. (d) Buried structure. (e) Homojunction with nonuniform doping. Indexes of refraction have values $n_3 > n_2 > n_1$. Light is confined to the grey areas.

semiconductor optical waveguide, the change of index of refraction can be obtained either by heterostructures of different materials or by nonuniform carrier concentrations. Typical examples are shown in Fig. 62.4, with the ridge-type (also called channel- or rib-type) being the most common. The index of refraction can also be increased by lighter doping, as in the case of Fig. 62.4(e), using doping compensation or by carrier injection with bias.[16] The latter is controllable by a voltage, and is called an active waveguide. They can be useful in routing light signals in waveguide switches.

REFERENCES

1. W. Franz, *Z. Naturforschg*, **13a**, 484 (1958).
2. L. V. Keldysh, "The effect of a strong electric field on the optical properties of insulating crystals," *Soviet Phys. JETP*, **34**, 788 (1958).
3. K. Tharmalingam, "Optical absorption in the presence of a uniform field," *Phys. Rev.*, **130**, 2204 (1963).
4. J. Callaway, "Optical absorption in an electric field," *Phys. Rev.*, **130**, 549 (1963).
5. J. Callaway, "Optical absorption in an electric field," *Phys. Rev.*, **134**, A998 (1964).
6. G. E. Stillman, C. M. Wolfe, C. O. Bozler and J. A. Rossi, "Electroabsorption in GaAs and its application to waveguide detectors and modulators," *Appl. Phys. Lett.*, **28**, 544 (1976).
7. D. S. Chemla, T. C. Damen, D. A. B. Miller, A. C. Gossard and W. Wiegmann, "Electroabsorption by Stark effect on room-temperature excitons in GaAs/GaAlAs multiple quantum well structures," *Appl. Phys. Lett.*, **42**, 864 (1983).

8. T. H. Wood, C. A. Burrus, D. A. B. Miller, D. S. Chemla, T. C. Damen, A. C. Gossard and W. Wiegmann, "High-speed optical modulation with GaAs/GaAlAs quantum wells in a *p-i-n* diode structure," *Appl. Phys. Lett.*, **44**, 16 (1984).

9. D. A. B. Miller, D. S. Chemla and S. Schmitt-Rink, "Electric field dependence of optical properties of semiconductor quantum wells: Physics and applications," in H. Haug, Ed., *Optical nonlinearities and instabilities in semiconductors*, Academic Press, Boston, 1988.

10. D. A. B. Miller, D. S. Chemla, T. C. Damen, A. C. Gossard, W. Wiegmann, T. H. Wood and C. A. Burrus, "Electric field dependence of optical absorption near the band gap of quantum-well structures," *Phys. Rev. B.*, **32**, 1043 (1985).

11. D. R. P. Guy, D. D. Besgrove and N. Apsley, "Multiple quantum well NIR optical modulators–A review of the potential for optical signal processing using III-V semiconductors," *Conf. Proc. Adv. Components Active Passive Airborne Sensors*, 3/1 (1990).

12. T. H. Wood, "Multiple quantum well (MQW) waveguide modulators," *J. Lightwave Technol.*, **6**, 743 (1988).

13. T. Y. Hsu, U. Efron, W. Y. Wu, J. N. Schulman, I. J. D'Haenens and Y. Chang, "Multiple quantum well spatial light modulators for optical processing applications," *Opt. Eng.*, **27**, 372 (1988).

14. T. H. Wood, C. A. Burrus, R. S. Tucker, J. S. Weiner, D. A. B. Miller, D. S. Chemla, T. C. Damen, A. C. Gossard and W. Wiegmann, "100 ps waveguide multiple quantum well (MQW) optical modulator with 10:1 on/off ratio," *Electronics Lett.*, **21**, 693 (1985).

15. Y. Noda, M. Suzuki, Y. Kushiro and S. Akiba, "High-speed electroabsorption modulator with strip-loaded GaInAsP planar waveguide," *IEEE J. Ligh. Tech.*, **LT-4**, 1445 (1986).

16. M. A. Mentzer, M. S. Wlodawski, R. G. Hunsperger, J. M. Zavada, H. A. Jenkinson and T. J. Gavanis, "Characterization and optimization of proton implanted optical (1.15 µm) GaAs waveguides," *Proc. SPIE*, **408**, 38 (1983).

CHAPTER
63

THERMISTOR

63.1 HISTORY

The name thermistor comes form thermally sensitive resistor. There is a long history of the observation of temperature-dependent resistance on different materials, dating back to the nineteenth century. Temperature thermometers using metals are called resistance temperature detectors, which are further discussed in Section 63.5.1. Thermistors usually imply semiconducting materials, and they are in two distinct classes: metallic oxides and single-crystal semiconductors. Negative temperature coefficient (NTC) was first observed by Faraday in silver sulfide in 1833. Commercial metallic-oxide thermistors were available in the 1940s. Understanding these oxide thermistors was greatly advanced by the works of Becker et al.[1] and Verwey et al.[2,3] in the late 1940s. Crystal germanium thermistors were studied by Lark-Horovitz et al. in 1946,[4] and by Estermann (also touched on Si),[5] Hung and Gliessman in 1950,[6] by Friedberg in 1951,[7] and later by Fritzsche[8,9] and Kunzler et al.[10] Silicon at low temperature was studied by Morin and Maita[11] and Carlson[12] in 1954–1955, and later by Johnston and Lindberg[13] and Herder et al.[14] Broom also studied a GaAs thermometer in 1958.[15] These crystal thermistors are not in competition with those of metallic oxides since they cover a different temperature range. For more in-depth discussion on thermistors, the readers can refer to Refs. 16 and 17.

63.2 STRUCTURE

Thermistors can be shaped into different forms, depending on the environment whose temperature is to be monitored. These environments include air ambient, liquid, solid surface, and radiation for two-dimensional imaging. Accordingly, the

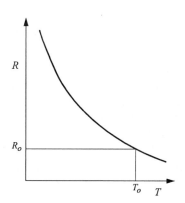

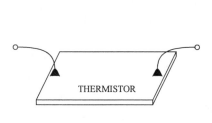

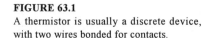

FIGURE 63.1
A thermistor is usually a discrete device, with two wires bonded for contacts.

FIGURE 63.2
General resistance-temperature characteristics of a thermistor.

thermistors can be in the form of beads, discs, washers, rods, and probes. Their sizes, small compared to other kinds of thermometers, are in the range of 0.2 mm to 2 mm. The representative structure and connection is shown in Fig. 63.1. Metallic-oxide thermistors are made from fine powders that are compressed and sintered at high temperature. The most common materials include Mn_2O_3, NiO, Co_2O_3, Cu_2O, Fe_2O_3, TiO_2, and U_2O_3. Single-crystal Ge and Si thermistors are doped to 10^{16}–10^{17} cm^{-3}, with compensating (opposite type) dopants in the order of a few percent.

The range of temperature sensing depends, for the first order, on the energy gap of the materials (larger E_g for higher temperature). Germanium thermistors, which are more common than Si, are used in the cryogenic range of 1–100 K. Silicon thermistors are restricted to below 250 K above which a positive temperature coefficient (PTC) sets in. Metallic-oxide thermistors are used in the range of 200 K to 700 K. For still higher temperatures, thermistors are made from Al_2O_3, BeO, MgO, ZrO_2, Y_2O_3, and Dy_2O_3.

63.3 CHARACTERISTICS

Since a thermistor is basically a resistor, the conductivity is given by the equation

$$\sigma = \frac{1}{\rho} = nq\mu_n + pq\mu_p \ . \tag{63.1}$$

Most thermistors operate in the temperature range in which the ionized concentration (n or p) is a strong function of temperature, given by the form

$$\text{CONCENTRATION} \propto \exp\left(\frac{-E_a}{kT}\right) \tag{63.2}$$

where the activation energy E_a is related to the energy gap and the impurity level. Qualitatively, as temperature goes up, the active doping level goes up, and resistance goes down. The decrease of resistance with temperature is called a negative temperature coefficient (NTC). Empirically, the net resistance can be described by

$$R = R_o \exp\left[B\left(\frac{1}{T} - \frac{1}{T_o}\right)\right] . \tag{63.3}$$

R_o is a reference resistance at T_o, and it is common to take room temperature as the reference. B is the characteristic temperature, and it lies in the range of 2000 to 5000 K. This factor B has actually a temperature dependence but is weak and can be ignored in a first-order analysis. The temperature coefficient of resistance α is given by

$$\alpha \equiv \frac{1}{R}\frac{dR}{dT} = \frac{-B}{T^2} . \tag{63.4}$$

The negative sign designates NTC. The change of resistance is the signal arising from a change of temperature ΔT,

$$\Delta R = R\alpha\Delta T . \tag{63.5}$$

A typical value of α is $\approx -5\%/K$ which is about 10 times more sensitive than the metal resistance temperature detectors. Qualitative characteristics of a thermistor are shown in Fig. 63.2. The resistance of a thermistor falls in the range of 1 kΩ to 10 MΩ.

At higher temperatures or in heavily doped devices, the dopants are fully ionized, and the decrease of mobility due to phonon scattering starts to dominate the temperature dependence. This gives rise to PTC. Generally, PTC is not as sensitive as NTC and is not utilized in thermistors.

Care has to be taken to avoid self-heating of the thermistor from too high a current. On the other hand, this self-heating can turn into advantages for specific applications which will be discussed later. The *I-V* characteristics resulting from self-heating are different with NTC and PTC. In thermistors with NTC, self-heating induces a drop in resistance and starts a positive feedback for a voltage source (Fig. 63.3(a)), leading to higher current. In thermistors with PTC, self-heating increases the resistance and results in negative feedback for a current source (Fig. 63.3(b)). These two curves are similar to negative differential resistance with S- and N-shape characteristics.

63.4 APPLICATIONS

The advantages of thermistors for temperature measurement include low cost, high resolution, and flexibility in size and shape. The absolute value of resistance is very high so that long cables and contact resistance are more tolerable. The slow response (1 ms to 10 s) is not a critical disadvantage in general applications. The applications of thermistors are summarized below.

1. **Temperature sensing and control:** Thermistors provide inexpensive and reliable temperature sensing for a wide temperature range. Practical examples range from fire alarms to tumor detection. For better precision measurement, thermistors are incorporated in a Wheatstone bridge. Sometimes a thermistor is part of an oscillator and the output frequency becomes a function of temperature.

2. **Compensation:** Most resistors and interconnects have PTC. A thermistor with NTC connected in parallel to those components can cancel the temperature dependence.

3. **As a thermal relay and switch:** These use the self-heating effects shown in Fig. 63.3. For example, characteristics with NTC (Fig. 63.3(a)) can be used for voltage regulation, and in delay and timing circuits. Characteristics with PTC can be used for surge protection.

4. **Indirect measurements of other parameters:** When a thermistor is self-heated, or when the thermistor is placed near a heat source, its rate of change in temperature depends on its surrounding. This can be used to monitor other quantities such as liquid level, fluid flow, vacuum level, etc.

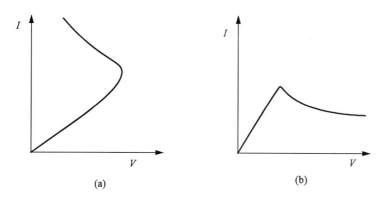

FIGURE 63.3
I-V characteristics of a thermistor with self-heating, (a) with NTC and (b) with PTC.

5. Long-wavelength detector: Application of a thermistor as a long-wavelength photodetector results in one of the thermal detectors–thermistor bolometer, to be discussed in Section 63.5.2.

63.5 RELATED DEVICES

63.5.1 Resistance Temperature Detector

The resistance temperature detector (RTD) is similar to a thermistor except it is made of metals. Because of this, it always has PTC and the α is much smaller, around 0.5%/K. Common metals used are platinum, nickel and copper, with platinum being the most widely used. The range of temperature these materials cover are: Pt, – 200°C to 630°C and up to 900°C with reduced accuracy; Ni, – 80°C to 300°C; and Cu, – 200°C to 200°C. The RTD is either in the form of wound wire or foil. It has a resistance of $\approx 100 \, \Omega$. Because of the low resistance, four-terminal measurement or a bridge circuit is needed to eliminate the connection resistance and the contact resistance.

63.5.2 Thermistor Bolometer

A bolometer is a thermal detector, as opposed to a quantum detector, for radiation. In a bolometer, radiation is absorbed by the material, the temperature is raised, and the resistance is changed and monitored. Metal bolometers were started as early as 1880 with platinum as the most common material. Thermistor bolometers are simply thermistors with a special coating for more efficient light absorption, especially in the far-infrared spectrum. Often a film of 200 Å of bismuth is used for this purpose. Long-wavelength response up to 1000 μm is possible. Metal-oxide thermistor bolometers first appeared in the 1940s. The use of single-crystal Ge and Si thermistor bolometers began in the 1960s. Currently, doped Ge devices are most practical.

In actual operation, since the thermistor bolometer is most suitable for wavelengths longer than a few μm, it is cooled, often down to 4 K, to suppress its own black-body radiation. The heat flow equation is given by

$$\eta P = H\frac{d\Delta T}{dt} + G\Delta T \tag{63.6}$$

where η is the absorption efficiency, P is the radiation power, H is the heat capacity (thermal mass), G is the thermal conductance, and ΔT is the temperature above the cooled environment. The major drawback of any thermal detector is the slow response governed by a thermal time constant

$$\tau = \frac{H}{G} \ . \tag{63.7}$$

For faster response, the heat capacity should be minimized and the thermal conductance maximized. Practical response time is similar to that of a thermistor (1 ms to 10 s).

With a constant current forced through the detector, the signal is a voltage variation given by

$$\Delta V = I \Delta R$$
$$= I \alpha R \Delta T$$
$$= I \alpha R \left(\frac{\eta P}{G} \right)$$

(63.8)

at steady state. Here again current has to be low to avoid self-heating. Measurement accuracy can be improved by incorporating the thermistor bolometer in a Wheatstone bridge. Also, the radiation can be modulated by a chopper in front of the detector to suppress background noise. Examples of applications are burglar and fire alarms, and the detection of terrestrial radiation.

63.5.3 Pyroelectric Detector

The pyroelectric detector is the latest development in the class of thermal detectors for long-wavelength radiation. The structure, as shown in Fig. 63.4, is simply a piece of pyroelectric material sandwiched between two conductive electrodes. These pyroelectric materials are also good insulators. Most common materials are triglycine sulfate, lithium tantalate and lead zironate titanate. The pyroelectric detector relies on some ferroelectric properties–the change of internal dipole moment with temperature, below the Curie temperature. This change of polarization induces a change in the surface charge which appears across the two electrodes. Using the equivalent circuit of Fig. 63.4(b), the

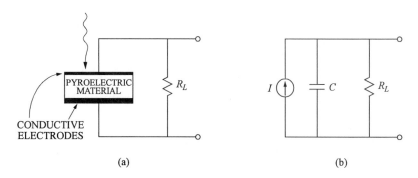

FIGURE 63.4
(a) A pyroelectric detector connected to an external resistor load, and (b) its equivalent circuit.

generation of a charge across the capacitor is supplied by a current source, given by

$$I = AC_p \frac{dT}{dt} \qquad (63.9)$$

where C_p is the pyroelectric coefficient. Typical values for C_p are $\approx 3 \times 10^{-8}$ C/cm^2-K. Equation (63.9) indicates that the signal only responds to a change of temperature, therefore, modulation of the light by a chopper or by other means is required. The current is fed to a large resistor load R_L whose value lies in the range of 10^9–10^{11} Ω. A large R_L optimizes the voltage signal, but the trade-off is reduced speed due to the RC time constant. This voltage signal is usually fed to an FET gate that has a higher input impedance than R_L, in order not to load the voltage.

The advantages of the pyroelectric detector are low cost, flat wavelength response up to 1000 µm, and uncooled operation. Most important, unlike other thermal detectors, the pyroelectric detector can operate at frequencies much higher than the thermal time constant allows. Operation frequencies much higher than 10 kHz are possible although with reduced output.

REFERENCES

1. J. A. Becker, C. B. Green and G. L. Pearson, "Properties and uses of thermistors–Thermally sensitive resistors," *Trans. AIEE*, **65**, 711 (1946).
2. E. J. W. Verwey, P. W. Haayman and F. C. Romeyn, "Semi-conductors with large negative temperature coefficient of resistance," *Philips Tech. Rev.*, **9**, 239 (1947/1948).
3. E. J. W. Verwey, P. W. Haaijman, F. C. Romeijn and G. W. van Oosterhout, "Controlled-valency semiconductors," *Phillips Res. Rep.*, **5**, 173 (1950).
4. K. Lark-Horovitz, A. E. Middleton, E. P. Miller and I. Walerstein, "Electrical properties of germanium alloys. I. Electrical conductivity and Hall effect," *Phys. Rev.*, **69**, 258 (1946).
5. I. Estermann, "Semiconductors as low temperature thermometers," *Phys. Rev.*, **78**, 83 (1950).
6. C. S. Hung and J. R. Gliessman, "The resistivity and Hall effect of germanium at low temperatures," *Phys. Rev.*, **79**, 726 (1950).
7. S. A. Friedberg, "Germanium-indium alloys as low temperature resistance thermometers," *Phys. Rev.*, **82**, 764 (1951).
8. H. Fritzsche, "Electrical properties of germanium semiconductors at low temperature," *Phys. Rev.*, **99**, 406 (1955).
9. H. Fritzsche and K. Lark-Horovitz, "The electrical properties of germanium semiconductors at low temperatures," *Physica*, **20**, 834 (1954).
10. J. E. Kunzler, T. H. Geballe and G. W. Hull, "Germanium resistance thermometers suitable for low-temperature calorimetry," *Rev. Sci. Instr.*, **28**, 96 (1957).
11. F. J. Morin and J. P. Maita, "Electrical properties of silicon containing arsenic and boron," *Phys. Rev.*, **96**, 28 (1954).
12. R. O. Carlson, "Electrical properties of near-degenerate boron-doped silicon," *Phys. Rev.*, **100**, 1075 (1955).
13. W. V. Johnston and G. W. Lindberg, "Silicon resistance thermometers," *Bull. Am. Phys. Soc.*, **10**, 719 (1965).
14. T. H. Herder, R. O. Olson and J. S. Blakemore, "Diffused semiconductor low temperature thermometers," *Rev. Sci. Instr.*, **37**, 1301 (1966).

15. R. F. Broom, "A low-temperature resistance thermometer using *p*-type gallium arsenide," *J. Sci. Instr.*, **35**, 467 (1958).
16. E. D. Macklen, *Thermistors*, Electrochemical Pub., Scotland, 1979.
17. H. B. Sachse, *Semiconducting temperature sensors and their applications*, Wiley, New York, 1975.

CHAPTER
64

HALL
PLATE

64.1 HISTORY

The Hall plate is also called the Hall generator. Its principle is based on the Hall effect which was discovered by E. Hall in 1879 on gold foil.[1] Since the Hall effect is very weak in metals, it was not practical until the realization of good semiconductor materials. Pearson first studied applying the Hall effect to detect magnetic field using germanium in 1948.[2] Commercial Hall plates were available as discrete sensors in the mid-1950s and as integrated sensors around 1970. For more details on the Hall plate, the readers can refer to Refs. 3 and 4.

64.2 STRUCTURE

The schematic structure of a Hall plate is shown in Fig. 64.1(a). It is simply a piece of semiconductor with four contacts. The Hall plate exists in one of three forms: (1) discrete bar, (2) thin film deposited on a supporting substrate, and (3) epitaxial film on an opposite-type substrate (Fig. 64.1(b)). The doping of the semiconductor should be minimized to maximize the Hall voltage as V_H is inversely proportional to the concentration. Common materials used are InSb, InAs, GaAs, Si, and Ge. Compound semiconductors are attractive for their high mobilities, while Si is more popular for integrated sensors because of its more mature technology.

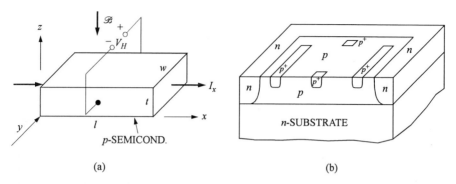

FIGURE 64.1
(a) Schematic representation of a Hall plate. (b) Structure of a Hall plate using an epitaxial layer. Surrounding n-regions form isolation.

64.3 CHARACTERISTICS

The Hall effect is the generation of a Hall voltage V_H when a piece of semiconductor is biased with a current and placed under a magnetic field that is orthogonal to the current flow. The Hall effect will be given here without proof, and the readers are referred to Appendix B8 for more details. The generated Hall voltage, assuming the Hall factor $r_H = 1$ and p-type semiconductor, is given by

$$V_H = R_H w J_x \mathcal{B} = w \mathcal{E}_x \mu \mathcal{B} \; , \qquad (64.1)$$

$$R_H \equiv \frac{1}{qp} \; . \qquad (64.2)$$

Note that to obtain a large signal, the carrier concentration must be minimized. This is the reason that the Hall effect is much more pronounced in semiconductors than in metals.

    The sensitivity of a Hall plate has various definitions, depending on whether it is current-related, voltage-related, or power-related. These are given by $\partial V_H / I \partial \mathcal{B}$, $\partial V_H / V \partial \mathcal{B}$, $\partial V_H / P \partial \mathcal{B}$, or simply $\partial V_H / \partial \mathcal{B}$. In any case, an efficient Hall plate should have low carrier concentration and small plate thickness t. Typical sensitivity is ≈ 200 V/A-T, but values up to 1000 V/A-T are possible.

    The length l should have a minimum value of $3 \times w$ so that the geometry effect does not diminish the Hall voltage substantially. Physically, it means that if l is too short compared to w, carriers reach the opposite terminal without a sufficient chance to be deflected to the sides to develope the full Hall voltage. This effect is accounted for by the geometric correction factor ($G < 1$) such that

$$V_H = G R_H w J_x \mathcal{B} = G w \mathcal{E}_x \mu \mathcal{B} \; . \qquad (64.3)$$

Obviously, G is a function of the l/w ratio, and is plotted in Fig. 64.2.

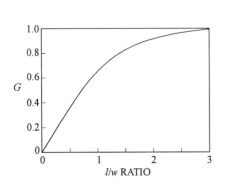

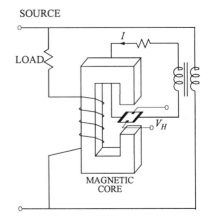

FIGURE 64.2

Geometric correction factor as a function of the l/w ratio. (After Ref. 4)

FIGURE 64.3

Schematic diagram for a Hall wattmeter. The bias current is proportional to the source voltage, and the magnetic field is proportional to the load current.

As a magnetic-field sensor, it is critical that V_H be proportional to $\mathscr{B}$ linearly and that V_H go to zero when $\mathscr{B} = 0$. In practice, there is often an offset voltage when $\mathscr{B} = 0$. The source of this offset is from both a geometric effect and a piezoelectric effect. The geometric effect is due to the fact that the two Hall taps are not exactly opposite to each other. If there is a misalignment Δx between them in the direction of the current flow, the offset voltage is given by

$$\Delta V_H = \mathscr{E}_x \Delta x \quad . \tag{64.4}$$

The piezoelectric effect is the generation of a voltage when a piezoelectric material is under stress. This is especially severe for thin-film Hall plates. Offset can also be due to piezoresistivity and temperature variation. The offset voltage can be eliminated by connecting two or four Hall plates together in a configuration that cancels the individual offset voltages, or by adding a fifth terminal as a control gate to inject current for compensation.

64.4 APPLICATIONS

The Hall plate is attractive for its low cost, simple structure, and compatibility with integrated-circuit technologies. Its main applications can be grouped into two functions–direct magnetic-field sensing, and position and motion sensing. An equipment to measure the magnet-field strength is called a magnetometer or gaussmeter. Special applications are pickup heads for magnetic tapes (including the magnetic strips in credit cards), magnetic disks, and bubble memories. Also, since a DC or AC current produces a magnetic field in the vicinity of the wire, the current can be detected indirectly. This is advantageous compared to the use of a regular ammeter, which has to be inserted in series with the wire. In the second group of applications, when a magnet is attached to an object, its position, displacement, and angular sensing is possible. Examples of applications in angular sensing are the tachometer, DC brushless motor, and for timing automobile engines for spark plugs. A contactless switch can be made from proximity sensing when a magnet is moved in and out of a Hall plate. Examples are switches for computer keyboards and closed-loop security systems. One application that is outside the above two areas is the analog multiplier. Since the Hall voltage is proportional to two independent quantities–the bias current and the magnetic field, it is an analog multiplier (Hall multiplier) of the two. This can be used as a power meter to monitor simultaneously voltage and current delivered to a load. The schematic diagram for such a wattmeter is shown in Fig. 64.3.

64.5 RELATED DEVICES

64.5.1 Magnetoresistor

The magnetoresistor is based on the magnetoresistive effect which is an increase of resistance in the presence of a magnetic field. The magnetoresistive effect arises from two independent mechanisms: (1) a physical magnetoresistive effect and (2) a geometric magnetoresistive effect. The first effect arises because carriers do not move with an identical velocity. The Hall voltage is set up to balance some average velocity, and carriers with different velocities from the average deviate from a straight path, as shown in Fig. 64.4(a). These longer paths

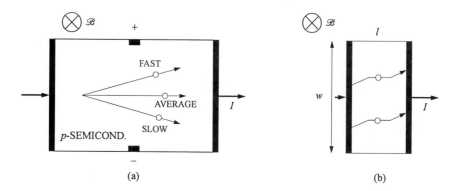

(a) (b)

FIGURE 64.4

(a) Physical magnetoresistive effect is caused by carriers having non-uniform velocities. (b) Geometric magnetoresistive effect occurs in samples with small l/w ratios. Carriers near the contacts move at an angle to the applied field.

lead to increased resistance. The geometric magnetoresistive effect occurs in samples with small l/w ratios. In this case, the full Hall voltage is not developed to balance the Lorentz force (Eq. (64.3) and Fig. 64.4(b)), and carriers near the contacts move at an angle, called the Hall angle, to the applied field. The longer path again leads to higher resistance. A magnetoresistor maximizing this effect is shown in Fig. 64.5 where conductive shorts are added and the structure is equivalent to many Hall plates in series, each having a small l/w ratio.

64.5.2 Magnetodiode

A magnetodiode is a p-i-n diode which contains a region of high recombination rate in the intrinsic layer (Fig. 64.6). When a p-i-n diode is under forward bias, the intrinsic layer has high concentrations of electrons and holes, and the current is controlled by recombination. Under a magnetic field, both electrons and holes are deflected toward the surface having a high recombination rate, and the recombination current is increased. A practical magnetodiode can be made from an SOS film where the bottom Si–Al$_2$O$_3$ interface naturally has a higher density of defects, for detection of a magnetic field parallel to the surface.

64.5.3 Magnetotransistor

A magnetotransistor, also called a magnistor, usually implies a bipolar transistor with multiple collectors whose current difference depends on the magnetic field.[3,5] These bipolar transistors can be lateral or vertical structures. Each can also operate in the deflection mode or injection-modulation mode. This combination of four schemes are represented by the top views and cross-sections

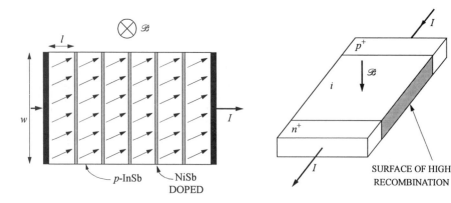

FIGURE 64.5
A magnetoresistor utilizing the geometric effect. NiSb shorts divide the sample into regions of small l/w ratio.

FIGURE 64.6
A magnetodiode is a p-i-n diode having one surface of high defect density.

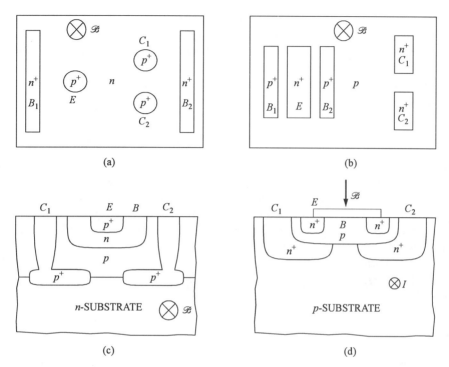

FIGURE 64.7

(a) (b) Top views and (c) (d) cross-sections of magnetotransistors. (a) Lateral magnetotransistor with deflection mode. Two terminals for the base are for driving the carriers through the base to higher velocity. (b) Lateral magnetotransistor with injection-modulation mode. (c) Vertical magneto-transistor with deflection mode. (d) Vertical magnetotransistor with injection-modulation mode. E = emitter, B = base, C = collector.

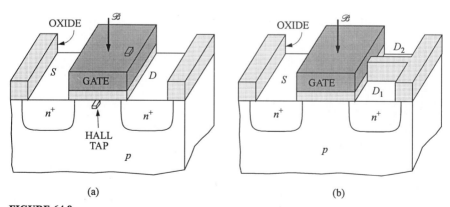

FIGURE 64.8

(a) A MAGFET using the inversion layer as the Hall plate. (b) A split-drain MAGFET.

in Fig. 64.7. In the deflection mode of operation, the injected carriers are deflected in the base by the magnetic field, and they get collected unevenly by the two collectors. In the injection-modulation mode, the base has two contacts and it acts as a Hall plate. Under a magnetic field, the base has unequal potential locally and it causes uneven emitter injection, also leading to uneven collector currents.

64.5.4 Magnetic-Field-Sensitive Field-Effect Transistor (MAGFET)

The MAGFET usually implies a MOSFET structure. It can operate in two modes. The structure in Fig. 64.8(a) is similar to a Hall plate where the sample thickness t is replaced by the induced inversion layer, and the output is the Hall voltage. The split-drain MAGFET, shown in Fig. 64.8(b), has two drains. Under a transverse magnetic field, carriers in the MOSFET channel are deflected toward one side, and the difference between the two drain currents is monitored.

64.5.5 Carrier-Domain Magnetic-Field Sensor

A carrier domain is a plasma of electrons and holes. It can be created, for example, by turning on a p-n-p-n structure (thyristor). A vertical carrier-domain magnetic-field sensor is shown in Fig. 64.9. Due to the symmetry of the device, the carrier domain is formed at the center. Under a magnetic field, the carrier domain is shifted laterally, imposing a change of currents in I_{p1} and I_{p2}, and in I_{n1} and I_{n2}. Other variations of horizontal and circular carrier-domain magnetometers have been studied.

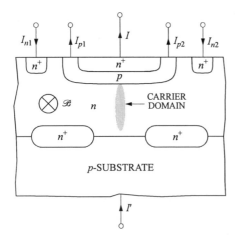

FIGURE 64.9
A carrier-domain magnetometer. Under a magnetic field, the carrier domain shifts laterally, and the differences as $I_{p1} - I_{p2}$ and $I_{n1} - I_{n2}$ are detected.

64.5.6 Magnetostrictive Transducer

The magnetostrictive effect is the change of material dimension under a magnetic field. The magnetic field can be detected indirectly by sensing the deformation. These magnetic transducers are made from nickel alloys and ferrites, and are used as acoustic-wave devices.

REFERENCES

1. E. H. Hall, "On a new action of the magnet on electric currents," *Am. J. Math.*, **2**, 287 (1879).
2. G. L. Pearson, "A magnetic field strength meter employing the Hall effect in germanium," *Rev. Sci. Inst.*, **19**, 263 (1948).
3. H. P. Baltes and R. S. Popovic, "Integrated semiconductor magnetic field sensors," *Proc. IEEE*, **74**, 1107 (1986).
4. S. Middelhoek and S. A. Audet, *Silicon sensors*, Academic Press, London, 1989.
5. S. Kordic, "Integrated silicon magnetic-field sensors," *Sensors Actuators*, **10**, 347 (1986).

CHAPTER
65

STRAIN GAUGE

65.1 HISTORY

A strain gauge (or strain gage) can measure the deformation of an attached object by monitoring its resistance change. When the strain gauge is elongated, two effects can change its resistance–a geometric effect due to longer length and smaller cross-section, and a piezoresistive effect due to a change in resistivity under strain. The latter effect only occurs in semiconductors and is much stronger than the geometric effect.

The change of metal resistance under strain was first realized by Lord Kevin in 1856. Strain gauges using carbon first appeared in the early 1930s. The metal-wire gauge started to be used in the late 1930s. When printed circuit-board technology emerged, in the 1950s, the metal-foil gauge began to dominate. The piezoresistive effect in the semiconductors Si and Ge was discovered by Smith in 1954.[1] This was subsequently pursued by Adams,[2] Mason and Thurston,[3] and Morin et al.[4] For a more in-depth study of the strain gauge, the readers can refer to Refs. 5–8.

65.2 STRUCTURE

A strain gauge can be made of metal and semiconductor material. The metal-foil gauge now replaces most of the older metal-wire gauge. It is typically laid out in a meander structure as shown in Fig. 65.1(a), and is bonded to an insulating backing material. The most common metals are copper-nickel alloys such as constantan. The semiconductor strain gauge can be a discrete bonded bar (Fig. 65.1(b)), a diffused or ion-implanted structure (Fig. 65.1(c)), or deposited

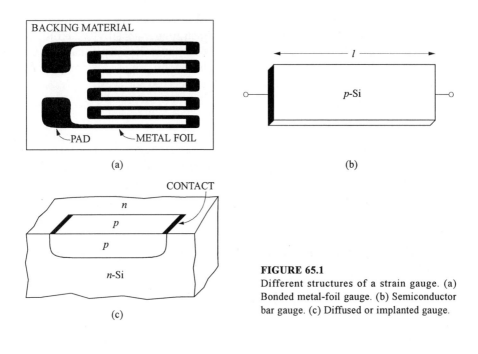

(a)

(b)

(c)

FIGURE 65.1
Different structures of a strain gauge. (a) Bonded metal-foil gauge. (b) Semiconductor bar gauge. (c) Diffused or implanted gauge.

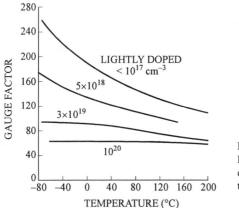

FIGURE 65.2
In semiconductors such as Si, the gauge factor decreases with doping level, but the temperature dependence is lessened. (After Ref. 9)

thin film. The diffused/implanted type is most common because it is compatible with integrated-circuit technology. The semiconductor gauge is usually made of p-type material because it has better sensitivity and linearity than n-type. It is heavily doped in the 10^{20} cm^{-3} range. Although higher doping decreases the gauge factor (discussed later in more detail), it improves another critical performance–the temperature independence. This trade-off is demonstrated in Fig. 65.2. Almost all commercial semiconductor strain gauges are made of silicon, although germanium has also been studied. Between semiconductor gauges and metal gauges, the former have much higher sensitivity and higher resistance for reduced power consumption, but the latter have advantages of less temperature dependence, better linearity, higher strain range (4% compared to 0.3%), and better flexibility for attaching them to curved surfaces.

65.3 CHARACTERISTICS

Since the measurand of the strain gauge is resistance, we first derive the relationship between strain and resistance. Strain S is caused by stress and is the ratio of the change of longitudinal linear dimension to its original length,

$$S = \frac{\Delta l}{l} \; . \tag{65.1}$$

The resistance of a bar or film with length l and cross-sectional area A is given by the equation

$$R = \frac{\rho l}{A} \; . \tag{65.2}$$

When the gauge is under strain, all three parameters l, A and resistivity ρ change, and

$$\begin{aligned}
\frac{\Delta R}{R} &= \frac{\Delta l}{l} - \frac{\Delta A}{A} + \frac{\Delta \rho}{\rho} \\
&= \frac{\Delta l}{l} \left(1 - \frac{\Delta A/A}{\Delta l/l} + \frac{\Delta \rho/\rho}{\Delta l/l} \right) \\
&= S(1 + 2v + P_z) \; .
\end{aligned} \tag{65.3}$$

Here v is the Poisson's ratio, and it relates the longitudinal strain to the transverse strain (linear dimension t perpendicular to l) by

$$v = \frac{-\Delta t/t}{\Delta l/l} \; . \tag{65.4}$$

The factor of two comes from

$$\frac{\Delta A}{A} \approx 2\frac{\Delta t}{t} \; . \tag{65.5}$$

P_z is a measure of the piezoresistive effect which distinguishes a metal gauge ($P_z = 0$) from a semiconductor gauge. It is given by

$$P_z = \frac{\Delta \rho/\rho}{\Delta l/l} = C_p Y \; . \tag{65.6}$$

C_p is the longitudinal piezoresistive coefficient and Y is the Young's modulus. The sum

$$G = 1 + 2v + P_z = \frac{\Delta R/R}{S} \qquad (65.7)$$

is called the gauge factor. It typically has a value of under 2 for metals, but for semiconductors it falls in the range of 50–200 and shows improved sensitivity by two orders of magnitude.

In practical operations, strain gauges are incorporated as part of a Wheatstone bridge so that a change in resistance can be detected accurately. The relationship between strain and resistance has to be calibrated. It is usually nonlinear and can be approximated by

$$\frac{\Delta R}{R} = C_1 S + C_2 S^2 \ . \qquad (65.8)$$

Also, calibration requires consideration of the temperature dependence of resistivity. It is especially severe for semiconductor gauges. A thermometer mounted near the strain gauge can provide additional data for adjustment. A better approach is to incorporate two or four similar strain gauges in the Wheatstone bridge for automatic temperature compensation, with only one arm exposed to the strain. Other considerations are resistance changes due to self-heating by the measurement bias, and changes due to the photoconductive effect when the gauge is exposed to light.

A strain gauge can be used for many useful mechanical transducers through the Hooke's law,

$$S = \frac{T}{Y} \qquad (65.9)$$

where T is the stress. Once the strain is measured, the pressure, force, weight, etc. can be deduced if the Young's modulus of the strained material is known. These applications will be discussed in the following section.

65.4 APPLICATIONS

Currently, the strain gauge is the most popular mechanical transducer. The applications of strain gauges can be divided into two types: (1) direct measurements of strain, deformation, and displacement, and (2) indirect measurements of pressure, force, weight, and acceleration through the Hooke's law. Major applications are listed below.

1. Direct strain measurements: For structural maintenance such as buildings and bridges, it is sometimes necessary to monitor the minute deformation such as bending, stretching, compression, and cracking. Figure 65.3(a)

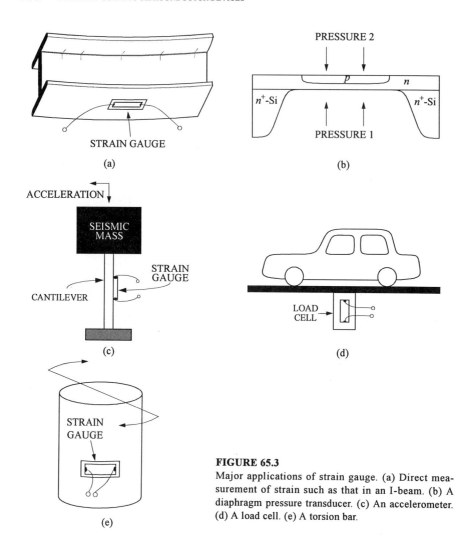

STRAIN GAUGE

(a)

PRESSURE 2

p n

n^+-Si n^+-Si

PRESSURE 1

(b)

ACCELERATION

SEISMIC MASS

STRAIN GAUGE

CANTILEVER

(c)

LOAD CELL

(d)

STRAIN GAUGE

(e)

FIGURE 65.3
Major applications of strain gauge. (a) Direct measurement of strain such as that in an I-beam. (b) A diaphragm pressure transducer. (c) An accelerometer. (d) A load cell. (e) A torsion bar.

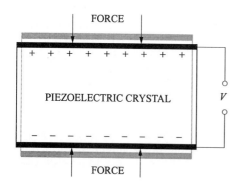

FORCE

+ + + + + + + +

PIEZOELECTRIC CRYSTAL V

− − − − − − − −

FORCE

FIGURE 65.4
In a piezoelectric transducer, strain produces charge and vice versa.

shows a strain gauge to monitor bending in an I-beam. Another area of application is in spacecraft and automotive bodies. The monitoring of strain is also mandatory for stress analysis. Measurement of displacement also falls into this category.

2. Pressure transducer: A popular pressure transducer for ambient and fluid is the diaphragm type shown in Fig. 65.3(b), made of a diffused gauge from silicon. The built-in diffused gauge monitors the deflection of the diaphragm under a differential pressure. The diaphragm is formed by chemical etching of the silicon substrate. This transducer is used successful in the medical field and the automotive field.

3. Accelerometer: Acceleration can be measured via the force (Fig. 65.3(c)) since

$$\text{force} = \text{mass} \times \text{acceleration} . \tag{65.10}$$

Acceleration perpendicular to the cantilever is monitored by bending, and that parallel to the strain gauge is by compression. Velocity can also be deduced from the integration of acceleration. Similar structures can be used to sense shock, impact, and vibration.

4. Load cell: The schematic of a load cell is shown in Fig. 65.3(d). The weight is deduced from compression or bending of a shaft. The load cells are used as heavy-duty truck scales as well as lightweight household electronic scales.

5. Torque transducer: The torque of a shaft (torsion bar) can be measured as shown in Fig. 65.3(e).

65.5 RELATED DEVICE

65.5.1 Piezoelectric Strain Gauge

A piezoelectric strain gauge is based on piezoelectricity, an effect that generates a charge when a piezoelectric crystal is under strain.[10] In operation it is very similar to a piezoresistive strain gauge except voltage is measured rather than resistance. Structurally, the piezoelectric crystal is sandwiched between two conductive electrodes as shown in Fig. 65.4. Under stress, the crystal is strained, and a charge or voltage is generated. The process is also reciprocal in that when a voltage is applied, strain and mechanical movement is induced. Good examples for this reciprocal process are piezoelectric microphone, where sound pressure produces voltage, and piezoelectric speaker, where voltage produces strain or mechanical movement.

The equations governing piezoelectricity are

$$S = \gamma T + dF , \tag{65.11}$$

$$\mathcal{D} = dT + \varepsilon F \tag{65.12}$$

where γ is the compliance and F is the force. These state that strain can be created by stress (T) and electric field, and charge (proportional to displacement $\mathcal{D}$) can be created by the same factors also. The piezoelectric charge constant d is given by

$$d = \frac{Q \ \text{per area}}{\text{pressure}} \ . \tag{65.13}$$

A piezoelectric transducer is self-generating in that no bias is required, and is dynamic in nature since charge is drained away gradually. For this reason, piezoelectric transducers are more useful in dynamic systems such as accelerometers, loudspeakers, microphones, phonograph pickups, ultrasonic cleaners, and for sensing shock, vibration, and impact. Other applications include the generation of ignition spark and the positioning of a laser mirror. (Static application is possible only in the strain-producing mode.) Common piezoelectric materials are quartz, zinc oxide, tourmaline, ceramics such as lead zirconate titanate and barium titanate. One disadvantage of the piezoelectric transducer is that the source impedance is high, so the first-stage amplifier that senses the voltage must have superior input impedance. Another useful piezoelectric transducer is the interdigital transducer for acoustic-wave devices (Chapter 66).

REFERENCES

1. C. S. Smith, "Piezoresistance effect in germanium and silicon," *Phys, Rev.*, **94**, 42 (1954).
2. E. N. Adams, "Elastoresistance in *p*-type Ge and Si," *Phys. Rev.*, **96**, 803 (1954).
3. W. P. Mason and R. N. Thurston, "Use of piezoresistive materials in the measurement of displacement, force, and torque," *J. Acou. Soc. Am.*, **29**, 1096 (1957).
4. F. J. Morin, T. H. Geballe and C. Herring, "Temperature dependence of the piezoresistance of high-purity silicon and germanium," *Phys. Rev.*, **105**, 525 (1957).
5. A. L. Window and G. S. Holister, Eds., *Strain gauge technology*, 2nd Ed., Elsevier Science, England, 1992.
6. R. L. Hannah and S. E. Reed, Eds., *Strain gage users' handbook*, Elsevier Science, England, 1992.
7. C. C. Perry and H. R. Lissner, *The strain gage primer*, 2nd Ed., McGraw-Hill, New York, 1962.
8. S. Middelhoek and S. A. Audet, *Silicon sensors*, Academic Press, London, 1989.
9. W. P. Mason, "Use of solid-state transducers in mechanics and acoustics," *J. Audio Eng. Soc.*, **17**, 506 (1969).
10. A. J. Pointon, "Piezoelectric devices," *IEE Proc.*, **129**, Pt. A, 285 (1982).

INTERDIGITAL TRANSDUCER

66.1 HISTORY

The interdigital transducer (IDT) is a surface-acoustic-wave (SAW) transducer. It converts an electrical signal to a mechanical SAW and vice versa, based on the piezoelectric effect. The piezoelectric effect was discovered by two brothers J. Curie and P. Curie in 1880. Shortly afterwards, surface acoustic waves were predicted by Rayleigh in 1885, and are now often referred to as Rayleigh waves. The IDT was invented by White and Voltmer in 1965,[1] replacing the older SAW transducers such as the wedge transducer and the comb transducer. In most applications, two IDTs are used, one in converting an electrical input signal to a SAW that propagates through a piezoelectric medium, and another in converting the SAW back to an electrical signal. These packages of two IDTs plus the medium are called SAW devices. The success of IDT led to the dominance of SAW devices over the bulk-acoustic-wave (BAW) devices. For more details on IDT and SAW devices, the readers can refer to Refs. 2–4.

66.2 STRUCTURE

The interdigital transducer consists mainly of interleaved metal fingers on a piezoelectric substrate as shown in Fig. 66.1. Alternating fingers are connected to one of two rails. The most critical dimension is the finger period d which determines the SAW wavelength λ. The linewidth l and space s of the fingers are usually similar, and are equal to $\lambda/4$. One common metal is aluminum, with a thickness typically in the 0.1–0.3 μm range; but it should, in any case, be less than $\lambda/2$. The overlap of the metal fingers W can vary even within one IDT. This is

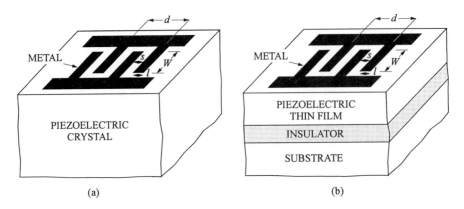

(a)   (b)

FIGURE 66.1
Structures of interdigital transducer (a) on bulk piezoelectric substrate, and (b) on deposited piezoelectric thin film. For the thin-film version, a thin ground plane may be used beneath the piezoelectric. An alternative is having the piezoelectric film deposited over the metal layer.

especially common in the output IDTs for signal processing, and such a structural approach is called apodisation. The number of finger pairs N depends on the application. Large N produces more efficient coupling between the electrical signal and the SAW, but the bandwidth also suffers, as discussed later. Common piezoelectric materials are quartz, $LiNbO_3$, ZnO, $BaTiO_3$, $LiTaO_3$ and lead zirconate titanates. These materials are good insulators. Less common piezoelectric materials are semiconductors such as CdS, CdSe, CdTe, and GaAs. A prerequisite of the piezoelectric effect is some degree of lattice order, and so crystalline or polycrystalline structures are required. For thin-film IDTs, the piezoelectric film thickness is in the order of the SAW wavelength, and ZnO is the most common material, deposited by sputtering. The piezoelectric thin film can be either under (Fig. 66.1(b)) or over the metal layer.

66.3 CHARACTERISTICS

The main function of an interdigital transducer is to interchange energy between an electrical signal and a SAW. To help visualize a SAW, one good analogy is the propagating ripple generated by throwing a stone into calm water, or by a moving boat. In a solid, a SAW is due to the deformation of the structure, or strain. Microscopically, atoms in a crystal are displaced from their equilibrium positions, and the restoring force, similar to that of a spring, is proportional to their displacement. For this reason, a SAW is also called an elastic wave. A SAW differs from a BAW in that it travels along the surface, with most of the energy confined within a wavelength of the surface. A SAW can be separated into a longitudinal wave where the atom displacement is parallel to the direction of

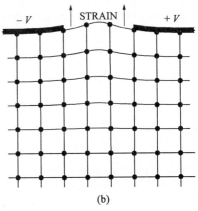

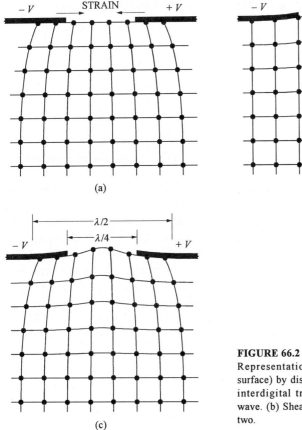

FIGURE 66.2
Representation of SAW (parallel to the surface) by displacement of atoms under an interdigital transducer. (a) Longitudinal wave. (b) Shear wave. (c) Composite of the two.

wave propagation, and a shear wave where this displacement is perpendicular to the wave propagation (Fig. 66.2). Whether the generated SAW is predominately a longitudinal wave or a shear wave depends on the piezoelectric properties and the crystal orientation. Figure 66.3 shows that in the piezoelectric effect, the relationship between polarization of the charge and strain depends on the crystal structure.

The velocity of the SAW propagation v depends on the elastic stiffness and the mass density of the medium. For all the practical piezoelectric materials mentioned above, it falls in the range of $1-10\times10^5$ cm/s, with most around 3×10^5 cm/s. The frequency response of an IDT centers at a frequency of

$$f_o = \frac{v}{\lambda} = \frac{v}{d} .$$

(66.1)

A small finger period d can therefore accommodate high-frequency operation, in spite of the low velocity. The frequency response of an IDT is given by

$$R(f) = C_1 \frac{\sin X}{X} \qquad (66.2)$$

where

$$X = N\pi \left(\frac{f-f_o}{f_o}\right) . \qquad (66.3)$$

This frequency response is shown in Fig. 66.4. The dependence of bandwidth on the finger-pair number is evident here.

The attractiveness of a SAW device is its low characteristic velocity, five orders of magnitude slower than an electromagnetic wave. Very large delay can be obtained with a reasonable size. A typical delay is ≈ 3 μs/cm. Slow velocity also translates into small wavelength and physical dimension (Eq. (66.1)). It is rather interesting to note that the state-of-the-art microwave circuit of ≈ 5 GHz requires the lateral transistor dimension be scaled to ≈ 0.3 μm, and such frequency of operation for an IDT also requires similar linewidth and space dimension. Other advantages of SAW devices include low attenuation, low dispersion (velocity variation with frequency), easy access of SAW, and compatibility with integrated-circuit technology. BAW devices lose some of these

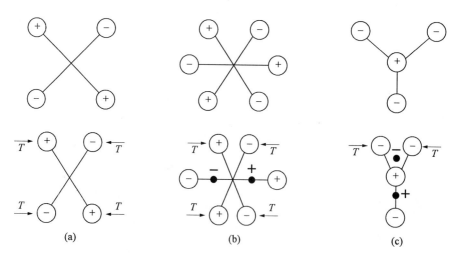

FIGURE 66.3

Origin of piezoelectric effect, showing polarization due to stress T. (a) Stress produces no polarization in a symmetric crystal. (b) Polarization parallel to stress. (c) Polarization perpendicular to stress. (After Ref. 2)

advantages. They are used only for frequencies below 10 MHz, which require unreasonably large SAW devices.

66.4 APPLICATIONS

The applications of SAW devices where IDTs play a critical role lie in two main areas: signal processing and sensing. For signal processing, the most common applications are delay lines and bandpass filters. The SAW devices for these purposes are shown in Fig. 66.5. Absorbers at the ends are needed because the SAW generated by an IDT is bidirectional. The absorber also costs a 3 dB loss of transmitted power. Other functional SAW devices include pulse-compressor (chirp filter), oscillator, resonator, convolver, correlator, etc. These SAW devices

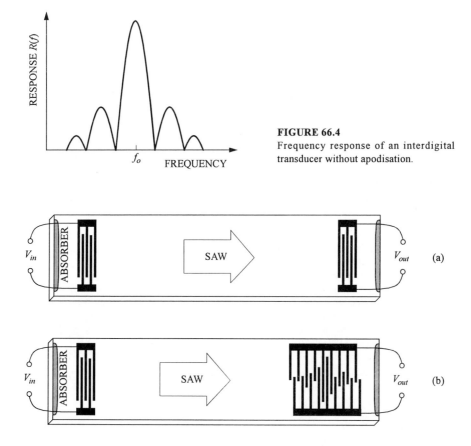

FIGURE 66.4
Frequency response of an interdigital transducer without apodisation.

FIGURE 66.5
Examples of SAW devices for signal processing. (a) Delay line. (b) Bandpass filter.

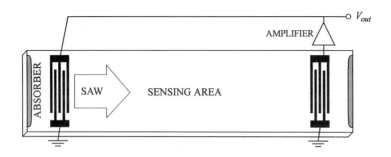

FIGURE 66.6
A typical SAW sensor is a delay-line oscillator where the oscillation frequency is monitored.

are useful in communication, radar, and broadcasting equipment such as TV receivers. A SAW sensor usually is composed of a delay-line oscillator as shown in Fig. 66.6.[5] The SAW velocity in the sensing area between the two IDTs is critical for the oscillation frequency, which is monitored to detect physical quantities such as temperature, moisture, pressure, acceleration, and stress. Detection of gas flow by sensing the cooling effect is possible. Also, if the central area is coated with a special absorbant, a SAW sensor is sensitive to certain chemicals and gases such as H_2, SO_2, NO_2, and NH_3.[6] When two IDTs are deposited on a surface, nondestructive testing on this surface for cracks and other defects can be performed. Finally, since SAW is a mechanical wave, light can be diffracted from the surface like a grating. This property is used in diagnostics, optical modulators, and light deflectors.

REFERENCES

1. R. M. White and F. W. Voltmer, "Direct piezoelectric coupling to surface elastic waves," *Appl. Phys. Lett.*, **7**, 314 (1965).
2. A. J. Pointon, "Piezoelectric devices," *IEE Proc.*, **129**, Pt. A, 285 (1982).
3. D. P. Morgan, *Surface-wave devices for signal processing*, Elsevier, New York, 1991.
4. S. Datta, *Surface acoustic wave devices*, Prentice-Hall, Englewood Cliffs, 1986.
5. A. D'Amico, "SAW sensors," *Sensors Actuators*, **17**, 55 (1989).
6. J. W. Grate, S. J. Martin and R. M. White, "Acoustic wave microsensors," *Anal. Chem.*, **65**, Part I, 940A, Part II, 987A (1993).

ION-SENSITIVE
FIELD-EFFECT
TRANSISTOR

67.1 HISTORY

The ion-sensitive field-effect transistor (ISFET) is one of the most common chemically sensitive field-effect transistors (CHEMFETs), which are covered more completely in Section 67.5. The ISFET was proposed and demonstrated by Bergveld, first in a brief communication in 1970,[1] followed by a more complete paper in 1972.[2] The inclusion of a reference electrode in contact with the electrolyte was reported by Matsuo and Wise in 1974,[3] and since then such an electrode is considered to be an integral part of an ISFET. The historical development of the ISFET is nicely captured in Ref. 4. For more details pertaining to the ISFET as well as other CHEMFETs, the readers can refer to Ref. 5.

67.2 STRUCTURE

Since the function of the ISFET is to detect ions, an electrolyte containing the ions has to be in contact with the device. In this arrangement, the electrolyte becomes the gate of a MOSFET (Fig. 67.1), replacing the conventional poly-Si or metal gate. The contact to the electrolyte gate is provided by a reference electrode, typically Ag-AgCl. The gate dielectric is a critical part of the structure, and often a multilayered gate dielectric is used. The dielectric in contact with the silicon substrate is usually a thermally grown oxide to achieve good interfacial properties. A barrier layer on top of SiO_2 is sometimes necessary to prevent ions from penetrating to the SiO_2–Si interface. The top layer of dielectric is chosen to

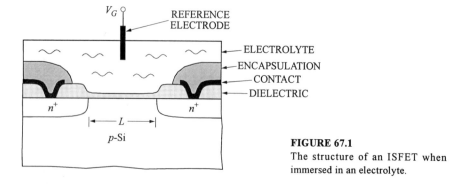

FIGURE 67.1
The structure of an ISFET when immersed in an electrolyte.

maximize the sensitivity as well as the selectivity of the ions of interest. Examples of these dielectrics, besides SiO_2, are Si_3N_4, Al_2O_3, TiO_2, and Ta_2O_5. A major concern in the design of an ISFET is the encapsulation which should prevent ions from penetrating to the rest of the circuitry. Typical dimensions of the channel length L and width W are in tens to hundreds of microns.

67.3 CHARACTERISTICS

To understand the operation of the ISFET, it is best to start with a conventional MOSFET (see Chapter 19). The electrical characteristics can be roughly divided into two regimes–linear and saturation, and their I-V characteristics are described by

$$I_{lin} = \frac{\mu C_i W (V_G - V_T) V_D}{L} \, , \tag{67.1}$$

$$I_{sat} = \frac{\mu C_i W}{2L} (V_G - V_T)^2 \, . \tag{67.2}$$

The criterion separating these regimes is given by the drain bias

$$V_{D, sat} = V_G - V_T \, . \tag{67.3}$$

An important parameter for any FET is the threshold voltage V_T. It is the gate voltage required to turn the transistor "on," and is given by

$$V_T = V_{FB} + 2\psi_B + \frac{\sqrt{2\varepsilon_s q N (2\psi_B)}}{C_i} \tag{67.4}$$

where

$$V_{FB} = \phi_m - \phi_s \qquad (67.5)$$

is the flat-band voltage. A metal work function ϕ_m is used since a metal gate is assumed. These $I\text{-}V$ characteristics are shown qualitatively in Fig. 67.2.

These equations are applicable to an ISFET with the exception of Eq. (67.5). The difference is explained with the energy-band diagrams in Fig. 67.3 at flat-band conditions. For an ISFET, it can be seen that

$$V_{FB} = \phi_{sol} - \phi_s + \psi_i - \psi_{sol} \qquad (67.6)$$

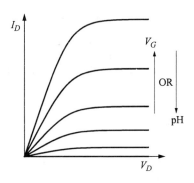

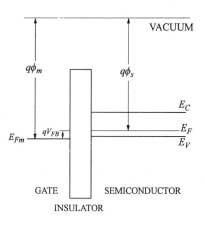

FIGURE 67.2
$I\text{-}V$ characteristics of the ISFET as a function of gate (reference electrode) voltage or pH concentration.

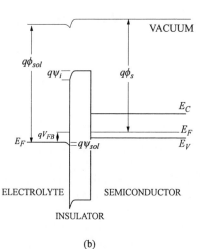

(a) (b)

FIGURE 67.3
Energy-band diagrams at flat-band conditions for (a) a conventional MOSFET, and (b) an ISFET in contact with an electrolyte.

where ψ_i is the surface potential of the insulator due to a dipole layer at the dielectric side of the electrolyte–dielectric interface, and ψ_{sol} is the potential drop at the solution side of the same interface. Furthermore, ψ_{sol} is insensitive to ions. The detection of ions relies on the change of ψ_i with ion concentration. In effect, ions get deposited on the insulator surface and change ψ_i, V_{FB}, V_T, and the FET current. The presence of ions is equivalent to a change of gate bias, as shown in Fig. 67.2. In practice, the ISFET is biased with a constant source-to-drain current I_D, and the change of gate voltage to sustain such current is the indicator. Examples of ions that are detectable are H^+ (pH), Na^+, K^+, Ca^{++}, Cl^-, F^-, NO_3^-, and CO_3^{--}. Typical values are 20–40 mV/pH for pH sensing.

67.4 APPLICATIONS

Compared to other electrochemical ion sensors, the ISFET has the advantages of small size, fast response, low output impedance, and low cost due to integrated-circuit technology. It is now commercially available. The main applications, currently, are in the biomedical field. For example, in blood and urine analysis, components such as pH, Na^+, K^+, Ca^{++}, Cl^-, glucose, urea, and cholesterol can be monitored. The limitations of long-term reliability and irreversibility are important concerns. Because of the nature in these applications, the ISFET sensors are mostly disposable.

67.5 RELATED DEVICES

67.5.1 Enzyme Field-Effect Transistor

The enzyme field-effect transistor (ENFET) is an ISFET with a gel deposited on top of the gate dielectric. This gel layer contains an immobilized enzyme, which reacts with ions to release a by-product such as H^+. The ions are detected indirectly since it is the by-product that changes the electrical characteristics. Chemicals to be detected in this manner include urea, penicillin, and glucose.

67.5.2 Ion-Controlled Diode

While the ISFET is similar to a MOSFET, an ion-controlled diode is similar to a gated diode (Fig. 67.4).[6] Here instead of using current as a monitor, the capacitance of a p-n junction is measured. By a proper choice of voltage on the reference electrode, the top Si surface can be inverted and the effective area of the junction is much increased, giving a larger capacitance. If ions are collected at the electrolyte–insulator interface, they change the Si surface potential and the surface inversion layer disappears, resulting in a much reduced capacitance. In practical operation, the capacitance is monitored at constant biases, or a change in reference electrode voltage is monitored to give the same capacitance. One advantage of this structure is that contacts are made at the back surface and encapsulation is less of a problem.

67.5.3 Semiconducting-Oxide Sensors

Gas sensors can be made from metal-oxide semiconductors such as SnO_2, ZnO, Fe_2O_3, and TiO_2, with SnO_2 being the most common.[7,8] These resistive gas sensors are either made from powders sintered at high temperature, or from deposition on some substrate by evaporation or sputtering. Often some noble metal such as Pd or Pt is added to improve their sensitivity. When exposed to a gas such as H_2, O_2, or CO, the resistance changes. The sensitivity of these semiconducting-oxide sensors can usually be improved by operating them above room temperature, in the range of 200–400°C. In spite of the non-ideal reproducibility, long-term stability, sensitivity, and selectivity, these metal-oxide gas sensors have a substantial commercial market because they are very inexpensive and simple to use. This resistive gas sensor has been applied to monitor home-utility gas leak.

The mechanism responsible for the change of resistance is believed to be due to reactions at the grain boundaries. A few models have been proposed. The most popular one states that these boundaries are oxygen rich, and potential barriers are formed that deplete the carriers surrounding them, and impede the current flow across them (Fig. 67.5). The gas to be detected can neutralize the adsorbed oxygen, reduce the barrier, and reduce the resistance. Another possible mechanism is, instead of barriers, the grain boundaries form a mesh of conductive paths. The gas reacts in these boundaries and affects the conduction.

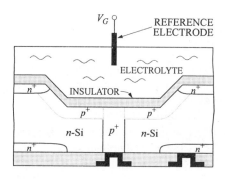

FIGURE 67.4
Schematic diagram of an ion-controlled diode with electrolyte.

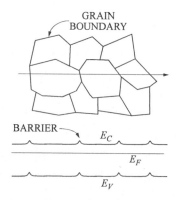

FIGURE 67.5
In a semiconducting-oxide sensor, the grain boundaries give rise to potential barriers. Energy-band diagram is shown for n-type material.

67.5.4 Catalytic-Metal Sensors

There is a group of sensors that utilize the change of work function of catalytically active metals when exposed to certain gases.[9] These devices are in the forms of:

1. MOSFET
2. MOS capacitor
3. MIS tunnel diode
4. Schottky-barrier diode

For a MOSFET, the catalytic metal is used as the gate material. The change in its work function changes the threshold voltage and, thus, the MOSFET current. For the MOS capacitor, since the capacitance varies with the gate bias (see Fig. 14.4), a change in work function causes a shift in the *C-V* curve. For the other two devices, the MIS tunnel diode and the Schottky-barrier diode, the barrier heights are modified and the forward currents are affected accordingly.

The catalytic metals can be Pd, Pt, Ir, and Ni, with Pd being, by far, the most successful. The most effective detection using this property is of hydrogen gas. The mechanism is believed to be due to the adsorption of H_2 gas by the catalytic metal. H_2 molecules then dissociate into H^+ ions and diffuse to the metal interface, which is in contact with the rest of the device, and a dipole layer is formed. This dipole layer changes the effective work function of the metal.

67.5.5 Open-Gate Field-Effect Transistor

The open-gate field-effect transistor (OGFET) was invented in the same year as the ISFET (1970) but is much less understood and less practical. Its main differences from an ISFET are the absence of the reference electrode and its use to detect gas, rather than ions in an electrolyte.

67.5.6 Adsorption Field-Effect Transistor

The adsorption field-effect transistor (ADFET) is an OGFET with a gate oxide reduced to less than 5 nm. This thin gate dielectric is used to improve sensitivity.

Both the OGFET and the ADFET, because of the open-gate configuration, present problems in electrical interference and instability. Two more devices were invented, which have a gate shielding the channel region. These are the surface-accessible field-effect transistor (SAFET) with an overhanging gate, and the suspended-gate field-effect transistor (SGFET) with a mesh gate.

67.5.7 Charge-Flow Transistor

The structure of the charge-flow transistor[10] is shown in Fig. 67.6. The gate has two regions of different conductivity. The middle portion over most of the channel

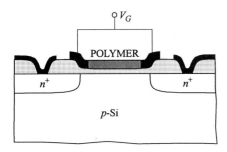

FIGURE 67.6

In a charge-flow transistor, the center of the gate is composed of material of high resistivity and is chemically sensitive.

is composed of a polymer or a glass layer of high resistivity, and is chemically sensitive. When a step voltage is applied to the outside edge of the gate, there is a time delay in the drain current until a complete channel is formed. This time delay is a function of the resistivity of the gate. When this charge-flow transistor is exposed to certain gases, the resistivity of the gate changes, and the change in the time delay can be used to detect the presence of the gas. This device has been used to detect humidity, gas, and smoke.

REFERENCES

1. P. Bergveld, "Development of an ion-sensitive solid-state device for neurophysiological measurements," *IEEE Trans. Biom. Eng.*, **MBE-17**, 70 (1970).
2. P. Bergveld, "Development, operation, and application of the ion-sensitive field-effect transistor as a tool for electrophysiology," *IEEE Trans. Biom. Eng.*, **MBE-19**, 342 (1972).
3. T. Matsuo and K. D. Wise, "An integrated field-effect electrode for biopotential recording," *IEEE Trans. Biom. Eng.*, **MBE-21**, 485 (1974).
4. A. Sibbald, "Chemical-sensitive field-effect transistors," *IEE Proc.*, **130**, 233 (1983).
5. M. J. Madou and S. R. Morrison, *Chemical sensing with solid state devices*, Academic Press, Boston, 1988.
6. C. Wen, T. C. Chen and J. N. Zemel, "Gate-controlled diodes for ionic concentration measurement," *IEEE Trans. Electron Dev.*, **ED-26**, 1945 (1979).
7. P. T. Moseley, "Materials selection for semiconductor gas sensors," *Sens. Actu. B*, **6**, 149 (1992).
8. S. R. Morrison, "Selectivity in semiconductor gas sensors," *Sens. Actu.*, **12**, 425 (1987).
9. I. Lundstrom, M. Armgarth and L. Petersson, "Physics with catalytic metal gate chemical sensors," *Crit. Rev. Solid State Mat. Sci.*, **15**, 201 (1989).
10. S. D. Senturia, C. M. Sechen and J. A. Wishneusky, "The charge-flow transistor: A new MOS device," *Appl. Phys. Lett.*, **30**, 106 (1977).

APPENDIX

A

SELECTED NON-SEMICONDUCTOR DEVICES

APPENDIX

A1

VACUUM TUBES

Vacuum tube is a generic name for the group of devices whose electrodes are surrounded by vacuum. The main types are the diode tube, triode tube, tetrode tube, and pentode tube, with the number of electrodes being 2, 3, 4, and 5, respectively. The diode tube was introduced in 1904, and the first amplifier, the triode tube, was realized in 1906. Vacuum tubes were the workhorses in the early radio and TV era. This changed abruptly when the solid-state transistor was invented in 1947. Today, vacuum tubes are obsolete except for some very specialized applications.

In a vacuum tube, the cathode, being the electron emitter, is the most critical electrode. Furthermore, heating is required to achieve sufficient electron emission for practical current levels. Typically the cathode temperature is in the range of 1000 K to 2600 K. The cathode can be of two forms, filament or cylinder. The filament type is self-heated by passing a current through it, and it is usually made of tungsten or thoriated tungsten. A cylinder cathode is indirectly heated by a buried heater inside (Fig. A1.1(a)), and it is usually made of nickel or nickel alloys, coated with barium oxide or strontium oxide. The physical structure of a vacuum tube, using a triode tube as an example, is shown in Fig. A1.1(b).

The operation of a vacuum tube is based on the thermionic emission of electrons from metal to vacuum, so all vacuum tubes have at least two electrodes, a cathode to emit electrons and a plate or anode for their collection. Electrical characteristics of a diode tube are shown in Fig. A1.2(a). The maximum current that can be extracted from the cathode by a thermionic-emission process is given by

$$J_{max} = A_E T^2 \exp\left(\frac{-q\phi}{kT}\right) \tag{A1.1}$$

where A_E is a characteristic constant of the cathode material, and ϕ is its work function. Of more interest is operation at a lower plate voltage V_{PL}. Generally, when current conduction is within a medium of low conductivity, and a vacuum is an extreme case, the current-carrying carriers modify the electric field and space-charge-limited (SCL) current results (see Appendix B4). All vacuum tubes operate in this regime. The diode tube current is given by the Child-Langmuir law

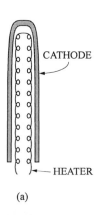

CATHODE

HEATER

(a)

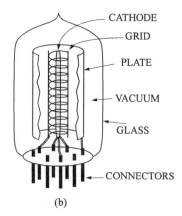

CATHODE

GRID

PLATE

VACUUM

GLASS

CONNECTORS

(b)

FIGURE A1.1
(a) Structure of an indirectly heated cathode. (b) Construction of a triode tube, representing typical appearance of a vacuum tube.

$$J = \frac{4\varepsilon_o}{9L^2} \left(\frac{2q}{m^*}\right)^{1/2} V_{PL}^{3/2} \tag{A1.2}$$

where L is the spacing between the cathode and the plate.

The triode tube is the first three-terminal amplifier, with a grid electrode placed between the cathode and the plate (Fig. A1.2(b)). The plate current can be described by

$$I_P = C_1 \left(\mu V_{GR} + V_{PL}\right)^{3/2} \tag{A1.3}$$

where μ is called the amplification factor and V_{GR} is the grid voltage.

A tetrode tube has an additional screen grid (Fig. A1.2(c)), in an attempt to reduce the large grid-plate capacitance in a triode tube. The resulting characteristics, however, have a peculiar dip due to secondary emission from the plate. This phenomenon is eliminated in a pentode tube, by a suppressor placed between the plate and the screen electrode (Fig. A1.2(d)). The characteristics of the pentode tube are similar to those of an FET.

The downfall of vacuum tubes was due mainly to their high power consumption from the necessary heating, and also their huge physical size, especially in light of the advanced integrated-circuit technology.

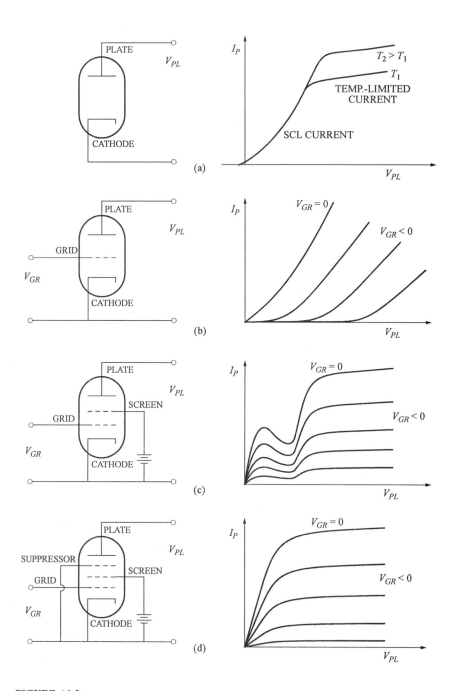

FIGURE A1.2
Schematic representations and electrical characteristics of (a) a diode tube, (b) a triode tube, (c) a tetrode tube, and (d) a pentode tube.

APPENDIX

A2

SUPERCONDUCTING DEVICES

Superconductivity was discovered by K. Onnes in 1911. A commonly accepted model for this phenomenon was presented by Bardeen, Cooper and Schrieffer (BCS model) in 1957, and they were awarded the Nobel prize in 1972 for their contribution. In this appendix, a discussion on superconductivity will be followed by a description of the Josephson junction and the superconducting quantum interference device (SQUID).

Superconductivity, as the name implies, is the state of zero resistance attainable below a critical temperature T_c (Fig. A2.1). For elementary metals and alloys, this T_c is typically below ≈ 20 K. In the 1980s, after much effort, the so-called high-temperature (high-T_c) superconductors were successfully realized, breaking the liquid-nitrogen barrier (77 K) to above 100 K. The newer materials are metallic oxide compounds such as YBaCuO. Zero resistance naturally implies zero electric field inside the superconductor. Another property is the expulsion of a magnetic field (Fig. A2.2). This phenomenon is not a consequence of zero resistivity in the Maxwell equations, and is called the Meissner effect. Microscopically, a magnetic field actually penetrates slightly into the superconductor, decaying exponentially with a characteristic depth. With an increasing applied magnetic field, the penetration depth increases and eventually superconductivity is destroyed. This critical magnetic field is a function of temperature (Fig. A2.3(a)), given by

$$\mathscr{H}_c(T) = \mathscr{H}_c(0)\left[1 - \left(\frac{T}{T_c}\right)^2\right] . \tag{A2.1}$$

Superconductors with these characteristics are called type-I. In a type-II superconductor, there are two critical magnetic fields (Fig. A2.3(b)). Between $\mathscr{H}_{c1}$ and $\mathscr{H}_{c2}$, zero resistance is preserved, but a magnetic field can exist inside in the form of fine threads, also called vortices. Above $\mathscr{H}_{c2}$, the superconducting properties again disappear. Consideration of the magnetic field has an interesting implication on the superconducting current (supercurrent). The supercurrent pattern follows that of the magnetic field penetration so it is a surface current only, different from a normal conductor. The existence of a critical magnetic field

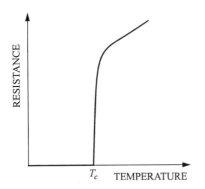

FIGURE A2.1
Resistance-temperature characteristics
showing the transition of superconductivity.

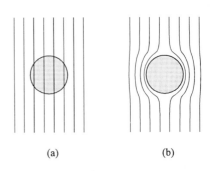

FIGURE A2.2
Magnetic-field pattern surrounding (a) a
normal conductor and (b) a superconductor.

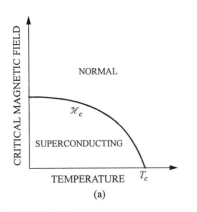

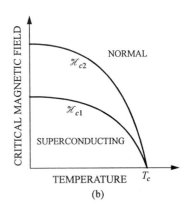

FIGURE A2.3
Critical magnetic field as a function of temperature for (a) type-I superconductor and (b) type-II
superconductor.

means that the supercurrent cannot exceed a level which produces such a
magnetic field value. The supercurrent therefore also has a limit.

Superconductivity is a quantum-mechanical phenomenon, and is explained
in the following by the formation of Cooper pairs, leading to an energy gap. The
resistance of a normal conductor is due mainly to phonon scattering and impurity
scattering. At a temperature below T_c, electrons rearrange themselves into Cooper
pairs. The formation mechanism is phonon related. Qualitatively, one electron
interacts with the lattice to produce a local deformation (phonon), and a second
electron is attracted to this phonon to form a Cooper pair. The energy of this pair
is lower than the individual electrons, by an amount called the energy gap
parameter Δ (Fig. A2.4). The BCS theory also suggests that free electrons have

this energy Δ above the Fermi level. As a result, an energy gap E_g of 2Δ appears. Since any scattering event must involve the exchange of energy, the existence of an energy gap inhibits scattering of the Cooper pairs. This is different from a normal conductor where an electron can gain any amount of energy. This energy gap has a value of $\approx 4kT_c$, and is on the order of a few meV for a T_c of ≈ 10 K. The existence of such an energy gap has been confirmed by optical absorption spectra.

In a Cooper pair, the two electrons have opposite spins and momenta. Their wavefunctions are also coherent such that they can be treated as one entity. In fact, in the superconducting state, all Cooper pairs and thus the whole superconductor can be described by a single wavefunction. This has an interesting consequence when the superconductor is formed into a ring. The phase difference around the ring must be a multiple of 2π. This leads to flux quantization

$$\Phi_r = \frac{N_i \pi \hbar}{q} \equiv N_i \Phi_o \qquad (A2.2)$$

where Φ_r is the total magnetic flux passing through the ring. This phenomenon is utilized in the SQUID.

The potential applications of superconductors are enormous. Having the property of zero energy loss, they will be useful for, to name a few examples, power transmission, electromagnets, and motors. Another area of application is IC interconnects for achieving minimum RC delay. The limitations of superconductors are a required low-temperature environment and a low-current capability.

The Josephson effect was named after its inventor who did this work in 1962 as a student, and he was awarded the Nobel prize in 1973. A Josephson junction simply consists of two conductors sandwiching a thin barrier layer of less than 20 Å, with at least one of the conductors being a superconductor. For the discussion here, both are assumed superconductors (Fig. A2.5). Since the barrier is thin, the two superconductors communicate and their wavefunctions overlap to give the following relationship

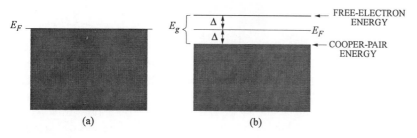

FIGURE A2.4
Energy-band diagrams for (a) a normal metal and (b) a superconductor.

$$J = J_c \sin\theta \tag{A2.3}$$

where θ is the phase difference, and J_c is the critical current density. Equation (A2.3) gives the maximum supercurrent for which the voltage across the Josephson junction V is zero. This is known as the DC Josephson effect. A second Josephson equation relates the phase difference to the applied voltage as follows:

$$\frac{d\theta}{dt} = \frac{2qV}{\hbar} \; . \tag{A2.4}$$

Substitution of Eq. (A2.4) into Eq. (A2.3) gives

$$J = J_c \sin\left[\left(\frac{2qV}{\hbar}\right)t\right] \; . \tag{A2.5}$$

The current is now a time-varying function and is known as the AC Josephson effect. The frequency of oscillation is controlled by the voltage, and is given by

$$f = \frac{2qV}{\hbar} \; . \tag{A2.6}$$

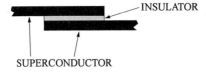

INSULATOR

SUPERCONDUCTOR

FIGURE A2.5
Schematic structure of a Josephson junction.

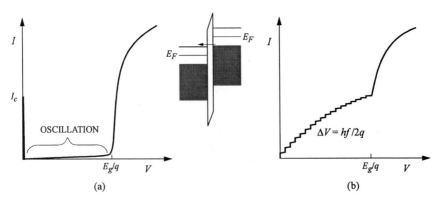

(a)   (b)

FIGURE A2.6
(a) DC characteristics of a Josephson junction, and (b) when exposed to microwave radiation. Insert is the energy-band diagram when bias is comparable to the energy gap.

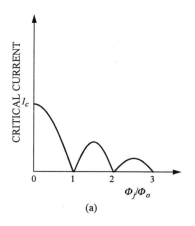 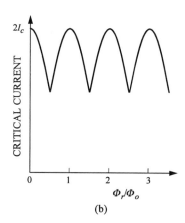

(a)　　　　　　　　　　　　　　　(b)

FIGURE A2.7

Critical current as a function of magnetic flux for (a) a Josephson junction and (b) a SQUID. Notice that since $\Phi_r \gg \Phi_j$ for the same magnetic field, the horizontal scales are vastly different.

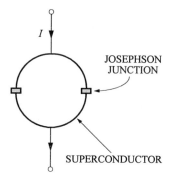

FIGURE A2.8

Schematic circuit diagram of a SQUID.

The DC characteristics of a Josephson junction are shown in Fig. A2.6(a). With $V = 0$, the supercurrent depends on θ and it has a maximum value of J_c. In the range $0 < V < E_g/q$, oscillation occurs but the DC value is near zero. Only a small DC tunneling current exits. At $V \approx E_g/q$, tunneling current rises rapidly. This condition is depicted by the energy-band diagram in the insert which shows that energy states are available for tunneling, analogous to a tunnel diode.

The Josephson junction has many applications. The DC switching characteristics of Fig. A2.6(a) can be used to implement logic and memory. The AC Josephson effect can be used not only as a microwave generator, but also as a detector. When exposed to a microwave of frequency f, the characteristics are shown in Fig. A2.6(b). There is a current step whenever

$$V = \frac{N_i hf}{2q} \tag{A2.7}$$

is satisfied. This quantization has been used as a standard for the ratio of the fundamental constants h/q, and also for the unit volt since frequency can be measured accurately.

As in the case of a superconductor, a magnetic field decreases the critical current of a Josephson junction. This critical current is a function of magnetic flux through the junction Φ_j, as shown in Fig. A2.7(a), and is given by

$$I_c(\mathscr{H}) = I_c(0) \frac{\sin(\pi\Phi_j/\Phi_o)}{\pi\Phi_j/\Phi_o} . \qquad (A2.8)$$

Such characteristics can presumably be used to detect a magnetic field. It will be shown in the following that the sensitivity can be much improved in a SQUID (superconducting quantum interference device).

A SQUID consists of two Josephson junctions connected in a ring as shown in Fig. A2.8. The magnetic field dependence of the total I_c is given by

$$I_c(\mathscr{H}) \approx 2I_c(0) \cos(\pi\Phi_r/\Phi_o) \qquad (A2.9)$$

and is shown in Fig. A2.7(b). Here Φ_r is the total magnetic flux through the ring. Comparing Fig. A2.7(a) to Fig. A2.7(b), the sensitivity to magnetic field of a SQUID over a Josephson junction is precisely the ratio of the ring area to the junction area. The SQUID is the most sensitive magnetic-field detector that exists. It has been used to detect waves coming from biological activities such as the brain and the heart. Because of its high sensitivity, a SQUID can also detect indirectly voltage or current, via the magnetic field they generate. Similarly, it can be used to implement logic, memory, and amplifying circuits, again with magnetic field as the input.

INDUCTOR AND TRANSFORMER

When a current flows in a wire, magnetic field is produced around the wire. This magnetic field has a circular pattern surrounding the wire, and the direction is determined by the right-hand rule as indicated in Fig. A3.1(a). The field strength also decays radially from the wire. An inductor is a wire bent in a particular shape designed to concentrate and store the magnetic energy efficiently. It is some form of a coil that gives the maximum magnetic field for a fixed current (Fig. A3.1(b)).

The impedance of an inductor is given by

$$Z_L = j\omega L \ . \tag{A3.1}$$

The term j indicates that the impedance is imaginary. For a sinusoidal waveform, the current leads the voltage by 90°. Equation (A3.1) also shows that the inductor has zero impedance at DC, and it is only active for a time-varying signal. For a variable current passing through an inductor, the voltage across it is given by

$$V = L\frac{dI}{dt} \ . \tag{A3.2}$$

This means that if there is a sudden change in current, the inductor develops some voltage to oppose the current surge. An inductor can thus stabilize the current passing through it, just as a capacitor can stabilize the voltage across it. The magnetic energy stored in an inductor is given by

$$E = \frac{LI^2}{2} \ . \tag{A3.3}$$

A single-layer coil like that in Fig. A3.1(b) is the simplest form of inductor. Its inductance can be approximated by

$$L = \frac{\pi\mu r^2 N^2}{l} \tag{A3.4}$$

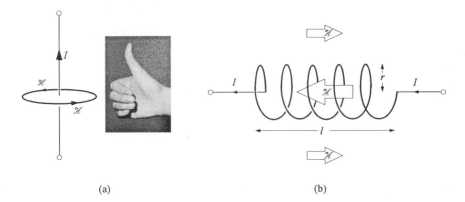

(a)   (b)

FIGURE A3.1
(a) Direction of magnetic field generated from a current is determined by the right-hand rule. (b) The structure of an inductor coil and its magnetic-field pattern.

where N is the number of turns and μ is the permeability of the medium. The inductance can also be increased by inserting a magnetic core of large permeability inside the winding. Practical materials are iron, nickel, and ferrites. The quality factor Q and power factor PF of an inductor are given by

$$Q = \frac{|Z_L|}{R_s} = \frac{\omega L}{R_s} \; , \tag{A3.5}$$

$$PF = \frac{R_s}{\sqrt{R_s^2 + (\omega L)^2}} = \frac{1}{\sqrt{1 + Q^2}} \; . \tag{A3.6}$$

Because of its physical structure, an inductor cannot be fabricated effectively in an integrated circuit. Although thin-film structures have been examined, they are not sufficient. IC designs usually avoid using inductors. Whenever inductors are unavoidable, they are used as discrete components attached to the circuit board, thereby consuming much space.

If a core is used in an inductor, there exists a loss mechanism due to an eddy current. This current circulates in a plane perpendicular to the magnetic flux, and is induced by changing current or magnetic flux. This eddy current results in power loss and heating. It can be minimized by laminating the inductor core, so that the thin layers of conductors are isolated by insulators.

An inductor in series can be used as a choke to limit current fluctuation. As such, it may be used to stabilize power supplies. Inductors are useful components in filters and resonant circuits. Since an inductor can generate a large magnetic field at its center, there is a group of devices that use a combination of inductor coil and magnet to transduce voltage or current into mechanical movement and

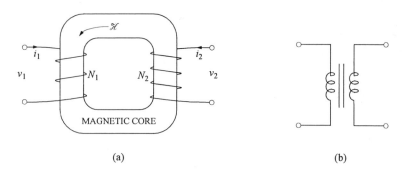

FIGURE A3.2
(a) Schematic structure of a transformer and (b) its circuit symbol.

vice versa. These include the loudspeaker and microphone, motor and power generator. Inductors are also the main ingredients of a transformer which is to be discussed next.

A common transformer consists of two inductor coils linked together by a donut-shaped magnetic core, as shown in Fig. A3.2(a). If the primary coil and the secondary coil have N_1 and N_2 turns of winding, respectively, the following relationship can be observed,

$$\frac{v_2}{v_1} = \frac{i_1}{i_2} = \frac{N_2}{N_1} \ . \tag{A3.7}$$

Lower case v and i represent small-signal amplitudes. The above equation also leads to

$$v_1 i_1 = v_2 i_2 \tag{A3.8}$$

which implies a power efficiency of 100%. In practice, due to eddy currents and hysteresis (nonlinear $\mathcal{H}$-$\mathcal{B}$ relationship), loss occurs, producing heat. A laminated core is often utilized to minimize the eddy current loss. The effective impedance of the primary Z_1, due to a secondary load Z_2, becomes

$$Z_1 = \left(\frac{N_1}{N_2}\right)^2 Z_2 \ . \tag{A3.9}$$

The transformer is used to step up or step down AC voltages, and also for isolation. It is often used in power applications. A practical example is the delivery of electrical power to buildings. The voltage in the street power lines is very high so that the current can be reduced to minimize $I^2 R$ power loss. A transformer is needed to step down the voltage before entering a building.

APPENDIX
A4

LIQUID-CRYSTAL DISPLAY

The liquid-crystal display (LCD) is a passive device, contrary to other displays such as the LED, plasma display, and fluorescent display in that it is not a direct source of light. Rather, it functions as a display device by controlling the transmission or reflection of light. Its main component is the liquid crystal. A liquid crystal is an organic compound with rod-shaped molecules that can be rearranged by an applied electric field so that its optical properties are changed. For this application, a liquid crystal has the ideal combination of the long-range order of a crystal and the flexibility of a liquid. Liquid crystals demonstrate three kinds of ordering in their molecular arrangement. These are nematic ordering, cholesteric ordering, and smectic ordering. Discussed in this appendix are three types of LCDs based on nematic ordering, and one on cholesteric ordering. All LCDs, however, share a similar structure having a liquid crystal confined between two plates, at least one of which is transparent glass. The outside surfaces of the transparent plates are coated with a transparent conductor such as SnO_2 or In_2O_3 to serve as electrodes for the applied field. The gap filled with liquid crystal is on the order of 10 μm, and it is hermetically sealed. LCDs can be transmissive or reflective. In the transmissive mode, a light source behind the LCD is needed. In the reflective mode, light comes from the same side of the viewer, and a reflecting coating is put on the back surface.

The most common LCD is the twisted nematic type. A nematic crystal is one where the molecule chains tend to align parallel to one another. The molecule orientation, represented by a vector called a director, can also be fixed by a grooved surface in contact with the liquid crystal. In a twisted nematic cell, as shown in Fig. A4.1(a), the two confining surfaces have grooves orthogonal to each other. This forces the director to rotate by 90°, gradually between the two surfaces. Light passing through this medium is forced to have a polarization change of 90°. With a proper pair of crossed polarizers, light is allowed to pass through. When an electric field is applied, molecules are turned parallel to the field, and light is blocked by the second polarizer. The contrast ratio can be improved in a super-twisted nematic cell where the rotation of the director between the two surfaces is increased, sometimes up to 270°.

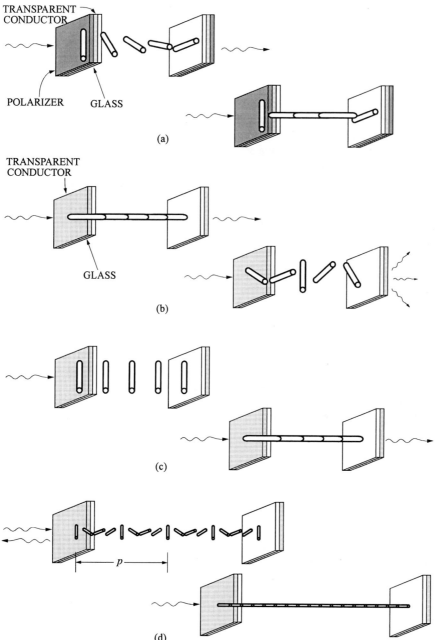

TRANSPARENT
CONDUCTOR

POLARIZER   GLASS

(a)

TRANSPARENT
CONDUCTOR

GLASS

(b)

(c)

p

(d)

FIGURE A4.1
Different versions of LCDs. Figures on the right are activated with voltage. (a) Twisted nematic cell.
(b) LCD using dynamic scattering. (c) LCD using guest-host effect. (d) Cholesteric LCD.

Another type of LCD operates by the mechanism of dynamic scattering. The structure (Fig. A4.1(b)) shows that when not activated, molecules are parallel to the light path. When a current is passed through the liquid crystal, ordering is disturbed by the turbulence and light is scattered. The LCD has a frosted-glass appearance when activated. The disadvantage of this mode is its higher power consumption.

The third type of LCD based on nematic ordering uses the guest-host effect. Pleochroic dye molecules are added to the liquid crystal and they follow the molecular alignment of the host (Fig. A4.1(c)). The modulation of light is due to anisotropic absorption of the dye molecules.

The last type of LCD discussed here is based on liquid crystals with cholesteric ordering. In this type of liquid crystal, the director is rotated naturally with respect to the adjacent layers, and has a pitch p (Fig. A4.1(d)). Light is reflected to the viewer by Bragg reflection whenever its wavelength λ satisfies

$$\lambda = \frac{p}{N_i} \ . \tag{A4.1}$$

This LCD is thus selective in color for a fixed p. When a field is applied, the cholesteric ordering is disturbed and reflection is cut off.

It is interesting to note that the above four kinds of LCDs all operate on different properties of light, namely polarization, scattering, absorption, and reflection. LCDs are attractive for their low power, low cost, slim profile, light weight, etc. They are widely used in watches, clocks, calculators, portable computer monitors, automotive dashboards, and numerous other equipment displays. The switching speed of a LCD is rather low, being in the range of 100–300 ms. For most applications, however, this is not a problem.

APPENDIX
A5

THERMOCOUPLE AND THERMOPILE

The thermocouple is based on thermoelectricity which is the interaction between thermal energy and electrical energy. There are three thermoelectric effects that are relevant to the operation and fundamental understanding of the thermocouple. These are the Seebeck effect, the Peltier effect and the Thomson effect, all named after the respective scientists who made their discoveries in the period of 1822–1847. In the Seebeck effect, when two dissimilar wires of conductor or semiconductor are joined together, and the two junctions are held at different temperatures, a current arises that flows around the loop (Fig. A5.1(a)). When this loop is broken, a voltage can be measured which is sometimes called the Seebeck voltage (Fig. A5.1(b)). It can be further demonstrated that this Seebeck voltage can be decomposed into components across each junction and each wire. The Peltier effect states that when a current is passed through a junction, heat is either absorbed or generated, depending on the direction of the current flow. This effect can indeed be used in refrigeration. In the open-circuit condition, a Peltier EMF (V_P) is developed across each junction, and it is a function of the temperature. The Thomson effect deals with similar heat exchange from a wire instead of a junction. For an open-circuit condition, when the wire has a temperature gradient along its length, a Thomson EMF is developed. It can be seen from Fig. A5.1(b) that the Seebeck voltage V_S is the sum of two Peltier EMFs and two Thomson EMFs, given by

$$V_S = (V_{P1} - V_{P2}) + (V_{TA} - V_{TB}) \ . \tag{A5.1}$$

If the junctions are at the same temperature, $V_{TA} = V_{TB} = 0$, $(V_{P1} - V_{P2}) = 0$, and $V_S = 0$. The Seebeck voltage is thus a measure of the difference in temperature of the two junctions.

A thermocouple is used as a temperature sensor. Since the output voltage depends on the difference in the junction temperatures, the temperature of one junction (the reference junction) has to be known. The other junction is then referred to as the sensing or measuring junction. A common reference temperature is 0°C which can be conveniently obtained by using ice. Room temperature can also be used as reference when accuracy is less critical. Common thermocouple

541

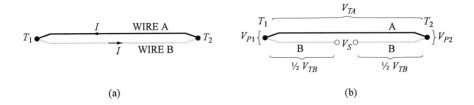

(a)   (b)

FIGURE A5.1

(a) In a closed thermocouple, when $T_1 \neq T_2$, a circulating current is formed. (a) When the circuit is open, a voltage is developed. This terminal voltage can be decomposed into Peltier EMF (V_P) across the junction and Thomson EMF (V_T) along the wire.

connections are shown in Fig. A5.2. The thermocouple wires are usually insulated, especially from touching each other, and they are only exposed at the junctions and the connectors. The relationship between temperature difference and voltage depends on the thermocouple materials. Lookup tables have been established for all thermocouples for this relationship. Common thermocouple types are summarized in Table A5.1. The techniques for forming the thermocouple junctions are welding, soldering, and brazing. The choice of thermocouple for an application depends on the suitability of the temperature range. The sensitivity also needs to be considered. It usually falls in the range of 5–90 µV/°C.

The thermocouple is widely used as a temperature sensor because it is robust, inexpensive, simple to use, and it covers a wide temperature range. The disadvantages are low sensitivity and accuracy, and the need for a reference temperature. The response time of a thermocouple is in the order of ms, but this low speed is generally not a problem for most applications.

A thermopile simply consists of multiple thermocouples connected in series, as shown in Fig. A5.3. The main purpose is to improve the sensitivity since the output voltage is now the sum of all the thermocouples. A thermopile is also

TABLE A5.1

Common thermocouples and their temperature range.

ANSI type	Composition	Temp. range (°C)
T	Cu–CuNi(constantan)	– 200 to 400
J	Fe–CuNi(constantan)	0 to 800
E	NiCr(chromel)–CuNi(constantan)	– 200 to 900
K	NiCr(chromel)–NiAl(alumel)	– 200 to 1200
R	Pt(13%Rh)–Pt	0 to 1400
S	Pt(10%Rh)–Pt	0 to 1400
B	Pt(6%Rh)–Pt(30%Rh)	800 to 1700

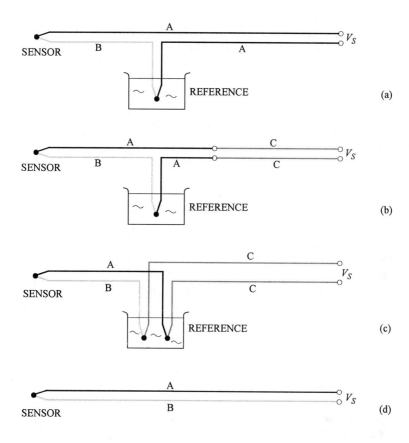

FIGURE A5.2
Different connections for thermocouples. In (b) and (c), regular extension wires substitute for the more expensive thermocouple wires. In (d), room temperature is the reference.

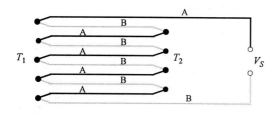

FIGURE A5.3
A thermopile consists of multiple thermocouples connected in series.

used as a photodetector for light of longer wavelengths (infrared and far infrared). It is in this case a thermal photodetector as opposed to a quantum photodetector. Light is absorbed at the thermocouple surface to produce heat which is monitored. The reference junction in the thermopile photodetector is usually inside the same housing, and is kept at the ambient temperature. It is shielded from the light source, and is sometimes coated with a reflecting surface. The exposure area is coated with a black film to maximize absorption. The unit is usually kept in vacuum or in an inert gas. Recent thermopile photodetectors are made from thin films for improved sensitivity and speed.

APPENDIX
A6

METAL-INSULATOR-METAL
DIODE

The metal-insulator-metal (MIM) diode has also been called a metal-oxide-metal (MOM) diode and a metal-barrier-metal (MBM) diode. Structurally it is a simple device where two metal layers are separated by a thin oxide. This thin oxide layer is usually a native oxide grown on one of the metals, and it is typically around 10 Å thick. The MIM diode structures are shown in Fig. A6.1. Early MIM diodes were the cat's whisker type, whereas recent structures are made of deposited metal films. Examples of materials are $Al–Al_2O_3–Al$ and Ni–NiO–Ni. Although the structure is very simple and does not require single-crystal semiconductors, it is very demanding in the reproducibility of thin insulator layers.

The conduction mechanism in an MIM diode is tunneling (see Appendix B7). The energy-band diagram indicating the tunneling through a trapezoidal barrier is shown in Fig. A6.2. This tunneling current is of the form

$$J = \frac{C_1}{x_{ox}^2} \{\phi_b \exp(-C_2 x_{ox} \phi_b^{1/2}) - (\phi_b + V) \exp\left[-C_2 x_{ox}(\phi_b + V)^{1/2}\right]\} \quad . \text{(A6.1)}$$

Qualitative I-V characteristics are shown in Fig. A6.3.

The MIM diode is mainly used as a microwave detector, based on its nonlinear I-V characteristics. The region of most interest lies in the applied voltage range of 100–300 mV where nonlinearity is at its maximum. In this voltage range, the characteristics are nearly exponential. Readers are referred to Appendix C1 for a more detailed discussion on microwave mixing and demodulation. Since tunneling is inherently a very fast process, the MIM diode has extremely high speed and can respond to electromagnetic waves into the 10^{15} Hz range, which is in the visible spectrum. The MIM diode can also be used as the select driver for LCDs in a flat-panel display.

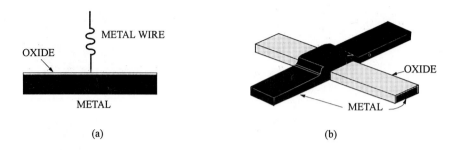

(a)

(b)

FIGURE A6.1
MIM diode structures. (a) Cat's whisker contact. (b) Deposited metal films.

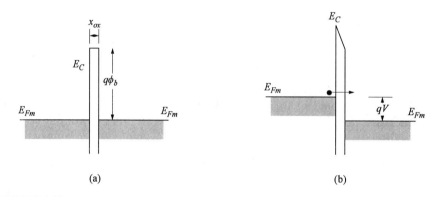

(a)

(b)

FIGURE A6.2
Energy-band diagrams of an MIM diode (a) in equilibrium and (b) under bias. Same metal materials on both sides are assumed.

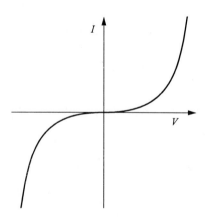

FIGURE A6.3
I-V characteristics of an MIM diode.

APPENDIX
B1

DRIFT VELOCITY AND MOBILITY

Electrons and holes under the influence of an electric field move with a net velocity called drift velocity v_d, and this movement of charge results in a drift current. The relationship between drift velocity and field is shown in Fig. B1.1. The concept of mobility applies to the low-field region where the drift velocity is proportional to the field, and the proportionality constant is the mobility. At high fields, the v_d does not increase indefinitely, but instead approaches a saturation velocity v_{sat}. The entire v_d–$\mathscr{E}$ curve can be fit by many empirical forms, and a simple one is given here as an example

$$v_d = \frac{\mu \mathscr{E}}{1 + (\mu \mathscr{E}/v_{sat})} \quad . \tag{B1.1}$$

At low field,

$$v_d = \mu \mathscr{E} \tag{B1.2}$$

and this mobility regime, for most part, describes drift current in semiconductors and metals well.

In order to understand mobility, the microscopic behavior of a carrier must be examined. Even without applied field, carriers are constantly moving with a high thermal velocity v_{th} which is given by the thermodynamic relation

$$\frac{1}{2}m^* v_{th}^2 = \frac{3}{2}kT \quad . \tag{B1.3}$$

The v_{th} at room temperature is about 10^7 cm/s. Furthermore, each carrier does not continue with a certain path indefinitely. A very important phenomenon called scattering occurs when a carrier collides with some scattering center. As shown in Fig. B1.2(a), each collision randomizes the direction of the thermal velocity. The net velocity averaged over time is zero, and therefore this thermal velocity does not contribute to a current. In this picture, the average distance between collisions is called the mean free path l_m, and the average interval is called the mean free time τ_m.

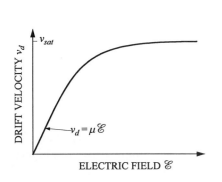

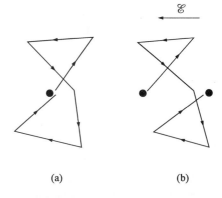

FIGURE B1.1
Drift velocity as a function of electric field for most semiconductors.

FIGURE B1.2
Trajectories of an electron. (a) Without electric field, the random thermal velocity has zero net v_d. (b) With an electric field, a net v_d is superimposed on the thermal motion.

Under an electric field, the carrier is accelerated by the field and a net drift velocity arises, superimposed on the random motion of v_{th} (Fig. B1.2(b)). It is important to note that if there were no scattering, velocity would go to infinity with time since the acceleration (force/$m^* = \mathcal{E}q/m^*$) is constant. In fact, it is usually assumed that just after each collision, the net v_d is randomized to be zero. The maximum v_d just before another collision is thus

$$v_d = \frac{q\tau_m \mathcal{E}}{m^*} \ .$$
(B1.4)

To obtain the drift current, some average v_d between collisions is more meaningful such as half of Eq. (B1.4). However, it turns out that by using a more rigorous derivation invoking statistical mechanics of the whole ensemble of carriers, or using a kinetic energy model, Eq. (B1.4) is actually the average drift velocity. From Eqs. (B1.4) and (B1.2),

$$\mu = \frac{q\tau_m}{m^*} \ ,$$
(B1.5)

and high mobility requires low m^* and long l_m (or long τ_m).

The scattering centers can be of many origins. They include (1) phonons, (2) ionized impurities, (3) neutral impurities, and (4) other carriers. Scattering can be generally divided into lattice (phonon) scattering and impurity scattering, and these, when considered separately, yield lattice mobility μ_L and impurity mobility

μ_I. According to Matthiessen's rule, the overall mobility is related to the individual mobilities by

$$\frac{1}{\mu} = \frac{1}{\mu_1} + \frac{1}{\mu_2} + \frac{1}{\mu_3}...$$

$$= \frac{1}{\mu_L} + \frac{1}{\mu_I} \ .$$

(B1.6)

This is useful to explain the temperature dependence of mobility shown in Fig. B1.3. For a typical semiconductor with moderate doping level, at higher temperature, mobility is dominated by lattice (phonon) scattering and it has a $T^{-3/2}$ dependence. At low temperature, mobility is controlled by impurity scattering, with a $T^{3/2}$ dependence. In this regime, μ_I rises with temperature because higher temperature means higher v_{th}, and faster carriers are less likely to be deflected by a scattering center.

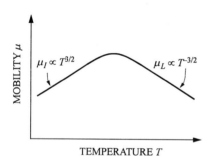

FIGURE B1.3
Temperature dependence of mobility can be separated into μ_I and μ_L.

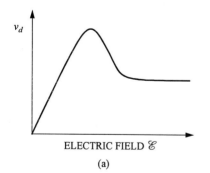

ELECTRIC FIELD $\mathscr{E}$
(a)

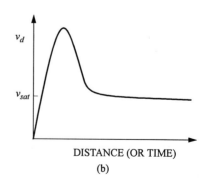

DISTANCE (OR TIME)
(b)

FIGURE B1.4
(a) Negative differential resistance from transferred-electron effect. (b) Velocity overshoot due to ballistic transport in ultra-small devices. Notice that the parameters for the abscissas are different.

At higher fields, the more energetic carriers, also called hot carriers, start to transfer energy to the lattice, creating optical phonons. Equation (B1.4) will be invalid when the carrier energy is higher than the thermal energy kT. In this case the carriers travel with a maximum speed of v_{sat} given by

$$v_{sat} = \sqrt{\frac{E_{op}}{m^*}}$$

(B1.7)

which typically has a value of $\approx 10^7$ cm/s at room temperature. It is coincidental and sometimes misleading that at room temperature, both v_{th} and v_{sat} have similar values. Their temperature dependence clarifies that they are not from the same origin. At lower temperature, v_{th} decreases while v_{sat} increases.

For the sake of completeness, we should point out some special cases that have different characteristics from those of Fig. B1.1. The characteristics shown in Fig. B1.4(a) are a result of the transferred-electron effect (Gunn effect), for materials that have low satellite valleys in their E-k relationship. With low fields, carriers are confined to the lowest conduction band, with a standard mobility. With higher fields, these carriers are excited to a satellite band which has a lower mobility and v_{sat}. This effect is the main mechanism for the negative differential resistance in a transferred-electron device discussed in Chapter 7. Another interesting deviation from the conventional drift process is the ballistic transport observed in devices whose dimensions are shorter than or comparable to the l_m. Since scattering does not occur, v_d is simply equal to $\mathscr{E}qt_t$ (transit time replacing the τ_m), which can be higher than the v_{sat}. Notice that the abscissa in Fig. B1.4(b) is distance or time rather than field. This phenomenon, also known as velocity overshoot, leads to drift velocities higher than v_{sat}, resulting in devices with much higher speed and current drive. Devices that operate with velocity overshoot are on the order of 0.1 μm in their critical dimension.

APPENDIX
B2

RECOMBINATION AND GENERATION

Under thermal equilibrium, the carrier concentrations in a semiconductor obey the mass-action law

$$pn = n_i^2 \ . \tag{B2.1}$$

When this thermal equilibrium is disturbed, net recombination or generation results. If excess carriers are introduced, either by light exposure or by carrier injection through a forward bias, $pn > n_i^2$ and net recombination occurs. On the other hand if carriers are depleted by a reverse bias in the space-charge region, $pn < n_i^2$ and net generation results. These recombination and generation processes are a means for the semiconductor to recover to the equilibrium condition when the disturbances are removed, and they are characterized by a parameter called minority-carrier lifetime τ. For example, in an n-type semiconductor, after light or bias is removed, the excess minority-carrier concentration Δp decays with time

$$\Delta p\,(t) \ = \ \Delta p\,(0) \exp\left(\frac{-t}{\tau_p}\right) \ . \tag{B2.2}$$

Also if Δp is introduced locally, the spatial variation from the injection source is given by

$$\Delta p\,(x) \ = \ \Delta p\,(0) \exp\left(\frac{-x}{L_p}\right) \ . \tag{B2.3}$$

where

$$L_p \ = \ \sqrt{D_p \tau_p} \ . \tag{B2.4}$$

As seen from Eqs. (B2.2) and (B2.3), the carrier lifetime is important not only for the response speed of a device, but it also determines the magnitude of the

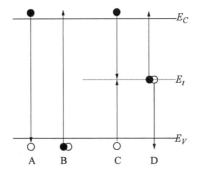

FIGURE B2.1
Recombination and generation of electron-hole pairs. A = direct band-to-band recombination. B = direct band-to-band generation. C = indirect recombination via traps. D = indirect generation via traps.

diffusion current, as well as recombination/generation current in a junction, which is to be discussed in more detail later.

We now derive the carrier lifetime from the semiconductor material properties. Electron-hole pairs are produced by generation and annihilated by recombination. There are two basic mechanisms for recombination/generation: (1) direct band-to-band transitions and (2) indirect transitions via bulk traps whose energy lies within the forbidden gap. These transitions are demonstrated in Fig. B2.1.

Band-to-band transitions are more probable for direct-energy-gap semiconductors. For this type of transition, the recombination rate is proportional to the product of electron and hole concentrations, given by

$$R = B_r \, pn \quad . \tag{B2.5}$$

The term B_r is called the recombination coefficient, and is related to the thermal generation rate by

$$B_r = \frac{G_{th}}{n_i^2} \quad . \tag{B2.6}$$

B_r is not only a function of temperature, but is also dependent on the band structure of the semiconductor. A direct-energy-gap semiconductor, being more efficient in band-to-band transitions, has a much larger B_r ($\approx 10^{-10}$ cm^3/s) than an indirect-energy-gap semiconductor ($\approx 10^{-15}$ cm^3/s). In thermal equilibrium, since $pn = n_i^2$, $R = G_{th}$ and the net transition rate $U \, (= R - G)$ equals zero. Under low-level injection, defined as the case where the excess carriers $\Delta p = \Delta n$ is higher in concentration than the minority carriers (for an n-type material, $p \approx \Delta p$), but lower than the majority carriers ($n \approx N_D$), the net transition rate is given by

$$U = R - G_{th}$$

$$= B_r(pn - n_i^2)$$

$$\approx B_r \Delta p N_D \equiv \frac{\Delta p}{\tau_p} \tag{B2.7}$$

where

$$\tau_p = \frac{1}{B_r N_D} \, , \tag{B2.8}$$

$$\tau_n = \frac{1}{B_r N_A} \, . \tag{B2.9}$$

However in some cases, especially in indirect semiconductors such as Si and Ge, the dominant transitions are indirect recombination/generation via bulk traps, of density N_t and energy E_t (Fig. B2.1). The net transition rate can be described by Shockley-Read-Hall statistics[1,2] as

$$U = \frac{\sigma_n \sigma_p v_{th} N_t (pn - n_i^2)}{\sigma_n \left[n + n_i \exp\left(\dfrac{E_t - E_i}{kT}\right) \right] + \sigma_p \left[p + n_i \exp\left(\dfrac{E_i - E_t}{kT}\right) \right]} \, . \tag{B2.10}$$

Without deriving this equation, some qualitative observations can be made on the final form. First, the net transition rate is proportional to $pn - n_i^2$, similar to Eq. (B2.7), and the sign determines whether there is net recombination or generation. Second, U is maximized when $E_t = E_i$, indicating for a spectrum of bulk traps, only the ones near the mid-gap are effective recombination/generation centers. Considering only these traps, Eq. (B2.10) is reduced to

$$U = \frac{\sigma_n \sigma_p v_{th} N_t (pn - n_i^2)}{\sigma_n (n + n_i) + \sigma_p (p + n_i)} \, . \tag{B2.11}$$

Again for low-level injection in n-type semiconductors,

$$U = \frac{\sigma_n \sigma_p v_{th} N_t \left[(p_{no} + \Delta p) n - n_i^2 \right]}{\sigma_n n}$$

$$\approx \sigma_p v_{th} N_t \Delta p \equiv \frac{\Delta p}{\tau_p} \tag{B2.12}$$

where

$$\tau_p = \frac{1}{\sigma_p v_{th} N_t} \tag{B2.13}$$

$$\tau_n = \frac{1}{\sigma_n v_{th} N_t} . \tag{B2.14}$$

As expected, the lifetime arising from indirect transitions depends on N_t, while in the previous case, the lifetime from direct transitions depends on the doping level (Eqs. (B2.8) and (B2.9)).

It will be shown in the following that when these bulk traps are present in the depletion region of a junction, such as a *p-n* diode or a Schottky diode, an additional current component arises. With forward bias injection, carrier concentrations are increased to

$$pn = n_i^2 \exp\left(\frac{qV_f}{kT}\right) . \tag{B2.15}$$

Also, with the assumption that $\sigma_n = \sigma_p = \sigma$, Eq. (B2.11) can be simplified to

$$U = \frac{\sigma v_{th} N_t n_i^2 \left[\exp\left(qV_f/kT\right) - 1\right]}{n + p + 2n_i} . \tag{B2.16}$$

Maximum U occurs at a location within the depletion region where $(n + p)$ is at a minimum. Since the product of n and p is fixed by the bias, the above condition occurs at $n = p \approx n_i \exp(qV_f/2kT)$. With this substitution,

$$
\begin{aligned}
U &= \frac{1}{2} \sigma v_{th} N_t n_i \left[\exp\left(\frac{qV_f}{2kT}\right) - 1\right] \\
&= \frac{n_i}{2\tau} \left[\exp\left(\frac{qV_f}{2kT}\right) - 1\right]
\end{aligned} \tag{B2.17}
$$

where

$$\tau = \frac{1}{\sigma v_{th} N_t} . \tag{B2.18}$$

The recombination current is thus given by

$$
\begin{aligned}
J_{re} &= \int_0^{W_d} qU dx \\
&\approx \frac{qW_d n_i}{2\tau} \left[\exp\left(\frac{qV_f}{2kT}\right) - 1\right] .
\end{aligned} \tag{B2.19}
$$

Notice that here the exponential dependence is $2kT$, as opposed to kT for diffusion current or thermionic-emission current. With a large amount of bulk traps, a p-n junction diode or a Schottky diode can exhibit mixed I-V characteristics as shown in Fig. B2.2(a) where low current or voltage has the $2kT$ dependence. Also, for a fixed V_f, the Arrhenius plot in Fig. B2.2(b) reveals how the current conduction can switch from one mode to another as the temperature is changed.

In the reverse-biased junction, within the depletion region both n and p are much smaller than n_i, and Eq. (B2.11) is reduced to (again assuming $\sigma_n = \sigma_p = \sigma$)

$$U = -\frac{1}{2}\sigma v_{th}N_t n_i \ . \tag{B2.20}$$

The generation current is simply given by

$$\begin{aligned} J_{ge} &= \int_0^{W_d} q\,(-U)\,dx \\ &\approx \frac{1}{2}q\sigma v_{th}N_t n_i W_d \\ &\approx \frac{qn_i W_d}{2\tau} \ . \end{aligned} \tag{B2.21}$$

The voltage dependence of J_{ge} is through modulation of W_d.

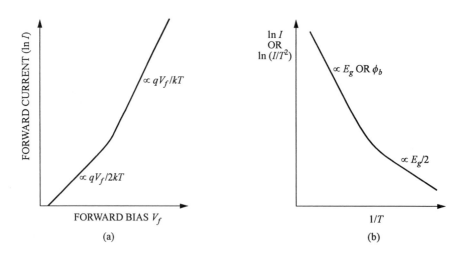

FIGURE B2.2
Forward current of a diode in the presence of recombination current. (a) I-V characteristics. (b) Forward current at a fixed bias as a function of temperature, showing the activation energy (Arrhenius plot).

The remaining topic to be discussed in this appendix is the enhanced recombination at the surface of a semiconductor due to additional interface traps, of density N_{it}. Because of this, the excess minority carriers at the surface, for example introduced by exposure to light, are reduced compared to the bulk, as shown in Fig. B2.3. Analytically, Eq. (B2.12) can be used with N_{it} replacing N_t and $p_n(0) - p_{no}$ replacing Δp,

$$U_s = \sigma_p v_{th} N_{it} [p_n(0) - p_{no}] \equiv S_p [p_n(0) - p_{no}] \ . \tag{B2.22}$$

S_p is equal to $\sigma_p v_{th} N_{it}$ and, having the unit of cm/s, is called the surface recombination velocity. Note that because N_{it} (cm^{-2}) has a different unit from N_t (cm^{-3}), the surface net recombination/generation rate U_s (1/s-cm^2) is different from U. To find the profile of $p_n(x)$ in Fig. B2.3, the continuity equation is used

$$\frac{\partial p_n(x)}{\partial t} = G_{op} - \frac{p_n(x) - p_{no}}{\tau_p} + D_p \frac{\partial^2 p_n(x)}{\partial x^2} \ . \tag{B2.23}$$

The boundary condition at the surface is provided by the necessity that the net recombination current is supplied by the diffusion current,

$$J_{re} = qS_p [p_n(0) - p_{no}] = qD_p \frac{dp_n}{dx}\bigg|_{x=0} \ . \tag{B2.24}$$

This, along with another boundary condition

$$p_n(\infty) = p_{no} + G_{op}\tau_p \ , \tag{B2.25}$$

gives

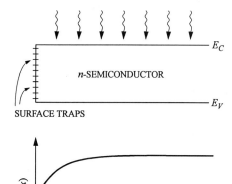

SURFACE TRAPS

$p_n(x)$

p_{no}

DISTANCE FROM SURFACE (x)

FIGURE B2.3
Profile of minority-carrier concentration near the surface when the semiconductor is exposed to light, showing the effect of surface recombination.

$$p_n(x) = p_{no} + G_{op}\tau_p \left[1 - \frac{\tau_p S_p \exp(-x/L_p)}{L_p + \tau_p S_p} \right] . \qquad (B2.26)$$

If the surface concentration is depleted ($pn < n_i^2$), as in the case of deep depletion under dark, the generation current is given by

$$J_{ge} = \frac{qn_i S_o}{2} . \qquad (B2.27)$$

REFERENCES

1. W. Shockley and W. T. Read, Jr., "Statistics of the recombination of holes and electrons," *Phys. Rev.*, **87**, 835 (1952).
2. R. N. Hall, "Electron-hole recombination in germanium," *Phys. Rev.*, **87**, 387 (1952).

APPENDIX
B3

IMPACT IONIZATION
AND
AVALANCHE

Impact ionization is the mechanism that leads to avalanche multiplication and eventually avalanche breakdown. These processes are important in many respects in device design and application. For example, avalanche multiplication is utilized as gain in the avalanche photodiode, and is also the main mechanism in the IMPATT diode. The avalanche breakdown is responsible for most device breakdown, and puts an upper limit on the operation voltage.

An impact-ionization event occurs when a carrier is placed in a high-field region. The carrier gains energy from the field, becomes a hot carrier, and when it collides with the lattice, loses its kinetic energy to generate an electron-hole pair. This process is depicted in Fig. B3.1(a) with a hole being the initial carrier. Notice that in order to excite an electron-hole pair, the kinetic energy of the hot carrier before collision has to be larger than the energy gap. After the collision, one primary hole gives rise to two holes plus one electron, thereby achieving a gain. Impact ionization is characterized by the ionization coefficient, α. It has the unit of inverse distance, and qualitatively indicates the number of electron-hole pairs generated per unit distance. It is a strong function of the electric field, as well as the energy gap. The ionization coefficient increases exponentially with field, and decreases with E_g. The overall generation rate G is related to the ionization coefficients and the number of carriers by

$$G = \alpha_p p v_p + \alpha_n n v_n = \frac{\alpha_p J_p}{q} + \frac{\alpha_n J_n}{q} \ .$$

(B3.1)

Avalanche multiplication is a result of multiple impact ionizations, and the gain is determined by the total number of ionization events. A high-field region of length L is shown in Fig. B3.1(b) which undergoes impact ionization by both electrons and holes. Assuming that hole current is injected from the left-hand side (positive bias) and electron current from the right-hand side, their respective gains are

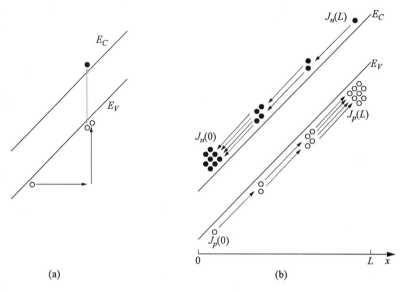

FIGURE B3.1
(a) An impact-ionization event starting with a hole results in two holes and one electron. (b)
Avalanche multiplication with impact ionizations from both electrons and holes.

$$M_p = \frac{J_p(L)}{J_p(0)} \quad , \tag{B3.2}$$

$$M_n = \frac{J_n(0)}{J_n(L)} \quad . \tag{B3.3}$$

Continuity of current requires that

$$J = J_p(x) + J_n(x) \quad . \tag{B3.4}$$

Since the change of currents is related to the generation rate by

$$G = \frac{dJ_p}{qdx} = \frac{-dJ_n}{qdx} \quad , \tag{B3.5}$$

Equation (B3.1) yields

$$\begin{aligned}
\frac{dJ_p}{dx} &= \alpha_p J_p + \alpha_n J_n \\
&= (\alpha_p - \alpha_n) J_p + \alpha_n J \quad .
\end{aligned} \tag{B3.6}$$

The solution of this partial differential equation gives[1]

$$M_p = \cfrac{1}{1 - \displaystyle\int_0^L \alpha_p \exp\left[-\int_0^x (\alpha_p - \alpha_n)\, dx'\right] dx} \quad . \tag{B3.7}$$

Similarly, it can be shown that

$$M_n = \cfrac{1}{1 - \displaystyle\int_0^L \alpha_n \exp\left[-\int_x^L (\alpha_n - \alpha_p)\, dx'\right] dx} \quad . \tag{B3.8}$$

Gain dominated by impact ionization from one type of carrier can be shown to be[2]

$$M_p = \exp\left(\int_0^L \alpha_p\, dx\right) \;, \quad \alpha_p \gg \alpha_n \;, \tag{B3.9}$$

$$M_n = \exp\left(\int_0^L \alpha_n\, dx\right) \;, \quad \alpha_n \gg \alpha_p \;. \tag{B3.10}$$

Another special case is that when $\alpha_n = \alpha_p = \alpha$, the gain is given by

$$M_p = M_n = \cfrac{1}{1 - \displaystyle\int_0^L \alpha\, dx} \quad . \tag{B3.11}$$

While avalanche breakdown will be discussed next, the multiplication below the breakdown voltage (the point at which gain equals infinity) is given by an empirical equation

$$M = \cfrac{1}{1 - (V_r / V_{BD})^n} \tag{B3.12}$$

where n varies with materials and is in the range of 3–6.

Avalanche breakdown is the condition when M_p or M_n becomes infinite. From Eqs. (B3.7)–(B3.8), this condition is met by

$$\int_0^L \alpha_p \exp\left[-\int_0^x (\alpha_p - \alpha_n)\, dx'\right] dx = 1 \tag{B3.13}$$

or

$$\int_0^L \alpha_n \exp\left[-\int_x^L (\alpha_n - \alpha_p)\, dx'\right] dx = 1 \;. \tag{B3.14}$$

It is interesting to note that avalanche breakdown needs impact ionization from both types of carriers. If α_n or α_p is zero, Eqs. (B3.9) and (B3.10) show that the gain is always finite. In other words, avalanche breakdown needs positive feedback of both types of carriers. One special case for breakdown is when $\alpha_n = \alpha_p = \alpha$, and the condition is given by

$$\int_0^L \alpha\,dx = 1 \quad .$$

(B3.15)

The impact ionization coefficients for electrons and holes in Si, Ge, GaAs, and GaP are shown in Fig. B3.2.

Finally, the breakdown voltages of one-sided step p-n junctions for different materials are shown in Fig. B3.3. They can be shown to fit an empirical formula[4]

$$V_{BD} \approx 60 \left[\frac{E_g \,(\text{in eV})}{1.1} \right]^{3/2} \left[\frac{N\,(\text{in cm}^{-3})}{10^{16}} \right]^{-3/4}$$

(B3.16)

where N is the concentration in the lightly doped side.

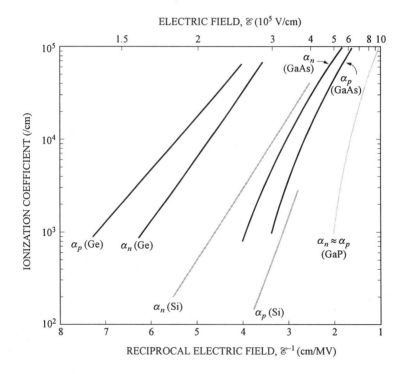

FIGURE B3.2
Ionization coefficients for electrons and holes in Si, Ge, GaAs, and GaP. (After Ref. 3)

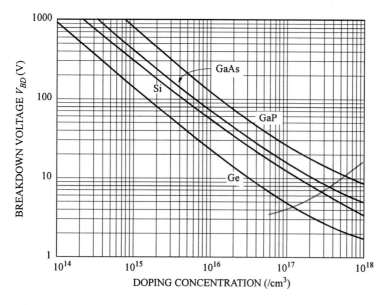

FIGURE B3.3

Breakdown voltage of abrupt one-sided *p-n* junctions for different materials. Dashed line indicates onset of tunneling due to high doping. (After Ref. 4)

REFERENCES

1. S. M. Sze, *Physics of semiconductor devices*, 2nd Ed., Wiley, New York, 1981.
2. M. Shur, *Physics of semiconductor devices*, Prentice Hall, Englewood Cliffs, 1990.
3. C. T. Sah, *Fundamentals of solid-state electronics*, World Scientific, Singapore, 1991.
4. S. M. Sze and G. Gibbons, "Avalanche breakdown voltages of abrupt and linearly graded *p-n* junctions in Ge, Si, GaAs, and GaP," *Appl. Phys. Lett.*, **8**, 111 (1966).

APPENDIX
B4

SPACE-CHARGE EFFECT AND SPACE-CHARGE-LIMITED CURRENT

The space charge in a semiconductor is determined by both the doping concentrations and the free-carrier concentrations,

$$\rho = (p - n + N_D - N_A)q \ .$$ (B4.1)

In the neutral region of a semiconductor, $n = N_D$ and $p = N_A$, so that the space-charge density is zero. In the vicinity of a junction formed by different materials, dopant types or doping concentrations, n and p could be smaller or larger than N_D and N_A, respectively. In the depletion approximation, n and p are assumed zero so that the space charge is equal to the majority-carrier doping level. Under bias, the carrier concentrations n and p can be increased beyond their values in equilibrium. When the injected n or p is larger than its equilibrium value as well as the doping concentration, space-charge effect is said to occur. The injected carriers thus control the space charge and the electric-field profile. This results in a feedback mechanism where the field drives the current which in turn sets up the field. The space-charge effect is more common in lightly doped materials.

In the presence of a space-charge effect, if the current is dominated by the drift component of the injected carriers, it is called the space-charge-limited current. Since it is a drift current, it is given by, in the case of electron injection,

$$J = qnv \ .$$ (B4.2)

The space charge again is determined by the injected carriers, giving rise to the Poisson equation of the form

$$\frac{d^2\psi}{dx^2} = \frac{qn}{\varepsilon_s} \ .$$ (B4.3)

The carrier velocity v is related to the electric field by different functions. In the mobility regime,

$$v = \mu \mathscr{E} \ .$$

(B4.4)

In the velocity-saturation regime, velocity v_{sat} is independent of the field. In the ballistic regime where there is no scattering,

$$v = \sqrt{\frac{2q\psi}{m^*}} \ .$$

(B4.5)

The space-charge-limited current can be shown to be

$$J = \frac{9\varepsilon_s \mu V^2}{8L^3}$$

(B4.6)

(Mott-Gurney law) in the mobility regime,

$$J = \frac{2\varepsilon_s v_{sat} V}{L^2}$$

(B4.7)

in the velocity-saturation regime, and

$$J = \frac{4\varepsilon_s}{9L^2} \left(\frac{2q}{m^*} \right)^{1/2} V^{3/2}$$

(B4.8)

(Child-Langmuir law) in the ballistic regime. L is the length of the sample in the direction of the current flow.

APPENDIX

B5

THERMIONIC EMISSION

There are many devices whose current conduction is via thermionic emission. The most common is the Schottky-barrier diode and it is used here for demonstration, but the results can be applied to other devices such as the planar-doped-barrier diode. Thermionic emission is always associated with a potential barrier height ϕ_b (Fig. B5.1). Due to Fermi-Dirac statistics, the density of electrons (for n-type substrate) decreases as the energy increases above the Fermi level. At any finite (non-zero) temperature, the carrier density at any finite energy is not zero. Of special interest here is the integrated number of carriers above the barrier height. This portion of the thermally generated carriers are no longer confined by the barrier and they contribute to the thermionic-emission current. In the following, this current is derived by two different approaches.

In the first approach, we start with the electron distribution as a function of energy,

$$n(E) = 4\pi \left(\frac{2m^*}{h^2}\right)^{3/2} \sqrt{E - E_C} \, \exp\left[\frac{-(E - E_F)}{kT}\right] \tag{B5.1}$$

where

$$E - E_C = \frac{1}{2}m^* \, (v_x^2 + v_y^2 + v_z^2) \quad . \tag{B5.2}$$

The symbols v_x, v_y, and v_z are the velocity components. When the diode is under forward bias (Fig. B5.1(b)), the potential barrier is voltage dependent. Those electrons with energy

$$\frac{1}{2}m^* \, v_x^2 \geq q \, (\psi_{bi} - V_f) \tag{B5.3}$$

can surmount the barrier and flow to the metal. Note that v_x is the velocity perpendicular to the interface so that only the relevant energy component is included. The total electron current from the semiconductor to the metal is given by[1]

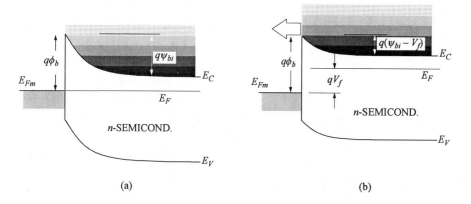

FIGURE B5.1
Energy-band diagrams of a Schottky barrier for derivation of thermionic-emission current. (a)
Equilibrium. (b) Under forward bias.

$$J = \int_{\frac{1}{2}m^* v_x^2 = q\,(\psi_{bi} - V_f)}^{\infty} q v_x n\,(E)\,dE$$

$$= \left(\frac{4\pi q m^* k^2}{h^3} \right) T^2 \exp\left(\frac{-q\phi_b}{kT} \right) \exp\left(\frac{q V_f}{kT} \right) \,.$$

(B5.4)

The opposite electron current from metal to semiconductor is determined by the
barrier height and is independent of bias. Taking this into account, the total net
current is given by

$$J = A^* T^2 \exp\left(\frac{-q\phi_b}{kT} \right) \left[\exp\left(\frac{q V_f}{kT} \right) - 1 \right]$$

(B5.5)

with

$$A^* = \frac{4\pi q m^* k^2}{h^3} \,.$$

(B5.6)

The effective Richardson constant A^* is a function of the effective mass. For
semiconductors with anisotropic effective masses, the consideration is more
complicated.[2] A^* can be further modified by quantum-mechanical tunneling and
reflection. The values of A^* for Si, Ge, and GaAs can be found in Table 3.2.

An alternative approach to derive the thermionic-emission current is the
following.[3] Without decomposing the velocity components, only electrons with

energy above the barrier will contribute to the forward current. This number of electrons above the barrier is given by

$$n = N_C \exp\left[\frac{-q\left(\phi_b - V_f\right)}{kT}\right] . \tag{B5.7}$$

It is known that for a Maxwellian distribution of velocities, the current from random motion of carriers across a plane is given by

$$J = nq\frac{v_{ave}}{4} \tag{B5.8}$$

where v_{ave} is the average thermal velocity

$$v_{ave} = \sqrt{\frac{8kT}{\pi m^*}} . \tag{B5.9}$$

Substitution of Eqs. (B5.7) and (B5.9) into Eq. (B5.8) gives

$$J = \frac{4\left(kT\right)^2 q\pi m^*}{h^3}\exp\left[\frac{-q\left(\phi_b - V_f\right)}{kT}\right] \tag{B5.10}$$

which is identical to Eq. (B5.4).

REFERENCES

1. S. M. Sze, *Physics of semiconductor devices*, 2nd Ed., Wiley, New York, 1981.
2. C. R. Crowell, "The Richardson constant for thermionic emission in Schottky barrier diodes," *Solid-State Electron.*, **8**, 395 (1965).
3. E. H. Rhoderick and R. H. Williams, *Metal-semiconductor contacts*, 2nd Ed., Clarendon, Oxford, 1988.

APPENDIX
B6

IMAGE-FORCE LOWERING

The image-force lowering, also known as the Schottky effect, occurs in a metal–nonmetal interface such as a metal–semiconductor junction (Schottky barrier), a metal–insulator junction or a metal–vacuum junction. In such junctions, a barrier exists that controls the emission of electrons (or holes) from the metal to its adjacent layer. It will be shown that the image-force lowering reduces such barrier height to allow for a larger flow of current, especially pertinent to the thermionic-emission current.

For simplicity, we start with a metal–vacuum junction, and the results are then applied to the more-common metal–semiconductor system. Figure B6.1 shows the electric-field configuration that occurs when an electron is placed near the metal. Such a system can be represented by an environment where the metal is replaced by an equal and opposite charge called an image charge. The electron experiences an attractive Coulomb force toward its image charge, given by

$$F = \frac{-q^2}{4\pi\varepsilon_o (2x)^2} \ .$$
(B6.1)

The energy of this electron, taken as $E = 0$ at $x = \infty$, is given by

$$E(x) = -\int_\infty^x F dx = \frac{-q^2}{16\pi\varepsilon_o x} \ .$$
(B6.2)

This expression indicates that for any metal–non-metal interface, the barrier is not abrupt (Fig. B6.1(c)), and this has an important consequence. (Although the expression implies that when x approaches zero, E approaches negative infinity. A simple calculation shows that for $x = 3$ Å, E has a value of only -1 eV.) In the presence of an external electric field, the total electron energy as a function of distance becomes

$$E(x) = -\left(\frac{q^2}{16\pi\varepsilon_o x} + q\mathscr{E}_x x \right) \ .$$
(B6.3)

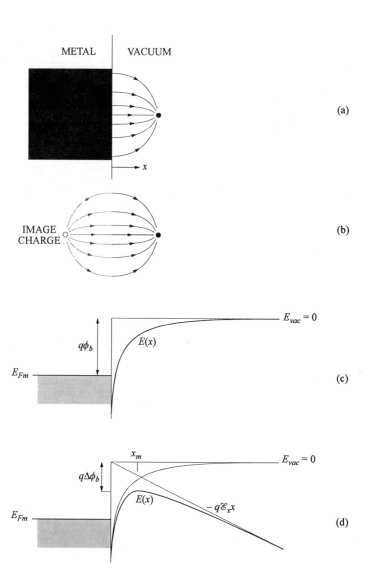

FIGURE B6.1
(a) Electric-field configuration when an electron is brought close to a metal. (b) This system can be represented by an image charge in place of the metal. Energy-band diagrams for electrons (c) without additional field and (d) with additional field.

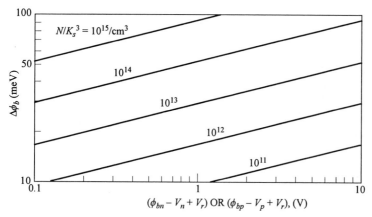

FIGURE B6.2
A plot of Eq. (B6.7) giving a quick estimate of the amount of image-force lowering.

It is seen in Fig. B6.1(d) that the barrier is now lowered by an amount $\Delta\phi_b$. It can be derived from Eq. (B6.3) that

$$\Delta\phi_b = \sqrt{\frac{q\mathcal{E}_x}{4\pi\varepsilon_o}} \tag{B6.4}$$

and the barrier maximum occurs at the location of

$$x_m = \sqrt{\frac{q}{16\pi\varepsilon_o\mathcal{E}_x}} \ . \tag{B6.5}$$

When these results are applied to a Schottky-barrier diode, slight modifications have to be made. First, permittivity in the semiconductor (ε_s) replaces that of vacuum (ε_o). Secondly, an electric field exists even without a bias and therefore image-force lowering occurs also in equilibrium. Although this field is not constant with distance, the value at the surface can be used as a good approximation,

$$\mathcal{E}_x = \sqrt{\frac{2qN_D(\phi_{bn} - V_n + V_r)}{\varepsilon_s}} \tag{B6.6}$$

where ϕ_{bn} is the original Schottky barrier (on n-type substrate) before image-force lowering. Substituting Eq. (B6.6) into Eq. (B6.4) gives

$$\Delta\phi_{bn} = \left[\frac{q^3 N_D (\phi_{bn} - V_n + V_r)}{8\pi^2 \varepsilon_s^3} \right]^{1/4}.$$
(B6.7)

This relationship is plotted in Fig. B6.2. A typical value for x_m is less than 50 Å. It should be added that the image force for holes is under similar consideration, and Eq. (B6.7) with appropriate parameters is applicable to hole barriers.

TUNNELING

Electron tunneling is a quantum-mechanical phenomenon. In classical mechanics, when an electron impinges on a barrier of higher potential (Fig. B7.1), it is completely confined by the potential wall. In quantum mechanics, the electron can be represented by its wavefunction. The wavefunction does not terminate abruptly on a wall of finite potential height, and it can penetrate through the barrier. The probability of electron tunneling through a barrier of finite height is thus not zero.

To calculate the tunneling probability, the wavefunction ψ has to be determined from Schrödinger equation,

$$\frac{d^2\psi}{dx^2} + \frac{2m^*}{\hbar^2}\left[E - U(x)\right]\psi = 0 \quad . \tag{B7.1}$$

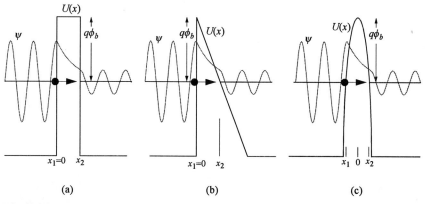

FIGURE B7.1
Wavefunction showing electron tunneling through barriers of different shapes. (a) Rectangular barrier. (b) Triangular barrier. (c) Parabolic barrier.

Simplification of Eq. (B7.1) is made by the WKB (Wentzel-Kramers-Brillouin) approximation if the potential $U(x)$ does not vary rapidly. The wavefunction is of the exponential form and it is attenuated by

$$\frac{|\psi(x_2)|}{|\psi(x_1)|} = \exp\left\{-\int_{x_1}^{x_2} \sqrt{\frac{2m^*}{\hbar^2}[U(x) - E]}\ dx\right\} . \tag{B7.2}$$

Equation (B7.2) is obtained by integration of Eq. (B7.1) after the WKB approximation. Qualitatively, the wavefunction outside the barrier has a general form of $\exp(ikx)$ where the wave vector is given by $k = (2m^*E/\hbar^2)^{1/2}$. Inside the barrier, $U(x) > E$ and the kinetic energy becomes negative, giving an imaginary k of $i\{(2m^*)[U(x)-E]/\hbar^2\}^{1/2}$. Here, the final form of the wavefunction becomes $\exp(-|k|x)$ which is the same as Eq. (B7.2).

Since the probability of the electron's presence is proportional to the square of the wavefunction magnitude, the tunneling probability is given by

$$T_t = \frac{|\psi(x_2)|^2}{|\psi(x_1)|^2}$$

$$= \exp\left\{-2\int_{x_1}^{x_2} \sqrt{\frac{2m^*}{\hbar^2}[U(x) - E]}\ dx\right\} . \tag{B7.3}$$

For the case of a rectangular barrier (Fig. B7.1(a)), the tunneling probability is given by

$$T_t = \exp\left(-2\sqrt{\frac{2m^* q\phi_b}{\hbar^2}}\ \Delta x\right) . \tag{B7.4}$$

For a triangular barrier (Fig. B7.1(b)), the potential is described by

$$U(x) - E = q\phi_b\left(1 - \frac{x}{\Delta x}\right) \tag{B7.5}$$

and the tunneling probability is given by

$$T_t = \exp\left[\frac{-4}{3}\sqrt{\frac{2m^* q\phi_b}{\hbar^2}}\ \Delta x\right]$$

$$= \exp\left(\frac{-4\sqrt{2m^*}\,q\,\phi_b^{3/2}}{3\hbar|\mathcal{E}|}\right) . \tag{B7.6}$$

For a parabolic barrier (Fig. B7.1(c)), with

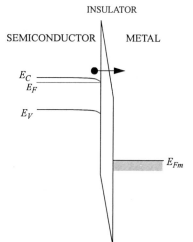

INSULATOR

SEMICONDUCTOR   METAL

E_C
E_F

E_V

E_{Fm}

FIGURE B7.2
Fowler-Nordheim tunneling of electron through a triangular barrier under large bias.

$$U(x) - E = q\phi_b\left(1 - \frac{4x^2}{\Delta x^2}\right) ,$$
(B7.7)

the tunneling probability is given by

$$T_t = \exp\left(-\frac{\pi}{2}\sqrt{\frac{2m^* q\phi_b}{\hbar^2}} \, \Delta x\right) .$$
(B7.8)

With known tunneling probability, the tunneling current is given by the simple function

$$J_t = -nv_{th}qT_t .$$
(B7.9)

Of particular interest is tunneling through the barrier created by a heterointerface between two semiconductors or an interface between a semiconductor and an insulator. Under large bias or high field, tunneling occurs through a triangular barrier as shown in Fig. B7.2. Such tunneling, where the width of the barrier becomes a function of applied voltage, is called Fowler-Nordheim tunneling and the current is described by the relation

$$J_t = C_1\mathscr{E}^2\exp\left(\frac{-C_2}{\mathscr{E}}\right) .$$
(B7.10)

For electron tunneling from silicon through silicon dioxide, the constants are $C_1 = 9.625\times10^{-7}$ A/V^2 and $C_2 = 2.765\times10^8$ V/cm. At lower voltages, tunneling is through a trapezoidal barrier and it is called direct tunneling.

APPENDIX
B8

HALL EFFECT

The Hall effect is named after the originator who made the discovery in 1879. Even today, it remains one of the most fascinating phenomena that is both fundamentally interesting and practical. Examples include the recent study of the fractional quantum Hall effect, and the application as magnetic-field sensors which are widely used in computer keyboards. The Hall effect is used in common practice to measure certain properties of semiconductors, namely the carrier concentration (even down to a low level of 10^{12} cm^{-3}), the mobility, and the type (n or p). It is an important analytical tool since a simple conductance measurement can only give the product of concentration and mobility, and the type remains unknown.

The Hall effect arises when a semiconductor or a metal is placed in orthogonal electric and magnetic fields. An example of a p-type semiconductor is shown in Fig. B8.1. The hole carriers moving in the x-direction are deflected by the magnetic field toward the y-direction. This results in unequal hole concentration at the two x-z surfaces, and a Hall electric field is generated. Once this Hall field $\mathscr{E}_H$ is fully established, moving carriers are no longer deflected sideway since the Lorentz force is balanced exactly by the Hall field. The Lorentz force is given by

$$\text{Force} = qv\mathscr{B} \quad . \tag{B8.1}$$

The carrier velocity v is related to the current density by

$$J = qv_{ave}p \quad . \tag{B8.2}$$

It should be noted that the v_{ave} in Eq. (B8.2) is an average value from a certain distribution, and is different from the individual v of a particular carrier needed in Eq. (B8.1). This difference is accounted for by the Hall factor r_H, to be discussed later ($v = r_H v_{ave}$). Since for each carrier the Lorentz force must be equal to the force exerted by the Hall field,

$$q\mathscr{E}_H = qv\mathscr{B} \quad , \tag{B8.3}$$

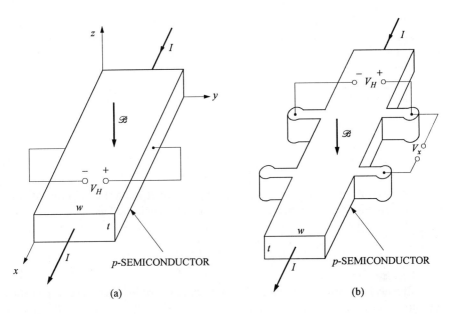

FIGURE B8.1
(a) Schematic diagram showing the basic structure for measuring the Hall effect. (b) A variation of the Hall structure where the conductivity can be measured simultaneously to give mobility in addition to the concentration.

$$\mathcal{E}_H = v\mathcal{B} = \left(\frac{r_H}{qp}\right)J\mathcal{B} \ . \tag{B8.4}$$

The Hall field $\mathcal{E}_H$ is shown to be proportional to J and $\mathcal{B}$, and the proportionality constant is referred to as the Hall coefficient

$$R_H \equiv \frac{r_H}{qp} \ . \tag{B8.5}$$

The Hall voltage V_H is a measurable quantity, given by

$$V_H = \mathcal{E}_H w$$

$$= R_H w J\mathcal{B} = \left(\frac{r_H}{qp}\right)w J\mathcal{B} \ . \tag{B8.6}$$

In order to obtain the concentration p, r_H needs to be known. It originates from

$$r_H \equiv \frac{\langle \tau^2 \rangle}{\langle \tau \rangle^2} \tag{B8.7}$$

where τ is the relaxation time (mean time between collisions). It is a complicated function of the magnetic field, the scattering mechanism, and the shape of the energy surface. It has a value of 1.18 for phonon scattering, 1.93 for impurity scattering, and generally it lies in the range of 1–2. At a very high magnetic field, it approaches a value slightly below unity. Equation (B8.5) also assumes conduction by a single type of carrier. A more general solution is described by

$$R_H = \frac{r_H}{q}\left[\frac{\mu_p^2 p - \mu_n^2 n}{(\mu_p p + \mu_n n)^2}\right] . \tag{B8.8}$$

It can be seen in the above equation that the sign of R_H and thus V_H reveals the majority type of the semiconductor. The Hall angle is defined as

$$\theta_H \equiv \tan^{-1}\left(\frac{\mathcal{E}_H}{\mathcal{E}_x}\right) = \tan^{-1}(r_H \mu \mathcal{B}) . \tag{B8.9}$$

Besides the carrier concentration and type, it is often necessary to measure the carrier mobility. Since

$$\sigma = q\mu_p p , \tag{B8.10}$$

the conductivity of the material has to be known. A structure more suitable for this purpose is shown is Fig. B8.1(b). Additional taps along the x-direction enable simultaneous and more precise measurement of σ by eliminating contributions from series resistance. Knowing σ, R_H, and r_H, the mobility is given by

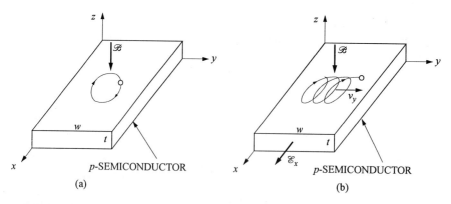

FIGURE B8.2
Hall effect in high magnetic field without scattering and (a) without electric field, and (b) with electric field $\mathcal{E}_x$.

$$\mu_p = \frac{\sigma}{qp} = \frac{\sigma R_H}{r_H} \ . \tag{B8.11}$$

If r_H is ignored ($=1$), a Hall mobility is obtained

$$\mu_H = \sigma R_H \tag{B8.12}$$

which obviously differs from the drift mobility by the factor r_H ($\mu_p = \mu_H/r_H$).

The resistivity of the material in the x-direction is known to increase with the magnetic field. This is called the magnetoresistive effect. Since carriers have a distribution of velocities, the ones that are different from the mean would not be exactly balanced by the Hall field, and they are deflected to travel along a longer path, leading to a higher resistance. (See Section 64.5.1.)

With high magnetic field and low temperature, a phenomenon known as cyclotron resonance can be observed. Additionally, if a structure containing a two-dimensional electron/hole gas is used, the quantum Hall effect occurs. These will be discussed in sequence.

Let us first consider the case where the applied electric field is zero, $\mathcal{E}_x = 0$. From the thermal velocity and the magnetic field, carriers go around in circles with cyclotron resonance frequency (Fig. B8.2(a))

$$\omega_c = \frac{q\mathcal{B}}{m^*} \tag{B8.13}$$

and radius

$$r = \frac{m^* v}{q\mathcal{B}} \ . \tag{B8.14}$$

When scattering is negligible such that the mean free path is longer than the circular path, the quantized states are distinctly separated,

$$E_n = \frac{\hbar^2 k^2}{2m^*} + \left(N_i + \frac{1}{2}\right)\hbar\omega_c \tag{B8.15}$$

where N_i is an integer. In a cyclotron resonance experiment, an electromagnetic wave with frequency close to ω_c is passed through the sample. When it exactly matches the quantized energy $\hbar\omega_c$, excitation between levels occurs and there is strong resonance absorption. This measurement is useful in obtaining the effective mass accurately.

Adding an electric field $\mathcal{E}_x$ will result in a spiral movement of holes in the y-direction (Fig. B8.2(b)). The center of this loop moves with a velocity

$$v_y = \frac{\mathcal{E}_x}{\mathcal{B}} \tag{B8.16}$$

and the Hall conductivity σ_{xy} is given by

$$\sigma_{xy} = \frac{J_y}{\mathscr{E}_x} = \frac{qpv_y}{\mathscr{E}_x} = \frac{qp}{\mathscr{B}} \ . \tag{B8.17}$$

Since $v_x = 0$, there is no longitudinal current J_x, and $\sigma_{xx} = 0$. This situation changes, however, if the Hall voltage is allowed to build up by an open circuit (letting $J_y = 0$). This Hall field leads to current flow again in the x-direction. The σ_{xy} in Eq. (B8.17) is still valid and can now be measured by $J_x/\mathscr{E}_H$.

The quantum Hall effect was first observed in 1980 by Klitzing who was awarded the Nobel prize in physics in 1985.[1] It is observable only on two-dimensional systems such as those in inversion layers or heterointerfaces. Schematically, t in Fig. B8.2 is below ≈ 100 Å. In a 2-D system, this dimension t can no longer be known precisely. It is more convenient to change the units of p, σ and R_H to $p' = 1/\text{cm}^2$, $\sigma' = 1/\Omega$, and $R'_H = \text{cm}^2/\text{C}$. With the added spatial confinement of carriers, not only is the energy quantized, but the number of carriers in each Landau level is also precisely known, giving a total density of

$$p' = \frac{mq\mathscr{B}}{h} \ . \tag{B8.18}$$

The Hall resistivity in this case depends on the number of Landau levels filled (m),

$$\sigma'_{xy} = \frac{I_x}{V_H} = \frac{qp'}{\mathscr{B}} = \frac{mq^2}{h} \ , \tag{B8.19}$$

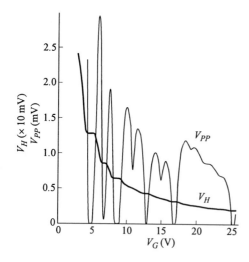

FIGURE B8.3
Characteristics of quantum Hall effects.
$V_H \propto \rho'_{xy}$, $V_{PP} \propto \rho'_{xx}$. (After Ref. 1)

and the Hall coefficient becomes

$$R'_H = \frac{V_H}{I\mathscr{B}} = \frac{1}{qp'} = \frac{h}{mq^2\mathscr{B}} \ . \tag{B8.20}$$

It is important to note that the measured quantity σ'_{xy} is a multiple of a fundamental constant q^2/h, and is independent of the sample size, applied fields, or the material itself. This quantum Hall effect is demonstrated in a MOSFET in Fig. B8.3 where the gate voltage V_G (sometimes $\mathscr{B}$) is used to scan the number of filled levels m. The Hall resistivity plateaus correspond to Eq. (B8.19) and they coincide with zero magnetoresistivity ρ'_{xx}. At these V_G values, the Fermi level is close to a Landau level, and scattering is minimal since there are no extended states. Outside these ρ'_{xy} plateaus, neither ρ'_{xy} nor ρ'_{xx} is quantized due to finite temperature and finite scattering.

The fractional quantum Hall effect was discovered in 1982,[2] shortly after the initial quantum Hall effect. It is based on the observation of fractional m in plots similar to Fig. B8.3. Values for m reported include 1/3, 2/3, 1/5, 2/7, 4/9, etc., and the theory is not yet well known.

REFERENCES

1. K. v. Klitzing, G. Dorda and M. Pepper, "New method for high-accuracy determination of the fine-structure constant based on quantized Hall resistance," *Phys. Rev. Lett.*, **45**, 494 (1980).
2. D. C. Tsui, H. L. Stormer and A. C. Gossard, "Two-dimensional magnetotransport in the extreme quantum limit," *Phys. Rev. Lett.*, **48**, 1559 (1982).

APPENDIX
B9

QUANTUM WELL AND SUPERLATTICE

When electrons are free to move in a semiconductor in all directions, their energy above the conduction-band edge is continuous, given by the relationship to their momentum

$$E - E_C = \frac{\hbar^2}{2m_e^*} (k_x^2 + k_y^2 + k_z^2) \ .$$

(B9.1)

In a quantum well, carriers are confined in one direction, say in the x-coordinate such that $k_x = 0$. It will be shown that the energy within this well is no longer continuous with respect to the x-direction, but becomes quantized in discrete levels.

The most important parameters for a quantum well are the well width a and the well height ϕ_b. The energy-band diagram shown in Fig. B9.1(a) corresponds to that of a heterostructure (composition) quantum well. The potential barrier is obtained from the conduction- or valence-band offset $\Delta E_C/\Delta E_V$. The solution for the wavefunction of the Schrödinger equation is

$$\psi(x) = \sin\left(\frac{\pi N_i x}{a}\right) \ .$$

(B9.2)

It should be noted that at the well boundaries, $\psi(x)$ is truly zero only when ϕ_b is infinite. With finite ϕ_b, carriers can "leak" out (by tunneling) of the well with certain probability. This is important for the formation of a superlattice discussed later. The pinning of nodes at the well boundaries leads to the quantization of bands, each has a bottom energy of (with respect to the band edges),

$$E_N = \frac{\hbar^2 \pi^2 N_i^2}{2m^* a^2} \ .$$

(B9.3)

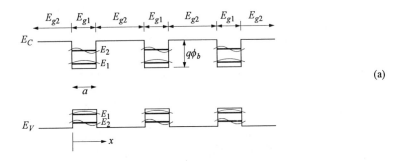

(a)

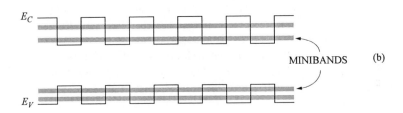

(b)

MINIBANDS

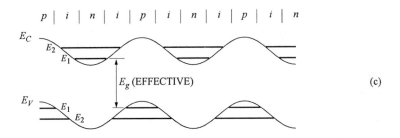

(c)

E_g (EFFECTIVE)

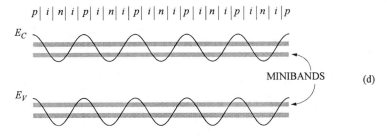

MINIBANDS

(d)

FIGURE B9.1
Energy-band diagrams for (a) heterostructure (composition) multiple quantum wells, (b) heterostructure superlattice, (c) doping (*n-i-p-i*) multiple quantum wells, and (d) doping superlattice.

With a as a variable, the definition of a quantum well can only be loosely defined. Although the minimum requirements should be that the quantized energy $\hbar^2\pi^2/2m^*a^2$ is much larger than kT, and a smaller than l_m. These do not take into account a finite barrier height.

When quantum wells are separated from one another by thick barrier layers, there is no communication between them and this system can only be described as multiple quantum wells. However, when the barrier layers between them become thinner to the extent that wavefunctions start to overlap, a heterostructure (composition) superlattice is formed. The superlattice has two major differences from a multiple-quantum-well system in that (1) the energy levels are continuous in space across the barrier, and (2) the discrete bands widen into minibands (Fig. B9.1(b)). The transition from multiple quantum wells into a superlattice is analogous to the formation of a regular lattice by pulling atoms together. The isolated atoms have discrete levels, whereas a lattice transforms these discrete levels into the continuous conduction band and valance band.

Another approach to form quantum wells is by spatial variation in doping, whereby the potential barriers are formed by space-charge fields (Fig. B9.1(c)). The barrier shape in this case is parabolic rather than rectangular. There are two interesting features in this doping (or n-i-p-i) multiple-quantum-well structure. First the conduction-band minimum and the valence-band maximum are displaced from each other, meaning electrons and holes accumulate at different locations. This leads to minimal electron-hole recombination and very long carrier lifetime, many orders of magnitude higher than the regular material. Secondly, the effective energy gap, which is now between the first quantized levels for the electrons and holes, is reduced from the intrinsic material. This tunable effective energy gap enables light emission and absorption of longer wavelength. This structure is unique in that it has an indirect energy gap in "real space," as opposed to k-space. When the doping quantum wells are close together, a doping (n-i-p-i) superlattice is again formed (Fig. B9.1(d)).

The confinement of carriers can be extended to being two-dimensional and three-dimensional, resulting in what are known as quantum-wire and quantum-dot structures.

GENERAL APPLICATIONS
OF
DEVICE GROUPS

APPENDIX
C1

APPLICATIONS OF RECTIFIERS

A rectifier is a specific type of diode that has the properties of low impedance (high current) under forward bias and high impedance (low current) under reverse bias. A diode is a more generic name for a two-terminal device that has non-linear DC I-V characteristics. A diode is not necessarily a rectifier. The tunnel diode is a good example (see discussions in Introduction). An ideal rectifier has characteristics shown in Fig. C1.1 and is used for most of the discussions in this appendix. The applications of a rectifier are listed below.

1. Half-wave rectifier: In general, when a waveform containing positive and negative voltage passes through a half-wave rectifier shown in Fig. C1.2, only one polarity is allowed to pass through. A symmetric waveform such as the sinusoidal becomes a "half-wave." When the output is passed through a low-pass filter, DC voltage can be obtained from the original AC voltage.

2. Full-wave rectifier: Here the circuit does not block negative voltage, but converts its polarity as shown in Fig. C1.3. It is a more efficient AC-to-DC converter than the half-wave rectifier. Two popular versions are the bridge rectifier and the configuration using a center-tapped transformer.

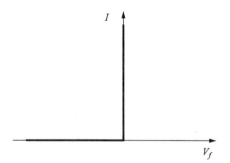

FIGURE C1.1
I-V characteristics of an ideal rectifier.

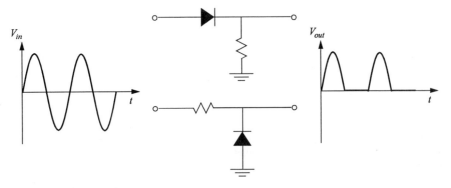

FIGURE C1.2
Half-wave rectifiers, series-connected diode (top) and parallel-connected diode (bottom), with input and output waveforms.

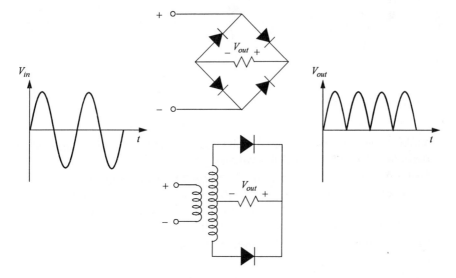

FIGURE C1.3
Full-wave rectifiers using a bridge configuration (top) and a center-tapped transformer (bottom).

3. **Clipper:** The circuit shown in Fig. C1.4 clips one polarity of the waveform to within a selected value, without distorting the rest of the waveform. When $V_o = 0$, it becomes a half-wave rectifier.

4. **Clamper:** The circuit shown in Fig. C1.5 shifts the DC level of the waveform without distorting its shape. Notice that the shifted waveform is of one polarity, with the minimum voltage at zero. This circuit can also be used in

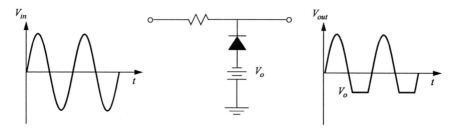

FIGURE C1.4
A clipper circuit with input and output waveforms.

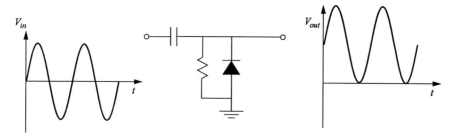

FIGURE C1.5
A clamper circuit with input and output waveforms.

an AC-to-DC converter as a "doubler" such that the DC value obtained is twice that from the original AC voltage.

5. Peak detector: A circuit shown in Fig. C1.6 detects the local peak value of a fast signal. It can be viewed as a half-wave rectifier with a low-pass filter. One practical example is the demodulation of AM broadcasting. The time constant of the output signal can be varied by R and C.

6. Logic: Simple OR and AND logics can be implemented as shown in Fig. C1.7.

7. The forward impedance changes with bias (see Eq. (C1.1) below) and the diode can be used as a varistor (see Section 12.5.1).

8. Microwave modulation, mixing, and detection: Although any nonlinear device, not necessarily rectifying, can theoretically perform these functions, the Schottky-barrier diode is most commonly used for this purpose because of the high-frequency capability. In systems such as broadcasting, the signals that contain the information are modulated with a much higher frequency, called the carrier frequency. The advantages of modulation to these higher frequencies are: (1) more efficient transmission through the atmosphere, (2) reduced antenna size, and (3) higher number of channels available. Popular

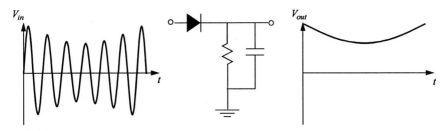

FIGURE C1.6
Peak-detection circuit with input and output waveforms.

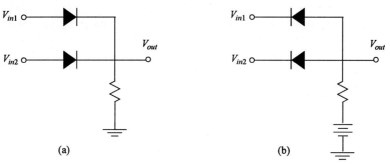

FIGURE C1.7
Logic realization for (a) OR gate and (b) AND gate.

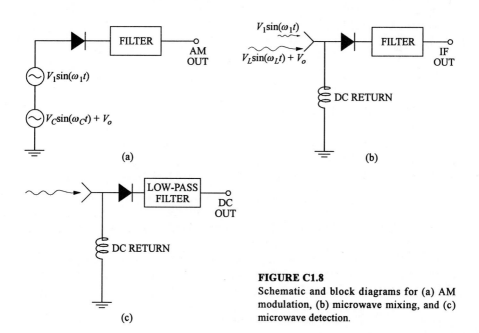

FIGURE C1.8
Schematic and block diagrams for (a) AM modulation, (b) microwave mixing, and (c) microwave detection.

modulation schemes are amplitude modulation (AM) and frequency modulation (FM).

For example, the circuit shown in Fig. C1.8(a) can produce AM. Starting with the forward characteristics of a diode,

$$I = I_o \exp (\beta_T V) \ , \tag{C1.1}$$

Taylor's expansion gives the following small-signal approximation on the current from an applied voltage which has a DC component V_o and an AC component v,

$$i \approx a_1 v + a_2 v^2 + ... \tag{C1.2}$$

For small-signal analysis, higher-order terms can be ignored. The sum of the carrier and the signal is the input to the diode,

$$v = V_C \sin (\omega_C t) + V_1 \sin (\omega_1 t) \ . \tag{C1.3}$$

The AC current is given by

$$i \approx a_1 v + a_2 v^2$$
$$= ... + 2 a_2 V_1 V_C \sin (\omega_1 t) \sin (\omega_C t) + ... \tag{C1.4}$$

which contains the AM output. The input and output waveforms are operated at the non-linear region of the diode characteristics as shown in Fig. C1.9(a).

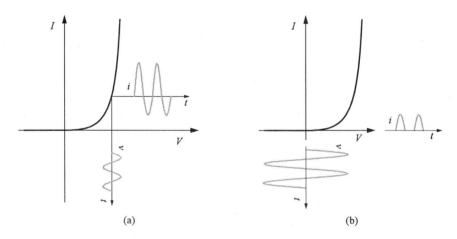

(a)   (b)

FIGURE C1.9
(a) Small-signal response in modulation, mixing, and detection. Note the non-linearity of the output current. (b) Large-signal response in a zero-bias detector.

A heterodyne receiver has a mixer followed by a detector. The function of the mixer is to down-convert the microwave frequency to a lower frequency, called the intermediate frequency (IF). This down-conversion also has three advantages: (1) less demanding on the amplifier, (2) easier for narrow-band filtering, and (3) by varying the local-oscillator frequency, the same system can be used for different carrier frequencies. In Fig. C1.8(b), the incoming signal is mixed with that from a local oscillator, and the mathematics are similar to the previous case,

$$v = V_1 \sin(\omega_1 t) + V_L \sin(\omega_L t) \ , \tag{C1.5}$$

$$
\begin{aligned}
i \approx a_1 v + a_2 v^2 \\
&= \ldots + 2a_2 V_1 V_L \sin(\omega_1 t) \sin(\omega_L t) + \ldots \\
&= \ldots + a_2 V_1 V_L \cos[(\omega_1 - \omega_L)t] + \ldots
\end{aligned}
\tag{C1.6}
$$

The down-conversion of frequency is apparent. Other unwanted frequencies are subsequently filtered out. The signal is shown to be proportional to the local-oscillator amplitude V_L. In practice, V_L is much larger than V_1.

A microwave detector can be operated in the small-signal regime or the large-signal regime. The schematic is shown in Fig. C1.8(c). For the small-signal analysis,

$$v = V_1 \sin(\omega_1 t) \tag{C1.7}$$

and similarly

$$
\begin{aligned}
i \approx a_1 v + a_2 v^2 \\
&\approx a_1 V_1 \sin(\omega_1 t) + a_2 V_1^2 \sin^2(\omega_1 t) \ .
\end{aligned}
\tag{C1.8}
$$

The last term is the important component as it has a non-zero DC value. Because its output is proportional to the square of the input signal, the device is often referred to as a square-law detector. For large-signal detection, there is no DC bias and the detector is sometimes called a zero-bias detector. The waveforms are shown in Fig. C1.9(b). This operation is similar to a half-wave rectifier. The output current is passed onto a low-pass filter to give a DC output.

APPENDIX
C2

APPLICATIONS OF NEGATIVE DIFFERENTIAL RESISTANCE

Negative differential resistance is referred to by two types of behavior. In transit-time devices like the IMPATT diode and BARITT diode, the negative resistance is dynamic in nature and only occurs in high-frequency operations. The negative resistance in these devices is characterized by having small-signal voltage and current that are out of phase in relation to each other. Only "static" negative differential resistance, which has a negative dI/dV region, is considered in this appendix. This type of negative-resistance devices can have an S-shape or N-shape I-V characteristics.

An example of an N-shape I-V curve is used. When a negative-resistance diode is connected in series with a resistor, the operation regime is determined by the conventional load-line analysis (Fig. C2.1). With proper choice of resistance and V_{DD} voltage, different intersections are possible. Points A and C in the figure are considered stable operating points while B is unstable. Switching circuits such

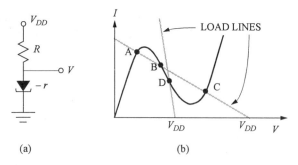

(a)　　　　　　　　(b)

FIGURE C2.1
(a) In the series connection of a resistor with a negative-resistance diode, intercepts depend on the resistance value and V_{DD}. (b) The intercepts A and C are stable operating points, while B is unstable and D is astable.

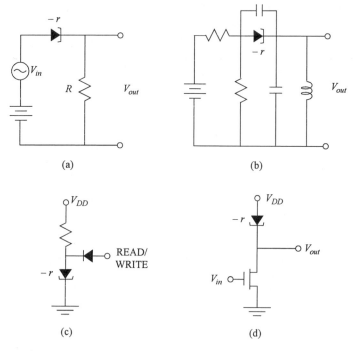

FIGURE C2.2
Circuit applications of negative differential resistance in (a) amplifier, (b) oscillator, (c) memory, and
(d) inverter.

as memory operate with this type of load line. With a different set of resistance
and V_{DD} voltage, D is the only intercept. It is considered astable and circuits such
as amplifiers and oscillators operate in this region. With this background, the
applications of negative differential resistance are listed below.

1. Amplifier: A simple example of series connection in Fig. C2.2(a) indicates
   that

$$\frac{V_{out}}{V_{in}} = \frac{R}{R + (-r)} \qquad \text{(C2.1)}$$

and it provides an AC voltage gain. Other versions of amplifiers are possible.

2. Oscillator: The circuit shown in Fig. C2.2(b) generates AC output with a DC
   input. The frequency can be tuned by L and C.

3. Pulse generator: A negative-resistance diode can also be used to realize a
   pulse-generator circuit.

4. Memory: In Fig. C2.1(b), the operating points A and C provide the bistable states in a memory. Figure C2.2(c) shows a simple memory cell.

5. Logic: Negative resistance can be incorporated in logic circuits. An example is the tunnel-diode-FET logic whose inverter is shown in Fig. C2.2(d).

APPENDIX

C3

APPLICATIONS OF TRANSISTORS

The name transistor comes from transfer-resistor because the resistance between the source and drain (emitter and collector) is controlled by the gate (base). The general applications can be digital and analog in nature. In digital applications, a transistor is used mainly as a three-terminal switch. In analog applications, it is used as an amplifier for AC signals. Specific applications are discussed below.

1. **Logic:** A digital computer needs logic building blocks such as OR, AND, NAND, NOT, etc., and a transistor is the primary component for these logic blocks. A simple logic inverter (NOT) is shown in Fig. C3.1. Based on these logic building blocks, other digital circuits such as a flop-flop, shift register, and memory can be formed.

2. **Control:** As a switch, a transistor controls the passage of a signal. An example is the multiplexer/demultiplexer circuit which enables multiple channels to be carried via a single transmission line (Fig. C3.2(a)). A transistor also selects the components in an addressable array. The example shown in Fig. C3.2(b) is applicable to a memory or a flat-panel display. As a

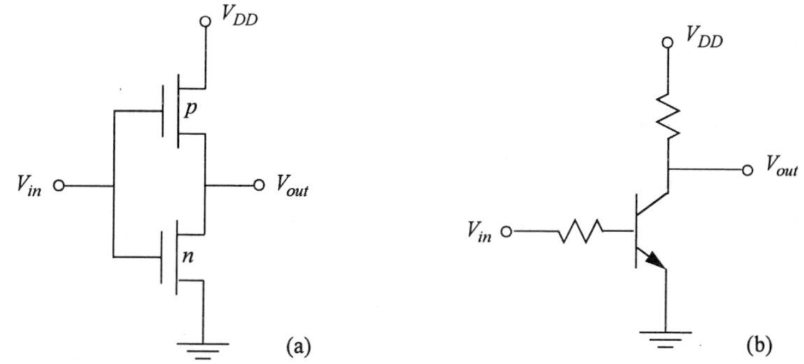

FIGURE C3.1
Inverter circuit using (a) complementary FETs and (b) a PET.

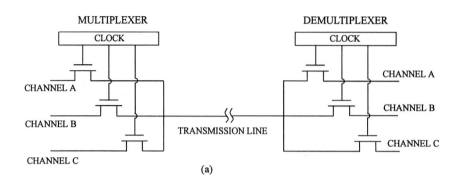

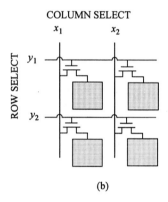

FIGURE C3.2
Using transistors as control devices in (a) a routing mechanism for an idealized multiplexer system, and (b) an addressable array such as memory or flat-panel display.

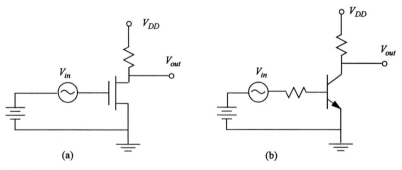

FIGURE C3.3
Amplifier circuits using (a) FET and (b) PET.

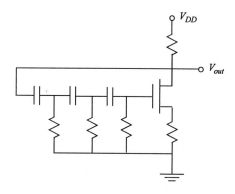

FIGURE C3.4
An example of transistor oscillator–phase-shift oscillator.

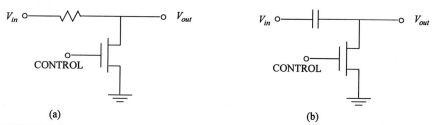

(a)   (b)

FIGURE C3.5
Using a transistor as a variable resistor for a (a) variable attenuator and (b) variable phase-shifter.

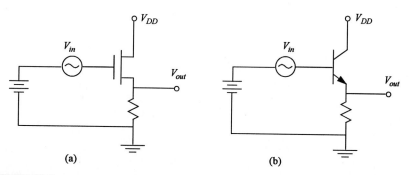

(a)   (b)

FIGURE C3.6
Impedance transformation using (a) source follower of an FET, (b) emitter follower of a PET.

power device, a transistor controls the power delivered to the load from a power source.

3. Amplifier: A transistor provides gain for an AC signal. Simple amplifier circuits are shown in Fig. C3.3. More complex circuits include differential amplifiers and operational amplifiers.

4. Oscillator: An amplifier with proper feedback can result in oscillation, such that a DC input can generate an AC output. A simple transistor oscillator is shown in Fig. C3.4.

5. Variable resistor: As an analog switch, a transistor provides variable resistance. Simple examples are variable attenuator and variable phase-shifter (Fig. C3.5).

6. Microwave applications: Being a non-linear device, a transistor can be used in microwave mixing, detection, and modulation. These operations are similar to those on diodes and they are described in more details at the end of Appendix C1.

7. Impedance transformation: The source follower and the emitter follower (Fig. C3.6) are special amplifiers where the voltage gain is approximately unity. The transistor transforms the output impedance of the signal to a much reduced value.

APPENDIX
C4

APPLICATIONS OF PHOTODETECTORS

There exists a large variety of photodetectors. To choose a photodetector for a specific application, the first criterion is the applicable range of wavelengths. Next, one has to consider speed, responsivity, and cost. The applications of photodetectors are listed below.

1. Object detection: A light source coupled to a photodetector forms a pair to detect an object that interrupts the light beam. This pair can be arranged in the reflection mode or direct mode. Examples are proximity detection, intruder alarm, liquid-level detection, tachometer, and range and speed finders.

2. Data retrieval: The light-detector pair is used to read stored optical data. Examples are compact-disc player and card reader.

3. Optical-fiber communication: An optical-fiber communication system is shown in Fig. C4.1. The main advantage compared to an electrical system is bandwidth. The light source can be either a laser or an LED. The choice of wavelength in this application is determined by the optical characteristics of the optical fiber. It is shown in Fig. C4.2 that for minimum attenuation, 1.5 µm is most suitable and for minimum chromatic dispersion, 1.3 µm is optimal. The repeater serves to boost up the signal and clean up the noise for a long-distant fiber. It consists of a detector, an amplifier, followed by a light source.

4. Opto-isolator. An opto-isolator (opto-coupler), as shown in Fig. C4.3, consists of a light source which converts an electrical signal to a light signal, and a photodetector which converts the light signal back to the electrical signal. The advantage is complete electrical isolation in case of circuit noise, or problem in impedance matching.

5. Chemical analysis: Chemical analysis is possible from the absorption spectroscopy of gas, liquid, and solid. An example is combustion control for automobiles.

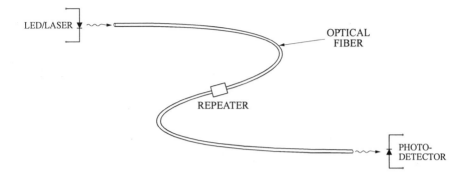

FIGURE C4.1
An optical-fiber communication system.

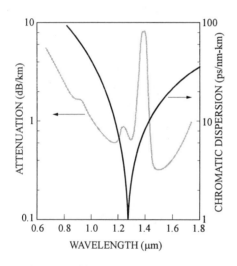

FIGURE C4.2
Wavelength dependence of attenuation and chromatic dispersion for a typical optical fiber. (After Ref. 1)

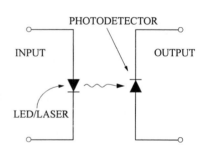

FIGURE C4.3
Schematic diagram of an opto-isolator.

6. Light-activated switch: A photodetector sends signal to a switch that controls the power to the equipment. Examples are automatic camera flashes and automatic controls for street lamps.

7. Light meter: A photodetector measures light power. Examples are the calibration of LEDs and low-power lasers, and light meters for photography.

8. Two-dimensional imaging: An array of photodetectors provides real-time two-dimensional imaging. There are numerous commercial and military applications. Examples are TV and camcorder cameras, astronomy, reconnaissance and surveillance, and tracking and guidance systems.

9. Thermal imaging: This is a special case of two-dimensional imaging that detects the blackbody radiation of an object which has higher temperature than the background. Usually it means infrared with wavelengths longer than a few μm. Applications are night vision, intruder alarm, medical diagnostics such as cancer detection, IC diagnostics, reconnaissance, weather forecast, and pollution monitoring.

10. Temperature measurement: A detector with a monochromator can profile the black-body radiation of an object, and thus determine its temperature.

REFERENCE

1. T. E. Bell, "Single-frequency semiconductor lasers," *IEEE Spectrum*, Dec. Issue, 38 (1983).

APPENDIX
C5

APPLICATIONS OF
BISTABLE OPTICAL DEVICES

Bistable optical devices have light as input and output, and they hold the potential for optical computing. These all-optical devices are attractive since they can be coupled directly to optical fibers, without converting to electrical signals. Besides, there is also a push for waveguide interconnect within the IC chip. These optical waveguides replace electrical interconnects whose speed is usually limited by capacitance. Without electrical wires, two-dimensional parallel processing with an array of bistable optical devices is much easier. This is important for 2-D image processing applications. Furthermore, using optical signals only, the bistable optical devices have much higher speed performance than electrical devices. First-order comparison between these is the speed of light (3×10^{10} cm/s) vs. carrier saturation velocity ($\approx 10^7$ cm/s). Optical switching also requires much less power. More specific applications of bistable optical devices include memory, logic, amplification, waveform clipping/limiting/shaping, and oscillation.

The memory application requires the hysteresis loop of the light in–light out characteristics (Fig. C5.1). For a range of L_{in}, there are two stable states (bistable) for L_{out}. The output state can be set by a positive light pulse or a negative light pulse.

Optical amplification can be obtained in the region of high dL_{out}/dL_{in} slope as shown in Fig. C5.2. A small signal superimposed on a DC level gives a large AC output. Similar idea can be applied with two input beams, resulting in an optical transistor or a transphasor (Fig. C5.3). The name transphasor comes from the adjustment of the phase of the reflected light inside the optical cavity of a bistable etalon. The phase relationship between the forward and the reflected beams causes destructive or constructive interference and is the basis for bistability (see Chapter 60–Bistable Etalon). In the transphasor, the bias beam has a large, constant intensity but is just below the switching threshold, and the control beam or probe beam is a small signal to be amplified. This control beam is equivalent to the gate/base of a conventional transistor.

A bistable optical device can perform different logic functions. A simple example of an AND logic is shown in Fig. C5.4. Here each of the two inputs are

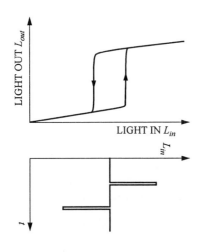

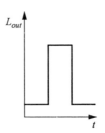

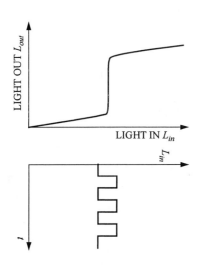

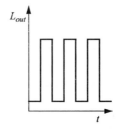

FIGURE C5.1
The bistable optical device can be used as a single-element static memory cell. The state of the light output is set by a positive or negative light pulse.

FIGURE C5.2
A bistable optical device used for optical amplification.

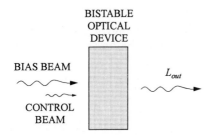

FIGURE C5.3
The transphasor has two optical input beams. The bias beam has higher, constant intensity and is slightly below the switching level. The control beam is to be amplified.

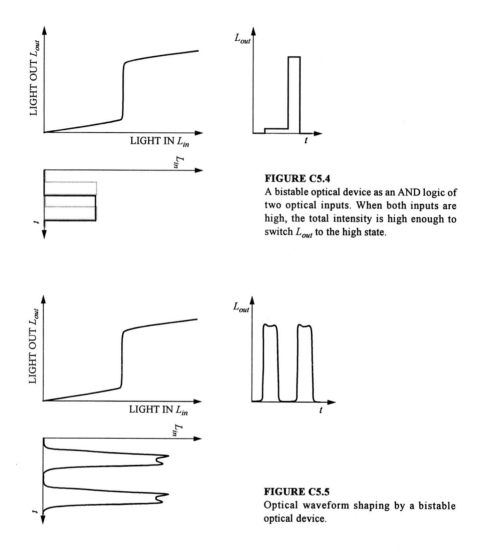

FIGURE C5.4
A bistable optical device as an AND logic of two optical inputs. When both inputs are high, the total intensity is high enough to switch L_{out} to the high state.

FIGURE C5.5
Optical waveform shaping by a bistable optical device.

smaller than the critical L_{in} to turn L_{out} high. If and only if both L_{in} are high, L_{out} is switched to a high state.

A bistable optical device can be used to reshape optical waveforms. An example is shown in Fig. C5.5. It can be seen here that in the L_{out} waveform, the rising and falling edges are much sharper, and also the noise at the peak is reduced.

SEMICONDUCTOR MEMORIES

The memory is an intricate part of a computer system. Memories can be divided into two major categories: magnetic and semiconductor. In the former category, they can be in the form of magnetic disk, tape, drum, or core. Semiconductor memories are further classified in Fig. C6.1, and are discussed in more detail in this appendix. The advantages of the semiconductor memories are higher density, higher speed in read and write, and no mechanical maneuver. The magnetic memories have larger total storage, and are more cost effective. For these reasons, semiconductor memories are used whenever they are in close interaction with the CPU or microprocessor, and magnetic memories are mainly used for data and file storage.

The first division of semiconductor memories, referring to Fig. C6.1, is based on their ability to maintain information when the power supply is disconnected. As the names imply, a volatile memory loses the content, but a nonvolatile memory does not need a voltage to maintain the data. A good example of nonvolatile-memory application is the storage of the start-up routine for a personal computer.

Before getting into each type of memory, we should also clarify the difference between a RAM and a ROM. RAM stands for random-access memory.

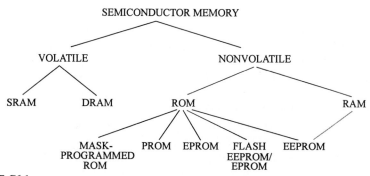

FIGURE C6.1
Classification of semiconductor memories.

It has an x-y address for each cell, which distinguishes it from other serial memories such as magnetic-type memories. Strictly speaking, a ROM (read-only memory) also has random-access capability since the architecture is similar. In fact, the read process of the RAM and ROM is almost identical. More appropriately, a RAM is sometimes called a read-write memory. The main difference between a RAM and a ROM is the ease and frequency of writing. A RAM has almost equal opportunity of write and read. A ROM in general has much more frequent read than write. It itself has a spectrum of writing capability, ranging from a pure ROM without any writing capability, to an EEPROM that has a lifetime endurance (write/erase) of more than 10^4 cycles. Because a ROM is smaller in size, and more cost effective compared to a RAM, it is used whenever frequent writing is not required. Typical examples are table look-up such as code conversion, character generation, trigonometry functions, etc. A ROM is also used to store logic functions (as programmable logic devices) and routine programs.

A semiconductor memory can be realized by either an MOS technology or a bipolar technology, and each has its own merits. An MOS memory has higher density, lower power, higher input impedance, and is less expensive. A bipolar memory is capable of higher speed. The MOS versions, which are much more popular, will be shown as examples in the following types of memories.

SRAM: The static RAM implies stability of data as long as the power supply is not interrupted. Each cell contains two inverters connected in anti-parallel. It is basically a flip-flop and has two stable states. Shown in Fig. C6.2 is an array of six-transistor cells. BL and WL represent bit-line and word-line respectively. The two p-channel devices are loads and since their current drive is not critical, they can be made of TFTs in order to save area. These loads can also be replaced with two-terminal devices such as depletion-mode transistors or resistors.

DRAM: The dynamic RAM relies on the charge stored in capacitors (Fig. C6.3). It is dynamic in the sense that the stored charge dissipates gradually through unavoidable leakage, and needs to be refreshed periodically. The time interval between refresh depends on the capacitance size as well as the leakage, and typically it is between 2–4 ms. Due to the smaller number of components in each cell, the DRAM has a larger cell count than the SRAM for the same technology, usually by a factor of four. The penalty is the requirement for refresh.

Mask-programmed ROM: As shown in Fig. C6.4, each cell is represented by a single transistor, and its state is determined by the connectivity (open or close) of the drain to the bit line. The memory content is fixed by the manufacturer and is not programmable once it is fabricated. Sometimes the mask-programmed ROM is simply referred to as ROM.

PROM: The programmable ROM is sometimes called field-programmable PROM or fusible-link ROM. The connectivity of the array is custom programmed by the customer, using the technique of fusing or anti-fusing. After programming, the memory array is similar to that of Fig. C6.4.

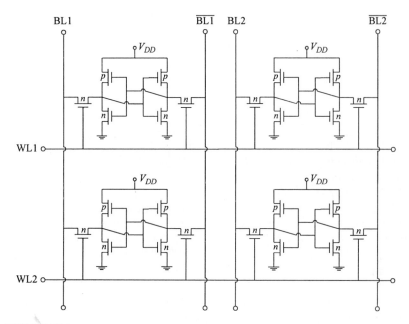

FIGURE C6.2

A 2x2 SRAM array. Note that for each cell, the bit lines have complementary data BL and $\overline{BL}$.

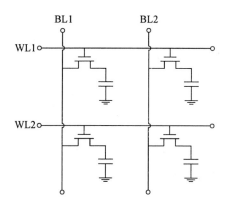

FIGURE C6.3

A DRAM array using one-transistor cells. Data are stored as charge across capacitors.

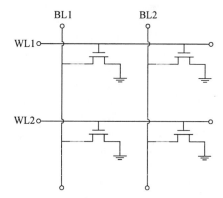

FIGURE C6.4

A mask-programmed ROM array. The connectivity of the drains to bit lines (dotted lines) are pre-determined by the fabrication process. For a PROM, the same connectivity can be field programmed by the customers using fuse or anti-fuse.

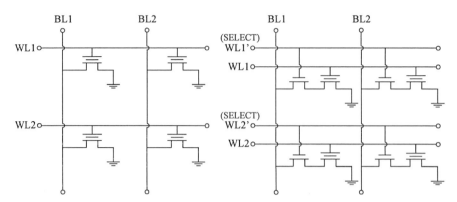

FIGURE C6.5
An EPROM usually implies cells using FAMOS transistors. A flash EEPROM also has similar arrangement.

FIGURE C6.6
An EEPROM array. Note that a select transistor is required for each cell, leading to a two-transistor cell.

EPROM: The electrically programmable ROM is generally referred to a memory with a FAMOS transistor array, shown in Fig. C6.5. Programming is performed by hot-electron injection or tunneling to the floating gate, and it requires high bias on both the drain (bit line) and the control gate (word line). Global erase is by exposure to a UV light or X-ray, but the chip usually has to be removed from the system. Selective erase is not possible.

EEPROM: In an electrically erasable/programmable ROM (also called electrically alterable ROM, EAROM), not only can it be erase electrically, but also selectively by byte address. In order to erase selectively, a select transistor is needed for each cell, leading to a two-transistor cell as shown in Fig. C6.6.

Flash EEPROM: A flash EEPROM (also called flash EPROM), as opposed to a full-featured EEPROM, can only be erased globally. It looses byte selectivity but maintains a one-transistor cell as shown in Fig. C6.5. It is thus a compromise between an EPROM and an EEPROM.

Nonvolatile RAM: This futuristic, ideal memory can be viewed as a nonvolatile SRAM, or an EEPROM with short programming time as well as high endurance.

APPENDIX

D

PHYSICAL
PROPERTIES

APPENDIX
D1

PROPERTIES OF SEMICONDUCTORS

	E_g (eV)	μ_n	μ_p	m^*_e	m^*_l	m^*_t	m^*_h	m^*_{lh}	m^*_{hh}	K_s	a (Å)
Elementary											
Si	1.12 (I)	1,500	500		0.98	0.19		0.16	0.50	11.8	5.431
Ge	0.67 (I)	3,900	1,900		1.64	0.082		0.04	0.28	16	5.646
C	5.47 (I)	1,800	1,600	0.2			0.25			5.7	3.567
Sn	0.082 (D)	2,500	2400				0.3				6.489
Te	0.33	1,100	560								
III-V											
AlAs	2.16 (I)	1,200	420	2.0				0.15	0.76	10.1	5.661
AlP	2.45 (I)	80						0.2	0.63	9.8	5.467
AlSb	1.63 (I)	200	500	0.12			0.98			12	6.136
BN	4.5 (I)									7.1	3.615
BP	2.0 (I)		300							11.6	4.538
GaAs	1.43 (D)	8,500	400	0.067				0.074	0.50	13.1	5.653
GaN	3.36 (D)	380		0.19			0.60			12.2	3.160
GaP	2.26 (I)	300	150		1.12	0.22		0.14	0.79	11.1	5.451
GaSb	0.72 (D)	5,000	1,500	0.042				0.06	0.23	15.7	6.096
InAs	0.36 (D)	33,000	480	0.023				0.025	0.41	14.6	6.058
InP	1.35 (D)	5,000	180	0.077				0.089	0.85	12.4	5.869
InSb	0.23 (D)	80,000	1,000	0.014				0.015	0.40	17	6.479
II-VI											
CdO	2.5	120									4.689
CdS	2.42 (D)	400	50	0.21			0.80			5.4	4.136
CdSe	1.7 (D)	800		0.13			0.45			10.0	4.300
CdTe	1.48 (D)	1,000	100	0.1			0.37			10.2	6.482
HgSe	0.30	20,000									6.082
HgTe	0.15	25,000	350				0.5				6.373
ZnO	3.35 (D)	200	180	0.3			1.8			9.0	4.580
ZnS	3.68 (D)	180	10	0.28						8.9	5.409
ZnSe	2.82 (D)	600	28	0.14			0.60			9.2	5.671
ZnTe	2.4 (D)	530	100	0.18			0.65			10.4	6.101

	E_g (eV)	μ_n	μ_p	m^*_e	m^*_l	m^*_t	m^*_h	m^*_{lh}	m^*_{hh}	K_s	a (Å)
Other compounds											
CdSb	0.45	300	2,000								
GaSe	2.05		20								
GaTe	1.66	14									
InSe	1.8	900									
PbS	0.41 (I)	800	1,000	0.22			0.29			17.0	5.936
PbSe	0.26	1,500	1,500							23.6	6.152
PbTe	0.32 (I)	6,000	4,000	0.17			0.20			30.0	6.462
SiC	2.42 (I)	400	50	0.60			1.00			10.0	4.360
TlSe	0.57	30	20								
ZnSb	0.50	10	350								

Note: Mobilities in cm^2/V-s. Effective masses in m_o. D/I = direct/indirect energy gap. All properties at room temperature.

APPENDIX
D2

PROPERTIES OF Ge, Si, AND GaAs

Properties	Ge	Si	GaAs
Atom/molecule density (/cm^3)	4.42×10^{22}	5.0×10^{22}	4.42×10^{22}
Atomic/molecular weight	72.60	28.09	144.63
Breakdown field (V/cm)	$\approx 10^5$	$\approx 3 \times 10^5$	$\approx 4 \times 10^5$
Crystal structure	Diamond	Diamond	Zinc-blende
Density (g/cm^3)	5.3267	2.328	5.32
Dielectric constant	16.0	11.8	13.1
Diffusion constant, intrinsic (cm^2/s)			
electron, D_n	100	39	220
hole, D_p	49	13	10
Effective density of states (/cm^3)			
in conduction band, N_C	1.04×10^{19}	2.8×10^{19}	4.7×10^{17}
in valence band, N_V	6.0×10^{18}	1.04×10^{19}	7.0×10^{18}
Effective mass (m_o), mobility			
electron, m^*_e	1.64 (m^*_l)	0.98 (m^*_l)	0.067
	0.082 (m^*_t)	0.19 (m^*_t)	
hole, m^*_h	0.044 (m^*_{lh})	0.16 (m^*_{lh})	0.074 (m^*_{lh})
	0.28 (m^*_{hh})	0.49 (m^*_{hh})	0.50 (m^*_{hh})
Effective mass (m_o), density-of-state			
electron, m^*_{de}	0.22	1.18	0.067
hole, m^*_{dh}	0.18	0.81	0.53
Electron affinity, χ (V)	4.0	4.05	4.07
Energy gap, E_g (eV)	0.67	1.12	1.42
Index of Refraction	4.0	3.4	3.3
Intrinsic carrier concentration, n_i (/cm^3)	2.4×10^{13}	1.08×10^{10} [#]	2.1×10^6
Intrinsic Debye length (μm)	0.68	24	2250
Lattice constant, a (Å)	5.64613	5.43095	5.6533
Linear coef. of thermal expansion (/°C)	5.8×10^{-6}	2.6×10^{-6}	6.86×10^{-6}
Melting point (°C)	937	1415	1238
Mobility (cm^2/V-s)			
electron, μ_n	3,900	1,500	8,500
hole, μ_p	1,900	500	400
Optical-phonon energy (eV)	0.037	0.063	0.035
Specific heat (J/g-°C)	0.31	0.7	0.35
Thermal conductivity (W/cm-°C)	0.6	1.5	0.46
Thermal diffusivity (cm^2/s)	0.36	0.9	0.44

Properties at room temperature. Most data from S. M. Sze, *Physics of semiconductor devices*, 2nd Ed., Wiley, New York, 1981. [#] M. A. Green, "Intrinsic concentration, effective densities of states, and effective mass in silicon," *J. Appl. Phys.*, **67**, 2944 (1990).

D3

PROPERTIES OF SiO_2 AND Si_3N_4

Properties	SiO_2	Si_3N_4
Density (g/cm³)	2.27	3.1
Dielectric constant	3.9	7.5
Dielectric strength (V/cm)	$\approx 1 \times 10^7$	$\approx 1 \times 10^7$
Electron affinity, χ (eV)	0.9	
Energy gap, E_g (eV)	≈ 9	≈ 5
Infrared absorption band (μm)	9.3	11.5–12.0
Melting point (°C)	≈ 1700	
Molecular density (/cm³)	2.3×10^{22}	
Molecular weight	60.08	
Refractive index	1.46	2.05
Specific heat (J/g-°C)	1.0	
Thermal conductivity (W/cm-°C)	0.014	
Thermal diffusivity (cm²/s)	0.006	
Thermal expansion coef., linear (/°C)	5.0×10^{-7}	
Resistivity (Ω-cm)	10^{14}–10^{16}	$\approx 10^{14}$

Properties at room temperature.

APPENDIX
D4

RESISTIVITY AND MOBILITY

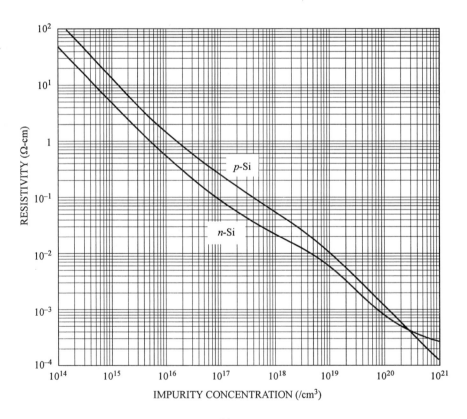

(a)

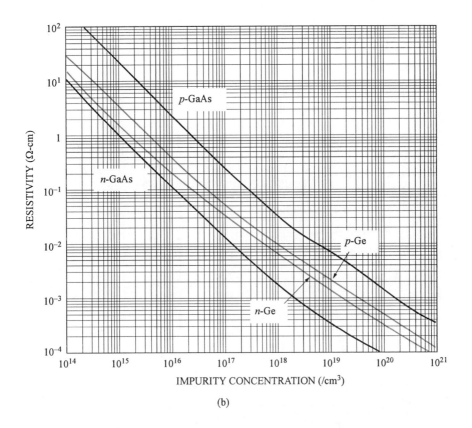

(b)

FIGURE D4.1
Resistivity of (a) Si and (b) Ge and GaAs as a function of doping concentration. (After Refs. 1 and 2)

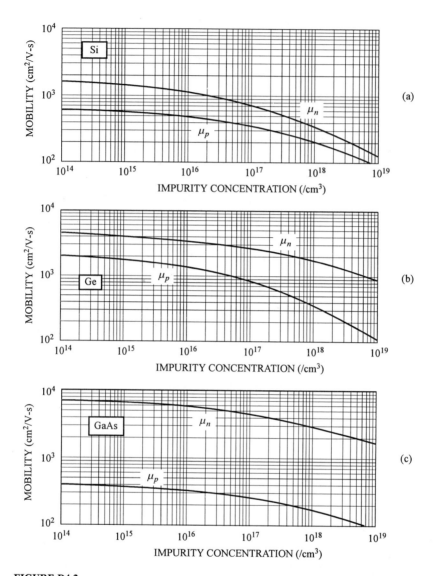

FIGURE D4.2
Carrier mobility as a function of impurity concentration for (a) Si, (b) Ge, and (c) GaAs at room temperature. (After Ref. 2)

REFERENCES

1. J. C. Irvin, "Resistivity of bulk silicon and of diffused layers in silicon," *Bell Syst. Tech. J.*, **41**, 387 (1962).
2. S. M. Sze and J. C. Irvin, "Resistivity, mobility and impurity levels in GaAs, Ge, and Si at 300°K," *Solid-State Electron.*, **11**, 599 (1968).

INTRINSIC CONCENTRATIONS AND FERMI LEVELS

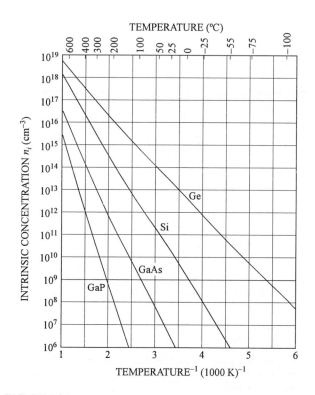

FIGURE D5.1

Temperature dependence of n_i for Si, Ge, GaAs, and GaP. (After Ref. 1)

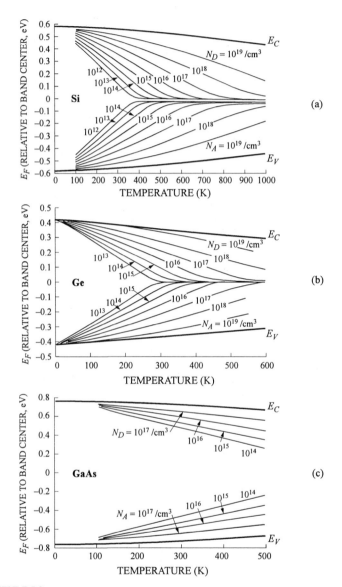

FIGURE D5.2
Fermi-level E_F as a function of doping and temperature for (a) Si (After Ref. 2), (b) Ge (After Ref. 3), and (c) GaAs (After Ref. 4).

REFERENCES

1. C. T. Sah, *Fundamentals of solid-state electronics*, World Scientific, Singapore, 1991.
2. W. E. Beadle, J. C. C. Tsai and R. D. Plummer, Eds., *Quick reference manual for silicon integrated circuit technology*, Wiley, New York, 1985.
3. A. K. Jonscher, *Principles of semiconductor device operation*, Wiley, New York, 1960.
4. A. G. Milnes, *Semiconductor devices and integrated electronics*, Van Nostrand, New York, 1980.

DEPLETION NOMOGRAPH

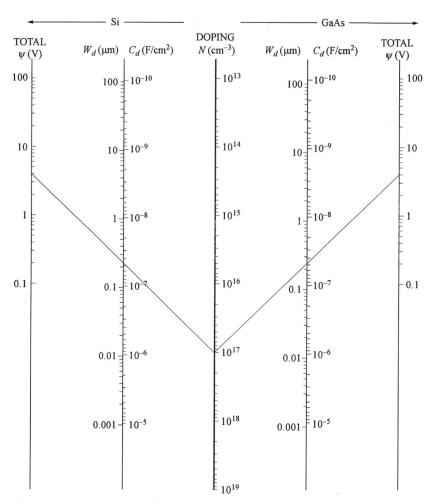

Note: Examples are for $N = 1 \times 10^{17}$ cm^{-3} and $\psi = 4$ V. There is also a quick way to estimate the depletion width. For most semiconductors, for $\psi = 1$ V and $N = 1 \times 10^{15}$ cm^{-3}, W_d happens to be around 1 μm. Since $W_d \propto (\psi/N)^{\frac{1}{2}}$ (Eqs. (E1.19)–(E1.20)), we can scale from this set of numbers. For example, with $N = 1 \times 10^{17}$ cm^{-3}, W_d becomes 0.1 μm. Changing $\psi = 4$ V would then increase the W_d to 0.2 μm.

APPENDIX
D7

ABSORPTION COEFFICIENTS

PHOTON ENERGY hv (eV)

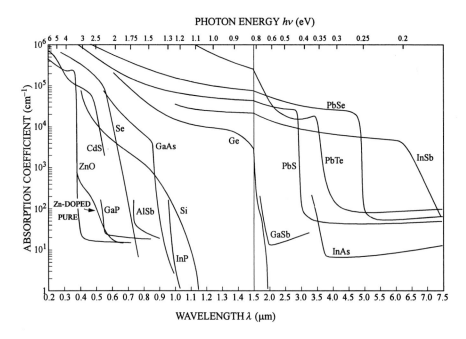

FIGURE D7.1
Optical absorption coefficient in semiconductors. (After Ref. 1)

REFERENCE

1. C. Belove, Ed., *Handbook of modern electronics and electrical engineering*, Wiley, New York, 1986.

SILICON OXIDATION RATES

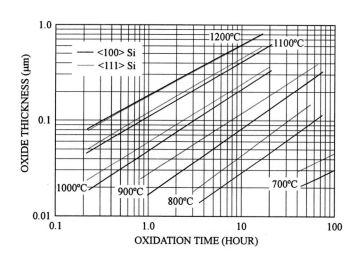

FIGURE D8.1

Oxidation rate in dry oxygen for <100> Si and <111> Si. (After Ref. 1)

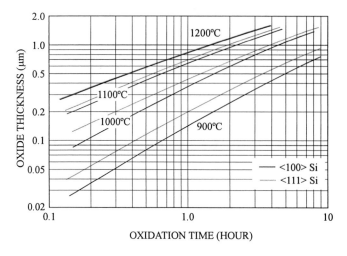

FIGURE D8.2
Oxidation rate in steam for <100> Si and <111> Si. (After Ref. 2)

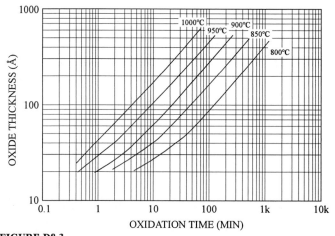

FIGURE D8.3
Thin-oxide growing rate of <100> Si in dry oxygen. (After Ref. 3)

REFERENCES

1. J. P. Meindl, R. W. Dutton, K. C. Saraswat, J. D. Plummer, T. I. Kamins and B. E. Deal, "Silicon epitaxy and oxidation," in F. Van de Wiele, W. L. Engl and P. O. Jespers, Eds, *Process and device modeling for integrated circuit design*, Noordhoff, Leyden, 1977.

2. B. E. Deal, "Thermal oxidation kinetics of silicon in pyrogenic H_2O and 5% HCl/H_2O mixtures," *J. Electrochem. Soc.*, **125**, 576 (1978).

3. H. Z. Massoud and J. D. Plummer, "Thermal oxidation of silicon in dry oxygen growth-rate enhancement in the thin regime," *J. Electrochem. Soc.*, **132**, 2685 (1985).

APPENDIX
D9

ION-IMPLANTATION RANGES AND STANDARD DEVIATIONS

$$N(x) = \frac{\text{Dose per area}}{\sqrt{2\pi}\Delta R_p} \exp\left[\frac{-(x - R_p)^2}{2\Delta R_p^2}\right] . \tag{D9.1}$$

TABLE D9.1
Ion implantation projected range (R_p) and standard deviation (ΔR_p) into Si.[1]

ENERGY (keV)	ANTIMONY R_p (μm)	ΔR_p (μm)	ARSENIC R_p (μm)	ΔR_p (μm)	BORON R_p (μm)	ΔR_p (μm)	PHOSPHORUS R_p (μm)	ΔR_p (μm)
10	0.0088	0.0026	0.0097	0.0036	0.0333	0.0171	0.0139	0.0069
20	0.0141	0.0043	0.0159	0.0059	0.0662	0.0283	0.0253	0.0119
30	0.0187	0.0058	0.0215	0.0080	0.0987	0.0371	0.0368	0.0166
40	0.0230	0.0071	0.0269	0.0099	0.1302	0.0443	0.0486	0.0212
50	0.0271	0.0084	0.0322	0.0118	0.1608	0.0504	0.0607	0.0256
60	0.0310	0.0096	0.0374	0.0136	0.1903	0.0556	0.0730	0.0298
70	0.0347	0.0107	0.0426	0.0154	0.2188	0.0601	0.0855	0.0340
80	0.0385	0.0118	0.0478	0.0172	0.2465	0.0641	0.0981	0.0380
90	0.0421	0.0130	0.0530	0.0189	0.2733	0.0677	0.1109	0.0418
100	0.0457	0.0140	0.0582	0.0207	0.2994	0.0710	0.1238	0.0456
110	0.0493	0.0151	0.0634	0.0224	0.3248	0.0739	0.1367	0.0492
120	0.0529	0.0162	0.0686	0.0241	0.3496	0.0766	0.1497	0.0528
130	0.0564	0.0172	0.0739	0.0258	0.3737	0.0790	0.1627	0.0562
140	0.0599	0.0183	0.0791	0.0275	0.3974	0.0813	0.1757	0.0595
150	0.0634	0.0193	0.0845	0.0292	0.4205	0.0834	0.1888	0.0628
160	0.0669	0.0203	0.0898	0.0308	0.4432	0.0854	0.2019	0.0659
170	0.0704	0.0213	0.0952	0.0325	0.4654	0.0872	0.2149	0.0689
180	0.0739	0.0224	0.1005	0.0341	0.4872	0.0890	0.2279	0.0719
190	0.0773	0.0234	0.1060	0.0358	0.5086	0.0906	0.2409	0.0747
200	0.0808	0.0244	0.1114	0.0374	0.5297	0.0921	0.2539	0.0775
220	0.0878	0.0264	0.1223	0.0407	0.5708	0.0950	0.2798	0.0829
240	0.0947	0.0283	0.1334	0.0439	0.6108	0.0975	0.3054	0.0880
260	0.1017	0.0303	0.1445	0.0470	0.6496	0.0999	0.3309	0.0928
280	0.1086	0.0322	0.1558	0.0502	0.6875	0.1020	0.3562	0.0974
300	0.1156	0.0342	0.1671	0.0533	0.7245	0.1040	0.3812	0.1017

TABLE D9.2

Ion implantation projected range (R_p) and standard deviation (ΔR_p) into SiO$_2$.[1]

ENERGY (keV)	ANTIMONY		ARSENIC		BORON		PHOSPHORUS	
	R_p (μm)	ΔR_p (μm)	R_p (μm)	ΔR_p (μm)	R_p (μm)	ΔR_p (μm)	R_p (μm)	ΔR_p (μm)
10	0.0071	0.0020	0.0077	0.0026	0.0298	0.0143	0.0108	0.0048
20	0.0115	0.0032	0.0127	0.0043	0.0622	0.0252	0.0199	0.0084
30	0.0153	0.0042	0.0173	0.0057	0.0954	0.0342	0.0292	0.0119
40	0.0188	0.0052	0.0217	0.0072	0.1283	0.0418	0.0388	0.0152
50	0.0222	0.0061	0.0260	0.0085	0.1606	0.0483	0.0486	0.0185
60	0.0254	0.0070	0.0303	0.0099	0.1921	0.0540	0.0586	0.0216
70	0.0286	0.0078	0.0346	0.0112	0.2228	0.0590	0.0688	0.0247
80	0.0316	0.0086	0.0388	0.0125	0.2528	0.0634	0.0792	0.0276
90	0.0347	0.0094	0.0431	0.0138	0.2819	0.0674	0.0896	0.0305
100	0.0377	0.0102	0.0473	0.0151	0.3104	0.0710	0.1002	0.0333
110	0.0406	0.0110	0.0516	0.0164	0.3382	0.0743	0.1108	0.0360
120	0.0436	0.0118	0.0559	0.0176	0.3653	0.0774	0.1215	0.0387
130	0.0465	0.0126	0.0603	0.0189	0.3919	0.0801	0.1322	0.0412
140	0.0494	0.0133	0.0646	0.0201	0.4179	0.0827	0.1429	0.0437
150	0.0523	0.0141	0.0690	0.0214	0.4434	0.0851	0.1537	0.0461
160	0.0552	0.0149	0.0734	0.0226	0.4685	0.0874	0.1644	0.0485
170	0.0581	0.0156	0.0778	0.0239	0.4930	0.0895	0.1752	0.0507
180	0.0610	0.0164	0.0823	0.0251	0.5172	0.0914	0.1859	0.0529
190	0.0639	0.0171	0.0868	0.0263	0.5409	0.0933	0.1966	0.0551
200	0.0668	0.0178	0.0913	0.0275	0.5643	0.0951	0.2073	0.0571
220	0.0726	0.0193	0.1003	0.0299	0.6100	0.0983	0.2286	0.0611
240	0.0784	0.0208	0.1095	0.0323	0.6544	0.1013	0.2498	0.0649
260	0.0842	0.0222	0.1187	0.0347	0.6977	0.1040	0.2709	0.0685
280	0.0900	0.0237	0.1280	0.0370	0.7399	0.1065	0.2918	0.0719
300	0.0958	0.0251	0.1374	0.0394	0.7812	0.1087	0.3125	0.0751

TABLE D9.3

Ion implantation projected range (R_p) and standard deviation (ΔR_p) into Si_3N_4.[1]

ENERGY (keV)	ANTIMONY R_p (μm)	ANTIMONY ΔR_p (μm)	ARSENIC R_p (μm)	ARSENIC ΔR_p (μm)	BORON R_p (μm)	BORON ΔR_p (μm)	PHOSPHORUS R_p (μm)	PHOSPHORUS ΔR_p (μm)
10	0.0056	0.0015	0.0060	0.0020	0.0230	0.0111	0.0084	0.0037
20	0.0090	0.0024	0.0099	0.0033	0.0480	0.0196	0.0154	0.0065
30	0.0119	0.0033	0.0135	0.0045	0.0736	0.0267	0.0226	0.0092
40	0.0147	0.0040	0.0169	0.0056	0.0990	0.0326	0.0300	0.0118
50	0.0173	0.0047	0.0202	0.0066	0.1239	0.0377	0.0376	0.0143
60	0.0197	0.0054	0.0235	0.0077	0.1482	0.0422	0.0453	0.0168
70	0.0222	0.0061	0.0268	0.0087	0.1719	0.0461	0.0532	0.0192
80	0.0246	0.0067	0.0301	0.0097	0.1950	0.0496	0.0612	0.0215
90	0.0269	0.0074	0.0334	0.0108	0.2176	0.0527	0.0693	0.0237
100	0.0292	0.0080	0.0367	0.0118	0.2396	0.0555	0.0774	0.0259
110	0.0315	0.0086	0.0400	0.0127	0.2610	0.0581	0.0856	0.0280
120	0.0338	0.0092	0.0433	0.0137	0.2820	0.0605	0.0939	0.0301
130	0.0360	0.0098	0.0467	0.0147	0.3025	0.0627	0.1022	0.0321
140	0.0383	0.0104	0.0500	0.0157	0.3226	0.0647	0.1105	0.0340
150	0.0405	0.0110	0.0534	0.0167	0.3424	0.0666	0.1188	0.0358
160	0.0428	0.0116	0.0568	0.0176	0.3617	0.0684	0.1271	0.0377
170	0.0450	0.0122	0.0603	0.0186	0.3807	0.0700	0.1354	0.0394
180	0.0472	0.0128	0.0637	0.0195	0.3994	0.0716	0.1437	0.0411
190	0.0495	0.0134	0.0672	0.0205	0.4178	0.0731	0.1520	0.0428
200	0.0517	0.0139	0.0706	0.0214	0.4358	0.0744	0.1602	0.0444
220	0.0562	0.0151	0.0776	0.0233	0.4712	0.0770	0.1767	0.0475
240	0.0606	0.0162	0.0847	0.0252	0.5056	0.0793	0.1931	0.0505
260	0.0651	0.0174	0.0918	0.0270	0.5390	0.0815	0.2094	0.0533
280	0.0696	0.0185	0.0990	0.0289	0.5717	0.0834	0.2255	0.0559
300	0.0741	0.0196	0.1063	0.0307	0.6037	0.0852	0.2415	0.0584

REFERENCE

1. W. E. Beadle, J. C. C. Tsai and R. D. Plummer, Eds., *Quick reference manual for silicon integrated circuit technology*, Wiley, New York, 1985.

IMPURITY DIFFUSION COEFFICIENTS

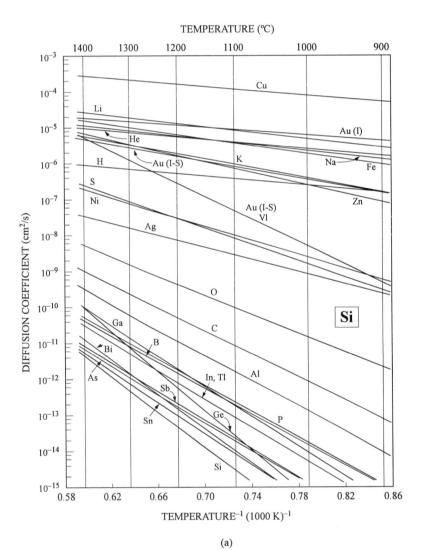

(a)

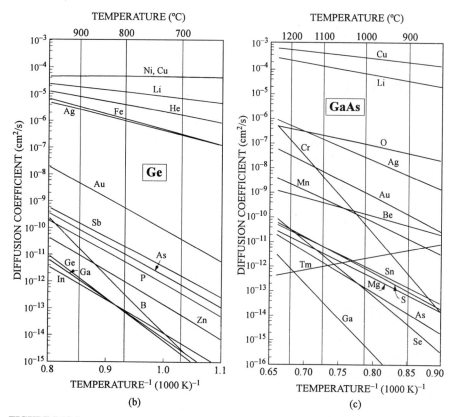

FIGURE D10.1

Impurity diffusion coefficients in (a) Si (I = interstitial, S = substitutional), (b) Ge, and (c) GaAs. (After Refs. 1–3)

REFERENCES

1. D. L. Kendall and D. B. De Vries, "Diffusion in silicon," in R. R. Haberecht and E. L. Kern, Eds., *Semiconductor silicon*, Electrochemical Society, New York, 1969.
2. D. G. Fink and D. Christiansen, Eds., *Electronics engineers' handbook*, 3rd Ed., McGraw-Hill, New York, 1989.
3. H. C. Casey, Jr. and G. L. Pearson, "Diffusion in semiconductors," in J. H. Crawford, Jr. and L. M. Slifkin, Eds., *Point defects in solids, Vol. 2, Semiconductors and molecular crystals*, Plenum Press, New York, 1975.

D11

IMPURITY ENERGY LEVELS

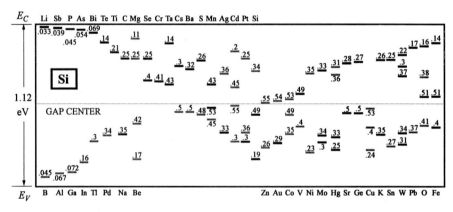

(a)

(b)

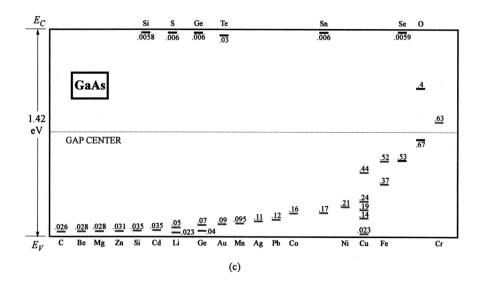

(c)

FIGURE D11.1

Impurity energy levels in (a) Si (b) Ge, and (c) GaAs. ━ Donor impurities. ━ Acceptor impurities. (After Ref. 1)

REFERENCE

1 S. M. Sze, *Physics of semiconductor devices*, 2nd Ed., Wiley, New York, 1981.

APPENDIX
D12

SOLID SOLUBILITIES

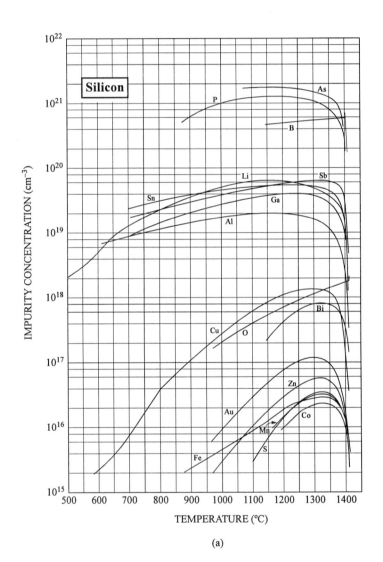

(a)

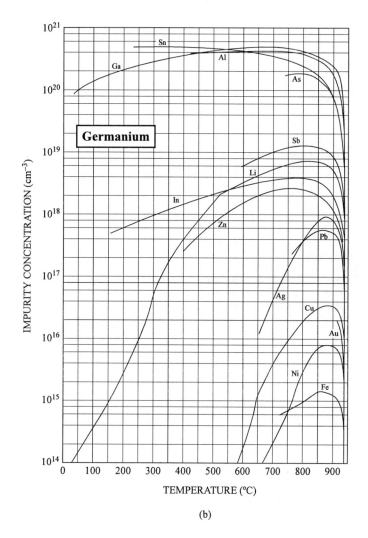

(b)

FIGURE D12.1
Solid solubilities of elements in (a) Si and (b) Ge at different temperatures. (After Ref. 1)

REFERENCE

1. F. A. Trumbore, "Solid solubilities of impurity elements in germanium and silicon," *Bell Syst. Tech. J.*, **39**, 205 (1960).

APPENDIX
D13

PROPERTIES OF
METALS AND SILICIDES

TABLE D13.1
Properties of metals.[1]

Metals	Melting point (°C)	Resistivity ρ (20°C) ($\mu\Omega$-cm)	Thermal coef. of ρ (ppm/K)	Density (20°C) (g/cm³)	Specific heat (J/kg-K)	Thermal conductivity (W/m-K)	Coef. of expan. (μ/K)
Aluminum	660.1	2.67	4500	2.70	917	238	23.5
Antimony	630.5	40.1	5100	6.68	209	23.8	8–11
Barium	729	60 (0°C)		3.5	285		18
Beryllium	1287	3.3	9000	1.848	2052	194	12
Bismuth	271	117	4600	9.80	124.8	9	13.4
Cadmium	320.9	7.3	4300	8.64	233.2	103	31
Calcium	839	3.7	4570	1.54	624	125	22
Cerium	798	85.4	8700	6.75	188	11.9	8
Cesium	28.5	20	4800	1.87	234	36.1	97
Chromium	1860	13.2	2140	7.1	461	91.3	6.5
Cobalt	1492	6.34	6600	8.9	427	96	12.5
Copper	1083.4	1.694	4300	8.96	386.0	397	17.0
Gallium	29.7			5.91	377	41.0	18.3
Germanium	937			5.32	310	56.4	5.75
Gold	1063	2.20	4000	19.3	130	315.5	14.1
Hafnium	2227	32.2	4400	13.1	147	22.9	6.0
Indium	156.4	8.8	5200	7.3	243	80.0	24.8
Iridium	2454	5.1	4500	22.4	130.6	146.5	6.8
Iron	1536	10.1	6500	7.87	456	78.2	12.1
Lead	327.4	20.6	4200	11.68	129.8	34.9	29.0
Lithium	181	9.29	4350	0.534	3517	76.1	56
Magnesium	649	4.2	4250	1.74	1038	155.5	26.0
Manganese	1244	144		7.4	486	7.8	23
Mercury	−38.87	95.9	1000	13.5	138	8.65	61
Molybdenum	2615	5.7	4350	10.2	251	137	5.1
Nickel	1455	6.9	6800	8.9	452	88.5	13.3
Niobium	2467	16.0	2600	8.6	268	54.1	7.2
Osmium	3030	8.8	4100	22.5	130	87.5	4.57
Palladium	1552	10.8	4200	12.0	247	75.5	11.0
Platinum	1769	10.58	3920	21.45	134.4	71.5	9.0

TABLE D13.1 (Continued)

Metals	Melting point (°C)	Resistivity ρ (20°C) ($\mu\Omega$-cm)	Thermal coef. of ρ (ppm/K)	Density (20°C) (g/cm³)	Specific heat (J/kg-K)	Thermal conductivity (W/m-K)	Coef. of expan. (μ/K)
Potassium	63.2	6.8	5700	0.86	754	104	83
Radium	700			5			
Rhenium	3180	18.7	4500	21.0	138	47.6	6.6
Rhodium	1966	4.7	4400	12.4	243	149	8.5
Rubidium	38.8	12.1	4800	1.53	356	58.3	9.0
Ruthenium	2310	7.7	4100	12.2	234	116.3	9.6
Silicon	1412			2.34	729	138.5	7.6
Silver	960.8	1.63	4100	10.5	234	425	19.1
Sodium	97.8	4.7	5500	0.97	1227	128	71
Strontium	770	23 (0°C)		2.6	737		100
Tantalum	2980	13.5	3500	16.6	142	57.55	6.5
Tellurium	450			6.24	134	3.8	
Thallium	304	16.6	5200	11.85	130	45.5	30
Thorium	1755	14	4000	11.5	100	49.2	11.2
Tin	231.9	12.6	4600	7.3	226	73.2	23.5
Titanium	1667	54	3800	4.5	528	21.6	8.9
Tungsten	3400	5.4	4800	19.3	138	174	4.5
Uranium	1132	27	3400	19	117	28	
Vanadium	1902	19.6	3900	6.1	498	31.6	8.3
Zinc	419.5	5.96	4200	7.14	394	119.5	31
Zirconium	1852	44	4400	6.49	289	22.6	5.9

TABLE D13.2
Properties of silicides.[2,3]

Silicides	Resistivity ($\mu\Omega$-cm)	Formation temp. (°C)	Å of Si per Å of metal	Å of silicide per Å of metal
$CoSi_2$	18–25	> 550	3.64	3.52
$MoSi_2$	80–250	> 600	2.56	2.59
$NiSi_2$	≈ 50	750	3.65	3.63
Pd_2Si	30–35	> 400	0.68	≈ 1.69
$PtSi$	28–35	600–800	1.32	1.97
$TaSi_2$	30–45	> 600	2.21	2.40
$TiSi_2$	14–18	> 700	2.27	2.51
WSi_2	30–70	> 600	2.53	2.58

REFERENCES

1. C. Belove, Ed., *Handbook of modern electronics and electrical engineering*, Wiley, New York, 1986.
2. S. P. Murarka, *Silicides for VLSI applications*, Academic Press, New York, 1983.
3. G. Georgiou, private communications.

APPENDIX

E

BACKGROUND INFORMATION

APPENDIX
E1

COMMONLY USED EQUATIONS

Equilibrium carrier concentration (non-degenerate),
(Under non-equilibrium conditions, E_{Fn} or E_{Fp} replaces E_F)

$$n = N_C \exp\left[\frac{-(E_C - E_F)}{kT}\right] = n_i \exp\left(\frac{E_F - E_i}{kT}\right) \tag{E1.1}$$

$$p = N_V \exp\left[\frac{-(E_F - E_V)}{kT}\right] = n_i \exp\left(\frac{E_i - E_F}{kT}\right) \tag{E1.2}$$

$$N_C = 2\left(\frac{2\pi m_e^* kT}{h^2}\right)^{3/2} \tag{E1.3}$$

$$N_V = 2\left(\frac{2\pi m_h^* kT}{h^2}\right)^{3/2} . \tag{E1.4}$$

Mass-action law,

$$np = n_i^2 = N_C N_V \exp\left(\frac{-E_g}{kT}\right) . \tag{E1.5}$$

Einstein relation,

$$\frac{D_n}{\mu_n} = \frac{D_p}{\mu_p} = \frac{kT}{q} . \tag{E1.6}$$

Drift properties,

$$v_d = \mu \mathscr{E} \tag{E1.7}$$

$$\sigma = \frac{1}{\rho} = n\mu_n q + p\mu_p q \ . \tag{E1.8}$$

Debye length and diffusion length,

$$L_D = \sqrt{\frac{\varepsilon_s kT}{q^2 N}} \tag{E1.9}$$

$$L_n = \sqrt{D_n \tau_n} \tag{E1.10}$$

$$L_p = \sqrt{D_p \tau_p} \ . \tag{E1.11}$$

Current equations (drift and diffusion),

$$J_n = q\mu_n n \mathscr{E} + qD_n \frac{dn}{dx} = \mu_n n \frac{dE_{Fn}}{dx} \tag{E1.12}$$

$$J_p = q\mu_p p \mathscr{E} - qD_p \frac{dp}{dx} = \mu_p p \frac{dE_{Fp}}{dx} \ . \tag{E1.13}$$

Continuity equations,
(G is external generation other than thermal, such as optical excitation)

$$\frac{\partial n}{\partial t} = G - \frac{n - n_o}{\tau_n} + \frac{1}{q}\frac{\partial J_n}{\partial x} \tag{E1.14}$$

$$\frac{\partial p}{\partial t} = G - \frac{p - p_o}{\tau_p} - \frac{1}{q}\frac{\partial J_p}{\partial x} \ . \tag{E1.15}$$

Displacement current,

$$J = \varepsilon \frac{d\mathscr{E}}{dt} \ . \tag{E1.16}$$

Poisson equation,

$$\frac{d^2\psi}{dx^2} = \frac{-d\mathscr{E}}{dx} = \frac{-\rho}{\varepsilon_s} = \frac{q\,(n-p+N_A-N_D)}{\varepsilon_s} \quad . \tag{E1.17}$$

Gauss' law,

$$\oint \mathscr{E}dA = \frac{Q}{\varepsilon} \quad . \tag{E1.18}$$

Depletion approximation,

$$W_{dn} = \sqrt{\frac{2\varepsilon_s\psi_n}{qN_D}} \tag{E1.19}$$

$$W_{dp} = \sqrt{\frac{2\varepsilon_s\psi_p}{qN_A}} \tag{E1.20}$$

$$\mathscr{E}_m = \sqrt{\frac{2qN_D\psi_n}{\varepsilon_s}} = \frac{qN_DW_{dn}}{\varepsilon_s}$$
$$= \sqrt{\frac{2qN_A\psi_p}{\varepsilon_s}} = \frac{qN_AW_{dp}}{\varepsilon_s} \quad . \tag{E1.21}$$

Light properties,

$$E = h\nu \tag{E1.22}$$

$$E\,(\text{in eV}) = \frac{1.24}{\lambda\,(\text{in }\mu\text{m})} \tag{E1.23}$$

$$p = \frac{h}{\lambda} = \hbar k \quad . \tag{E1.24}$$

APPENDIX
E2

ACRONYMS

AC	Alternating current
ADFET	Adsorption field-effect transistor
AM	Amplitude modulation
AM0	Air mass 0
AM1	Air mass 1
APD	Avalanche photodiode
ASCR	Asymmetric silicon-controlled rectifier
BARITT	Barrier-injection transit-time
BAW	Bulk acoustic wave
BBD	Bucket-brigade device
BCCD	Buried-channel charge-coupled device
BCS	Bardeen-Cooper-Schrieffer
BICFET	Bipolar inversion-channel field-effect transistor
BiCMOS	Bipolar complementary metal-oxide-semiconductor
BiFET	Bipolar field-effect transistor
BSIT	Bipolar-mode static-induction transistor
C^3	Cleaved-coupled-cavity
CCD	Charge-coupled device
CCIS	Charge-coupled image sensor
CHEMFET	Chemically sensitive field-effect transistor
CHINT	Charge-injection transistor
CID	Charge-injection device
CMOS	Complementary metal-oxide-semiconductor
COMFET	Conductivity-modulated field-effect transistor
CTD	Charge-transfer device
CTIS	Charge-transfer image sensor
CW	Continuous wave
DBR	Distributed-Bragg reflector
DC	Direct current
DDD	Doubly diffused drain
DF	Dissipation factor
DH	Double-heterojunction

DHBT	Double-heterojunction bipolar transistor
DHFET	Double-heterojunction field-effect transistor
DIAC	Diode AC switch
DMOS	Double-diffused metal-oxide-semiconductor
DOES	Double-heterostructure optoelectronic switch
DOVATT	Double-velocity avalanche transit-time
DOVETT	Double-velocity transit-time
DRAM	Dynamic random-access memory
EAROM	Electrically alterable read-only memory
EEPROM	Electrically erasable/programmable read-only memory
EMF	Electromotive force
ENFET	Enzyme field-effect transistor
EPROM	Electrically programmable read-only memory
ESD	Electro-static discharge
FAMOS	Floating-gate avalanche-injection metal-oxide-semiconductor
FE	Field emission
FEFET	Ferroelectric field-effect transistor
FET	Field-effect transistor
FLOTOX	Floating-gate tunnel-oxide
FM	Frequency modulation
GATT	Gate-assisted-turn-off thyristor
GEMFET	Gain-enhanced metal-oxide-semiconductor field-effect transistor
GRIN-SCH	Graded-index separate-confinement heterojunction
GTO	Gate-turn-off
HBT	Heterojunction bipolar transistor
HEMT	High-electron-mobility transistor
HET	Hot-electron transistor
HEXFET	Hexagonal field-effect transistor
HFET	Heterojunction field-effect transistor
HIGFET	Heterojunction insulated-gate field-effect transistor
IC	Integrated circuit
IDT	Interdigital transducer
IGBT	Insulated-gate bipolar transistor
IGFET	Insulated-gate field-effect transistor
IGR	Insulated-gate rectifier
IGT	Insulated-gate transistor
IMPATT	Impact-ionization-avalanche transit-time
ISFET	Ion-sensitive field-effect transistor
JFET	Junction field-effect transistor
LASCR	Light-activated silicon-controlled rectifier
LCD	Liquid-crystal display
LDD	Lightly doped drain
LED	Light-emitting diode
LIGT	Lateral insulated-gate transistor
LOC	Large-optical-cavity

LPCVD	Low-pressure chemical-vapor deposition
LRTFET	Lateral resonant-tunneling field-effect transistor
LSA	Limited-space-charge accumulation
LSI	Large-scale integration
MAGFET	Magnetic-field-sensitive field-effect transistor
MAOS	Metal-alumina-oxide-semiconductor
MBE	Molecular beam epitaxy
MBM	Metal-barrier-metal
MESFET	Metal-semiconductor field-effect transistor
MIM	Metal-insulator-metal
MIMIM	Metal-insulator-metal-insulator-metal
MIMS	Metal-insulator-metal-semiconductor
MIOS	Metal-insulator-oxide-semiconductor
MIp-n	Metal-insulator-p-n
MIS	Metal-insulator-semiconductor
MISFET	Metal-insulator-semiconductor field-effect transistor
MISIM	Metal-insulator-semiconductor-insulator-metal
MISM	Metal-insulator-semiconductor-metal
MISS	Metal-insulator-semiconductor switch
MIST	Metal-insulator-semiconductor thyristor
MITATT	Mixed-tunnel-avalanche transit-time
MNOS	Metal-nitride-oxide-semiconductor
MOCVD	Metallo-organic chemical-vapor deposition
MODFET	Modulation-doped field-effect transistor
MOM	Metal-oxide-metal
MOMOM	Metal-oxide-metal-oxide-metal
MOMS	Metal-oxide-metal-semiconductor
MONOS	Metal-oxide-nitride-oxide-semiconductor
MOp-n	Metal-oxide-p-n
MOS	Metal-oxide-semiconductor
MOSFET	Metal-oxide-semiconductor field-effect transistor
MOST	Metal-oxide-semiconductor transistor
MS	Metal-semiconductor
MSM	Metal-semiconductor-metal
NEA	Negative electron affinity
NERFET	Negative-resistance field-effect transistor
NTC	Negative temperature coefficient
OGFET	Open-gate field-effect transistor
P^{2}CCD	Profiled-peristaltic charge-coupled device
PCCD	Peristaltic charge-coupled device
PDB	Planar-doped-barrier
PEM	Photoelectromagnetic
PET	Potential-effect transistor
PF	Power factor
PRESSFET	Pressure-sensitive field-effect transistor

PROM	Programmable read-only memory
PTC	Positive temperature coefficient
PUT	Programmable unijunction transistor
QWBRTT	Quantum-well-base resonant-tunneling transistor
QWIP	Quantum-well infrared photodetector
QWITT	Quantum-well-injection transit-time
RAM	Random-access memory
RBT	Resonant-tunneling bipolar transistor
RCT	Reverse-conducting thyristor
RF	Radio frequency
RHET	Resonant-tunneling hot-electron transistor
ROM	Read-only memory
RST	Real-space-transfer
RTBT	Resonant-tunneling bipolar transistor
RTD	Resistance temperature detector
SAFET	Surface-accessible field-effect transistor
SAGM-APD	Separate-absorption-graded-multiplication avalanche photodiode
SAM-APD	Separate-absorption-multiplication avalanche photodiode
SAW	Surface acoustic wave
SBS	Silicon bilateral switch
SCCD	Surface-channel charge-coupled device
SCH	Separate-confinement heterojunction
SCL	Space-charge-limited
SCR	Silicon-controlled rectifier
SCS	Silicon-controlled switch
SDHT	Selectively doped heterojunction transistor
SEED	Self-electrooptic-effect device
SGFET	Suspended-gate field-effect transistor
SIPOS	Semi-insulating polycrystalline silicon
SISFET	Semiconductor-insulator-semiconductor field-effect transistor
SIT	Static-induction transistor
SIThy	Static-inductor thyristor
SMS	Semiconductor-metal-semiconductor
SOI	Silicon-on-insulator
SONOS	Silicon-oxide-nitride-oxide-semiconductor
SOS	Silicon-on-sapphire
SQUID	Superconducting quantum interference device
SRAM	Static random-access memory
SUS	Silicon unilateral switch
TE	Thermionic emission
TEA	Transferred-electron amplifier
TED	Transferred-electron device
TEGFET	Two-dimensional electron-gas field-effect transistor
TEO	Transferred-electron oscillator
TETRAN	Tunnel-emitter transistor

TFE	Thermionic-field emission
TFT	Thin-film transistor
THETA	Tunneling hot-electron-transfer amplifier
TRAPATT	Trapped-plasma avalanche-triggered transit
TRIAC	Triode AC switch
TUNNETT	Tunnel-injection transit-time
ULSI	Ultra-large-scale integration
UMOS	U-groove metal-oxide-semiconductor
VCSEL	Vertical-cavity surface-emitting laser
VFET	V-groove field-effect transistor
VLSI	Very-large-scale integration
VMOS	V-groove metal-oxide-semiconductor
VMT	Velocity-modulation transistor
WKB	Wentzel-Kramers-Brillouin

APPENDIX
E3

ELECTROMAGNETIC SPECTRUM

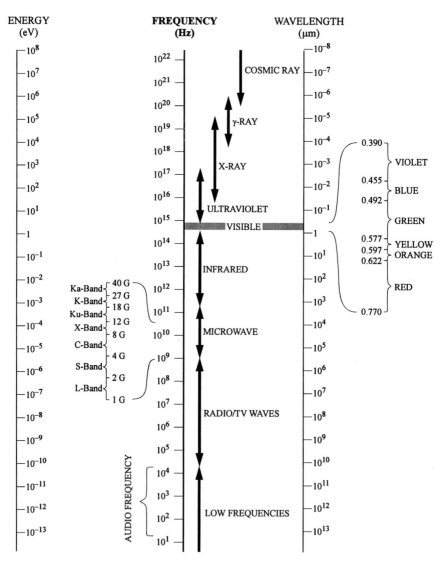

APPENDIX
E4

PERIODIC TABLE

TABLE E4.1
Portion of the periodic table relevant to elementary and compound semi-conductors.

II	III	IV	V	VI
	B	C	N	
Mg	Al	Si	P	S
Zn	Ga	Ge	As	Se
Cd	In	Sn	Sb	Te
Hg		Pb		

TABLE E4.2
Periodic table of the elements. The number above the element symbol is the atomic number, and that below is the atomic weight.

IA	IIA	IIIB	IVB	VB	VIB	VIIB	VIII			IB	IIB	IIIA	IVA	VA	VIA	VIIA	VIIIA
1 **H** 1.00797																	2 **He** 4.0026
3 **Li** 6.941	4 **Be** 9.01218											5 **B** 10.81	6 **C** 12.011	7 **N** 14.0067	8 **O** 15.9994	9 **F** 18.9984	10 **Ne** 20.179
11 **Na** 22.9898	12 **Mg** 24.305											13 **Al** 26.9815	14 **Si** 28.086	15 **P** 30.9738	16 **S** 32.064	17 **Cl** 35.453	18 **Ar** 39.948
19 **K** 39.0983	20 **Ca** 40.08	21 **Sc** 44.956	22 **Ti** 47.90	23 **V** 50.942	24 **Cr** 51.996	25 **Mn** 54.9380	26 **Fe** 55.847	27 **Co** 58.9332	28 **Ni** 58.69	29 **Cu** 63.546	30 **Zn** 65.38	31 **Ga** 69.72	32 **Ge** 72.59	33 **As** 74.9216	34 **Se** 78.96	35 **Br** 79.904	36 **Kr** 83.80
37 **Rb** 85.47	38 **Sr** 87.62	39 **Y** 88.905	40 **Zr** 91.22	41 **Nb** 92.906	42 **Mo** 95.94	43 **Tc** 98.906	44 **Ru** 101.07	45 **Rh** 102.905	46 **Pd** 106.4	47 **Ag** 107.868	48 **Cd** 112.40	49 **In** 114.82	50 **Sn** 118.69	51 **Sb** 121.75	52 **Te** 127.60	53 **I** 126.904	54 **Xe** 131.30
55 **Cs** 132.905	56 **Ba** 137.33	71 **Lu** 174.97	72 **Hf** 178.49	73 **Ta** 180.948	74 **W** 183.85	75 **Re.** 186.2	76 **Os** 190.2	77 **Ir** 192.2	78 **Pt** 195.09	79 **Au** 196.967	80 **Hg** 200.59	81 **Tl** 204.37	82 **Pb** 207.19	83 **Bi** 208.980	84 **Po** 210.05	85 **At** 210	86 **Rn** 222.00
87 **Fr** 223	88 **Ra** 226.02	103 **Lr** 262	104 **Rf** 261	105 **Ha** 262													

Lanthanide series (rare earths)

57 **La** 138.91	58 **Ce** 140.12	59 **Pr** 140.907	60 **Nd** 144.24	61 **Pm** 145	62 **Sm** 150.4	63 **Eu** 151.96	64 **Gd** 157.25	65 **Tb** 158.925	66 **Dy** 162.50	67 **Ho** 164.930	68 **Er** 167.26	69 **Tm** 168.934	70 **Yb** 173.04

Actinide series

89 **Ac** 227.027	90 **Th** 232.038	91 **Pa** 231.036	92 **U** 238.03	93 **Np** 237.048	94 **Pu** 239.13	95 **Am** 243.13	96 **Cm** 247	97 **Bk** 247	98 **Cf** 251	99 **Es** 252	100 **Fm** 257	101 **Md** 258	102 **No** 259

APPENDIX
E5

SYMBOLS FOR ELEMENTS

Actinium	Ac	Hafnium	Hf	Promethium	Pm
Aluminum	Al	Helium	He	Protactinium	Pa
Americium	Am	Holmium	Ho	Radium	Ra
Antimony	Sb	Hydrogen	H	Radon	Rn
Argon	Ar	Indium	In	Rhenium	Re
Arsenic	As	Iodine	I	Rhodium	Rh
Astatine	At	Iridium	Ir	Rubidium	Rb
Barium	Ba	Iron	Fe	Ruthenium	Ru
Berkelium	Bk	Krypton	Kr	Samarium	Sm
Beryllium	Be	Lanthanum	La	Scandium	Sc
Bismuth	Bi	Lawrencium	Lr	Selenium	Se
Boron	B	Lead	Pb	Silicon	Si
Bromine	Br	Lithium	Li	Silver	Ag
Cadmium	Cd	Lutetium	Lu	Sodium	Na
Calcium	Ca	Magnesium	Mg	Strontium	Sr
Californium	Cf	Manganese	Mn	Sulfur	S
Carbon	C	Mendelevium	Md	Tantalum	Ta
Cerium	Ce	Mercury	Hg	Technetium	Tc
Cesium	Cs	Molybdenum	Mo	Tellurium	Te
Chlorine	Cl	Neodymium	Nd	Terbium	Tb
Chromium	Cr	Neon	Ne	Thallium	Tl
Cobalt	Co	Neptunium	Np	Thorium	Th
Copper	Cu	Nickel	Ni	Thulium	Tm
Curium	Cm	Niobium	Nb	Tin	Sn
Dysprosium	Dy	Nitrogen	N	Titanium	Ti
Einsteinium	Es	Nobelium	No	Tungsten	W
Erbium	Er	Osmium	Os	Uranium	U
Europium	Eu	Oxygen	O	Vanadium	V
Fermium	Fm	Palladium	Pd	Xenon	Xe
Fluorine	F	Phosphorus	P	Ytterbium	Yb
Francium	Fr	Platinum	Pt	Yttrium	Y
Gadolinium	Gd	Plutonium	Pu	Zinc	Zn
Gallium	Ga	Polonium	Po	Zirconium	Zr
Germanium	Ge	Potassium	K		
Gold	Au	Praseodymium	Pr		

APPENDIX
E6

INTERNATIONAL SYSTEM OF UNITS (SI UNITS)

Quantity	Unit	Symbol	Equivalence
Length	meter*	m*	
Mass	kilogram	kg	
Time	second	s	
Temperature	kelvin	K	
Current	ampere	A	C/s
Frequency	hertz	Hz	1/s
Force	newton	N	kg-m/s^2, J/m
Pressure, stress	pascal	Pa	N/m^2
Energy	joule*	J*	N-m, W-s
Power	watt	W	J/s, V-A
Electric charge	coulomb	C	A-s
Potential	volt	V	J/C, W/A
Conductance	siemens	S	A/V, 1/Ω
Resistance	ohm	Ω	V/A
Capacitance	farad	F	C/V
Magnetic flux	weber	Wb	V-s
Magnetic flux density	tesla	T	Wb/m^2
Inductance	henry	H	Wb/A

* It is more common in the semiconductor field to use cm for length and eV for energy. (1 cm = 10^{-2} m, 1 eV = 1.6×10^{-19} J)

E7

UNIT PREFIXES

Prefix	Multiple factor	Symbol
exa	10^{18}	E
peta	10^{15}	P
tera	10^{12}	T
giga	10^{9}	G
mega	10^{6}	M
kilo	10^{3}	k
hecto	10^{2}	h
deka	10	da
deci	10^{-1}	d
centi	10^{-2}	c
milli	10^{-3}	m
micro	10^{-6}	μ
nano	10^{-9}	n
pico	10^{-12}	p
femto	10^{-15}	f
atto	10^{-18}	a

APPENDIX
E8

GREEK ALPHABET

	Lowercase	Uppercase
Alpha	α	A
Beta	β	B
Gamma	γ	Γ
Delta	δ	Δ
Epsilon	ε	E
Zeta	ζ	Z
Eta	η	H
Theta	θ	Θ
Iota	ι	I
Kappa	κ	K
Lambda	λ	Λ
Mu	μ	M
Nu	ν	N
Xi	ξ	Ξ
Omicron	o	O
Pi	π	Π
Rho	ρ	P
Sigma	σ	Σ
Tau	τ	T
Upsilon	υ	Y
Phi	φ	Φ
Chi	χ	X
Psi	ψ	Ψ
Omega	ω	Ω

APPENDIX
E9

FUNDAMENTAL CONSTANTS

Quantity	Symbol	Value
Avogadro constant	N_{Av}	6.0221×10^{23} /mol
Bohr radius	a_B	0.52917 Å
Boltzmann constant	k	1.3807×10^{-23} J/K
		8.6174×10^{-5} eV/K
Electron rest mass	m_o	9.1094×10^{-31} kg
Elementary charge	q	1.6022×10^{-19} C
Gas constant	R_o	8.3145 J/K-mol
Magnetic flux quantum ($h/2q$)	Φ_o	2.0678×10^{-15} Wb
Permeability of vacuum	μ_o	1.2566×10^{-8} H/cm
Permittivity of vacuum	ε_o	8.8542×10^{-14} F/cm
Planck constant	h	6.6261×10^{-34} J-s
		4.1357×10^{-15} eV-s
Proton rest mass	m_p	1.6726×10^{-27} kg
Reduced Planck constant ($h/2\pi$)	$\hbar$	1.0546×10^{-34} J-s
		6.5821×10^{-16} eV-s
Speed of light in vacuum	c	2.9979×10^{10} cm/s
Thermal potential (kT/q) at 300 K	ϕ_T	0.025852 V

APPENDIX
E10

LIST OF SYMBOLS

Symbol	Description (unit)
A	Area (cm^2)
A^*	Effective Richardson constant (A/cm^2-K^2)
A^*_n	Effective Richardson constant for electrons (A/cm^2-K^2)
A^*_p	Effective Richardson constant for holes (A/cm^2-K^2)
a	Lattice constant (cm)
$\mathcal{B}$	Magnetic-flux density (Wb/cm^2, V-s/cm^2)
B_r	Recombination coefficient (cm^3/s)
$C_1, C_2 \ldots$	Constants
C	Capacitance (F)
C_A	Capacitance per unit area (F/cm^2)
C_{BC}	Base-collector capacitance (F)
C_{BE}	Base-emitter capacitance (F)
C_D	Diffusion capacitance (F/cm^2)
C_d	Depletion-layer capacitance (F/cm^2)
C_{FB}	Capacitance at flat-band (F/cm^2)
C_G	Gate capacitance (F)
C_i	Insulator capacitance (F/cm^2)
C_{it}	Interface-trap capacitance (F/cm^2)
C_{ox}	Oxide capacitance (F/cm^2)
C_p	Parallel capacitance (F)
C_{par}	Parasitic capacitance (F)
C_s	Series capacitance (F)
c	Speed of light in vacuum (cm/s)
D	Diffusion coefficient for carriers or impurities (cm^2/s)
D_a	Ambipolar diffusion coefficient (cm^2/s)
D_{it}	Interface-trap density (/cm^2-eV)

Symbol	Description (unit)
D_n	Diffusion coefficient for electrons (cm^2/s)
D_p	Diffusion coefficient for holes (cm^2/s)
$\mathscr{E}$	Electric field (V/cm)
$\mathscr{E}_H$	Hall field (V/cm)
$\mathscr{E}_m$	Maximum electric field (V/cm)
E	Energy (eV)
E_a	Activation energy (eV)
E_C	Conduction-band edge (eV)
E_F	Fermi level (eV)
E_{Fm}	Metal Fermi level (eV)
E_{Fn}	Quasi-Fermi (imref) level for electrons (eV)
E_{Fp}	Quasi-Fermi (imref) level for holes (eV)
E_g	Energy gap (eV)
E_i	Intrinsic Fermi level (eV)
E_{op}	Optical-phonon energy (eV)
E_t	Trap energy level (eV)
E_V	Valence-band edge (eV)
E_{vac}	Vacuum energy level (eV)
F	Force (N, kg-cm/s^2, J/cm)
F_{ph}	Photon flux density (/cm^2-s)
f	Frequency (Hz)
f_T	Cutoff frequency (at which the short-circuit current gain is unity) (Hz)
G	Conductance (S)
G	Generation rate (/cm^3-s)
G_N	Gummel number (/cm^2)
G_{op}	Optical-generation rate (/cm^3-s)
G_{th}	Thermal-generation rate (/cm^3-s)
g_m	Transconductance (S)
$g_{m,lin}$	Transconductance in the linear region (S)
$g_{m,sat}$	Transconductance in the saturation region (S)
$\mathscr{H}$	Magnetic field (A/cm)
h	Planck constant (J-s)
$\hbar$	Reduced Planck constant, $h/2\pi$ (J-s)
I	Current (A)
I_B	Base current (A)
I_C	Collector current (A)
I_D	Drain current (A)

Symbol	Description (unit)
I_E	Emitter current (A)
I_h	Holding current (A)
I_{ph}	Photocurrent (A)
I_s	Switching current (A)
I_{sat}	Saturation current (A)
I_{sc}	Short-circuit current in response to light (A)
i	Intrinsic (undoped) material
J	Current density (A/cm^2)
J_f	Forward-current density of rectifier (A/cm^2)
J_{ge}	Generation-current density (A/cm^2)
J_n	Electron-current density (A/cm^2)
J_p	Hole-current density (A/cm^2)
J_{ph}	Photocurrent density (A/cm^2)
J_{re}	Recombination-current density (A/cm^2)
J_{sc}	Short-circuit-current density (A/cm^2)
J_T	Threshold-current density (A/cm^2)
K	Dielectric constant, $\varepsilon/\varepsilon_o$ (unitless)
K_i	Dielectric constant of insulator (unitless)
K_{ox}	Dielectric constant of oxide (unitless)
K_s	Dielectric constant of semiconductor (unitless)
k	Boltzmann constant (J/K)
k	Wave vector (/cm)
L	Length (cm)
L	Inductance (H)
L_c	Effective channel length (cm)
L_D	Debye length (cm)
L_n	Diffusion length of electrons (cm)
L_p	Diffusion length of holes (cm)
l	Length (cm)
l_m	Mean free path (cm)
M	Multiplication factor (unitless)
m_o	Electron rest mass (kg)
m^*	Effective mass (kg)
m^*_e	Electron effective mass (kg)
m^*_h	Hole effective mass (kg)
m^*_{hh}	Effective mass for heavy hole (kg)
m^*_l	Longitudinal effective mass for electron (kg)
m^*_{lh}	Effective mass for light hole (kg)

Symbol	Description (unit)
m^*_t	Transverse effective mass for electron (kg)
N	Doping concentration (/cm^3)
N_A	Acceptor doping concentration (/cm^3)
N_C	Effective density-of-states in conduction band (/cm^3)
N_D	Donor doping concentration (/cm^3)
N_i	Integer number (unitless)
N_{it}	Interface-trap density (/cm^2)
N_t	Bulk-trap density (/cm^3)
N_V	Effective density-of-states in valence band (/cm^3)
n	Net electron concentration (/cm^3)
n	Of n-type (negative charge) conductivity
n	Ideality factor of rectifier under forward bias (unitless)
n_i	Intrinsic carrier concentration (/cm^3)
n_n	Electron concentration in n-type semiconductor (majority carriers) (/cm^3)
n_o	Electron concentration in equilibrium (/cm^3)
n_p	Electron concentration in p-type semiconductor (minority carriers) (/cm^3)
n_{po}	Electron concentration in p-type semiconductor (minority carriers) in equilibrium (/cm^3)
n_r	Index of refraction (unitless)
P	Pressure (N/cm^2)
P	Power (W)
p	Net hole concentration (/cm^3)
p	Of p-type (positive charge) conductivity
p	Momentum (J-s/cm)
p_n	Hole concentration in n-type semiconductor (minority carriers) (/cm^3)
p_{no}	Hole concentration in n-type semiconductor (minority carriers) in equilibrium (/cm^3)
p_o	Hole concentration in equilibrium (/cm^3)
p_p	Hole concentration in p-type semiconductor (majority carriers) (/cm^3)
Q	Charge (C)
Q	Quality factor of capacitor and inductor (unitless)
Q_A	Charge density (C/cm^2)
Q_f	Fixed oxide charge (C/cm^2)
Q_{it}	Interface-trap charge (C/cm^2)
Q_m	Mobile ionic charge (C/cm^2)
Q_{ot}	Oxide trapped charge (C/cm^2)
q	Unit electronic charge (C)

Symbol	Description (unit)
R	Resistance (Ω)
R	Recombination rate (/s-cm^3)
R_c	Specific contact resistance (Ω-cm^2)
R_L	Load resistance (Ω)
R_p	Parallel resistance (Ω)
R_s	Series resistance (Ω)
$R_\square$	Sheet resistance per square (Ω/$\square$)
r_H	Hall factor (unitless)
S	Strain (unitless)
S	Subthreshold swing (V/decade)
S_n	Surface recombination velocity for electrons (cm/s)
S_o	Surface recombination velocity (cm/s)
S_p	Surface recombination velocity for holes (cm/s)
T	Absolute temperature (K)
T	Stress (N/cm^2)
t	Time (s)
t_t	Transit time (s)
U	Net recombination/generation rate, $U = R - G$. Positive/negative value implies net recombination/generation (/s-cm^3)
U_s	Net surface recombination/generation rate (/s-cm^2)
V	Applied voltage (V)
V_B	Base voltage (V)
V_{BD}	Breakdown voltage (V)
V_{BE}	Base-emitter voltage (V)
V_C	Collector voltage (V)
V_{CE}	Collector-emitter voltage (V)
V_D	Drain voltage (V)
$V_{D,sat}$	Drain voltage at the onset of saturation (V)
V_{DD}	Supply voltage (V)
V_E	Emitter voltage (V)
V_{FB}	Flat-band voltage (V)
V_f	Forward bias of rectifier (V)
V_G	Gate voltage (V)
V_{GR}	Grid voltage (V)
V_H	Hall voltage (V)
V_h	Holding voltage (V)

Symbol	Description (unit)
V_n	Fermi level from conduction-band edge in n-type semiconductor, $(E_C - E_F)/q$. Negative for degenerate material (V)
V_{oc}	Open-circuit voltage in response to light (V)
V_P	Punch-through voltage (V)
V_p	Fermi level from valence-band edge in p-type semiconductor, $(E_F - E_V)/q$. Negative for degenerate material (V)
V_{PL}	Plate voltage (V)
V_r	Reverse bias of rectifier (V)
V_S	Source voltage (V)
V_s	Switching voltage (V)
V_{sub}	Substrate voltage (V)
V_T	Threshold voltage (V)
v	Velocity (cm/s)
v_d	Drift velocity (cm/s)
v_n	Electron velocity (cm/s)
v_p	Hole velocity (cm/s)
v_{sat}	Saturation velocity (cm/s)
v_{th}	Thermal velocity (cm/s)
W	Device width (cm)
W_d	Depletion width (cm)
W_{dm}	Maximum depletion width (cm)
W_{dn}	Depletion width in n-type material (cm)
W_{dp}	Depletion width in p-type material (cm)
x	Distance (thickness) (cm)
x_i	Insulator-layer thickness (cm)
x_{ox}	Oxide thickness (cm)
Y	Young's modulus, modulus of elasticity (N/cm^2)
Z	Impedance (Ω)
α	Optical absorption coefficient (1/cm)
α	Common-base current gain (unitless)
α	Ionization coefficient (1/cm)
α_n	Ionization coefficient for electrons (1/cm)
α_p	Ionization coefficient for holes (1/cm)
α_T	Base transport factor (unitless)
β	Common-emitter current gain (unitless)

Symbol	Description (unit)
β_T	Reciprocal of thermal potential, q/kT (1/V)
γ	Emitter injection efficiency (unitless)
Δn	Excess electron concentration beyond equilibrium ($1/\text{cm}^3$)
Δp	Excess hole concentration beyond equilibrium ($1/\text{cm}^3$)
ε	Permittivity (F/cm, C/V-cm)
ε_i	Permittivity of insulator (F/cm, C/V-cm)
ε_o	Permittivity of vacuum (F/cm, C/V-cm)
ε_{ox}	Permittivity of oxide (F/cm, C/V-cm)
ε_s	Permittivity of semiconductor (F/cm, C/V-cm)
η	Quantum efficiency (unitless)
λ	Wavelength (cm)
μ	Drift mobility ($\text{cm}^2/\text{V-s}$)
μ	Permeability (H/cm)
μ_H	Hall mobility ($\text{cm}^2/\text{V-s}$)
μ_n	Electron drift mobility ($\text{cm}^2/\text{V-s}$)
μ_o	Permeability of vacuum (H/cm)
μ_p	Hole drift mobility ($\text{cm}^2/\text{V-s}$)
ν	Frequency of light (/s)
ν	Poisson's ratio (unitless)
ρ	Resistivity (Ω-cm)
ρ	Charge density (C/cm^3)
ρ_m	Mobile-ionic-charge density (C/cm^3)
ρ_{ot}	Oxide-trapped-charge density (C/cm^3)
σ	Conductivity (/Ω-cm)
σ	Capture cross-section (cm^2)
σ_n	Capture cross-section for electrons (cm^2)
σ_p	Capture cross-section for holes (cm^2)
τ	Minority-carrier lifetime (s)
τ_D	Dielectric relaxation time (s)
τ_m	Mean free time in scattering (s)
τ_n	Minority-carrier lifetime for electrons (s)
τ_{nr}	Carrier lifetime due to nonradiative recombination (s)

Symbol	Description (unit)
τ_p	Minority-carrier lifetime for holes (s)
τ_r	Carrier lifetime due to radiative recombination (s)
Φ	Magnetic flux (Wb, V-s)
Φ_o	Magnetic flux quantum, $h/2q$ (Wb, V-s)
ϕ	Work function (V)
ϕ_b	Barrier height (V)
ϕ_{bn}	Barrier height for electrons (V)
ϕ_{bp}	Barrier height for holes (V)
ϕ_m	Metal work function (V)
ϕ_{ms}	Work function difference between metal and semiconductor, $\phi_m - \phi_s$ (V)
ϕ_{ph}	Photon flux (/s)
ϕ_s	Semiconductor work function (V)
ϕ_T	Thermal potential, kT/q (V)
χ	Electron affinity (V)
χ_{ox}	Electron affinity for oxide (V)
χ_s	Electron affinity for semiconductor (V)
ψ	Wavefunction (unitless)
ψ	Semiconductor potential, $-E_i/q$ (V)
ψ_B	In bulk, Fermi level away from intrinsic Fermi level, $\lvert E_F - E_i \rvert /q$ (V)
ψ_{Bn}	ψ_B in n-type material (V)
ψ_{Bp}	ψ_B in p-type material (V)
ψ_{bi}	Built-in potential of junction at equilibrium (always positive) (V)
ψ_n	Potential at n-type boundary with respect to n-type bulk (band bending in n-type material, positive when bending down in the energy-band diagram) (V)
ψ_p	Potential at p-type boundary with respect to p-type bulk (band bending in p-type material, positive when bending down in the energy-band diagram) (V)
ψ_s	Surface potential with respect to bulk (band bending, positive when bending down in the energy-band diagram) (V)
ψ_T	Total potential variation (V)
ω	Angular frequency (Hz)

INDEX

(Page numbers in **boldface** indicate major sources, when there are many entries.)